WITH
Honor

WITH
Honor

MELVIN LAIRD

*in War,
Peace,
and Politics*

Dale Van Atta

THE UNIVERSITY OF WISCONSIN PRESS

The University of Wisconsin Press
1930 Monroe Street, 3rd Floor
Madison, Wisconsin 53711-2059

www.wisc.edu/wisconsinpress/

3 Henrietta Street
London WC2E 8LU, England

Library of Congress Cataloging-in-Publication Data
Van Atta, Dale.
With honor : Melvin Laird in war, peace, and politics /
Dale Van Atta ; foreword by Gerald R. Ford.
p.   cm.
Includes bibliographical references and index.
ISBN 0-299-22680-8 (cloth : alk. paper)
1. Laird, Melvin R. 2. Cabinet officers—United States—Biography.
3. United States. Dept. of Defense—Officials and employees—Biography.
4. United States—Politics and government—1963–1969. 5. United States—
Politics and government—1969–1974. 6. Nixon, Richard M. (Richard Milhous),
1913–1994—Friends and associates. 7. Vietnam War, 1961–1975—United States.
8. Legislators—United States—Biography. 9. United States. Congress.
House—Biography. 10. Legislators—Wisconsin—Biography. I Title.
E840.8.L25V36   2008
355.6092—dc22
[B]
2007040159

TO THE

AMERICAN SOLDIERS, SAILORS, AIRMEN AND WOMEN

who served our country courageously and honorably in Vietnam.

CONTENTS

FOREWORD

Jimmy Carter once said: "Of all the cabinet officers who served in the first Nixon term, Mel Laird, with his quiet and somewhat modest demeanor, as well as absence of self-promotion, was the most underestimated." Henry Kissinger and I often remarked how underrated and certainly underappreciated have been the enormous contributions of this remarkable man. This book is long overdue since no respectable historian tracing the evolution of this country during the second half of the twentieth century can afford to overlook the life and legacy of this "Man from Marshfield" who so thoroughly changed the course of America's history.

Without Melvin Laird as our country's tenth secretary of defense, there likely would have been no end to the Vietnam War during the Nixon administration, no end to the draft, no steady military modernization during the country's most virulent antimilitary years, and no arms control treaties with the Soviet Union. This laudatory list does not include all that the Honorable Melvin Laird did in the sixteen years before becoming defense secretary.

I was not surprised on that January 1953 day in the House Chamber when Speaker Sam Rayburn swore in this thirty-year-old political prodigy from central Wisconsin. Months earlier, members of the Wisconsin delegation—Johnny Byrnes and Glenn Davis—had tipped me off to an outstanding young state senator from Marshfield whom they were absolutely convinced would be elected in the House in 1952. For Mel, it was the first of nine triumphs at the polls; over the next sixteen years, he more than lived up to the advance billing given to me.

From the outset, Mel was a highly effective member of the House Committee on Appropriations, serving on both the Defense and Health Subcommittees, which together controlled two-thirds of the federal budget. I was his seatmate on the Defense Appropriations Subcommittee, where I was the ranking member, and he was right behind that. With his quick mind and endless capacity for hard work, Mel quickly became one of the best-informed House members on military affairs. He was our sharpest and most relentless interrogator of the defense establishment when they came testifying. Mel was the only congressman who so rattled Defense Secretary Bob McNamara that he lunged across the witness table when Mel called him out on a lie. He was a tower of strength for us on that subcommittee.

But his best work was on the Health, Education, and Welfare Subcommittee. As the senior member on the Republican side, he won the respect and confidence of the members on both sides of the political aisle. Long before today's talk of a health crisis in America, Mel Laird was legislating in hopes of averting such a crisis. Among many significant achievements, he and the chairman, Rep. John Fogarty, worked closely to legislate a vast and rapid expansion of the National Institutes of Health. It's no exaggeration to refer to health care's renaissance from 1953 through 1969 as the Fogarty/Laird Years.

Though Mel often exemplified the epitome of bipartisanship, he was a committed, progressive Republican who was always intensely interested in electing a Republican majority so we would have a Republican Speaker of the House. In the late 1950s, when a group of so-called young Turks joined forces to overthrow Joe Martin in favor of Congressman Charlie Halleck of Indiana, Mel and I were a part of that group. Then, in the wake of the Goldwater debacle in 1964, history repeated itself. Only this time around, these by-now middle-aged Turks were looking for a candidate to challenge Halleck. Mel urged me to run, and thanks in no small part to his efforts, I won that election by the landslide margin of 73 to 67.

Mel became the Republican conference chairman. For the next four years, we worked in tandem on legislative programs that helped revitalize the Republican Party and elect Dick Nixon president in 1968.

To Mel, politics is the "art and science of government." More than almost anyone I've known, Mel has the political equivalent of perfect pitch; he has a long-range view of what's going to happen, and he knows what to do about it. He's a prodigious worker. He was abrasive at times, and enjoyed scheming—not for any sinister reason but to keep the pot boiling. He is an idea man; he pushed hard, and I responded to that kind of challenge. Ours was a good combination: we respected one another and confided in one another. We were the closest of friends; we played together, and often prayed together. I never made a serious move in the House or the White House without consulting this friend and partner.

I well remember a day in December of 1968 when we found ourselves in Palm Springs, California, attending a Republican governors' conference. It was there I learned that Nixon intended to appoint Mel as his secretary of defense. I felt sadness for my friend and myself. It would be a grisly job for him, coming at a terrible time of trauma in American history. And I didn't look forward to the House without him. But knowing of his impressive military record in the Navy in World War II and his subsequent service with me on the Defense Appropriations Subcommittee, I believed that Mel would be of enormous help to President Nixon and get us out of the morass of Vietnam honorably. In my judgment, Nixon was very, very lucky to have Mel working with him and Henry Kissinger to extricate us from Vietnam.

With due credit to Henry for the Paris Accords, it was Mel who really brought our troops home. He unilaterally began withdrawing them faster than Nixon and Henry wanted to, but slower than Mel wanted to. There was not a single month while he was secretary of defense that the number of American troops in Vietnam increased. Mel was lampooned by editorial cartoonists as a "missile head," while too many missed the fact that he was adroitly doing the heavy lifting in the Nixon administration on all things military. He deftly negotiated the crosscurrents of the views of the uniformed military leadership, the White House, the Congress, and the American public. To keep American defense strong in the face of the Soviet military threat while ending the draft and conducting myriad other initiatives was no small feat.

At a time when our returning soldiers were being spat upon by their fellow Americans, and some on Capitol Hill seemed to have lost their common sense, Mel stood strong for the defense of America and never lost one vote in Congress. At a time when obsessive secrecy in the Nixon administration was actively undermining the good it would do, Mel was the most open, candid, and fearless of the cabinet officers. At a time when it was not easy to hold onto one's integrity and honor and pride, Mel was able to do that not only for himself but all who served with him. Few public servants were so tested by events as Mel Laird in those days of tumult and challenge, and fewer still came out unblemished.

Mel announced during his confirmation hearings that he would serve only one term as secretary of defense; the taxi to take him home was already ordered. But by then he was Washington's Indispensable Man, and Nixon immediately drafted him as Presidential Counselor for Domestic Affairs when the unraveling Watergate scandal forced the resignation of John Ehrlichman and H. R. Haldeman. During his year at the White House, as Mel kept the necessary budget-making gears of government working, he once again stood out as a model of personal and political integrity.

The October 1973 resignation of Vice President Agnew touched off speculation over who Nixon might choose to replace him, and it was Mel behind the scenes who maneuvered Nixon to choose me. Two days after Agnew's departure, my wife, Betty, and I were at home in Alexandria, Virginia, having a quiet family dinner, when the telephone rang. It was Mel. He told me that the Democrat-controlled House and Senate were very unlikely to confirm Nelson Rockefeller, Ronald Reagan, or Nixon's favorite choice, John Connally, for the job. He asked whether I would be interested. My ambition was to be Speaker of the House, not vice president, but that evening, Betty and I agreed those three and a half years as vice president would be a nice way to end my political career in the nation's capital. I assumed that would be history's footnote for me.

But history doesn't stop for anyone—not for Mel, and not for me. I became president and Mel a key member of my unofficial "Kitchen Cabinet." He has been quietly but forcefully advising every president and secretary of defense since. He exemplifies a magical blend of principle and pragmatism that is sorely needed in our country today. In fact, it is what Americans want. Most Americans are pragmatists. We want to make things work. We value authenticity at least as much as ideology. As far as Mel and I are concerned, there are no enemies in politics—just adversaries who disagree with you on one vote and might be with you on the next. We've always thought that you had to listen before you could lead, and it's hard to listen if you're screaming at one another. It's even harder to hear the voice of those who sent you to Washington in the first place.

Political partisanship offends most Americans because the partisans have forgotten that ours is a representative democracy. To many voters—and even more nonvoters—parties today are suspected of being decidedly unrepresentative. At worst, they appear as little more than conduits for special interest money. Our parties will never regain confidence of the voters until they look beyond the consultants and the tracking polls. At the end of the day, no leader worth his salt will take comfort in the polls he conducted or the tactical victories he may have racked up. Anyone can take a poll; only a leader can move a nation. All his life, Mel has been that kind of leader.

In the words of the *Reader's Digest*—the magazine Mel has served for more than three decades now—I count Mel Laird among the "most unforgettable characters" anyone could ever have the privilege of meeting. He remains today what he has always been: a model public servant; a can-do conservative who went into politics because he liked people; a man who reflects honor upon Washington and the people who sent him there; a patriot before a partisan. This thoroughly researched biography by Dale Van Atta bringing to life the lessons of Mel's life and service couldn't come at a better time. The reader who peruses these pages of history will soon come to understand how those of us who have known him are so much better for it, as is this country.

GERALD R. FORD JR.
December 2006

ACKNOWLEDGMENTS

Mel Laird never intended to write a book about his life, and it took me three long years to talk him into letting me write an authorized biography. My first approach to Laird was in early 1994. We crossed paths at the *Reader's Digest* Washington, D.C., office where he was (and is) the senior counselor for international affairs, and I was (and am) a contributing editor. In several conversations with Bill Schulz, the *Digest* Washington bureau chief, I became intrigued with his accounts of how former Secretary of Defense Laird had survived, honor intact, from the Nixon administration. As I looked deeper, it became clear to me that Laird was largely responsible for ending U.S. involvement in the Vietnam War.

My two other chief mentors at the time were also surprisingly high on Laird. One was Dick Brown, a longtime friend and top official with the General Accounting Office. He could not say enough good things about Laird, whom he had come to know through his boss, GAO Comptroller General Chuck Bowsher, who had worked under Laird at the Pentagon. And there was Jack Anderson, my partner on a nationally syndicated column. Jack had won a Pulitzer Prize uncovering the duplicity of Richard Nixon and Henry Kissinger over the Indo-Pakistan war, and he was at the top of Nixon's enemies list. When I mentioned I was thinking about a Laird biography, Jack slapped my back and said, "Do it!" He told me Laird was one of the most honest, effective, and yet unheralded politicians the country has seen in the last century.

Sy Hersh, the well-prized *New York Times* reporter and author of the Kissinger biography *The Price of Power,* vouched for Laird's integrity. David Broder of the *Washington Post* and CBS's Bob Schieffer were equally effusive.

Both said Laird's contribution to American history had been too long overlooked. Dozens of others of all political stripes, from Hillary Rodham Clinton to Dick Cheney to Colin Powell, said the same.

Finally, in 1997, when Mel turned seventy-five, Bill Schulz and I finally persuaded him it was time. It took another two years to secure enough funding to begin the project on solid ground. That came from Laird's beloved Marshfield Clinic, whose nonprofit Heritage Foundation generously agreed to back the project. Once Laird was in, he was all in. His memory was extraordinary, as was his attention to detail. He had a long list of people to interview, and a huge cache of material about the Nixon administration that had never before been made public. The fact that it took so many years to finish the book had as much to do with Laird's insistence on fairness and perfection as with my personal commitment to tell his whole story well and accurately.

When a book project lasts more than a decade, the list of those who should be thanked is voluminous. At the top of the list are five individuals who were with this project from the beginning and without whom it would have been impossible: Mel Laird; Robert Froehlke, who is Laird's oldest and closest friend and served him as secretary of the Army; Robert Pursley, Laird's military assistant at the Pentagon; Daryl Gibson, my friend and colleague for thirty-five years and a freelance book editor; and Kathy Weaver, Laird's executive assistant.

Reed Hall, executive director of the Marshfield Clinic, has been a champion of this work in recent years. His loyalty to Laird has been both touching and tenacious as numerous obstacles to the book's final publication arose. The Laird family was also gracious and unswervingly helpful, beginning with his wife, Carole Howard Laird. His three children—John, Alison, and David—and his stepdaughter, Kimberly, were also cheerfully helpful and encouraging. He is justifiably proud of all of them.

More than three hundred people were interviewed for this book, and I am grateful for all their contributions. Former presidents Gerald Ford, George H. W. Bush, Jimmy Carter, Ronald Reagan, and Bill Clinton all offered their insights on Laird, as did Dick Cheney. Also granting interviews out of respect for Laird were ten former secretaries of defense—Robert S. McNamara (1961–68), Clark M. Clifford (1968–69), Elliot L. Richardson (1973), James R. Schlesinger (1973–75), Donald H. Rumsfeld (1975–77, 2001–6), Harold Brown (1977–81), Caspar Weinberger (1981–87), Dick Cheney (1989–93), William J. Perry (1994–97), and William S. Cohen

(1997–2001). Many of the military leaders of those various eras, including the Joint Chiefs of Staff, also contributed.

Among the other hundreds interviewed, those who went above and beyond in their assistance included but are not limited to (alphabetically): Senator John Chafee, who granted an interview two days before he unexpectedly died; former Secretary of State Larry Eagleburger, a fellow Wisconsinite and loyal friend; Jerry Friedheim, whose anecdotes and "lists" of things the book should cover were superb; Laurie Hawley, Laird's congressional and Defense Department executive assistant, who thankfully preserved all the appointment books; Henry Kissinger, who gave time even though he knew some of the book's themes would be critical of him; Jack Mills, raconteur and Laird buddy; former Japanese Prime Minister Yasuhiro Nakasone; former West German Chancellor Helmut Schmidt; Donna Shalala, former Clinton Health and Human Services secretary; and Senator John Warner, one of Laird's favorite protégés and friends.

A debt is also owed to various historians, among them David Horrocks of the Gerald R. Ford Presidential Library and Dr. Alfred Goldberg and Stuart Rochester, historians for the office of the secretary of defense. There were also Barbara Constable, Dwight D. Eisenhower Presidential Library; Carol Hegeman, Eisenhower National Historic Site; as well as archivists at the John F. Kennedy Presidential Library, Lyndon Baines Johnson Presidential Library, Richard Nixon Library, and the Nixon Presidential Materials section of the National Archives. The folks at my local Loudoun County library in Ashburn, Virginia, were unstintingly helpful and understanding as I spent many months at the corner table that became my satellite office. The bibliography of this book includes many journalists and historians who are long-standing experts on Laird's period in world history, and whose work prepared me with countless words of background. Among the most notable are military historians Lewis Sorley and Bruce Palmer.

The folks at the University of Wisconsin Press—acquisitions editor Gwen Walker, interim director Sheila Leary, and managing editor Adam Mehring— were as helpful and insightful as they were tough and professional. The readers and I have been well served by them.

Finally, no author can work more than a decade without help from friends, a few of whom I acknowledge here: the aforementioned Dick Brown and his wife, Hazie, Mike Binstein, Lynn Chapman, Clark and Kathy Kidd, Ryan McIlvain (my unpaid "intern"), Shad and Tiffany McPheters, Phil and Joni Broderick, Warren and Anne Cordes, and Paul Smith.

The most miraculous thing about my wife, Lynne, is that I am still privileged to call her my wife at the end of this project, which had its shares of ups and downs. She unfailingly supported me with love and patience.

The final miracle of this book is the greatest tribute this world-weary and cynical investigative reporter can offer Mel Laird: after exhaustively reviewing his life, I respect and admire him more at the end of this process than when I began.

WITH

Honor

Prologue

THE LAST JOB CONGRESSMAN MELVIN LAIRD wanted in the fall of 1968 was that of secretary of defense. The Vietnam War was at its bloody apex, and public support for the war was at its nadir. Richard Nixon had just been elected president of the United States based on a rumored "secret plan" to end the war. But Laird knew his old friend Nixon had no such plan. The only plan was to scour the ranks of the unwilling and find someone to be secretary of defense, someone who would then figure out how to pull the United States from the Vietnam quagmire.

Laird had just been elected to his ninth term in Congress representing his beloved state of Wisconsin, and there was no place he would rather be than in the House of Representatives. Since the election, Nixon had leaned heavily on Laird to help him find a defense secretary, preferably a Democrat for the sake of interparty relations. Laird proposed Senator Henry "Scoop" Jackson of Washington. He was a hawkish advocate of strong military power as well as conservative about national security. Jackson was willing to consider the job, but when he went to a Democratic retreat in Hawaii and told some of his friends about it, Senator Edward Kennedy tore into him. Kennedy and the others wanted a free hand to thrash the Republican prosecution of the war. Having one of their own heading the Pentagon was unthinkable. And, they told him, do this and it will be the political kiss of death: you'll never be president yourself.

Jackson phoned Nixon from Hawaii with his regrets. It was December, and the press was clamoring for Nixon's cabinet slate. He turned his wrath on Laird over the Jackson debacle and ordered Laird to come to the annual meeting of the Republican Governors Association at Palm Springs, California,

3

where the two of them would work on the problem. "You got me into this mess. You're going to damn well *fix it!*" Nixon told Laird.[1]

Following Nixon off the plane in Palm Springs, Laird knew he was firmly planted in the proverbial hot seat, and it had nothing to do with the desert heat. If Laird couldn't find another option, Nixon would force the job on him. At a cocktail party before dinner that night, Laird was not himself. He tried to stay out of sight, since he had told Wisconsin reporters he would be in his hometown of Marshfield all week. One of them spotted Laird and asked him to step outside the hotel suite for a word. After Laird joked about the ill-fitting dinner jacket he had rented, since he hadn't had time to pack, the reporter asked him how Nixon's cabinet was shaping up. "I can't talk to you," Laird replied with uncharacteristic discomfort. "I'm sorry, I've talked too much already."[2]

Saturday, December 7, was one Pearl Harbor Day anniversary Laird would never forget. He decided golf would clear his head; as he played, he formed a strategy to parry Nixon's unwelcome plans for him. Laird would come up with a precondition to acceptance that was plausible yet so odious that Nixon would never accept it. Halfway through the eighteen holes, Laird's game was interrupted by a call from the House Republican leader, Jerry Ford, a close friend. Ford reported that he had just come from lunch with Nixon, who was talking about naming Laird as defense secretary.

Laird was in the greatest quandary of his life as he boarded Nixon's jet for the return trip to D.C. Ford was on the plane, as was veteran political operative Bryce Harlow, whom Nixon had named as his legislative affairs liaison. Harlow had joined Laird in lobbying for Jackson for defense secretary, and Nixon's opening blast was directed at both advisors. "You sons of bitches!" Nixon sputtered. "You talked me into this thing with Scoop and now he's backed out." Then he turned on Laird. "There's only one way to fix this—I'm going to announce YOU for defense secretary!"

"The hell you are!" Laird countered. "I'm not going to leave Congress." During an extended debate on the cross-country flight, Laird outlined reasons why it would be better for the new administration if he remained in Congress. Nixon's response is summed up in a letter he later wrote to Laird: "I made the hard sell—even though a friend was involved. I know this was a terribly difficult decision for you to make, but you were the indispensable man—the right man for the right place, at the right time."[3]

Less than an hour away from Andrews Air Force Base, Laird, mellowed by a Manhattan or two, appeared to give in, but it was only an illusion. He had waited to reveal his trump card, the one condition to which Nixon would never agree. "Well now, I'll tell you," Laird wound up, "if you give me a firm, positive commitment that no one in your administration, or you, will ever interfere with any appointment, military or civilian, that is made in the Department of Defense while I serve as secretary, I might consider doing it."

Laird was confident in his belief that no president would surrender that power to a cabinet secretary. He was so sure of himself that he promised conclusively: "If you give me that kind of commitment, you can count on my doing it."

Nixon thought for a moment, and then replied, "Mel, you have my word on it."

Laird had been outfoxed. In a last grasp for clemency, Laird asked Nixon to put it in writing on a cocktail napkin. Nixon did, and signed the napkin.

If a genie had given the new defense secretary three wishes, complete control of his appointments would still have been first, second, and third on the list. The Defense Department had almost five million employees and was the nation's largest employer. Its annual budget was $80 billion, more than the total government expenditures of every nation in the world except the Soviet Union. At the top of this center of power were more than one thousand prized political appointments. Those coveted spots were traditionally saved to repay presidential political debts, reward friends, and install a cadre loyal to the president. Laird knew Nixon well, and he was beginning to get an inkling of the kind of manipulative staffers the new president would employ as his palace guard. If Laird was going to run the Defense Department his way, he needed to be surrounded by his own cadre.[4]

The two most important people in Laird's life, his mother, Helen, and his wife, Barbara, could not believe what he had agreed to do. Helen, a savvy political strategist in her own right, was opposed to the Vietnam War and didn't want her son tar-brushed by it. Barbara avoided the limelight for herself and their three children. Her response to the news was to take her phone off the hook. She harbored a prescient distrust of Nixon and, like Caesar's wife, cautioned Laird about getting too close.

Laird was not a complex man. He knew that the defense post at the height of the war could spell the end of his political career, but he was also confident that he could end the draft and the war, even if Nixon proved reluctant to do either. Laird's sense of honor and duty to country drove him to finally accept the onerous position. "My decision to accept the post . . . was the most difficult decision of my political life," he said in his first official statement. "I did not seek the post of secretary of defense. I did everything I could to promote other individuals for that office, [but when] the final decision had to be made, I could not tell the president-elect of the United States that I would not serve my country in this most important post."[5]

It was also destiny by default, Laird said later. "Nixon couldn't find anybody else who wanted the damn job."

1

The Man from Marshfield

It was the first bright and sunny day after two weeks of dark squalls and heaving seas, but the crew of the USS Maddox *didn't see the kamikaze until it was too late.*

The 2,200-ton American destroyer was part of Admiral "Bull" Halsey's Third Fleet in early 1945. Her complement of 359 men was exhausted. Along with the other ships of Task Force 38, the Maddox *had just completed a daring eleven-day, 3,800-mile mission in the South China Sea, running a gauntlet through Japanese-occupied positions.*

Now, the Maddox *had taken up a new position, within sight of the Japanese-held island of Formosa. This time it was thirty-five miles from the center of the task force, assigned to rescue pilots who had splashed down, and direct airborne pilots back to their home ships. The returning planes were supposed to circle the* Maddox *for inspection before being allowed to pass. Wily Japanese airmen had learned that American planes had blind spots below and behind them, so the Zeros had been slipping undetected into American aircraft formations and tagging along, back to the most valuable Navy target of the war—the aircraft carriers.*

Sunday afternoon, January 21, the supply officer nicknamed "Pay" sat down for a sandwich at his usual place in the wardroom, a few feet from the starboard bulkhead. Over the ship, the first three of a dozen returning Hellcats (F6Fs) circled for inspection; suddenly the middle plane dropped out of formation. Too late, several men on deck realized it was not a Hellcat but a deadly black Japanese Zero, which was now diving steeply toward the Maddox, *guns blazing. The kamikaze leveled off just aft of the radio antennae and crashed through the top deck of the ship, releasing a 132-kilogram bomb that exploded behind the wardroom's starboard bulkhead. "Pay"—Ens. Melvin Laird—was closest to the blast, taking the brunt of the shrapnel that pierced the air of the wardroom.*

The ship's doctor, Malcolm Burris, rushed to the wardroom. He saw blood on the hatch before he stepped into the conflagration. The scene was eerily quiet; not one of the wounded officers was screaming or crying. After a quick once-over of all the wounded, Doc Burris was relieved that none had been hit by shrapnel in the head or the chest. Laird had been particularly lucky; the steel back of his chair had shielded him. He had been hit in dozens of places along his left side, down his thigh and leg, and in his lower back and buttocks. The Maddox had suffered eight dead and thirty-two wounded. It took two hours to ferry the wounded in stretcher baskets by a line strung from the Maddox to the battleship Wisconsin. The following morning the Maddox buried her dead at sea, each wrapped in a mattress cover and weighted with five-inch projectiles.

The doctors on the Wisconsin, named after Laird's home state, carved thirty-eight pieces of shrapnel out of his body, but they couldn't reach them all. More than a dozen pieces would work their way out through his skin over the next six decades—while he served in Congress, while he became a friend and confidante to heads of state, while he guided the military as secretary of defense, while he brought an end to the most unpopular war in American history.[1]

~

At the age of ten Mel Laird decided what he wanted to be most of all was a U.S. Navy officer. Or, at least, wear the uniform. The dream was born on a sunny morning in 1932, when he rounded a corner in downtown Marshfield, Wisconsin, and came face to face with the first U.S. Navy officer he had ever seen. Cdr. John McCain Sr., in brilliant dress whites with gold trimmings, was visiting an uncle who owned a dry goods store in Marshfield. The boy trailed the man for most of the day, pestering him with questions about the Navy and basking in the reflected glow of that bright white uniform twinkling with brass buttons.

A few years later, during World War II, the boy and the man would share a beer in the South Pacific, where Admiral McCain Sr. was the commanding officer of a naval task force and Laird a lowly ensign in that command. More than three decades later, McCain's son, Adm. John S. McCain Jr., would be commander of the Pacific Fleet during the Vietnam War, reporting to Secretary of Defense Laird. They would work together to free Navy Cdr. John S. McCain III from a prisoner-of-war camp—not guessing then that the third John McCain would become a U.S. senator and presidential candidate.[2]

The encounter between the ten-year-old boy and the Navy officer was the stuff of Laird's Norman Rockwellian childhood. His maternal grandfather

William Duncan "W. D." Connor had come to the Wisconsin frontier from Canada at the age of eight. As an adult, William took over the family's banking, farming, and retail empire, which had grown to include a significant share of the state's hardwood forests. In 1895 W. D. moved his home and headquarters to a fast-growing city that impressed him, Marshfield. He served on the city council, the Wood County Board, as state Republican party chairman, and finally as lieutenant governor.

W. D.'s daughter Helen married a young Presbyterian minister named Melvin Robert Laird. Two sons—William Connor and Richard, known as Connor and Dick—were born while Melvin Sr. was a minister and Presbyterian college president in Lincoln, Illinois. World War I interrupted Rev. Laird's career, and he enlisted in the Army as a chaplain, serving in France. After the war, Rev. Laird moved his family to another pastorate, this time the Westminster Presbyterian Church in Omaha, Nebraska, where his third son and namesake, Melvin Robert Laird Jr., was born on September 1, 1922.[3]

After four years of raising three boys and tending to the duties of a minister's wife, far from her Connor family home, Helen was drained, physically and emotionally. Rev. Laird set aside his career to take his wife home to Marshfield for recuperation. There was no full-time ministerial assignment there, so he accepted his father-in-law's offer to become secretary-treasurer of Connor Lumber Company. W. D. bought them a house at 208 South Cherry Street, right across from his own. If it was a bitter pill for Rev. Laird to swallow, he never voiced it. It certainly changed young Mel Jr.'s life for the better. All the values and interests he later demonstrated in life were culled from that town and its people.

Home was safe, solid with oak hardwood floors on two levels, French doors opening out to the porch. Most meals were eaten at home, and Sunday night supper was served on a tea cart near a fireplace in the living room, where the family laughed and talked into the night. And there was a baby brother, David, to fuss over—the fourth and last child.

Melvin Sr. would hold court every morning at the Coffee Cup Restaurant, planning important town affairs or arguing Greek mythology with Greek immigrants. Like his father-in-law, he was elected to the Wood County Board, serving for a dozen years, the last two as chairman. And nearly every Sunday, there were requests from towns to fill in for their absent Presbyterian pastors. But no matter how busy he was, he always made time to be home each day at noon to have lunch with Mel.

In those days, family and close friends called Laird Jr. by a nickname that stuck—"Bom." (His lifelong friends had to be discreet about the nickname when Laird became secretary of defense.) His aunt Marion Connor was an opera singer who went to Italy for training. In one letter home she asked, "How is our little bambino doing?" The family took to calling Mel "bambino" and then shortened it to "Bom." In kindergarten he met his best friend and lifelong confidant, Robert Froehlke, who would later serve with him in the Pentagon. Bom's second grade teacher gave him an "F" in conduct, and his sixth grade teacher cracked him with a rubber hose to instill obedience.

When Bom was young, there were as many horses as cars in Marshfield. But that began to change after the first concrete road came through town and became part of the "Yellowstone Trail," a tourist route to the national park. Bom's fascination with autos and the folks who drove them came to cost him dearly. When he was eight, a car ran over his left knee, breaking his kneecap. He confessed that he hadn't seen the car because he and a young girlfriend were busy stealing fresh peas off a passing wagon. The accident prevented him from excelling at sports, although he regularly competed.

Laird's family was part of the town's elite, but they didn't display their wealth. If Bom wanted spending money he had to earn it himself. He started at about age six selling can openers door-to-door with his brother Connor and then went into business for himself. For several years in grade school he was a middleman for farmers, selling corn, potatoes, and tomatoes to a list of regulars.

As Laird grew into his teenage years, he became aware of ethnic, racial, and religious divisions in his hometown. Marshfield had been built and financed by Protestant Yankee settlers, and the labor had come mostly from German and Austrian immigrants, who were Catholic or Lutheran. The Presbyterians and the Episcopalians were at the top of the pecking order; the Methodists, Baptists, and Lutherans floated around the middle; and the Catholics were toward the bottom of the economic scale. It was as much a rich-versus-poor as it was a religious debate, and it simmered for decades, occasionally breaking out in "gang wars," as Marshfield *News-Herald* accounts called them.

The many issues of the day—from union organizing to a Ku Klux Klan rally in Marshfield—were fodder for active discussion and debate at the Laird home. In the late 1930s the family helped German Jewish refugees, Dr. Stephan Epstein and his wife, Elsbeth, learn English by reading with them night after night, occasionally stopping to hear Epstein's account of the growing threat of Adolf Hitler. Epstein took a special interest in Bom and greatly influenced his future course.

All the Lairds were voracious readers. Mel's mother, Helen, had learned in her father's house and at the university to value intelligent opinions well expressed. "Knowledge Is Power" was one of W. D.'s favorite maxims, and his $2,500 gift made possible the Marshfield Public Library. Helen followed in his interests, becoming president of the city library board. She invited educators and religious and political leaders to Sunday teas, hosting the meek and the mighty, from a second grade teacher to presidential candidate Wendell Willkie.

But in those early years, Bom most valued discussions with his father. No subject was forbidden, not even questioning Rev. Laird's core belief in God. "You make up your own mind on that, Bom," Melvin Sr. would say. "I think it's fine for you to question. Always question. You've got to come to your own conclusions on this thing, but here's what I believe."

The first time Bom drank beer, at a tavern called Strikey's when he was about sixteen, guilt took him to his teetotaling father's confessional the next day. His father said the decision whether to drink or abstain was up to Bom, but he would prefer that his son didn't imbibe. Bom was careful after that to drink only in moderation.

At Marshfield Senior High School Bom was a leader on the winning debate team and editor of the yearbook, but he never let school stand in the way of making a living. He was at his entrepreneurial peak during his senior year. He had many enterprises, one of them as the booking agent for "Earl Ostrander and His Musical Mutineers—That Ten Piece Band from the Dairyland," getting them prom gigs in surrounding towns. In another venture, he talked several classmates into signing a thirty-day note for a $100 loan from a bank to put on a dance. The dance did well, but he had to do some quick borrowing elsewhere when the bank's cashier breathlessly pulled him out of class, insisting on payment two weeks ahead of time because a bank examiner on their premises was not likely to favor loans to a teenager.

The coup de grace for foresight occurred at the state basketball championships. Marshfield had a dream team of sorts in Bom's senior year. They lacked height and experience, but they pulled off a Cinderella story. The team went all the way to the state championships, where they lost in the final showdown by only one point. Somehow, Laird foresaw the team's success early, and booked a room at a Madison hotel with two twin beds. As the Marshfield team got nearer to the regional finals, desperate local fans couldn't find a room in Madison for any price. So Laird and his buddy Jack McDonald slept for free in the beds while five classmates slept on the floor and paid the hotel bill.

Laird graduated an unimpressive thirtieth out of a class of 165. The graduation speaker was his father, who gave a rousing address on "Eternal Verities"—faith, hope, and charity. Reverend Laird's optimism worked its magic on his son. Despite ominous war clouds over Europe that spring of 1940, he left the graduation ceremony convinced he could make his own way in the world.

⌇

A coin toss brought Laird to Carleton College, in Northfield, Minnesota, in the fall of 1940. The previous June he and friend Bill Copps had locked themselves in a room with six bottles of Coke, a can of popcorn, and five college catalogues. After two hours of debating the pros and cons, and coming to no clear decision, the boys flipped a coin. Copps went to the University of Wisconsin and Laird went to Carleton.[4] The four-year liberal arts college is in a small town best known for stopping the Jesse James gang with a hail of gunfire after they robbed a local bank.

Laird came to Carleton without a plan. His career preferences were teacher, engineer, minister, or journalist, but a Carleton professor, Larry Gould, turned him to science. As a boy he had dreamed, with the alchemists, that he could change carbon to gold. In a college essay he wrote, "Who knows? Maybe I will." College classes never received Laird's full attention, however. He ran a laundry service for students—not doing the dirty work himself but franchising it out to other students and taking 20 percent off the top. He also jumped quickly into a new "Co-operative Social" program at Carleton, which provided entertainment and dances for members. Mel's favorite duty for the co-op was traveling to Chicago to book bands through the William Morris Agency, including the famous Cab Calloway band. He also dabbled in politics and was elected president of the freshman class. At the first freshman mixer, he met a bright, pretty girl from Indianapolis, Barbara Masters. They hit it off immediately and dated no one else during their freshman year.[5]

On December 7, 1941, in the first semester of Laird's sophomore year, the Japanese attacked Pearl Harbor, and every young man had a choice to make. Laird was anxious to join the Navy immediately, but a college dean persuaded him to wait several months. During that time, it was hard to concentrate on his studies, so he decided to join the Carleton equivalent of a fraternity, the Phillo Society. Initiation was a scavenger hunt, sending Laird and fellow pledges scurrying around Northfield and beyond for items on a list. One of them was a standing ashtray from the Nicolett Hotel, where the pledges were spotted by the police, nabbed, and taken to the local precinct for questioning. The fraternity was soon disbanded. No record was kept by police of the theft, but the college dean, Lindsey Blayney, gave an account of it, at Laird's insistence, to the U.S. Navy Recruiting Office in early spring 1943 when Laird was ready to enlist. He was called into the Naval Reserves office for a physical and, though he had been honest about his scrape with the law, he fudged the truth about other things that could have disqualified him—his bad knee and a weak right eye. He managed to hide the knee problem, but dissembling about his eyesight required a clever deception.

"Put your hand up to your right eye, and read the chart," the optometrist commanded. Laird put his left hand up to his right eye, and read it flawlessly.

"Alright, let's try the other eye."

Laird dropped his left hand, and put his right hand over the same eye. And he read it perfectly again. The sleight of hand was good enough to win him admission into the U.S. Naval Reserves Officers Training Program.[6]

By December 1942, the terrible machinery of war had chewed up boys who were close to Laird. His brother Connor had learned of the Pearl Harbor attack when he was in Chicago with his friend, Walter Kohler, a future three-term governor of Wisconsin and the son of the bathroom fixture company's founder. The pair went to the Navy recruiting office on the morning of December 8 and joined up. By early 1943, Ens. Connor Laird was one of twenty-nine men assigned to a minesweeper, *YMS-133*, operating out of Coos Bay, Oregon. *YMS-133* was one of dozens of such minesweepers assigned to the Pacific Ocean, from the California coast to the western Pacific. Almost as dangerous as the mines was a hidden sand bar in the bay, formed where the Coos River empties into the ocean. On February 20, 1943, in turbulent weather and high seas, the inexperienced skipper of the *YMS-133* tried to turn the ship around and, in the process, put it broadside to the swells. A twenty-five-foot wave washed over it and rolled the ship twice, filling it with water and sand. Eight men died, including the skipper and Ensign Laird.[7]

With the news of his brother's death, Mel Laird put off marriage to Barbara and pushed the Navy to give him orders for active duty. In August 1943 he reported to St. Mary's College in Winona, Minnesota, for the Navy's V-12 training courses. In December Laird was transferred to Harvard for final, specialized classes in supply, disbursement, and paymaster practices.[8] But Harvard ran out of room, so Laird and more than two hundred other midshipmen were assigned to two dormitories and Supply Corps classes at the all-female Wellesley College. (Thus Laird became one of the few *men* in America then who could say he attended Wellesley.) Laird was appointed morale officer—the easiest job he would ever have in the Navy, given that there were more than two thousand women at the school.

Carleton College accepted his credits from St. Mary's and Wellesley, and he earned his diploma. Before he was to report to a new destroyer being built in Bath, Maine, Laird was given a short leave. He met Barbara in Marshfield and he proposed, using a ring his mother had given him from her grand-mother. Barbara accepted. Laird was willing to be *engaged* but not to risk marriage yet in case he did not return.

～

To inlander Melvin Laird the USS *Maddox* was impressive at first sight. The latest of the new Sumner-class 2,200-ton destroyers, she had been built at the Bath Iron Works in less than six months. Her captain, James S. Willis, was a quiet man not given to levity. He had under him a crew of 338 with twenty officers.[9] Ensign Laird was designated the ship's Supply and Disburs-ing Officer. He was quietly reflective that Sunday, August 27, 1944, when the *Maddox* sailed past the Boston light for the last time on the way to the war zone. Many of the sailors cheered. They had been grousing ever since the Nor-mandy invasion in June that it was taking too long to get into the war. With all the patriotic naïveté of the uninitiated, the men were anxious to be off to war before it was over. The veterans knew better, and so did Laird. Having already lost a brother, he was anxious to do his duty but would have no com-plaints about "missing the war" if peace were declared before he got there.

The *Maddox* stopped at Norfolk, Virginia, to join two other destroyers to escort a new aircraft carrier, the USS *Ticonderoga*, to the Pacific theater. The crew settled down to the serious task ahead of them. They crossed through the Panama Canal and, on September 24, entered Pearl Harbor and passed the remains of the USS *Arizona*, a sobering reminder of the Japanese attack three years earlier.[10] On October 6, as the *Maddox* sailed from Pearl Har-bor, the men did not suspect it would be a full year before they would return. And not all of them would come back.

～

The first stop was Ulithi, an atoll in the far western Pacific and the anchorage for the largest naval armada ever assembled. In late summer, the Third Fleet commander, Adm. William "Bull" Halsey, had selected the atoll as the ideal strategic naval base for the invasion of the Philippines and the final push against Japan's home islands. Ulithi's deep lagoon could accommodate more than seven hundred naval vessels. The *Maddox* was assigned to Task Force 38, the Third Fleet's renowned "fast carrier task force." Halsey named an old sea dog to head the task force, the irascible Vice Adm. John "Slew" McCain, now sixty years old, and the same man who had left such an indelible im-pression on Laird when he was a youngster. (During beers shared at Ulithi, McCain provided details from his own memory to several members of the *Maddox* crew of the pesky boy who shadowed him that day.)

As the American fleet pushed its way across the Pacific, island by island, battle by battle, its victory seemed inevitable—except to the Japanese. The national Shinto religion implied that Japan was fated to rule the world. They believed that Emperor Hirohito was the "Son of Heaven," and the forces of nature themselves would be harnessed, if necessary, to defeat the invading infidels. After all, it had happened before. In 1281, a large Mongol fleet sent by the great Kublai Khan was bearing down on a far smaller Japanese naval force. Another barbaric victory for the Mongols seemed unavoidable. At a propitious moment, heaven intervened and sent the legendary *Kamikaze*— "Divine Wind"—against the Mongols. This monstrous typhoon destroyed the Khan's fleet. Later, when Japan's suicide air corps pilots needed a name, they became the modern kamikazes, a new Divine Wind that would save the empire from the largest fleet assembled in the history of mankind.

By mid-December 1944, Admiral Halsey had been fully apprized of the destructive force the kamikaze pilots could cause. He made alterations to his battle strategy and armament to meet the threat. But Halsey failed to adequately prepare for nature's original kamikaze—a monster typhoon. For Melvin Laird and the *Maddox*, the ordeal began four days earlier with a series of pilot rescue attempts that had depleted the ship's fuel supply. Escorting a carrier task force was a fuel-intensive business, so on December 16 Admiral Halsey instructed all 132 vessels of Task Force 38 to meet at a rearward replenishment rendezvous the following morning. He was unaware that a furious storm was blanketing an area of eight thousand square miles and headed for the same rendezvous point.[11]

At 5 a.m. on Sunday, December 17, the storm conditions in the Philippine Sea reached the right pitch to become the full-fledged Typhoon Cobra. Five hours later, the first of the Task Force's ships began arriving at the refueling point through heavy seas and rain. The thirsty *Maddox* pulled alongside the battleship *Wisconsin* but was hampered by the storm and zero visibility from getting hoses from one ship to the other.

In the afternoon, Vice Admiral McCain relayed Halsey's orders to discontinue fueling and head for a calmer fueling rendezvous the next morning. The *Maddox* was one of only three ships ordered to stay put and continue trying to refuel. McCain recognized the desperate need of these three destroyers to fuel immediately. The *Maddox* maneuvered alongside the tanker *Manatee*, and for an hour Ensign Laird on the bridge watched as the fueling crew on the heaving deck managed to get three hoses over from the tanker. All of the hoses snapped; a fourth hose was manhandled into the fuel tanks, and the *Maddox* was able to fuel for seven minutes. Then, according to the ship's diary, a huge wave surged between the ships, causing the *Maddox* to veer sharply to port, ripping the hose beyond its limit. A second wave tossed the two ships so close that the sailors could almost reach out and touch the tanker. One man with an axe hastily chopped the tow line to separate the ships. With no more hoses, the *Maddox* and the *Manatee* parted company.

At 3 p.m. on Sunday, Halsey ordered the task force to still another rendezvous point, putting it on a course parallel to the typhoon's track. Then before midnight Halsey canceled the fueling rendezvous coordinates and set a new one for the next morning, farther to the northwest. Captain Willis on the *Maddox* felt instinctively that it was the wrong course, but he was under orders.[12] Few on the *Maddox* could sleep that night. When the ship made headway, it would impale itself on each wave, forcing the twin screws out of the water, where they would spin and shake the ship with tremendous force. Pipe handholds on the bridge gave Ensign Laird something to hang on to as his feet swung out from under him with each roll and the *Maddox* leaned on its side. Down below, he crouched between walls or clung to pipes during the rolls. In sick bay, Doc Burris used a how-to manual to perform his first emergency appendectomy on a sailor. With the help of two pharmacists mates holding the small intestine during the rolls, the procedure, which should have taken thirty minutes, went on for several hours.[13]

By dawn on Monday, December 18, the waves were thought to be reaching heights of eighty feet. At 7:10 a.m., Task Force 38 was ordered to change course a sixth time.[14] By 8 a.m., the *Maddox* was at the center of the typhoon. The fleet was ordered to make the seventh course change, each of which had taxed the fuel of the small ships. A light aircraft carrier, the *Monterey*, was in serious distress. Airplanes tied down on her hangar deck had broken loose, slammed against each other, and exploded into flames. Two men were washed overboard and were lost. A third man, on his way to help put out the fire, was saved by a thin miracle—his slide overboard was stopped by a thin ridge on deck. It was a touch of destiny for which Laird was later grateful. He didn't yet know the lucky officer, Lt. Gerald R. Ford, but the two men would one day become close friends.

At 11:23 a.m., the destroyer *Spence* sank. Belatedly, Halsey directed the task force ships to scatter, with each captain allowed to take the safest course for his own ship. At noon, the destroyer *Monaghan* sank, followed to the bottom within seconds by the destroyer *Hull*. By 3 p.m. Monday, the peak of Typhoon Cobra had finally passed, but it took hours for the winds to abate. In all, 778 men were lost at sea. A naval Court of Inquiry was conducted on the fleet's Christmas return to Ulithi. The court concluded that Admiral Halsey was solely responsible for the loss of life and damage to the ships, but that his "errors in judgment [stemmed] from a commendable desire to meet military requirements."[15]

~

After its minimal typhoon damage was repaired, the *Maddox* was judged fit to sail out of Ulithi with Task Force 38. Late on the evening of January 9, the Third Fleet began an unprecedented foray into the South China Sea. More than one hundred warships, including the *Maddox,* made this daring raid. The mission was spectacularly successful for Halsey's fleet. They launched a series of deadly strikes against Camranh Bay, Saigon, Cape San Jacques, Hong Kong, and Formosa.[16]

After the kamikaze attack on January 21 when Laird was wounded, the *Maddox* was ordered to return to Ulithi in company with two light cruisers and two destroyers, all assigned to escort the damaged carrier *Ticonderoga.* By early February 1945 Laird had recovered from his more serious wounds and was released for duty aboard the *Maddox.* While the ship was at Ulithi, Captain Willis was promoted to Destroyer Division commander and the *Maddox* got a new commander, Capt. Selby Santmyers. The ship underwent repairs for seven weeks at Ulithi, missing the recapture of Manila and Corregidor, and the February 19 amphibious landing on an eight-square-mile volcanic island known as Iwo Jima. By mid-March, the fleet had a new commander, Adm. R. A. Spruance, and was renamed the Fifth Fleet. It had 617 ships in anchorage at Ulithi, readying to support the invasion of Okinawa.

After the eighty-eight-day battle for Okinawa was over—the bloodiest land conflict of the Pacific war—the *Maddox* rested in the Philippines and then set sail into Japanese waters for the final assault on Japan. The most memorable foray for the *Maddox* in those last weeks of the war was a high-speed run into Tokyo Bay in July 1945 in advance of the heavier fleet ships. With eight other destroyers, the *Maddox* slipped into the bay to scout the enemy fleet and ended up sinking two, possibly three, Japanese merchant ships carrying supplies to the enemy, and damaging their Japanese naval escort, all in less than fifteen minutes. It was the final surface engagement of the Pacific war.[17]

On August 6, the United States dropped the first atomic bomb on the southern Honshu city of Hiroshima. The official estimate of dead—before radiation effects were known—was eighty thousand. The second bomb, on August 9, decimated Nagasaki and, by official estimate, killed sixty thousand. Japanese army and navy chiefs implored Emperor Hirohito to continue with the war. He overruled them, probably because he was convinced, by the combination of firebombing and atomic bombs, that the Allies would, if necessary, kill every Japanese citizen to achieve "unconditional surrender."

V-J Day (Victory in Japan) was August 15, 1945. At 1 p.m. Admiral Halsey broadcast to the entire fleet that Japan had surrendered. A shout went up on the *Maddox* and was echoed in a wave from ship to ship. The *Maddox* continued in a protective screen position outside Tokyo Bay for two weeks. On August 30 they had the proud task of escorting nine American submarines into Tokyo Bay to witness the official surrender. As the peace papers were signed aboard the USS *Missouri* on September 2, the *Maddox* was assigned as a communications link ship, patrolling the entrance to Tokyo Bay.

At noon on September 20, the *Maddox* began sailing for home. The men knew they weren't the bravest to ship out to war, and maybe not the most skillful, but they were definitely among the luckiest. Now it was time to plan for the rest of their lives. One day, the junior officers were doing just that. "We were philosophizing about what we were going to do after we got out," remembered Ens. Dorsey Thomas.[18] Tony Kane said he was going back into law enforcement; Frank Feeney planned to go to college on the GI Bill; Tom Thorstensen was intent on earning his PhD; Zeke Monsell was going back to work as a manager for Atlantic Richfield Oil Company. It was Laird's turn now. Speaking plainly and directly, he said, "I'm going back to Wisconsin and be a politician."

The men were a little stunned, since they didn't hold the profession in particularly high regard. "Why that?" they choused.

"Because, goddamn it, I think I can do some good!"

⌇

Barbara had passed the war writing letters to her fiancé, earning a masters degree in education from Northwestern University, and becoming a teacher. She had frequently visited her future in-laws in Wisconsin, and they decided she was a good match for their son. Ten days after Laird landed in San Francisco, Barbara and Mel were married at the Fourth Presbyterian Church in Indianapolis on October 15, 1945. None of Laird's brothers could make the wedding, nor any of his Marshfield friends including Bob Froehlke, because many of them were still in the service. Melvin Laird Sr. stood with his son as best man. Laird still had a few months to serve in the Navy and he was assigned as disbursing officer in the family allowance division of the Navy's National Bureau of Supplies and Accounts, headquartered in Cleveland.

In early March 1946 Laird's parents went to the Mayo Clinic in Rochester, Minnesota, for their annual physicals. The doctors found colon cancer in sixty-eight-year-old Melvin Laird Sr. and recommended immediate surgery. Both parents decided not to alarm their children until they knew whether the surgery was successful. Eight days after what was deemed to be a "successful" operation, Laird senior died of a pulmonary embolism. Helen Laird's call to inform her three surviving sons of their father's death came as a bolt out of the blue. Lieutenant Laird rushed to Marshfield. His older brother Richard was in British Columbia and could not come home, so at the age of twenty-three, Melvin shouldered the family burden. Within hours after hearing of his father's death, Laird decided he would move to Marshfield immediately to take care of his mother. His request for a hardship discharge was granted.[19]

At the time of his death, Melvin Laird Sr. was a Wisconsin state senator and the only clergyman in the Senate. His colleagues respected him, and his name had been whispered for a possible run for governor.[20] At least one of Mel Laird's uncles and several friends urged him to run for his father's state senate seat and finish the two years left on his second term. Laird didn't dawdle over the decision. Once Barbara had agreed to marry him, he threw his hat into the ring less than two weeks after the funeral.

The real battle was the Republican primary in August 1946. Whoever won that was usually victorious in the November general election. Laird's opponent was a friend—an older, far more experienced state assemblyman, Walter Cook. But that didn't cow Laird. (Froehlke, who helped on the campaign, recalled how wily his friend could be. At the end of one speech in Neillsville campaigning for his father before the war, Laird had looked at his watch and said: "I'm very sorry that I can't stay. I would like to stay and greet all of you, but there's a vitally important meeting in Port Edwards that I must just rush off and attend this evening." As they left, presumably for the town on the opposite end of the district, Froehlke was puzzled: "Gee, Mel, I didn't know we're going to Port Edwards." "Just wait" was all Laird said, with a smile. After driving only a mile or so, Laird pulled the car off the road, turned off the lights and waited. Within minutes, the opponent barreled past them on the road, headed on a wild good chase to Port Edwards.[21])

Laird was not mustered out of the military until mid-May, so much of his campaigning was done in uniform, which his opponent unwisely criticized. Each time Cook brought up the subject of the uniform, Laird responded that, being fresh from the war, he hadn't had time to buy civilian clothes. It was a regular excuse for Laird to bring up his service record. Laird won the primary and general elections handily, giving credit to his father's good name more than his own efforts. At twenty-four, he became the youngest man ever to serve in the Wisconsin state senate.

~

There was another Wisconsin Republican primary race that year that captured national attention. The highly revered U.S. senator Robert La Follette

Jr., was being challenged by a brash former circuit court judge and Marine Corps officer, Joe McCarthy. The historical background that led to that critical primary is important in understanding Laird's political background and the unique Wisconsin brand of Republicanism. Many historians believe the Republican party was born in a little white schoolhouse in central Wisconsin, when fifty-four of the town of Ripon's one hundred registered voters gathered in March 1854 to fight slavery. Alvan Bovay, an ardent abolitionist, called the meeting to protest attempts by the Democratic majority in Washington, D.C., to spread slavery into the Kansas and Nebraska territories.[22] Disaffected Whigs came to the meeting, tired of their own party's compromises on the issue. They wanted a party that would stand up to the Democrats—whom some dubbed "slavocrats"—and on that night they decided to form their own party, the Republicans.[23]

A year after the Republican Party was formed in Ripon, Robert Marion La Follette was born in the small town of Primrose, southeast of Ripon. He would change both Wisconsin and national politics. By 1885 La Follette was a U.S. congressman on his way to bigger things. By the turn of the century, however, he had become alarmed at the stranglehold wealthy industrialists had on the Republican party and the state, and determinedly wrested the party from them under the banner of "Progressive Republicanism." In 1900 he ran a victorious campaign for governor, supported in a pivotal way by Laird's grandfather, W. D. Connor, who was then the chairman of the Wisconsin Republican Party.

As governor, and then as a U.S. senator, La Follette and his Progressive leadership, assisted by Connor and many other able Wisconsinites, transformed American politics and social policy. What was often dubbed under the umbrella rubric "the Wisconsin Idea" soon became Washington policy. In 1904 Wisconsin instituted America's first mandatory primary elections, to replace selection of candidates by political machines. The Progressive Republicans were also important advocates of the direct election of U.S. senators. Until 1913, senators were chosen by governors or state legislatures. Under Progressive Republicans, social services in Wisconsin expanded rapidly, including America's first unemployment and workers' compensation benefit laws.[24] In 1920 Wisconsin became the first state to ratify the Nineteenth Amendment for women's suffrage. A year later, Wisconsin became the first to eliminate all legal discrimination against women. State historians refer to the Progressive Republican Wisconsin era, which continued up to World War II, as "the Golden Age."

Progress was not without a price. La Follette became known as "Fighting

Bob" because he split the Republican Party between "old guard" and Progressives. W. D. Connor broke with La Follette in 1912 when the senator would not support Teddy Roosevelt's presidential candidacy because he wanted to run himself on a Progressive Party ticket. Instead, Roosevelt himself became the Progressive Party's first presidential nominee. A dozen years later, in 1924, Senator La Follette formally broke with the Republican Party and ran as the Progressive candidate for president. He had the most impressive third party showing to date with almost five million votes, but it was not enough. Within a year, "Fighting Bob" died. His son, Robert Jr., known as "Young Bob," held a senate seat for more than two decades, a good portion of it as a member of the Wisconsin Progressive Party. But that party became moribund after World War II, and Young Bob formally dissolved it in March 1946, urging its members to return to the Republican fold. That meant La Follette could run for reelection as a Republican. Party bosses, however, put their support behind a young opportunist, Joe McCarthy, who had been a Democrat himself until he realized that Democrats didn't get elected in Wisconsin.[25]

Laird, who considered McCarthy an unprincipled man, could not in good conscience support his candidacy, so he actively campaigned for Young Bob La Follette. But La Follette had too long neglected his Wisconsin constituent base, and he also had a drinking problem. More than once in that primary campaign, Laird, a Republican candidate himself for state senate, covered for La Follette. The official explanation for La Follette's virtual absence from the state during the primary was that he was too busy with important matters in Washington.

The triumph of the unknown McCarthy over La Follette was not only an upset, but also the passing of an era.[26] It was the first time in more than forty years that no La Follette family member held prominent office in Wisconsin.[27] More than fifty years later, Donna Shalala, Secretary of Health and Human Services during the Clinton administration, paid tribute to the role Wisconsin professors and politicians had played in the social services and environmental movements. "Most of the ideas that came out of Wisconsin," she said, "are in fact programs that defined this century and what kind of country we wanted to be."[28]

⌇

The Wisconsin state senate had thirty-three members, compared to the assembly's one hundred. Both legislative houses were dominated by Republicans, so twenty-four-year-old Laird began in a good starting position. Laird loved the legislature from the beginning; he felt born to it. He was assigned to three committees—education, veterans, and labor. He immersed himself in the work and quickly rose to prominence. One measure of his power came in 1948 when Laird twice faced down Sen. Joe McCarthy and beat him both times. In the first case, it was in Laird's capacity as the chairman of the state Young Republicans during their convention. Behind the scenes, there was a struggle for who would be elected at the convention as state chairman. The party and McCarthy backed Jack Mills, the Milwaukee County Young Republicans chair. Laird, never having met Mills, already favored a different young man, so he summoned Mills to come to his hotel suite to give him the bad news.

Mills was put off from the get-go—first at being summoned, and then at Laird's pasha-like appearance in the room, seated in a high-backed chair on a dais, smoking a cigar. "He looked like a king or something," Mills said. After minor pleasantries, Laird came out with it: "I don't want you to run for chairman this year. I will support you in two years."

"You're kidding, right?" Mills blurted out.

"No, I'm not kidding."

Mills had McCarthy and party bosses in his corner, and he wasn't going to let Laird stop him on his own drive to become governor. So he threw down the gauntlet: "Senator, with Milwaukee County alone, I've got 42 percent of the votes. I'm going to carry it completely. All I need is one other county. And you're asking *me* not to run this time? I'll tell you what: I'll support *your* candidate next time."

Laird was miffed. A splotch of red started at his forehead and crept across his whole pate. He shook a finger at Mills: "Mills, let me tell *you* something. You can't get elected with just Milwaukee and McCarthy. If you run, you're going to lose!" Mills recalled later, "I ran and I lost. I didn't get one other county. And that was the end of Jack Mills, as far as progressing in the party. I hated him. The bastard! I hated him."[29] (He did learn to respect Laird's political ability, and not long after the two became friends for life.)

On the national scene in 1948, a friend of the Laird family, Harold Stassen, the young forty-year-old governor of Minnesota, decided to make a run for the Republican presidential nomination. (Stassen had signed up for the Navy with Laird's older brother, Connor, and Walter Kohler, the day after the Pearl Harbor attack.) The April 6 Wisconsin primary was considered pivotal for presidential primary candidates, and the race was wide open. Gen. Douglas MacArthur, a native of Wisconsin, ran for the nomination, although he didn't bother to come home from Tokyo to campaign. California governor Earl Warren was also a candidate, and he sent an earnest emissary to Wisconsin to try to win over Laird and other delegates. The emissary was Richard Nixon.

Laird was suitably impressed with him at their first meeting but not enough to switch his support from Stassen, who won the Wisconsin Republican presidential primary. (New York governor Thomas Dewey eventually won the Republican nomination and was then defeated by Harry Truman.)

The next vote among the Republican leadership in the state was for chairman of the Wisconsin delegation. McCarthy should have been a shoo-in, but two of the Stassen delegates, Laird and his mother, stood in his way. Mel disliked McCarthy and Helen didn't trust him—together they successfully backed their friend Walter Kohler Jr. in a humiliating loss for McCarthy. Kohler, the son of a popular former Wisconsin governor, was the Lairds' pick for Wisconsin's next governor.

Many of Laird's campaign speeches in those early years centered on principled politics. He had been disheartened, he told one Rotary Club audience, that a recent Gallup poll found nine out of ten parents "do not want their children to go into politics because they regard it as a messy, crooked business with no future."[30] That was not the way he saw it or practiced it. He developed his own oft-repeated credo: "Politics is the art and science of government; politics is what men and women make it; we the people are the government."[31]

Laird's work in the state senate was wide ranging and reflected broad interests. He was instrumental in making much-needed improvements to Wisconsin's education system, as well as its mental health and general health institutions. He sponsored legislation allowing medical groups to practice on a corporate basis. At the time, doctors' salaries were low, and they had no retirement and few other benefits. Laird thought it was vital to allow facilities such as his hometown's Marshfield Clinic to operate in a more business-like manner and attract quality doctors, as well as encourage young people to go into the medical profession.

Senator Laird also became a prominent state tax authority, chairing the legislative council committee on taxation. He pushed forward Wisconsin's pioneering "revenue-sharing" approach to taxation, another "Wisconsin Idea" that became federal policy when Laird was instrumental in persuading President Richard Nixon to adopt the concept. On a federal level, it meant returning some of the federal income tax to the states to use as they saw fit. On the state level, when Laird was a legislator in Wisconsin, it meant sharing state income tax funds with local and county governments, believing that those who live in the community know better how to use tax funds locally.

It was in Wisconsin that Laird learned the value of friendships across party

lines, and he cultivated among those friends Democratic state senator Gaylord A. Nelson, who went on to be a popular Wisconsin governor and then
a U.S. senator. Nelson recalled that, "Fraternizing between Republicans and
Democrats in those days was not seen as a treasonable offense. A sense of
good will seemed to anoint most political discourse. The political playing
field was more user-friendly than it is today. . . . I did most of the debating
on the Democratic side, and Mel was the best debater on their side—maybe
the best debater in the state senate. He would contest things vigorously, but
he was always civil. He had strong convictions and great integrity, decency,
compassion. We would debate all day long, and argue on the floor, and then,
at sundown, sensibly move to the nearest pub to continue our friendly dis-
putations into the night. Every so often, Mel would come home with me for
dinner, or we'd go to DiSalvo's Spaghetti House. It was more civilized in
those days."[32]

By 1951, after only four years as a state senator, Melvin Laird was clearly
a star headed for greater things. Besides his own native skills and maturity,
he had also backed the right horse for governor, Walter Kohler Jr. The previous March, Laird had taken a sentimental journey with Governor Kohler
as a member of a small state delegation to Portsmouth, Virginia, for the
recommissioning of the USS *Wisconsin*, the ship on which he had recuper-
ated from severe shrapnel wounds.[33] After the ceremonies were over, Laird
and others decided to come home by way of Washington, D.C. It was Laird's
first visit to the capital, and he made an appointment with friends and mentors, Wisconsin Republican congressmen John Byrnes and Glenn Davis.
Before their meeting, he wanted to see Davis in action on the floor of the
House of Representatives. After Laird took a gallery seat, he was pleased to
observe Davis in the middle of a debate supporting a colleague, Republican
congressman Gerald Ford from Michigan, who was only in his third year in
Congress. Ford was arguing against an appropriations bill that was loaded
with expensive goodies for the districts of congressmen on the Appropriations
Committee. What impressed him most was that here were three idealistic
men for whom their conscience was their primary constituent. Washington
began to look like a great place to be in the company of such men.

2

Guns and Butter

Burning Tree Club in suburban Bethesda, Maryland, has long been a gathering place for the powerful men of Washington, D.C. It was an eighteen-hole enclave of camaraderie in early 1953, when a powerful foursome arrived to play a round of golf. An hour before tee time, a call came from the White House to the club's pro, Max Elbin. The Secret Service soon followed to establish a command post in the clubhouse. The buzz started at the "nineteenth hole," the club bar where members and guests nursed drinks and played cards. The new president of the United States—Dwight D. Eisenhower—arrived that Wednesday afternoon, under a slightly overcast sky, with the two men he knew best from Capitol Hill—the new House majority leader Charles Halleck, and Sen. Robert A. Taft, whom Ike had beaten for the GOP presidential nomination.[1] To their mutual surprise, less than six months after engaging in intense political battle, Taft and Eisenhower had become good friends.

The president had chosen Halleck for his golf partner that day and let Taft choose a fourth golfer. Taft's first choice had been the new congressman from Wisconsin, Melvin Laird, but Laird had a sprained ankle, so he suggested that Taft instead invite Jack Westland, another freshman congressman from Washington state, who had spent his boyhood in Laird's congressional district in Wisconsin. (Westland had recently won the National U.S. Amateur Golf Championship.) Laird went along as scorekeeper. That afternoon, both newcomers were introduced to the members relaxing in the stately Tudor clubhouse. On the fast track to leadership, Laird had already been given an almost unprecedented appointment for a freshman congressman—a seat on House Appropriations Committee—and now he was golfing with the president. Although Eisenhower lost the game that day, the president was impressed with his affable young companions.

After six years in the Wisconsin legislature, Laird had decided in 1952 that Congress was where he wanted to be. The congressman for the Seventh District of Wisconsin, Reid Murray, had died in April while still in office, and Laird had jumped into the open race. Two men opposed Laird in the September Republican primary, but Laird was a popular, accomplished state senator who had the support of every daily newspaper in the district and almost every weekly paper. In the primary he collected more votes than both of his opponents did.

Republicans old and young aimed for an electoral sweep of state, congressional, and presidential elections in 1952. Among the youngest Republicans working on Laird's campaign was thirteen-year-old David Obey, who would later represent Wisconsin in Congress as an ardent liberal Democrat. Four decades after his time "as a wayward teenager," Obey sheepishly displayed his "Laird for Congress" button and acknowledged that in 1952 he had enthusiastically "circulated the literature to one-third of the households in the city of Wausau for Mel, and for Ike, and for Nixon, and for Joe McCarthy."[2]

The Republicans got their sweeping victory in November—control of the Senate, House, and White House. Eisenhower, with Richard Nixon as his running mate, won with 55 percent of the vote. Laird won his first election to Congress with a record-setting 95,049 votes, the largest vote ever cast for a candidate in the Seventh District. It was 72.3 percent of the vote and a resounding defeat for his Democratic opponent. At the age of thirty, Laird headed to Washington as the youngest Wisconsin man elected to Congress.

The president's friendship and that of Robert Taft provided Laird with rare informal access and, more important, influence by association. His recent appointment to the House Appropriations Committee meant that many senior members of Congress sought to befriend him; he was thus in a good position to help drive the issues of the Eisenhower era, and the issues close to Wisconsin's heart.

If all the milk produced in Wisconsin for a year were packaged in one-quart cartons and stacked side by side, it could form a highway twenty-eight lanes wide from New York to San Francisco. The state's license plate logo "America's Dairyland" is no idle boast; Wisconsin is a leading producer of milk, cheese, and butter. When Laird went to Washington, more than half of Wisconsin's land was in farming, and at least a third of the state's labor force was involved in the production or marketing of farm products. The young congressman was acutely aware that his district was the largest milk- and cheese-producing district in the entire country, and 1953 was not necessarily a good time to be representing those interests.

American agriculture was still recovering from the effects of the Depression, now coupled with the loss of male labor during World War II. Middlemen were grabbing more and more of the dairy dollar, and farmers were being squeezed out of their land because of low prices for their products. In recognition of that problem, Congress had passed the Agricultural Act of 1949, which mandated payments by the Commodity Credit Corporation for surplus products based on "parity" prices. Parity was the price the government declared by law to be fair, based on what a farmer had to pay for farm and consumer products. Using a base period from the relatively prosperous 1910–14 years, the government calculated what price it would take in the 1950s to equal that purchasing power. Simply put, if the sale of one hundred gallons of milk bought so many Sunday neckties back in the old days, parity would be the price those one hundred gallons would need to sell for in order to buy the same number of ties in the 1950s. The government, however, could not afford to pay a 100 percent parity price to the farmer for his surplus, so a maximum of 90 percent was authorized.

During the 1952 campaign, Eisenhower had supported 90 percent parity, and he won the farm vote. On the other hand his secretary of agriculture, Ezra Taft Benson, believed that federal aid to farmers smacked of socialism, and he made that clear in straight-talking speeches.[3] In early 1954 Laird began to get indications that Benson might drop the parity rate to the legal minimum of 75 percent. He had private meetings with Benson and felt assured that any change would happen gradually. Then came the February 15 announcement that beginning April 1, the price would be 75 percent of parity; an uncounted number of dairy farmers would go bankrupt that year.

After failing to change Benson's mind or stop him with legislation, Laird pulled rank. He secretly applied to Eisenhower, using the White House's congressional liaison, General Wilton B. Persons. Persons reported back to Laird that Ike had promised parity would drop only to 82.5 percent, a compromise Laird could live with. But before he could publicly crow about this, another call came: Benson had informed the president that if he insisted on a compromise he would have to find a new agriculture secretary. Eisenhower capitulated.[4] Disheartened, Laird faced a storm of criticism in his first campaign for reelection, having been undercut by his own party's administration. Out of his nine successful campaigns for Congress, 1954 was Laird's toughest. But dairy ire was not enough to overcome his solid reputation. He won with 59.1 percent of the vote.[5]

∽

In early 1954, an unusual visitor, who would soon become a friend, dropped by Laird's home for an animated discussion—seventy year-old Roger Baldwin, founder and national chairman of the American Civil Liberties Union. The ACLU inevitably took on a liberal tint from the hue of most of its clients and was considered an enemy of the Republican party.[6] But as was often the case, Congressman Laird, from progressive Wisconsin, found himself to the left of his party. When Baldwin heard through his niece, who was Laird's next-door neighbor, that he would be welcome at Laird's home, the amiable aristocrat, in his usual rumpled suit, knocked on Laird's door one evening. He had come to discuss an "urgent matter"—Laird's sponsorship of a bill to add the words "under God" to the Pledge of Allegiance.

The original pledge was written in 1892 by Baptist minister Francis Bellamy, a self-described Christian Socialist. It was only twenty-three words long: "I pledge allegiance to my Flag and to the Republic for which it stands; one nation indivisible, with liberty and justice for all."[7] In the 1920s the pledge was changed, replacing "my Flag" to "the flag of the United States of America." By the mid-1930s, reciting the pledge was compulsory for most American school children, and it was often done with a straight-arm salute that subsequently went out of favor when the same gesture was used to salute Hitler.

In 1942 Congress officially recognized the pledge on its fiftieth birthday and added it to the Flag Code of the United States. No change could be made to it without legislation, which is why Laird needed a bill in 1954 to amend the pledge to read "one nation under God." In their first evening together, Baldwin pleaded with Laird to see the danger of adding "under God" to the pledge. Baldwin argued courteously but heatedly that Laird's resolution violated the First Amendment's tenet of separation of church and state. Baldwin was eloquent, but Laird, the son of a Presbyterian minister, stood firm. Even though Laird wouldn't drop the bill, Baldwin found him affable and open on civil rights issues dear to Baldwin, so they continued as friends.

Laird was not alone in his belief that the words "under God" belonged in the pledge. Representative Oliver Bolton of Ohio was also outspoken about the urgent need for the addition. In those days, the House did not allow more than one sponsor's name on a bill, so the only way to "co-sponsor" legislation was to offer identical bills under individual names. Now, not only was there a Laird resolution but a Bolton one, as well as at least thirteen others, including one by Democrat Louis Rabaut of Michigan, who had been the first to introduce the idea legislatively in Congress the year before.[8]

Laird appeared before the House Judiciary Committee on May 6 and testified that it was a long overdue change.[9] He noted that in the constitutions of forty-seven of the states, the authority of God is recognized and declared. Every poll taken at the time showed that as many as 97 percent of all Americans believed in a Supreme Being, as did the Founding Fathers. Although God was not mentioned in the Constitution, the Declaration of Independence referenced God or the "Creator" four times. And, Laird dramatically concluded, what better time than on Lincoln's 145th birthday to follow the lead of the president who had uttered in the concluding words of the Gettysburg Address: "that we here highly resolve that these [Civil War] dead shall not have died in vain; that this nation, *under God,* shall have a new birth of freedom; and that government of the people, by the people, for the people, shall not perish from the earth."

The Senate passed the bill first, and the House was ready to do the same, but pride of authorship sparked a lengthy debate. Congressman Rabaut fought to have the House pass his bill instead of the Senate's version—which would mean the Senate would have to swallow its pride and vote again on the identical House bill. Republican floor leader Charlie Halleck begged Rabaut to back off, so that the legislation could be signed a few days later on National Flag Day. But Rabaut refused, so the House, including Laird and other cosponsors, passed the Rabaut resolution by voice vote on Monday, June 7, 1954. The following day, the Senate obligingly signed off on the House bill. Laird was so pleased that he passed out small cards to children in his district that reelection year with the new pledge printed on them, along with a small note that Laird was the co-sponsor of the new pledge.

At that time of religious revival in America, when parents worried almost as much about materialistic consumerism as they did about the godless Communists, Laird did not stop with the pledge reform. He pushed successful legislation that directed the architect of the Capitol to designate a prayer-and-meditation room in the building, where members of Congress could come to spiritually consider their work.[10]

Laird also was instrumental in making "In God We Trust" the national motto. Its original author was Lincoln's secretary of the treasury Salmon P. Chase, who first put those words on coins in 1864. Nine decades later, in 1956, Laird helped steer passage of the bill through the House and the Senate making the motto official. The following year, the new national motto appeared for the first time on paper money.[11]

More deeply than golf-and-bridge interests, more profound in some ways than their mutual Republican principles, Laird's and Eisenhower's shared Presbyterian faith encouraged a closeness that might not otherwise have existed. Being so in sync with Eisenhower on core moral issues, Laird became a favorite of the president, who often served as both a mentor and father figure for the young congressman who had lost his own father.

Some of Laird's speeches in the Eisenhower era reveal the religious touchstone that drove both men—the place of a Christian in politics: "Only those people with the highest altruistic motives [should] have any business in politics. There ought not to be any room for other folks. They ought to be crowded out by the people who believe in the highest ideals, and who work for the best interests of all men." Laird postulated: "If Providence has placed self-government in the hands of the people, the better people had better take over, lest the reins of administration fall into the hands of the improvident." So, "when people ask me, 'Ought a Christian go into politics?,' my answer has been, '*How can a Christian stay out?*'"[12]

During the Eisenhower era, Laird's primary base of power came from what was then the most powerful and hardest-working committee in Congress— House Appropriations (HAC). No government project can become a reality without money, and no dollar can be spent unless the HAC appropriates it. No other committee in Congress came close to the number of hours that the HAC spent in session. Laird's load on the committee was among the heaviest. At one point, he was assigned to four subcommittees: Health, Defense, Military construction, and Commerce.[13] When asked by another congressman why Laird had so many assignments, ranking Appropriations Committee member John Taber replied: "Mel Laird likes hard work."[14]

Despite his lack of seniority, Laird soon became influential within the committee itself because of his ability to absorb large amounts of information, analyze it, and then use it to buttress a Republican argument or challenge a witness. These abilities grew over the years and came into high relief when he was secretary of defense. Alarmed about the $267 billion national debt when he came into office, Laird was a bona fide budget-slasher. He made it a practice to vote for every reduction that came through his committee and often found himself in the minority on some of those votes.[15] With a Republican-controlled Congress and White House, Laird and the HAC efficiently turned the tide of government spending in the first year.[16] The Eisenhower era was highlighted at one point with three consecutive years of balanced budget and one year in which surplus money was actually used to pay down the national debt. There were two years of recession, but overall the eight-year Eisenhower period saw the Gross National Product rise by almost 50 percent to more than $500 billion. This golden era was the birth of America's affluent society.[17]

~

Richard Nixon was a vice president who never quite came in from the cold of the Eisenhower Oval Office. Eisenhower had a cabinet full of millionaires, and Nixon was a professional politician, not a self-made businessman. Eisenhower had many friends among the high-ranking military, and Nixon, with his lackluster war record, did not qualify in that category either. The president also favored amiable, game-loving raconteurs; if Nixon ever tried to be the life of a party, the strain was evident.

Initially, Eisenhower had wanted someone else as his vice president, and that desire accelerated after he suffered his first heart attack in September 1955, in Denver. It brought into painful relief the very real possibility of Nixon becoming president by default. The thought made Eisenhower uncomfortable, and he made a move the day after Christmas to replace Nixon. In an Oval Office discussion, the president made the case to Nixon that his presidential prospects would be better if he were in the cabinet—preferably secretary of defense. Ike noted that Nixon's popularity had not improved in three years, and that he probably needed administrative experience in another position. Not knowing the president's ulterior motive, Nixon initially took the suggestion to be a "friendly and sincere one." But at the same time, he suspected Ike's friends had "been sowing doubts in his mind . . . that I might be a drag on the ticket."[18]

Word that Nixon needed a public boost quietly went out to his closest friends—including Laird—all of whom were members of an exclusive, secretive Republican group called the Chowder and Marching Club. The society, which had nothing to do with soup or Sousa, was a fraternity of fifteen Republican members who gathered together in March 1949 to oppose a multibillion dollar veterans bonus bill. Many Republicans, then in the minority, opposed the handout to every veteran, regardless of need. Among them were Representatives Glenn Davis from Wisconsin and Don Jackson from California who enlisted thirteen other younger members in their cause. Among the charter members were then Representatives Nixon and Ford.[19] These fifteen Republican upstarts, most of whom were veterans themselves (including one congressman who had lost both legs in the war[20]), unanimously opposed the Democratic giveaway and managed to successfully kill the bill.

In the process, Chowder and Marching (C&M) became an incubator for future presidents. Some authors specializing in psychohistory have suggested that Nixon's political genius created the group to use as a kind of secret Opus Dei to promote his presidential ambitions.[21] The facts belie such theories. As Nixon once mused, C&M was "the most ill-organized, disorderly organization I know."[22] Davis and Jackson were the de facto leaders, but the club was never formally organized; it had no officers, rules, or even a clubhouse. The group met every Wednesday at the congressional offices of the members in alphabetical rotation. The club's name is something of a mystery even to members: "We never ate chowder and we never marched," Ford recalled.[23] Congressman Jackson whimsically put the name on the notice for C&M's second meeting, and it is likely it came from a 1933 Cary Grant movie in which one C&M charter member, John Lodge, played a bit part. At one point in the movie, a banner is held up that states: "The O'Brien Chowder and Marching Club."

While Laird was still a state senator, he first heard tales of the group from Glenn Davis and Johnny Byrnes, who pushed to put Laird in C&M as soon as he came to Congress, but there was no opening for him until a year later, in 1954. By secret ballot, C&Mers usually voted on a prospective member based on his personality, early indications that he was a "comer," and because he was assigned to a committee not already represented in the club. At every Wednesday meeting, each active C&Mer gave a brief report on what had occurred in the executive sessions of his committee. Information is power in Washington, and C&M became a unique repository of political insight.

With the elevation of C&Mer Nixon to vice president, and others who were appointed to the Eisenhower administration, the club grew to mythological stature. Though small in number, they were able to lure cabinet members, the Joint Chiefs of Staff, civilian service chiefs, and federal judges to give them private briefings at the Wednesday-morning breakfasts. The CIA chief invited them to Langley headquarters for an unprecedented intelligence briefing, and Eisenhower invited the club to the White House for a special off-the-record breakfast.[24]

In 1952, when Eisenhower had previously considered dropping Nixon from the ticket, the entire Chowder and Marching Club rallied to Nixon's defense. Facing a similar prospect in 1956, they planned a highly visible show of support in the guise of a birthday party for the vice president on January 9. Laird took the lead in arranging the costly soiree. He leaned on gifted national fund-raisers Jack Mills and Victor Johnson—both friends from Wisconsin—to come up with more than $10,000 in private contributions for the event at the National Press Club.[25] More than five hundred attended, including most of the Republican luminaries of the day. As hosts, Laird and fellow C&Mers donned chef's hats and striped butcher's aprons as they brought out the large birthday cake.

Nixon was visibly moved. Three days later he wrote to Laird, "It was [a] superb party." The highlight was when, "I saw members of our group wheel out that beautiful cake with its 43 candles. [It] will never be exceeded as a mountain-top experience." He counted Laird and all "my fellow members of the Chowder and Marching Club my closest political and personal friends in this world."[26] It was rare for Nixon to use such emotional hyperbole, but he meant every word of it. And Nixon knew the subtext of the birthday party was a powerful statement to the president that he could ill afford to "fire" a man with such friends.

At the 1956 Republican National Convention, Mel Laird was named a member of the Platform Committee, chaired by Sen. Prescott Bush, father and grandfather of future presidents.[27] The platform for Eisenhower's reelection sparked little controversy and passed easily without dissent. Laird had time to relax, including playing the first of many rounds of golf with Senator Bush. He also had time to chat with one of the Bush sons, George H. W., who hustled around with messages and platform drafts as a page for the committee. After the convention, Laird traveled with Eisenhower and Nixon to several campaign stops and otherwise acted as an energetic member of Ike's "truth squads." These were senators and representatives assigned to follow key Democratic speakers and hold alternative press conferences to debunk Democrats' assertions about the national Republican ticket.

On the home front, Laird also faced a repeat opponent, who unexpectedly died a few days before the Democratic primary. The man's widow then became one of only twenty-seven women in the United States running for Congress that year, taking up the campaign for the office.[28] But she had little chance against Laird. One newspaper noted that Laird had "boom[ed] around the countryside," averaging more than a speech a day, covering every community in the ten-county Seventh District twice and eating at as many as three church picnics in a single afternoon. "Despite his great energy, Laird appears older than his years," the reporter added, pointing out a bullet-head pate that would be the delight of future editorial cartoonists: "Partly bald and his remaining hair cropped, he has a deacon-like fringe over his dome."[29] The voters didn't hold his hair loss against Laird; his victory margin was two to one.

The Eisenhower-Nixon ticket also swept to a landslide victory but with coattails so short that a Democratic House and Senate were returned to Washington. It was only the second time in American history that the majority had voted for a president of one party and given control of Congress to the opposition.[30]

Joe McCarthy had reached the zenith of his influence and also plummeted to his exile from power during the first two years of the Eisenhower administration. When Republicans were in the majority those first two years, McCarthy

could have become chairman of the powerful Senate Appropriations Committee. He chose instead to chair the Committee on Government Operations, a
watchdog investigative committee, which was likely to garner him more publicity. He named himself chairman of the Permanent Subcommittee on Investigations, which became a platform for his infamous Communist witch hunts.

While it was expected that McCarthy would continue to ride herd on State
Department bureaucrats who were suspected subversives, it came as something of a surprise to loyal Republican leaders that he took on his own party's
White House appointees. That set Eisenhower's teeth against McCarthy, but
he refused to publicly criticize the senator, believing that McCarthy fed on
publicity.[31] Laird was of the same mind but had a different dilemma; not
only was McCarthy the senator from Wisconsin, he was also a member of
Laird's party. Tradition dictated that Laird give him the benefit of the doubt,
and there were plenty of doubts. "I understood what a phony he was, and
a lot of people didn't. A lot of people in Wisconsin didn't. A lot of conservative people didn't," Laird recalled. Even in Laird's hometown, McCarthy
was a hero. In May 1951, about eight hundred residents had packed the local
armory to have dinner with McCarthy and hear his "Report From Washington" speech.[32] Laird, as a state senator, was one of the thirty-one guests on
the dais, but he made sure that he was at least five chairs removed from
McCarthy. One of the reasons to be wary was that McCarthy was frequently
drunk. "I would be with him sometimes when he would order a malted milk
for breakfast, and he'd pour half of it out and put almost half a pint of booze
in it. I never admired that," Laird said.

McCarthy elevated to national notoriety his two most subservient aides:
the venal chief counsel to the Permanent Subcommittee on Investigations,
Roy Cohn, whose natural cockiness was inflated into gross arrogance by the
helium of McCarthy's power; and Gerard David Schine, a dreamy-eyed millionaire's son, heir to great hotels and theaters, night club habitué, and escort
of Hollywood starlets. The "Katzenjammer Kids," as they were derisively called
behind their backs, took a rampaging trip throughout Europe in 1953. There
they denounced as subversive the Voice of America and the U.S. overseas
information program, causing libraries to be closed and books to be burned
in their fearful wake.

Their next target was the U.S. Army. Schine had been drafted into the service, which occasionally didn't treat him as he felt he deserved, so the young
pair declared war on the Army. With McCarthy as the assault leader, this
unlikely cabal had the Army on the run for a while. The televised "Army–
McCarthy Hearings" hearings ran from April 22 to June 15, 1954, and captured

the nation's attention. In a May 5 letter to his constituents, Laird called it a "three-ring circus," and lamented the fact that it "diverted attention . . . from many important decisions and activities taking place in our Capital."[33] Two days later, Laird repeated the complaint in a speech at a two-day Marathon County, Wisconsin, Republican rally. He noted that only "four or five reporters were present the other day" during action on a $73 billion defense appropriations bill, while "there were more than 200 over in the Senate office building [covering the] three-ring circus."[34]

McCarthy also appeared at the Republican rally, which gave the *Wausau Daily Record-Herald* a chance to contrast the Wisconsin senator with the congressman: "Wisconsin's junior senator is one of the most controversial figures in the nation, both among members of his own party as well as among the Democratic opposition. Most people are either strongly for him or just as strongly against him, with few sitting on the fence. . . . Unlike Sen. McCarthy, Rep. Laird is not passionately hailed either as a great hero or a villain. But he does evoke universal esteem and high respect for his deep sincerity, integrity, devotion to duty and level-headedness whether or not one agrees with his views on any particular issue."[35]

The nadir of the hearings, and the tolling of the bell for McCarthy, came on June 9, 1954, when the grand inquisitor finally met his match in Joseph Welch, the Army's special counsel. When McCarthy viciously maligned a junior partner in Welch's law firm, Welch scarcely raised his voice in response. "Until this moment, Senator," he began sadly, "I think I never really gauged your cruelty or your recklessness. . . . If it were in my power to forgive you for your reckless cruelty, I would do so. I like to think that I am a gentleman, but your forgiveness will have to come from someone other than me."

It was as if the nation collectively hushed, as did the Senate hearing room. Stung, McCarthy began sputtering out another attack, but Welch silenced him: "Senator. You have done enough. Have you no sense of decency, sir, at long last? Have you left no sense of decency?" The Senate Caucus Room audience of 700 spontaneously erupted into applause, and the hearing was thrown into recess.[36]

Still, it took the rest of the year for McCarthy's demise to play out. Less than a week after the hearing, McCarthy received overwhelming support at the state Republican Convention, chaired by an unhappy Mel Laird. He knew that many anti-McCarthy delegates, expecting a fanatic show of home-state support from his fans, sat out the convention. It so happened that only one delegate, Polk County Republican chairman Harold Michael, dared to speak out against a resolution praising McCarthy. Laird gave him time to make his case, but Michael's words could barely be heard over the roar of boos, catcalls, and shouted insults such as, "Throw the Communist out!" "Shut the microphone off!" "Go back to Russia!" Laird tried without success to gavel them to silence.

The convention was watched closely by the U.S. Senate, whose majority hoped that Wisconsin would punish its own man. When that didn't happen, it was up to the Senate to act. On December 2, 1954, the Senate voted 67 to 22 to condemn McCarthy for conduct unbecoming a U.S. senator—labeling his behavior "contemptuous, contumacious and denunciatory." A faint effort was made by his friends to press the Wisconsin congressional delegation, including Laird, into sponsoring a House resolution condemning the Senate's action, but there were no takers.

McCarthy died in May 1957. He had been hospitalized previously for alcoholism and most probably succumbed to cirrhosis of the liver. The Senate allowed a funeral service in the Senate Chamber at the request of his widow. His body was flown to Wisconsin where thirty thousand Wisconsinites filed through an Appleton church to view the open casket. One of those present for the service was Melvin Laird. Until that day, he had lived up to his pledge of never missing a roll-call vote.[37]

Jerry Ford later said that Laird had taken an appropriate arms-length attitude toward McCarthy. It had been no small thing, Ford observed, that neither Laird nor the more senior Wisconsin congressmen Glenn Davis and Johnny Byrnes, ever supported McCarthy's anti-Communist campaign. "The three of them, Mel, Glenn and John were just privately embarrassed by McCarthy's demagoguery and his conduct generally," Ford said. "Now, they had a very narrow path to follow, because McCarthy was popular in Wisconsin. I think Mel handled the McCarthy problem very skillfully. He stayed outside of the McCarthy envelope, so to speak."

～

Agricultural discontent in Wisconsin was the primary reason William Proxmire won McCarthy's seat in a special election in August 1957 after McCarthy's death. Proxmire was a relatively unknown Democratic politician whose opponent was the popular Republican governor Walter Kohler. In twenty-five years, no Democrat had won a seat for the U.S. Senate from Wisconsin. If Kohler had won, the Senate would have been evenly split, 48 to 48—Alaska and Hawaii were not yet states—and Nixon would have had the tie-breaking vote, automatically reverting the Senate to Republican control. That change would have greatly diminished the chances of the ambitious Senate majority leader Lyndon Johnson from becoming a national politician. But so great was the rancor toward Ezra Taft Benson in Laird's home state that Proxmire won the upset election primarily by hammering on the secretary of agriculture, instead of Proxmire's opponent.[38]

In the 1958 election, an analysis of the anti-Benson vote by *Congressional Quarterly* concluded that Benson had cost "one-third of his Republican supporters representing Midwest farm districts;" Their seats went to Democratic challengers.[39] Laird was one of the lucky ones, winning reelection with 60.5 percent of the vote.

Supporters back home dubbed Laird "Dairyland's Best Friend." It was more than campaign rhetoric, because Laird did much more than fight against precipitous parity price drops. He was fairly successful in limiting the import of cheaper, substandard dairy products. In his first year, he prompted President Eisenhower to invoke a section of the 1949 Agriculture Act to cut imports of cheese. The first one-on-one meeting between Ike and Laird in the Oval Office had been a "victory" meeting; a beaming Ike was photographed receiving a ten-pound piece of prime Wisconsin longhorn cheese.[40] The battle against foreign imports continued into the Kennedy and Johnson administrations, and Laird was unflagging in his efforts. He was most incensed when the United States allowed Communist Bulgaria to flood the American market with "Colby cheese," named after the Wisconsin town in his district where it had been created.[41]

Laird also decried a frustrating set of trade barriers that existed between American states. Intent on protecting their own farmers' products, states with limited dairy production set up a series of fake inspections, out-of-state taxes, and bogus shipping requirements that effectively prevented delivery of cheaper milk from states with a surplus. Wisconsin produced 85 percent more milk than was consumed in the state, so its farmers were greatly hurt by the interstate barriers. Laird spearheaded "free flow of milk" legislation aimed at setting up a uniform national standard for milk. He was only moderately successful in this effort, which continually foundered on the shoals of "states' rights" advocates.

None of this was enough to get farmers out of the vicious cycle of declining prices and increased production. No matter what Laird or Congress did, they could not repeal the basic economic law of supply and demand. Laird reckoned that people simply had to drink more milk and eat more butter and cheese. First, he scored several victories in the never-ending conflict between butter and margarine producers. Incensed that the military was buying "butter substitutes" for mess halls, Laird mounted a patriotic-sounding campaign to allow America's service members and veterans to have the best—

butter—when they asked for it. And he had an irrefutable bit of logic on his side: why should the military and Veterans Administration pay for margarine when they could draw from the huge butter surpluses the federal taxpayer had already purchased? The common-sense approach won the day for dairy and resulted in major contracts signed by the Commodity Credit Corporation with the VA and Defense Department.[42]

Laird was an indefatigable promoter of milk as well, encouraging packagers to put milk in small cartons that could be dispensed in vending machines. He placed Washington's first milk dispensers prominently in the Republican and Democrat cloakrooms of the House, and he presided at the "christening ceremony" for the vending machines, encouraging every member of Congress to "drink an extra glass of milk a day."[43]

But he was not done. Laird realized that the best use of the surplus milk would be to offer it at low- or no-cost in the School Lunch Program. The School Milk Program was created by legislation Laird co-sponsored in 1954, spreading the product far and wide.[44] The federal program quickly grew, delivering enormous amounts of milk to public and parochial schools, nonprofit nursery schools, child-care centers, and summer camps.

⁓

Congressman Laird's introduction to defense issues was a clumsy one. The first time the future secretary of defense went to the Pentagon for a military briefing he literally got lost through no fault of his own. The colonel escorting him led him through a maze of corridors before admitting that he didn't know where he was either.[45] That Laird would merit this personal escort and briefing by top military brass in only his sixth week as a congressman is evidence of his early specialty with defense appropriations work.

Eisenhower came to office with a zeal for cutting the military budget. The former top general knew that the services' requests for funds were too extravagant, and ordered the Joint Chiefs of Staff to take a "new look" at all of it. The "New Look Program" frowned upon large standing armies of American soldiers stationed around the world. Instead, its emphasis was on atomic weapons and guided missiles.[46] Early in his first term, Laird worked with Ike to cut $5 billion from the Air Force budget by reducing the number of combat wings. That change set the tone for tough choices on defense in the following years. Laird turned out to be even more parsimonious than Eisenhower, refusing to approve money for some defense programs and taking heat from the Republican Party and voters back home.

Laird felt that "the malignant effects of inter-service rivalry" were costing Americans billions in unnecessary duplication.[47] He fought hard, but not always successfully, for the consolidation of bases. And he butted heads with other members of Congress when he tried to eliminate or move military operations to places that made the most sense—not necessarily the places that pleased the most voters.

Jerry Ford and Mel Laird first bonded as friends on the Defense Appropriations Subcommittee. Ford was nine years older and had been in Congress two terms before Laird was first elected. The Laird and Ford children grew up together, and the two families often vacationed together. The two men shared an almost fanatical interest in golf and were partnered at many tournaments at Burning Tree Country Club. Ford's friendship with Nixon was older, and he once calculated that he was about "as close [to Nixon] as anybody got. But there was never the complete intimacy that I have, for example, with Mel Laird."[48]

"Even though we were on the same side politically, we also had some differences on that defense subcommittee," Ford recalled. "But the differences were always very straightforward. There was never any hangover."[49] Ford treated Laird as the "idea man" and chief lieutenant. The Eisenhower White House quickly learned to negotiate the House defense budget with the Democrat leadership and with the Ford-Laird team.

Laird was often sent over to the Senate to argue for the House version of defense bills. His command of facts and figures and his common sense cut through the dross and won the many inter-House debates. It was in those sessions that Laird had animated discussions with Lyndon Johnson, a member of the Senate Armed Services Committee who, in only one term, had become Senate majority leader. "I had many occasions to work with him as a legislator, and I had great respect and admiration for his ability as a legislator," Laird told interviewer David Frost.[50] Mel had chosen his words carefully, because he did not consider Johnson a man of integrity, which meant they could never be close friends.

For Laird, one telltale measure of Johnson's lack of integrity was his golf game. Burning Tree golf pro Max Elbin said Johnson was the poorest player of all the presidents: "He couldn't hit a bull in the ass with a bass fiddle."[51] But that was not the reason for Laird's disdain. Johnson had a tendency to cheat at golf; if he didn't like where he had hit a ball, he would drop another one and try again, or place it where he would have liked the first ball to land.

A more serious tip-off that Johnson would not be a worthy friend was his penchant for using his position to make money. During Johnson's time in the House and Senate, he became the multimillionaire owner of a galaxy of radio and TV stations, which was possible only because he had used his political

influence to strong-arm the Federal Communications Commission into giving him favorable licenses, permits, and rulings. Following Johnson's signals,
many lobbyists knew the way to buy political influence with him was not
through the outright campaign contributions, but by paying high rates for
advertising on his stations. Laird knew this because the Wisconsinite he had
promoted to become an Eisenhower FCC commissioner and later chairman,
John Doerfler, had uncovered the evidence in FCC files and shared it with
Laird.[52] Armed with that information, though not referring directly to it,
Laird, in a speech on the House floor, courteously but pointedly questioned
Senator Johnson's improper use of congressional influence. Laird's speech
didn't get much attention, but Johnson noticed and Laird felt it tainted their
relationship.

Only twice in the twentieth century did the younger members of a U.S. political party rise up against their party leader in Congress and mount a successful coup. In both cases, Laird was a leader of these "young Turks." It first
occurred after the 1958 election, when the Democrats won forty-seven additional seats in the House, and thirteen more in the Senate, giving them close
to a two-thirds majority in both chambers. Nixon tried to be upbeat in a
pep-talk letter to Laird: "While we have suffered a major loss, nationally I
think the Republican Party came out of this campaign stronger than when
it went in because of the very fact that we went down fighting."[53] That was
nonsense, and Laird knew it. New blood was desperately needed at the party's
leadership level.

The pragmatic Laird did not set out at first to replace House minority
leader Joe Martin of Massachusetts. No speaker or minority leader had ever
been deposed in the twentieth century because the risk of mounting such an
effort was great; instigators would be punished with poor committee assignments and loss of many other perks. So Laird set his sights lower. He thought
that if his friend Johnny Byrnes of Wisconsin became chairman of the Republican Policy Committee—a job Martin also held—new ideas and a new image
for the party might be possible from that perch. When Martin resisted, the
upstarts decided that there was no other choice; Martin himself, the Republican House leader for twenty years, had to go. Laird and Rep. Glenard Lipscomb of California took two surveys among the House Republicans. The
first found a majority would back a coup, and the second poll showed support for three names: Johnny Byrnes, Jerry Ford, and Charlie Halleck, who
was Martin's number two man. (In deference to these three more senior
Republicans, Laird did not add his own name to the poll.)

Byrnes proved the most popular choice, and Ford came in second.[54] But Halleck had the support of the president, so Laird and his fellow young Turks had no choice but to back Halleck. The Republican caucus met on January 6, 1959. Laird had counted heads beforehand and was confident that Halleck would beat Martin by four or five votes. On the first secret ballot, Halleck won by only one vote, 73-72. "I learned that there are a lot of liars when it comes to secret ballots," Laird ruefully observed. "People give you a commitment and you can't really count on it. You always want a few extra votes in your pocket." An objection was made to the first tally because there was one uncounted vote that had been illegible. In a second ballot Halleck won by four.

Laird crowed a little in public about what he foresaw as the positive results of this historic revolt. Instead of a reputation as naysayers to popular government programs, Republicans would be seen as the "party of fiscal responsibility" that would only support programs when the money was there to pay for them. However, in the back of Laird's mind remained the thought that Halleck had not been his first choice, and, in a few short years, Halleck's leadership would prove increasingly inept, prompting Laird and friends to rise again in revolt.

∽

Although Mel Laird considered Ike a mentor and friend, he did not vote for all of the president's programs. On average, Laird voted for Eisenhower's proposals about two-thirds of the time, according to a calculation of the relevant eight Eisenhower years by *Congressional Quarterly*.[55] Laird favored Ike's domestic programs more than his foreign programs; he voted against half of Eisenhower's foreign policy–related legislation. And no administration effort earned Laird's disapprobation more consistently than foreign aid, which came under the rubric of "Mutual Security Program." Eisenhower had inherited the effort from the Truman administration, and was convinced it was vital to U.S. national security. He also knew it would be tough going to persuade Americans that foreign aid was really a defense issue. Laird supported mutual security in principle, but not in price.

Laird had joined the Congress in believing foreign aid was excessive, and his first congressional trip abroad confirmed it. In late 1953 he was one of a five-man fact-finding committee that traveled through Europe. When he returned, Laird pronounced emphatically that the time had come to wean Europe away from U.S. aid. The Marshall Plan, which Laird had favored because it aimed at building Europe to prewar levels, had done such a good job that by 1953 European nations were economically better off than they were before the war. Yet they were still eager to receive American aid at a time when the U.S. national debt of $273 billion was far in excess of the combined indebtedness of all the countries the U.S. was helping. Laird firmly believed that the defense burden in particular should be shared with America's allies, and later, as secretary of defense, he instituted that as a bedrock of the "Nixon Doctrine."

A review of all Laird's votes reveals that he never once voted for an Eisenhower mutual security appropriation unless it had been substantially cut, as in 1956 when the House cut foreign aid by $1.1 billion. Those votes were one of the few areas of disagreement between Laird and Ford. Part of Ford's support was parochial—he had served on the Foreign Operations Appropriations Subcommittee, which had recommended the expenditures. On that subcommittee, Ford was also part of the subgroup that reviewed the CIA's cloak-and-dagger activities—many of which mesmerized the committee but turned out to be foreign policy disasters.[56]

One of the foreign trouble spots that received Laird's scrutiny was the Middle East. In 1953 he visited Jordan, Turkey, Lebanon, Iraq, and Egypt. He was appalled at the condition of the Arabs living near Israel. Some 900,000 Arab refugees, driven out of Palestine, were subsisting on meager rations in United Nations refugee camps. But they were better off than those living in their own villages near the Israeli border and thus not eligible for U.N. aid; Laird saw some of them eating grass. Meanwhile, Israel was flouting conditions under which it was created as a state, which included failing to compensate Arabs for their homes or permitting them to return. Yet American assistance paid for two-thirds of Israel's budget, allowing it to finance a well-equipped army while the Arab nations had substandard military strength.

At a Tel Aviv dinner with the prime minister Moshe Sharett, Laird raised some of these points with Sharett, who unapologetically agreed, "Yes, we have great support in the United States." Laird cautioned him that it might not always be the case if Israel's course diverged from American foreign policy interest. "There's one thing that I don't want you to underestimate—my Jewish friends are certainly loyal to Israel, but they're loyal to our country first," he added.

"Young man," Sharett smiled, patronizingly, "I think you've got a lot to learn."

In a speech to a service club when he got back home, Laird recounted his observations and the Sharett conversation, and lamented the disproportionate amount of foreign aid going to Israel instead of its Arab neighbors. After the meeting, his friend and political advisor Bob Froehlke took him aside: "Mel, you just lost every Jewish vote and dollar in the Seventh Congressional

District. You may have picked up a few Arab votes, but the bad news is that there isn't one Arab in your district and there are a lot of Jews." Laird's response was the first time Froehlke heard him utter a maxim that would become a mantra: "Bob, I have to live with my conscience longer than my constituents."[57]

Dwight Eisenhower declared in one interview after his presidency: "The United States never lost a soldier or a foot of ground in my administration. We kept the peace. People asked how it happened—by God, it didn't just happen, I'll tell you that."[58] Eisenhower sidestepped U.S. intervention in several regional skirmishes, which suited Laird just fine. He preferred diplomacy over shooting. But now, the greatest temptation for American military combat intervention would come from a country on the Indochina peninsula called Vietnam.

The French had been trying to hold onto their colony by force of arms against a Communist insurgency led by Ho Chi Minh. On the condition that the French would eventually grant Vietnam its independence, Roosevelt, Truman, and Eisenhower all financially supported the French military. After an increase by Ike of $60 million in aid in mid-1953, the United States was funding three-quarters of the French war effort, but they wanted more—including ground forces. Eisenhower talked with the British prime minister Winston Churchill, who said that his people hadn't supported a military effort to hold onto their own colony of India, so they weren't about to back a military effort on behalf of a French-held colony. Besides, Churchill added, sending Western ground troops after guerrillas in a tropical jungle would be like going into the water to fight a shark. Unable to secure an international U.N.-related force, Eisenhower proved extremely reluctant to send American troops to Asia so soon after securing an armistice in Korea. It was a position that Laird enthusiastically supported.

In early 1954, as the French were building up a jungle fortress at a place called Dien Bien Phu, 170 miles west of Hanoi (in what would later be called North Vietnam), Eisenhower sent ten bomber aircraft along with mechanics, who became the first American soldiers to assist the French. When Republican leaders pressed him about the commitment, he pledged the Americans would be pulled out by June 15, which they were.[59]

The Viet Minh forces, which would number more than one hundred thousand men, began a massive attack and siege of the sixteen thousand French soldiers at Dien Bien Phu on March 14, 1954. For fifty-five days there was terrible loss of life on both sides. As the French began losing the battle, the pressure for U.S. ground troops to save the French was great, but Eisenhower would not approve the American involvement without other countries' assistance. At an April 7 news conference, Eisenhower made his most famous speech about Indochina, which became known thereafter as "the domino theory." Asked about the strategic importance of Indochina, the president said there were "broader considerations that might follow what you would call the 'falling domino' principle." If the United States abandoned Southeast Asia, that could result in the loss to Communist forces of all Indochina, then Burma, Thailand, Malaya, and Indonesia—and probably the additional loss of Japan, Formosa (Taiwan), and the Philippines, at which point Australia and New Zealand would be threatened.

Such real concerns made Eisenhower more susceptible at that time to pressure from military leaders and right-wing politicians to enter the war. While Laird was opposed to such a move, his C&M buddy Nixon was hawkish. On April 16, 1954, before the American Society of Newspaper Editors, Nixon said that if sending American forces was the only way to avoid further Communist expansion in Asia, he believed that "the Executive Branch of the government has to take the politically unpopular position of facing up to it and doing it, and I personally would support such a decision." He appeared to be enunciating a new administration policy, contrary to what Eisenhower had ever said, and the statement made headlines around the globe.

Dien Bien Phu finally fell to Ho Chi Minh's forces (under General Nguyen Giap) on May 7—the same day Laird declared pointedly in Athens, Wisconsin, "Indochina is no place for American soldiers to fight."[60] Twelve days later, on May 19, Laird was heartened to hear the president express the same view. The occasion was a White House breakfast for the C&M Club. At one point, Eisenhower said, "America should never get involved with a land war in Asia." Laird never forgot and frequently quoted Eisenhower's words over the years. Laird also remembered that Nixon had a distinctly different viewpoint, and that Eisenhower "took him to the woodshed" regarding his more hawkish remarks.

Almost seven years later, Eisenhower completed his term as president and had held the line against American troop involvement in Vietnam. A total of only 773 military advisors were then in South Vietnam, according to Laird. The number was so infinitesimal when looking not only at the total number of U.S. forces but also at larger involvement in dozens of places around the world that Eisenhower supporters could boast about his Republican administration, "He got us out of Korea and he kept us out of Vietnam."

3

A House Divided

H R. HALDEMAN STEPPED OFF THE PLANE on a chilly November Sun-
. day in central Wisconsin, fashionably warmed by a cashmere coat
with velvet collar. The advance man for Vice President Nixon made an unforgettable first impression on Bob Froehlke, who met him at the airport. Mel
Laird had asked Froehlke to host Haldeman in his home for the evening, and
Haldeman was in town to pave the way for Nixon's appearance at a party
honoring Laird—an occasion that became the Great Kennedy-Nixon Cranberry Debate of 1959.

After six years in Congress, Laird's popularity was such that his friends
and supporters had independently planned a formal affair for him—the "Melvin R. Laird Appreciation Night" on November 12. Nixon, gearing up to run
for the presidency, agreed to be the keynote speaker but insisted that his
appearance be nonpartisan; no local politicos would be invited to sit on the
dais with him to boost their own campaigns. Still, Nixon could not ignore
the fact that Wisconsin would be a crucial presidential primary state only a
few months later. He was also fully cognizant that his potential opponent,
Sen. John F. Kennedy, was scheduled to speak in Laird's hometown of Marshfield on the same night, just thirty-two miles from the Laird dinner in Wisconsin Rapids. Nixon felt his appearance needed to be well advanced, so
Haldeman was sent four days ahead.

Dinner at the Froehlkes' that night was their usual Sunday supper tradi-
tion—hot dogs roasted in the fireplace. When informed of the evening menu,
Haldeman, who was described later as having "a gaze that would freeze
Medusa," brusquely asked: "Do you always cook hot dogs in your fireplace?"
He eventually caught the spirit of the occasion and seemed to enjoy himself.[1]

But the bucolic beginning for the quasi campaign event did not extend past Monday morning when Health, Education, and Welfare secretary Arthur S. Fleming started America's first big food scare. The San Francisco office of the Food and Drug Administration had discovered that a batch of Oregon cranberries was contaminated with the weedkiller Amitrole, which was potentially toxic for humans. At a press conference in Washington, Fleming announced that 9 percent of the Oregon and Washington crops might be contaminated—but that the majority of cranberries, which were grown primarily in Wisconsin and Massachusetts, had shown no contamination. A reporter pressed him: Can a "housewife" feel safe in buying *any* cranberries at the supermarket? "To be on the safe side," Fleming said, "she doesn't buy."[2]

Only two weeks before Thanksgiving, Fleming was the grim reaper. Cranberries disappeared from supermarket shelves across the country and from the menus of many restaurants. Laird quickly jumped into the fray. His great-grandfather had been the first man to grow the fruit in Wood County, and the crop had taken off to the point that nearly one third of all cranberries in America were grown in Laird's district.[3] Within hours of Fleming's press conference, Laird called FDA administrator George Larrick and demanded quick action to clear innocent Wisconsin cranberries. As the ranking member of the HEW Appropriations Subcommittee, Laird held the purse strings and Larrick knew it. "If there is any way of getting clean berries to the public in time for Thanksgiving, we will certainly do it," he promised.

The scare had been prompted because rats that were fed Amitrole in concentrations of one hundred parts per million had developed thyroid cancer. To duplicate that consumption, a human being would have to have digested fifteen thousand pounds of contaminated cranberries every day for a number of years. But it was too late to calm the public with such facts. The best Laird could get was an immediate dispatch of one hundred inspectors and sixty chemists to cranberry-producing areas to examine and quickly pronounce the majority of the crop clean.[4] By the time Nixon and Kennedy arrived in Wisconsin for their speeches, the crimson crisis was Topic A. Senator Kennedy, from the cranberry-producing state of Massachusetts, ceremoniously drank two glasses of cranberry juice as he spoke to fifteen hundred Democrats assembled in Marshfield. As he sipped, Kennedy denounced the Eisenhower administration—and by association, Nixon—for inflating the scare.

With all the photographers at the Laird banquet, the largest dinner ever held (with two thousand guests) in central Wisconsin, the congressman whispered to Nixon that he damn well better eat all his cranberries and ask for seconds. "I'm going to watch you eat them first," Nixon smiled back at Laird.

So Laird downed a man-sized portion, and then Nixon started on his cranberry sauce, eventually consuming four helpings pressed on him by Laird's wife and mother.

Nixon aide Herb Klein remembers the cranberry competition between Nixon and Kennedy as "the first debate." If consumption was the measure, Nixon certainly out-ate Kennedy. But the pro-Kennedy *Madison Capital-Times* declared the "cranberry duel" a "dead heat." Yes, "Nixon ate the most cranberries," they pronounced, but "Kennedy got in the best licks"—rhetorically.[5] Laird saw the episode as a harbinger of things to come: his earnest, hard-working candidate, Nixon, bested by a more charismatic Kennedy, heavily favored by the press traveling with him.

Laird liked Kennedy, a fellow U.S. Navy and World War II veteran, and a fellow young Turk on the other side of the aisle. Their first meeting had been in the White House on a memorable occasion. A Polish pilot, Lt. Franciszek Jarecki, had defected on March 5, 1953, flying his plane into Denmark. It was the first time the West had a chance to look at a high-performance Soviet MiG. The CIA had promised Jarecki cash and American citizenship; Kennedy and Laird (with Ford) were responsible for pushing a bill through their two houses "For the Relief of Franciszek Jarecki." Eisenhower invited Jarecki, Kennedy, Laird, Ford, and several others to the White House on July 29 for the ceremonial signing.[6] Laird chatted with Kennedy, congratulating him on his engagement only a month before to Jacqueline Bouvier.

But the first substantive conversation between Kennedy and Laird occurred at a private Democratic dinner, during which he defended Kennedy to the senator's senior party leadership. Laird had been invited to the dinner by Democrat John Fogarty, with whom he'd become close while working on the Health Appropriations Subcommittee. What Laird most remembered was that Kennedy's ambition was the butt of criticism for the small gathering of senior Democrats. His upstart campaign for the Democratic presidential nomination in 1960 was not generally supported by the party leadership.

~

For a man with few disappointments in his political life up to that point, Laird's selection by Nixon as the vice chairman instead of chairman of the 1960 Republican Platform Committee was a small setback. After the 1958 midterm election debacle for Republicans, Eisenhower thought a nonpolitical, charismatic outsider such as Charles Percy, an Illinois businessman and Eisenhower protégé, would put a better face on the party as chairman. The press speculated that Nixon had wanted someone more liberal than himself, handsomer, younger, and photogenic, and Percy was all that. (At thirty-seven,

Laird was actually three years younger than Percy, but his balding pate versus Percy's fulsome blond mane gave a different impression.) Laird publicly said he was "highly honored" to be appointed vice chairman.[7] He later learned that Nixon passed him over in an attempt to curry favor with New York's governor Nelson Rockefeller.

In 1960, if America had a royal family, it was the Rockefellers. Their business and philanthropic enterprises affected every facet of American life. Nelson Rockefeller was a force that Nixon had to co-opt if he wanted to be president, and Charles Percy moved in Rockefeller's circles. But Nixon had miscalculated. Around the time of the Percy appointment, it was becoming evident that even though he had not campaigned in the primaries, Rockefeller hoped the Republican delegates would draft him as their presidential nominee at the July convention.

What imbued Rockefeller with such new quixotic obstinacy was his conviction that America had fallen behind in the nuclear missile race. He was not alone. One of his protégés, Harvard professor Henry Kissinger, had written a book that presumed the Soviets were ahead in that race. Senator Kennedy had expressed alarm about the "missile gap" in August 1958, and it was clear that he would make it a major charge against the Eisenhower-Nixon administration in the campaign.

Nixon knew that if he was going to beat Kennedy, he had to have the more liberal Eastern Republican establishment with him, and that required Rockefeller's endorsement. Nixon sent a rapid series of offers to Rockefeller: Would he like to be the vice presidential nominee? No! Would he chair the Republican National Convention? No. Would he please give the keynote address? No—he might not even attend. On May 25, 1960, Rockefeller announced he was making himself available for a presidential "draft."

Nixon was still hoping to mollify Rockefeller through emissaries, and he saw Percy as his best hope. Percy met with Rockefeller for three hours in New York on July 6 and was given a nearly six-thousand-word memo of what Rockefeller thought should be included in the Republican Platform. Then Nixon caught a plane to New York to negotiate the fine print with Rockefeller in his penthouse apartment on Fifth Avenue. To the governor's surprise, Nixon was willing to compromise on almost every point. What Rockefeller didn't know, and Laird did, was that Nixon did not think the platform was sacred, so he was willing to compromise with Rockefeller, who held platforms in higher regard.

At 10:30 p.m., after Nixon and Rockefeller had been negotiating for a couple of hours, a five-way telephone conversation between New York and

Chicago was arranged to bring other key players into the process. In Chicago, from their rooms in the Sheraton Blackstone Hotel, Laird and Percy came on the line. Roswell Perkins, a Rockefeller deputy at another hotel, also came on. Broken only by an accidental twenty-minute disconnection by the operator, the five spoke on this "party line" for more than three hours. Although Laird was able to mask it somewhat, he was the primary dissenter. Rockefeller was getting what he wanted, and Nixon was getting what he most wanted, which was Rockefeller's support. But Laird didn't like it, because he knew what a furor the amended platform would prompt from several quarters that Nixon could ill afford to anger. At one point, he presciently cautioned the four other parties: "There is one person missing in this conversation: the president."

After the call ended at 2 a.m., Nixon stayed another hour and a half, finalizing the press release about the agreement on "specific and basic positions" that would be issued in Rockefeller's name; he flew back to Washington at 3:30 a.m. The statement, which outlined seven points each on domestic and foreign policy, was promptly dubbed by journalists who received it after dawn as the "Fourteen-Point Compact of Fifth Avenue."[8]

Republican conservatives and moderates were furious, believing Nixon had sold them out. Many of the 104 Platform Committee delegates were up in arms as well. They had worked hard to produce a platform draft of which they were proud. It was insulting that Nixon had paid court to Rockefeller who had been allowed to dictate a rewrite. Then came an eruption of volcanic anger from President Eisenhower. On Saturday morning, after learning of the accord while at his Newport, Rhode Island, vacation spot, Eisenhower chose to take out his rage on Laird. The president had learned from Bryce Harlow that Laird was really running the Platform Committee, not Percy. The language in the Rockefeller platform about needed domestic and national security changes might be construed as criticizing Eisenhower administration policies. There was no small talk in the call from Eisenhower to Laird. The compact was a personal affront to him. "Mel, that Park Avenue accord that Dick Nixon has agreed to with Rockefeller is a load of rubbish," Eisenhower began. (The president mixed up the avenues, always referring to it as the *Park* rather than *Fifth* Avenue compact.) What made Ike seethe most were the words about national defense, which implied that it had been insufficient under his watch. "Mel, I know more about the Defense Department than Nixon and Rockefeller will ever know," the president sputtered. "I personally reviewed the defense budget, and I stand by it as 100 percent adequate. It doesn't need another $3.5 billion like Rockefeller says. Just because Kennedy is out there talking about a missile gap doesn't mean there is one."

Laird could do nothing but agree. The president concluded the call with instructions to Laird. "I want you to go see Dick and tell him I consider this a *personal* thing. They are questioning my leadership. That accord is not in the best interests of the Republican Party, nor of the country. If some of those words get in the platform, especially in the defense section, I cannot support the platform or the candidate. Tell Dick he has to back off, or else I cannot support him. He's got to decide whether he wants my support or Rockefeller's!"[9]

Laird met privately with Nixon shortly after he arrived in Chicago and delivered the tough message. Nixon was shocked. He had thought that he had cut out the language that might offend Eisenhower. Now he was hearing it was not enough, so he leaned on Laird to fix it. "Mel, do what you have to do," Nixon said. "*You* handle it. Take over the committee and run it." But both of them knew Nixon couldn't publicly back away from Rockefeller, having made the Fifth Avenue Compact in good faith. He was depending on Laird to block enough of the language from getting into the final platform so Eisenhower would be mollified.[10]

For four days, from Saturday to Tuesday night, Laird got little sleep. Percy, in over his head for this political fight, was willingly sidelined to work on a film about the Eisenhower administration and the platform that would be aired during the nationally televised convention.[11] For his friend Rockefeller, the best Percy could do at this point was promise that "I would weave the fourteen points of the compact into sort of a voice-over narration in the film," he recalled.

The final 12,485-word platform, which passed on a convention voice vote July 27, had a generally moderate political tone, having been adroitly massaged by Laird so that the three primary players—Nixon, Rockefeller, and Eisenhower—signed off on the whole platform without rancor. Contemporary press accounts suggested that the compact had skewed the platform into Rockefeller's corner, but a close analysis suggests that in substance there was little change from the original platform draft.

Laird received praise for pulling a rabbit out of the hat, considering the many directions from which the Fifth Avenue Compact had received fire.[12] Percy later thanked Laird for getting him through "the first real battle that I had—my introduction into the infighting of national politics."[13]

Nixon won the Republican nomination on the first ballot. Among the few men Nixon considered for the vice presidential nomination—after Rockefeller's refusal—was Jerry Ford. But he chose, instead, to go with a Massachusetts Republican, ambassador to the United Nations and former senator,

Henry Cabot Lodge, who would bring along the Eastern intellectual wing of the party.

Laird was fairly secure in his district, which he won that November with two-thirds of the vote. So he devoted substantial energy and time, when Congress was not in session, to campaigning for Nixon. During the campaign, the rumor was rife that if Nixon won, he would tap Laird as his secretary of defense. When questioned about it, Laird expressed his sincere disinterest.[14]

Not so energetic in the Nixon campaign was President Eisenhower. Privately he regretted that in 1951 his own party, reacting to Roosevelt's four terms, had helped push the Twenty-second Amendment, limiting a president to two terms. If not for that—and even though he turned seventy in October, which made him the oldest president—Eisenhower would have run for a third term and probably would have defeated Kennedy. Instead, he watched an underling, with whom he was not close and about whom he was ambivalent, run for his Oval Office. He made only four major appearances for Nixon, and any good that he did unraveled with the constant quoting of a press conference statement Eisenhower made. When asked to name a major idea Nixon had contributed to the Eisenhower administration, Ike had snapped: "If you give me a week, I might think of one. I don't remember."[15]

Even so, the Kennedy-Nixon race was very close. Kennedy received 49.72 percent of the vote, while Nixon garnered 49.55 percent. Out of 68.8 million votes, Nixon lost by only 114,673. Not given to pessimism, Laird looked for positive signs in the Republican net gain of twenty-one House and two Senate seats. With the Republican standard-bearer Eisenhower on his way out, and Nixon unemployed and relegated to inactive Republican leadership status, there was room for new blood at the top of the party. Laird, having acquitted himself with distinction during the convention and campaign, was destined to hold a prominent place in the post-Eisenhower party.

~

John F. Kennedy came to the presidency shining with charisma and glowing with promise. But the "New Frontier" did not have any magic solutions. The Cold War was growing so much colder that before the year was out, backyard bomb shelters were a thriving industry. The Republican minority, with Laird as one of their emerging leaders, felt it was critical to provide modified or alternative solutions, as well as balance. As a counterpoint to the new Democrats, Laird deftly began defining himself as a *creative conservative.*

While Laird was tentatively testing the waters as loyal opposition spokesman during the JFK presidential honeymoon, one man was noticeably silent—Nixon. He had been devastated by the election loss, though he tried to mask it for his friends. Nevertheless, even during the festive farewell bash he gave for his Chowder and Marching Club pals Nixon seemed down-hearted.[16] After he left the vice presidency, he remained silent about the new Kennedy administration. "In view of my position as the opposing candidate I should allow a reasonable time to pass before saying anything that could be interpreted as critical of my successful opponent," he explained to Laird in an April 11 letter. Since candidate Kennedy had ambitiously promised to do more in his first ninety days than he actually accomplished, Nixon felt that he "should break this self-imposed silence" with a May speaking tour. He asked Laird for speech ideas.[17] Laird responded: "Somehow or other, we must find a means of dramatizing to the American public the difficulty which the new president has in making big decisions and in standing by these deci-sions once they have been made."[18]

There could be no better case-in-point than the Bay of Pigs fiasco. Ken-nedy had authorized a CIA effort to overthrow Fidel Castro using Cuban exiles who would "invade" the island. When they were ambushed, Kennedy refused to send air support, fearing to awaken a Soviet response. More than 100 of the Cuban exiles were killed and 1,113 were dragged off to prison. In the immediate wake of the disaster, Kennedy asked Republican leaders to hold their tongues and present a united front. He sent a military aircraft to pick up Laird in Wisconsin so he could participate in the White House brief-ing on the Bay of Pigs.[19] The Republicans agreed to a temporary morato-rium on finger-pointing in the interests of national unity, but they could not keep silent for long. Two months after the invasion, with the gloves finally off, Laird observed, "The invasion fiasco was caused by the failure of our Commander-in-Chief to carry out the original plans [which] included mil-itary air support."[20]

No single foreign policy action irked Laird more than Kennedy's dealings and missteps over Laos. The 1954 Geneva Accords, which primarily dealt with Vietnam, had also guaranteed Laos neutrality. During the next six years, how-ever, an off-and-on civil war caused three factions to vie for power. When one of them, the Communist Pathet Lao, threatened to overtake the others, a decision had to be made by the new president on whether to commit U.S. troops to back the pro-Western forces. At a dramatic March 23, 1961, press conference, Kennedy squarely blamed the Soviet Union for priming the crisis and swore to protect Laos and the region from a fall to Communism. Some troops in the Pacific area were then moved around to give the impression that military muscle would back the president's rhetoric, but it was all bluff. Kennedy was secretly determined to push for a coalition Lao government, which would include the Communists. In early 1962 he strong-armed America's Laotian allies into an agreement sharing power with the Communists and neutralists. That agreement was called the Declaration and Protocol on Neutrality in Laos. It was signed on July 23, 1962, by the United States and fourteen other nations.

Laird was incredulous. He felt that Kennedy's failure to keep his promise to get the Communists out of Laos had "gravely weakened" the president's credibility and respect in the region. Laird warned that the Pathet Lao would never live up to the agreement nor would the North Vietnamese, whose forces did not withdraw from Laos, although they had promised to do so in signing the agreement. Laird observed that the Kennedy administration had engineered "an arrangement whereby the communists [are] enabled to take over Laos through political means rather than military means."[21]

As Laird had predicted on numerous occasions, by 1964 the agreement on Laos was a cruel charade. The Pathet Lao pulled out of the coalition and continued the civil war for territory in Laos, aided by the North Vietnamese and Soviets, all brazenly violating the 1962 agreement. Meanwhile, Kennedy withdrew American military advisors and decreased financial support. His successor, Lyndon Johnson, would later take the battle underground to avoid the appearance of violating the neutrality pact. The CIA, State, and Defense Departments prosecuted what came to be called "the secret war in Laos" to keep the Communists in check.

Laird—not suspecting then how the story of Southeast Asia would become his own political history in a few short years—strongly believed in the value of military alliances and felt "neutralism" in certain countries was an open invitation for a Communist takeover.

Even in retirement, Dwight D. Eisenhower was the closest thing the Republican Party had to a leader in the early 1960s, but the grand old man of the GOP was not a font of new ideas for Republicans. Presidential candidates and others who sought him out came away disappointed. Somehow, Eisenhower's popularity never transferred to other Republicans, as the party's congressional losses of 1954, 1956, and 1958 proved.

Some Republicans felt that Richard Nixon was the party's future. He had lost the White House to Kennedy by a nose, but in the process had helped Republicans gain congressional seats in the 1960 election. On leaving office, Nixon sent Laird a vice presidential ash tray as a souvenir, with a note promising to let Laird know "where I will be and what I will be doing [as] soon as I make a final decision with regard to my plans for the future."[22]

It didn't take him long to decide. In mid-1961, Nixon met with his C&M friends to ask their opinion about his running for governor of California in 1962. "We *all* recommended that he not do it—almost unanimously," Laird recalled. "I didn't think he could win. And if he ever wanted to come back and run again for president, I thought it would be a mistake to get defeated in California." In a few weeks, Nixon announced he was going to run anyway, rejecting the considerable wisdom of the C&M and offending them in the process. "We all thought, 'Why the hell did he come out here and ask for our opinions?' We were all down on him after that." (Laird never let Nixon forget. Years later, on a couple of occasions when Nixon asked Laird for advice, if Laird was convinced Nixon had already made up his mind, Laird would say, "Well, I remember when you asked for advice on running for governor." Nixon would laugh and say, "Oh, you son of a bitch!")

With Nixon in the doghouse and Eisenhower in ideological retirement, Laird quickly fashioned himself as the party's fresh-ideas man. He first decided to follow through on a suggestion made in the early 1950s by the American Political Science Association. The group had proposed that each party draft a declaration of policy in the off-presidential election years to update the party platforms. Laird started working behind the scenes to form a committee to do just that.

Laird wanted unanimous consent from all top national Republicans on the document. So all sixteen Republican governors were consulted, as were Nixon and other potential 1964 Republican presidential candidates. Laird pressed Ike for assistance, and he agreed to consult after the first draft was done.[23] The final 2,400-word document from the "1962 Joint Committee on Republican Principles" was approved by both the House and Senate Republican conferences. The document began with the enunciation of the "basic beliefs" of all Republicans, which still have some currency today—limited government, and an emphasis on individual rights. The statement then reviewed what it called the Kennedy administration's general failure in the cause of freedom at home and abroad. The Democratic domestic program was flawed by the thinking that "Government must protect individuals from foolish spending by taking their money and spending it for them." The strongest condemnation dealt with Kennedy's foreign policy: "Despite this Nation's position as the most powerful on earth, the bankruptcy of its leadership was shown at critical times in the past year. . . . It has demonstrated neither the wit nor the will to meet effectively the assault of international communism on freedom."

Communism gave Laird the fodder for his first book, published in 1962.

The genesis of the volume had come from a course titled How To Be A Communist, which Laird had taken from Notre Dame professor Gerhard Niemeyer, who also lectured on the subject at the National War College. Laird was stimulated by the classes, held in Washington and Chicago, where he became acquainted with George Shultz, later a Nixon budget official and Ronald Reagan's secretary of state.

Laird's special assistant Bill Baroody Jr. and his friend Karl Hess, working with Laird for a year, produced the book. The title, A House Divided, signified a world that was then as America had been during the Civil War, half-slave (under the Communist thumb) and half free. Subtitled "America's Strategy Gap," the volume dissected Kennedy's foreign policy as an "underdog strategy" that seemed to pursue peace-at-any-price, and claimed victory any time a nuclear war did not occur. In Laird's opinion, the administration had failed to understand the Communist will, its disinterest in true negotiation, or the cunning nature of its leader, Nikita Khrushchev.[24]

Laird recognized that until the 1960s, conservatives had been regarded as the low ideology on the intellectual totem pole. His strategy for reinventing the Republican Party included putting a more scholarly patina on conservatism. Even though Laird himself was not known as a deep thinker, he understood the relationship between ideas and politics, and he mounted a successful assault on the liberal ivory tower through several approaches, including publication of A House Divided. Laird became the point person for the rejuvenation of the top conservative think tanks of the twentieth century: the American Enterprise Institute for Public Policy Research, the Center for Strategic and International Studies, and the Heritage Foundation.

The story of his backstage role begins in 1953 with Laird's first connection to the American Enterprise Institute. Its founding purpose was to be a conservative counterweight to the Brookings Institution, but it was dismissed by many as another megaphone for business interests. One of those men who thought it had greater possibilities was Carl Jacobs, president of Wisconsin-based Hardware Mutual Casualty (later Sentry Insurance) where Laird's childhood friend Bob Froehlke worked. Jacobs had been a significant supporter in all of Laird's campaigns for the state senate.

At a Washington dinner party just a few days before Eisenhower's inauguration, a core group met for the first time aiming to energize what was then called the America Enterprise Association (AEA). Jacobs had brought along Laird, and also asked a bright young U.S. Chamber of Commerce staff economist William J. Baroody to join them. Laird took to Baroody immediately. He instinctively recognized a can-do kindred spirit who could transform the faltering AEA, but Baroody didn't want to leave his Chamber of Commerce job. In 1954, Laird hosted a luncheon on Capitol Hill to impress Baroody. He invited the A-list of Republicans, including Ford. Laird used the lunch to complain about the lack of conservative academics to testify in Congress on issues dear to the party's heart. The liberal think tanks, including the Brookings Institution, dominated the brain trust. Laird and his peers proved persuasive, and Baroody was hired to transform the AEA, under its new name, the American Enterprise Institute. Baroody's son Bill Jr. worked for Laird at the House Republican Conference and regularly cross-fertilized projects between AEI and Congress. He would later succeed his father as AEI president.

The Georgetown University Center for Strategic and International Studies (CSIS) was a direct stepchild of AEI.[25] Laird sometimes complained to Baroody that while AEI was producing great economic and domestic policy material for Congress, there was a need for a conservative foreign policy think tank. He and Baroody agreed that the man for the job was David Abshire, a decorated Korean combat veteran AEI had hired only a year before on Laird's recommendation. In 1962, when it appeared it was better for Abshire to found his own institute, independent of AEI, Laird was instrumental in lining up retired Admiral Arleigh Burke, the longest-serving chief of naval operations and a World War II legend, as cofounder with Abshire of CSIS. As was so often the case, Laird didn't leave fingerprints when he influenced events from behind the curtain, but evidence of Laird's involvement is substantive in his private files.

As for the Heritage Foundation, its most important and visionary cofounder in 1973, Edwin Feulner Jr., was a Laird protégé. As such, he worked at the CSIS, then on Laird's congressional staff, and then for Secretary of Defense Laird at the Pentagon. Along the way he saw the need for a rapid-response think tank that could jump quickly into legislative debates in Congress by preparing position papers. With money from conservative Colorado brewer Joseph Coors, Feulner founded the Heritage Foundation, which became the cutting-edge advocacy institute that leaped to prominence during the Reagan presidency.[26]

In his book *A House Divided*, Laird implied that freedom would be the most important issue of the 1962 campaign. Nowhere was that more urgent, he thought, than in Cuba, which by late summer was transforming into a bristling outpost of the Soviet Union. Intelligence briefings Laird received in the Defense Appropriations Subcommittee hearings estimated that an average of 120 anti-Castro and others were being slaughtered by Castro each week, and the dictator was brutally stifling his people's attempts to flee the country. The Cuban militia had about 350,000 men, and "arms received [by Cuba] were enough to equip 600,000 men—which meant that the extra arms were intended to . . . promote the growth of Communism in other Central or South American countries," according to Laird's assessment of U.S. intelligence reports.[27]

In late August, Laird called on President Kennedy to blockade Cuba.[28] Laird knew that if the president imposed such a blockade, the Soviet Union would rattle some serious sabers, but the proper response would be to ignore them. In his book, written before the Cuban Missile Crisis, Laird had predicted that "the most dangerous situation conceivable would be to leave all questions to the hour of crisis, when a group of presidential advisors . . . would hover around the President, and seek to influence him. Only doctrine— firm and carefully reasoned in advance—can prevent such an eventuality." Laird feared that because of Kennedy's withdrawal of air support during the Bay of Pigs invasion, "the Communists—instructed by observing our confusion—will create future crises in which our leaders will be forced to make sudden decisions."[29]

The famous "Thirteen Days" of the October 1962 Cuban missile crisis unfolded in a similar manner. Publicly announcing the existence of nuclear missile sites under construction in Cuba, and proving it with reconnaissance photos, Kennedy vowed the sites would not be completed. He instituted a U.S. Navy blockade of Cuba, and for a tense week the world stood on the brink of nuclear war. Khrushchev "blinked" when it became clear Kennedy was willing to go as far as he needed, even with nuclear weapons. After an October 28 agreement, the Russians dismantled the missile bases in return for U.S. pledges not to invade Cuba, to end the blockade, and to remove U.S. nuclear missiles from Turkey, which was already planned.

While it is true that too often the party not in power professes to know how best to run things, in this case the record shows that Laird had been right about the blockade. "It is too bad that this nation did not listen to Congressman Laird several months ago," one Wisconsin newspaper editorialized in the direct aftermath of the crisis. "If [Laird's] advice on a 'peace blockade' had been followed, Mr. Khrushchev would have backed down from his Cuban plans long before he reached the dangerous situation of aiming nuclear missiles at U.S. cities." The paper praised Laird for his support of crucial weapons programs: "[H]ad it not been for an amendment sponsored by Cong. Laird several years ago, only two nuclear submarines would be on duty now." Instead, "today there are six Polaris submarines, each equipped with 16 nuclear missiles roaming the seas. They could be no small reason why Mr. Khrushchev backed down on his Cuban adventure."[30]

One thing Kennedy gained by delaying strong action was to postpone the settlement of the crisis until just before the midterm 1962 elections, and that earned his party a "rally-round-the-flag" bonus. Instead of expected Republican gains, both parties maintained the status quo. "The biggest issue—whether the President was doing enough in Cuba—evaporated before election day," one respected publication wrote in review. Congressman Laird and many other Republicans felt that way. The Republican Congressional Committee chair charged that his party's chances for big gains had been "Cubanized."[31]

One man who believed he was terribly hurt by Kennedy's strong handling of the crisis so close to election day was Richard Nixon, who had lost the California governor's race that year. He was privately convinced that Kennedy had manipulated the crisis for the benefit of the Democratic Party. An early hint of this classic Nixon paranoia can be read between the lines of a letter from Nixon to Laird: "While the overall results in California were disappointing, the Republican showing generally in the nation was most encouraging, particularly in view of the fact that the Cuban blockade took place just when our campaign was beginning to reach its peak."[32]

Laird easily won his sixth term in Congress, racking up a two-to-one vote against his Democratic opponent. This occurred, as before, because Democrats not only voted for him but also campaigned for him. Kennedy's own secretary of health, education, and welfare, John Gardner, came to Wisconsin to help drum up the vote for Laird. Years later, Laird's congressional successor, Democrat David Obey, who as a child had campaigned for Laird, offered something of a confession that testified to Laird's 1960s crossover appeal. "In 1962, I was on the ballot running [as a Democrat] for the [Wisconsin] legislature. And I have to be honest about it; we had a turkey on our ticket running against Mel for Congress. I have to admit I voted for Mel."[33]

Getting along with Democrats, and receiving some of their support, did not obligate Laird to support the majority of the Kennedy administration's initiatives. A *Congressional Quarterly* study of key 1961–63 roll-call votes shows that Laird voted with the president only 28 percent of the time—more often on domestic issues than foreign ones.[34] The *Congressional Quarterly* reports had looked at just a small number of critical floor votes. When Laird added up his committee votes, he reported to his constituents that he had supported Kennedy two-thirds of the time—almost as much as he had Eisenhower.[35]

Laird's most influential voting came in the Appropriations Committee, where he often found himself in agreement with Kennedy in his two specialty areas, health and defense.

One of the difficulties Eisenhower and the Republicans had in keeping defense spending relatively stable was the growing armaments industry lobby. Eisenhower's famous TV and radio farewell address spelled out the problem: the arms makers in search of profits, the military services in search of 100 percent security, and colluding congressmen anxious to keep defense jobs in their districts had set up a powerful advocacy group. Eisenhower gave the lobby a name, "the military-industrial complex."[36] By adding that label to the American lexicon, it made a powerful warning from the former supreme commander of World War II.

Laird agreed wholeheartedly with Eisenhower that the fight against Communism called for vigilance, but not necessarily inflated spending. [37] He and Ike both felt strongly that Kennedy's campaign charge of a missile gap between the United States and the Soviets had been overstated. They expected the new president to try to exceed Eisenhower's last defense budget. But Kennedy didn't, at first. Unquestionably the missile gap issue was a ruse that helped elect Kennedy. In classified briefings while a candidate, JFK was given the facts and figures that clearly demonstrated there was no gap. When Kennedy took office, he knew that no gap existed, and some of his officials admitted it. Only three weeks after the inauguration, JFK's new defense secretary Robert S. McNamara acknowledged to reporters that he had found no missile gap.[38] In fact, as Laird knew from the highly classified briefings he received in 1961 and 1962, the United States had at least a four-to-one, perhaps even a five-to-one, advantage over the Soviets.[39]

The most significant part of the advantage was the Polaris submarine and missile system, which Laird pushed heavily as "the most nearly invulnerable weapon in the history of warfare."[40] Kennedy agreed and increased the Polaris program funding by 50 percent in his first year—part of a $5.9 billion increase over the Eisenhower budget. JFK had not initially intended to hike the defense budget so much. But all that was changed by the building of the Berlin Wall and the increasing Cold War stakes.

Laird became a champion and House expert of some high-dollar defense programs including the Polaris submarine and missile system, the Navy's antisubmarine warfare program, and the X-20 manned military space glider called Dyna-Soar (for dynamic soaring). He frequently differed with Defense Secretary McNamara on spending issues, and the two developed a rivalry that would occasionally flare in public. In December 1963, after McNamara

unilaterally cancelled the Dyna-Soar project, Laird was needled on that decision by a television talk show host, Ann Corrick, who began, "Secretary
McNamara has been in combat with Congress over a number of things [such
as] the cancellation of the Dyna Soar . . . how would you assess him as a
Secretary of Defense?"

With some congressional courtesy, Laird answered that, so far, McNamara had been "a good Secretary of Defense. I don't believe, however, that
the Secretary of Defense can be the *sole judge of every decision* that must be
made in the Pentagon. And I think that . . . Secretary of Defense McNamara
has . . . spread himself rather thin on many of the decisions that needed to
be made in the Department of Defense."[41]

~

The line of demarcation between Laird and McNamara turned from fuzzy
to unmistakable over the Vietnam War. As a senator, Kennedy had approved
all of Eisenhower's decisions regarding Vietnam. He was impressed with the
leadership of South Vietnam's president, Ngo Dinh Diem, who had adroitly
knitted together his population into a viable nation and, with about $250
million in annual U.S. economic aid, brought social and economic stability
to the south. At the end of 1960, South Vietnam controlled more than 80
percent of its own land area, and the indigenous Viet Cong guerrillas answering to Hanoi numbered fewer than six thousand. The American military mission numbered around 773, and none had been killed in combat. But after
Kennedy's election, North Vietnam—possibly to test the mettle of the new
president—increased its Viet Cong numbers and activities to the point that
Diem declared in October 1961: "[This is] no longer a guerrilla war but a
real war waged by an enemy who attacks us with regular units."

The first step toward the American quagmire came at the end of April 1961
when JFK decided to increase the number of American military advisors
to more than the ceiling set by the 1954 Geneva accords. Even though the
United States had not been a signatory, American leaders had pledged to
abide by the accords. Kennedy's executive decision to abrogate the agreement was done in secret—neither congressional leadership nor American
allies were informed. The second step came after the return of an October
fact-finding mission led by General Maxwell Taylor, who recommended that
eight thousand U.S. combat troops could be slipped in under the guise of
flood assistance and quietly stay on afterward as military advisors.[42] Kennedy
did not sign off on the subterfuge and was disinclined to authorize such a
large increase in military advisors; nevertheless, he sent in more. By the end
of 1961 there were 1,364 of them, and the first American advisor/soldier had

been killed in Vietnam combat. He and other advisors regularly traveled and fought alongside South Vietnamese units. Though they were clearly engaging in battle, Kennedy refused to confirm it. In a January 1962 press conference, when pointedly asked if U.S. soldiers were fighting in Vietnam, he answered with a resounding: "No!"

It soon became apparent to newsmen and the more astute military advisors accompanying South Vietnamese troop units that the Viet Cong had the upper hand, despite official U.S. pronouncements to the contrary. After a trip to Vietnam in May 1962, McNamara, a former corporate executive who believed numbers told the story, reported that "every quantitative measurement . . . shows that we are winning the war." Two months later McNamara again stated: "Our military assistance in Vietnam is paying off. I continue to be encouraged. There are many signs indicating progress."

At the same time, Laird had a far less rosy view. He wrote in *A House Divided* that the "counter-measures to defeat the Communist attack on South Vietnam will not be easy nor will they produce quick results," especially if the enemy was allowed consistently to slip back after battles into the sanctuary of North Vietnam and Cambodia. "The prime means of penetrating an active sanctuary is to launch counter-offensives behind enemy lines, recognizing no borders." In other words, unless the war was taken into North Vietnam, it would not end.[43]

Diem welcomed American dollars and military arms, but refused to be dictated to by the Americans. He ignored their behind-the-scenes protestations that the secret police tactics employed by his brother, the head of the secret police, Ngo Dinh Nhu, were too repressive. The tough Diem was always an authoritarian leader, using iron-hand techniques such as torture and imprisonment of political enemies to stay in power. Kennedy stomached those reports until 1963 when South Vietnam's Buddhists and students started rebelling, beginning with a religious ritual and followed by acts of self-immolation by priests, which Diem's sister-in-law, Madame Nhu, ridiculed as inconsequential "barbecues." Diem's troops raided Buddhist pagodas in response to antigovernment demonstrations, and Kennedy publicly denounced this reaction as a human rights violation. Privately, he told Diem that the Nhus had to go.

Diem could not agree to sack his most loyal brother, whose control over the secret police was pivotal to Diem's continued rule. When his intransigence was clear, Kennedy gave the green light for South Vietnamese generals to plot a coup. When the CIA-assisted coup ended in the assassination of Diem and Nhu, Kennedy was said to be "shocked" by the news. Kennedy's true role in the assassination is lost to history, as less than a month later he was himself felled by an assassin's bullet.

A tale repeated by Kennedy aide Kenny O'Donnell and Senate majority leader Mike Mansfield maintains that the president had told them in the spring of 1963 that he fully intended to completely withdraw all U.S. troops after the 1964 election. In a subsequent conversation with O'Donnell, he reportedly added that if he did it before the election, there would be a "wild conservative outcry" against his reelection. Even if he pulled out the troops after a presumed victory, he predicted to O'Donnell: "I'll become one of the most unpopular Presidents in history. I'll be damned everywhere as a Communist appeaser. But I don't care. If I tried to pull out completely now [1963] from Vietnam, we would have another Joe McCarthy Red scare on our hands, but I can do it after I'm re-elected. So we had better make damned sure that I *am* re-elected."[44]

Whatever Kennedy's intentions, he and McNamara had deployed a total of 16,575 troops to South Vietnam by the end of 1963—a more than 2,000 percent increase over the Eisenhower administration's complement. And the coup, carried out with Kennedy's complicity, created such chaos in South Vietnam, along with commensurate Viet Cong gains, that new president Lyndon Johnson felt even more U.S. troops were needed there, in short order.

And so began the tragedy that Melvin Laird would later feel morally and politically compelled to end.

4

Laird Also Rises

THE BUSY WEEK WAS WINDING DOWN, and Mel Laird was looking forward to the weekend. At the Rotunda Restaurant on Capitol Hill he had lunch that Friday, November 22, 1963, with a close Democrat friend, Congressman John Fogarty of Rhode Island. The laughter and consultation ebbed as they checked their watches about 1:45 p.m., and then headed back to an Appropriations Committee meeting. As they walked between the Cannon and Longworth congressional office buildings, the news rippled through the crowds on the street: "Kennedy has been shot!" The two swiftly reached the committee hearing room, and Fogarty announced the session was cancelled. Both men returned to their offices to field phone calls. Laird issued a short public statement. He decried the "dastardly blow at the very heart of our Republic," and conveyed his "deepest sympathy" to the Kennedy family.[1]

Laird liked Kennedy, but he had been mystified, as was his mentor Eisenhower, about the nation's adoration of this president while he was in office. They both considered him to be a man who epitomized the triumph of style over substance. Laird had been asked to make some satirical remarks about Kennedy a month hence on December 23 at a Gridiron Club Dinner. The club had been organized by Washington journalists in 1885 to host politicians and roast them with good humor. As a top Republican leader, Laird was scheduled to speak before press spokesman Pierre Salinger. "We really have to admire the job that Pierre's doing," he had planned to say. "Imagine trying to keep the press interested in a guy with a $90 billion budget, a beautiful wife, a pair of cute kids, and a whole bathtub full of aircraft carriers." He had also planned to acknowledge Arthur Krock of the *New York Times*, who was celebrating his fiftieth year with the Gridiron, and then add: "You know it kind of makes me think—a little wistfully perhaps—when we remember that Art was first elected to this fine club some three years before the second coming. You know, before Jack was born."[2]

The loss of Kennedy threw the 1964 presidential election campaign into a tailspin. Vice President Lyndon Johnson would now be the incumbent, and the Republicans were struggling to find someone to challenge him. As early as 1963 Laird himself had been promoted as presidential material by Eisenhower himself. The president had been in Europe in August filming a special for CBS, *D-Day Plus Twenty Years.* On his return voyage aboard the USS *United States,* he spoke with journalists about the Republicans best qualified to run against Kennedy in 1964. Two congressman were on his list of eleven names—Laird and Jerry Ford. Richard Nixon did not make the cut.[3]

More than once in subsequent private meetings, Eisenhower would repeat the endorsement, and Laird would change the subject. He thrived on the political stimulation of the House and aspired to nothing higher. He had achieved party leadership by patient and persistent steps. The pivotal one was manipulating the removal of House Republican leader Joe Martin in 1959, followed by his vice chairmanship of the 1960 Platform Committee, and then leadership of the 1962 joint House-Senate Committee producing an interim platform statement. Early in 1963, another move was made that advanced his influence.

After the poor Republican showing in the 1962 elections, Laird pressed Ford, then forty-nine, to make a bid at the beginning of the next Congress to replace sixty-seven-year-old Charles Hoeven of Iowa as chairman of their caucus, the House Republican Conference. It was the view of younger members of Congress that Hoeven's leadership was lackluster, and that the conference, which rarely met, was in need of rejuvenation. Once again, Laird worked in concert with younger Republican members of the House to oust an old-guard leader.

Laird's three primary congressional cohorts were Charlie Goodell of New York, Robert Griffin of Michigan, and future defense secretary Donald Rumsfeld of Illinois, all of whom were in their thirties. This new quartet of young Turks went about so efficiently and quietly collecting votes for Ford that the coup was not publicly known until the day before the January 8 vote. Ford became the third-ranking House Republican on an 87 to 78 secret vote, and the younger members also increased their representation on the Republican Policy Committee chaired by Johnny Byrnes. Hoeven privately warned party leader Charlie Halleck to watch his back because he might be next. Halleck knew from personal experience how formidable Laird could be, because it was Laird who had pulled strings once before to get Halleck his job.[4]

As the 1964 presidential election season dawned, the Republican leadership had a problem. The two front-running presidential candidates, Nelson Rockefeller and Barry Goldwater, appeared to be poles apart, which threatened to split the party. While Rockefeller gave due obeisance to the Republican old guard, Goldwater had no talent for reaching out to moderate and liberal Republicans. The party needed a platform that would bridge the gap, and Laird was chosen to create it as the platform chair for the convention.

Meanwhile, Eisenhower was ambivalent. Seeking a signal from him, Republican leaders found he was unwilling to endorse either Rockefeller or Goldwater. Instead, Eisenhower pushed hard for others to run—first Henry Cabot Lodge, then Pennsylvania governor William Scranton. At the time, Laird thought Rockefeller was the man who had the best chance of defeating Johnson. Goldwater did not help his chances when he voted against the Civil Rights Act of 1964 because he believed part of it was unconstitutional, and because he didn't like the proposed expansion of federal over state authority. Some called Goldwater's vote courageous since it was not to his political advantage. Laird, who voted for the bill, defended Goldwater for voting his convictions.

Coming on the eve of the 1964 Republican Convention, the fallout from Goldwater's vote made Laird's job as platform chair much more difficult. He had begun preparation for the job many months before he was even named chairman of the committee. He had tapped great minds of the day—a promising Harvard professor, Henry Kissinger, and thirteen other educators, scientists, and economists—to contribute to a book of essays to be titled *The Conservative Papers*. One purpose of the book was to serve as a riposte to *The Liberal Papers,* a 1962 book of essays collected by a group of House Democrats. Laird was appalled to discover that the Democrats' book had become required reading in political science courses at several colleges he visited. When he protested, the professors responded that they would also gladly teach from a conservative collection, but there was none. Laird promised to correct that.

Recalling the times, columnist Robert Novak said that Laird was intent on "trying to revive a moribund party. He was trying to provide some intellectual fervor for the Republicans, an intellectual revival."[5] Laird asked eight other representatives, including Ford, to join him on an ad hoc committee to call for scholarly papers.[6] Published in March 1964, *The Conservative Papers* had heft. Besides Kissinger, contributors on subjects from nuclear energy to foreign policy to food issues included Edward Teller, a University of California physicist and the "father of the H bomb"; Harvard economist Gottfried

Haberler; University of Chicago economist Milton Friedman; former president of the United Nations General Assembly and Security Council Charles Malik of Lebanon; and Karl Brandt of the Stanford Food Research Institute. Reviewers across the political spectrum praised the book. Not only did it sell well, but it was included in college curricula across the country. It also provided some of the timely groundwork for the 1964 platform, as Laird had intended.

Laird himself was a human vacuum cleaner of policy issues. Columnist Mary McGrory reported from the San Francisco Cow Palace as Laird prepared to convene the Platform Committee: "A bulky, round-faced, balding 42-year-old who looks older, he is an old hand with the gavel and he has a mania for the stuff of platforms. He devours position papers, he reads the fine print, he loves documents, disputes and policy discussions. He has dispatched crates of material that would bore anybody else in San Francisco, and he has read every word of it."[7]

The platform work was the place where Laird gained an early respect for Henry Kissinger and thus began a relationship, which is of no small historical moment. Later, it would be Laird whose urging would encourage president-elect Nixon to name Kissinger as his national security advisor in 1968. But in 1964 Kissinger was still on the learning curve when it came to politics, and Laird would prove to be one of his teachers. After Kissinger's work on *The Conservative Papers* in 1963, Laird borrowed him from his mentor Rockefeller to work on the 1964 platform.

A platform chairman is pulled in many directions, particularly when the potential candidates are at different ends of the party spectrum. Laird didn't aim to please any of them. He had four rules: don't tarnish the reputation of America or its people; don't dodge the tough issues; don't equivocate; and don't make promises that the party can't keep.[8]

At the convention, the most heated platform disagreement between pro- and anti-Goldwater delegates focused on three issues: civil rights, control of nuclear weapons, and extremism.[9] From the beginning, Laird planned to include a firm endorsement of the Civil Rights Act in the platform, which he did, even though Goldwater thought it redundant. The second assault on the platform by anti-Goldwaterites was their insistence that it include a statement that only the president or someone he designated could decide to use nuclear weapons. Goldwater, who never could sidestep tough questions, had already said he thought the American commander of NATO should be able to decide to push the button if necessary.[10] Eisenhower secretly called Laird up to his hotel suite to tell him that no wording of any kind should appear in the platform about delegating nuclear authority. Both men knew what few others did—a highly classified fact that made the whole issue moot but couldn't be publicly acknowledged. Laird knew from briefings for the Defense Appropriations Subcommittee that the NATO commander had already been given nuclear "pre-delegation authority" during the Eisenhower administration. As they discussed the issue one-on-one, Eisenhower firmly told Laird the secret could not even be hinted at. (The information was declassified four decades later.)

The last nettlesome issue was extremism. In 1964 the term "extremist groups" in the media generally referred to one on the Left, Communists—and two on the Right—the Ku Klux Klan and the John Birch Society. It was the "Birchers" that caused contentious debate at the Republican convention. They were natural supporters of Goldwater, although he neither joined nor favored them. Many Republicans were concerned, however, about the growing Birch influence within the party and wanted to take a stand. Governor Scranton demanded the Republican platform repudiate political extremism in general, and name names.[11] Laird successfully opposed the amendment.

"The most important thing about a platform is you gotta have guidelines," Laird had written in a short satire for the Gridiron Club. "The first principle [is that] the platform must be short—no more than fifty words. The second guideline is that the platform must deal with principles, not programs—[such as] motherhood and sin." A third principle is that it "must spell out what a party is *against*." Therefore, the title of his "ideal platform" was "Building a Better America Under the Auspices of the Republican Party Because History Has Demonstrated That Democrats Lack Spunk, Leadership, Direction, Understanding, and Rural Support." That chewed up twenty-five words. The platform itself was: "Mother Love and Love of Mother Presents Us with a Challenge and Challenges Us with the Present. Republicans Denounce Sin and Democratic Rule; Elect Republicans."[12]

Although he wrote it as a spoof in late 1963, Laird essentially followed those guidelines for the real platform months later. The 1964 Republican platform, titled "For The People," did concentrate more on principles than programs. One of its four sections denounced the Democratic Party and presidencies (though not by name) for what it called their domestic and foreign policy failures.[13] And while it was not fifty words, the 8,500-word platform was, as Laird had pledged in advance, not even half as long as the Democratic platform, which tipped the scale at 22,000 words.

On the Tuesday evening of the convention, July 14, Laird took the podium at 6:58 p.m. and as a *New York Times* columnist recounted, "He astounded the thousands and sent a groan across the nation when he announced that members of the committee were so proud of their work that they would read it [entirely] for the enlightenment of mankind. Tradition holds that platforms are written not to be read, and when Mr. Laird started, the delegates at last began doing the things that delegates do at less revolutionary conventions. This included milling in the aisles, stretching, scratching, yawning, waving at cameras and at other delegates, and sneaking out for beer and hot dogs. . . . The platform reading ended at 8:47 p.m., one hour and forty-one minutes after it had started."[14]

Some commentators thought this was a shrewd move by Laird to delay acrimonious debate until after prime-time TV audiences went to bed. A much smaller viewing audience saw the later spectacle of an erudite Rockefeller trying to offer an amendment while repeatedly being interrupted by boos and catcalls from the galleries. All amendments were rejected.

Lyndon Johnson had the advantage of incumbency and the sentiment of the legacy left by John F. Kennedy, making his victory a sure thing in 1964. He beat Goldwater with 61 percent of the vote, the largest popular vote margin in American history. Wisconsin was among the states in the pro-LBJ column, giving him 62.1 percent of the state vote. And Melvin Laird, aided in part by canny campaigning and careful cultivation of the Democratic voters, was reelected with 61.8 percent of the votes in his district.

~

As one of the strong Republicans left standing after the devastating election, Laird was anxious to rebuild the party. He got the party leadership to create a Republican National Leadership Council—a collective of the party's best minds to rejuvenate it. Then he focused his sights on Republican House minority leader, Charlie Halleck of Indiana. Laird and friends had put Halleck in six years before, and now it was time to take him out. The coup was not an ideological one. It had more to do with age and style. At the age of sixty-four, Halleck was tired, and neither forceful nor bold.

There was, in addition, a hidden issue: Halleck was an alcoholic. It was not discussed publicly at the time, but it was a prime topic of private Republican conversation. In early 1964, after an obviously inebriated Halleck came to the House floor, Laird had been appointed by a group of embarrassed Republicans to take him aside and deliver an ultimatum. "Charlie," Laird began emphatically, "if you ever come to the floor like this again, I've been commissioned by my colleagues to tell you that we won't reelect you at the start of the next Congress." When Halleck ignored the warning, Laird felt morally and politically justified in mounting a coup.

The question, reeking of implications for the future, was this: Who should challenge Halleck as minority leader? The *New York Times* answered the question after the November election: "The potential challengers are Mr. Ford and Mr. Laird. . . . Each has publicly disclaimed his candidacy but has privately indicated that he would be available if a majority of his colleagues wanted him."[15] Some suggested that Laird's occasional "abrasiveness" and his links to Goldwater made him less electable than Ford. In reality, some of the young conservatives who finally went for Ford would have preferred the more aggressive Laird, if he had just given them the green light.[16] But once Ford confirmed that he was interested, Laird stepped aside.

Laird was in charge of securing the votes for Ford, and experience had taught him not to count on promises before a secret ballot. At one point, Rep. Donald Rumsfeld told Laird the election was sewed up for Ford, but Laird sent Rumsfeld back to get more commitments. On January 4, 1965, all 140 Republicans met on the House floor in their caucus (officially known as the House Republican Conference) and elected Ford as their minority leader by a margin of thirteen votes and chose Laird as the new conference chair, Ford's old job. Charlie Halleck was a gentleman in defeat and served two more terms in Congress. Laird kept Halleck's friendship. Several years after Halleck retired, he was on a fishing trip in Montana with his wife, Blanche, when she fell out of the boat and drowned. Distraught, Halleck called Laird, then the secretary of defense, through the Pentagon Command Center at 3:30 a.m.. "I'm out here in the wilderness," he wept over the phone. "I have to get Blanche home to Rensselaer [Indiana]. Can you help me?"

"Of course, Charlie," Laird responded. "I'll help you anytime." Halleck and the body of his wife were helicoptered off the Madison River, and an airplane was provided to fly them back to Indiana the next morning.

～

Long before Ronald Reagan coined the phrase, "Let's get the government off the backs of the people," Laird developed the same resolution. One day he looked up the heading, "United States Government," in the Milwaukee telephone book and counted 240 entries. A quick check of the state government directory revealed only 166.[17] He decided to do something about it, and his inventive "revenue sharing" proposal became one of the most far-reaching federal spending reforms of the twentieth century.

The more Laird investigated, the more sure he became that the monster middleman of federal relations with local governments was the "categorical grant" program. It didn't make sense to him that local taxpayers would send their money to Washington, only to have it sent back to programs in their towns with strings attached. The roots of the program went back to the Great Depression of the 1930s when Americans had looked to Washington for relief, and Franklin D. Roosevelt had obliged with federal grants for public works projects that employed or gave financial relief to out-of-work Americans. By the time Laird came to Washington, members of Congress had become hooked on the programs, considering them vital for reelection. They fought for a portion of the grant money so they could prove to their constituents that they could bring home federal dollars—in reality the citizen's own taxes coming back to them, minus the federal administrative cut. Laird was not immune to the exercise, but he soured on it early. One federal grant for improvement of an airport in central Wisconsin, which Laird had worked to get, had the ironic effect of turning him into a zealous reformer. It was 1958 and Washington had a $30 million pot for local airports. Congressmen, including Laird, scrambled for some of the dollars for the folks back home. But when he snagged $230,000 for his district's airport, he began receiving irate letters from constituents who thought the money could be better spent on something else.

As a state senator, Laird had helped develop a formula to give state income tax money directly to the towns and counties where the taxpayers lived. Under the innovative Wisconsin tax-sharing program, state tax dollars were divided so that fifty cents of each dollar went back to the city or town where the taxes had been raised, ten cents to the county, and the remaining forty cents to the state. Wisconsin didn't tell the local governments how to spend their money. The logic of translating this idea from the state to the federal level so Washington could return a flat percentage of the tax dollars each state had sent to the capital seemed so sound that Laird didn't feel it could be refuted. The plan would use the federal government's talent for doing what it did best—raising revenue—and then pass that money back to the states and cities to do what they did best—providing services.

Other members of Congress were not immediately persuaded by his arguments. To them it looked as if Laird was trying to take away one of the gauges they used to measure their own success. If their congressional districts got flat amounts of money automatically, how could the representatives take credit for delivering that money? But Laird was undeterred. He re-introduced a bill on revenue sharing every year, and every year he was turned down.

Laird came the closest to winning passage for his bill during the Johnson era. LBJ had inflated federal categorical grants to an all-time high, and while most Johnson aides were not interested in sending tax dollars back to the states without a set of instructions attached, one particular influential official was. Walter Heller, a University of Minnesota economics professor, was chairman of Johnson's Council of Economic Advisors and a proponent of revenue sharing. In 1964 he began pushing revenue sharing so hard that it was labeled the "Heller Plan," even though Laird had begun the idea.[18] Johnson initially pledged support, but then changed his mind.[19]

Laird's enthusiasm was not dampened. By the time he left Congress, he had delivered more than 350 speeches on the subject to a wide variety of groups, but he never got a bill passed.[20] After he left Congress, Laird continued to lobby for revenue sharing, and he found Nixon a receptive ear. Still, he faced the same old resistance from members of Congress who enjoyed playing Santa Claus in their districts. The specific roadblock was the House Ways and Means Committee where Wilbur Mills the chairman of the committee and a Democrat from Arkansas, and John Byrnes, a Republican from Wisconsin, adamantly opposed the resolution.[21] It took sixteen months to wear them down and required the critical help of two men—Governor Nelson Rockefeller and Defense Secretary Laird. A review of the Oval Office tapes shows that in almost every discussion of revenue sharing, Laird was either in the room or his involvement and help were referenced by the participants.

While Rockefeller rallied the nation's governors and whittled down Rep. Mills, Laird worked on his friend Byrnes. The offensive worked, and Laird's fourteen-year-long dream of a revenue-sharing revolution was finally signed into law in October 1972. From 1972 to 1986, federal revenue sharing dispensed $85 billion back to the states, cities, and communities. President Reagan ended it because he was running hefty federal deficits, and he wanted to end anything that smacked of grant give-backs to the states. But by the time Reagan shut it down, Laird's brainchild had a subtle but powerful side effect of restructuring and rebuilding Republicans as the party that let local governments keep their own money. With his concept of revenue sharing, Laird was instrumental in changing more than federal expenditures and the Republican Party voter base: he used it to resurrect and transform the game of football.

~

If any sports team and its fans exemplify the independent, rugged American spirit, it is certainly the Green Bay Packers, the only nonprofit, publicly owned team in professional sports. Although the team did well on the field, its financial underpinnings were precarious in the early years. The Packers were bailed out through various local business loans, playing intrasquad games for the extra admission receipts and even passing the hat during halftime. But the biggest bailout came in 1950, when fans rescued the bankrupt team by selling $25 shares of stock in the team and raising $118,000. The primary provisions of the unique sale were that the shares would never earn dividends, could never increase in value, and if the team were ever sold, the proceeds would be used to build a war memorial at the local American Legion hall, whose members march in to "present the colors" before each Packers' game.[22]

The "cheeseheads" had saved the team, but more support was needed at the beginning of the television age. As the various NFL franchises negotiated local and national TV contracts with newly interested broadcast executives, it became apparent that the bigger cities, which could command larger viewing audiences, would soon outpace the smaller ones in TV revenue and, thus their ability to attract competitive players would be greater. At this point, two of the Packers' greatest fans and patrons, Congressmen Mel Laird and Johnny Byrnes, went to work on the problem. They wound up saving the Packers *and* the NFL.

The first step was winning the support of the new NFL commissioner, Pete Rozelle, who then got an agreement from the owners that the NFL would negotiate as one with television networks and share the revenue equally among the teams. In early 1961 CBS signed a single-package deal with the NFL paying $4.65 million for exclusive 1961 season broadcast rights; each of the NFL's fourteen teams was to receive an equal share.[23] Within months, a U.S. district judge in Philadelphia ruled that the agreement "eliminated competition" and was a violation of federal antitrust laws.[24] Laird, Byrnes, and Rozelle had anticipated the ruling and worked hard to secure a congressional antitrust exemption for the NFL.[25]

Laird and Byrnes got their second major opportunity at football history in 1966 when, after secret negotiations between the NFL and the fledgling American Football League, a merger was signed ending a costly bidding war between the two rivals. From the judicial branch came the same hue and cry over monopoly. But Laird and others were again working to exempt the NFL from antitrust laws. Laird discovered a way to end the resistance that was holding up the legislation allowing a merger. Senator Russell Long, a Louisiana Democrat, was the most formidable opponent. At one point, Long revealed what was really bothering him: "You know, Mel, I've been trying to get a team in New Orleans for a long time. I haven't made any progress and I can't get Pete Rozelle to listen to me on how important it is."

Laird said cannily, "Well, I'll tell you what, Russell. If we get it worked out so that we can get you a team in New Orleans, will you get that bill out and be a promoter of it on the floor?" Long agreed, and the deal was struck. Almost immediately after the meeting, Laird called up Rozelle and said, "You better damn well give him his team if you want this to pass." Rozelle hustled up to Capitol Hill and made the promise on behalf of the NFL.[26]

The same dance worked for another Louisiana Democrat, Rep. Hale Boggs; all he wanted was a Louisiana team, too. Boggs and Rozelle met an hour before the final House vote on the AFL-NFL merger bill. When Boggs asked him if the New Orleans team was firm, Rozelle equivocated: "It still has to be approved by the owners. I can't make any promises on my own." Boggs mused, and then told Rozelle he would hold up the vote until Rozelle had checked with all the owners. "That's all right, Hale," Rozelle corrected himself, "you can count on their approval."[27] Several weeks after Congress approved the AFL-NFL merger, Rozelle, with Long and Boggs at his side, announced the formation of a sixteenth NFL franchise, the New Orleans Saints. Rozelle said that New Orleans had beaten out six other cities competing for an expansion team. Only a few people knew the backroom deal that led to its creation.[28]

The 1961 and 1966 antitrust waivers engineered by Laird "may have been the two most important things that happened in pro football," observed Joe Horrigan, vice president of the Pro Football Hall of Fame. The football historian C. Robert Barnett agreed that it was a sport-saving move when NFL team owners "legislated themselves into parity."[29]

At the same time he was lobbying for pro football, Laird had tried to get baseball and other sports organizations to do the same thing—revenue sharing. He promised antitrust waivers for them, too, but none ever took him up on the offer. (However, baseball officials were so impressed with the congressman that Los Angeles Dodgers owner Walter O'Malley was authorized in 1968 to offer Laird the job of baseball commissioner, which he declined. Bowie Kuhn accepted, and was commissioner from 1969 to 1984.)

Among Laird's neighbors in the Washington suburb of Chevy Chase was an inquisitive teenager named David, who loved to argue politics. David was the son of a Democratic former congressman from Oklahoma, but he would castigate Laird for being "too liberal" and otherwise make a nuisance of himself (including accidentally walking through Laird's glass back door). Nevertheless, Laird spent many hours mentoring the teenager. After David studied at Oxford University on a Rhodes Scholarship, he visited Laird to get advice regarding his future. Laird advised him to return to his father's home county, register as a Democrat, and in good time run for state office, just as Laird had. David Boren followed his mentor's advice, eventually becoming governor of Oklahoma and then a U.S. senator. Boren recalled Laird's tutelage with appreciation and when asked at different times what his political identity was, he would proudly call himself "a Laird Democrat."[30]

Laird's interest in the young man was not just because he thought Boren might make a good politician, but because he had the potential to become a leader in any field he chose. Laird made a side vocation of seeking out young people who buzzed with the kind of promise he had felt at their age. In 1965 he invited major national and state leaders to the Wisconsin State University (later the University of Wisconsin) at Stevens Point for a day-long discussion with top juniors and seniors from the sixty-four high schools in his district. This was no ordinary high school field trip. As the ranking member of the Appropriations Subcommittee that controlled the federal education budget, Laird could command the best speakers in the field. The commissioner of education Francis Keppel was the keynote speaker at the first of many such gatherings; the workshop subjects included the Vietnam War, civil rights, and morality in a changing society. Using resources from the Library of Congress, Laird sent the high schoolers advance material so the exchange of ideas would be more productive. Keppel effusively told Laird that it was the best discussion he'd had with students since becoming commissioner three years earlier.[31]

"Laird Youth Leadership Day" took on a life of its own. Over the next three decades, Laird induced nearly every national education commissioner and, after 1979, education secretary to visit the Stevens Point campus, along with many other national and state luminaries.[32] One repeat guest, *Washington Post* columnist David Broder, participated in part because he was likely to meet talented "comers" there such as Elizabeth Hanford, a consumer advisor in the Nixon White House. She later married Bob Dole and was selected in 1983 as President Reagan's transportation secretary. Broder noted in his column that he knew Liddy Dole was destined for big things since he had "met her at a [1971] Wisconsin high school forum arranged by Melvin R. Laird."[33] The forums were a chance to take part in "a free exchange of ideas" with intelligent and informed students, as Laird pitched it to invited guests.

Laird knew that many of these students, from low- or middle-income families, could not afford to attend even a state university. Beginning in 1957, he dispensed college scholarships through the "Laird Youth Leadership Foundation," funded in its early days with honorariums from his speeches. More than 375 high school graduates in his district received scholarships from the foundation in the ensuing years.

≈

The Menominee Indians of Wisconsin faced one of their most formidable showdowns with the white man in 1954 in the halls of Congress. The experience won them a friend for life in their congressman, Melvin Laird. Prominent voices in Congress in 1954 were calling for the "termination" of federal support for the Menominee tribe.[34] While most Native Americans had been forced off or bought off their land, the Menominees had held steadfastly to their ancestral claim on Northern Wisconsin. In the 1800s, efforts to force the Menominees west of the Mississippi River had been met with fierce and diplomatic opposition. Realizing they were outnumbered and outgunned by the government, the Menominees chose peace talks over war. Chief Oshkosh successfully negotiated several treaties with Washington. In exchange for much of their land, the Menominees were allowed to stay in Wisconsin and were given the promise of eternal government protection.

The 1954 Termination Act was a pilot project aimed at eventually weaning all Indian tribes off federal wardship. A few select tribes deemed fit for self-government were chosen for the experiment. Of these tribes the three-thousand-member Menominee was by far the largest. The Termination Act was to repeal the Menominees' reservation status, making them, among other things, subject to state and federal taxes. Utah senator Arthur Watkins, a staunchly conservative Republican, introduced and spearheaded the bill. He believed the Menominees could be self-sustaining based on the lucrative timber holdings on their 234,000-acre reservation.

Laird did not agree and warned the Menominees about the potential downside of the Termination Act. Nevertheless, the tribe agreed to support the act after Senator Watkins visited the reservation. During an informal meeting, Watkins essentially gave the Menominees an ultimatum: they had to either accept termination or lose their claim to a multimillion dollar settlement over government mishandling of tribal lands. Armed with a dubious mandate from the tribe, Watkins went back and steamrollered Congress. Laird resisted until the Menominees asked him to withdraw his opposition and support the legislation on their behalf. Eisenhower signed the Termination Act in June of 1954.

The intervening years saw Laird continually postponing the actual date of termination, since the majority of tribal members came to believe they had been snookered. The Native Americans learned they could depend on Laird and respect him. "It was just his manner, his way of doing things," remembered tribal artist James Frechette. "He didn't have any hidden agenda, and wasn't pulling any strings you couldn't see. The people in the tribe were so used to dealing with bureaucrats that they could spot that kind of crap."

Laird was adopted into the tribe as an honorary chief and given a new name which means "Chief Lawmaker." The grateful tribe also observed an annual "Melvin R. Laird Day" powwow to honor his work on their behalf.[35]

As the years wore on, there remained the quiet, ominous drumbeat of an impending termination date that Laird could not postpone forever. In 1961, after seven years of stalling tactics by Laird, the bill finally took effect. Menominee County was officially born, the eleventh county in Laird's district.[36] On the eve of its "emancipation" from federal control, Menominee County was considered the poorest in Wisconsin. It was immediately declared a "depressed area" to qualify it for federal aid. The county welfare director described one house in which twenty-two people were living on one income.[37] The Menominee forest land, expected to be a wellspring of revenue, proved to be a millstone around the tribe's neck. In a few short years, the Menominee treasury went bust, unemployment soared, and more than 70 percent of the population fell below the poverty level. In a desperate attempt to raise money, the Menominee leaders began selling off lakefront vacation property.

Laird did everything he could to get aid for the foundering tribe. Over the course of several years he secured millions of dollars in federal support, but the tribe continued its downward trajectory. Although the Menominees remained doggedly optimistic—even putting up a sign at the entrance to the reservation that read, "We Will Make It"—their prospects were grim. Ultimately, the U.S. government abandoned its designs for an across-the-board termination policy, and in the early 1970s President Nixon promised continued federal protection to all tribes as then constituted. The Menominees, however, were no longer a tribe.

When Laird had visited at the Menominee reservation for a ceremony in 1953, by his side had been a young Menominee girl, Ada Deer. Daughter of a white mother and a Menominee father, she grew up in Keshena, the village heart of Menominee country. In the 1960s, Deer became the first woman in her tribe to earn a college degree when she graduated from the University of Wisconsin. She went on to earn a master's degree in social work from Columbia University and was en route to a law degree when the aftereffects of the Menominee "termination" finally boiled over. Ada Deer was appalled at how her tribe was being forced to sell off land to increase its tax base. It was like "burning down your house to keep warm in a blizzard," Deer said. "Indians look upon land with a sense of spirituality—the mother earth. There's one bumper sticker that says, HOW COULD YOU SELL YOUR MOTHER?"[38]

Inspired to action, Deer dropped out of law school and went to lobby for her tribe in Washington, advocating the passage of a Restoration Act to undo what the Termination Act had done; it would allow the Menominee tribe to regain its unique autonomy as a reservation while once again exempting it from state and federal taxes. Deer worked to build a coalition of support within the Nixon administration, which was tough going since she was a very vocal Democrat. The man who helped bridge the difference was Mel Laird, the former congressman for the Menominee. By that time, in 1973, Laird had resigned as defense secretary but had returned to Washington politics as domestic counselor for Nixon.

"I called Mr. Laird's office," Deer said. "That was the only call I ever made to him—that was all that was needed."[39] According to Menominee expert and author Nicholas Peroff, "Laird's role was confirmed by a senior BIA [Bureau of Indian Affairs] official, who commented that the former Wisconsin congressman 'was the mover behind the scenes who formed the White House position on restoration.' Former Congressman Laird's contacts both in the administration and with his former congressional colleagues opened many doors for Ada Deer and other restoration lobbyists."[40] In June 1999, with a nudge from Laird, the Senate passed a bill giving $32 million to the Menominee tribe as compensation for mishandling their tribal funds in the 1960s.[41] More than twenty years removed from public political life, Laird was still looking out for his constituents.

5

Cloud Riders

Dᴜʀɪɴɢ Mᴇʟᴠɪɴ Lᴀɪʀᴅ's ʟɪꜰᴇ of public service, he always had a clear view of what was most important to him—and it was not in the defense arena, for which he would become best known. Laird liked to quote American philosopher William James: "The great use of life is to spend it for something that will outlast it." For all the money he earmarked to the Defense Department, the military hardware would rust and become outdated, and the best use of nuclear missiles was no use at all. The deep-seated idealism at the core of the Wisconsin pragmatist inevitably drove Laird toward work that would save lives by attacking a host of human diseases.

His seat of power to effect change was as the ranking member of the Health, Education and Welfare Appropriations Subcommittee for more than a decade. Working through three administrations—Eisenhower, Kennedy, and Johnson—he often forced substantially larger health budgets than the presidents had in mind. With so many demands on the taxpayer dollar, not the least of which was the arms race, could America afford to earmark large amounts for medical research, which promised no guarantees? Laird postulated that the question needed to be reversed: How could America afford *not* to spend whatever was needed to speed up medical research? Although he normally fancied himself a realist about budgets, Laird was, in the words of a fellow legislator, a "cloud rider," a zealot of the highest order when it came to funding health programs and research.

When most of America was enthralled with the space race, Laird pounded the podium in the House for more health funds with these words: "I, for one, would rather see this nation first in health, than first on the Moon."[1] The result of his zealotry was multifold, including the transformation of the National Institutes of Health into the world's foremost medical research entity, and the establishment of the Centers for Disease Control and Prevention. One man familiar with Laird's role, Dick Cheney, lauded his "amazing achievements in the field of medical research and improvements in the health and welfare of military and civilian citizens alike."[2] And in 1997, Jimmy Carter pronounced in tribute, "I don't know of anyone who has done more in his service in the Congress, and even subsequently, to promote the strength of the National Institutes of Health, the Centers for Disease Control, and to spread America's technical and scientific knowledge of health processes around the world."[3]

The driving force behind Laird's efforts can be traced to his childhood, his hometown, and an institution that has always been at the epicenter of his pride, the Marshfield Clinic. It was the place where doctors watched over Laird's own health from infant to octogenarian. The clinic was founded by six general practitioners in the horse-and-buggy days of 1916. Group medical practices were then a new notion and not highly regarded by the American Medical Association, which referred to them as late as 1937 as "Medical Soviets."[4] Under Laird's guardianship the Marshfield Clinic grew into one of the largest private, not-for-profit multispecialty group practices in the United States, and one that has given the Mayo Clinic in neighboring Minnesota a run for its reputation.

In 1923 one of the early patients to the group practice was little "Melvie," an infant with an earache. Laird's family had been visiting from Nebraska, but they soon returned to live in Marshfield and the clinic's doctors became an integral part of their lives. "These young doctors became my friends," Laird recalled. The most influential of them was Dr. Stephan Epstein. The son of a prominent German dermatologist, Epstein was advancing up the medical ladder in Breslau when the Nazi regime came to power. Epstein saw the handwriting on the wall for Jews and sailed to America. Through referrals, he arrived in Marshfield in the winter of 1935 where he intensively studied English so he could pass the state medical boards and work for the Marshfield Clinic. He spent many hours with the Lairds, and Melvin, then a high school senior, read English aloud with Epstein. Young Laird found in him a fine mentor, whose role increased exponentially with the death of Laird's father in 1946.[5]

Their discussions ranged far and wide. It was Epstein who first educated the future secretary of defense on the importance of the nuclear deterrent in maintaining peace, as well as the necessity to control nuclear weaponry through negotiation. And he pressed on Laird the preeminence of good health care. He preached that an individual politician could do more good than any single doctor. That appealed to Laird, and as a Wisconsin state senator he sponsored legislation, opposed by the state's medical society and others, which legalized the corporate practice of medicine in the state. It allowed the Marshfield Clinic and others to attract and retain doctors through the promise of higher salaries and retirement programs. When Laird headed off to Washington, Dr. Epstein advised him to get a seat on the HEW Appropriations Committee.

The freshman congressman followed this advice. When he was assigned to the Appropriations Committee in 1953 by its Republican chairman John Taber, he was allowed to focus on health issues. He was in on the 1953 creation of the cabinet Department of Health, Education, and Welfare. In 1957 Taber assigned himself and Laird to the HEW-Labor Subcommittee and told the young congressman to act as its ranking member. "You serve here for a little while, and then I'm going to step down," Taber told him. In 1959, as promised, Taber left the subcommittee, making Laird "ranking" for the minority side, or officially the subcommittee's second-most important member. He immersed himself wholeheartedly into the subcommittee's work, remarking at one point that he had spent so much time with doctors and on medical issues that he began "to feel that the MC [member of Congress] behind my name should be changed to MD."[6] By 1968 he had outlived or out-served all his early committee colleagues. "There is no one else left on the HEW committee in either the Senate or the House that has served ever since the department was created," he said a bit whimsically in November 1968. "This makes me sound like a very old man, but I really consider myself still very young [and] I'm not ready to leave this job yet."[7] Within weeks, not out of his own personal choice, he was named defense secretary by president-elect Nixon.

Laird never forgot his roots in the Marshfield Clinic. His old friend Dr. Epstein became one of the most influential directors of the clinic and also the chief architect of its conversion from a group of general practitioners to specialists, including a burgeoning medical research department enhanced with federal grants delivered by Laird from his appropriations perch. Laird also pressured the clinic to develop an advanced finance program, the Security Health Plan, which was one of the first HMO's available in the country—and the first to get HEW approval.

Laird's attention to the clinic was minuscule compared to the overall picture of medical history he influenced through congressional funding. But he did not do it alone. Like Laird, John Edward Fogarty was a "boy wonder" who made a big mark on Congress—but there the similarities ended. Fogarty was a New Englander, a Democrat, and an ardent unionist without a college education. He was a bricklayer, like his father and older brother, and was only twenty-three when he was elected president of Bricklayers Union No. 1 of Rhode Island. With little political experience, he was first elected to Congress in 1940 at the age of twenty-seven.[8]

Fogarty knew that to help his home state he needed a seat on the Appropriations Committee. After two years of trying, he finally netted an appropriations assignment in 1947. He did not, however, get the military subcommittee he wanted. To his great disappointment, Fogarty was assigned to the Subcommittee on Labor and Federal Security Agency (the HEW predecessor). While the labor portion of subcommittee work intrigued Fogarty, the health segment bored him. At one point as he perused a newspaper during a hearing, subcommittee chairman Frank Keefe banged his gavel and admonished, "Mr. Fogarty, this is important business we're considering here; you ought to pay attention and maybe you'll learn something!"[9]

Exactly when Fogarty finally started paying attention is unclear, but Laird thinks it was a battle over the cost of streptomycin that made Fogarty a convert. The new drug was introduced to the market in 1947 as an effective treatment for tuberculosis, but it cost $250 a gram. Chairman Keefe enlisted Fogarty in a successful fight to appropriate $3 million for the manufacture of synthetic streptomycin so it could be sold for $10 a gram. When the Democrats took back the House in 1949, Fogarty became the new Labor-HEW Appropriations chairman. And when Laird joined the subcommittee, there was an immediate bond between the two men.

"There was nothing artificial about this man," Laird said. "He was so open; everything was on the table with him, so we hit it off very well." Laird came to love almost everything about Fogarty, large and small—his robust handshake, his love of bricks, steak cooked in his brick fireplace at home in Harmony, Rhode Island, his joy in a good joke but self-consciousness about telling any himself, his unhurried approach that sometimes caused him to miss airplane connections, the way he made it difficult for anyone else to pick up the check at a restaurant, his complete loyalty to and trust in his friends, and his great pride in anything Irish. (He wore a bright green tie as if it were a coat of arms.)[10]

Laird didn't need conversion to the cause of medical research, as Fogarty had. From the first, he signed on to stand strong with Fogarty on appropriations. Because he was the subcommittee chairman, Fogarty was often credited with funding that led to major medical advances of the period, but those advances were possible because the minority leader on the subcommittee,

Laird, was his energetic partner. "My father was a very quiet, unassuming man," said Mary Fogarty McAndrew. "He never gave the impression he did it alone. Having someone from the other side—Mel—right there with him, and being able to work so closely with him, was a huge advantage."[11]

One man who witnessed their work up close was Rep. Hugh Carey, later the Democratic governor of New York. By the time Carey came to the House in 1961, Fogarty and Laird were already inseparable on appropriations. Carey, as a fellow New Englander, Irish Catholic, and Democrat, was quickly brought into Fogarty's fold, and he proved companionable enough to join Fogarty and Laird for evening drinks in Fogarty's first-floor office. Fogarty would frequently complain when Carey arrived a couple of drinks behind schedule. "I can't help it, John," he'd mumble. "I'm on the top floor; you're down here in a prime office on the first floor. It takes me longer to get here than Mel." In short order, Carey found himself in an office next to Fogarty, a favor to the latter from the speaker of the House. "[Fogarty] had me moved so I wouldn't be late for drinking hour with him and Mel."[12]

Carey watched with wonder as Fogarty and Laird took on fellow subcommittee members, full committee members, the House, the Senate, and three successive presidents to ram through hefty annual increases in medical research appropriations. The two men manipulated their subcommittee hearings like master puppeteers. The most effective technique was to press HEW officials to admit that they could use more money than the president's Bureau of the Budget had told them they could request. It infuriated Eisenhower, Kennedy, and Johnson, in succession, but the pair was unrelenting. During the Eisenhower era Laird would be called to the White House for tongue-lashings, but he wouldn't budge. During the Kennedy and Johnson administrations Fogarty similarly was denigrated by his party's presidents, but he also refused to cut the HEW budget.

Fogarty-Laird hearings were a carefully choreographed steamroller: they recruited expert witnesses because they would vouch for what the two congressmen already wanted. They picked only those professionals who could drop the medical jargon and speak passionately. Fogarty and Laird were so prodigiously knowledgeable about the subjects, having immersed themselves in medical minutiae, that no bureaucrat or politician of either party could best them in debate. When their bills went to the full House, the pair was a bulwark that could not be broken. Not once did they accept an amendment to an HEW appropriations bill; every challenge was beaten back.

In the Senate, their ally was the courtly Democrat from Alabama, Lister Hill. His father had been a pioneering heart surgeon, and the story goes that young Lister couldn't follow in his father's surgical boots because he couldn't stand the sight of blood. Hill became a lawyer, but it was medicine that was closest to his heart. As chairman of the Labor-HEW Appropriations Subcommittee and the Labor and Welfare Committee in the Senate, he had responsibility for all substantive health legislation. The tactics he employed mimicked the Fogarty-Laird techniques, but with a southern tinge. In a familiar routine, he would lean over the table and ask an administration witness courteously: "Are you shuah, Doctuh, that you're asking for enuff for these wunnnderful programs?"[13]

Fogarty and Laird couldn't afford to lose each other, so that meant campaigning for one another across party lines. In September 1964, for example, Fogarty was the featured speaker at a Marshfield Clinic Foundation party in Laird's hometown. He told the crowd he had met only five Democrats in his visit "and they are all going to vote for Mel Laird." Then he added, in a remark that brought down the house: "I would too, if I lived here. . . . [I]f you want good health and better educational opportunities for your children, I would hope you will vote for Mel Laird in November."[14]

Laird soon returned the favor. Fogarty had built a small brick library behind his house, and he added a fancy brick outhouse, complete with the traditional half-moon cutout in the door. The Bricklayers Union sponsored a dedication of the outhouse as a fund-raiser, with tickets selling at $250 apiece. Laird was featured on the invitation as the dedicatory speaker. Republican governor John Chafee of Rhode Island was furious when he received the invitation. "Why are you coming up here giving Fogarty all this publicity and campaign help?" Chafee demanded to know.

"Well, John, I would do anything for Fogarty if he asked me to do it— almost anything. I wouldn't cheat, or rob, or kill, but when he asks me for a favor like this, I will certainly do it. We have a relationship that goes far beyond partisan politics. And, John, you had to get a lot of Democratic votes to get elected governor. The smartest thing you could do is attend this dedication and show you're above partisan politics, too." Chafee said he took Laird's advice and attended the dedication "of what Mel liked to call the John Fogarty Brick Shithouse—which was actually quite artistically done."[15] Laird's favorite part of the dedication: Fogarty had rigged each toilet seat so that when someone sat down, a voice would boom from below: "Please move over; I'm still painting down here."

Although Chafee came to accept the Fogarty-Laird mutual admiration society—later even working for Secretary of Defense Laird as his secretary of the Navy—others in Laird's party of fiscal conservatives had ongoing concerns about his collusion with a big-spending Democrat. Gerald Ford thought Laird pushed too hard because he raised the Eisenhower and Kennedy-Johnson budgets by millions of dollars each year. For the sake of his conservative reputation, the record shows that Laird occasionally appeared to oppose Fogarty on the Floor, only to quietly capitulate later as part of their ongoing political choreography.

Perhaps Fogarty-Laird's finest monument is the National Institutes of Health in Bethesda, Maryland. The NIH began with a single doctor in a one-room laboratory at Staten Island, New York. In 1887 that doctor, Joseph Kinyoun, was given a $300 grant from the predecessor of the Public Health Service to establish a small Laboratory of Hygiene. With the money, he found the bacterial cause of cholera. In 1930 his lab was moved to Washington and renamed the National Institute of Health. (The name was pluralized to National *Institutes* in 1948 when the National Heart Institute was created and joined the already-existing National Cancer Institute as part of the organization.) As it expanded, the NIH moved to Bethesda. The institution grew at a progressive pace until 1955, a year that almost threatened to bury its good works but instead transformed the organization.

In postwar America, there were few more dread diseases than poliomyelitis, and leading the fight against it was the National Foundation for Infantile Paralysis, sponsor of the original March of Dimes. By 1953 Dr. Jonas Salk had discovered his miraculous polio vaccine and begun testing. With thousands of children contracting the disease every year, the vaccine was pressed into service in April 1955. The first sign of trouble was a call to the NIH two weeks later; a vaccinated Chicago baby had contracted polio. The next day another call came, this one from Napa Valley, California, reporting that a four-year-old vaccinated child had contracted polio. As more cases poured in the Public Health Service identified the culprit as Cutter Laboratories in Berkeley, California. Safe vaccine was produced when the live polio virus was made inactive by a process using formaldehyde. Cutter employees failed to adhere to the right procedures, sending out active polio virus in its vaccine. The Cutter lab was shut down on May 7, but by then almost eighty vaccinated children had been infected, and they had spread the polio to another 120 playmates and relatives. Eleven children died, and three quarters of the group were paralyzed.[16]

When the non-Cutter vaccine was determined to be safe, the public clamored for universal distribution. Until then, the federal government had distanced itself from the vaccine's distribution, letting the polio foundation purchase and distribute it. When members of Congress, including Laird, pushed for a federal purchase, HEW secretary Oveta Culp Hobby resisted. Such a program could lead to "socialized medicine by the back door," she countered. Congress ignored her and enacted a $34 million federal purchase program for massive vaccination of all infants and children through the second grade. Within one year polio deaths were cut by 50 percent, and in time the disease was almost totally eradicated.

The horror of the Cutter fiasco, and then the federal foot-dragging over distribution meant heads had to roll if the Public Health Service and NIH were to recover quickly. Oveta Hobby resigned, as did others, including the NIH director. The new director, Dr. James A. Shannon, became the founding father of the modern NIH with a mission to create a world-class health research institution. When some of his scientists would boast of their pure science work, he would bring them up short: "This is not the National Institutes of *Science*. It is the National Institutes of *Health*." In Shannon, the triumvirate in Congress—Congressmen Fogarty and Laird and Senator Hill—finally had a director who shared their vision, and who could spend whatever they sent his way. In hearings Shannon was their best witness. Fogarty and Laird would secretly script how much money Shannon would "reluctantly" agree to settle for. Then in a good show, they would appear to be tough with him in the public hearings. "It was all part of a strategy," remembered Dr. Carl Baker, former National Cancer Institute director.[17] "It looked like they were clobbering Shannon but it was all arranged ahead of time."

The result of their collaboration was evident in Shannon's first year as director, when Fogarty, Laird, and Hill more than doubled his annual budget, from $98 to $213 million.[18] Thus began a sustained pattern of consistently large annual increases for the NIH as fast as Shannon could justifiably spend the money. During the 1953–69 period, when the Fogarty-Laird-Hill triumvirate was in operation, NIH's budget increased some twenty-eightfold.[19] More than a dozen buildings were constructed or begun, some of them brick, at Fogarty's insistence. The most important, in Laird's view, was the $7.3 million National Library of Medicine. To the NIH's already-existing seven institutes another three were added: the National Institute of Child Health and Human Development (1962), General Medical Sciences (1962), and the National Eye Institute (1968). By 2004 the number of NIH's institutes had reached twenty.[20]

By 1959 some journalists were identifying Laird as the most important "swing" vote on medical research funds. Fogarty and Hill were expected to support NIH fund hikes, but Laird was starting to look like he had some misgivings, partly reflecting concerns of the president. In a private letter to Laird, Eisenhower complained about an attitude that "wherever a prudent investment of the taxpayers' dollars is found to be in the public interest, greater and greater spending for the same purpose will be even more in the public interest. This unsound thinking seems to be particularly applicable to [HEW] appropriations." Ike called it a "fallacy . . . that a cascade of tax-payers' dollars will guarantee progress in research."[21] Laird agreed that Con-gress should not force feed NIH more money than it could soundly use, but he had a hard time finding anything in the appropriations that looked to him like waste.

And so he pressed on. Mel's championing of dental research and fluori-dation, at a time when some thought it was a Communist conspiracy to poi-son Americans, earned him an honorary doctor of dentistry degree. His brother, Dr. David Laird, a former English department chairman at Cali-fornia State University (Los Angeles), needled Mel at one point, expressing amazement at "the range and diversity of the robes and honors," but the dental one was the most curious. "Are we to suppose that it is in recognition of Mel's unquestionable skill in the art of oral implantation—the art, that is, of putting words in other people's mouths?"[22]

The National Mental Health Association named Laird its Man of the Year in 1960, out of gratitude for the tens of millions of dollars he had earmarked for mental health research and the construction of community mental health facilities. He was also intent on the swift production and broad distri-bution of kidney dialysis machines. He fast-tracked research on the develop-ment of artificial heart and heart-related devices by appropriating special money to the NIH over the objections of Dr. Shannon, who thought it was moving too fast. In 1966 Laird reported with justifiable pride that he had closely followed the story of a thirty-seven-year-old woman who walked out of a Houston, Texas, hospital, and flew home to Mexico as the first person in medical history whose life was saved with a man-made heart pump. The heart pump, developed and used by Dr. William DeBakey, had been made possible by federal funds.[23]

Before the Environmental Protection Agency (EPA) was created, the purse strings for most federal ecology programs were held by Laird and Fogarty in HEW.[24] Seeing more links between pollution and disease, Laird pushed NIH to create the Environmental Health Sciences Center. The effort was held up during the Kennedy administration because the president wanted it to be located in the D.C. area. Laird was convinced that federal science would benefit from geographical distance from Washington politics. The first step was finally achieved in 1964 when Laird, in conference with the Senate, agreed to appropriate money for the center only on condition "the facility would not be located within 50 miles of the District of Columbia."[25] It ended up in North Carolina as the National Institute of Environmental Health Sciences. Its studies on cancer-causing agents, lead poisoning, asbestos exposure, dust mite infestation, and the like have formed the basis for government regulatory policy.

Four years after Laird left Congress, reflecting on his large-scale NIH empire-building era with Fogarty, he concluded in a 1973 speech before a group of surgeons: "John Fogarty and I worked as a team, as partners in progress. Together we delivered the rationale and the votes that raised the NIH from a shoestring operation to one of the most preeminent biomedical research complexes on earth. That is the way to make progress, I believe—by focusing on partnership rather than partisanship."[26]

~

Surgeon general Luther Terry lit up a cigarette in the chauffeured government car taking him to a packed State Department auditorium on January 11, 1964. He was to stand before more than two hundred reporters and deliver the first-ever surgeon general's report. Terry had been in the post less than three years but had somehow summoned up the courage to defy the weight of American tobacco manufacturers to produce a damning 387-page antitobacco report, unassumingly titled, *Smoking and Health: Report of the Advisory Committee to the Surgeon General of the United States.* Dr. Terry's aide, along for the ride, delicately observed that the first question reporters would ask him would be: "Do you smoke?" No, they won't ask, Terry countered; reporters would be interested in the weighty scientific conclusions, not his personal habits.

As Terry delivered the conclusions of the report to the journalists, the atmosphere was electrifying. His report stated flatly that "cigarette smoking is causally related to lung cancer in men; the magnitude of the effect of cigarette smoking outweighs all other factors." Not only that, but cigarette smoking was "the most important cause" of chronic bronchitis, and probably was a significant contributor to heart disease. At the time he said this, 46 percent of American adults smoked. The link between smoking and both cancer and heart disease had been apparent to scientists for decades. Now the surgeon general had finally declared it an undeniable fact. The air was heavy with the weight of the moment in the smoke-filled room as newsmen, government officials, and tobacco industry lobbyists puffed self-consciously on their cigarettes. Soon enough, a reporter who knew Terry baited him with the question:

"Do you smoke, Dr. Terry?"

Terry turned to the inquisitor, smiled with resolve, and responded simply: "No."

"Dr. Terry, when did you quit?"

"About 30 minutes ago," he said. Terry never smoked again.[27]

Laird was also a cigarette smoker, and Terry had badgered him to quit smoking during the previous year as Terry became alarmed over mounting scientific evidence of its danger. It was a gutsy move since Terry was still then smoker himself and was also trying to curry favor for his budget at Fogarty-Laird subcommittee hearings. One night in late 1963, after a grueling hearing over cancer funding and more pestering from Terry, Laird announced to his family at the dinner table that he wasn't going to smoke cigarettes any more. Though he remained an intermittent cigar smoker for ten years, Laird succeeded in quitting cigarettes cold turkey. (His wife of more than forty-five years was unable to quit and died of cancer in 1992.)[28]

The surgeon general's report advised that "cigarette smoking is a health hazard of sufficient importance . . . to warrant appropriate remedial action." Laird and a majority of Congress soon responded with a law that put warning labels on cigarette packages beginning in 1966. Then, when Laird joined the Health Appropriations Subcommittee, he became committed to funding cancer research. He was a consistent supporter of the National Cancer Institute, the primary agency through which the government supported cancer research. Again, there were opponents, one of whom suggested in a hearing that NCI researchers should slow down and "proceed a little more cautiously." A witness at the hearing, Dr. Harry Weaver of the American Cancer Society, was quick to respond, "I know of no single disease . . . that was ever controlled by proceeding cautiously."[29]

One of the institutions seeking a large NCI grant was in Laird's back yard, the McArdle Laboratory for Cancer Research on the Madison campus of the University of Wisconsin. Bursting at the seams in a small building, the facility needed more space fully dedicated to cancer research. The university couldn't come up with the matching funds that NCI required, so McArdle's director, Dr. Harold Rusch, asked if Laird could help. Rusch went to Washington and met with John Fogarty and Laird. Fogarty and Rusch hit it off, partly because Rusch had once been an apprentice bricklayer. As they walked near the Capitol, they appraised the brickwork of various buildings in passing. At one point, Fogarty asked the doctor how he had handled the pinpoint bleeding spots that beset bricklayers. "I bandaged my fingertips with adhesive tape or wore canvas gloves, but they were usually worn through before the end of the day." Fogarty, a master bricklayer, smiled and confided: "We urinated on our fingers and that stopped the bleeding. Doc, how do you explain that?" Rusch couldn't.[30]

As a "mate" in masonry, Fogarty was more receptive to Rusch's plea for federal construction funds without the required matching money, especially when he found it was a national problem. Rusch wrote to thirteen other university cancer research centers and discovered they were in the same fix—their affiliated universities weren't able to help them with expansions. So when Laird offered an appropriations amendment in 1960 providing $30 million in start-up construction funds for fourteen regional cancer research centers under the National Cancer Institute, Fogarty was Laird's greatest backer for the amendment. During the full Appropriations Committee hearing, a friend and Wisconsin colleague of Laird's, Rep. Glenn Davis, strenuously objected. He was appalled at the huge price tag for the NCI-affiliated regional centers. Laird recalled that Fogarty took him on. "He said, 'I can't understand the gentleman from Wisconsin [Davis] raising Cain with these regional cancer centers that we're authorizing around the country. We're only gonna do three a year or so, and then we'll end up with 14 of them. And those are the ideas of your colleague from Wisconsin. THESE ARE *LAIRD-ETTES!*'" Fogarty fairly shouted. The name stuck and the bill passed.[31]

Among the first to qualify were the Farber Cancer Research Center in Boston, North Carolina Medical Center in Durham, Sloan Kettering in New York, the University of Wisconsin Medical Center in Madison, the M. D. Anderson Clinic in Houston, and the Stanford University Medical Center.

⁓

An envelope arrived at the Capitol Hill office of Senator Tom Daschle in October 2001 with a white substance inside. Within days, four postal workers employed at the Washington, D.C., Postal Processing and Distribution Center who had likely handled the envelope were hospitalized with breathing difficulties; two died. Coming shortly after the 9/11 attack on the World Trade Center, bio-terrorism was suspected. The Centers for Disease Control closed down the mail center and identified the powder as anthrax—the first reported outbreak caused by occupational exposure since 1957.[32] The quick containment and identification of the anthrax was due in large part to the CDC. One of its patron saints who got a thank-you note after the incident was Melvin Laird. Dick Cheney wrote the note to thank Laird for his "long list" of "legislative successes"—in particular, for "helping to establish the Centers for Disease Control."[33]

Legionnaires Disease, AIDS, Lassa Fever, Hanta virus, Ebola virus, and smallpox are on the short list of epidemics and maladies tackled by the CDC, which owes its existence in large part to Laird and Fogarty. The CDC, based in Atlanta, has its roots in military efforts to control malaria during World War II. By the early 1950s, its future was uncertain because of competition from other agencies and inadequate funding.[34] That was when the Fogarty-Laird team began operating with muscle, ensuring the CDC's permanence and expanding it through funding, just as they did with NIH. CDC historian Dr. Elizabeth Etheridge said that the Fogarty-Laird era is still "looked on nostalgically as the 'good old days' insofar as getting money out of Washington was concerned."[35] Between 1953 and 1969, Fogarty and Laird escalated CDC appropriations more than 1,000 percent, from an annual $5.9 million budget to $62.1 million.[36]

Besides rapidly escalating the CDC's funding, they also shrewdly pressured the Public Health Service to start shifting some of its larger divisions close to Atlanta—venereal disease, tuberculosis, immunization, and other functions. Throughout the 1950s, despite the growth in duties and prestige, the CDC had remained in ramshackle buildings scattered in several cities. Its various offices were a health hazard unto themselves—labs without germ-proof walls, no air conditioning in the summer or inadequate heat in the winter, dilapidated fire-trap buildings, and animal facilities that were impossible to secure. (One routine duty of the officer-of-the-day was escaped-monkey retrieval).[37] The CDC desperately needed a modern headquarters, which came into being only because of the three congressional benefactors of the era, Fogarty, Laird, and Hill. In 1947 the Atlanta-based Coca-Cola Company gifted the CDC with fifteen acres of land next to Emory University to build a headquarters. Within a few years Congressman Laird went to Coca-Cola for more land and a building for the national headquarters of the Boys and Girls Clubs of America, of which Laird was a trustee. The $13 million-plus CDC complex in Atlanta didn't get built until Fogarty and Laird made it a funding priority. The six-floor main building, spread out to five interconnected buildings with just what the doctors had ordered: offices, labs, and secure animal rooms in abundance. At the insistence of Senator Hill, who was a die-hard segregationist, the building had separate restrooms for blacks and whites. But shortly after the 1960 dedication, with a quiet okay from Fogarty and Laird, the CDC took down the "Colored Only" signs, and converted the surplus bathrooms to labs.

The decade of the 1960s—when Fogarty and Laird wielded the magic money wand—turned the CDC into a first-class agency. The CDC's involvement in eradicating smallpox is a prime example. A vaccine for smallpox was discovered in the late 1700s, but it required vaccination of every possible human host to rid the planet of the disease. Only when the CDC joined the effort in 1966 did the vaccination campaign sponsored by the World Health Organization escalate rapidly. Not the least of the problems was that in many of the areas where the disease was most virulent, people suspected it was their gods' way of punishing sinners. In Latin America, for example, the smallpox god was Obaluaye. Through careful education, and often after persuading tribal leaders to set the example by receiving the first inoculation, the CDC methodically overcame resistance.[38] The CDC also developed more effective vaccine delivery systems, which brought about the total eradication of the disease.

As Congressman Laird monitored and encouraged the CDC's smallpox participation, he met opposition from others in Congress who questioned the expenditure of millions of American dollars abroad, since by the time the CDC joined the effort, smallpox was nonexistent in the United States. Laird countered their concern by pointing out a central fact of the modern era: "A disease such as smallpox in this age of fast travel can be spread to countries half a world away in just a few hours."[39] Laird firmly believed that the health of every individual was precious and that was his guiding philosophy in nurturing CDC's rapid growth.

~

Late Monday afternoon, January 9, 1967, Laird was laying it on thick with Fogarty. They had shared many good times as traveling companions; they had visited Pope John XXIII together in Rome and attended four different World Health Assemblies in Geneva. Laird was proposing one more trip. "Let's skip the congressional opening ceremony tomorrow and go to Los Angeles and see the Green Bay Packers play in the Super Bowl on Sunday. We'll sign the [congressional] oath of office in L.A." Fogarty felt it was important to take the oath in the House, so he persuaded Laird to postpone their trip for a day. Fogarty never made the ceremony. The next day, January 10, the fifty-three-year-old congressman suffered a heart attack and died at his desk.[40]

The eulogies multiplied swiftly and eloquently. Dr. Howard Rusk wrote in the *New York Times:* "With his bright green tie and his Irish accent, he was a circuit rider for health, a teacher, a preacher, a fearless foe to any challenger who stood in the way of his crusade. He died on the field of battle. His friends from the scientist to the sick mourn his loss and call him blessed."[41]

Laird, using his influence as ranking member on the Defense Appropriations Subcommittee, secured a Pentagon plane to take any colleagues who wanted to attend, Republican or Democrat, to Fogarty's funeral in Rhode

Island. Laird, choking with emotion, delivered one of the eulogies: "I have spent more time with John Fogarty than with any other man in public life [so] when I speak of John Fogarty, I am speaking of a man whom I not only loved and admired as much as any man I have ever known, but I am also speaking of a man I knew as well as any man on this earth . . . I [will] never forget his great sympathy for anyone, especially children and old people, with a mental or physical disability; his love of God and faith in the Catholic religion that was simple and pure, and completely free from ostentation."[42]

Fogarty, the reluctant convert to health issues, had taken the work with Laird so seriously that he had passed up opportunities to become the governor of his state, or senator, or secretary of health, education, and welfare—a job president-elect Kennedy had offered him. The attendant respect that fellow Democrats gave Fogarty had naturally overflowed to Laird, his Republican partner.

Early in Laird's congressional career, House Speaker John McCormack, a Democrat, decided to mentor the young Republican. He spent hours tutoring Laird in the ways of the House, partly out of gratitude for the nonpartisan spirit Laird demonstrated in his partnership with Fogarty. After one speech of Laird's in support of a health science bill, McCormack complimented him: "That was a terrific speech today. You're coming along fine." Then, arm around Laird, McCormack ushered him to a little room just off the Members' Dining Room on the House side of the Capitol building. "I want you to have this room. It's your own private dining room or meeting room for whatever you need to do."

Laird beamed. Capitol rooms were scarce, and this was a very rare assignment of exclusive space from the House Democratic Party leader to a Republican. "The most coveted status symbol in Congress [is] the Capitol hideaway," the New York Times noted. There are only about fifty such secret offices possible in the Capitol itself, and "such refuges are more scarce in the House. Party leaders have them, but not many others." When word of Laird's plum spot leaked out, howls were heard from more senior members of McCormack's party. But the Speaker stood fast, and Laird kept the private dining room throughout his government service, using it even when he was secretary of defense.[43]

Another unusual byproduct of the Fogarty partnership with Laird was an invaluable memento from a Democratic White House. John F. Kennedy suffered from chronic back pain, and in 1955 he finally found a physician, Dr. Janet G. Travell, who relieved his pain with a series of prescription medications. In addition, in Dr. Travell's New York office, Kennedy discovered a perfect chair for his back, a custom-designed rocking chair. He subsequently ordered one from the small North Carolina company that made it. When he became president, Kennedy appointed Travell as his personal physician, and she made sure the "Kennedy rocker" was available wherever he might land—in the Oval Office, on Air Force One, or on vacation.

Kennedy also gave away some of the rocking chairs to friends. One went to Fogarty, who was described by Senator Bobby Kennedy at Fogarty's funeral as "a great friend of President Kennedy and of the entire Kennedy family." At the same time Fogarty received a chair, so did Laird. The president had been particularly grateful for Laird's work with Fogarty on mental retardation—an issue dear to Kennedy, whose sister struggled with the condition.

Laird undoubtedly would have traded the rare rocker, the private dining room, and other "perks" to work with Fogarty just a little longer. His death in early 1967 left a large hole in the HEW Appropriations Subcommittee that could not be entirely filled by successor Daniel Flood, of Pennsylvania. And when Laird was named defense secretary-designate in December 1968 it meant that the last of the big four was gone. Senator Hill had declined to run for reelection in 1968, and Dr. Shannon had retired from the NIH.

On the occasion of Laird's appointment to the Nixon cabinet, *Washington Star* columnist Judith Randal observed a political irony: "By a strange quirk of politics, Nixon's choice of Laird as Secretary of Defense may have wider repercussions on the medical front than his selection of Robert H. Finch for the HEW cabinet post. In fact, some observers of the health research scene see in Laird's departure from Capitol Hill a situation that is little short of disaster."[44]

6

Into the Quagmire

Sunday, August 2, 1964, at 3:40 a.m., the Klaxon sounded "general quarters" aboard the USS *Maddox*. Mel Laird's old World War II destroyer was under surprise attack, this time twenty-five miles off the coast of North Vietnam, in the Tonkin Gulf. The *Maddox* had been patrolling international waters in a conflict, which was not yet officially an American war but was about to become one.

Three North Vietnamese torpedo boats moved toward the *Maddox* at high speed, spraying the destroyer with machine-gun fire and launching torpedoes. There was no running away from the fight because the small boats could travel nearly twice as fast as the bulky destroyer. The *Maddox* dodged two torpedoes and sank one of the Soviet-built patrol boats. The other two sped away. *Maddox* Captain Herbert L. Ogier radioed the Seventh Fleet and reported the attack, which lasted about thirty minutes. It was the first direct combat between the United States and North Vietnam—the true beginning of the ten-year conflict known as the Vietnam War.

A sailor picked up some enemy shell fragments off the deck of the *Maddox*. Those souvenirs, and a tiny hole in the *Maddox*'s aft gun-sighting platform would later provide needed proof to Washington that the attack had really happened. At the Pentagon, the top brass were puzzled. What had prompted North Vietnam to go on the offensive against an American ship in international waters? Was it a mistake, or was it an act of war by Hanoi that demanded retaliation? President Lyndon Johnson huddled with his advisors, and they decided to let the attack pass. Johnson had an election to worry about and it was no time to start a war; he ordered the *Maddox* to pull farther out to sea. Another destroyer, the *Turner Joy*, was dispatched to pair up with the *Maddox,* and an aircraft carrier, the *Ticonderoga,* was alerted to provide air cover for the two destroyers should they need it.

What happened two days later remains one of the great mysteries of American warfare. At 7:40 p.m. on August 4, the *Maddox* radioed that it was again under attack—or at least the radar operators on the destroyer thought it was. On a pitch-black night, with zero visibility, they picked up radar signatures from North Vietnamese patrol boats and radar spotting of more than twenty torpedo launches against the *Maddox* and the *Turner Joy* over a four-hour period. In the middle of the confusion, the *Maddox* received an intelligence intercept from electronic eavesdroppers at the National Security Agency. North Vietnamese radio chatter had hinted that an attack on both destroyers was "imminent."

The destroyers began zigzagging through the dark seas trying to dodge the unseen torpedoes. The *Turner Joy* locked its guns on what it thought was a patrol boat radar signature and fired. Someone aboard the destroyer reported seeing a column of smoke in the direction of the target. The *Ticonderoga* dispatched two F-8E Crusaders and two A-4 Skyhawks. In less than an hour the four planes were circling the two destroyers, the pilots trying to sort out the frantic radio messages from spotters on the ships. The pilots peppered the water with rockets but never saw an enemy ship.[1] By midnight, officers on the *Maddox* were beginning to doubt whether there had been any torpedoes in the first place and sent a message to that effect to direct superiors in Hawaii.[2]

The remaining mystery was the intercepted enemy message threatening an attack. It would be several years before investigators figured out that the message probably referred to the first attack on the *Maddox* two days earlier. But on that August day in 1964 in Washington, alarm bells were going off in the White House and the Pentagon. One attack could be written off as a rash act, but two were too many for President Johnson to ignore. He needed to know if it was one or two, and he needed to know fast.

Defense Secretary Robert McNamara cobbled together spotty reports of sightings from the destroyers, and, with the recommendation of Admiral U. S. Grant Sharp (the commander of the Pacific command, or CINCPAC), he reported to the president that there had probably been two attacks. Twelve hours after the bizarre and probably one-sided "battle" in the Tonkin Gulf, Johnson ordered pilots from the aircraft carriers *Ticonderoga* and *Constellation* to begin retaliatory bombing runs over North Vietnam. In four hours, the Navy planes flew sixty-four missions, blowing up naval bases, oil depots, and patrol boats. One Navy pilot, Lieutenant Richard Sather, was killed, the first casualty in Vietnam; another, Lieutenant Everett Alvarez, was shot down and became the first American prisoner of war in Vietnam. It would be eight and a half years before he was released.

The war between North and South Vietnam had been joined by the United States in a haphazard manner. Nearly five years later when Laird occupied the office once held by McNamara, he reviewed the reports of the Tonkin Gulf affair and judged it to be "a phony operation." Not that the evidence of a second attack had been trumped up; Laird eventually came to believe it was badly mishandled and that the details were hyped when reported to him and other members of Congress. But in 1964, based on this faulty information, Laird was full of the same chest-thumping outrage against the North Vietnamese enemy as the rest of Congress.

Johnson went on national television at 11:37 p.m., August 4, to announce the American bombing of North Vietnam. The next morning McNamara took a resolution to the Senate asking congressional authority "to take all necessary steps, including the use of armed force" to protect South Vietnam from its enemies. It was the closest thing to a declaration of war the Vietnam conflict would ever get, and it would stand until Congress repealed it in 1971. (In 1973, Congress passed the War Powers Act hoping to prevent history from repeating itself. The act limited the power of the president to make war.)

With reports of the audacious attacks in the headlines, the Tonkin Gulf Resolution eased through Congress. Laird supported it, but in a speech on the House floor he cautioned that the resolution did not add up to a policy. America still had to decide whether to dally in Southeast Asia or take "whatever steps are necessary to win the war in that beleaguered area within a reasonable period of time. . . . We must develop and announce to our friends as well as to the Communists what our policy in Southeast Asia is as we face the future." Talking to reporters, Laird said the United States had to adopt a "winning policy in Vietnam, or get out."[3] For the next five years, there would be no winning policy, just an alarming escalation of American troop numbers until Laird became secretary of defense and pulled the plug.

In retrospect, Laird felt he and others had been strong-armed on the Tonkin Gulf Resolution. He reserved his most bitter criticism for McNamara. In Laird's mind, McNamara was either a dissembler or a fool on that subject; a dissembler for twisting the inconclusive reports into an excuse for war, or a fool if he believed those same reports. By the time Laird himself was in McNamara's shoes, he had developed a firm policy about military intelligence reports on any given incident: Never believe the first report, be skeptical about the second, and question the third. He was always cautious about single reports from the three agencies that were funded secretly in the defense budget—CIA, DIA, and the service intelligence branches.

⌒

As memories of the Cold War grow dim, so fades the reason the United States intervened in Southeast Asia in the first place. The area had long been overrun by one world power after another, including China in the first millennium, France in the 1800s, and Japan during World War II. After that war, a Vietnamese Communist, Ho Chi Minh, moved into the vacuum of leadership to consolidate North Vietnam under a Communist-style rule. France tried to reestablish a foothold in South Vietnam, supporting a non-Communist regime there. The result was the Indochina War, which ended with the fall of the French garrison at Dien Bien Phu in May 1954. The French made a last-minute appeal to the United States to intervene with a massive air strike against North Vietnamese forces around Dien Bien Phu, but the United States refused. France was out of Indochina, and the specter of a Communist takeover of South Vietnam, and perhaps all of Indochina, loomed large. President Eisenhower likened the region to a "row of dominoes" ripe for a fall to Communism.

Representatives of nine nations, including the United States, were meeting in Geneva in the spring of 1954 when the French were run out of Vietnam. The Geneva delegates, including those from both Vietnams, "temporarily" divided Vietnam into two nations, North and South, with a timetable set for elections in 1956 to join them under one government. Those elections never happened, and civil war gradually escalated between the two Vietnams; the United States eased, almost unthinkingly, into the role of protector of the South.

Laird tried to steer the Republican agenda toward a winning policy in Southeast Asia. At a dinner for Republicans in rural Wisconsin in March 1964, Laird said that the United States had three choices: continue the half-hearted and creeping escalation by the Johnson administration; leave Vietnam and support neutrality by outsiders, which he personally believed would open the door to Communists; or, his favored option, "step up the war effort. This would include accepting troops from nations willing to contribute troops to the operations and making greater contribution of our own materials and supplies." Laird warned that Americans should be willing to fight by the same rules that the North was using—specifically crossing into North Vietnam and blockading its marine resupply routes, which implicitly meant mining Haiphong harbor. A week later, in a similar speech, he predicted that unless this was done, the Vietnam War might "drag on for ten years."[4]

In May, Laird stepped up pressure on the Johnson administration to adopt a winning strategy. When McNamara appeared before the Defense Appropriations Subcommittee in executive session on May 21, Laird hammered him with Vietnam questions and arguments; Jerry Ford also joined in. After noon, an exhausted McNamara was quizzed about the morning session by Johnson, one of many conversations LBJ secretly taped:

> "I had Ford and Laird . . . all trying to make hay out of [our Vietnam policy]," McNamara recounted.
> "What are they poking at you about?" the president queried.
> "Oh, a 'no win' policy," McNamara responded. He went on to summarize the litany of criticism from the subcommittee that Johnson wasn't fighting to win.
> "Who tried to do it?" the president pressed. "Laird?"
> McNamara told him it was mainly Laird, Ford and two others. Asked by the president whether they could hurt the administration, McNamara assessed: "Jerry Ford and Laird are dangerous."[5]

Evidence of their political agility came ten days later when Laird trapped LBJ. It was vintage Laird, and an example of the early use of a technique he would employ four years later to help elect Nixon president. The essence of it was to put Johnson in the position of having to deny that he had a plan to end or win the war. In this case, Laird wanted Johnson and McNamara to deny that they were about to make a move that Laird thought should be made: an attack into North Vietnam. Laird's opening gambit came during a May 31 appearance on a national radio program. "The administration's position is to move north [allow U.S. troops to cross into North Vietnam] and we are now preparing to move north. This is a preparation which has been going on for several months," Laird announced, adding that his Defense Appropriations Subcommittee in the House was gearing up to support the move with money. "We feel that we should be prepared to move into North Vietnam. I have felt this for some time and I am happy to say that the administration takes the same position."[6]

Johnson was cornered at a press conference and tried to quip his way out of it: "I know of no plans that have been made to that effect," he said. "I would say that Mr. Laird is not as yet speaking for the administration. He might next year some time," referring to the upcoming November presidential election.[7]

Laird launched into a speech of umbrage on the House floor after Johnson's press conference. Johnson was trivializing a serious issue, he said. Laird knew the administration had contingency plans including a move into North

Vietnam if necessary. Feigning surprise at Johnson's denial of invasion plans, Laird said the president had made a serious tactical mistake in telling the enemy that there was no such plan.

Johnson continued to steam about it and raised the matter in two phone calls late in the afternoon to McGeorge Bundy, his national security advisor, and Secretary of State Dean Rusk. Both were with McNamara and the rest of the LBJ national security team in Hawaii conferencing about Vietnam policy. "Laird is saying that McNamara has [a] plan for invasion of the north," Johnson reported to Bundy. "Well, all I said was that I knew of no such plan. I don't mean that we haven't got plans for any contingency, but I approved no plan to invade anything." Bundy tried to calm the president down and advised that the best thing was just to ignore Laird this time: "I'd just leave it alone. I wouldn't get in an argument with Laird—he's too small."[8]

In June 1964, Rep. Melvin Laird was neither "too small" as Bundy suggested, nor as "dangerous" as McNamara characterized him. Johnson had effectively co-opted opposition in the Senate by winning Senate minority leader Everett Dirksen's compliance on the president's Vietnam policies. But now the president could neither control nor afford to ignore the Ford-Laird tag-team opposition. As chairman of the House Republican Conference, Laird was technically number three in the House Republican leadership—after minority leader Ford and minority whip Les Arends. But he was de facto number two in power and authority. Laird deliberately fuzzed the chain of command by telling constituents and others that he was "chair of the House Republicans," which, however factual, suggested to the uninitiated that he was number one.

Johnson had won the 1964 presidential election by painting his opponent Barry Goldwater as a warmonger who would expand U.S. involvement in Vietnam. It was a duplicitous game cynically played against the American voters. In September 1964 White House strategy sessions reached a consensus that air attacks against North Vietnam would probably have to be launched. But it was not advisable to do so until after the election. On September 25, Johnson said, "There are those that say you ought to go north and drop bombs, to try to wipe out the supply lines, and they think that would escalate the war. We don't want our American boys to do the fighting for Asian boys. We don't want to . . . get tied down in a land war in Asia." On October 21 in Akron, Ohio, he made an even more emphatic campaign pledge: "We are not about to send American boys nine or ten thousand miles away from home to do what Asian boys ought to be doing for themselves."[9]

On Sunday, November 1, two days before the election, the Vietcong shelled a U.S.-supported air base at Bien Hoa, destroying six B-57s and killing five

Americans. This was a more serious challenge to the United States than the Gulf of Tonkin provocation in which no Americans were killed or armament damaged. But this time Johnson did nothing. He was shaping his new peace-maker persona, possibly with the hope that his inaction over Bien Hoa would be a signal to the North Vietnamese of his willingness to negotiate peace.

After the election Laird and Ford became the Republican Party's only formidable critics on Vietnam. Laird distinguished himself as an exceptional prognosticator of Johnson's Vietnam War moves. As Laird had predicted during the 1964 election, Johnson took the war into North Vietnam with an order to begin sustained bombing in late February 1965. The campaign, called "Operation Rolling Thunder," continued for three and a half years and became the vehicle for Johnson and McNamara to notoriously micromanage the war—poring over maps, choosing largely insignificant targets, putting key strategic targets off limits, and overriding the wisdom of their military commanders in the Pentagon and on the scene half a world away. While Johnson waged a gradual and limited war, aimed at persuading the North Vietnamese into peace talks, the military men chafed at the restrictions they believed kept them from victory. Laird knew this, not from the White House briefings for Republican leadership but from his Defense Appropriations Subcommittee work and his sources at the Pentagon. He considered the president's briefings to be mere photo opportunities with no opening for input from the members of Congress.

Laird stormed home after the first such briefing and told his family he wasn't going to be photo fodder for Johnson anymore.[10] He soon issued an ultimatum to McNamara in a secret subcommittee hearing that unless the president allowed Republicans to offer their ideas on the Vietnam War in future foreign policy briefings, he would no longer attend. Johnson didn't change the format, and Laird stayed away. At the same time, the White House boasted that there had already been twenty-one hours of "give-and-take" between the president and members of Congress in White House briefings and receptions.[11]

March 8, 1965, marked the day the first American ground troops were officially sent to Vietnam. Two Marine battalions landed on the beach at Da Nang, greeted by a welcome sign, flashbulb-popping photographers, and bikini-clad South Vietnamese sunbathers. Johnson insisted they weren't there for combat but to defend the air base. In a speech Laird complained, "In Southeast Asia, we continue a policy that has caused thousands of South Vietnamese and American casualties, with no effective plan in sight to end this conflict. We continue the fiction that it is a South Vietnam war, that we are only there as advisors."[12]

Laird knew better because his friends at the Pentagon had shared some of Johnson's Vietnam secrets. So while the American public did not know for some time that Johnson made the decision on April 1 to use American ground troops for offensive action, Laird learned as much within a week. He found that Pentagon officials and the U.S. commander in Vietnam, Gen. William Westmoreland, were pushing for tens of thousands more troops. Johnson hadn't determined a number, but he decided he wanted a very public show of support from Congress for whatever his Vietnam policy would be. He asked for a $700 million supplemental appropriation in May. Members of Congress who might have questioned his policy felt forced to vote in favor of the funds needed to support already-deployed "advisors" in Vietnam, as Johnson described them. Laird voted in favor of the appropriation, along with 407 other representatives; only seven voted against. The Senate ratio was 83 to 3. The three were Democrats: Wayne Morse of Oregon and Ernest Gruening of Alaska (the two who had voted against the Tonkin Gulf Resolution the previous year); and Laird's friend and fellow Wisconsinite Gaylord Nelson.[13]

The strain of the war began to show on Johnson in June and July 1965. General Westmoreland insisted he was going to need substantially more troops before long, and the president had to make a decision that could portend disaster for his presidency and the country. If he decided to deploy many more ground troops, he knew America would soon be in the Vietnam quicksand up to its neck. Still, he continued to maintain the fiction that the United States was not in combat in Vietnam.

Laird was livid. "We may be dangerously close to ending Republican support of our present Vietnam policy," he vented in a statement for the press on June 14. "This possibility exists because the American people do not know how far the administration is prepared to go with large-scale use of ground forces in order to save face in Vietnam." Laird urged Johnson to allow the bombing of more strategic targets and blockade North Vietnam's Haiphong Harbor to stop shipment of war supplies. And he predicted that escalating the ground war would cost American lives. Johnson was under-utilizing American sea and air power, while entangling men in a guerrilla war on the ground.[14]

Coming as the statement was from "one of the most influential Republicans in the House," the *New York Times* called it the "first significant sign of potential Republican opposition to the Administration's Vietnam policies." But for the moment, Laird appeared to be the only prominent Republican willing to challenge Johnson. Senate minority leader Everett Dirksen immediately kowtowed. "We are going to uphold the President's hand [in the Senate]. What else can you do in a situation like this?" he said.[15] Ford was unaccountably silent, and Johnson must have sensed a schism between Ford and Laird, which meant Johnson might be able to isolate Ford. In an evening phone call three days later, Johnson probed Ford on that, as well as the extent of Republican support for his Vietnam policy.

Ford bluntly asked him, "How much are we going to use the ground forces?"

"Only when and if and as necessary to protect our national interest," Johnson ambiguously responded, before allowing that they would inevitably be involved in some combat.

Ford responded, "The only thing, if we're going to do more offensively on the ground, then I think we all ought to sit down and talk about it."

"I'll be glad to do that," Johnson obliged, "if it can stay out of the papers." LBJ launched into a tirade about recent press reports. Then the president moved onto his final point, testing whether Laird was speaking for himself or for a wider Republican opposition which might include Ford.

"I think you ought to get a muzzle on Laird," Johnson said. "Make him quit telling me that I can't have ground troops I need to protect my airplanes, because I can't bomb like he wants to if the goddamned Vietcong are destroying my airplanes on the ground."

Ford failed to take the bait and criticize his partner, so Johnson ended the call.[16]

At this time, Johnson's "Rolling Thunder" aerial bombing campaign and his Vietnam policy were popular, according to the polls. Laird had to explain to his constituents in a late June 1965 letter why he was beginning to speak strongly about a growing need to alter that policy. The president had stated that his goal was a negotiated settlement with North Vietnam, not a military victory, and had even hinted that Communist elements might be allowed to stay in South Vietnam as part of any truce, Laird explained. Was that something Americans should die for? "Republicans in Congress have supported the President's recent actions but his decision to enlarge the ground war and commit as many as one hundred thousand or more American ground troops is causing us to raise certain questions about our future role in that war-torn country. . . . It is my view that if a negotiated settlement is our goal, we should not endanger large numbers of American troops," he told his constituents.[17]

Ford turned up the volume on his own rhetoric, matching Laird's, at a

July 1 press conference and an appearance on a Sunday television talk show two weeks later. Ford had come to believe that it was time to speak out. Later that day, he went public with the warning that if the "rumors" were true that Johnson was about to commit major ground forces, including a call-up of Reserves, the president ought to get a congressional endorsement for that.

The next day, Eisenhower phoned LBJ to echo that sentiment, advising Johnson that he ought to consult with the House and Senate leadership before making a big move. But Johnson disagreed. Instead, he said, "I'll tell Dirksen [to tell] Mel Laird and Jerry just not to get excited." Eisenhower said he, too, hoped "to calm these people down by telling them I talked to you."[18] Neither Dirksen nor Eisenhower, however, could silence Laird and Ford. The issue was too important and the moment too pivotal. Five days later, on the evening of July 27, 1965, Johnson called congressional leaders of both parties to the White House for a heads-up about the Vietnam speech he would deliver the next day. Laird did not attend, in keeping with his no-briefing policy.

As far as Laird and Ford were concerned, the decision Johnson made was a terrible mistake. And it was a policy that would reverberate through the history of American warfare. The president would be using the draft, not the Reserves and National Guard, to continue the buildup of troops in Vietnam. The next day Johnson announced as much at a press conference; the troop complement in Vietnam would be raised to 125,000 by doubling the draft numbers. This meant that draft boards could pluck reluctant warriors out of the American heartland one at a time and send them to Vietnam, instead of sending Reserve units that had trained together and would leave together. At this time, Johnson had already, secretly, approved another 100,000 troops by year's end, and another 100,000 in 1966.[19]

The next day, at Laird's regular weekly luncheon with a half-dozen reporters, Ford joined him for an off-the-record briefing. The journalists reported afterward that unnamed "congressional sources" had spilled the story about what really had happened in the briefing at the White House—that Johnson had planned an emergency call-up of the Reserves and a request for $5 billion to expand the war, but that he had changed his mind at the last minute; and that Senate majority leader Mike Mansfield had interrupted Johnson's carefully choreographed meeting by reading a three-page statement warning LBJ of a public backlash if the Reserves were called up.[20]

By the time the news of Johnson's private meeting hit the headlines, he was on vacation at his Texas ranch. He boiled over not only at the breach of confidence about his meeting with the congressmen but also at the implication that he had made his decision about the draft based solely on political advantage. The reports that Democratic congressmen had talked him off a ledge on the issue of troop deployment were "untrue and perhaps malicious," Johnson said. Someone had "broken" his confidence and "distorted" his intent. On its own, the leak from the White House briefing should not have riled the president, but this was the last straw by Ford and Laird as they tried to force him to change his Vietnam policies.[21] In a news analysis, the *Los Angeles Times* opined that while some assumed the president blamed Ford, who had been at the White House briefing, "in reality, however, the President's greatest animosity is aimed at Rep. Melvin Laird of Wisconsin."[22]

Jerry Ford knew it was time for Republicans in the House to stand strong together, particularly since the Senate Republicans, under Dirksen, had failed to step up to the plate. Thus was born the party's first white paper on Vietnam—a collection of facts and charts showing in stark terms the buildup of American troops, and an implication that Johnson's tepid approach to the war had misled the enemy regarding America's resolve. As chairman of the Republican Conference, Laird commissioned the report. The conference research director Bill Prendergast and Dr. John Bibby of the University of Wisconsin wrote the first six-thousand-word draft. Alerted about the upcoming Republican white paper, Johnson had ordered a competitive report, *Why Vietnam?*

When the Republican report *Vietnam: Some Neglected Aspects of the Historical Record,* was issued, Johnson implied at a press conference that the party was playing politics with national security.[23] Three hours later, Ford, Laird, and Rep. Charles Goodell had their own press conference to defend the right of Congress to differ with the president. "We shouldn't be muzzled," Ford maintained, using the same word that Johnson had used in asking him to silence Laird a month before. "We shouldn't be smothered. We shouldn't be muted."[24]

⁓

The day after Lyndon Johnson announced that he would feed the war by means of the draft, four hundred demonstrators in New York City marched from City Hall Park to the local Army induction center. There, several of them became the first anti-Vietnam protestors to burn their draft cards. They were not, however, the first to protest with fire. Norman Morrison, a thirty-one-year-old Quaker, had carried his one-year old daughter Emily to the lawn of the Pentagon on November 2, 1965. He doused himself with kerosene, struck a match on his shoe, and burned himself to death. In the last instant before flames engulfed him, he tossed Emily to safety in the direction of a crowd of stunned onlookers. A twelve-foot-high pillar of fire reached within view of the office of the Secretary of Defense McNamara, whose window was only forty feet away. Morrison had left a letter with his wife explaining that he had to do something to protest napalm bombings of villagers in Vietnam.

The first significant protests against American involvement in the war began after the late February 1965 launch of the "Rolling Thunder" bombing campaign. As it continued throughout the spring, the "teach-in" was born. College campuses cancelled classes for a day or more (or students would boycott classes), and students would attend seminars debating and protesting the war. The first major national antiwar demonstration was organized by the Students for a Democratic Society on April 17, 1965, in Washington; it drew twenty thousand marchers.

The demonstrations disturbed Rep. Laird because he feared they would encourage the enemy to doubt American resolve. At the time Laird could be described accurately as a "hawk" about the war, as was the majority of Congress. But Laird was a very specific type of hawk—he thought the United States should quickly and massively pound the enemy into submission by air and sea power—not by the use of ground troops. Laird postulated to journalists in a speech on November 20, 1965, in Fresno, California, that perhaps it was time for Johnson to ask Congress to formally declare war. One reason to support a declaration of war, he said, would be because the enemy could then be compelled to treat POWs humanely under the Geneva Conventions. "That's the only reason why I would support it," he concluded, but "I don't think we in Congress should push [the White House] into it."[25] A few days later, he told *New York Times* reporter David Broder: "The fact is sinking in that we are actually in a war there, without one ever being declared. [T]he President should have the courage to come to Congress and ask for authorization to fight a war if that is what this is."[26]

The purpose behind many of Laird's political moves was not always evident from the opening gambit but was usually unveiled over time. Laird knew there was no chance Johnson would ask for a declaration of war. Laird's rhetorical probes were aimed at producing something close but importantly different. He did not believe the United States was involved in an "illegal war," which required a formal declaration. But he also did not think that the Gulf of Tonkin Resolution should be a blank check for Johnson. Laird wanted an open debate.

In Laird's mind, there were several options that made more sense than the Johnson strategy. For example, Laird had been calling for trade restrictions and a naval blockade against North Vietnam since March 1964. In 1965 Laird began pushing a blockade plan with repetitive urgency. Ford wholeheartedly agreed with him on this point, and together they managed to persuade the Republican Coordinating Committee—made up of Republican legislators, governors, presidential candidates, and Eisenhower—that it was the right policy for their party to support. On December 13, 1965, the GOP committee came out with a strong unanimous statement urging "maximum use" of American air power against all "significant military targets" in North Vietnam and an immediate naval quarantine against the enemy.

Behind Laird's push for a more aggressive approach was his lingering suspicion that the president was holding back to buy time until the enemy agreed to come to the negotiating table. In the process, American lives were being lost on the ground by fighting a guerilla war for which they had little training, and this was unthinkable to Laird because the United States had superior air and sea power. It was also unthinkable to the military men who tried to advise Johnson. While Laird and others lobbied publicly for a powerful air war over North Vietnam, the Joint Chiefs of Staff tried to lobby the president privately for precisely the same thing.

They were finally allowed to meet with Johnson on the subject in November 1965. It was an extraordinary meeting, revealing the extent of Johnson's intractability and intemperance over Vietnam, even with his own military leadership. The substance was revealed years later by retired Lt. Gen. Charles G. Cooper in an essay for the Naval Institute titled, "The Day It Became the Longest War." At the time of the meeting, Cooper was a Marine major and aide to Adm. David McDonald, chief of Naval Operations. The first indication it was going to go badly, Cooper recalled, was that Johnson made his visitors stand, signaling that the meeting would be brief.

Gen. Earle Wheeler, the new chairman of the Joint Chiefs, got to the point. "The essence of Gen. Wheeler's presentation," Cooper wrote, "was that we had come to an early moment of truth in our ever-increasing Vietnam involvement. We had to begin using our principal strengths—air and naval power—to punish the North Vietnamese, or we would risk becoming involved in another protracted Asian ground war with no definitive solution. Speaking for the chiefs, Gen. Wheeler offered a bold course of action designed to avoid the threat of protracted land warfare. He proposed isolating the major port of Haiphong through naval mining, blockading the rest of the North Vietnamese coastline, and simultaneously beginning a B-52 bombing offensive on Hanoi."

Johnson asked all the chiefs if they agreed, and they did. "Seemingly deep in thought, President Johnson turned his back on them for a minute or so, then suddenly, losing the calm, patient demeanor he had maintained throughout the meeting, he whirled to face them and exploded," Cooper recalled.

The president shouted obscenities, called the top brass insulting names, and ridiculed them for trying to use a military solution to a political and diplomatic problem, and said they had no idea of what it was like to be in his position. "He told them he was disgusted with their naive approach toward him, that he was not going to let some military idiots talk him into World War III. . . . It ended when he ordered them to 'get the hell out of my office!'"[27]

In public, Laird was saying the same thing to the president as the Joint Chiefs tried to say in private—blockade the coast, mine the harbor, and bomb the most vital strategic targets. Ironically, Johnson hoped his "limited warfare" approach would bring the enemy to the negotiating table. But it was not until 1972, when Laird was defense secretary and Nixon was president, that the plan of blockading and bombing became the tool that finally forced Hanoi to agree to a truce.

7

Fight Now, Pay Later

WASHINGTON LOVES A GOOD FEUD. When the evenly matched Congressman Laird and Secretary of Defense McNamara locked horns, it was juicy fodder for cocktail parties and political columnists. There were few public exchanges—most of their clashes occurred behind closed doors during Defense Appropriations Subcommittee hearings—but the news frequently leaked out. At first, Laird had considered McNamara a brilliant defense secretary who had laudably established civilian control at the Pentagon in his first years there. But Laird came to believe that McNamara had outlived his usefulness after one term. When Laird became convinced that McNamara had not told the whole truth about the Tonkin Gulf incident, the gloves came off. The media took note, frequently describing Laird as McNamara's toughest critic. As one writer for the Scripps-Howard newspapers put it, Laird took on McNamara while most of Washington still believed he was "the greatest thing to hit town since standup drinking."[1]

The most memorable dustup between the two men came during closed-door budget hearings in early 1966. Laird began pressing McNamara about his pattern of grossly underestimating the budget needs for the war. McNamara got testy, and Laird continued to press. "I think the secretary is tired and overworked," Laird said, with a hint of sarcasm. "He has engaged in short-tempered outbursts recently. I think he needs a good rest—at least a week or two away from the desk."

A furious McNamara exploded with a profane remark, jumped up, and appeared to lunge across the table at Laird. Rep. George Mahon interceded with a quick rebuke to McNamara for his words and body language: "Mr. Secretary, we don't use that kind of language in this room, and we don't have that kind of reaction to questions asked by a member of this committee. Mr. Laird has the perfect right to suggest that maybe you're tired and worn out."[2]

The contretemps was over, but Laird refused to retreat, even though some members of Congress on both sides of the aisle and White House aides asked him to back off. The following March 1967, when McNamara was back to remedy another budgeting shortfall, Laird got under his skin again, demanding to know how he had made yet another multibillion dollar error. "Okay, you've got the knife in me," McNamara reportedly protested at one stage. "Just don't twist it."[3] Laird was convinced that McNamara was a broken man, barely hiding his injured psyche under a veneer of bravado.

As one of the nation's top defense appropriations experts, Laird was furious about the duplicitous way Johnson had financed the Vietnam War. Reasonable people could and did differ on tactics for prosecuting the war, but Laird felt that the funding should be a matter of hard numbers in an open book. In 1965 Laird began hammering Johnson for the accounting sleight of hand that left the public in the dark about how much the war was costing. Johnson and McNamara established a pattern of submitting an annual defense budget that grossly underestimated the actual cost of the war. The administration would then come back to Congress with supplemental requests to pay for the war. Laird called it a "fight now, pay later" policy, which would finance the war "on the installment plan."

The defense budget Johnson submitted in early 1965 didn't include a single dollar for increased American activities in Vietnam. Instead, he financed it first with two supplemental appropriations—$700 million in May and an "emergency" $1.7 billion in September added on as a late part of the 1966 fiscal year budget. On the floor of the House Mel Laird called it a "fraud" to suggest that, even with the extra $1.7 billion, the war was fully funded. He predicted Johnson would come back in January and ask for billions more, to cover the cost of the fifty-thousand-plus extra troops deployed to Vietnam. Just as Laird had predicted, in January 1966 the Johnson administration asked for $13.1 billion more, which was approved in March. By logical calculation, the president and McNamara had seriously underestimated the Vietnam War cost for fiscal year 1966 by almost $15 billion.

In October 1966 Laird again predicted the White House would approach Congress after the election and request an emergency supplemental war appropriation somewhere between $12 and $16 billion.[4] "Laird doesn't know what he's talking about," McNamara told the press. But three months later, McNamara was back, securing a $12.2 billion supplemental for the war.[5]

Laird felt that the Johnson method of war financing—trying to feed his "Great Society" social programs and fight a war—was wrong on every count. "No nation has ever been able to finance a large war and expand domestic services without seriously injuring its own economy," Laird argued. "This fact must be remembered by those who insist on 'business as usual' here at home while the war effort continues abroad."[6] The president was trying to get both "guns and butter," and that wasn't possible—although Laird, as a representative from a dairy district, generally avoided using that nineteenth-century expression for nations at war that had to choose between the two. (He occasionally said it was a "guns and oleo" issue.)[7] Even though Laird knew how Johnson was fudging on the budget, he could not bring himself to vote against any Vietnam budget request. "For me not to support the funding of the troops that our President has committed to Vietnam would be irresponsible, and, for me, unthinkable. . . . [W]hen the American flag has been committed in a military action, it is the duty of the Congress to see that the American men who are sent into battle will have all the support our nation can provide to do an effective job with a minimum of casualties," Laird wrote in a newspaper column.[8]

Laird was also accurate in predicting the manpower needs for Vietnam, over and above McNamara's low-ball figures. Each time the president raised the troop complement, Laird accurately guessed a higher number would be deployed. In 1966 he began using his own numbers—numbers that included those men Johnson admitted were on the ground in South Vietnam, and those the president didn't mention who were on ships and on air bases in other Asian nations, all supporting the war. When Johnson raised the ground troop numbers to 300,000 in August 1966, Laird said the number was really 385,000. When Laird took over as defense secretary in 1969, Johnson was claiming there were 540,000 troops in the war. In reality, Laird said, the number including the sailors and airmen was more than one million.

In 1966 it looked as if Laird might have a tougher reelection race than usual. He was running against an incumbent legislator for the first time, Norman Myhra. Myhra was a double hand-amputee World War II veteran with a zeal for campaigning. It was clear he hoped to either win the election for Congress or get appointed as the postmaster in Stevens Point, whichever came first. Word was out that the Democrats had promised him the postmaster job if he would run as their "sacrificial lamb" against Laird. To run, Myhra had to give up his assemblyman office, so he decided to give it his all. Democratic senator Gaylord Nelson remembered driving with Myhra during the campaign and having to listen to his rhetorical attacks on Laird. Nelson had agreed to campaign for a day and lend his coattails to a fellow Democrat, but it was a day that he hated to remember. "I guess he [Myhra] thought the nastier you were, the better your chances," Nelson recalled. "His attacks on Mel were absolutely embarrassing to me. It was dumb politics, and inaccurate. It was mean-spirited. He got the hell beat out of him."

Laird won the election handily, with 65 percent of the vote. At that point Nelson stated that Laird demonstrated the strength of his character. Instead of seeking political revenge for Myhra's bitter campaign, Laird called Nelson and told him that if Myhra were nominated to be Stevens Point postmaster, Laird would not stand in the way. "Anybody that got the treatment Mel did generally wouldn't bother to affirmatively call. Most people would say, 'to hell with him,'" Nelson related. Instead, Laird was offering to help in overcoming any objections to Myhra for the appointment. Setting the tone of the campaign aside, Laird argued that Myhra had served honorably in World War II and as an assemblyman. "He's paid his dues," Laird concluded to Nelson, who was reluctant to support Myhra after his personal experience. But Laird persuaded him, and Myhra was made postmaster.[9]

Laird picked up a new protégé on the political playing field during the 1966 campaign. Dick Cheney had been raised in Casper, Wyoming, and got bachelor's and master's degrees in political science from the University of Wyoming. Cheney intended to be a professor, as did his wife Lynne, and they enrolled in doctoral programs at the University of Wisconsin in the fall of 1966. Before school started, Cheney snagged a summer job as an aide to Wisconsin governor Warren Knowles, who was running for reelection. Knowles had been friends with Laird since they were seatmates in the Wisconsin state senate, so they campaigned together that summer, with twenty-five-year-old Dick Cheney in tow. Knowles borrowed a popular Laird campaign technique—taking a Polaroid picture of himself with voters and giving it to them; Cheney was the governor's designated photographer.[10] Laird saw Cheney as a true comer, bright, anxious to learn, and a good listener. He spent time on the campaign trail teaching the young student the political ropes. More than a mentor, however, Laird became Cheney's first important patron in Washington.

What Cheney remembered most from that summer of campaigning was a long conversation about Vietnam on a late-night trip on a small plane between northern Wisconsin and Chicago. "This was before there was a lot of opposition to the war—especially in political circles. But I can remember on that plane ride that night, Mel raising serious questions about the judgments and decisions that had been made during the Johnson administration in terms of getting into Vietnam. I remember him cautioning the governor to be careful about what he said about Vietnam—that all was not right with the policy there."[11]

~

In the fall of 1966, the House Republican leadership issued a second white paper on Vietnam, this one more scathing than the one the previous year. The document's main theme was that LBJ had made the United States a "full-fledged combatant in a conflict that was becoming 'bigger than the Korean War.'"[12] A significant new theme was the administration's lack of candor about casualties, both allied and enemy. The white paper argued that Johnson had no clear idea of how to get out of Vietnam and didn't possess the courage to tell the American people the truth.[13]

Laird had found that the most effective campaign oratory tapped into a national suspicion that Johnson and the Democrats were heavy-handedly dictating domestic and foreign policies without listening to some wise voices of dissent urging more centrist policies. The Republican victories of the 1966 midterm election were a testament to the effectiveness of the new Ford-Laird House Republican leadership, which had been the driving force behind national Republican policy. With financial and political support, they targeted up to one hundred House seats held by those Democrats who appeared most vulnerable. If they secured seventy-eight, Republicans would be the majority party in the House. Laird estimated Republicans would gain anywhere from thirty-one to sixty seats in the November election.[14] When the votes were tallied, they had a net gain of forty-seven seats. The gains were "a victory for all Americans because two-party government was restored to our nation's capital," Laird declared.[15]

The victory might have been slightly sweeter for the Republicans had Johnson not stolen the spotlight on the eve of the election in order to bolster the Democrats' position. The president arranged a summit in Manila in late October with six allies—South Vietnam, Thailand, South Korea, the Philippines, Australia, and New Zealand. From abroad he issued a unilateral peace offering, promising that the allies would withdraw their forces within six months after Hanoi withdrew its own troops "and the level of violence subsides."[16] Although the resolution was vague and badly flawed, it gave Johnson and his party an eleventh-hour appearance of being peacemakers, which helped stem Democrat losses a bit in the 1966 congressional election.

Laird had played such a prominent role in the Republican electoral victories in 1966 that in early 1967 it was inevitable that the media would speculate about his displacing Ford as minority leader. "A searing row has developed

among House Republicans," one columnist opined. There were Laird supporters who were pushing for a coup because they viewed Laird as "a tougher,
smarter political operative than Ford, and what the party needs in the House
for the next two years is not a good-looking but ineffectual guy ." The columnist observed that "the Laird-Ford ruckus has yet to surface."[17] In reality, there never was a Laird-Ford split, and the two men remained fast friends
and close political allies.

Ford needed Laird's idea-a-minute personality. Because insiders knew just
how cunning and manipulative Laird was behind the scenes, some Republicans bragged that he was "our Lyndon Johnson."[18] Other comparisons were
made; one from a *Los Angeles Times* political journalist said that Laird, the
man "widely viewed as the gray eminence of Congressional Republicans,"
had established "a role now likened to that of the French monk Francois le
Clerc du Tremblay who, with Cardinal Richelieu, was the power behind the
throne of Louis XIII."[19] But the most frequently used appellation to describe
Laird was "Midwest Machiavelli," a man of "subtlety and cunning."[20]

Ford himself sometimes used the word "schemer" to describe his friend.
"He's the greatest schemer, and he knows that we all know that he does it.
That's his nature; he's always got to be scheming. He doesn't scheme for any
sinister reason; he just likes to keep the pot boiling. I never got mad at it
[because] Mel Laird is one of the brightest political people that I ever knew.
He had exceptional political perceptions as to issues, candidates, conflicts.
He was, in my judgment, one of the shrewdest political operatives ever—
and I say that in the right sense, not as a critical comment. He loved politics, and he absorbed himself in politics."[21]

For his part, Laird felt Ford had two primary liabilities. One was that he
didn't "catch on as rapidly as he should to the political significance of an event
or an issue. Once he understands it, there's no problem—but it does take
him time." The second was that he was a laid-back leader. "You had to kick
him in the ass usually to get him to do something," Laird said. Ford appreciated Laird's goading. "He's a pusher, and I respond to that kind of challenge. So it was a good combination; we worked together very well."[22]

The one aspect of the Ford-Laird partnership that Laird most disliked was
that he necessarily had to be cast as the heavy. They both knew that somebody had to crack the whip and keep Republicans in line with the leadership,
and the genial Ford was better suited to be the good cop. He was older and
gave off a more vigorous physical appearance than the balding Laird. "Even
Laird admirers fear that his overbearing manner and devilish look—eyes

gleaming, cigar waving—may keep him from attaining any higher elected party post," the *Wall Street Journal* suggested.[23]

For many reasons, the Laird-Ford partnership withstood erosion from external forces. As members of several social groups, such as the Chowder and Marching Club, they partied together. Laird and Ford shared a great love for golf, which often put them together on the links. Their families celebrated birthdays and holidays with one another. And there was one more key reason for their unbreakable bond that outsiders did not know: Laird and Ford prayed together every week.

The gathering every Wednesday in a little room on the House side of the Capitol was begun by Republican Rep. Al Quie, later the governor of Minnesota. A Lutheran anxious to make a spiritual connection with some House members, Quie said he pondered whom he should approach. He thoughtfully considered the New Testament story of the divine selection of Saul, a Jew who was also a Roman citizen well versed in Greek philosophy. Wanting to follow that example, he asked himself, "Who is the best politician in Congress?"

"The answer was obvious: Mel Laird was the best politician," Quie recounted. "So I thought, I've gotta talk to him—but I never got around to it." He was afraid of being rebuffed on the prayer invitation, but at one point, when he was seated in the front row of the House chamber with Laird behind him, Quie prayed for the strength to raise the delicate issue. Twice he tried to speak, but could not. "God, I can't do this," he prayed. "You're going to have to get someone else to do it; I just can't."

At that moment, as another member droned on with a speech, Laird leaned forward and said, "Al, I've been thinking we ought to get together some time for prayer and invite some of our friends to pray with us." Quie said that "from that moment on, I never doubted the power of the Holy Spirit." Repairing to the Speaker's Lobby, Laird and Quie worked out the details. The group needed to be small, they agreed, so each of them would invite one friend only. Laird said he would invite Ford; Quie wanted to approach their mutual friend Charlie Goodell. By the next night, when they found each other at a Chamber of Commerce gathering, the excitement was still palpable. Ford and Goodell had agreed. "This has to be of God," Laird said.

From that point on—whenever it was possible on Wednesday around noon—the four met for vocal prayer and reflection. In a weekly rotation, one would say the first prayer, and each of the three others would follow. They would close saying the Lord's Prayer in unison. Certainly it might have been viewed by outsiders as a Republican "power group" since Ford was the minority leader, Laird the Republican Conference chair, and Goodell and Quie both key committee leaders for the conference, but they didn't see it that way. "We never made a big thing about it," Laird noted. "We didn't wear our religion on our sleeve, so we didn't talk about it with others. It was informal, comfortable, and a very private thing for all of us."

When Goodell was appointed in 1968 to the Senate to replace the late Bobby Kennedy, John Rhodes of Arizona took his place in the small group. The Wednesday prayer group continued through to the end of Ford's presidency in 1977, and all through that time Laird served as defense secretary, White House domestic counselor, and then as a senior counselor for *Reader's Digest*. But if he was in town on Wednesday, Laird would find his way back to the small House prayer room and enjoy the spiritual repast once more with his old friends.[24]

⌁

March 18, 1967, could arguably go down in history as the day that broke the will of the Johnson administration concerning Vietnam. The precipitating act happened entirely behind the scenes when Gen. William Westmoreland, the commander of U.S. forces in Vietnam, insisted that he needed another 200,000 American troops, which would raise the total number of ground troops to 670,000. The general also wanted to expand the war into Cambodia and Laos, increase the bombing of North Vietnam, and invade from the sea through the demilitarized zone. The price tag would have been $10 billion more a year for a war that was already costing $25 billion annually.

Johnson and McNamara were stunned. The Westmoreland memo sat like dead weight on the president's desk and was never answered. It marked a turning point for McNamara. He urged the president to reject the escalation and then two months later wrote his own memo, which proved to be the beginning of the end as defense secretary. In that memo McNamara advised Johnson that the approach they were taking was wrong: Expecting the North Vietnamese to come to the bargaining table was a pipe dream; Hanoi would bide its time hoping that the 1968 election would unseat Johnson; Westmoreland's request for more troops would throw Congress and the American people into a "bitter" debate. "The picture of the world's greatest superpower killing or seriously injuring 1000 noncombatants a week, while trying to pound a tiny backward nation into submission on an issue whose merits are hotly disputed is not a pretty one," McNamara wrote.[25]

A second memo from McNamara to Johnson six months later sealed the defense secretary's fate. On November 1, 1967, responding to more pressure from the Joint Chiefs to escalate the war and seek military victory, McNamara advised Johnson to halt the bombing of North Vietnam and begin turning the war over to the South Vietnamese. "Continuation of our present course of action in Southeast Asia would be dangerous, costly in lives, and unsatisfactory to the American people," McNamara wrote.[26] The president had a military establishment urging him to pull out all the stops, and a defense secretary telling him to pull back. He was not willing to do either. By the end of November Johnson had arranged a new job for McNamara as president of the World Bank. Three months later, Clark Clifford moved into McNamara's office.

Looking back on that time, McNamara insisted there was no feud with Laird. He "was a terrific congressman, an extraordinary congressman," and the Defense Appropriations Subcommittee was "one of the best committees in Congress. I testified before him and Jerry Ford for years and years and years. They were Republicans and I was in Democratic administrations under Kennedy and Johnson." When asked if he thought Laird was tough on him, McNamara said, "Well, you know, he was tough in the sense that he was so well informed that you had to be on your toes when you went up there, and keep your hands in your pockets!" He chuckled, remembering. "But he was damn, damn good. I admired and respected him."[27]

Laird also downplayed the notion of a feud. McNamara was one of the first people Laird called on after being nominated as secretary of defense. At a press conference Laird said, "I did disagree with him on his estimates as far as Vietnam War costs. Only the disagreements seem to make news [but] I was in agreement with him more often than I was in disagreement with him."[28] Laird was referring to all aspects of the defense budget, including manpower policies, weapons procurement, and the vast array of Pentagon issues that went beyond Vietnam.

Although he still regarded McNamara with respect, Laird was critical of McNamara's 1995 memoir, *In Retrospect,* in which McNamara finally admitted mistakes that Laird had pointed out as they occurred in the 1960s. In the book, "McNamara never really pays tribute to the men and women who gave so much to their country, died for it." Laird said. "You cannot just turn your back on those young men and women who went out there. You owe them a lot. Right or wrong, you owe them a lot." He said in a later interview, "McNamara was a brilliant man in many, many respects. He was really a whiz kid; there's no question about that. But I don't think he had the feeling or concern for people that you need if you're going to be secretary of defense."

$\sim$

As a congressman, Laird had some personal perspective on the human cost of the war. Jim Albertson was no soldier, but he died in Vietnam while undertaking a mission Laird had urged upon him. Dr. Albertson was the president of Wisconsin State College (later University of Wisconsin) at Stevens Point, and Laird trusted his judgment. When Laird learned the Agency for International Development (AID) was putting together a team to study higher education in South Vietnam in order to prepare that country for a peaceful future, he thought Albertson was just the man for the job. The team flew to Vietnam in January 1967 to begin a study of the three public universities of Saigon, Can-Tho, and Hue. It took some courage for these educators, since all of South Vietnam was effectively a war zone. But the forty-one-year-old Albertson, a World War II veteran who served two years in the Pacific, shrugged it off. On March 23 the Air America twin-engine plane ferrying Albertson and his team around Vietnam landed at an airfield north of Da Nang to wait out a tropical storm. Anxious to get them to their next stop, the pilot decided that the weather had cleared up enough to fly. But after takeoff the plane slammed into the side of the mountain. Dr. Albertson, the pilot, an AID official, and seven educators from Harvard, the University of Illinois, and colleges in Wisconsin and Minnesota were killed.[29]

Laird was devastated when he heard the news. He struggled to console Albertson's widow and five children. After returning from speaking at Albertson's funeral and thinking it over for weeks, Laird offered heartfelt words in the House chamber about the loss of the selfless volunteers: "These men with Jim Albertson as their leader were frontline soldiers in the long-range war of ideas. Their weapons were books instead of bullets. Their objective was to help develop universities in which young people of Southeast Asia could seek truth to guide them in deciding their own destiny." After praising Albertson, Laird moved on to the larger tragedy of the soldiers, sailors, and airmen who never returned from the war. "The war in Vietnam has brought tragedy and loss to thousands of American families from coast to coast," he said. "For hundreds of these boys, we will never know what contribution they might have made to their communities and their nation had their lives not been cut short by the cruel and indifferent consequences of war."[30]

A few weeks after that speech, the name of one of those "boys" appeared on the June 23 roster of the dead—someone Laird knew intimately from back home in Marshfield. Second Lt. Charles Leo Johnson was killed in action in Chu Chi while simultaneously directing his men in an attack and trying to drag his wounded radio operator to safety. He had been in Vietnam only six weeks. The lieutenant, who was awarded a posthumous Silver

Star for his gallantry, was one of eleven children of Herbert and Adele Johnson, the family that lived in the house behind Laird family home for many
years. Thirty years later, a published Marshfield history reported that the
Johnson family believed Charles's death in mid-1967 helped transform Laird
from a hawk to a dove on the Vietnam War.[31]

The buzzwords "hawk" and "dove" were too simplistic to describe Laird
and most of his generation. They had fought and won a world war, and had
paid a dear price for victory. They were not afraid to stand up against tyranny,
but experience had taught them that the end had to justify the sacrifice. In
Vietnam Laird was pretty sure the American public didn't know what the
"end" was supposed to look like, and he strongly suspected the president
didn't know either.

In a February 1967 letter to Johnson, Laird pleaded for clarification. The
president had recited lofty goals about security and freedom for South Vietnam but was dropping hints of compromise in negotiations with the enemy.
"Our country is a great country and our people a great people," Laird wrote.
"They are willing to make whatever sacrifices are necessary in time of war
to insure honorable success for their country's cause. I pray that you, as our
nation's leader, will take them into your confidence and lay before them a
full and detailed report on the foreign policy of the United States."[32]

An internal White House memo called the Laird letter "a thoughtful piece
of work . . . he is right in saying that the matters he has raised are among
those things which do trouble a number of our people." An LBJ aide said
that Laird had suggested that the president should make it the subject of a
major message, and the aide was prepared to work on the first draft.[33] (Laird
only knew that the White House sent him a standard-issue reply assuring
him that his letter was receiving the "most serious consideration.")

Among issues Laird addressed in his letter to the president was the failure to restrict trade to North Vietnam, as Laird had so often urged. This time
Laird was prepared to make a full-court press on the trade issue. A few days
before Johnson got Laird's letter, the president received a heads-up memo
from a White House aide, Douglass Cater, who had discussed the issue with
Laird at a dinner the night before. "He thinks that the Administration is not
facing up to the fact that in Vietnam it is not the Communist Chinese (but
the Soviets) who are providing the support that permits North Vietnam to
continue the war."[34]

On March 23 Laird introduced a resolution declaring to be "the sense of
Congress" that future expansion of trade with the Soviet Bloc be contingent
upon "demonstrable evidence that their actions and policies with regard to

Vietnam have been redirected toward peace and an honorable settlement." Laird charged that the Johnson administration had deliberately misinformed Americans by suggesting that the Chinese were the main suppliers to North Vietnam when, in reality, it was the Soviets.[35] That fact was admitted by the administration in highly classified briefings not then available to the American public. Two months later, the rest of the Republican leadership caught up with Laird. At a meeting on May 25, the top Republican Senate and House leaders agreed it was time to back Laird's position. After the meeting, speaking for the Senate Republican leadership, Everett Dirksen began his statement with a question: "Have you heard of a single Russian who was reported as a casualty in Vietnam? You haven't and you won't. [Today] the U.S. Command reported that total American casualties were in excess of 70,000 [including] 10,253 dead. . . . How were they killed? For the most part by Red Russian weapons and Red Chinese weapons in the hands of the Red Viet Cong [and] there are more weapons to come. . . . These are the people with whom we are asked to turn the cheek of compassion and embark on a policy of East-West trade. Is trade so sweet and profits so desirable as to be purchased at the price we now pay in death and agony?"[36]

Laird was glad to have his fellow Republicans on board, but it was already too late for reasonable success in Vietnam. In March he laconically told a Chamber of Commerce breakfast meeting in his hometown that he saw "no real chance for a U.S. military victory in Vietnam."[37] In a February news column Laird—who had advocated an embargo and blockade three years before—concluded: "Had we used trade as one of the most effective weapons of war at the outset, I am convinced that the agonizing losses both in man and material would not have been as large and the duration of the war would have been materially shortened."[38]

~

The freshman Republican class of the Ninetieth Congress was a large one, with fifty-nine newly elected Republican members of the House beginning their first terms in 1967. They looked to the leadership for guidance, and Laird became a mentor to many of them, as he had to others before them. The new class included George Herbert Walker Bush. Shortly after the election, Bush wrote then-minority leader Ford to make a "strong plea" for a coveted seat on the Appropriations Committee, which he acknowledged was a "grandiose request" for a freshman. Laird himself was one of the few ever to win a seat on the powerful committee in his first term. Ford advised Bush that the man to see about the request was Laird. Laird thought Bush had merit, but there was no appropriations seat available. So he conferred with his Republican colleague from Wisconsin, Johnny Byrnes, who, as ranking member of the equally powerful Ways and Means Committee, agreed to give Bush a coveted seat there. While the two were "not intimates," Bush said he respected Laird and was "grateful" for Laird's role in getting him on the Ways and Means Committee. The fact that Laird "reached out" to the freshman from Texas was important since "we had such a huge freshman class in those days."[39]

In his 1987 autobiography George H. W. Bush wrote that Laird and Ford, as well as the Democratic leadership of the House, taught him what he called the four fundamentals of "leadership in a free legislative body:"

> 1. No matter how hard-fought the issue, never get personal. Don't say or do anything that may come back to haunt you on another issue, another day.
> 2. Do your homework. You can't lead without knowing what you're talking about.
> 3. The American legislative process is one of give and take. Use your power as a leader to persuade, not intimidate.
> 4. Be considerate of the needs of your colleagues, even if they're at the bottom of the totem pole.[40]

While Bush was particularly appreciative that Laird embraced Rule 4, he suggested that sometimes Laird would bend Rule 3—that is, he would *strongly* lean on Bush and others in the freshman class to vote with the Republican leadership. "He was always very pleasant to me," Bush laughed, "but Mel was kind of a disciplinarian, a strict guy."[41]

Another in that freshman class was one of Laird's Wisconsin protégés, William (Billy) Steiger, who at twenty-eight was even younger than Laird had been when he first began to serve in Congress. Dick Cheney was looking for a job in Washington, and Laird asked Steiger to put Cheney on his staff as a congressional fellow. (Laird would have preferred to take Cheney under his own wing but had no openings at the House Republican Conference.)[42] Another in their circle was Rep. Donald Rumsfeld. Later during the Nixon administration, Rumsfeld headed the Office of Economic Opportunity, and Cheney became his key aide. In the Ford administration, Rumsfeld was tapped as chief of staff and asked Cheney to work for him again. Cheney succeeded Rumsfeld as Ford's chief of staff. Always, behind the scenes, was Laird steering Cheney to the next move. Two years after Gerald Ford was defeated for reelection, Laird encouraged Cheney to run for Wyoming's single House seat, which Cheney won in 1978. Within a few years, following Laird's example, Cheney engineered a fast rise up the House Republican leadership ladder. "You were Chairman of the House Republican Conference, so I strove for that same goal," Cheney later reflected to Laird. "When struggling with the obstacles and frustrations of trying to get anything done while in the minority, I would wonder to myself, 'Now, how would Mel have handled this can of worms?'"[43]

One recurrent "can of worms" with which any Congress deals is corruption. The Congress is empowered to conduct hearings up to and including impeachment proceedings against judges, and the president and vice president of the United States. For a minority party, it becomes a matter of sensitive strategy just how much to press the issue of corruption, particularly when the president himself is involved.

Lyndon Johnson was not a man afflicted with an overworked moral compass. Beginning in 1948 when he bought votes and rigged the ballot-counting to win a seat in the Senate, Johnson seemed to justify his ethical lapses as necessary steps to reach the presidency and engineer his vision of a Great Society. One of Johnson's most flagrant abuses as a public servant was to "make a fortune by owning, while in government, government-regulated television," recalled George H. W. Bush. "But almost nobody back in those days said it was wrong." Laird was a legitimate exception in a day when political ethics were fairly elastic. In Bush's view, Laird had the moral high ground to raise questions about LBJ's fortune built on Federal Communications Commission variances and other questionable dealings. "There was never any question about Laird's integrity," Bush said. "Laird was tested by fire. He had plenty of chances to go awry as a congressman. Plenty of people would love to have bought influence with him by giving him illegal money, but he didn't operate that way."[44]

Lyndon Johnson, by contrast, operated in shades of gray. Johnson had the reputation of being an inveterate womanizer. FBI director J. Edgar Hoover loved to gossip about it in private breakfast meetings with Rep. Glenard Lipscomb, the ranking member of the subcommittee that handled the FBI's budget. Laird, who counted Lipscomb among his closest friends in Congress, was often invited to those breakfasts. Hoover apparently felt he could curry favor with Lipscomb by offering such details, but since neither Laird nor Lipscomb encouraged the talk, Hoover didn't go into salacious details.

As a leader of the opposition party, Laird declined to use Johnson's bedroom as a relevant subject for public debate. But Laird did feel he ought to be able to take a close look at the special White House perks that were paid for by the Pentagon. Johnson stonewalled and hid his costly use of the presidential yachts, helicopters, and airplanes from Laird, the inquiring ranking member of the Defense Appropriations Subcommittee. In February 1966 columnists Rowland Evans and Robert Novak approached Laird because they had heard one of Johnson's three presidential yachts, the *Honey Fitz,* was being remodeled at a cost of nearly $1 million. Laird looked into it and, since the information was not classified, he reported back to Evans that the cost was actually $100,000. After the columnists printed the figure, a furious Johnson personally ordered a clampdown on such information and a full investigation of Laird. Tipped off to this, Laird wrote Johnson's press secretary Bill Moyers that "things have come to a sorry pass indeed if a Member of Congress cannot be furnished public information from individuals in our Defense Department without fear of reprisal by the White House." He laid out his role, and said that when such information was not openly provided to the taxpayers, there is a great "disservice to the Congress as well as to the Executive Branch. I have never been a 'nit-picker' on any White House spending requests funded by our Defense Appropriations Subcommittee."[45]

The president called McNamara and asked him to make Laird back off the perks issues. According to McNamara's memo to Johnson, he called Laird and told him on several occasions that Johnson had issued instructions eliminating "all unnecessary frills or luxuries" on the yachts and aircraft, and that all data relating to them was public record.[46] The wily Laird decided to test the president's word on this, and it came up false. Laird had the General Accounting Office (GAO) inquire about renovations to one of the presidential aircraft. Bill Gulley, who would serve in the White House Military Office for eleven years, including as its chief, said when the GAO came calling for the information Johnson responded, "Tell the bastards no!"[47]

Detecting this LBJ sore spot, Laird made it a point to repeatedly inquire about various aspects of Pentagon perks for the president. Gulley wrote in his memoirs that Johnson was quite distracted by Laird's probing on these small matters. For example, he wanted to know exactly how many helicopters the taxpayers were funding for the president. "Tell 'em I have one helicopter," Johnson finally grunted to Gulley. "I can only ride one helicopter at a time, so tell the bastards one's all I've got."

"So we only had one helicopter, one pilot and two crewmen," Gulley said. "Of course, we really had thirteen helicopters, with a crew of three for each and an additional one hundred ground crew to maintain them, but Johnson never let us report more than one helicopter and three crew."[48]

⁓

In the spring of 1964 Laird began observing "excessive use of the Pentagon's censorship," in the name of national security. Much of the censorship was done to make McNamara and the administration appear more capable than had been shown during the intense scrutiny of the actual congressional hearings held behind closed doors. In one hearing on defense spending, Laird questioned McNamara for the better part of several days. When Laird later read the transcript of the hearing, it had been censored in a way that misrepresented his questions.[49] During the next three years, Pentagon censorship of the hearing transcripts went from bad to worse, especially as McNamara tried to cover up the tragically failing U.S. military effort in Vietnam. In one closed-door hearing, Gen. Earle Wheeler, chairman of the Joint Chiefs of Staff, ruefully observed, "The war will not be lost in Vietnam. This war, if it is lost, will be lost here in Washington." When the transcript was printed, his remark was cut to read simply, "The war will not be lost in Vietnam."[50]

At another closed-door hearing in March 1967 Laird spoke to the assembled military witnesses criticizing the ability of the South Vietnamese to govern themselves at that point. "I just don't think it's possible," he said. It was a shorthand assessment of his concerns about America taking over the war and making South Vietnam a dependent nation. After the Pentagon's editing, the transcript was released in May, and Laird's remark was suspiciously absent. He demanded an accounting from McNamara about the censorship during an open hearing in May. McNamara explained, "I think it is a mistake to tell the people of South Vietnam today that you lack confidence in their ability to learn how to govern themselves. I do not see how this can possibly improve the relations of our nation with theirs."[51]

Laird let the drama play out in the press without much comment. McNamara was roundly criticized in newspaper editorials for setting himself up as a judge of what Americans had the right to hear. McNamara's "defense is indefensible" and "indicates a Pentagon attitude of superior authority over Congress," the *Milwaukee Sentinel* editorialized. "If McNamara wants to make such judgments, let him resign as Secretary of Defense and then run for Congress. He can, if elected, then help to shape policy instead of, as he is supposed to be doing now, merely carrying it out."[52]

As 1967 wore on Laird was approaching his threshold of support for Johnson's Vietnam War policy, whether Ford or other Republicans agreed with him or not. Vietnam had become the third largest war in American history, having surpassed Korea. Its costs were ranging from $2.4 billion to $2.7 billion a month, and that ignored a figure-fudging McNamara-Johnson technique: they stripped American troops in NATO countries and elsewhere of machinery and ordnance, which allowed them to understate the cost of American military materiel expended in Vietnam.

In July 1967 Laird traveled to Chicago to address the Lions International Convention with a hard-hitting speech that became his treatise on Vietnam. The event was all the more significant when put in context—a Republican congressman protesting the war to a conservative, middle-aged audience from middle America. "I consider myself neither a 'hawk' nor a 'dove,' but a pessimist," he said. Johnson and McNamara had "Americanized" the war. "American casualties have now mounted to such an extent that they are out-running South Vietnamese casualties by roughly two to one. . . . Precisely what is the end result we are striving to attain? What is the shooting all about? What is it in Southeast Asia that justifies a kill rate of ten thousand Americans annually and possibly fifty thousand wounded?"

The president had said that the goal was freedom, and the GOP had supported him. But Johnson was in danger of losing that support, Laird warned, in large part because of the October 1966 Manila pronouncement agreeing to withdraw American troops only after North Vietnam withdrew its forces. "It is my own deep conviction [that] the president's commitment in Manila, if carried out, would ultimately lead to a takeover of South Vietnam by the Communists. If this remains the ultimate prospect of our sacrifices in Vietnam, no American in good conscience would want to support anything more than an immediate unilateral withdrawal of American troops before another drop of American blood is needlessly spilled."[53] With that speech, Laird was allying himself with the moderate-to-left wing of his party.

By the fall of 1967 Laird was ready for a major move on the issue of Vietnam. He chose to do it in an address to the American Mining Convention in Denver on September 11. In a lengthy discourse, Laird made a point-by-point assessment of how he had come to the unusual decision as a conservative Republican in the middle of an undeclared war to withdraw support from the White House for its Vietnam policy. One statement summed up the anguish that led to Laird's break: "If the choice is between turning South Vietnam over to the Communists in 1969 or right now in 1967, we might as well do it now and prevent further American casualties."[54]

One Republican who didn't like Laird's disaffection with Johnson's Vietnam policies was Senate minority leader Everett Dirksen. He was a man of iron will and old values who was absolutely committed to supporting the president in time of war. In a showdown with Laird and Ford in Dirksen's office, the patrician senator demanded that a strong resolution on Vietnam, putting the party wholly behind Johnson's conduct of the war, must be proposed and passed at the December 11 meeting of the Republican Coordinating Committee (RCC). Ford and Laird responded that the presidential election was less than a year away, and the Republican Party should be developing its own position on Vietnam instead of blindly following Johnson. If Dirksen dared propose such a resolution, Ford and Laird would not sign off on it.[55] Dirksen backed down.

Laird's transformation into a kind of "closet dove" was evolving. In January 1968 he stated that it would be better to negotiate with the Viet Cong, who at least lived in South Vietnam, than to talk to Hanoi. Laird had quietly postulated since 1966 that it might be possible to give the Viet Cong's political arm, the National Liberation Front, a place in an elected coalition government of South Vietnam. He hit the issue hard in early 1968, and it was a significant departure for a Republican leader.[56] As chairman of the House Republican Conference, Laird was tacking his own party's ship to get control of the war debate.

The North Vietnamese had an agenda of their own for the 1968 election, and thus the machinations of the war were inseparably connected with the political scene in Washington. Since the spring of 1967, Hanoi had been putting together a plan for a massive offensive called "General Offensive, General Uprising." It would eventually be known as the Tet Offensive, named for the Vietnamese New Year's holiday. Over the course of a few weeks, 84,000 enemy troops attacked more than one hundred towns in South Vietnam, including Saigon where sappers penetrated the U.S. Embassy grounds. In the end the offensive failed to conquer South Vietnam, but the cost in casualties on both sides was high. An estimated 45,000 of the enemy—more than half of the invading force—were killed, the South Vietnamese military had 2,300 fatalities, and the United States suffered 1,100 dead.[57]

Back home, the public was shocked. Johnson had too often pronounced that the United States was near victory, and the unexpected, massive, and coordinated attack by the enemy inside South Vietnam seriously eroded American support for the war and the president. By March 1968 Johnson's approval rating had sunk to 26 percent, and he nearly lost the New Hampshire primary to an antiwar candidate Sen. Eugene McCarthy. Exhausted, demoralized, and out of steam, Johnson announced on March 31 that he would not seek reelection. With the incumbent president out of the election picture, the Republicans were looking at a whole new ball game—and Laird was primed to play.

8

The Resurrection of Richard Nixon

CONGRESSMAN JOHN CULVER OF OHIO spotted Mel Laird at Chicago's O'Hare Airport in early 1968, and stopped for a chat about the upcoming presidential primary elections. Although the two men were of opposite parties they were friends, and Culver wanted Laird's opinion.

"Well, Mel, who's it going to be for your party? Nixon?"

Laird grimaced. "Nixon? We would never give you Nixon!"

"What do you mean?" Culver asked.

"We'd lose our ace in the hole in the campaign—the fact that no one trusts Johnson," Laird explained. "The trouble is nobody trusts Nixon, either, so why would we give that advantage away?"[1]

Nixon had the lingering odor of damaged goods. He had lost one presidential election already, in 1960, and he had been warned by his friends in the Chowder and Marching Club not to run for governor of California in 1962—a race he lost by a humiliating three hundred thousand votes. In what was supposed to be his swan song, Nixon told reporters, "As I leave you, I want you to know—just think how much you're going to be missing. You won't have Nixon to kick around anymore, because, gentlemen, this is my last press conference." Yet the intervening six years had been kind to Nixon in some ways. He had ingratiated himself with Republican leaders across the country and was ready to call in those markers as he began quietly planning for his second presidential bid.

In 1968 Laird avoided publicly endorsing any candidate until after his state primary on April 2. Wisconsin went overwhelmingly for Nixon, and from that moment on the party-loyalist Laird was a Nixon man all the way. By then Lyndon Johnson had announced that he would not seek reelection. That made antiwar candidate Sen. Eugene McCarthy the Democratic front-runner, with

Sen. Robert Kennedy and Vice President Hubert Humphrey as formidable competitors. Less than a month later, the picture changed yet again, becoming darker. The Reverend Martin Luther King Jr. was assassinated on April 4 in Memphis. African Americans erupted in America's cities with grief and riotous rage. Parts of D.C. were soon in flames. As violence escalated, Nelson Rockefeller, who had already dropped out of the Republican race, decided the country needed him and announced his presidential candidacy a second time on April 30.

The Republicans pushed toward their August nominating convention in Miami Beach, and Laird eschewed his traditional role as chairman of the committee that would write the party platform. "I'm through with it," he groused when the laurel was proffered again.[2] Everett Dirkson got the assignment instead, but no one in the party leadership believed Laird would stay in the wings. Never a man to go through the front door when a side door would do, he got a hotel suite in Miami for the House Republican Conference staff and began ghostwriting the platform for Dirksen.

A month before the convention, Laird had published a new book, a sequel to his 1964 *Conservative Papers.* This one, *The Republican Papers,* was edited by a more pragmatic Laird who intended to use it to make his party proactive rather than reactive. Among the twenty-eight essay contributors was a constellation of academic stars such as the University of Chicago's Milton Friedman, Harvard's Gottfried Haberler, and Washington University's Murray Weidenbaum, as well as other Ivy Leaguers. Daniel P. Moynihan, who had served in the Kennedy and Johnson administrations, added a liberal essay, using Laird's book to reason with his fellow Democrats about the need for bipartisanship.[3]

The five-hundred-page book was a hit. It was a particularly hot seller on American campuses where conservative students, starved for academic discourse, snapped it up. Radical students also bought it to differ with its authors point-by-point at forums, teach-ins, and demonstrations. Some colleges and universities made it required reading for political science courses, which also boosted sales. All proceeds were earmarked to pay salaries and boost the staff work of the House Republican Conference.

At a July 3 press conference at which *The Republican Papers* was released, Laird cautioned that it should not be regarded as a "platform document." Yet, several of the people who contributed to the book were members of the Platform Committee, and each committee member was provided an advance copy for "consideration" in their work. By the time Laird appeared as a witness before the Platform Committee on its first day of hearings, he had dropped all pretense. Holding up the book, he said, "These positive proposals, Mr. Chairman, *must* be included in the 1968 Republican Platform document."[4] In addition to providing a template for the platform, *The Republican Papers* enhanced Laird's image, revealing a more centrist Republican than many had realized him to be.

During the week of the Republican Convention in Miami, 173 more men were killed in Vietnam. Nearly 20,000 Americans had died in the war, and another 150,000 were wounded. Every twenty minutes, the United States was spending a million dollars on the war.[5] It was naturally the most important item on the Platform Committee's foreign policy agenda—and potentially the most divisive. Laird's appearance on the first day of platform hearings a week before the official convention began was much anticipated; he was expected to set the tone. Regarding Vietnam he told the assembled 106-member Resolutions Committee in the Fontainebleau Hotel that the platform should establish first that it was Democrats who had gotten the United States into the war.[6] Mindful of the contentious 1964 platform debate that had hobbled their candidate, all wings of the Republican Party compromised on the Vietnam plank, seasoning it with words of wartime resolve and future peace. Once the full week of platform hearings was complete and the convention begun, all disagreements on every platform issue had been settled. In a rare show of Republican unity, there was no convention debate over the platform, and not a single dissenting vote was recorded when the 11,500-word document was accepted by the delegates.

As to the contest for the nomination itself, Nixon won it before the convention began. Laird had concentrated months before the convention on who would be the vice presidential pick, pressing Nixon to choose someone who would enlarge the party's coattails to include Republican House and Senate candidates. Besides Ford, who had told Laird he didn't want to be considered, high on Laird's list was Nelson Rockefeller.[7] But Nixon had his own theory about running mates. Laird believed Nixon was looking for a yes-man, and Nixon indeed selected the man his counselors were least enthusiastic about—Spiro Theodore "Ted" Agnew, the governor of Maryland.

Nixon was impressed with the way Agnew had handled the Baltimore riots after the King assassination. Then, Agnew had called a conference of about one hundred black leaders. When they arrived expecting to work with the governor to quell the discontent, Agnew blamed them for the riots, accusing them of "circuit-riding, Hanoi-visiting . . . caterwauling, riot-inciting, burn-America-down type of leadership." Nixon liked that show of bravado.[8] When he announced Agnew as his running mate, the Republican Party, including Laird, was in a state of shock that quickly turned to resistance. Still, Laird soon argued that they should vote for Nixon's choice on grounds of party unity, which they did. Laird, however, could not bring himself to personally vote for the lackluster Agnew, so he left his seat on the floor when the vote was taken.[9]

Laird would soon understand what his instincts were telling him. None of the Republicans at the convention, including Nixon, had any idea that they had nominated a governor and former county executive who was secretly taking kickbacks on county and state construction projects—thousands of dollars in cash bribes in little white envelopes, first delivered to Agnew in Maryland and then later to the White House when he was vice president.[10]

Among the many Republicans instinctively upset at the choice of the relatively unknown Agnew was a young woman with Coke-bottle glasses named Hillary Rodham, who had gone to the convention to work for Rockefeller while she was an intern on Laird's payroll. She had come from the affluent conservative suburb of Park Ridge near Chicago's O'Hare Airport and throughout her high school years her politics had been her father's—bedrock Republican.[11] Rodham's horizons began to expand when she went to Wellesley College in 1965. She established herself quickly and became president of the Young Republicans Club during her freshman year. Several months into that year she wrote a confessional letter to her Methodist minister back home saying she found herself "leaning left." Each summer, the Wellesley College Internship Program sent ten women to Washington as interns. Rodham's political science professor Dr. Alan Schechter was responsible for finding her a good assignment. He knew she was by then only a nominal Republican but thought one of the best places for independent-minded Rodham was with the quasi-academic atmosphere of Laird's Republican Conference.[12]

Laird's first memory of Rodham was that he joked with her that he had been one of the first men to attend Wellesley (during World War II), and she laughed heartily. Then she moved the talk to the Vietnam War and her opposition to it. He found her to be unusually outspoken for a college junior. When it came time for Laird to put together a speech that was critical of Johnson's fight-now pay-later conduct of the war, he asked Rodham to help out.[13]

Of her work for Laird, Hillary Rodham Clinton later recalled that Laird gave his interns serious assignments and introduced them to influential party members.[14] She particularly prized a photo taken of her with Laird and Ford, which she sent to her father. "He had it hanging in his bedroom when he died," she said.[15] Her strongest memory of Laird that summer came from an intern group discussion on Vietnam at which she spoke her mind. They debated a little with Laird, who carefully challenged some of her more naive observations. But he treated her as an equal, she remembered. "He was without pretense. He was down-to-earth. He was a very powerful member of the Congress who was willing to engage in a back-and-forth with a kid who was only moderately well informed, I'm sure he thought. But at least he took me seriously."[16]

Rodham was not chosen to go to the convention with the Republican Conference, but she was invited by Rockefeller's staff. Her disappointment that Nixon, not Rockefeller, was nominated, drove her farther from the party of her father. Yet after she became more radically antiwar on her return to Wellesley, she had no hesitance in contacting Defense Secretary Laird. At one point she told a student protestor from Biafra that she knew Laird and thought he would be glad to hear the student's concerns about the African civil war. A meeting was set up without any difficulty.

When Hillary Rodham Clinton officially switched parties and became an ardent Democrat, Laird still maintained their friendship. Laird's Pentagon military assistant Gen. Robert Pursley suggested that genuine bipartisanship stemmed from Laird's "ability to keep contact with people in his expanding universe of relationships. He could have easily dropped Hillary Rodham, a mere intern, out of that universe, and forgotten her. But he maintains all those relationships and the universe just keeps on expanding. And nobody ever drops out that I can tell."[17]

The 1968 Democratic National Convention in Chicago was marred by violent clashes between police and antiwar demonstrators. Lyndon Johnson forced adoption of a Vietnam War plank that took a harder line than the Republican policy and was a slap at the large Democratic antiwar forces led by Eugene McCarthy. In an unprecedented move for Democratic conventions, a minority plank was presented by McCarthy, partnered with South Dakota senator George McGovern and Massachusetts senator Edward Kennedy. Their peace plank barely lost in the voting.

The worst night was Wednesday, August 28, which should have been Hubert Humphrey's evening of triumph as he sealed his party's nomination for president. Television images of the savage police beatings flooded the nation shortly before Sen. Abraham Ribicoff of Connecticut rose to nominate his "peace" candidate, McGovern. At one point, seeing some of the bloody scenes on TV monitors, Ribicoff turned to Mayor Daley and said: "With George McGovern, we wouldn't have Gestapo tactics on the streets of Chicago." Daley erupted, and the convention was in pandemonium as the mayor shouted obscenities that the TV audience couldn't hear—but they could read his lips. The convention never fully settled down again. After Humphrey won the first ballot, the traditional call from the dais was made to make it unanimous. The Democratic convention managers declared it to be unanimous even as hundreds of delegates could be heard by the press and TV viewers shouting, "No!"

Hobbled as he was coming out of the convention, Humphrey still had a good chance if he declared independence from the president's policy on Vietnam. His first opportunity arose in Philadelphia on September 9, the formal opening day of his campaign, when he made an attempt to step away from Johnson's stifling control. In a question-and-answer session with college students, Humphrey dropped a headline-making statement: "I would think, negotiations or no negotiations, we could start to remove some of the American forces [from Vietnam] in early 1969 or late 1968."

President Johnson was meeting with congressional leaders when he read Humphrey's prediction off the news ticker. His famous temper boiled over, and the next day he went out of his way during a speech at an American Legion convention in New Orleans to say: "We yearn for the day when our men can come home, but no man can predict when that day will come." It silenced Humphrey for several critical campaign weeks. Laird later believed that if Humphrey had stood up for his beliefs on Vietnam, he would have won the election.[18]

As Humphrey was ramping up his campaign, Laird was personally advising Nixon on his own campaign. Laird continued to worry that Humphrey would wise up and veer away from Johnson to win the election, so he needed to find a way to check any Humphrey movement in that direction. He was on the campaign plane on September 24 when, in Bismarck, North Dakota, he had a brainstorm that he shared with Nixon. He was going to switch to the press plane for the next leg of the trip to Boise, Idaho, and give the reporters an earful about LBJ's "secret plan" to begin withdrawing troops from Vietnam.

As a member of the Defense Appropriations Subcommittee, Laird knew Congress had been briefed on such a contingency plan in the event of a withdrawal. It was a secret timetable Laird had seen for orderly withdrawal should a peace agreement be signed, with an activation date that Johnson's people called "T-Day" (for "termination") of the hostilities reached by a peace treaty. But Laird, the wily politico, was going to gloss over the part about a peace treaty being a prerequisite. Nixon warmed to the idea immediately. "Mel, get back on the press plane and go," he ordered, smiling with new cheer in the middle of an exhausting campaign.

Laird did his job adroitly on the press plane from Bismarck to Boise, and the media, weary of Nixon's stock speeches, swallowed it whole. By the time the plane touched down in Boise, the headlines had already been made. Laird said Humphrey would announce a planned cutback of up to ninety thousand ground troops in the first six months of 1969. He indicated his belief that Humphrey would be announcing such a program the following week. One stop later in Seattle, Laird held a press conference to repeat his predictions, and now the news was rebounding through the Johnson administration. Their response couldn't have been better had Laird scripted it himself.[19]

"I've never heard of it," said the White House press secretary.

"I know of no plan which has been developed within the Department of Defense nor submitted to the Department of Defense which would reduce the troop ceiling in South Vietnam beneath the previously announced figure of 549,500," said the Pentagon spokesman.[20]

Laird relished the reports he heard in response to his tactic: Johnson had warned that if Humphrey wanted the support of the president, he had better not mention anything about planned withdrawals from Vietnam. Johnson called Defense Secretary Clark Clifford and told him to go on record saying there was no withdrawal plan. Reluctantly, Clifford, who wanted to begin a withdrawal as badly as Humphrey did, issued a statement the next day saying that he was still "building toward" a troop level of 549,500 and was about fifteen thousand men short of that. "We have no intention of lowering that level, either by next June or at any time in the foreseeable future," he said.[21]

Clifford later confided to Laird that Johnson was still fuming and had "bullwhipped" Clifford into going on TV and making an even stronger statement, which he did on *Meet the Press* the following Sunday, September 29: "I believe it is important that the American people not be misinformed about our plans. The Defense Department has no plans at this time for the return of any troops. The level of combat is such that we are building up our troops, not cutting them down."[22]

Few politicians could work smoke-and-mirrors magic like Laird could; he had the Democrats where he wanted them—denying that they had any plans for bringing American soldiers home from the jungles of Vietnam. And Laird was able to pull this off without Nixon ever having to define his own plans for ending the war.

One of the greatest myths of the presidential campaign of 1968 is that candidate Nixon once said, "I have a secret plan to end the war." He made no such statement. The roots of the false quote trace to a remark Nixon made in Nashua, New Hampshire, while campaigning on March 5, 1968: "I pledge to you the new leadership will end the war and win the peace in the Pacific." Reporters pestered him with questions about how he would do that. When he refused to elaborate, journalists began talking about his "secret plan."[23]

On the other hand, Nixon began to think the myth of his "secret plan" wasn't a bad one. His strategy was to make no reference to such a plan, nor to correct reports that alluded to it. Laird recalled, "I always knew he didn't have a plan. There was no plan." On the day Nixon nominated him for secretary of defense, Laird pointedly asked if he had a plan to share. Nixon said that he did not. He asked Laird to come up with one, and Laird already had a good idea of what he wanted to do, based on the Vietnam plank he coauthored for the Republican platform—to "de-Americanize" the war as quickly as possible and bring the troops home.[24]

A turning point for Hubert Humphrey's electoral fortunes came with his nationally televised speech from Salt Lake City on September 30. That morning, he had met with Utah Democrats and said, "If the elections were held today, we wouldn't have a prayer. You know it and I know it." It was time for him to stand on his own, to step out from the drag of LBJ's Vietnam policy. When he spoke on TV that day, no vice presidential seal was evident and he was introduced not as vice president but as the Democratic Party's candidate for president. He then offered a three-point Vietnam plan that included a unilateral bombing halt as a way to see if the North Vietnamese would seriously negotiate. It was only slightly different from Johnson administration policy, but he made it sound like a major departure.[25]

Humphrey had found his footing, and Laird was alarmed that if he continued on that course, Nixon might lose. Partly to stir the Johnson pot, hoping LBJ would slap Humphrey down again, Laird called the White House at 9 p.m. that Monday night and tweaked the president's congressional liaison Harold Barefoot Sanders. "He asked if the Humphrey speech represented the new Administration policy on Vietnam," Sanders reported in a memo to President Johnson. "I told Mel I was not advised about this—I was just not going to say one way or another."[26]

Johnson handed Humphrey a surprise gift just six days before the election—an apparent breakthrough in the peace talks. On October 31, Johnson announced that he was halting the bombing of North Vietnam as a boost to the Paris peace talks. The expected bump in the polls for Humphrey was more muted when Saigon made it clear that they would not be a party to the talks. Besides Saigon's quick repudiation of the peace talks, there was a suspicion among many voters that Johnson had cynically pulled the rabbit out of the hat just to thwart Nixon's election.

Laird rightly suspected Johnson's electoral eve political motivations, but even he could not predict what a curse Johnson's bombing halt would prove to himself personally and to Nixon. Once halted, the bombing would prove to be a political nightmare to restart. For the next four years Nixon and Laird would have to live with what came to be called the "understandings" with North Vietnam over the bombing. In reality, there was misunderstanding and backpedaling instead. Johnson agreed to stop bombing North Vietnam if the North would stop shelling South Vietnamese cities and would not increase their movement of weapons and men through the demilitarized zone. The United States also said it would retain the right to fly armed reconnaissance missions over the North. But nothing was put into writing. Hanoi violated the unwritten pact repeatedly and began to see the U.S. reconnaissance flights as thinly disguised bombing missions.

While the agreement was not put on paper, it was cast in stone in American public perception, and resumption of the bombing became a political impossibility. That was inevitable for a deal that was cut for purely political reasons. While Laird, as a congressman, supported the bombing halt, he later said that he never believed it had any practical benefit for the Paris talks, as Johnson claimed it would.

For four years Nixon would hold back from resumption of wholesale bombing in the North. Instead Laird would order isolated strikes as retaliation for attacks on the reconnaissance planes and occasional diversionary attacks which he referred to as "protective reaction" over the North. Not until late 1972 was Nixon able to set aside the "understandings" completely and launch an all out air war over the North that would force Hanoi back to the bargaining table and bring an end to the U.S. combat role in the war.

～

Nixon, a two-time electoral loser, won the presidency in 1968 by less than half a million votes. His once-strong lead had been systematically whittled down by Humphrey's Salt Lake City speech, the bombing halt, and the strength of third party candidate, former Alabama governor George Wallace. Congressman Laird had his own reelection race to run in 1968, but as in past contests, his opponent never had a chance. Laird was reelected with 64 percent of the vote. He had worked hard to get Nixon elected, and he needed a break. What better place to duck the pressures of the presidential transition than in a leper colony? Laird invited his friend, tobacco lobbyist Jack Mills, to join him on a little working vacation to inspect the National Leprosarium in Carville, Louisiana. It was a pet project in Congress of Laird's and John Fogarty's, and Laird had promised to keep an eye on the place.

Some of Nixon's aides found Laird's disappearing act inconvenient in late November. Nixon was seeking Laird's advice almost daily on cabinet appointments and strategy for the new administration. Laird was expected to spend every spare minute at Nixon's headquarters at the Pierre Hotel in New York City. Instead, Laird was cutting the rug at the weekly dance at the leper colony. The phonograph was blaring a Caribbean beat, and Laird was stepping to the music with gusto. Mills hung back from the patients, many of whom were disfigured. Laird had visited plenty of hospitals, so the scene didn't faze him and he knew that leprosy was one of the least contagious of diseases. He strode up to one woman and requested a dance—the first of many with the patients—until it was time to call it a night. Laird and Mills returned to their room at the Roosevelt Hotel in New Orleans and opened a deck of cards for gin rummy.[27]

About 8 p.m., as Laird was on his way to winning $38, the game was interrupted by a call from New York City. "Dick Nixon," the caller identified himself. He was thinking about his reform plans for programs of the Health, Education, and Welfare Department, and he needed a secretary who was strong, someone who knew Congress, and who was respected by the members. He'd concluded that Laird was the best man for the job.

"Absolutely not, Dick," Laird immediately retorted. "Not under any circumstances! I do not want to go over there, and I will not go over there." As ranking Republican on the committee that oversaw that department, Laird felt that he was already running HEW. He was also a senior member on the Defense Appropriations Subcommittee, which, combined with the Health Subcommittee, gave him significant influence over two-thirds of the federal budget. On top of that, he was chairman of the House Republicans, on the fast track (just behind Jerry Ford) to becoming Speaker of the House, if the Republicans gained control of the House again. He hung up the phone and relayed the conversation to Mills, who was annoyed by Laird's refusal. It would have been convenient for the tobacco lobbyist to have a friend at HEW.

Nixon wasn't finished with Laird yet. The congressman served only sixteen days of his ninth term because Nixon succeeded in doing what Democrats had been unable to do for sixteen years: remove Laird from his beloved Wisconsin Seventh District. The new assignment was as secretary of defense—a job which Laird said he got because no one else wanted to take responsibility for the Vietnam War. In the month following the election, Laird had done his best to field other candidates, but there had been no takers among the most qualified options. Laird himself had refused loudly and often, but his final gambit had failed on the airplane ride home from the Republican Governors Association meeting in Palm Springs in early December. He had told the president-elect that he would accept the cabinet post only if Nixon did not interfere with any staff appointments. Against all political logic, Nixon agreed—and Laird was stuck.

On December 11, 1968, Nixon staged the first-ever en masse rollout of a new cabinet on coast-to-coast television; he was the only speaker and he used no notes. Acting as a master of ceremonies, he stood on a raised platform behind a simple podium, backed by bright blue curtains in the ornate Palladian Room of Washington's Shoreham Hotel. Facing him, seated in white chairs on a red carpet—for a red-white-and-blue motif—were the twelve cabinet designees and their wives. As he named each of them, the camera panned to their faces.[28]

Originally, at least six of them had been suggested for their positions by Laird: George Shultz (Labor), David Kennedy (Treasury), George Romney (Housing and Urban Development), Walter Hickel (Interior), John Volpe (Transportation), and William Rogers (State). But the most important man Laird suggested was not a cabinet officer. This was Henry Kissinger. Laird had worked closely with the Harvard professor during the 1964 Republican Platform Committee deliberations and was impressed with his foreign policy expertise. He had kept in touch with Kissinger. Laird pegged him as a perfect candidate for national security advisor. When Nixon protested because he had never even met the man, Laird arranged a meeting. Nixon made the offer, and Kissinger accepted.[29]

As the first defense secretary recruited from Capitol Hill, Laird was seen as a powerful antidote to the McNamara years when the Pentagon was run on a corporate model. Laird's Pentagon would be run on a political model. The newspapers were quick to point out that Laird had a Purple Heart, and still carried the shrapnel from a Japanese kamikaze attack. As McNamara's biggest adversary in Congress, Laird could signal a potent turnaround on Vietnam policy. Above all, it would be a mistake to underestimate Mel Laird. A journalist who knew him well said: "He looks as bland as Wisconsin cheese, but he is as sharp as Vermont cheddar."[30]

Laird had been forced into assuming the post at the worst possible time, and he had no illusions about just how tough the job would be. The first secretary of defense, James Forrestal, tormented by critics and weighed down after only two years on the job, had leaped to his death from a tower room in Bethesda Naval Hospital within months of resigning. Knowing the dangerous shoals ahead, Laird sought counsel from the man he respected most.

Since mid-May 1968, Dwight Eisenhower had been a full-time resident of Ward Eight of Walter Reed Army Hospital in Washington, the victim of seven heart attacks. He stayed in the "presidential suite" with an adjoining room for his wife, Mamie. Ike held on against the odds, celebrating Nixon's victory in November. Although Eisenhower was frail, he agreed to see Laird on Friday, December 13, to offer congratulations and counsel. Laird was not expecting much, and he certainly hadn't anticipated so quickly angering Ike that the patient would rally for an hour-long advisory session.

"Mel, have you been down to see President Johnson?" Eisenhower asked.

"No, Mr. President," Laird responded. "I haven't been down there. You know, Dick just nominated me the other night." Eisenhower nearly came out of the bed, wires and all.

"'Dick?'" he said with disgust. "Mel, what do you mean by calling him 'Dick?' He's 'Mr. President' to me, and he's certainly 'Mr. President' to you! I never want to hear you referring to him as 'Dick' again."

Laird was speechless and while he regained his composure, the newly animated Eisenhower picked up his bedside phone and asked for the Oval Office. "Mr. President," Eisenhower respectfully addressed Johnson. "I've got Mel Laird here and he tells me he hasn't arranged to see you. I think you ought to have a visit with him. I was surprised that he hadn't called you."

Laird could not hear how LBJ responded, but Ike was soon lecturing Johnson: "I know you've got a history with Mel on those conference committees over appropriations. Sure, you've been on different sides of many issues, but he's taken on a big job and responsibility and I want him to come down there and talk to you—get briefed by you so he's fully up to date on what's going on with Vietnam and all."

A pregnant pause followed, as Eisenhower nodded on the phone in agreement. "Well, when do you want him down there?" An appointment was made.

It hadn't occurred to Laird to seek an audience with LBJ, but Eisenhower set him straight. "Mel, you should have gone to see the president first. You should be down there at the White House right now. He is the commander in chief of our forces now, and you're the designated secretary of defense, soon the second man in command. You should be getting a full briefing from President Johnson."

With that settled, Eisenhower offered his own counsel, as Laird remembered it: "As you know, Mel, I don't think we should have ever been on the ground in Vietnam to the extent we find ourselves. It's going to be your job to extricate us, but you must disengage us honorably. If you don't do it honorably, the trust and credibility of the United States will not be worth a red cent anywhere in the world."[31]

~

On the same Friday he visited Eisenhower, Laird paid an afternoon call on Clark Clifford. Laird and Clifford already had a bipartisan friendship and mutual respect, having known each other for years, including multiple appearances by Clifford before Laird's Defense Appropriations Subcommittee. Still, Clifford later admitted "an initial wariness" when he sat down with Laird. Part of that wariness came from Johnson's blustering denunciation of Laird at lunch with Clifford the day before. "He [Johnson] spent much of the time analyzing Nixon's new cabinet," Clifford recalled in his memoirs. "He was disappointed by the choice of Laird, he told me, whom he considered 'one of the ablest' but also one of the 'meanest and most partisan' Republicans in the House." Clifford took the assessment with a grain of salt, coming as it was from a Democrat who had his own reputation for mean partisanship.[32]

Clifford's first meeting alone with Laird turned out to be comfortable. In office a scant ten months under a president who wouldn't hear of withdrawal from Vietnam, Clifford confessed to Laird that he would have liked to stay another year or two under a fresh administration; Laird had advised Nixon to keep Clifford, but to no avail.

Laird's event-filled Friday ended with a press conference, arranged by Clifford. Laird's most-quoted remark was a hope that the war in Vietnam would be over before he had to put together the first Nixon administration defense budget, by 1970. There was also some talk of staffing.

"Sir, would you favor the appointment of a Democrat as your deputy?"

"Well, I favored the appointment of a Democrat as Secretary of Defense," Laird smiled. The remark brought down the house. All the journalists were aware of Laird's behind-the-scenes maneuvers to persuade Nixon to choose either Clifford or Senator Henry "Scoop" Jackson.[33]

~

Johnson did not want to meet with the Nixon administration's secretary of defense; the much-feared Texas tornado was somewhat afraid of Laird. He had been a pugnacious partisan adversary to the president, which earned him respect from Johnson. Laird was a fiscal conservative who railed against the waste of taxpayer money, which made him an enemy of Johnson's generous Great Society and his open-ended Vietnam War. Laird also had occasionally raised questions about the president's spending on White House perks such as the presidential yacht, and that had infuriated Johnson. Mostly, though,

Johnson had been fearful that Laird's snooping might uncover the $3.7 million that the president had secretly siphoned out of the military budget to improve his Texas ranch. A man who watched this interplay closely, Bill Gulley, disclosed some of the details in a memoir of his years as head of the White House Military Office. Gulley offered an insider's account of Johnson's reaction to the selection of Laird as the defense secretary. Johnson was in his bedroom perusing the front page of the *Washington Post* when he read the first report that Laird might be nominated. "Melvin Laird—goddamn it!" the president reportedly cursed. "That son of a bitch'll lock us all up. We're all going to jail now." Gulley knew immediately that Johnson "was thinking about all the military hardware he had down at the ranch."[34]

On Monday, December 23, at 5:37 p.m., Laird was ushered into the Oval Office.[35] Not knowing what was on the president's mind, Laird anticipated a briefing on Vietnam and discussion of other vital national security matters, including the control of nuclear weapons. The visit turned out to be neither as Eisenhower had billed it nor what Laird had hoped for.

"Well, Mel," the president drawled, smiling and clapping Laird on the back as they greeted each other. "I know we've had a lot of disagreements, and we've had some agreements over the years on the Appropriations Committee. But now there are a few things that we've got to have an understanding about."

"If you have any advice, I'd appreciate it," Laird, said, ready to be handed the keys to the Pentagon . . . the secrets in the presidential safe . . . the real story behind the Vietnam War.

Then Johnson began with the important business at hand. "I've got this valet who's assigned to me from the Department of Defense. I also have a cook who's assigned to me from the Department of Defense that's been very good. I want both of them assigned to me down at the ranch."

Laird respectfully nodded, while his mind reeled and Johnson continued. "I'm having a problem, too, with that heliport down there. I want to get that improved and I've got to get some communication and some good radar in there. Can you handle that?"

"Well," Laird stalled, rolling it over as if he were seriously and fully considering the requests, while he was really trying to recover his composure. He was new at this cabinet secretary business, but he was pretty sure it wasn't the Pentagon's job to give a former president a GI valet-for-life or assign an Army cook permanent KP duty at the LBJ spread in Texas. The heliport and communications improvements sounded much more doable in the name of security.

"I'll look into it," Laird promised.

Only after the president's prime concern about his perks was addressed did he turn the conversation to affairs of state. But it was another letdown for Laird, since the president offered no insights or information that Laird didn't already know. Johnson complained about how the press had painted the 1968 Tet Offensive as a huge defeat for the United States. He was right about that; the enemy took the biggest losses in that offensive. In fact, Tet was a huge military defeat for the North Vietnamese and Viet Cong, but the press had turned it into a more important psychological victory for the enemy. If anything, it was the credibility gap caused by the consistently rosy Johnson and McNamara pronouncements about Vietnam that had caused the press to question the administration when it characterized Tet.

Referring to the recent presidential campaign, Johnson tweaked Laird for implying that the administration had a withdrawal plan for Vietnam. "You got a little out there, Mel, during the campaign," he said. Laird mostly listened. He reflected later that he didn't see any point in arguing.

There was one piece of advice that Laird took to heart because he had seen the evidence himself. Johnson told him that various people would try to drive a wedge between the Defense and State Departments. LBJ advised that the best way to prevent such divisiveness was for Laird to cultivate his own friendship with the new secretary of state William Rogers, maybe playing golf with him once a week. Laird agreed and the two ended up playing frequently at Burning Tree.[36]

Johnson may have wasted this opportunity to advise Laird more thoroughly because he did not think Laird would be much of a player. Johnson thought Rogers, who was closer to Nixon, would be the strongman in the new administration. Clifford wrote that Johnson confided as much to him, which would partially explain why Johnson had given a substantive briefing on the war to Rogers before he met with Laird. Clifford later recounted to friends, and also partially in his memoirs, that Johnson and others of the outgoing administration seriously underestimated the influence Laird and Kissinger would have. And they "seriously overestimated the role Rogers would play as Secretary of State," he wrote.[37]

The curious presidential "briefing" ended at 6:37 p.m. Laird had been cautious with Johnson because he knew the conversation probably was being taped.[38] Johnson had microphones everywhere. They were in the Oval Office, in his bedroom, in the situation room, at Camp David, and at his ranch in Texas.[39] Laird knew before the meeting that military officers were running the White House taping system under the auspices of the White House

Communications Agency. Laird had told Nixon he would not allow the military to be involved in the surreptitious practice, whatever Nixon decided after he became president. Laird removed all the equipment and military signal corps operators by mid-February 1969 with Nixon's concurrence. When Nixon later changed his mind in early 1971, he knew better than to ask Laird to bring back the signal corps men. He didn't even want Laird to know the taping system was up and running again because he knew Mel would protest that it was unethical. So he had the Secret Service set up the system and keep it secret.

∽

Laird had thirty-seven days to fill the top staff positions for the 4.8 million-member Defense Department. Operating from a suite at the Carlton Hotel, Laird decided to diagram the task. The chart covered all four military services, the National Security Agency and twelve intelligence agencies. An early appointee in the public affairs office, Richard Capen, described the diagram: "One entire wall was filled with this organization chart. It was huge; it must have been twenty feet across. It was so terrifying to look at that thing. I couldn't imagine how this congressman who had been running less than two dozen people in his Capitol Hill office was now going to manage five million."[40]

Laird spent twelve to fourteen hours every day, including the Christmas holidays, filling in that chart. He might have been overwhelmed were it not for the fact that, from his many years on the Defense Appropriations Subcommittee, he knew most of the top players at the Pentagon in addition to the hopefuls who wanted jobs there. He appointed his friend in Congress, Glenard Lipscomb, as his transition chief. Both men were so adept at reading people that no applicant was able to steamroller either of them into making a Pentagon appointment they might regret.

What made Laird's appointments singular—like no other secretary of defense before or since—is that his civilian and military choices could not be vetoed by the president, unless Nixon were to break the promise made on the cocktail napkin. Those who assisted Laird in the selection process—including Robert Froehlke and congressional aides Bill Baroody, John Dressendorfer, and Ed Feulner—all recalled there was great pressure from people Nixon had chosen to be his White House staff. Laird's most trusted backstop against patronage appointments was Carl Wallace, his congressional administrative assistant who followed him to the Pentagon. Wallace or Froehlke would politely agree to look at applications sent over by Nixon's people and conduct interviews, but that was no guarantee of a job. John Warner, who was on the Nixon transition team, said he couldn't "think of a single person who was ever foisted on Mel Laird."[41]

From the beginning, the Pentagon was going to be a place apart, ruled solely by Laird. Later, when White House officials below the president tried to interfere, Laird reminded them that he had a deal with Nixon. A few times he would produce the handwritten Nixon napkin and remind them of the promise. Since political patronage was off the table, Laird was free to concentrate on merit. This infuriated some Nixon aides who placed loyalty to Nixon during the campaign as the most vital prerequisite for appointment. As the staffing process continued into the first months of the administration, peeved Nixon aides frequently called Laird's staffers over to the White House for a dressing-down.

One early indication that the Defense Department might be peppered with Democratic appointees was Laird's friendship with Paul Warnke, who was one of Clifford's closest colleagues and a pariah to the Republicans. Laird asked him to stay on as head of the Pentagon's foreign policy department, the International Security Affairs (ISA), for a few months to help the him prepare for trips to Vietnam and NATO meetings, and assist in the opening of arms control talks with Moscow.[42] Nixon's team and top military brass were stunned. Immediately after Laird was named defense secretary, a private memo had been sent urgently to him conveying the "advice" of Air Force chief of staff Gen. John McConnell, who was "speaking for [all] the Joint Chiefs," that, above all "Paul C. Warnke & his *entire staff* . . . ALL ABSOLUTELY MUST GO."[43]

Laird also respected Clifford's Deputy Secretary of Defense Paul Nitze; he appointed him as a consultant and representative to the strategic arms limitation talks. Nitze played a pivotal role in the negotiations of SALT I and II until he resigned in 1974. Both Warnke and Nitze were men Laird had known from his congressional work. But there were others from the Clifford regime that he wanted to get to know, too. He was pleased on the first weekend after his appointment to be invited to the Cliffords' home for a dinner party. It was a chance to size up some of the people who had been running the Pentagon. General Earle "Bus" Wheeler, the chairman of the Joint Chiefs of Staff was there. There were still a few months left in Wheeler's term, and Laird had to decide whether to reappoint him or go with someone else.

In the vestibule of the home, Laird bumped into Robert Pursley, then a brilliant young Air Force colonel who had been the military assistant to both McNamara and Clifford. Mistaking Pursley for someone else, Laird said "I'm sorry you're leaving," and after some small talk walked away. "Well, that takes care of that," Pursley said to himself, assuming he had just been fired. But once Laird figured out who Pursley was and spent some time with him, he asked the colonel to stay on as his closest military advisor—a man who would become so close to Laird that Kissinger would later tap Pursley's phones to keep track of what Laird and Pursley were up to.

Laird also kept two Johnson administration men—Dan Henkin and Jack Stempler—to head his public affairs and legislative affairs divisions, respectively. Henkin, a Democrat, had a long history with the Pentagon. Stempler, who called himself a political independent, was nevertheless surprised to keep his job. (He would later serve in the same position for the Carter administration.) Dr. John Foster was McNamara's director of Defense Research and Engineering, and Laird asked him to continue in the post, which he did for Laird's full term. Robert Moot, Clifford's Pentagon comptroller, was a Democrat, having voted and worked for both Kennedy and Johnson. But Laird appreciated his credible testimony during subcommittee hearings, and asked him to continue in the post. Moot became one of the people Laird counted on most for running the Pentagon on a day-to-day basis.[44] Laird felt Barry Shillito was underutilized by Clifford as logistics chief for the Navy. So Laird promoted him to head up logistics for the whole Defense Department. Shillito, an ardent Democrat, was as surprised as the others. He had already made plans to go into private business, but he agreed to stay.

Laird's appointments for service secretaries were no different. For secretary of the Air Force he wanted MIT professor and deputy administrator of NASA Robert Seamans, but Seamans said he couldn't come until he finished the semester at MIT, so Harold Brown (later, President Carter's secretary of defense) agreed to stay on in the position until Seamans was available.[45] As for secretary of the Army, Nixon had promised the position to two different men—William Casey and former congressman Howard "Bo" Callaway. Laird wanted neither of them. He wanted Bob Froehlke, but knew he first needed his friend as assistant secretary of defense for administration for at least a year. So he asked Stan Resor, who had been Army secretary since 1965, to stay on.

The position of secretary of the Navy was the most coveted Department of Defense post among Nixon supporters. Toiling away on the Nixon transition team, John Warner had decided it was time to throw his own name in the hopper for a permanent job. Laird was aware of Warner's keen interest, due in no small measure to the lobbying efforts of Warner's father-in-law, billionaire Republican contributor Paul Mellon. But Laird finally told Warner the job was going to John Chafee, and Warner would be his undersecretary.

"Nixon hates him!" Warner protested. "He's a Rockefeller man. Don't you understand that? He's a Rockefeller liberal! You can't have that guy in there! I'm the guy that worked with Nixon for eight years!" Warner was about to learn, as the whole country would soon figure out, that Laird had no objection to a liberal service secretary because Laird himself had "a liberal streak up his back," as Warner affectionately put it. Laird told him that he and Chafee would make a great team. "Not only will you learn to like this guy, you'll learn to love him." And Warner did.[46]

Nixon was not happy about Laird's bipartisan hiring, but he couldn't do anything about it except cajole. Eight months into his new administration, the White House requested that Froehlke send over a list identifying the party affiliation of the Pentagon's top positions. It was a humorous and painful survey for some of Laird's staff to take. Navy Assistant Secretary Robert Frosch remembered Chafee calling him one day. "Bob, I'm gonna ask you a question, but it embarrasses me a little to ask you. Are you enrolled as a Democrat or a Republican?"

"John," Frosch laughed, "you know I'm a congenital Democrat."

"Yeah, I knew that," Chafee said, sighing. "Shit! You're the third one today."[47]

The final tally showed that of the sixty-eight top positions that had been filled at the Pentagon, a little more than half (thirty-six) were Republicans. Fifteen were Democrats, nine described themselves as "independents," and the political affiliation of eight was "unknown," with no further explanation.[48]

~

No appointment for the secretary of defense is more important than that of deputy secretary, yet rarely do secretaries get to make that choice. Because of his napkin deal with Nixon, Laird had a free hand to pick his own man. In his search for the right person, Laird consulted three former secretaries of defense, dozens of university presidents, and quite a few civic and business leaders. The name that kept coming up was David Packard, cofounder of Silicon Valley's premier electronics firm, Hewlett-Packard. Laird and Packard had worked together in the past on issues of funding university research when Packard was on the Stanford board of trustees. In the year prior to Nixon's election, Hewlett-Packard had done $100.7 million in business with the federal government, including the Pentagon. It was a conflict-of-interest hurdle that should have prevented Laird from asking Packard to serve, but Laird was intent on having him as deputy secretary. Laird called Packard on the pretext of soliciting his recommendations for Pentagon appointments. Packard wrote in his short memoir that he agreed to meet with Laird at the Carlton Hotel. "After a few hours of discussion, he said he wanted me to join him as his deputy secretary. This sounded intriguing, but the conflict-of-interest requirements were very strict."[49]

No Pentagon official was allowed to have more than $10,000 worth of stock in a company that did business with the military. At the time Packard owned more than $300 million in Hewlett-Packard stock. But Laird didn't give up. The day after Christmas, at Laird's request, Packard flew east again to meet with Laird. That meeting would be a full-court press. Laird asked former HEW secretary John Gardner, a close friend of both Laird and Packard, to join them for breakfast at the Carlton. Gardner arrived first, and Laird buttonholed him. "John, this breakfast is all about one thing, to persuade David to be my deputy. You've got to help me do that." Gardner argued it couldn't be done because the Senate would never confirm Packard unless he sold the stock, which Packard could not do. "Mel, you'll never be able to work out the details."[50]

Packard joined them at the table, and Laird made his pitch. "This country's been awfully good to you, and it is payback time," he said. He told Packard he could persuade Congress to grant an exception—to allow him to keep his stock if Packard put all the dividends and appreciation into charities while he was a public employee. The loss to Packard might be in the millions of dollars, but it was doable.

Gardner chimed in then: "Dave, you can tell him, 'Yes.' Mel can never work that out." So Packard gave a qualified "Yes."

Laird hastened to Capitol Hill and explained his plan to Sen. Richard Russell of Georgia, the Democratic chairman of the Senate Armed Services Committee, which would have to approve Packard's nomination. "Mel, no one's that important to you," Russell laughed.

"Yes, Dave Packard is that important to me."

Russell picked up the phone and summoned four other committee members: Democrats Stuart Symington and John Stennis, and Republicans Margaret Chase Smith and Milton Young. In less than an hour they had assembled in Russell's office where he spelled out the problem and the solution: Packard's defense-related stock would be put into a trust, with all income and appreciation from it to be distributed among various charities. Incredibly, they all agreed to Laird's terms and said they could deliver the votes of the rest of the committee.[51]

"Congratulations," Laird reported back to Packard. "You're the new deputy secretary of defense. You told me 'yes' at breakfast, and today I have delivered the package." That night the Packards and the Lairds celebrated the new management team with dinner at a Washington restaurant.

On December 30, Laird held a press conference to introduce Packard to the media. Packard said he had agreed to make the sacrifice to become deputy secretary because he thought "it was about time that I [did] something in return for my country." Then he outlined his income, which amounted to $1 million a year, much of which he would have to forgo if the Senate signed off on Laird's proposal.

"Mr. Packard," one reporter asked, "what will your salary be in your new job?"

"I don't know," Packard asked. "I didn't ask that."

After the laughter had subsided, Laird informed his new appointee and the press: "His salary will be $30,000."

"It is safe to assume, then, that you are taking a cut?" a reporter asked, to continued laughter.

Packard, also chuckling, responded, "Yes, I am taking a helluva cut!"[52]

Packard never seemed to regret his decision to serve in the Pentagon. He mentioned his financial loss only once, Laird recalled, and that was in a congressional hearing. Texas congressman Jack Brooks took Packard to task over the expense of a kitchen and caterer in the Pentagon where Packard would lunch with dignitaries. "Tell me, Secretary Packard, what did your lunch cost yesterday?"

Without missing a beat Packard replied, "I'll tell you, Chairman Brooks. As near as I can calculate in my mind right now, that lunch cost me $325,000."

9

Looking for an Exit

THE MAN WHO TOOK OVER RESPONSIBILITY for the Vietnam War on January 20, 1969, might have tripped a metal detector—if there had been one—when he walked through the door of his new office. Laird's body still carried shrapnel from the Japanese kamikaze attack on the USS *Maddox* during an earlier, different war. He bore the metal fragments proudly and considered them only a minor annoyance when they occasionally worked their way through to the skin and had to be surgically removed. It was the small price a serviceman paid for a big victory.

Now his primary mission for his country was getting it out of another war, probably without victory—and possibly without honor. He had no illusions about the job. The slippery slope on which the United States slid into the Vietnam War would prove to be a treacherous incline when it came time for an orderly exit. When Laird inherited the war in 1969 there were more than half a million American troops in South Vietnam and another 1.2 million supporting the war from U.S. Navy ships and nearby allied countries. Americans were dying at a rate of two hundred a week. The United States had lost 31,000 men and women; South Vietnam had lost three times that many. The enemy's dead were harder to count, but it was a safe bet that the 1968 Tet Offensive and other campaigns that year alone cost North Vietnam some 289,000 men.[1] Putting the horror of casualties aside, at $24 billion a year—one third of the total military budget—the U.S. Treasury could ill afford the war, which was draining money from domestic programs and diverting U.S. military assets from other hot spots around the world.

Laird sized up his office suite that first day. He had been in it several times before as a congressman, but as he stepped off the elevator—the only private one in the Pentagon—he inhaled the fact that it was now his. On one side, two secretaries, Laurie Hawley and Thelma Stubbs, guarded the gate and screened visitors, mindful of the light on the door that indicated if someone was with him or if he was open to visitors. On another side was a private dining room and just beyond it the office of the deputy secretary. Nearby was a bed Laird used for spending the night during crises.

Laird's private office itself was cavernous, filled with chairs and couches for holding meetings and welcoming VIPs. One magazine called it "Laird's Little Acre." The centerpiece was the imposing glass-topped desk the size of a conference table, which had once belonged to Gen. John "Black Jack" Pershing. Three in-and-out boxes attempted to hold the flow of documents requiring his review and signature. In front of the desk was an expensive oriental rug, which had been added by Clark Clifford's wife and marred by burns from ashes flying out of Deputy Secretary Paul Nitze's pipe. Clifford had eventually covered it with Plexiglas. Directly across from the desk, on stands framing a space for photo-taking, were two flags—the American flag and the secretary of defense's own ensign, a red, white, and blue flag with an American eagle, wings outstretched, four crossed arrows, and five stars.

Behind the desk hung a portrait of James Forrestal, the first defense secretary, a man who was driven to suicide by the job. McNamara had hung the painting in this place of honor, and Laird, who felt a personal connection to Forrestal (who had been secretary of the Navy during World War II when Laird was a Navy officer) decided to keep it. (The Forrestal painting would remain through several more secretaries, but it was removed by Caspar Weinberger at the beginning of the Reagan administration in 1981.) Near the painting in Laird's day was a ship's bell that chimed the hours, and below the painting was a credenza with a bank of telephones—hotlines to the president, David Packard, the Joint Chiefs of Staff, and the commanders in Saigon and Hawaii.[2]

The secretary's suite also had a large walk-in vault full of classified documents including, as Laird knew before he arrived, a request from General Westmoreland for 205,179 more troops—many of them reservists—to raise the U.S. contingent in Vietnam to more than 700,000. Westmoreland, as commander of U.S. forces in Vietnam, wanted to exploit North Vietnam when it was at its weakest point, *after* the 1968 Tet offensive. It made tactical sense to a military commander who wanted to win, but at a time when the Johnson administration was trying to soft-pedal Tet as a huge defeat for the enemy, the troop request had a look of panic about it, as if the allies had been tromped by Tet and needed to call in the Reserves.[3]

The request had been in Clifford's office since February 1968 when

Westmoreland had submitted it through Gen. Earle Wheeler, chairman of the Joint Chiefs. Laird believed Westmoreland was oblivious to the fact that the American public no longer cared about winning the war, and the general was disdainful of any political pandering to that public opinion. But the facts behind the troop request were more subtle than that. It was General Wheeler who had seen Tet as a turning point that could be capitalized on, and he had needled Westmoreland to ask for enough reinforcements to trigger the call-up of reservists, something President Johnson had been unwilling to do. Westmoreland had gone along, even settling on the exact figure that Wheeler had suggested. Then Wheeler had taken the case to Johnson and Clifford.

Clifford had been appalled; Johnson had said he would think it over. When he did, he realized it was time for Westmoreland to come home from Saigon. His replacement was Gen. Creighton Abrams, a gruff World War II tank commander with a much dimmer view of the prospects in Vietnam. Abrams had been Westmoreland's second in command in Saigon, but his skirts were unsullied by the troop request because, inexplicably, no one had told him about it.[4]

The administration lived in fear that the troop request would be leaked to the press. Two days before the 1968 New Hampshire primary, the *New York Times* spilled the story on the front page, blaming Westmoreland, who then felt he had been ambushed. The White House parried the news with a half-truth: the request had never reached the president's desk. Yet, a year later when Laird entered office, the request had not yet been rejected officially because to do so would have set America on a path Johnson was not ready to take—the road that would bring American soldiers home before a peace treaty was signed.

Now Laird, a master at reading and heeding public opinion, was secretary of defense, and Westmoreland was the new Army chief of staff. As one of Laird's first acts in office, he formally killed the old troop request, although he would raise it frequently in conversations with Clifford over the next four years, especially when Clifford roiled the waters by publicly calling for faster troop withdrawals from Vietnam. "You left me a request for 200,000 more troops for Vietnam and you didn't have the guts to turn it down. Why the hell did you leave that work for me?" Laird railed. According to him, Clifford responded, "Well, Mel, you have to understand that the president didn't want me to get involved with anything like that."

⌇

The 1964 selection of Wheeler as the sixth chairman of the Joint Chiefs had marked a distinct break with the past; some called it the "end of the age of

heroes." In the previous seventeen years, the five men who held the post—
Gen. Omar Bradley, Adm. Arthur Radford, Gen. Nathan Twining, Gen. Lyman
Lemnitzer, and Gen. Maxwell Taylor—had been famous combat commanders in World War II and Korea. Wheeler was not a household name, and he
had never served as a combat commander.[5] Johnson picked him for the military's top man in uniform because he was politically adept and an honest
broker between the military and civilian leadership. He was careful to express his own strong personal opinion only when asked by the president or
secretary of defense, and otherwise confined his views to the meetings of
the Joint Chiefs.[6]

Battling the civilian leadership, and keeping the Joint Chiefs together
during the Johnson administration wore down Wheeler, who already had a
bad heart. He had at least one heart attack in 1967, which was kept secret,
and possibly a second. Yet he would end up serving six years as chairman,
longer than anyone before or since. By law, the chairman of the Joint Chiefs
was allowed to serve a maximum of four years, which for Wheeler should
have ended in the summer of 1968. But Johnson wanted Wheeler to finish
out the administration and provide a stable transition for the next president.
Wheeler reluctantly agreed, and an act of Congress made it legal.[7]

Laird was determined to keep Wheeler on for a sixth year, but Nixon
didn't agree and suggested that Marine Corps Commandant Gen. Leonard
F. Chapman Jr. be the new chairman. Laird knew that the only reason Nixon
urged that promotion was so he could appoint a general who had been his
military aide when he was vice president, and whom he considered a close
friend. Laird said no, and invoked the cocktail-napkin promise. He respected
Wheeler as a loyal officer who knew the territory and would carry out orders,
even if Wheeler didn't agree with them. Those orders, as far as Laird was concerned, would be to begin taking Americans out of Vietnam as quickly as
possible. Nixon did not put up too much of an argument about the Wheeler
extension because the president thought he was one general who had not
lost hope of victory in Vietnam: Nixon liked that can-do spirit. Wheeler had
forcefully made a case for his own retirement, but Nixon wouldn't hear of
it. Wheeler was surprised by Nixon's insistence and didn't realize then that
it was actually Laird's idea to keep him.[8]

The terms of the other service chiefs were fixed, and Laird did not tamper
with them. He kept the conservative and cunning Adm. Thomas Moorer as
chief of Naval Operations. Laird was happy to have General Chapman stay
on as commandant of the Marine Corps, and considered him to be "probably the most brilliant of the four-star generals that were in the military at

that particular time." He did not feel the same about Westmoreland who had been Army chief of staff for only seven months, but Laird chose to live with him. Westmoreland later complained in his memoirs that Laird never listened to him as a member of the Joint Chiefs. That wasn't true, Laird said; he listened . . . but he rarely agreed. Westmoreland's views about aggressively prosecuting the war were not shared by the other chiefs, and the general also had lost his influence with Congress.

Westmoreland was not thrilled to have a politician for a boss. Laird frequently had to lecture him on politics. "Politics is not a bad thing, Westy," Laird would say. "That's the art and science of government. We have to make our government work. You have to have support of people. People are important in this country." As was typical of Laird, he still respected the man with whom he differed. Their sons were friends at prep school, and the two men amicably crossed paths at school events. Laird often said the striking Westmoreland looked more like a soldier than any military man he had ever met: "When he'd get dressed up in his uniform, I always felt like saluting."

The man who had been Air Force chief of staff for four years, Gen. John McConnell, also stayed on but was already a psychological casualty of the Vietnam War. A World War II combat pilot (China-India-Burma theater), McConnell had become brigadier general at the age of thirty-six. He was a fast-rising star who could not conceive of fighting a war in which victory was not the goal. Consequently, the Johnson-McNamara manipulation of the military destroyed him. As his Air Force pilots flew over North Vietnam, dodging surface-to-air missiles and antiaircraft flak, McConnell was furious that they were not allowed to bomb the best targets. A sign on his door said, "Our job is to fight and win. Don't you forget it."[9]

To a man, the chiefs were wary of Laird. Although they had known him to be generally supportive of the military in Congress, that experience could not predict how he would act as their boss. He had always voted for the military budget, but only after he held their feet to the fire in attempts to hunt out waste and urge the military to economize where it could. And what would he do with Vietnam?

Laird's first meeting with the chiefs, on January 22, 1969, was on their turf, in "the Tank." Windowless, guarded, soundproofed, shielded from eavesdropping, and restricted to a very small group, the Tank was the Pentagon's inner sanctum for the thrice-weekly meetings of the chiefs. No briefcases, tape recorders, or other devices were allowed. Note taking was often forbidden. By tradition, the secretary of defense attended the meeting once a week. As the chiefs convened at 2 p.m. on that January day, they could not help but feel history about to unfold. The familiar surroundings, the thick gold carpet and gold drapes (an alternate nickname was the "Gold Room"), the neatly placed papers in front of them, the sharpened pencils, and small bowls filled with hard candy gave them some sense of comfort. They were also reassured when General Wheeler informed them that they "will have to put up with me for another year." Wheeler gave an account of his meeting with the new president, and then informed them that the new defense secretary had requested to meet with them and would now be brought in. Laird entered and circled the room, shaking hands all around. Then he sat at the head of the table in silence, appearing to wait for permission to speak. When Wheeler nodded to him, Laird began with an apology. "I want to thank you for inviting me here today, and I'm sorry to take this time to interrupt your work."

Opening the lone folder in front of him, Laird offered a thirty-minute review of where the new administration stood on most things military. Without showing all his cards on Vietnam, Laird let them know that he knew the issues but welcomed a healthy give-and-take between the chiefs and himself. Then he shook everyone's hand again and walked out of the room. Mark Perry's definitive book on the history of the Joint Chiefs, *Four Stars,* recounts what happened next:

> Following the predictable stunned silence, there was an almost palpable sense of relief around the table as well as a chilling realization that an enormously self-confident and adept politician was in control. Laird had accomplished in a few minutes what most officers believed would take years to gain: he had won the trust of a disenchanted high command that was more than willing to mistrust any Defense Secretary, regardless of his policies.
>
> It was no less than a revolution in civilian-military relations, a commentary on what officers prize above all else. In the history of the JCS, the Laird introduction of January 22, 1969, stands out as the primary example of just how a civilian leader can both dampen military mistrust and gain military allegiance for controversial foreign policy initiatives that run counter to traditional military beliefs. . . .
>
> [O]f all the secretaries who have served at the Pentagon, Laird remains among the most respected, not because he agreed with military programs and policies (he very often didn't), but because he was willing to compromise on JCS positions and accord the chiefs the respect they thought they deserved. Perhaps Laird, with eight terms in Congress under his belt, could not have acted any other way; nevertheless, his intuition to treat members of the JCS as intelligent

political equals rather than warmongering subordinates worked wonders in transforming the Pentagon from a battlefield to a demilitarized zone.[10]

On the power scale, Laird and National Security advisor Henry Kissinger were evenly matched in the first years of the Nixon administration. "Henry always told me I was more Machiavellian than he was," Laird said. "I'd say, 'No, I'll give you that award.'" A title more frequently applied to Laird was the "cheese country Richelieu," after the crafty seventeenth-century French cardinal. Laird had the ability to manipulate Congress, and Kissinger held similar sway over the president. Each used the skills of the other to strengthen their combined position. Laird knew from the beginning it would be a mistake to alienate the man whose office was located closest to the president's.

The National Security Council was Kissinger's power base and the place where he and Nixon chose to centralize their control over the State and Defense Departments. Laird couldn't stop Kissinger and Nixon from reorganizing the NSC, but he could avoid entangling himself in its machinations in order to preserve what he called his "freedom of movement." He rarely went to NSC meetings unless the president was going to be there. Under the Johnson administration, the NSC had a reputation for not paying much attention to the military. But Laird knew Kissinger and Nixon would be different. Knowing Nixon's nature, and suspecting Kissinger's, Laird correctly predicted both would try to establish a separate channel to the Joint Chiefs that bypassed him. By law, the chain of command goes from the president to the secretary of defense, and from him to what were then known as the commanders in chief (CINCs) of the various commands around the world.

For the prosecution of the Vietnam War, the command chain went from Nixon to Laird to the commander in chief of the Pacific Forces (CINCPAC) in Hawaii, Adm. John McCain Jr. McCain was an aggressive, can-do commander who occasionally had to be cooled down by his superiors. (Even as Laird was taking office and preparing to withdraw U.S. troops from Vietnam, McCain was being quoted in an interview with *Reader's Digest* as saying, after the 1968 Tet offensive, "We have the enemy licked now. He is beaten. The enemy cannot achieve a military victory; he cannot even mount another major offensive.") From McCain, the command chain went to General Abrams in Saigon, the commander of the Military Assistance Command Vietnam, MACV, or "MacVee" as it was called in Pentagon shorthand. Abrams was gaining a reputation as the realist who would not doctor the grim news about the war.

That chain of command did not include the Joint Chiefs—not even the chairman. In theory, they were there to advise the president, but that was not the practice. Since the Joint Chiefs chairman was in charge of the National Military Command Center (NMCC) from which operational military orders flowed, he acted as if he were part of that chain, just under the secretary of defense. The command center was also the place into which all information on what was going on around the world was funneled. From the beginning, because NMCC staffers reported to the Joint Chiefs chairman, Laird was concerned that the command center could become a black hole in a crisis. If, for example, a North Korean fighter jet shot down a U.S. spy plane—as would happen just three months later—the deputy for operations in the command center was supposed to inform Wheeler. Over in the White House Situation Room, aides to the president would get the same intelligence. Dozens of people could learn of the incident and rally a response before anyone remembered to tell the secretary of defense.

Given the personalities of the Nixon players, Laird couldn't let that happen. He insisted that he interview and approve all deputy directors assigned to run the NMCC. In addition, Laird and his top military assistant, Col. Robert Pursley, would frequently drop in on the command center, befriending the senior officers and inserting themselves into the NMCC command chain that otherwise could have left Laird out.

During Laird's four years as secretary of defense, both Nixon and Kissinger would actively work to sideline Laird, who was not always in agreement with their agenda. The pair energetically tried to co-opt the chiefs as well as General Abrams. They cultivated "back channels" behind Laird not just to glean military advice and scuttlebutt but to convey secret orders. The myth grew up around Laird that he had been bypassed several times by Nixon and Kissinger on critical Vietnam decisions, including bombing targets. The truth was, however, that even if Laird was not a party to an order, he knew about it within hours after it was given and usually before it was carried out. Since he had earned the chiefs' loyalty, and also proved he could protect them and most of their pet programs from Congress, the chiefs and Abrams kept Laird fully informed.

In fact, Laird encouraged the chiefs to meet with Kissinger and the president, just as long as they reported back to him. The chiefs could be valuable lobbyists for defense programs at the White House, Laird felt. They also became Laird's eyes and ears, along with David Packard, on the various NSC committees Kissinger established in his attempt to control the national security and foreign policy apparatus. When one of the chiefs neglected to report on a meeting at the White House, Laird always learned about it from

someone else and then there was hell to pay. In his memoirs Adm. Elmo
Zumwalt, who in 1970 became chief of Naval Operations, reported at length
on Kissinger's attempts to turn him into an NSC courtier. At first, Zumwalt
was flattered. But then, Laird became "infuriated" when he learned from another source about an unreported meeting between Zumwalt and Kissinger.

The next time Zumwalt visited Kissinger, the admiral said he was obliged
to report back to Laird. Kissinger suggested they could call their appointments "nonmeetings" and he would take responsibility for what happened
there; Laird wouldn't have to know. "Nevertheless I soon concluded, "Zumwalt
wrote, "that professional ethics compelled me to pass along the substance
of our conversations to Laird." Within weeks, it became more than a matter
of ethics for Zumwalt, who came to view Kissinger as duplicitous, intellectually arrogant, and dangerously elitist. Conversely, he saw Laird as a straight-
shooter who deserved Zumwalt's loyalty.[11]

The same was true for the rest of the chiefs. While they valued separate
time with Kissinger (and even more so with the president), they trusted
Laird. Pursley said this discernment on their part saved the careers and reputation of those men. "Normally, the chiefs, when they hear the president
say something, are almost immediately going to click their heels, 'Yes sir,' and
go try to implement it," Pursley said. "If that had happened during the Nixon
administration, it would have been a wild and crazy world. President Nixon
was keen on issuing orders that were impetuous, petulant—and a number
of other adjectives—which weren't really intended to be implemented . . .
Mel Laird protected the chiefs and Abrams from those kinds of things."[12]

~

Richard Nixon had set the agenda for his national security apparatus at a
meeting in Key Biscayne, Florida, on December 28, 1968, before he was inau-
gurated. He had invited those who would, by statute, be members of or
advisors to his National Security Council—Laird, Secretary of State Rogers,
Vice President Agnew, and Kissinger. David Packard was also there along
with Bryce Harlow, who was Nixon's pick for congressional relations liaison,
former ambassador Robert Murphy, who was the chief Nixon transition
representative at the State Department, and Gen. Andrew J. Goodpaster, former national security advisor in the Eisenhower administration, who also
acted as Nixon's principal transition national security advisor.[13]

One month earlier, the agenda for the meeting had been set when Nixon
met Kissinger at the Pierre Hotel in New York and offered him the job of
assistant to the president for national security. At that meeting, the two men
realized they had something in common, a vision of the way U.S. foreign

policy should work—run out of the White House by the National Security Council instead of the State Department. It was a natural for Nixon, who wanted tighter control over policy, and for Kissinger, who was national security advisor.

Key to Kissinger's plan was the creation of a revised NSC system, including the National Security Study Memorandum (NSSM) and National Security Decision Memorandum (NSDM) process. Study memos would order departments to look into something in which the president was interested; decision memos would be the president's instructions, through Kissinger, to take action. Within days of his own appointment, Kissinger had the first three NSDMs drafted, all of which shifted power to the NSC and to himself.

Before the Key Biscayne meeting, Kissinger had drafted a plan for revamping the NSC to subtly slide the power away from the cabinet secretaries and into the White House staff. It wasn't very subtle for Laird and Rogers, who recognized a coup when they saw one. In his memoirs, Kissinger relates that Nixon had already approved his plan before the December 28 meeting, but he set up the agenda to make it appear as though there would be a healthy give-and-take to get everyone's opinion on the changes before they were approved.

There wasn't much give-and-take. Nixon quickly gave up the charade and declared the Kissinger plan a fait accompli. Disagreement was discouraged as much by Nixon's emphatic support of the plan as by the setting in the screened porch of his Florida villa, where the breezes off Biscayne Bay deliberately encouraged the illusion of tranquillity. Laird and Rogers kept silent at the meeting, waiting to make their objections to Kissinger on their return to Washington.

Kissinger's critics have often portrayed this first bold move of the Harvard professor as a calculated grab for power. "This is what they always say," Kissinger protested in an interview. "But the reorganization of the NSC was actually not my idea. That was Eisenhower's and Goodpaster's. I was a bystander on that one. . . . He and I called on Eisenhower [who] had absolutely stern views that the State Department [should] not chair interdepartmental machinery, and that's why we put everything into the NSC. This was not my idea."[14] In the same interview, Kissinger portrayed himself as an early innocent with few or no friends in Washington.

He had only one client: Nixon. All of Kissinger's power flowed from that one man whom he aimed to please. "You have to remember that I came in as a Rockefeller man . . . [Nixon] didn't know me from Adam." To have gone against Nixon's wishes—or to persuade the president to do something he

would later regret—was self-destructive. "I would be losing my only con-
stituency," he emphasized. Certainly Nixon wanted to bring foreign policy
power back to the White House through the NSC, and he needed no persuading from Kissinger. "It was what Nixon wanted," confirmed Lawrence
Eagleburger, who worked as an aide to Kissinger during the transition. But
Kissinger wanted it, too, Eagleburger said. "I love Henry Kissinger; he's
my dearest friend. But let us not necessarily believe that Henry was pushed
any more than he did the pushing. There was method in his madness, shall
we say."[15]

Laird had not objected at Key Biscayne to the new NSC power because
he had known Nixon long enough to see when his mind was made up. But
Laird also knew he could change some of the details in one of Kissinger's
proposed National Security Decision Memoranda before it was signed. In
his memoirs Kissinger humorously recalled: "The first to be heard from was
Laird, who in the process initiated me to his patented technique of bureaucratic warfare: to throw up a smoke-screen of major objections in which he
was not really interested but which reduced the item that really concerned
him to such minor proportions that to refuse him would appear positively
indecent."[16]

Kissinger and Laird had dinner together and worked out their differences,
mostly in Laird's favor. Kissinger had written the CIA director out of the
NSC, but at Laird's insistence the CIA was brought back in. Laird didn't like
the implication in NSDM 2 that only the NSC could initiate policy and
strategic studies; Laird felt that the Defense and State Departments ought to
be able to propose studies, and Kissinger agreed. Laird lost on one important
issue. He unsuccessfully proposed that Nixon shut down the liaison office
between the Joint Chiefs and the NSC. Colonel Pursley had warned Laird that
keeping the position was just asking for trouble. It could be used improperly
as a way for the Joint Chiefs to circumvent the secretary of defense or, in
the reverse, for the president to work around the secretary and deal directly
with the Joint Chiefs. Both Pursley and Laird were right to worry; by 1971
the new chairman of the Joint Chiefs, Adm. Thomas Moorer, would manipulate the liaison office to spy on the president, using a military aide to sur-
reptitiously photocopy and steal White House national security documents.[17]

Laird could hardly complain about Kissinger's first bureaucratic moves. He
was the primary advocate for putting Kissinger in as national security advisor, yet he had no illusions about Kissinger. John Warner remembered Laird
taking him aside—before Kissinger's overweening ambition reared its head—
and saying, with a smile: "Watch out. Henry is gonna try to run it all."[18]

After the Key Biscayne meeting, Laird observed to Kissinger that he was "reaching out for too much authority, and too much power," Laird recalled. None of this bothered Laird too much because the power Kissinger was trying to co-opt was not Laird's but Rogers's as secretary of state. Rogers recognized the problem, too, and made similar objections but not very strenuously or effectively. He didn't relish confrontation unlike Laird who thrived on it. Laird and Kissinger became worthy adversaries, arguing about something on the phone almost daily. Despite the full backing of the president for much of what he did in the early years, Kissinger knew he had to be very careful with Laird, a man with powerful friends on Capitol Hill and in the media whom neither he nor Nixon could count on to side with them.

Imbued with self-confidence, and understanding Kissinger's strengths and weaknesses, Laird cared little during or after the Key Biscayne meeting about how Kissinger *thought* he would run the show, because Laird intended to run his own Defense Department, no matter what. In addition, Vietnam was to him a far more pressing issue than bureaucratic in-fighting.

When Laird flew to the Key Biscayne meeting, he had a primary goal in mind: to plant the seed of "de-Americanizing" the war in Vietnam. With each man there so concerned about his own agenda, it is not surprising that neither Kissinger nor Laird mentioned the other's agenda when they recalled the fateful meeting. Kissinger's memoirs dwell heavily on how he was able to finesse his NSC memo. Laird remembered the meeting as an amicable one, focused on how the new administration would approach Vietnam. "They decided that I'd go to Vietnam as soon as possible after the inauguration, and that I would come back and report to the president with a program," recalled Laird. At that time Laird didn't know the details, but he already knew what the "program" would be—he was going to pull American troops out of Vietnam as fast as he safely could. As was his backdoor style, he didn't say it in so many words at the meeting. "I brought up the fact that in order to maintain the defense budget and maintain any degree of support in the Congress, we're going to have to de-Americanize that situation over there and turn over more responsibility to the South Vietnamese. I reminded them that this was called for in the Republican platform."

Not yet wise to Laird's shrewd footwork, the others at the meeting were nevertheless suspicious. Withdrawing troops could be seen as a sign of weakness at the Paris peace talks, but Laird didn't have much patience left for those endless talks. Laird believed passionately that Nixon had won the election because of the Vietnam War. The American people were fed up with it, and unless Nixon started pulling American soldiers out of Vietnam, and quickly, he would not be reelected four years hence. Thus the new defense secretary girded himself for the loneliest political battle of his life, one that would pit him against the Joint Chiefs, Kissinger, and at times, Nixon himself.

⁓

The day after the inauguration, Nixon convened the first meeting of the National Security Council, which by Nixon and Kissinger's grand design was to supplant the State Department as the preeminent base of foreign policy power. At the brief meeting, everyone was handed a homework assignment from Kissinger. During the previous two months he and his staff had been energetically pulling together a Vietnam options paper. At Kissinger's request the president and two experts of the Rand Corporation, a government-affiliated think tank, had flown to New York City to meet with Kissinger at the Pierre Hotel on Christmas Day 1968 to help outline the options. Kissinger was quite impressed with Daniel Ellsberg, one of the Rand experts. One anecdote Ellsberg conveyed to Kissinger stuck with him. The young consultant mentioned that when McNamara became defense secretary he had tied the Defense Department bureaucracy in knots by asking them, on paper, to answer ninety-six penetrating questions. This maneuver established fairly quickly who was in charge, and it unearthed for the record the differences between the military and competing civilian agencies on key issues. Kissinger seized on the idea, which became the genesis of National Security Study Memorandum 1 (NSSM 1) or "Nissum One" in NSC jargon.

With the help of Ellsberg and others, Kissinger produced a paper for the first NSC meeting, which asked seventy-eight questions about Vietnam. As the new officials of the Nixon administration began scanning through the six-page, single-spaced assignment, Kissinger explained that the president wanted each agency (Defense, State, CIA, Joint Chiefs, etc.) to answer the questions and send them back separately to the NSC. Aside from the bureaucratic (and autocratic) designs of Kissinger, NSSM 1 was nevertheless a valuable questionnaire and one that would inevitably give a freeze-frame picture of the war from the viewpoint of each agency. The parties at that first meeting, including Laird, accepted the marching orders without remonstration. There was very little talk revealing where they stood, with each keeping his opinion close to the vest until Kissinger's questionnaires were returned.[19]

The day after Kissinger distributed the questions, he issued another memo with "Vietnam Policy Alternatives." There were seven of them, ranging from an all-out military assault until the victory was won to an immediate, unilateral withdrawal of U.S. troops. When the answers to NSSM 1 rolled in, the divisions on the Nixon team were glaring. The Joint Chiefs, Adm. John

McCain, and the U.S. Embassy in Saigon waxed enthusiastic about the war and the potential for victory. The CIA and the new defense secretary were dubious. There were a few things everyone agreed on: North Vietnam had enough men in reserve to outlast any loss of troops; the enemy was calling all the shots as to where and when the fighting would occur—and thus controlled the casualty numbers for both sides; and finally, even though decimated by the Tet Offensive, the North Vietnamese regular army could still mount major offensives.

At the Defense Department, the most pessimistic voice was that of Paul Warnke, assistant secretary for International Security Affairs. Once all the answers to NSSM 1 were in, Warnke wrote Laird a grim analysis. Hanoi had not come to the bargaining table in Paris because it wanted to negotiate peace, Warnke wrote. The Communists were in Paris because they had figured out it would take too long to wear out their enemies on the battlefield alone, and they were hoping to wear them out at the negotiating table, too. The enemy's pool of men was seemingly bottomless. In 1968 alone, 291,000 North Vietnamese soldiers had either died, deserted, or been so badly wounded that they were out of commission. Yet in 1969 all of those losses had been replaced. General Abrams had estimated in his response to NSSM 1 that North Vietnam could enlist 300,000 new soldiers every year. At that rate, the allies would have to kill 25,000 of them a month to stem the tide—something Abrams said the allies could do if called upon. The key point, Warnke concluded, was that the North Vietnamese were able and willing to suffer casualties at unexpectedly high and sustained levels, and could still do substantial damage.

Upgrading the South Vietnamese army and then turning the war over to them was Laird's exit plan, but Warnke did not soft-pedal the enormity of that task. He reminded Laird of a month-old CIA assessment that said without the help of the Americans, the South Vietnamese army "would rapidly disintegrate under a heavy and sustained communist offensive." The CIA was doubtful that the South could make a better showing "any time soon." This was not consistent with General Abrams's vision, but it was a sobering thought.[20]

Warnke's caution about the folly of trying to pursue a military victory over North Vietnam was a position he had held for some time. His memo to Laird was a warmed-over version of one he and Colonel Pursley had written for Clark Clifford nearly a year earlier. Clifford had given them these instructions: "I want to impress upon the President [Johnson] that our posture is basically so impossible that we have got to find some way out. . . . We should come up with a memo that makes the case for a disengagement on our part as a matter of transcendent importance for this country."[21] Warnke and Pursley had produced such a memo, and Clifford had agreed heartily with their conclusions, but the memo ended up being for Clifford's eyes only. Johnson was not interested in the news it bore. In Laird's hand, the same information reinforced what he already believed about the war, and unlike Clifford, Laird had the power to do something about it.

~

There was certainly plenty of blame to go around in January 1969 for the way the war had turned out. The American public, which will rally for a crisis but often ignores creeping problems, had paid scant attention to the incremental buildup in Vietnam. America slid into the war with little thought for how it might end. First, the United States sought to defend French colonial rights in the region against rising nationalism. By the time colonialism became politically incorrect, a new reason to make a stand in Vietnam had come to the fore, and the word was "hegemony"—the possibility that the Soviet Union and China might combine their Communist agendas to take over the world. Under that theory Vietnam was a domino—if allowed to fall, it would knock over the entire region. Never mind that the Chinese and the Vietnamese despised each other, and that China barely lifted a finger to help its neighbor North Vietnam, and would have been safer with a divided Vietnam than a border nation united in Communism and allied with the Soviet Union. Never mind that the war was almost entirely funded by the Soviets. Never mind that Chinese and Soviet Communism were a twain that would never meet.

Laird, as common man, was disdainful of the Ivy League buzzwords Kissinger tossed around like "hegemony" and "detente." Laird saw things in simpler terms: stay or go, win or lose, in or out. When hegemony began tarnishing as an excuse for American troops to be in Vietnam, there was nothing left but the noble goal of self-determination for South Vietnam, if indeed that was what the South Vietnamese wanted. By 1969 even that wasn't clear. South Vietnamese politics were in upheaval, and its economy was built on sand. The Communist cause had caught the fancy of an indigenous army of South Vietnamese guerrillas, the Viet Cong.

America's allies who occasionally joined her in Vietnam, at America's expense, began souring on the war and limiting their support. Even Japan was starting to complain about the use of Okinawa as a base for the B-52s that pummeled North Vietnam. By 1969 it was too late to make a friend out of Ho Chi Minh and try to influence his brand of Communism in the North. The United States had the equivalent of eleven combat divisions, nine tactical air wings, and seven divisions of "advisors" telling the people of South Vietnam how to fight their war.

Laird's razor-sharp political instincts told him what Americans wanted to hear: if South Vietnam wanted independence from the North, then it was their battle to fight. And if they didn't have the will to fight and win, then so be it. The United States had, bit by bit, "Americanized" the war, crippling the South by treating it as the grunt on the battlefield, suited to take orders but not to command. Aside from war-weariness, Laird had another reason for wanting to get out of Vietnam as quickly as possible. The war was destroying the U.S. military. While in Congress, Laird had begun to harp on McNamara, accusing him of robbing Peter to pay Paul—underestimating the cost of the war to get Congress to go along with his budget, and then taking money from other defense programs, such as NATO, to pay for the shortfall in Vietnam. Meanwhile, the drain was allowing the Soviet Union to narrow the gap between U.S. and Soviet weaponry.

Johnson chose not to call up reservists to do the jobs for which they were trained—but used the draft instead to ship hastily trained, often unwilling soldiers to the front. The readiness of the Reserves suffered dearly for Johnson's choice. Not only were they deprived of the chance to use their training and hone their skills in real combat, but their resources were siphoned off by the war. Meanwhile, the draftees, who comprised one third of those deployed, were demoralized by jungle warfare, dissipated by readily available drugs, torn by racism on the job, and scorned by their countrymen when they came home. Laird saw his mission as no less than the salvation of the U.S. military.

U.S. Navy Ensign Melvin R. Laird, c. 1945.

The USS *Maddox*, on which Laird served in World War II. The *Maddox*, along with the USS *Turner Joy*, later played a central role in the August 1964 Gulf of Tonkin incident that led to the escalation of the Vietnam War.

Newly elected to the U.S. House of Representatives, Laird (R-WI) presents President Dwight D. Eisenhower with a sample of Wisconsin cheese and an early invitation to return to Minocqua, Wisconsin, for another fishing trip, 1953.

Campaigning for reelection to Congress, 1954.

With his children John, David, and Alison, 1957.

With wife, Barbara, prior to raising a new flag from the Capitol at Laird's home office, 1959.

Vice President Richard M. Nixon passes a dish of cranberries to Laird after the great "cranberry scare" in 1959. This first nationwide food panic was triggered by the announcement that domestic cranberry products contained trace elements of a weed killer known to cause cancer when fed to laboratory animals in massive amounts.

With Carl Wallace, Leon Parma, and Jack Mills at a gathering of the Chowder and Marching Club, 1956.

With Congressman John E. Fogarty (D-RI), on the right, at the World Health Organization in 1959. During the 1950s and '60s, Laird and Fogarty worked in a bipartisan manner on a number of initiatives in the field of medical research and education, including the National Institutes of Health, the Centers for Disease Control, twelve regional cancer centers, and the National Library of Medicine.

Viewing a model of the McArdle Cancer Research Center at the University of Wisconsin–Madison, one of the twelve regional cancer centers initiated with Laird's active support. Pictured with Laird, from left to right: McArdle director Harold Rusch; Dr. Kenneth Endicott, director of the NIH Cancer Institute; and University of Wisconsin president Fred Harvey Harrington, 1962.

On a canoe trip with daughter, Alison, on the Wolf River on the Menominee Indian Reservation in Wisconsin, 1968.

Laird fields questions from high school students on Laird Youth Leadership Day at the University of Wisconsin–Stevens Point. Laird began the program in 1958 to promote leadership among young people from central and northern Wisconsin. In addition, Laird endowed the Helen C. Laird Theater at the University of Wisconsin–Marshfield.

"WELL, WHAT DID YOU EXPECT THE SECRETARY OF DEFENSE TO LOOK LIKE?"

"AN' THE KREML-INS 'LL GIT YOU EF YOU DON'T — WATCH — OUT!"

Upon becoming secretary of defense in January 1969, Laird became a popular subject for political cartoonists, who often depicted his head in the shape of a missile. (Above: © 1969 by Bill Mauldin, reproduced with permission of the Mauldin Estate. Left: A 1969 Herblock Cartoon, © 1969 by the Herb Block Foundation, reproduced with permission.)

Responding to questions at a press conference, June 1969.

Secretary of Defense Laird with President Nixon at Vietnam discussions in the White House Cabinet Room, September 1969. U.S. Ambassador to Vietnam Ellsworth Bunker and Secretary of State William Rogers are seated to the left.

With newly appointed Deputy Secretary of Defense David Packard, 1969.

With then Air Force
Colonel Robert
Pursley, who served
as Laird's military
assistant from
January 1969 to early
1972. Pursley was
later promoted to
lieutenant general.

Laird threw himself behind the Go Public Campaign, launched in March 1969 to pressure North Vietnam into treating prisoners of war humanely. At this June 1969 press conference, he is joined by the wives of POWs in an effort to raise the awareness of the American public about the extent of the prisoners' mistreatment.

In May 1969 cartoonist Bob Stevens depicted Laird's efforts as a ray of hope to prisoners of war. The results of the Go Public Campaign became clear only several years later, when returning POWs reported an improvement in their treatment in mid-1969. (Reprinted with permission of Bob Stevens and Copley Newspapers.)

10

Off the Menu

EVEN BEFORE NIXON TOOK OFFICE, Gen. Creighton Abrams, seeing the writing on the wall, had delicately approached South Vietnamese president Nguyen Van Thieu with the possibility that the United States would begin a process of withdrawing its forces. On January 17, 1969, Abrams and U.S. ambassador Ellsworth Bunker went to Thieu's palace in Saigon and told him they were going to recommend that the Ninth Infantry Division be sent home from the Mekong Delta. It was a logical place to begin; there were no North Vietnamese units there, only Viet Cong, and the South Vietnamese army could handle them. Abrams reported back to the new administration that Thieu wanted to know if a withdrawal of some troops would be "well received" in the United States, indicating he knew withdrawals were calculated to please the American public.[1]

Now it was Laird's turn to go to Saigon and be more blunt with Thieu. Laird had promised a trip as soon as he had settled into his office. On March 5, he had breakfast with Nixon and then headed to Andrews Air Force Base to board a plane for Saigon. Laird was not given to introspection, nor was he one to overanalyze what the trip was all about. In his mind it was simple. He needed to know how long it would take to train the South Vietnamese army to handle the war themselves, and he needed to know how quickly he could withdraw U.S. troops while that was happening. "I never was a great supporter of the Vietnam War," Laird recalled. "I was a great supporter of getting the hell out of there." The media knew this about Laird. The previous December, before the Nixon administration came into office, *Business Week* predicted that Laird would "rapidly 'de-Americanize' the fighting," while the *Wall Street Journal* observed that Laird was "eager to liquidate the U.S. effort there on any seemingly honorable terms."[2]

Laird was aware that others who had made the pilgrimage to Saigon before him had come back optimistic about the war—being in the presence of the military brass in Saigon had that effect on visitors. Johnson, as vice president, had gone to Vietnam and come back convinced the war was noble and winnable. George Romney, while a presidential candidate, made the trip and afterwards declared the war was "morally right and necessary." When confronted with political reality, he later said he had been "brainwashed." For Laird such tales were hogwash: "I think they were there to listen to how much more U.S. support they needed. I was there to listen to how much more they could get along without. I was looking at a different strategy—one that substituted South Vietnamese capability for that of the United States and, in the process, reduced U.S. military presence."

Laird had urgent problems to mull over on the trip. North Vietnam, in a blatant slap in the face to Nixon and the nascent peace talks, had launched another Tet-season offensive in February, shelling South Vietnamese cities in violation of the unwritten "understandings" tacitly agreed to when the United States had halted the bombing of the North just three months earlier. In the first week of the new offensive, 453 Americans were killed—the worst losses in ten months. General Abrams had initially pushed for a resumption of the bombing in retaliation for the attacks, but Nixon was stuck with those "understandings." Abrams's second option was to hit the North in a place that would hurt almost as much—Cambodia.

North Vietnamese troops had virtually taken over a swath of Cambodia along the South Vietnamese border, kicking out the locals and establishing "sanctuaries" from which the troops launched cross-border attacks. Logic would dictate that those nests should be wiped out. But there was a roadblock: the United States officially recognized Cambodia as neutral in the war, and any attacks over the border would bring antiwar rioters into the streets of America protesting the expansion of a war that Nixon had promised to shrink.

On February 9 Abrams cabled General Wheeler to share fresh intelligence about the location of the North Vietnam headquarters in Cambodia (the Central Office for South Vietnam, or COSVN). Abrams said it could be taken out in an hour of B-52 strikes, and the likelihood of hitting any Cambodians was nil, since they had all fled the area. On February 18 Abrams sent two colonels to Washington to brief Laird, Kissinger, and Rogers on the plan. Since the group met in Laird's office during breakfast hours, the operation was given the code name "Operation Breakfast."

Laird immediately saw the political downside. He understood the logic of going after the enemy in its lair, but Laird knew instinctively there was no way of selling that logic to the American public or the Democratic Congress. But Nixon was itching to retaliate against the North for the new Tet offensive, and he warmed immediately to the idea of bombing a North Vietnamese headquarters, even one in Cambodia. His solution to the public relations problem was simple—don't tell anyone. Laird found the notion of secrecy to be naive to the point of stupidity. Nixon was leaving to make the diplomatic rounds in Europe and was talked out of making any decision on Cambodia until he returned, if for no other reason than it would look cavalier for the United States to be bombing Cambodia while the president was globetrotting.

Then, on the plane to Brussels, Nixon changed his mind. Angry over increased attacks on cities in South Vietnam, he ordered the immediate bombing of the sanctuaries in what was called the "Fish Hook" region of Cambodia, named for its geographic shape. Kissinger and his military assistant, Col. Alexander Haig, flew to Brussels to work out the details of how to keep the bombing a secret. Back in Washington, Laird stewed about the deception and cabled Kissinger that it was a bad idea. Once again Nixon cancelled the order. Then he capped the confusion by sending two cables to Saigon— one to Ambassador Bunker telling him to inform Abrams that the Cambodia bombing was off, and a second to Abrams telling him to ignore the cable to Bunker and go ahead with the planning. Bunker's boss, Secretary of State Rogers, was opposed to the bombing, fearing the effect it might have on the peace negotiations. Nixon found it easier to keep his old friend Rogers out of the loop instead of telling him the truth. This dissembling became a pattern for Nixon. Although he was the most powerful man in the world, he hated to cross other powerful men and would do anything to avoid them rather than giving a direct order.

It was in this charged atmosphere that Laird arrived in Saigon for the first time. With him were General Wheeler, assistant defense secretary Bob Froehlke, Pentagon press chief Dan Henkin, Paul Warnke, and Robert Pursley. To greet Laird, the North Vietnamese peppered Saigon with rockets. No sooner had Laird gotten off the airplane than the press contingent waiting at the airfield asked what he was going to do about this obvious violation of the 1968 "understandings." Would the United States resume the bombing of the North? "I do not want to issue warnings nor make any threats," Laird responded. "I do want, however to state unequivocally that if these attacks continue unabated, an appropriate response will be made." He wouldn't say what he had in mind.

Laird's first stop was Abrams's headquarters. After some preliminaries, Laird set out his position. This is how he recalled it: "Now Abe, I don't want to hear anything about increases. I just want to talk about our withdrawal program and when we're going to start. How good are the South Vietnamese forces? How quickly can they improve? How soon can they assume larger and more important combat roles?" Abrams was not offended by Laird's tough talk; he had confidence in the South Vietnamese. That day marked the beginning of a mutual respect between the two men.

Laird spent part of his first night in Saigon in an underground bomb shelter in the backyard of the U.S. Embassy, while the enemy fired with small arms into a cemetery next door. Laird, Bunker, and Pursley had retreated there after dinner when the firing came too close for comfort. Unruffled, they talked business for two hours until it was deemed safe for them to re-surface. Laird and Bunker came to call each other friends over the ensuing four years, but they didn't always agree on Vietnam policy. As a full-time resident of Saigon, Bunker was close to President Thieu and would frequently take his side in debates about the pace of U.S. troop withdrawals. Although Bunker never spoke up in meetings between Laird and Thieu, he would make his case later to Laird and then cable his bosses at the State Department complaining that Laird was being too rough on Thieu. Their response would be to send someone to Saigon to hold Thieu's hand and occasionally give him false hope. Then Laird would have to send another emissary to get Thieu back on track.

On day two in Saigon, Laird headed for the presidential palace to deliver his first round of bad news to Thieu. Laird gave him the courtesy of a home court because the message would be a hard one to swallow. Amid the pomp and honor guards, Laird got down to business, unhampered by the subtlety that others might use in dealing with Asians. "I told him what would take place and he'd better get going on his program. He needed to get going on the modernization of his troops. They had to realize that they were going to take a more responsible role and it wasn't going to be Americanized any longer." Thieu protested with a hint of authority in his voice that this was not what he had been promised by McNamara and Johnson. That prompted Laird to give him a "civics lesson" in American government.

While in Saigon, Laird secretly dispatched Froehlke to Thailand to warn its leadership about a possible bombing campaign in Cambodia. Normally this would have been a diplomatic job left to the ambassador, but Laird didn't trust that channel. "We had several important air bases in Thailand and I didn't want them to be threatened in any way. I couldn't rely on the State Department to do it. I thought they would make too much of a deal out of it and it would be all over the papers," Laird recalled.

As would become his habit on successive trips to Vietnam, once the business in Saigon was done Laird went out into the field, visiting various Army corps headquarters and dining with the troops. He gave them little hope that they would stay for a military victory. At a stop in Danang, the press called on him to account for headlines in the *New York Times* claiming that Marines were that very day fighting for control of a slip of land, the A Shau Valley in Laos, supposedly a neutral country. In fact, that campaign in Laos, called "Operation Dewey Canyon," had been going on since the day after Nixon's inauguration, costing 125 American and 1,600 enemy lives. The command in Saigon had earlier announced the operation, but only the part of it carried out on the South Vietnamese side of the border in the Quang Tri province. No mention had been made when the action spilled over into Laos. And it wasn't the first time U.S. troops had violated Laotian neutrality by crossing the border to harass the enemy supply lines along the Ho Chi Minh Trail. The Johnson administration had authorized such incursions in February 1968 "in emergency situations . . . in exercise of the right of self-defense against enemy attacks."[3]

There were also two U.S. air campaigns ongoing in Laos at the time of Laird's first visit to Saigon. One, code-named "Barrel Roll," used fighters for isolated attacks on Communist Pathet Lao rebels. The second and more crucial, "Steel Tiger," used B-52s to bomb North Vietnamese supply lines running through Laos.

Laird dodged the questions about Laos in Danang, but the next day in Saigon, while boarding his plane to leave, he had more to say. In what sounded like an off-handed response to a reporter's question about Cambodia and Laos, Laird said American troops were allowed to cross the border to protect themselves, and he made it sound as if that had always been the policy. In reality, Laird had just given that order to Abrams. Laird called it "protective reaction"—as opposed to "hot pursuit," which was not allowed—and it opened wide the door for ground and air attacks into Laos, Cambodia, and North Vietnam on the smallest provocation from an enemy stronghold there. Back in Washington, the State Department recognized Laird's veiled statements for what they were—new policy.[4]

"Protective reaction" was the one bit of good news that the military got from Laird's visit. As the brass bid him farewell in Saigon that day, they knew that he was not going to help them win the war.[5] He was only going to keep as many Americans alive as he could while he worked to bring them all home.

Laird's party made a two-day stop in Hawaii where they could find seclusion to write a report to Nixon about their findings. Laird also had another mission there—to rein in the commander of the Pacific forces, Adm. John McCain Jr. The February issue of *Reader's Digest* included an upbeat interview with McCain, who was an unregenerate optimist about the war and never lost an opportunity to say so. His briefing charts for visiting dignitaries in Hawaii were the stuff of legend—maps of Vietnam with the Russian bear brooding over the whole of Southeast Asia, its fangs dripping blood over the region. Laird's staff came to call these theatrical sessions the "big red arrow briefings." The diminutive admiral would pace back and forth waving a cigar at the blood and the arrows, describing troop movements and aggressive strategies that would stop the advance of the Big Bear. Laird privately believed that McNamara had encouraged such talk by his own rose-colored reports to Congress in the early years of the war.

When subjected to a McCain briefing, Laird learned to listen respectfully and then say what he had come to say. This time, in a four-hour meeting with the admiral, he told McCain to tone down his public gushing. This was the son of the first Navy officer that Laird had ever seen, decked out smashingly in his white uniform that day more than thirty years earlier in Marshfield. Laird had great respect for the McCain military tradition, from the grandfather down to the grandson, Commander John McCain, who was at that moment a prisoner of war in Hanoi. But Laird couldn't have Adm. McCain spouting off about the winnability of the war at this time. McCain's response was a loyal recognition of the chain of command: "Aye, aye, sir."

Holed up at a military beach compound on Oahu, Laird, Paul Warnke, Dan Henkin, and Robert Pursley spent eighteen hours crafting a report to Nixon. It would form the foundation of the new administration's Vietnam policy. Laird privately told the president in that report that Abrams did not need any more troops; resuming the bombing of the North would get the United States nowhere; the United States had already dropped 2.8 million tons of bombs in the war (compared to 2.6 million tons for World War II and the Korean War combined) and the result was still a stalemate; the rules limiting cross-border raids should be eased up (something he had already taken the liberty of doing); South Vietnam was making surprisingly slow progress toward assuming more responsibility for the war, and the U.S. military had no satisfactory program to hurry that up. Laird's punch line was this: The United States should withdraw fifty thousand to seventy thousand troops from Vietnam before the end of 1969. It was Laird's first card placed on the table, his opening of negotiations with the president, Kissinger, and the Joint Chiefs about the pace of withdrawal, the beginning of the end.

~

While Laird had been away, Nixon had issued another order to bomb Cambodia, this one to take effect on March 9, 1969. But Rogers protested and, with Laird still in Vietnam, Nixon backed down again. Finally, on March 15, after another brutal shelling of Saigon, Nixon called Kissinger and said he was ready to hit back, but that Rogers was not to be told until it was too late to call the bombers back. On Sunday, March 16, Nixon had calmed down enough to summon Laird, Rogers, Kissinger, and Wheeler to the Oval Office, ostensibly to discuss the pros and cons of hitting Cambodia. At least two people in the room, Laird and Kissinger, understood how Nixon's mind worked and knew the meeting was a charade. Nixon had already made up his mind but could not bring himself to be direct with Laird or Rogers, both of whom opposed the plan for different reasons. Nixon wanted to make them think he was still open to their suggestions.

Rogers was worried about damaging the peace talks and offending Cambodian ruler Norodom Sihanouk, who could protest the bombing of his country. Sihanouk had already privately hinted to American diplomats that he would welcome any help they could give him in wresting part of his country back from the occupying North Vietnamese. But publicly, if the bombing came to light, he would have to protest and demand an apology. Thus Rogers conceded if the bombing was inevitable, it must be kept a secret.

Laird wanted to support the Joint Chiefs in this first test of their authority under his administration, even though he didn't share their enthusiasm for bombing campaigns in general. He wanted this bombing because the *chiefs* wanted it, and because it made some sense as a tactic. Then, too, the chiefs would owe him when he asked for their support of his troop withdrawal plan. Laird still objected to the secrecy, as did Wheeler. Laird believed that the minimal benefit gained from the Cambodia bombing would be a waste of what little public support there was left for the war when the secret was discovered.

At each meeting on Operation Breakfast—the Cambodia bombing—Laird would turn to Wheeler and say, "How many people will know about this?" Wheeler would promptly supply the answer that Laird wanted, "At least twelve thousand." That was the number of military men and women it would take to mount the offensive, from the ground crews that gassed up the B-52s in Guam to the lowly message senders in the Pentagon and Saigon. But, after a couple of hours of debate that Sunday, Nixon said he had decided to go ahead anyway. Fine, said Laird, but he personally refused to order the B-52 pilots to lie on their flight logs. Wheeler left the White House and went back to the Pentagon to cable the bombing orders to Abrams. Kissinger also sent a top-secret cable to the embassy in Saigon with orders for the military to lie about the bombing. The deception involved sending two sets of targets to the pilots. Their instructions on takeoff were to hit targets in South Vietnam near the Cambodian border. But once the planes were in the air, new orders were sent diverting them to Cambodia. Some diversionary hits were made in South Vietnam, but the majority of the pilots flew on to Cambodia. When they returned, the pilots were ordered to file false reports of their targets.

Operation Breakfast had been launched March 18, 1969, initially to take out the North Vietnamese command in Cambodia—COSVN—in one strike. As Laird had suspected, the "headquarters" of the enemy was not a sitting duck. In fact, COSVN was an elusive, mobile collection of people and equipment that no single bombing run could wipe out. But the door had been kicked open to Cambodia, and it would not be easily closed. Operation Breakfast was soon renamed "Operation Menu," with successive raids, each being given a different meal as a code name: lunch, dinner, supper, dessert, snack, and the like. In the next fourteen months, 3,600 B-52 sorties dropped 100,000 tons of bombs on Cambodia. The North Vietnamese said nothing, because to do so would be to admit that they were in Cambodia in violation of that country's neutrality. The Cambodians said nothing because none of their people were left in the region to get hit. Despite his objections, Laird kept his lips sealed, except to tell a few select members of Congress. Still a politician at heart, he felt strongly that the Senate and House leadership on the defense committees had a right to know what was going on. Plus, Laird assumed they would find out eventually, and he wanted his own skirts to be clean.

It took seven weeks before the secret bombing campaign was a secret no more, but the public reaction was so mild and the news media so restrained in its reporting that the incident remains one of the public relations puzzles of the war. Laird had predicted a huge public outcry once the bombing was exposed. That outcry was years in the unfolding. The immediate explosion was internal—at the White House.

On May 9, *New York Times* reporter William Beecher, in a front-page story, announced that B-52s were pounding North Vietnamese supply caches in Cambodia. Beecher said the news had been confirmed by "Nixon administration sources." Suspicion fell immediately on the man most opposed to the secrecy, Laird. He was enjoying a round of golf with his friends Jack Mills, Jerry Ford, and Bob Michel at Burning Tree Country Club when he was summoned to the clubhouse to take a phone call from Kissinger. "I just want you to know you'd better get in touch with the president," Laird recalled Kissinger telling him. "He's mad as hell that you leaked that story to the *New York*

Times." Laird told Kissinger to "Go to hell," hung up on him and went back to the golf game. It was not the first time and it would not be the last time that Kissinger and Nixon suspected Laird had spilled secrets to the press. Laird sometimes was guilty as charged, but not this time.

As events unfolded, it was never a mystery to Laird how Beecher got his story. A week earlier, a reporter from the *London Times* had flown over Cambodia in a small plane and noticed huge potholes in the ground below. A small story was buried in the London paper and got no attention. Although Laird wasn't sure if Beecher had another source, he knew that Beecher had called Pentagon public affairs chief Dan Henkin and confronted him with the information. Henkin's response had been that the story was "speculative" and that he couldn't confirm or deny it.[6] As one of the twelve thousand people who knew about the bombing, Henkin did not exactly lie to Beecher. Although several other reporters took a stab at the secret bombing story, none of them hit real pay dirt, and it dropped from the headlines within a few days.

That did not, however, assuage the anger of Nixon and Kissinger. Determined to find the leaker, the president and Attorney General John Mitchell took their problem to a master—FBI director J. Edgar Hoover. Hoover fell back on his old standby, wiretapping. Nixon, with Kissinger's knowledge, authorized tapping the telephones of seventeen news reporters and administration officials, including some NSC staffers whose loyalty Kissinger doubted. They didn't have the nerve to tap Laird's phones, which would have been discovered immediately as Laird ordered regular "sweeps" for bugs. Instead, they tapped the home phone of the man Laird was most likely to talk to after hours—his military assistant Pursley. The tap was kept on his phone for a month, then reinstated a year later—on both Pursley's home and office phones—and kept for almost a year after that. Neither Laird nor Pursley found out about the taps for nearly four years.

There were various excuses for listening in on Pursley's conversations: suspicions that he was leaking advance notice of troop withdrawals or spilling news about an allied invasion of Cambodia in 1970, and the outside chance that Nixon and Kissinger could glean some intelligence on what Laird was up to. But thousands of hours of tapes produced nothing, except complaints from Pursley's wife and children that there was something chronically wrong with their phones.

The bombing of Cambodia continued with little media attention until April 1970 when it became just part of the backdrop of a U.S. ground invasion into Cambodia, which was not a secret. It was that invasion that finally triggered a public outcry about expansion of the war into a "neutral" country, the most tragic domestic result of which was the shooting of student protestors at Kent State University.

In the spring of 1969, when the bombing was still a secret, Laird did what he could to prepare Congress for the reality of extending the war into the enemy's sanctuaries in Cambodia and Laos. In mid-March, in a hearing to ask the Senate Armed Services Committee for more money to upgrade the South Vietnamese army, Laird mentioned in passing that Laos and Cambodia were becoming increasingly more troublesome as enemy bases. Laird reminded the senators that Nixon had threatened some form of retaliation should the attacks on South Vietnamese cities continue. Most of the committee members already knew what Laird was talking about, but the American public did not.

At the same hearing, Laird asked for more money for Vietnam operations; he was careful to tell the senators that the funds were not for exit operations, since that would signal a need for less money. "I do not wish to mislead this committee on what I am talking about here. I am not talking about the withdrawal of American troops at the present time," Laird said.[7] He was cagey with Congress because he believed in letting the president deliver good news. The announcement about the first withdrawal of troops was already planned for a meeting between Nixon and Thieu on Midway Island in June. But before then, there was plenty of dickering to be done over specific numbers. Laird's dodge was not just a courtesy to the president, however. It was part of a carefully calculated strategy to make sure Laird himself came out on top in that dickering.

The Sunday after Laird's appearance on Capitol Hill, he was a guest on NBC's *Meet the Press*. He continued to sidestep the specifics of a troop withdrawal, but for the first time he put a name to his program for ending the war: "I believe we can move toward *Vietnamizing* the war by the program that I outlined to the Armed Services Committee," Laird said. From that moment on, "Vietnamization" was the buzzword that would define Laird's four years in office.[8]

The next morning when Kissinger, Nixon, and the Joint Chiefs picked up the *Washington Post*, they got a little lesson in Laird-style politicking. Buried on page twenty-five was a column by Laird's friends Rowland Evans and Robert Novak announcing his strategy. They wrote that Laird was not satisfied with the old plan to train the South Vietnamese to take on just the home-grown Viet Cong rebels. He had in mind a second phase of training to make them capable of fighting the North Vietnamese army, too, "thus creating the proper psychological climate for the start of U.S. troop withdrawal."[9]

The Evans and Novak column sent Kissinger "up the wall," according to Laird, who admitted years later that he had indeed been the source of the leak to the columnists. As was Laird's habit when he was the leaker, he called Kissinger to shift the blame. "I called Henry immediately and told him, 'Damn it, Henry, quit leaking this stuff.'" Kissinger was neither appeased nor fooled, but the leak accomplished its purposes for Laird. It put the public on notice as to his plan, and it let his critics in Congress know that he really was planning a withdrawal, even if he couldn't yet announce it himself. Laird could live with the repercussions over at the White House because he felt he had done the right thing. "I'm always a team player," he explained. "That was in the best interests of the team. But they may not have known it at the time."

Nixon indirectly alluded to his initial resistance toward Laird's Vietnamization program in his memoirs, writing: "Mel Laird had long felt that the United States could 'Vietnamize' the war—that we could train, equip, and inspire the South Vietnamese to fill the gaps left by departing American forces. It was *largely on the basis of Laird's enthusiastic advocacy* that we undertook the policy of Vietnamization."[10]

Kissinger opposed Vietnamization as well. In a private memo to Nixon, he complained that Laird's troop withdrawal program would become like "salted peanuts to the American public: The more U.S. troops come home, the more will be demanded." This would be unilateral withdrawal, and he was "deeply concerned" about that prospect. "I don't know when Henry *ever* would have been prepared to see withdrawals start," recalled Lawrence Eagleburger, one of Kissinger's aides and a future secretary of state. To Kissinger, every American boot taken off South Vietnamese ground weakened his negotiating position with the North Vietnamese.[11]

"Nixon and Kissinger were in an entirely different frame of mind," remembered Robert Pursley, Laird's military assistant. "They thought: 'We'll win this war. We'll hang the coonskin on the wall. Military victory—U.S.' But Laird was pushing withdrawal. It was clear that Laird's strategy was the logical one to pursue, but it was damned hard for a president and a guy like Kissinger to swallow."[12]

Nixon actually may have been more realistic than Kissinger, the political novice, about Laird's behind-the-scenes balancing act. At a meeting of the National Security Council two days after the Evans and Novak column appeared, Nixon passed Laird a handwritten note: "Mel, you've done a great job up there [Capitol Hill] and in your press appearances. RN." Two days later, on March 28, at the next meeting of the NSC, Nixon all but threw out Johnson's 1966 Manila accord, which had promised no U.S. troop reductions until a peace agreement was signed. Nixon issued National Security Decision Memorandum 9, which stated there would be no de-escalation of the war, but the United States "should be prepared to withdraw all combat forces from South Vietnam if Hanoi meets specific conditions of a mutual withdrawal agreement." The major condition was withdrawal of enemy troops from Laos, Cambodia, and South Vietnam. As it turned out, the notion of mutual withdrawal was just words on paper. Three days later, Laird wrote a memo to the Joint Chiefs telling them how they should interpret the meeting: "There must be alternatives to mutual withdrawal. The principal alternative to be planned for is Vietnamizing the effort."[13] The American troops would come home even though there would be no corresponding withdrawal by Hanoi.

And almost before the ink was dry on Nixon's de-escalation order, on April 1 Laird ordered the number of B-52 bombing raids cut by 10 percent, for "budgetary reasons." Laird was a skeptic when it came to the capabilities of air power as it was being used in Southeast Asia. He neither asked nor told the president about the cutback until after he had ordered it. Nixon's directive of March 28 had been ignored.

As Laird, Nixon, and Kissinger walked out of that meeting, the White House physician Dr. Walter Tkach had approached them and said, "Mr. President, President Eisenhower just died." The man who had warned against any U.S. entanglement in an Asian war, the mentor whom Laird had counted on to advise him through the tough times ahead, was gone.[14]

~

The phone beside Laird's bed rang before dawn on Tuesday, April 15, 1969. It was Colonel Pursley who had been up since 1:45 a.m. gathering enough information to justify waking the boss. The news Pursley delivered was Laird's first bona fide national security crisis. Two North Korean MiG fighter jets had shot down an American military spy plane apparently on a routine mission over international waters the night before. The plane, an EC-121, and its thirty-one crew members were missing in the Sea of Japan. The way Laird and Nixon responded to the crisis over the next two weeks would illustrate differences in leadership style and, ultimately, how national security operations would play out. The president was about to find out just how shrewd and sure-footed his defense secretary could be.

The EC-121 was an unarmed propeller plane bristling with six tons of electronic listening equipment. It had taken off from the Naval Air Station at Atsugi, Japan, the evening before with instructions to collect data over the Sea of Japan and land at an air base in South Korea, and it was to come no closer than fifty miles to North Korea, well clear of the twelve-mile limit that

North Korea claimed as its territorial waters.[15] When the plane disappeared off the radar at 11:50 p.m., the word was quickly passed to the White House Situation Room and from there to Kissinger's military assistant, Col. Alexander Haig, who made a courtesy call to Pursley. Thus was avoided one of Pursley's worst nightmares: that the defense secretary would be the last to know about a crisis because of the convoluted chain of command.

The official North Korean radio station, Radio Pyongyang, announced that MiGs had shot down an American spy plane because it crossed into North Korean air space. As day broke over the Sea of Japan, the third report came in; an American patrol plane had spotted debris from the EC-121 floating about one hundred miles off the coast of North Korea. The patrol plane radioed two Soviet destroyers, which were the closest ships in the area, and asked them to begin the search for bodies.

Laird immediately ordered all U.S. reconnaissance flights to stand down from missions near China, Cuba, and the Soviet Union, and over the Mediterranean until the Pentagon could figure out if those flights were indeed critical, and if so, whether armed escorts were required as part of their routine. The action made so much sense to Laird, that he didn't think it necessary to ask the president, or even inform him in any detail.

Kissinger wanted the Pentagon to come up with options for retaliation, and he also wanted to know how to keep the North Koreans from plucking any survivors out of the water and taking them prisoner. Pursley fired a quick memo back to Kissinger: "Mr. Laird has serious reservations . . . about whether we would want to prevent anyone from picking up the survivors." Pursley tactfully added that since the water temperature was about forty degrees, the Pentagon could be none too picky about who came to the rescue.[16] As it turned out, there were no survivors, and only two bodies were ever recovered.

The National Security Council met on Wednesday to look over a horrific set of retaliatory options drawn up quickly by the Pentagon at Nixon's request: shoot down a North Korean plane over the ocean; bomb the airfield where the offending MiGs were based; bombard the coast of North Korea from U.S. ships; invade North Korea across the demilitarized zone; use American submarines to attack North Korean ships; blockade North Korean ports; mine North Korean waters; seize North Korean assets abroad.[17] Nixon was steamed that the options presented were so dire, and he complained that he wasn't given enough alternatives. By that time Laird knew from other intelligence sources, and had told Nixon, that the decision to shoot down the EC-121 was probably made by a jittery pilot who had not sought approval up the chain of command. Laird also had learned the EC-121 mission had value but was not critical. That tempered Laird's enthusiasm for retaliation, but not Nixon's.

In reality, Laird saw little real value, but major substantial risks, in payback, but he wasn't about to say so to the president who was itching for a way to look tough. Laird enlisted the help of General Wheeler, who was as reluctant as Laird to start a fight with North Korea. In a good-cop/bad-cop ploy, Laird urged restraint while Wheeler appeared to back the president's desire for action. But, Wheeler advised, a military response would take time to mount. It was the time Laird needed to let tempers cool.[18] Kissinger recorded in his memoirs that Nixon decided at that moment never again to trust either Laird or Rogers, who had sided with Laird: "He would get rid of Rogers and Laird at the earliest opportunity; he would never consult them again in a crisis."[19]

Author Mark Perry, in *Four Stars*, a history of the Joint Chiefs, hinted at how that new distrust may have manifested itself. Within a few days of the EC-121 crisis, Kissinger "reportedly approached Wheeler with a suggestion that the NSC and the JCS cooperate in sharing foreign policy and military information outside the government's usual lines of communication." The implication was that Nixon did not trust Laird, but he did trust the chiefs. Perry wrote that Wheeler never took the bait.[20]

On Thursday, three days after the EC-121 went down, the frustrated Nixon ordered the toughest response he could, given the constraints—the EC-121s would henceforth fly with armed escorts—except that there were no EC-121s flying over the Sea of Japan, or anywhere in the world, because Laird had grounded them. And he didn't want them flying again until he was finished with his safety review. Kissinger and Nixon hounded Laird for weeks to resume the flights. Using his old standby excuse—these things take time—Laird delayed the resumption of flights until May 8 when he had finished his review.

As for the issue of whether the EC-121 had violated North Korean air space, Laird has remained tight-lipped, even more than three decades later. While the incident was ancient history in the United States, it remained a powerful propaganda weapon in the quiver of the North Koreans. "Our government has said they were in international waters. That's the position we continue to take," Laird said. He acknowledged that there had been times when similar reconnaissance flights had strayed "a little closer than they should have been." Of the flight that was shot down, Laird would only say, "They were not over territorial waters of the Koreans—the twelve miles—*at the time they were shot down*. I can guarantee you that."[21] In fact, Laird truthfully reported to a closed-door session of the House Armed Services Committee within hours of the incident that the North Koreans had shot down the EC-121 ninety miles from their coastline.[22]

Nixon was so eager to prove the United States right in the episode that he spilled a closely guarded secret and sent the National Security Agency (NSA) into apoplexy. At an April 18 press conference defending the mission of the EC-121, Nixon announced that he knew the plane had not been shot down over North Korean air space, and he knew that the North Koreans knew it too. As proof, Nixon boasted that the NSA had been reading the North Korean radar even as it was tracking the EC-121. And, Nixon elaborated, the United States could do the same with Soviet radar. Until then, that tracking ability had been top secret. It was the same technology that allowed the Defense Department to track every test missile firing in the Soviet Union and China, and it clued Laird in when the Soviets began putting multiple warheads on their missiles. Oddly enough, although there were ways for the Soviets to quickly scramble their telemetry so it could not be tracked, they were slow to do that even after Nixon's unwise boast.

American spying wizardry had given Laird another heads-up in the EC-121 case. The communications from the attacking MiGs were monitored, and they showed that the pilots apparently acted impulsively without seeking the order to fire from their superiors. In Laird's mind, that made the difference between a deliberate act of war and pilot error. Nixon knew that, too, but was determined to retaliate anyway. "The problem was, Nixon's philosophy was that he wanted to show what some labeled the 'madman' theory. He wanted people to think he might do anything," Laird explained. It was an image that Nixon had told both Laird and Kissinger he wanted to project to America's enemies, to keep them off balance.

In this case, Laird stopped the so-called madman by using delaying tactics and thus weathered his first national security crisis. Laird never regretted his machinations in the EC-121 crisis. He felt he had kept the United States out of a skirmish, maybe even a war, with North Korea. But Kissinger considered the whole experience a fiasco. He determined to batten down the hatches at the National Security Council. From the framework of the team that had worked on the crisis, he created the Washington Special Actions Group within the NSC to handle future international crises. Laird appointed David Packard to serve on this group.

Meanwhile, Nixon took a military action that he did have some control over. In frustration over the lack of retaliation against North Korea, he ordered another "Operation Menu" bombing of Cambodia. And for nearly a year he had the Pentagon produce reports about how the United States might react should North Korea pull another stunt. At one point the Pentagon turned over to the White House a thirty-eight-page list of targets in North Korea and methods for taking them out should the need arise.[23]

~

The closest congressional vote on a defense issue in 1969, Laird's first year as secretary, was not over the Vietnam War. It was the decision about whether the United States should build and deploy an antiballistic missile (ABM) defense system to block a Soviet or Chinese nuclear attack. The ABM debate dominated the headlines in the first seven months of the Nixon administration. "Stop the ABM" became a frenzied incantation against the Pentagon— a backdoor punishment for miscalculation in Vietnam and squandering billions of dollars on wasteful defense programs. Laird had looked down the road and felt sure that the United States would not prevail in arms reduction talks with Moscow unless, like the Soviets, the United States had an active ABM system to put on the negotiating table. He worked with prodigious energy to fund a defensive system that he fully intended would be bargained away in return for Soviet agreement to limit nuclear weapons.

The possibility of a shield against nuclear missiles was first considered in the 1940s and remained controversial into the twenty-first century. In the closing months of World War II, a project was begun to develop antiaircraft missiles to shoot down bombers. Within a decade it had grown into something larger—the Nike family of radar-guided missiles with the potential to shoot down not just planes but eventually incoming nuclear missiles also. The Russians outstripped U.S. missile development in 1957 when one of their rockets boosted into space the world's first orbital satellite, Sputnik. Military analysts worried that if the Russians could launch a satellite into space, they could launch a nuclear payload as well. Thus was born the race to field an ICBM, an intercontinental ballistic missile, which is fired into space on a trajectory that takes it to a target on the other side of the globe. Congress, including Representative Laird, responded with increased funding for America's missile programs—the offensive ICBM and defensive ABM programs.

Johnson and McNamara had opposed an American ABM system because they felt it was too costly and would never be adequate to protect the United States. Finally Johnson decided to deploy a scaled-down ABM system, and he ordered a reluctant McNamara to do it. The ABM plan, which Laird inherited when he became secretary of defense, was called Sentinel—a proposed system of radar and missiles to detect and shoot down incoming nuclear missiles. After the inauguration he told Nixon he needed a little breathing room to consider the ABM options, and on February 6, 1969, Laird ordered a halt to all construction work on ABM sites. As he examined his own deepest thoughts on the matter, one thing became abundantly clear to him: despite the legislative battle it would spark, the Nixon administration needed to have an active ABM system to use as a bargaining chip in arms talks with the Russians.

On March 1, Laird transmitted his secret recommendation to Nixon—that they go ahead with a modified Sentinel program to defend America's nuclear weapons cache instead of its cities.[24] Laird had never liked the idea of defending cities with any ABM system. No system could be perfect, and millions of Americans might be killed, even with a defense system in place. Laird thought it was better to defend probable targets—such as the ICBM silos in the northern United States. If the ABM system could protect enough retaliatory, second-strike nuclear weapons, then the Soviets might not be tempted to try a first strike. When Nixon announced Laird's new plan, he used the word "safeguard" repeatedly; the press picked up on it and began calling it the Safeguard system to distinguish it from LBJ's Sentinel program.[25]

What loomed large in Laird's mind during the 1969 ABM debate was more than one hundred feet tall—the Soviet SS-9 missile, which was first deployed in 1967. At first, American intelligence experts presumed it was an incremental advance for Russian strategic forces, which were still technologically behind the United States. Then, in early 1969, intelligence reports caused some alarm among the few men cleared to read the highly classified documents, including the new defense secretary. The SS-9 was significantly more accurate than previous Soviet missiles. The CIA deduced that it could hit within a half-mile of a target on the North American continent. It was also estimated that in a second modification of this two-stage behemoth, the Russians had placed a warhead with a yield of up to twenty-five megatons, which was more than 150 times the destructive power of the Hiroshima bomb.

In one of many consultations with Nixon over the ABM program, Laird convinced the president that some of the highly classified reports on the SS-9 should be made public to buttress the case for the ABM. Nixon authorized Laird to declassify whatever he felt was necessary for his first public ABM testimony before the Senate Armed Services Committee in mid-March. But when Laird shared the data with the Senate and the TV viewing audience, Sen. William Fulbright accused him of scaremongering. Fulbright refused to ask Laird any questions, saying that the wily Laird would use questions as an opener to filibuster. Sen. Albert Gore (father of the future vice president) offered a hypothetical scenario: "Say a watchman from a farm in Montana calls up the president and says, 'Four and a half minutes ago three missiles were picked up on radar . . . which buttons do I push?'"

"The panic button!" Senator Fulbright interjected, and the gallery erupted in laughter.

"This is not a laughing matter," Laird admonished. "It is a deadly serious question, and it gets right down to the heart of the discussion here today. I can tell you that if I were . . . President I would like to have an ABM to launch—and not have to press the button for the [retaliatory] strike."[26] It was a telling comeback, and a favorite for replay on TV network news programs. Journalists began referring to the ABM system as "the second button"—an opportunity to save the United States without being forced to kill millions of Russians in retaliation.

Another secret driving Laird's support for the ABM was something he could only hint at during the Senate hearings. Intelligence intercepted at a National Security Agency listening post in northwest Turkey had confirmed that the Soviets were testing MIRVs (multiple independently targeted vehicles) on their nuclear missiles. Instead of using a single warhead to target a population center in the United States, the Soviets could deploy multiple warheads to take out smaller military targets, such as our missile silos. Laird immediately understood that the MIRVs gave the Soviets a "first strike capability," meaning they could launch an unprovoked attack on multiple U.S. missile silos and take them out without huge loss of life. There would be less risk of raising world anger over such an attack, and our ability to retaliate would be crippled.

When Laird used veiled terms to describe this new "first strike capability" during the hearings on the ABM, Senator Fulbright demanded to know more. All the other accepted intelligence estimates of the day from the CIA and Defense Intelligence Agency had concluded that the Soviets were not contemplating a first strike, and Fulbright suspected Laird was stretching the truth to suit his stance on ABM. But Laird could not reveal all that he knew from the secret NSA intercept out of Turkey. (It carried the highest "code word" level of classification.) Eventually, Laird did share the NSA secrets with the CIA, and the intelligence estimates were updated. But for a time Laird stood alone, even taking flak from some parts of the intelligence community, for claiming that the Soviets might be developing a first-strike capability.[27]

After the Fulbright-Gore hearing, Laird's mother called him from Wisconsin where she had been watching the proceedings on TV, and she complained about his testimony. She hated hearing her son elaborate on these terrible destructive weapons. "It is not the most pleasant subject to talk about," she scolded "Bom." "You're scaring everybody!"[28] She was right to be concerned because it soon became clear that Laird, as the primary ABM spokesman, was the lightning rod for ABM critics, more so than Nixon. Commentary on Laird painted him as a hard-liner whose provocative ABM hard-sell was out of step with the president's conciliatory language toward the Soviet Union. Behind the scenes, the president was not wholly supportive of Laird's tough stand in the Senate. Nixon sent Laird a copy of his inaugural address with this passage underlined: "We cannot learn from one another until we stop shouting at one another."

While Laird was arguably the best lobbyist for the ABM system, the president himself was one of the worst. Laird realized that Nixon had a habit of making members of Congress feel that he was smarter than they were. "You can't get a vote if you start appealing to people from that kind of a pedestal," Laird said. It was not unusual for aides to hear Nixon grousing angrily about senators that "they are just a bunch of pygmies down there—a bunch of god-damned pygmies!" And while Nixon could fume and spout threats when he was alone with aides, he was too often without spine or force in one-on-one efforts to lobby legislators. On the ABM issue, Laird said, "You couldn't count on Nixon for help to get a vote through the Congress. He just didn't think it was as important as I did. More than once, I'd have to remind him: 'By God, we have to win on this thing or you're not going to have any bargaining chips as far as strategic arms limitations are concerned.'" To contemporary observers, it was evident that Laird had been left to "carry the Administration load in the ABM controversy," as the *Washington Post* characterized it.[29]

The full Senate took up the military authorization bill—including the ABM funding—on July 8, 1969. The debate lasted twenty-nine days and was the longest in the Senate concerning a military matter since World War II.[30] In late July, with the opposition claiming at least fifty-one votes against ABM, it looked as if Laird and the Nixon administration were going to lose. But Laird was a master vote counter, and his tally said the outcome would be 50-50. He needed one more vote for the ABM; he set out to secure a pledge from the Senate's lone woman, Margaret Chase Smith of Maine, because he knew it was in his power to do something nice for someone she cared about, her executive assistant William Chesley Lewis Jr.

The Republican senator and her assistant had a long, working relationship that had blossomed into a friendship, and possibly a romantic relationship, although neither admitted to that. Partly due to Smith's patronage, Bill Lewis had advanced to the rank of brigadier general in the Air Force Reserves. When Laird became secretary of defense, he found General Lewis was fulfilling his annual training requirement in the secretary's Legislative Affairs Division, which was something of a conflict of interest. That office was responsible for lobbying members of Congress and their staffers on defense matters. Several weeks each year Lewis was a lobbyist, and the rest of the time, as a Senate staffer, he was the one being lobbied. Laird's legislative team was not fond of Lewis, in part because he had advanced so far in the Reserves without having served in combat or commanded men. Laird legislative chief Dick Capen recalled Lewis was "bothered" that he didn't have more medals. Another legislative aide, Brig. Gen. James Lawrence, said that Senator Smith would quietly buttonhole him and urge, "You know, it'd be nice if Bill got another ribbon or something."[31]

In the summer of 1969, Laird floated a rumor intended to reach Smith's ears to the effect that he was thinking of changing Lewis's training post to somewhere less convenient. Then, at the right moment in late July, Laird arranged a meeting with the senator to talk to her about her anti-ABM vote. This is how he remembered the conversation:

"Isn't there something I can do or say to you to change your mind?" Laird cajoled.

"No," she responded. "There is nothing."

"Well, I'm sorry, Margaret, I just thought there might be something that you really needed. This is a very important vote, because if we stop the ABM, I think arms reduction and arms control will go down the drain."

She understood his point, but added that there was one beef she had against Laird when he was in the House. He had not supported Lewis's promotion to brigadier general. Laird had his opening. He reminded her that he currently had some control over General Lewis's military career. "There must be SOMETHING I can do for you now about that, Margaret." There was a long pause. "Well, Mel, maybe there is. I'm a little worried about Bill. He wants to keep his Reserve mobilization assignment with your legislative office."

"Consider it done," Laird said. "And maybe he needs another medal?" "That would be nice," she smiled.

The historic vote on the ABM funding took place on August 6, 1969. Laird had counted the votes and knew he needed one extra.[32] As the debate began at 11 a.m., Senator Fulbright intoned: "I have been in the Senate twenty-five years . . . I do not believe [any] Senator can cite a single case in which a serious challenge has been made on the floor of the Senate to any military program, since World War II, over $1 trillion. I have never heard a serious debate take place on it. This is the first time."[33]

In a series of amendments crafted by her aide General Lewis, Smith was able to give Laird the vote he needed to secure funding, while at the same

time maintaining her public opposition to the ABM. Her vote provoked a
gasp across the Senate floor and caused speculation in the press for weeks, but
Laird kept the backstory a secret for decades. And he made good on his promise to her. Lewis remained with the Legislative Affairs Division when doing
his Reserve duty, and he received a "Meritorious Service Medal" in 1969, then
a "Joint Services Commendation Medal" in 1971 from Secretary Laird, and a
"Meritorious Service Medal" from Army Secretary Froehlke. In photos when
the medals were awarded Senator Smith stands beaming at the general's side.

Laird's instinct proved correct; the only way to slow down Soviet missile
production was by treaty, and the only way to get a treaty was by having a
viable American ABM system to offer up. Nixon and Kissinger agreed, in
retrospect. "I am absolutely convinced that had we lost the ABM battle in
the Senate, we would not have been able to negotiate the first nuclear arms
control agreement in Moscow in 1972," Nixon wrote in his memoirs.[34] The
man who negotiated that agreement, Kissinger, confirmed the judgment in
his own memoirs: "When the SALT [Strategic Arms Limitation] talks started
in November [1969], contrary to the dire predictions of arms controllers, the
Soviets proved eager to negotiate on ABM. . . . The trade-off of Soviet willingness to limit offensive forces in exchange for our willingness to limit ABMs
was the essential balance of incentives that produced the first SALT agreements three years later."[35] Neither Nixon nor Kissinger gave credit to Laird.

During the five hundred days of the 1969–72 Strategic Arms Limitation Talks
(SALT), the president was fairly removed from the process, except to make
the major decisions that, more often than not, Kissinger had already for-
mulated for the president's approval. Within the administration, points of
view tended to form on two sides—those reluctant to give away any weapons advantage (the Pentagon) and those more willing to compromise in the
quest for peace (the State Department and the Arms Control and Disarmament Agency, or ACDA). While all had input and were crucial to the process,
the Pentagon held the power Nixon worried about.

"If the Pentagon refused to support a SALT agreement," Nixon wrote in
his memoirs, "the domestic political consequences would be devastating."[36]
In fact, ratification by the Senate would have been unlikely. Nixon was lucky
to have in Laird not only someone who could bring the Joint Chiefs in line
on major issues but someone who would be extremely effective in selling
SALT on Capitol Hill. In effect, the U.S. position during the negotiations was
primarily the result of negotiation and compromise between Kissinger and
Laird. Kissinger has admitted as much. "You can read stories that I would go

off and, on my own, negotiate these agreements. And I pulled these [arms] numbers out of the air in excesses of megalomania—which are not unknown [for me]," he recalled with a smile. "But I can tell you what really happened: I would go to Mel Laird and I'd say, 'I have to do this. We're going to negotiate it. Tell me what you can *really* live with in the Defense Department. *You* give me the numbers.' And *those* are the numbers I worked from."[37]

Laird had promised Nixon he would deliver a fully supportive Pentagon for the arms talks. The financially draining Vietnam War had forestalled U.S. strategic weapons programs at the same time as the Soviet Union was engaged in a massive buildup—producing up to 250 land-based and 128 submarine-based nuclear missiles a year.[38] Laird felt that anything that could slow down the Soviet pace was a good thing. "Nothing concentrated the minds of American leaders on the advantages of SALT as much as the clear and present danger of one-sided arms control in the form of congressional cuts in U.S. defense budgets," agreed Gerard Smith, who headed the U.S. SALT delegation. "The changing popular and congressional mood about strategic arms was not lost on such an astute politician as Secretary of Defense Melvin Laird."[39] He was unusually qualified to act as well.

Laird's military assistant, Bob Pursley, who had served the two predecessor defense secretaries, observed: "There weren't many other defense secretaries who were as knowledgeable or even as interested in arms control as Mel was. It was unusual to have a politically based secretary who was that incisive about what the arms control issues were, and his influence on the talks was seminal."[40] From his first days in office, Laird intuitively knew four things about arms control: it was vital to get a congressional vote supporting America's ABM program, which he was able to narrowly accomplish; second, the vote would compel the ABM-fearing Soviets to come to the arms talk table; third, he had to have his own man as part of the U.S. delegation; and fourth, he needed a man who would be more knowledgeable and better at negotiating than any other player on either side of the table. That is why Laird asked Paul Nitze to become his arms control representative on June 26, 1969, six weeks before the ABM vote was held and fully four months before the Soviets even agreed to begin the SALT talks.

It was a major coup for Laird, but not an easy one. Nitze was a long-time Democrat who had served as deputy secretary of defense and secretary of the Navy during the Kennedy and Johnson administrations. When Laird wanted Nitze to serve in a high-level post on the Laird-Packard team, Sen. Barry Goldwater vowed he would block the confirmation. Goldwater believed Nitze had been the brains behind Johnson's successful caricature of Goldwater as a warmonger during the 1964 presidential election that Goldwater lost. Laird also knew that Nixon would be suspicious of a man who had been such a close advisor to his late archenemy, JFK. So, instead, he appointed Nitze as his personal representative for arms control, which did not require confirmation, and ensconced him in an office down the hall from the secretary's office.

Nitze, known as the "silver fox" for his white hair and shrewdness, was sixty-eight at the time. An East Coast aristocrat, he had abandoned investment banking for government service beginning with the Roosevelt administration. He was a key member of the team President Truman sent to survey the effects of the atomic bomb on the people and geography of Hiroshima and Nagasaki, which made him the only man on either side of the SALT talks who knew firsthand the horrors of nuclear holocaust. He was an instrumental player behind the creation of the Marshall Plan, which resurrected Europe, and the North Atlantic Treaty Organization, which defended it. Nitze was also the principal author of NSC 68, the famous 1950 Truman policy document that outlined the U.S. Cold War policy of "containment" of the Soviet Union. In it, Nitze declared: "The Soviet Union . . . is animated by a new fanatic faith, antithetical to our own, and seeks to impose its absolute authority over the rest of the world."[41]

When the SALT talks officially began on November 17 in Helsinki, the final U.S. delegation was named with Gerard Smith as chairman. The four other principal delegates were to be representatives for the secretary of defense (Nitze), secretary of state (Ambassador Llewelyn Thompson), Joint Chiefs of Staff (Maj. Gen. Royal B. Allison), and a civilian scientist, Harold Brown, a former Air Force secretary who was then president of Cal Tech. Not one delegate on the U.S. side or Soviet side measured up to Nitze for his combination of experience, tenacity, and intelligence. John Newhouse, the chief chronicler of SALT, stated flatly that Nitze had by then "accumulated more experience with the affairs of U.S. security than anyone alive."[42] Nitze was extremely effective *representing* Laird, Brown recalled, but he was also "the principal influence *on* Laird."[43]

Both Laird and Kissinger were wary of Gerry Smith. Smith was a staunch advocate for arms control to the point of going on record as supporting a ban on ABMs and a moratorium on MIRVs. Neither was a useful position because the Soviets would never agree to them, nor would Laird and the Pentagon. While it would have greatly slowed down the arms race to ban placement of multiple warheads on existing missiles, no one felt such a ban could ever be verified since, at that time, the Soviets would never agree to on-site inspection. Smith's more liberal views encouraged him to explore these and other potential positions with the Soviets. "He was agile in drafting instructions for himself that permitted his nominal superiors [Nixon and Secretary of State Bill Rogers] only a minimum of influence over his discretionary powers," Kissinger wrote in his memoir. "He was not unskillful either in interpreting directives he did not happen to agree with to make them conform to his preferences."[44]

Laird viewed Smith as a fundamentally decent and honorable man who, nevertheless, needed to be reined in. On June 1, 1970, he wrote to Smith's boss, Secretary Rogers, that Ambassador Smith was out of control because he was treating Washington consensus negotiating instructions "as suggestions without force." Rogers wrote back the next day defending Smith as "stay[ing] well within authorized policy." Three days later, on June 5, Laird fired back that Smith, as part of well-intentioned efforts to flush out the Soviets had been "misleading" and given "mistaken impression[s]" about U.S. positions. Laird addressed a memo to the president on the same day, concluding: "I am concerned that the U.S. delegation, in its eagerness to move towards some agreement, has in effect been implying new options to the Soviets which we have not approved." The delegation was privately admonished, and Laird came to an accord of sorts with Smith during a June 11 breakfast meeting in Brussels with Smith and Nitze. The campaign had served its purpose to demonstrate who was calling the shots in SALT—Laird and, more important, Kissinger, who had agreed with the plan to hobble Ambassador Smith.[45] One of the delegates, Harold Brown, who would later be President Carter's secretary of defense, watched this bureaucratic battle with intense interest. His conclusion was that the real debate on U.S. positions was between Laird and Kissinger. Kissinger spoke for Nixon and Laird for the military. Both ACDA, in the person of Smith, and the State Department were without critical influence. "Laird and Kissinger had differences, but because there was agreement between them in the end, SALT I was signed."[46]

The most important issue on which Laird would not budge was that the U.S. should *never* agree to sign only an accord dealing with defensive strategic weapons, or ABMs. A concurrent offensive arms freeze must be in place at the same time. Soviet pressure for ABM-only was intense. "Moscow . . . had little reason to negotiate on offensive weaponry, since the Americans were not building more strategic weapons," Newhouse summarized.[47] More than any other issue, this standoff stalemated the talks from 1969 until spring 1971. At different points, nearly everyone involved except Laird flirted with capitulation. In July 1970, anxious about the upcoming congressional elections, Nixon told Kissinger that he was willing to have a summit on ABM-only and deal with offensive arms later. Nixon knew that the public supported this position, because they were anxious for the progress toward peace this would seem to represent. But Laird was adamant against this, and Kissinger knew it would be a fatal mistake to go ahead without Laird's approval since he represented the U.S. military's national security interests.

When further recommendations from the SALT delegation and others came that perhaps they could simply sign some kind of nonbinding agreement for SALT while having a full-fledged ABM treaty, Laird said no again. "We should not accept a formal agreement on defensive systems only, even with an informal agreement on offensive systems," Laird wrote Nixon in a private memo on March 9, 1971.[48] Three days later, Nixon got a message from the Soviets insisting once again on ABM-only. But by this time Nixon was sold on the importance of the pair together, so he directed Kissinger to obtain an agreement that committed the Soviets to negotiate on both agreements. Kissinger did, and secured that commitment from Brezhnev himself, which was announced by Nixon on May 20 on national television. It was this breakthrough that set the stage for the Moscow summit the following spring.[49]

But Kissinger, who was not as brilliant a negotiator as has often been portrayed, had mistakenly told Brezhnev at the same time that the submarine-launched ballistic missiles (SLBMs) did not need to be part of SALT agreement. Neither Nitze nor Laird could believe he had made so haphazard a tradeoff. Still, it was not in writing. A chagrined Kissinger spent the next year trying to recant this oversight with the Soviets, who continued to avoid real negotiations on offensive weapons systems. In a series of private eyes-only memos to Kissinger, Laird complained mightily about this:

> I believe that the time has come to inform the Soviets that the next three weeks at Helsinki should be spent in thorough discussion of offense limitations. The Soviets have so far avoided discussion of our offense proposal, except to reject inclusion of submarine-launched missiles in the freeze! This is intolerable in view of the fact that they would already have a numerical advantage in [SLBMs] with the proposed freeze. . . . The major bargaining chip we have with the Soviets is the Safeguard [ABM] program. Our major concern is with the momentum of their offensive buildup program. We have bargained Safeguard down [from twelve] to a marginal two sites. We have not yet begun to discuss their offense program seriously. Out of the first 15 plenary and mini-plenary sessions, the U.S. discussed ABMs 11 times and offenses 3 times. The Soviets discussed ABMs 15 times and offenses never except to reject limitations on SLBMs.[50]

Almost two months later, on October 29, Laird reiterated to Kissinger:

I am . . . deeply concerned that the Soviets are succeeding with their tactic of splitting an ABM agreement from any real consideration of strategic offensive limitations. We have, in effect, offered to give up our right to strategically sig-nificant defense of our ICBMs without asking for or obtaining offensive limits that would justify this sacrifice. I believe that we are in danger of losing sight altogether of the relationship between the offensive threat and the survivabil-ity of our retaliatory forces. We must re-establish [now] this offense-defense linkage. We should not freeze ourselves into an ABM position that has neither long term strategic utility nor leverage on the Soviets to continue meaningful offense negotiations.[51]

Kissinger acceded on both points, and Nixon had finally become firm on the same position as Laird. The submarine missile issue became the last major SALT I obstacle, and it was Laird who came up with what Kissinger called an "ingenious solution" to end the stalemate. In a January 18, 1972, memorandum to Nixon, Laird urged that it was vital to speed up the strate-gic offensive negotiations, and toward that end he was prepared to allow the Soviets to continue building their submarine missiles, but at a slower rate. Also, the Soviets must *dismantle* either an older submarine or land-based missile once their submarine missiles had passed an agreed-upon baseline number. Nixon directed Kissinger to float this idea through his "back chan-nel" with Soviet Ambassador Anatoly Dobrynin. "I did this on March 9, 'thinking out loud' as if it were my own idea for breaking the deadlock." Dobrynin didn't respond, but during a secret meeting with Brezhnev on April 22, the Soviet leader handed Kissinger a paper which "in effect accepted Laird's formula."[52]

Brezhnev also agreed to a second Laird position, from which he had refused to move during the entirety of the SALT talks. To Laird, it was vital that the Soviet offensive program be frozen to the agreed-upon numbers for five years. The Russians initially had countered with an eighteen-month term for SALT I, and later suggested a compromise of three years. No deal, Laird said, and Kissinger held firm. In the second major Soviet concession of the Kissinger-Brezhnev meeting, Brezhnev agreed that the "Interim Agreement . . . on Cer-tain Measures with Respect to the Limitation of Strategic Offensive Arms" (or SALT I), would last for five years.[53]

Alone among cabinet officials, Laird knew about these secret Kissinger con-ferences soon after they occurred. Laird had various ways of keeping track of Kissinger. One of his best sources on Kissinger's meetings was Nitze. When the latter had a pro forma meeting in 1969 with President Nixon (and Kissinger) about his appointment as a SALT delegate, the president had asked Nitze to spy on the rest of the delegation for the White House. According to Nitze's memoirs, Nixon told him: "I have no confidence in [Bill] Rogers nor do I have complete confidence in Gerry Smith. I don't think they understand the arms control problem. So I want you to report anything you disapprove of directly to me." Nixon described a back-channel JCS communications method Nitze could use. "I told Mr. Nixon that I could not do what he was asking."[54] Nevertheless, Nitze was the man Nixon and Kissinger most respected on the delegation, so Kissinger kept Nitze privately informed of his secret SALT talks with the Soviets. And Nitze was Laird's man, so Nitze dutifully reported all this to the secretary of defense who was, then, never caught by surprise at Kissinger's machinations.

At the culminating 1972 summit, which was the first-ever visit of a U.S. president to Moscow, Nixon and Brezhnev signed two key agreements on May 26. One was the five-year agreement on limiting strategic nuclear weapons, which was popularly named by Laird as SALT I, and the ABM Treaty.[55] Together, they were the landmark first step in halting and ultimately reversing the nuclear arms race and were contemporaneously viewed as significant achievements boosting Nixon's reelection chances and his historical standing. However, approbation for the SALT/ABM success should be shared by Kissinger, Laird, and Nixon.

If Laird had not been such an effective secretary, particularly on Capitol Hill, it's likely the accords would have been more to the Soviet's advantage. Ambassador Smith's cables were replete with references that the chief Soviet negotiator, Vladimir Semenov, was making to one of his alarming speeches outlining Soviet perfidy and huge military buildup despite all their talk about peace.[56] Both Smith and Kissinger found Laird's influence and harder-line position on arms control useful and believable in achieving Soviet concessions. "I know of no instance where unilateral American restraint elicited a significant or lasting Soviet response," Kissinger wrote in his memoir.[57] Indeed, it was axiomatic with Laird that the U.S. must never negotiate with the Soviet Union except from a position of strength. That was the main reason he secured White House and congressional approval for an accelerated Trident strategic submarine program, a system that was part of what Laird promised the Joint Chiefs in return for their support of the accords.[58]

Laird had "provided crucial leadership by presenting the President with constructive proposals and realistic assessments of potential [SALT] agreements, and by keeping in perspective the goals of security and stability rather than ease of negotiation or popularity," wrote Gardiner Tucker, Laird's systems

analysis chief, in a January 1973 overview memorandum. "We have been influential because we have been realistic rather than extreme, and because we
have been able to pull the Department of Defense together on the essential
issues." Without Laird's leadership, "unwise agreements might well have been
reached."[59]

In the end, the SALT I agreement and ABM Treaty were imperfect documents.[60] They left for later key issues such as the definition of a "heavy"
missile and inclusion of strategic nuclear weapons-carrying bombers and
"theater" or shorter-range nuclear weapons located in Europe and the Warsaw Pact. Nevertheless, the two accords were vital forerunners of the many
agreements that followed, which would truly limit and reduce the nuclear
arsenals of each nation.[61] The ABM Treaty itself was in force for thirty years,
until President George W. Bush withdrew the United States from the treaty
in 2002.[62]

Kissinger has received well-deserved notice for his pivotal role in these
negotiations, and it could not likely have been accomplished if the firmly
anti-Communist Nixon had not been a president who saw the wisdom of
arms control. However, Laird was the equally vital third leg of this stool upon
which arms control success rested, a point that has not been understood by
historians because he has not written his own memoir and his private memoranda and documents have not been available to outside review. "SALT I
and the ABM Treaty, which could not have happened without Mel's leadership, were incredibly important steps in the progression of arms control
within the national security fabric of this country," summarized Pursley. "And
it is one of the brightest stars in Mel's crown."[63]

11

Going Public

THE MIDWAY ISLAND CONFERENCE on June 8, 1969, was publicly billed as a meeting where two presidents, Richard Nixon and Nguyen Van Thieu, would debate and decide how many U.S. troops would leave Vietnam in the first round of withdrawals. But in truth, Thieu's opinion was irrelevant, and the number had already been decided by Nixon, with some careful manipulation by Laird.

On April 10, Nixon, through Kissinger, had issued National Security Study Memorandum 36, asking for a timetable for turning the war over to the South Vietnamese. The president wanted options to accomplish the plan in one to four years. The next day columnists Evans and Novak published a report that Nixon was planning a "massive reduction" of two hundred thousand troops from Vietnam in an effort to persuade the North Vietnamese to do the same. Laird said he was not the source of that leak, which was off the mark on at least two points. According to Laird, Nixon never really believed the North would respond to a U.S. troop withdrawal by scaling down its own forces. And the plan was not to withdraw just two hundred thousand men, but all of them, five hundred thousand plus.

Laird later told Evans and Novak that "We had to go ahead with withdrawal regardless of what North Vietnam did in response, because we did not have domestic support." That was Laird's mantra for the next four years, that the U.S. participation in the war was doomed because the folks at home were fed up with it. Kissinger, ever scornful of politics, never agreed. Nixon would come around only as the 1972 election drew closer. Until the president saw the light, Laird had to fight tooth and nail for each soldier he brought home.

Ten days before the Midway meeting, the Joint Chiefs delivered their formal recommendation—withdraw 50,000 troops by the end of 1969 and a total of 244,000 troops in three and a half years, leaving more than 300,000 Americans behind indefinitely as advisors and support to the new and improved South Vietnamese army.[1] Laird passed along the memo to Nixon, agreeing with the 50,000 figure for 1969 but remaining deliberately vague about the rest of the plan. He hadn't told the chiefs yet, but he had no intention of having any American combat troops still in Vietnam by his last day in office. He was keeping that plan a secret from the chiefs so as not to alienate them from the beginning. Far from being discouraged by the chiefs' initial figures, Laird respected the commanders for taking one baby step away from the war in which they had so much invested.

General Wheeler eventually signed off on the fifty thousand figure, but he argued against the number until the eleventh hour—the weekend before the Midway Island summit meeting between Nixon and Thieu where the first withdrawal number was to be announced, ostensibly in a show of harmony between the two presidents. That weekend, Wheeler made a trip to the presidential retreat at Camp David where Laird was vacationing with his family. (Laird was always quick to educate the uninformed about Camp David—that it was a Defense Department facility, which was loaned on demand to the president, not the other way around.) Wheeler's trip was for naught because Laird's mind was made up. His political instincts told him that if he could just get that first contingent of troops out, it would be impossible for Kissinger or Nixon or the commanders to stop the momentum.

The "problem," as Kissinger recalled seeing it, "was that once you established the principle of withdrawal, you were in a situation like salted peanuts—every six months we would have to do more" to satisfy the public's hunger for withdrawals.[2] In addition, Kissinger saw little value in troop withdrawals as a way to end the war. He put his hopes in the peace talks. One of his early tactics was to link U.S.–Soviet relations to a settlement of the war, since the Soviet Union was bankrolling the enemy. Using the State Department to deliver the message, Kissinger let Soviet ambassador Anatoly Dobrynin know that talks about the arms race and other bones of contention might go more smoothly if the Soviets put pressure on Hanoi to cooperate in any peace talks. Laird nearly spilled the beans about this approach at a Senate hearing in mid-March. When pressed to come up with some progress on the Vietnam front, Laird didn't want to talk about his withdrawal plans; instead he offered up Kissinger's plans for secret talks. As always with Laird, it was not an accidental slip of the tongue but a deliberate attempt to put pressure on the Soviets to respond to the overtures. They never did—more evidence to Laird that the solution would not be found through diplomacy.

Nixon and Laird stopped in Honolulu en route to Midway to refuel and break the withdrawal news to General Abrams and Admiral McCain. On the flight over, Laird was still unsure which withdrawal number Nixon would accept. When the two talked on the plane, Laird fell back on his old standby argument that would appeal to Nixon: the political situation in the United States was such that Nixon couldn't afford *not* to withdraw some troops.

Laird, William Rogers, Kissinger, Wheeler, Ambassador Bunker, and Henry Cabot Lodge, the chief peace negotiator in Paris, attended the briefing in Hawaii. There were as many opinions as there were men, but Nixon took Laird's advice. The first phase would bring home twenty-five thousand troops in the summer, with another twenty-five thousand withdrawn by the end of the year. When Laird briefed Nixon in Hawaii, he made it clear that Vietnamization might get messy. His preparatory notes for the briefing say, "These forces [the South Vietnamese army] are improving slowly, and with the right kind of help from us, continuing improvement can be expected. However, even with additional equipment and significantly increased combat support provided by our forces, they are not likely to be able to stand alone against the current North Vietnamese *and* VC [Viet Cong] threat. Any withdrawal of U.S. forces from South Vietnam must take this into account. Yet improvement in the South Vietnamese forces is also related to morale, commitment and motivation. In this regard, U.S. troop reduction, if carefully balanced, can have a positive effect by making the South Vietnamese realize they must do more." In other words, if America didn't back off, the South Vietnamese would never take the initiative to fight their own war.

The next day, Sunday, the Nixon party continued on to Midway Island, arriving a few minutes after Thieu's plane landed, contrary to the protocol that Thieu had insisted on. He wanted to arrive second and cement the impression that it was Nixon's party and Nixon's agenda, not his own. While Nixon headed off to the meeting with Thieu at the home of the American commander of the military facility on the tiny atoll, Laird indulged himself in some politicking. He shook hands with every dignitary and underling at the airfield.

Over at the commander's house, things were delayed a moment while Thieu traded the small chair assigned to him for one that was as big as Nixon's. The meeting lasted about four hours, and when they were finished, Nixon announced to the waiting press, "As a consequence of the recommendation by the President [Thieu] and the assessment of our own commander in the field [Abrams], I have decided to order the immediate redeployment from Vietnam of a division equivalent of approximately twenty-five thousand

men." Nixon also perpetuated the fiction that the criteria for continued withdrawals remained in place: progress in training the South Vietnamese army;
progress at the Paris peace talks; and a reduced level of enemy activity on
the battlefield.[3]

With the formal announcement made, Laird was impatient for the show
to end. His daughter, Alison, was graduating from high school in Washington the next morning, and he was the commencement speaker. A KC-135
tanker airplane was waiting for him on the runway. Air Force One would
take Nixon home by way of Hawaii and California because it would need to
refuel, but the tanker could take Laird nonstop to Washington. As the summit dragged on, Laird did everything he politely could to get the president
to wrap things up. Then, with Nixon and Thieu still standing on the tarmac
going through the formalities of parting, Laird sat in the KC-135 on the runway checking his watch. Finally he ordered the pilot to get the plane in the
air, the noisy takeoff drowning out some of the diplomacy on the tarmac.

The plane deposited Laird at Andrews Air Force Base at 7:30 the next morning, where he hastily told the waiting reporters that Nixon had made a historic decision at Midway. Then, begging off more questions, Laird said he
had something important to do and drove to the high school, arriving with
ten minutes to spare. The *Time* magazine photo of proud father and graduating daughter still graced Laird's desk three decades later with the caption
summing up the day: "What happiness is."

The public reaction to the announcement of the first withdrawal was less
than ebullient. Clark Clifford—whom Laird was fond of describing as the
defense secretary who never took one soldier out of Vietnam—criticized the
withdrawal plan as too slow. In an article in *Foreign Affairs* in mid-June,
Clifford called for the removal of all American ground combat forces within
eighteen months.[4] Peeved by this armchair quarterbacking from the Johnson gang, Nixon went on television to remind Americans of just how many
men had *not* come home during their watch. Clifford's meddling secretly
pleased Laird; Clifford's quick withdrawal plan was not realistic, but Laird
believed it helped to have a Democrat in his corner.

⁓

Not content with sliding out of Vietnam the way America had slid in, Laird
wanted a concrete change in MACV's mission statement for the war, in addition to a firm plan for troop withdrawals. On July 7 he was aboard the presidential yacht *Sequoia* to meet with Nixon and Kissinger. There he announced
to the surprise of the other two men that he had changed the wording of the
mission statement from applying "maximum pressure" against the enemy

to pledging "maximum assistance" to the South Vietnamese army. Nixon, who hated face-to-face confrontations, agreed initially. He later changed his mind but still was not willing to order a change back to the old mission statement. That was fine with Laird, who thought it was the defense secretary's call anyway.

Three days after the meeting on the *Sequoia,* the first of the twenty-five thousand homebound troops arrived in Seattle. The plan was to have each wave of soldiers parade through the streets of the towns where their units were based, hopefully to the welcoming applause of the grateful home crowd. An official Army history of the first returning unit tells the upshot of that public relations debacle. Leaving Saigon, one soldier raised his fist in a "black power" salute. Another complained that the ceremony was just for show, and still others worried aloud to reporters that they were being sent home ignominiously without winning the war. Antiwar demonstrators greeted the plane in Seattle. A *New York Times* article noted that on the day the 814 men arrived home, another one thousand men had been sent over. It would be the first and last formal welcome-home ceremony for the returning troops.[5]

Beginning with that first homecoming, it took four years to evacuate about half a million American ground troops from Vietnam. The same number of soldiers, sailors, and airmen were pulled out of Saudi Arabia, Kuwait, and Iraq at the end of the 1991 Persian Gulf War in less than six months. In that particular case, the objective was independence for Kuwait. With the pullout accomplished, all that remained were logistics—the ratio of departing troops and materiel to available transports. In the minds of many Americans in 1969, particularly those in Congress who wanted to best Richard Nixon in the political arena, the Vietnam War formula was just that simple—order as many planes and ships as needed, and bid good riddance through the rearview mirror.

But even after Laird set the military on a homeward-bound course, there was no quick exit strategy available. Nixon was determined to end U.S. involvement in the war, but he vowed not to go down in history as the first American president to lose a war. Laird and Kissinger were keenly aware of the dishonor that came in international diplomatic circles to a nation that reneged on its commitments and walked away from its allies. The upgrading of South Vietnamese forces could not be instantaneous. Vietnamization was going to take time; the missteps of the past could not be corrected overnight.

But among the myriad Vietnamization issues there was one unique problem. There were estimates of about fifteen hundred American soldiers, sailors, and airmen missing in action or known to be prisoners of the enemy. They could not be left behind when the last unit boarded the plane for home, no matter how successful Vietnamization had become. Laird had little faith in the negotiation process in Paris as a way to end the U.S. involvement in Vietnam, but when it came to the POWs, negotiations could be a key element in freeing them. The peace negotiations were under the control of the State Department, and the same was true of the POW issue until Laird came along. For liaison with POW families, the Defense Department had maintained a small staff reporting to the assistant secretary for International Security Affairs. Laird bolstered that staff, brought in an energetic staffer, Roger Shields, and made the issue a personal priority.

With the State Department in charge of policy, the POWs had become the unmentionables in the Paris negotiations. American diplomats were afraid that by demanding release of the prisoners, or even insisting on better conditions for them, the country would signal its desperate concern for those men and thus increase their value as a bargaining chip for Hanoi. Even the families of the POWs had been under strict instructions to keep their silence, lest the North Vietnamese figure out just how much those men were worth back home. Laird had no patience with such timidity. Credible reports were accumulating in the Pentagon of torture, starvation, disease, and death in the POW camps. Laird quickly realized that those MIAs and POWs constituted a powerful tool, which the United States could use to shame Hanoi around the world and, in the process, possibly save the lives of the prisoners. Laird saw the aggrieved families as partners in that campaign. The wives and mothers of the POWs were tired of stifling their opinions. If they were going to explode, Laird wanted them on his side.

He also felt strongly that the POWs were the Pentagon's responsibility, not to be defaulted to the diplomats. From the beginning, Laird would go through the motions of consulting and informing the State Department on POW policy, but he would not wait for their permission to shake up the status quo.

The prisoners held in the North were, for the most part, career Air Force and Navy pilots and crewmen shot down in bombing raids. They were kept in established camps where camaraderie with other prisoners, their military training, and patriotic bent helped them to resist and endure. As bad as conditions were in North Vietnam for American prisoners, the picture in the South was worse. Prisoners of the Viet Cong tended to be young, immature, poorly prepared enlisted men who had been captured in ground combat or taken when they ventured too far from their units. They were forced to travel with the Viet Cong like nomads, carried in bamboo cages or dragged from camp to camp without the company of other prisoners. Many died from the complications of untreated wounds, exposure, starvation, disease, and brutal treatment.

In February 1969 Averell Harriman called on Laird at his Pentagon office after hearing rumors of Laird's plan to go public on the POW-MIA issue. Ambassador Harriman, former Vietnam peace negotiator in Paris, urged Laird not to go forward with his plans. Laird was noncommittal; he soon assigned Richard Capen in his Public Affairs office to review the current intelligence and report back on May 3 at a Defense Department staff weekend retreat at Airlie House in Virginia. When he heard Capen's findings at the conference, Laird bellowed, "By God, we're going to go public." Thus, on that weekend, what officially became known as the "Go Public Campaign" came into being. No more would the POWs get the silent treatment from their own government. "We were going to show photos and we were going to show facts to illustrate that the men were being tortured, that they were being denied medical treatment, that they were not being identified, and that they were not allowed to get mail, in violation of the Geneva Conventions," said Capen.[6]

The civilians at the Pentagon quickly got on board, but the military officers were more reluctant, fearing that by humiliating North Vietnam publicly over the POW issue, Laird might further endanger the lives of the prisoners. Capen took his case to one among the military hierarchy who had the most to lose should that happen, Adm. John McCain, whose son had been a prisoner in North Vietnam since October 26, 1967. "Whatever you feel is right, do it," the admiral told Capen. "Don't let me influence you." It was typical of the tack the admiral would take in the future whenever Laird visited CINC-PAC headquarters in Hawaii and inquired about the young pilot. The admiral would show appreciation for Laird's concern and then quickly change the subject lest it appear he wanted any special consideration for his son.

Kissinger was not enthused about the plan to go public, fearing it would complicate the peace talks. The State Department, from Secretary Rogers down to the negotiators in Paris, thought it was a gamble. The president was noncommittal, but Laird pressed on. Capen and his staff scheduled a press conference for May 19, 1969, and carefully prepared and rehearsed their presentation on inhumane treatment of the POWs. Reporters, expecting little more than a dog-and-pony show without any news, stirred when Laird himself walked into the briefing room.

"The North Vietnamese have claimed that they are treating our men humanely. I am distressed by the fact that there is clear evidence that this is not the case," Laird began. He detailed the known offenses—failure to release prisoner lists, refusal to deliver prisoner mail, use of the prisoners in propaganda films. Then Laird turned the press conference over to Capen, who distributed a packet of forty-six photos (most of them circulated on the black market in North Vietnam) that showed injured American prisoners, some with limbs atrophied from untreated wounds, some in solitary confinement.[7]

The news got a small splash in the next day's headlines, but the reverberations were bigger in the arena that mattered. On May 20 the North Vietnamese delegate to the Paris peace talks blustered that his government had no intention of releasing even a list of prisoner names, let alone prisoners themselves, until the United States took its troops out of Vietnam. Within two weeks Radio Hanoi began a series of broadcasts in which speakers who claimed to be American POWs waxed grateful about their humane treatment at the hands of the enemy. In one such radio broadcast on June 5, a man claiming to be Lieutenant Commander McCain admitted that he had bombed civilian targets before his capture and praised the North Vietnamese for "good medical treatment," which had enabled him to walk again. At the time, the real McCain had been beaten and tortured to the point that he attempted suicide to resist his captors' demands that he sign a confession of war crimes. The broken arm that the radio broadcast claimed his captors had so skillfully healed had in reality been rebroken by his torturers.

The next step for Hanoi, on July 3, was to announce the release of three POWs in honor of the Fourth of July holiday. It took thirty-two days before the three were actually released and allowed to celebrate *their* independence—time that their captors spent trying to persuade them that the price of their freedom was to tell the folks back home about the humane treatment they had received. The chosen three were Air Force captain Wesley Rumble, Navy lieutenant Robert Frishman, both pilots, and Navy seaman Douglas Hegdahl who had been swept off his ship during a storm and picked up by the North Vietnamese. Each of the three had lost anywhere from twenty to sixty pounds while in captivity. Rumble, suffering from a back injury, had to be helped off the plane in New York, and reporters were told that he could not speak. He was immediately put on another plane to an Air Force hospital in California.

Frishman and Hegdahl were taken to Bethesda Naval Hospital outside Washington, D.C., where Laird met with them and happily learned that they were not about to be used by Hanoi as poster boys for a propaganda campaign. They had memorized the names of hundreds of POWs and insisted on verbally downloading their lists before answering any other questions in their debriefings. For Capen, that list alone made the Go Public Campaign a success.[8]

Support from the White House for the campaign remained lukewarm, but one unexpected ally emerged. Vice President Agnew was incensed by the way Hanoi had handled the release of the three—in particular the fact that the POWs were turned over to high-profile American antiwar activists who had escorted them home and who had praised Hanoi for its "humanitarian" policy toward POWs.[9] Agnew sent a top-secret memo to Laird speculating on the negative effect that selective POW releases into the hands of the "far left wing" could have on the remaining prisoners.

A month later Laird followed his hunch that Agnew might be a strong ally in the White House. He wrote Kissinger to suggest that, given the differences of opinion between the State and Defense Departments, the vice president be designated as "the principal authority on all issues of policy" concerning POWs. It took Kissinger two months to respond that Nixon had vetoed the Agnew idea.[10]

Laird was not surprised. The State Department and the National Security Council wanted to downplay the issue, and Agnew would have outranked them. Laird didn't give up on Agnew and continued to draft the vice president into the cause whenever he could. When Agnew made a tour of several nations in December 1969, Laird asked him to drop the POW issue into the conversation with any head of state who would listen.

Laird's special POW Task Force went fishing in the private sector for help. At its urging, in October 1969 the American Red Cross started a "Write Hanoi" campaign, and in November *Reader's Digest* published a story about the treatment of POWs and inserted a detachable postcard for readers to send as part of the Red Cross effort. Laird used his personal connections at the magazine to secure that article. He had cultivated a friendship with owner DeWitt Wallace, who occasionally tried to lure Laird away from politics with offers of a position in the magazine's executive ranks. (Laird would eventually accept Wallace's offer upon resignation from the Nixon administration in 1973.) More than 679,000 *Reader's Digest* postcards filled the mail bags that were sent to Hanoi.[11]

When Laird's POW Task Force enlisted the help of H. Ross Perot, Laird found the sharpest burr to put under the saddle of Hanoi. The indomitable Texas millionaire had not yet made his reputation in politics, but in the millionaires club he was known as one who would hang on to a cause like a bulldog on an ankle bone. Capen came up with the idea of having Perot fund a shipment of Christmas gift boxes to the POWs. Volunteers packed thirty tons of food, clothing, and medical supplies, and loaded them on a plane nicknamed "Peace on Earth." Perot had asked permission to land with his packages in North Vietnam, but he didn't wait for that approval before giving the order for the plane to take off. With a flurry of publicity at each refueling stop along the way, the plane finally arrived in Vientiane, Laos, where Perot got word that Hanoi had turned him down. Any Christmas packages, they said, would have to be sent through Moscow by regular mail, within ten days, in small boxes weighing no more than 6.6 pounds each.

If the North Vietnamese thought that would deter Perot, they didn't understand the American entrepreneurial spirit. Perot ordered the plane to Anchorage, Alaska, where volunteers were assembled in short order to break down the crates of supplies into smaller boxes, each addressed to the Hanoi post office, via Moscow. "Peace on Earth" got as far as Copenhagen before the Soviets refused permission for the plane to land in Moscow. In all, the plane carried its cargo more than thirty-five thousand miles, irritating the North Vietnamese at every stop.[12]

Perot, keenly aware of the publicity value of his attempts to tweak Hanoi, continued the barrage in 1970 with an offer to buy the POWs' freedom for $100 million in food and medicine for the North Vietnamese people. Hanoi did not take Perot up on the offer. Then he collected a planeload of reporters and took them to South Vietnam for a tour of prison camps where captured North Vietnamese soldiers were held. Perot filmed the enemy prisoners and collected letters for their families, then petitioned Hanoi for permission to fly there to deliver the missives. Again Hanoi refused. Undaunted, Perot continued to find ways to keep the POWs in the public eye. He testified before Congress, built replicas of POW cells and put them on display in the Capitol rotunda, paid for public opinion polls to track awareness of the issue, and repeatedly financed POW advocates in travel to foreign countries to make a case for the prisoners.

◇

Without much cooperation from the White House, Laird doggedly pressed Nixon to appoint a "special presidential emissary" on POW issues. His first nominee was the Reverend Billy Graham, whom Laird would have loved to see go head-to-head with the double-talking North Vietnamese delegates in Paris. But the White House quashed the idea. Then Laird turned to former astronaut Frank Borman, commander of Apollo 8 on a lunar orbit mission. By 1970 when Laird was looking him over, Borman was a vice president at Eastern Airlines—not the high-profile celebrity Laird had hoped for but a respected businessman and a big name in the space program. With Nixon's approval, Borman was given the assignment and took off on an around-the-world mission to buttonhole twelve heads of state. When he returned, he testified before Congress in an attempt to stir them and the public to show more concern for the POWs. Borman's mission was not a huge success, but Laird was grateful for every small step in the Go Public Campaign. There was never another special emissary appointed.

Although in retrospect Laird spoke fondly of Nixon's support for the Go Public Campaign, in reality the president remained mostly detached from the POW issue, in part because of Kissinger's worries about the peace talks. But Laird never eased the pressure on Nixon. He hounded the president in memos to include the POWs in presidential speeches and remarks at press conferences. Something as simple as having the president meet with aggrieved POW wives required weeks of negotiations between Laird and the White House. When that meeting finally came off on December 12, 1969, it produced the first public speech Nixon had made in office specifically about the POWs. In six short paragraphs, Nixon praised the wives and reproved the North Vietnamese: "Insofar as the treatment of prisoners is concerned, it would probably not be inaccurate to say that the record in this war is one of the most unconscionable in the history of warfare."[13]

The visible elements of the Go Public Campaign must have seemed like baby steps to those who didn't understand the delicate dance going on between Laird and the White House. Gradually more prisoner lists were released, more mail allowed, and a few prisoners released. But it was not until all the POWs came home in 1973 that Laird knew the full effect of the Go Public Campaign. The men spoke and wrote of a change that came about slowly, beginning in mid-1969, when their treatment improved, torture lessened, and most importantly, they were grouped together in common cells more often than in solitary confinement. While some speculated that the death of Ho Chi Minh in 1969 changed the rules, Laird was convinced the improved treatment was due in large part to his insistence that the POW issue be brought out of the shadows and into the glare of worldwide public scrutiny.

So passionate was Laird about the American POWs that in late 1970 he gave the go-ahead for a gallant rescue attempt, which was at once a spectacular success and a disappointing failure. The target was a prison camp called Son Tay deep in North Vietnam, just twenty-three miles west of Hanoi. Since May 1968, American POWs had been held at Son Tay under harsh conditions of torture and deprivation. Hoping that U.S. reconnaissance planes might overfly the camp occasionally, the prisoners methodically spelled out a coded appeal for a rescue in the arrangement of rock piles and ditches they worked on around the camp. They even hung their laundry in patterns that would call attention from a bird's-eye view. Their coded message was that fifty-five men were housed at Son Tay, and they wanted someone to come and get them. (Laird said the Son Tay prisoners also got their appeal out using another method, which is still classified.)

Their plea was decoded at the Pentagon in the spring of 1970, and Laird authorized planning to begin for a rescue raid on the camp. Search-and-rescue operations for downed pilots were common within hours after crashes, but never had U.S. soldiers crossed into North Vietnam to shoot up a POW camp and take the prisoners home. In South Vietnam there had been just under one hundred attempted raids on Viet Cong camps to rescue American and allied prisoners, but they had netted only one U.S. soldier, and he died two weeks later of wounds sustained from enemy gunfire during the rescue.

The secrecy around the Son Tay raid would be so tight that not even the president would be told until four months into the planning. Laird and Adm. Tom Moorer of the Joint Chiefs, along with Colonel Pursley, were the only ones in the top tier at the Pentagon who knew what was going on. Moorer did not tell the rest of the chiefs. Even the fifty-nine men who pulled off the raid trained for three months and were not told the nature of their mission until the day before they took off in helicopters bound for Son Tay. Air force brigadier general Leroy Manor commanded the overall operation, and Army colonel Arthur "Bull" Simons led the search-and-rescue team.

On September 24, 1970, General Manor told Laird that the team was close to being ready. It was time for Laird to tell the president. Five days later Nixon and Laird were on a trip to Europe and had concluded an audience with Pope Paul VI at the Vatican when they retired for the night to the *Saratoga*, an aircraft carrier in the Mediterranean. It was there that Laird took Nixon aside and explained the plans for the Son Tay raid. In typical Laird fashion, he did not directly ask permission. He told Nixon that absent a presidential objection, he would go ahead with the plan. Nixon's reply, as Laird remembered it, was, "I think it's just fine. Go ahead."

On November 18, with the Son Tay raiders already on their way to Southeast Asia, Admiral Moorer came to the Oval Office with his briefing charts and faced Nixon, Kissinger, Laird, Rogers, and CIA director Richard Helms. After Moorer presented the military aspects of the raid, Laird briefed Nixon on what was known about the conditions the POWs endured. Nixon asked a few questions and said he had to think about it. The next day, at a meeting of the National Security Council in a room full of people who knew nothing about the raid, Nixon passed a note to Laird telling him to go ahead with the mission. "Mel, as I told Moorer after our meeting yesterday regardless of results, the men on this project have my complete backing and there will be no second guessing if the plan fails. It is worth the risk and the planning is superb. I will be at Camp David Saturday. I would like for you to call me as soon as you have anything to report." The note was unsigned.[14]

The outcome of the Son Tay raid was already cast in stone, but no one in Washington knew it. The prisoners had been moved out of the camp in July because of a flood on a nearby river. The day before the raid, the DIA got word from a sometimes-reliable agent in North Vietnam that the prisoners had indeed been moved, but that information was countered by the most recent reconnaissance flights over the camp that showed a resurgence of activity at Son Tay. Laird weighed the new information and informed Nixon. Together they decided the risk was worth it. The raid would go ahead. Laird had always told Simons and Manor that there was at best a fifty-fifty chance that POWs were in the camp, and the two military men said that was enough for them to go ahead.

On November 19 the helicopters carrying the Son Tay raiders took off from Thailand at 11:25 p.m. for the three-hour flight over Laos and into North Vietnam. Simultaneously, in what would be a more controversial play than the raid itself, Navy jets from aircraft carriers in the Tonkin Gulf took off for the first large-scale bombing raid over North Vietnam since Johnson halted such bombing two years before. The jets that buzzed Hanoi carried only flares, but planes that flew farther south dropped live bombs. It was a diversion to draw attention away from the helicopters coming into North Vietnam from the west.

The diversion worked. The arrival of the American helicopters at Son Tay at 2 a.m. was a complete surprise to the soldiers guarding the compound. One helicopter was deliberately crash-landed into the center of the camp so the raiders could clear away the first resistance from inside. Then the other helicopters landed outside the fence, and the American forces stormed in, mowing down their stunned enemy. It took just over twenty minutes for the raiders to search the camp, determine that there were no POWs, and leave the way they came.

A message, "negative POWs," was flashed to General Manor waiting at a command post in South Vietnam, and from there relayed to the Pentagon's National Military Command Center. Laird had been waiting in his office one floor above the command center along with CIA director Helms. A squawk box in the office picked up communications from downstairs, and when the first message came through that the raiders were all coming out alive, Laird and Helms hurried to the command center to learn more. When they arrived, they were told there were no prisoners. Stonefaced, Laird called Nixon at Camp David and reported the outcome.

As Laird walked back to his office, his stoic demeanor belied the strategy already roiling in his head. He had to get on top of the public reaction and turn the perception from failure to the heroic and compassionate effort he genuinely believed the mission had been. As far as he was concerned, the raid had been a success. The raiders had done their job perfectly, and with no casualties. The fact that there were no POWs at Son Tay was of only secondary interest to Laird at that moment. "I was absolutely relieved," he later recalled. "I thought [the raiders] might all be shot up."

Laird never thought of Son Tay as a public relations disaster. Even thirty years later, as he prepared for a reunion with the Son Tay raiders, he bristled at the idea that the outcome of the raid might have been tough to justify. "I didn't have any problem with explaining it to the public. I'd have gone any place to talk about what those men did. It really threw the North off base that we could come in that close without being detected. I loved that. As long as those people got out safe, I just loved it." Of the raiders, Laird said emotionally, "They're my boys."

Not only was he proud of what the men had done, but at the time he knew it would be impossible to keep it a secret. Colonel Simons and General Manor returned to Washington, and the two reluctant soldiers were escorted by Laird into the Pentagon press room. They stood by with squared shoulders and grim faces while Laird explained the rescue attempt. The reporters deluged Simons and Manor with questions, many of which were answered gruffly with, "I can't answer that." Laird had brought them to the press to showcase their heroism, but the two were having none of it. They were paid to keep secrets and weren't about to discuss the raid in any detail, nor did they appreciate the attention, especially when they had no POWS to show for their effort. The fearsome looking and aptly nicknamed "Bull" Simons by his mere appearance discouraged the questioning. After a few minutes of watching the officers growl, "Yes," "No," and "I can't answer that," Laird stepped in to give the reporters some complete sentences and paragraphs they could quote.[15]

Laird's antiwar nemesis on the Senate Foreign Relations Committee, William Fulbright, called the next morning, demanding that Laird appear before the committee the following week and explain what had gone wrong. Unwilling to let a week go by in which the surprise in Congress would foment into rage, Laird said, "I'm available now."

"I can't do it now," Fulbright responded.

"Well, I can't come up next week," Laird said. "I'm just going to tell the press that I offered to come up today to be before your committee and you refused."

Fulbright capitulated, and Laird hurried up to the Senate for one of the more caustic confrontations he would have with Fulbright during his four years as defense secretary. With uncharacteristic passion, Laird said, "As it became clear to me that Hanoi, week after week, month after month, and year after year, was rebuffing our efforts at Paris . . . I could not ignore the fact that our men were dying in captivity. Mr. Chairman, I want this committee to know that I have not faced a more challenging decision since I have been Secretary of Defense. I concluded that there was no other acceptable alternative than to recommend that the volunteer force . . . should be authorized to make a valiant attempt to save their fellow Americans. I have said and I want to repeat today, that it is my firm belief that if there had been prisoners of war at Son Tay, they would be free men today."

Fulbright berated Laird for allowing the raid of an empty POW camp and blamed faulty intelligence for the outcome. The intelligence was just fine, Laird came back. The raiders knew the location of the camp, the layout of the buildings, the location of surface-to-air missiles nearby, the closest military installations, and the capability of the enemy's radar. "The intelligence for this mission was excellent, except for our not having a camera that would see through the rooftop of buildings," Laird said. He would repeat the quip many times in the next few days whenever he was challenged about the quality of the intelligence. Fulbright didn't want to hear Laird's recitation of intelligence successes. "I do not think this is relevant," he said. "There weren't any prisoners there. What difference does it make?"

"What we have done here has shown all of these prisoners in North Vietnam that America does care," Laird replied.

Fulbright bristled. "Was there any doubt that America cares about them? I did not know that there was any doubt."

"Yes, there was a doubt," said Laird.[16]

Laird was battered for weeks over the raid by the press and opponents on Capitol Hill, and for a time he seemed to stand alone in his support of the raid. Even the CIA, which had been in on the planning from the beginning, floated the story that it had not been informed, thus brushing off the accusations of faulty intelligence about the camp. But Laird stuck to his story that he had a duty to the POWs. As he told Fulbright, "If this country is willing to abandon its military men to death and captivity, we will have truly lost our national morality and our humanity . . . I have no regrets about [the raid] being recommended. My only regret is that we did not bring out any prisoners."

12

Dueling Machiavellis

IN ANY POLITICAL ADMINISTRATION the question of who gets credit and who takes blame looms large. Power is often maintained through illusion and manipulation. During the Nixon years, the masters of the game were the equally matched Laird and Kissinger. In the first year they quickly became each other's favorite sparring partner. Theirs was a vigorous competition for turf and just plain one-upmanship. "Laird acted on the assumption that he had a Constitutional right to seek to outsmart and outmaneuver anyone with whom his office brought him into contact," Kissinger later wrote. "This was partly a game and partly the effort of a seasoned politician to protect his options." The highly adroit National Security advisor observed that Laird's "maneuvers . . . were conducted with all the artistry of a Kabuki play, with an admixture of the Florentine court politics of the fifteenth century."[1]

Kissinger once told a gathering honoring Laird in Wisconsin,

> No one man can handle Mel Laird. So I always had some deputy who had to do the preliminary skirmishing so that I might find out at least where the battlefield was. And there were a number of guidelines I gave to my associates:
>
> Guideline One: Mel Laird is extremely smart.
>
> Guideline Two: he *knows* he's extremely smart.
>
> Guideline Three: he will let *you* know he's extremely smart.
>
> Guideline Four: it is much less painful to do what he wants than to refuse what he wants.[2]

What Laird wanted was quite often the same as what Kissinger wanted, but four major exceptions became evident in the first year. Laird wanted (1) sizable and swift American troop withdrawals from Vietnam; (2) national acknowledgment of the POWs and international pressure for more humane treatment; (3) unhesitating movement from the draft to an all-volunteer force; and (4) a commitment to open government, which fully informs the public on all important matters. That Laird won on the first three goals was the more historically significant because it was not only Kissinger but Nixon who opposed him. Laird's loss on the issue of "open government" became a painful one. The paranoid penchant for secrecy that led Nixon and Kissinger to lie about the bombing of Cambodia and other actions redounded to the administration's discredit and later made Nixon's resignation inevitable.

The battle lines were effectively drawn when Kissinger moved to strengthen the National Security Council as the engine of national security policy. Although he said it was not his intention at first, every subsequent move by Kissinger was an attempt to make him the majordomo of national security. By tradition and portfolio, the secretary of state is supposed to be the president's chief foreign policy advisor, and the secretary of defense his chief military policy advisor. As the administration began, political observers reckoned that Laird would become the dominant advisor. "You've got to get up awful early in the morning to outmaneuver him," observed a Democratic opponent in the *New York Times*. "You'd better have a strong Secretary of State to balance him."[3] But no prognosticator had yet divined the talent, brilliance, and design for power that the little-known Henry Kissinger would so effectively employ. As it turned out, it was Secretary of State Rogers who became the casualty.

"Henry was very smart, but Mel was smarter," observed George Shultz, who was a chief budget official in the Nixon administration and later President Reagan's secretary of state. "Mel enjoyed the bureaucratic in-fighting and was a match for Henry."[4] James Schlesinger was another eyewitness to Kissinger-Laird relationship because he was the White House budget official who specialized in national security and later served Nixon as CIA director and then secretary of defense. "Henry was just totally frustrated by Mel because Henry could manipulate almost everybody—but when he got to Mel, Mel outsmarted him as frequently as Henry was able to work with him," Schlesinger observed. "Henry—what shall I say—*handled* Bill Rogers over at State very effectively and had him handcuffed. But Mel was too damn slippery to be handcuffed."[5]

Kissinger became so unsettled with his inability to "handle" Laird that he frequently lost his temper over it. "The guys on the White House staff used to think that Laird's first name was, 'Son of a Bitch!' because [with Kissinger] it was 'Son of a bitch Laird did this!', or 'Son of a bitch Laird did that!'," recalled Ivan Selin, an assistant defense secretary under Laird.[6] White House chief of staff H. R. Haldeman's diary entries are replete with references to an unnerved Kissinger spouting oaths about Laird. One day in October 1969 Nixon confided to Haldeman that he was quite concerned "about K's [Kissinger's] attitude and wants to be sure we keep him upbeat. Can't let him overreact to each little aberration [from] Laird. K argues that you have to maintain tight discipline on the little things or you can't control the big ones. P [president] feels you should lose the ones that don't matter and save your strength and equity for the big battles that really count." Four days later, Nixon told Haldeman that the problem was becoming untenable. Kissinger was no longer able to effectively deal with Laird, and this "has become an issue. Wants me to make all this clear to K. Hard to do. [Kissinger] injects himself too much into everything, between P and cabinet officers, and they just won't buy it. So he becomes ineffective even at getting them to do what they already were ready to do."[7]

Laird's friend Jack Mills, who often traveled with him, recalled Kissinger's frequent telephonic interruptions of their golf games and other outings. "Mel and Kissinger always argued on the telephone. I could only hear one side, but it would go something like this: "'Henrrry. HENry. Now wait a minute, Henry. Don't give me that crap, Henry. You don't have to worry about that, Henry. You're acting like a child, Henry. Don't worry about it! Goddamn it, Henry, I said don't worry about that!'"[8]

Some of Kissinger's favorite appellations for Laird were "Machiavellian" and "devious." Kissinger wasn't alone in using such terms about Laird. In his memoirs, Nixon quoted Eisenhower telling Nixon in 1967 that of all the Republicans on the national scene, Laird was "the smartest of the lot, but he is too devious."[9] A "sneak" was the worst term Nixon aide John Ehrlichman remembered the president applying to Laird.[10]

"Mel enjoyed being devious," said former defense secretary Caspar Weinberger, a White House budget official during the Nixon administration, who was repeatedly outmaneuvered by Laird on defense budget issues. "If there were two ways to go to a particular destination, and one path was straight and the other went around many curves, Mel always picked the one that went around many curves."[11]

Kissinger was inevitably won over by Laird, primarily using humor and midwestern forthrightness. At one gathering to honor Laird, Kissinger concluded, "I think of him with *enormous* affection, only slightly tinged with exasperation."[12] In an insightful description of Laird in his memoirs, Kissinger wrote: "[W]hile Laird's maneuvers were often as Byzantine in their complexity or indirection as those of Nixon, he accomplished with verve and surprising goodwill what Nixon performed with grim determination and inward resentment. Laird liked to win, but unlike Nixon, derived no great pleasure from seeing someone else lose. There was about him a buoyancy and a rascally good humor that made working with him as satisfying as it could on occasion be maddening."[13]

Laird confessed he deliberately goaded Kissinger—in part because it was so much fun, and in part because he didn't think it was healthy for Kissinger to take himself so seriously. From his corner of the ring, Kissinger summarized the sparring in this way: "Provided he was allowed some reasonable range for saving face by maneuvering to a new position without embarrassment, Laird accepted bureaucratic setbacks without rancor. But he insisted on his day in court. In working with him, intellectual arguments were only marginally useful and direct orders were suicidal. I eventually learned that it was safest to begin a battle with Laird by closing off insofar as possible all his bureaucratic or congressional escape routes, provided I could figure them out, which was not always easy. Only then would I broach substance. But even with such tactics I lost as often as I won."[14]

In one attempt to get Kissinger's goat, Laird and his military assistant Robert Pursley had a stamp made that spelled out "BULLSHIT" in big letters. Both had noticed that when Kissinger came for breakfast meetings at the Pentagon, he would rubberneck trying to read Laird's private notes. So they stamped several memoranda Kissinger had sent Laird with the bright red BULLSHIT and then strategically placed the papers among others in Laird's notebook for the next breakfast meeting. "We thought Henry would see it and say, 'What is that?' And Mel was going to say, 'Why, we stamp all your stuff that way!'" explained Pursley. "Sure enough, when Mel turned to the first page, Henry saw it but didn't say a word. Not one word. Mel went over to the next one and so on, another Kissinger memo stamped BULLSHIT."[15] Kissinger didn't smile; he was clearly not amused. Larry Eagleburger, who was a longtime friend to both men, said, "That [story] is part of the whole Laird character that I like so much—namely, he could be serious, but he also had a playful streak that could, on occasion, lessen the tension."[16]

One more attribute of Laird's that bedeviled Kissinger was a certain obtuseness on Mel's part. "When Laird employed one of his favorite phrases, 'See what I mean?' there was no possible way of penetrating his meaning," Kissinger recounted. In fact, it became another guideline to his staffers for dealing with the defense secretary: "Guideline Five is, when Mel Laird says to you, 'You know what I mean?', there is no conceivable way you can possibly know what he means." In his own memoir, Kissinger wrote, "Laird would think nothing of coming to a White House meeting with the Joint Chiefs of Staff, supporting their position, then indicating his reservations privately to the President and me, only to work out a third approach later with [Congress.]"[17]

Many who worked with Laird remembered his "you-know-what-I-mean" patter. Barry Shillito, Laird's assistant secretary of defense suggested in retrospect that Laird himself didn't always know why he made one political move over another. "He always says, 'You know what I mean? You know what I mean? You know what I mean?' Nine times out of ten you may not have a clue as to what the hell he means," Shillito chuckled. "And often, I'm not sure he knows what he means either, but he's trying to get it out of you."[18]

Laird's canniness and his solid friendships made him one man in the administration who could not be fired, no matter how much he might circumvent the White House on issues. "Henry was particularly taken—almost mesmerized—by the power that Mel had with the Congress," Pursley said. "It was something that Henry couldn't dream of having, and the president himself didn't have. But Mel had it in spades, not only because Mel came from Congress, but because he continued to cultivate it on both sides of the aisle."[19] Ehrlichman, who was no friend of Laird's, underscored this point in his memoirs: "From time to time Henry Kissinger complained bitterly to Nixon, Haldeman and me about Laird's unscrupulous tactics. But Henry didn't demand Laird's firing, as he did Secretary of State William Rogers'. Laird was so effective with his old congressional cronies . . . that everyone realized he was irreplaceable."[20]

Indeed, Laird's influence in the Nixon administration was stronger in 1969 than Kissinger's. For all Kissinger's vaunted foreign policy expertise, it was Laird who was the more likely author of the defining foreign policy doctrine of his administration, the so-called Nixon Doctrine, which was unveiled at a presidential press conference in the South Pacific on July 25, 1969.

In July 1969 two Americans had landed on the moon. John F. Kennedy precipitated the race to the moon, and Lyndon Johnson and NASA's best made it happen, but Richard Nixon fully intended to bask in the glory of it as president. He wanted to witness the splashdown and greet the astronauts on their return to Earth, so he met them on the aircraft carrier USS *Hornet,* 950 miles southwest of Hawaii. For Nixon, it was the first stop of a twelve-day round-the-world tour. The next stop was the island of Guam, where Nixon held a "background" press conference on July 25. In an expansive mood,

Nixon told reporters that in order to ensure "no more Vietnams," the United States would reorder its foreign policy in Asia. America would keep all treaty commitments but would no longer furnish arms and men to friends who were fending off aggressors unless those friends first provided their own manpower to defend themselves. The exception was if that ally were attacked with nuclear weapons, then the United States would respond with nuclear weapons.

The announcement, which reporters dubbed the "Guam Doctrine," caught Kissinger by complete surprise. He and Nixon had discussed Asia strategies in preparation for a speech, but Kissinger was not the author of the Guam Doctrine, as some historians have suggested.[21] Laird was neither surprised nor upset when he got news of Nixon's unilateral announcement of a new Asia policy, because it was a policy he had been urging upon Nixon since 1967. The principles Nixon espoused in the doctrine were an outgrowth of the Vietnamization policy Laird had first called "de-Americanization" when he had it inserted in the 1968 Republican Party platform. Laird himself said he promoted the basis of the doctrine in memoranda to Nixon prior to the pronouncement in Guam.[22]

When the first news of Nixon's unexpected pronouncement reached Washington, Laird seized upon it to promote his Vietnamization program. He had his public affairs aides hold a press conference and firmly pin the Guam Doctrine on the president by renaming it the "Nixon Doctrine." They further fleshed out the doctrine with three "pillars" that Nixon had not precisely uttered; strength, partnership, and a willingness to negotiate. The Nixon Doctrine, as polished by Laird's staff, meant that the United States was committed to strengthening its own defense, helping its allies only if they were willing to help themselves, and negotiating a way out of combat whenever possible.

The Nixon Doctrine might well have been called the Laird Doctrine for its most dogged sponsor. He drove it home, almost ad nauseam, at his Monday meetings with the Joint Chiefs and top staff, inserting it in many of their discussions. Laird also pounded the pulpit for the Nixon Doctrine whenever he was asked to make a speech. And when he forgot to mention it, his staff would remind him. They once ordered a two-layer birthday cake for him with three pillars holding up the top layer. If Laird told staffers that he was at a loss for words at any particular speaking engagement, they would enthusiastically reply, "Give them the Pillars Speech!"

Laird pointed out in speeches that the Nixon Doctrine meant that the era of interventionism, which President Truman had begun, had been replaced

by a new pragmatic era of limits. "America will no longer try to play policeman to the world," he would say. "Instead, we will expect other nations to
provide more cops on the beat in their own neighborhoods."[23] One of Laird's
practical initiatives to further that goal was a program to "loan" ships to poorer
allies such as Turkey, Greece, and the Republic of China (Taiwan). Taiwan
willingly took over from America the patrolling of the straits between their
nation and mainland China after the loan of three submarines and other
American ships. One of those ships was the destroyer USS *Maddox*. Laird
learned that the *Maddox* was to be decommissioned in 1972; instead of having it "scrapped for razor blades," he transferred it to Taiwan as both a strong
personal and political symbol of his commitment to the new Nixon Doctrine.
(Renamed the *Po Yang*, the storied destroyer patrolled the Straits of Taiwan
until 1985.)[24]

Kissinger's stock in trade was the secret deal, which meant keeping even cabinet secretaries in the dark. The first of the "back channels" Kissinger opened
in international negotiations came under the cover provided by Nixon's
round-the-world trip in the summer of 1969. After stops in the Pacific area,
India, Pakistan, and Romania, Kissinger split off from the president and went
to Paris. There, on August 4 he secretly sat down with Hanoi's representative,
Xuan Thuy, in a private apartment using the multilingual military attaché
at the embassy, Gen. Vernon Walters, as his interpreter. Walters's boss, the
secretary of defense, was not to be told.

The fact that Nixon and Kissinger deliberately kept Laird out of the loop
did not mean he was not "in the know." Laird had an extensive circle of friends
throughout the administration. He also tended to inspire loyalty for his square
dealings. Neither Kissinger nor Nixon could make a significant national security move without involving any military assets or without using an individual who was likely to report back to Laird.

A month after Kissinger's Paris meeting, the extent of Laird's reach became
apparent to Nixon and Kissinger. On September 12, after dinner at Camp
David, Nixon had a free-ranging discussion with White House staffers about
an incident in Vietnam where some Green Berets had been charged with
murdering a purported North Vietnamese spy. Haldeman recorded in his
diary: "Tried to call Admiral McCain to get his view, and Laird found out,
and called K, very upset that we hadn't gone to him instead." Haldeman later
added to his diary: "The fact that Laird apparently knew immediately of our
attempt to call McCain from Camp David gave us something new to worry
about. Were the Camp David phones tapped for the Defense Department?"[25]

John Ehrlichman elaborated on the spasm of paranoia that gripped Nixon and Kissinger: "The Camp David operators were all Army enlisted men and their supervisors were Army officers. The only question was: how closely did Mel Laird monitor the President and the rest of us at Camp David when we called someone on his Army telephone system? Did he just keep track of whom we called, or did he also know what was said?"[26] While Laird does not remember how he learned of the attempted contact with McCain, it was not because he had the Camp David phone system bugged. He never wiretapped anyone—unlike Kissinger, who not only wiretapped his own aides but one of Laird's, too.

Not long after he had ferried Nixon around the world in the summer of 1969, Col. Ralph Albertazzie, the pilot of Air Force One, got an interesting call from Col. James D. (Don) Hughes, chief of the White House Military Office. "Wander down here to the White House," Hughes advised his subordinate. "Act like you're just visiting people. Don't let anybody know that you're on any particular mission. But eventually show up in the Roosevelt Room about 2 o'clock." Albertazzie followed the instructions and seated himself at the mahogany table in the room near the Oval Office. Hughes was already there, as was Alexander Haig. When Kissinger arrived, it was evident that he had called the meeting. He revealed that he was in the process of secretly negotiating peace with the North Vietnamese. For future talks, he needed Albertazzie to clandestinely fly him to Europe in Air Force One or its backup plane.

"The president does not want the secretary of the defense or the Joint Chiefs to know about these trips or talks," Kissinger said, his eyes boring into the military pilot. Nor was the secretary of state or the CIA director to be informed. It was up to Albertazzie and Hughes to figure out how that could be accomplished, Kissinger challenged, before leaving the room. Albertazzie didn't question the orders he had received from his commander in chief via Kissinger. But how to accomplish the task was something else altogether. "Well, Ralph, all you have to do is concoct the perfect alibi for the world's best known airplane," Hughes smiled as they walked to the door. "It better be good."

Albertazzie soon came up with the answer. The Johnson administration had installed a $25 million voice-scrambler system aboard Air Force One that needed substantial testing before the president could rely upon it. So the cover story became that the trips to Europe were training missions to test the long-distance voice-scrambler communications capability.

Starting in February 1970 Albertazzie flew Kissinger in the presidential planes to France, Germany, and England, on thirteen clandestine missions.[27] While both Albertazzie and Hughes have insisted they did not tell Laird about the flights, Laird himself said he knew about every one of them because he had more than one "source" who informed him about how his military planes—the presidential planes were part of the Defense Department—were being used.

Laird not only knew about every one of Kissinger's flights, but he knew precisely what Kissinger and the North Vietnamese had said in each secret meeting. Laird's ace-in-the-hole was the National Security Agency, a huge Department of Defense communications espionage agency headquartered at Fort Meade, Maryland. The NSA routinely intercepted messages sent from North Vietnam's Paris offices to Hanoi. Each time Kissinger clandestinely spoke or communicated with the North Vietnamese, they would dutifully report what had occurred back to their superiors in Hanoi. What few knew— even in the highest levels of government—was that the NSA's geniuses had cracked the North Vietnamese code and could read everything transmitted by Hanoi's representatives at the peace talks with Kissinger. Because it needed to be a closely held secret, Laird ordered Admiral Noel Gayler, the head of NSA, to send a man to Laird's office with every such decoded intercept as soon as it was ready.

When Kissinger was privately informed of this in early 2001, he was astonished. He never knew the NSA had decrypted intercepts of the North Vietnamese reports of his talks, so he had never seen the transcripts. Trying to keep his composure, Kissinger pointedly asked: "It raises the interesting question: Why did he [Laird] never send those reports over to the White House?"

Kissinger later called Laird to complain. "I thought you always shared with me, Mel." Laird responded that it was not his responsibility to provide NSA intelligence to Kissinger. After he had read the transcripts, Laird had regularly sent the NSA courier to the Oval Office to wait while the president personally read the intercepts. So it was Nixon who had not shared the critical intelligence with his national security advisor. "Goddamn that Nixon!" Kissinger half-sputtered and half-laughed. "That son of a bitch just wanted to have these so he could check up on me!"

The tale of the NSA intercepts adds to evidence that Nixon and Kissinger could never significantly ignore Laird, even though he might sometimes oppose their maneuvers. And any expectation that they could keep him in the dark was folly.

~

The Nixon administration's penchant for secret machinations spilled over into the antiwar movement. Protests were sometimes triggered by an exposure of secrets, and the public came to mistrust Nixon as much as he himself mistrusted anyone outside his tight circle. In contrast, Laird seemed almost to embrace the "great unwashed" culture of America's youth in the 1960s.

By the time Laird became secretary of defense in 1969, the majority of America's young people were against the war. None of Laird's own three children were happy about his acceptance of the job of secretary of defense. "I think you're taking the worst job in the world," his oldest son John told him on the phone. Attending Wisconsin University in Eau Claire, John was already active in the local antiwar movement.[28] Mel's daughter, Alison, in her senior year of high school, was feeling the first stirrings of activism against the war. Characteristically, their father had encouraged the children to follow their consciences. David Frost asked Laird in late 1970 what he would be doing if he were twenty, like his son John, and opposed to the war. "I would speak out," Laird responded. "I told my son that I expected him to speak out on the way he felt about the various issues of the day. This is something that we have discussed in our family on many occasions. We have heated discussions."[29]

Alison recalled, "One of the most important things he taught us was to believe in yourself and do what you believe. Speak out. You can't sit there and tell everybody that you think everything is terrible that's happening if you're not going to do something about it. He made you very much an activist and a volunteer." At her chosen schools, Virginia Intermount in Bristol, Virginia, and then the University of Tennessee, her name cost her friendships despite her own protest of the war. The war "was very unpopular around the college campus, and it got personal. There were friends and people that came to me and were angry because their brothers or boyfriends . . . had died in Vietnam." So they blamed her father, and Alison by extension.

Laird's youngest child, David, was not silent either. *Avante-Garde* magazine asked high school newspaper editors in Washington to query thirty children of prominent Nixon administration policymakers on their opinions. Twenty declined to comment; only one of the ten who did comment—the son of Laird's assistant secretary for International Security Affairs Warren Nutter—favored the war. The magazine's editor held a press conference on the lawn of the Laird home, handing out copies of the survey titled, "The Sins of Their Fathers." Among the ten who offered an opinion was David Laird, who said: "I'm against the war in Vietnam. I think the United States has learned that it shouldn't get into another war like this ever again."[30]

As his family and closest friends knew, Melvin Laird had a genuine love for America's youth—however outspoken, and that allowed him to understand and even sympathize with the youthful antiwar movement. His affection and respect would be shown time and again in his years at the Pentagon. Of the triumvirate running the Vietnam War—Nixon, Kissinger, Laird—the secretary of defense was the only one to bridge the generation gap. "I happen to believe that the generation gap is a vastly overrated phenomenon," Laird said in an April 1971 speech. "Most young people do not reject the values that our nation has proclaimed since the beginning of its history. Rather, they complain that our actions too often violate these principles—or that we are moving too slowly to realize them. . . . Most young people . . . understand the difference between dissent and disruption. They know the difference between reasoned argument and unreasoning violence."[31]

For security reasons, Alison and David Laird attended private schools while their father was secretary of defense. And as a regular recipient of death threats, Laird had reason for security concerns about his family. At the Pentagon, and when Laird traveled, the man in charge of his security, Lt. Col. Joe Zaice, remembered the first half of 1969 as fairly safe. Zaice, who served nine secretaries of defense, said, "The first time my life was threatened was when I went out to Marshfield with Secretary Laird and he drove."[32] Laird had gone home for Mother's Day, and Zaice and advance man Julian Levine had attended Presbyterian services with the Lairds. ("Being a nice Jewish boy, and Joe Zaice a nice Catholic boy, we used to enjoy going to the Presbyterian church in Marshfield," Levine remembered with a laugh.[33]) After the services, Laird insisted on driving home. "I offered to drive, but he wouldn't let me," Zaice recalled. "It was a macho thing. We got in the car, and he ran through three stop signs without ever seeing them. That was an exciting time. I was in the back with Mrs. [Helen] Laird, who was a lovely woman, a delight and a card. But she was screaming and yelling at him. I just kept my mouth shut. Yes, that was the first time my life was ever threatened."[34]

That spring of 1969 there was one truly life-threatening incident. It also had to do with transportation, not a demonstration. The occasion was an April 26 speech at small Saint Leo College near Dade City, Florida. Laird enjoyed going to colleges and "mixing it up" with students. After the speech, an Army Huey helicopter lifted off with the secretary and his party—a half-dozen passengers including two congressmen and high-level military officials. About twenty miles north of Tampa, Zaice saw—and thought he smelled—smoke. As a precautionary measure, the crew set the helicopter down on the median strip of a busy interstate, I-75. They couldn't locate the trouble, which was later determined to be a short circuit.[35] At the time, the crew and passengers concluded that Zaice had mistakenly cried "fire" when it was only smoke from a passenger's pipe.

Within minutes, they were in a very dangerous situation as the helicopter lifted off again. Laird and Zaice recall an explosion and sparks shooting through the inside of the helicopter, lighting up the dark night air as the helicopter rotors struck some power lines. The Huey lurched sideways and nearly flipped over before the crew was able to bounce it to the ground near a ditch. At that point, the passengers unceremoniously bolted off the crippled craft, order of military rank be damned. A nearby escort helicopter took them to safety, with everyone concerned that the first copter might explode.

"We were all running, to be perfectly honest with you," Zaice said. A fairly fit Laird somehow got in the lead, and Zaice wasn't sure the secretary could see he was about to run into the blades of the second chopper. "I yelled to him, but nobody could hear me. The blades on both choppers were running. So I just ran after him and tackled him." A dazed Laird got up and carefully walked around the blades, boarded the helicopter, and continued safely to MacDill Air Force Base for the plane ride back to Washington.[36] Zaice was convinced the if he had not acted, Laird might have been beheaded.

⁓

On October 7, 1969, Laird became the first secretary of defense ever to address a national convention of the AFL-CIO. He had a two-decade relationship with its chief George Meany, and thus had been invited to speak at the convention in Atlantic City, New Jersey. "I cannot promise a miraculous end to the war," Laird told the labor leaders. "I cannot tell you how or when the war in Vietnam will end. It has been my policy in office not to make optimistic forecasts—there have been too many of those." When he finished, he was given a standing ovation. Then the convention's one thousand delegates, representing thirteen million AFL-CIO members, passed a resolution supporting the Laird-Nixon plan of Vietnamization and diplomatic negotiation to end the war. Only one delegate voted against it. Afterwards, Meany remarked a bit wryly to his friend that this was the one group in America that understood the necessity of negotiating from strength.[37] (The next day, Laird received a thank-you note from Nixon for "the strong and exceptionally effective explanation of our Vietnam policy you gave to the AFL/CIO," which he felt was "right on the mark."[38])

The Nixon administration was now bracing for a planned nationwide protest on October 15, 1969, fashioned by organizers as a Vietnam Moratorium Day. The work of the moratorium was being done by thousands of volunteers who were inspiring involvement in hundreds of communities across the country, including Eau Claire, Wisconsin, where one of the student leaders, John Laird, got more attention than he wanted. With sensitivity for his father's position, he had originally intended to keep a low profile. A political science professor alerted the local press that the secretary of defense's own son would march against the war on the fifteenth.[39] John Laird told a local newspaper, "I think everybody should be against the war." Did his father know he'd be marching? Yes, and he hadn't objected. What about his father's position? John said his dad "is doing the best job I think he possibly can. He thinks we're under a commitment [to South Vietnam] and he is trying to fulfill that commitment as well as he can."[40]

Moratorium Day was a spectacular success for the organizers, marred only by a general lack of live TV coverage. The coast-to-coast event was declared the largest public protest against the war to date. In Eau Claire, John Laird marched with thousands of fellow students and townspeople, a *Newsweek* reporter in step behind him. "He thought he was going to get this great big story," John said, but young Laird kept it low key. On Moratorium Day, the *Washington Post* ran a feature story on John's dissent. The newspaper acknowledged that he had been "reluctant to even talk" to them because he had been "hounded by television, newspaper and magazine reporters" trying to find a "big generation gap, father-son conflict," which didn't exist.[41] After Moratorium Day, John turned down lucrative offers from colleges to speak. He routinely told them that if they wanted a war protestor to speak, they could ask students on their own campuses.

Melvin Laird says he was never offended by his children's antiwar activities. "I got demonstrated against. I got blood thrown at me. But not by my kids. I think John was very responsible in his objection to certain parts of the war. I understood that. Besides, they always defended the old man. They've always been very supportive." John Laird learned something from his brief celebrity status: "I have friends that really haven't talked to their parents since the late 1960s, early 1970s. The Vietnam War divided their family so much that they still really haven't talked to each other." Not so with his father. "My Dad's been my best friend pretty much all my life. He still is."

Nixon was intent on making it appear that his administration was not cowed but was conducting business as usual on Moratorium Day. He held a National Security Council meeting at 10 a.m. and then asked the secretaries of defense and state to stay behind. The president was privately concerned about their "softness," even though he did not voice that to them. According to H. R. Haldeman's notes, Nixon's intent after the meeting was "to try to get them in line about Vietnam and [the] November 3 speech." (Nixon had previously announced that he would give a major policy speech about the war on that date.) Both Nixon and Kissinger, though, knowing John Laird would be marching against the war that day, made the mistake of needling the defense secretary about his inability to muzzle his own son. "I told them it was none of their business," Laird recalled. "I said that's the way John felt and I supported him. They never brought it up again."

That evening Laird got away from the office early enough for dinner with his wife. The protestors happened to plan their first Moratorium Day on his wedding anniversary, and Laird wasn't about to let a national demonstration get in the way of celebrating twenty-four years of marriage.

The distance between the Nixon-Kissinger-Agnew condemnatory axis and the Laird-Rogers conciliatory mind-set was starkly evident on October 19 and 20. At a New Orleans Republican fund-raising dinner on October 19, Agnew charged that the moratorium had been "encouraged by an effete corps of impudent snobs who characterize themselves as intellectuals." He warned that the next protest scheduled for November would be "wilder [and] more violent" because of the "hard-core dissidents and professional anarchists" within the antiwar movement. On the twentieth, at an awards dinner, Secretary Rogers praised many of those who participated, who "wished principally to register dramatic but dignified expression of their deep concern for peace in Vietnam."[42]

In late October 1969 Laird took his Vietnamization show on the road to his biennial "Laird Youth Leadership Conference" for high school students meeting at Wisconsin State University at Stevens Point. Laird had begun hosting the conferences when he was in Congress, and he used his influence to attract speakers from the highest ranks of government. So wide was the gap between the Nixon administration and the nation's colleges, that the *Washington Star* declared in advance "it will be the first time a high official closely connected with the Nixon administration's Vietnam war policy has exposed himself to such a forum." Added the *Wall Street Journal*, "the stage was set . . . for a unique showdown between young critics and old politician Laird . . . a rare opportunity for tomorrow's leaders to take pot shots at today's."[43]

As Laird entered the university field house on October 27, he smiled and nodded a greeting to the three dozen antiwar protestors sporting homemade signs, such as "Nixon-Laird, Blood Brothers." Laird's mother, who was with him that day, was upset that her son was being labeled a murderer, but Laird seemed energized by the protestors. As expected, the dominant subject of the hour-long question-and-answer period with the 250 top high school students was Vietnam. The students were prepared with earnest, often well-informed questions and criticisms. Laird reminded them that as their congressman, he had opposed large-scale U.S. involvement in Vietnam. "I want you to know that I will judge whether I have been a success as Secretary of Defense on the basis of whether this war is ended and whether these sacrifices and these deaths can be stopped."[44]

Three days later, Thursday, October 30, Laird was part of a unique brainstorming session at the White House. The president wanted help on his upcoming speech, so he summoned Laird, Rogers, and Attorney General John Mitchell, picking their brains for two hours. One of Laird's main points was that Nixon should focus on the positive aspects of Vietnamization and peace talks in Paris. The televised address, which Nixon personally wrote and fretted over for weeks, became known as the "Silent Majority" speech.[45] In Nixon's view, it was a raging success. Knowing that polls had consistently shown the majority of Americans favored his Vietnam War policies, Nixon offered no new proposals. Instead, he issued a direct plea to "the great silent majority of my fellow Americans" for support. They responded, flooding the White House with eighty thousand telegrams, calls, and letters of support. A Gallup poll taken among those who watched the speech found that 77 percent supported Nixon's view.[46]

But the president had accomplished this by deliberately alienating America's youth in one of the most divisive addresses any president has ever made. In essence, he depicted the antiwar demonstrators as an enemy who must be silenced. "North Vietnam cannot defeat or humiliate the United States. Only Americans can do that," the president said, and there was no mystery as to what Americans he was talking about. To the silent majority, he pledged not "to be dictated [to] by the minority who hold that point of view and who try to impose it on the nation by mounting demonstrations in the street." If he allowed "a vocal minority, however fervent its cause, [to] prevail over reason and the will of the majority, this nation has no future as a free society."

~

The organizers of the first Moratorium Day decided they would hold one every month. At Laird's November 10 staff meeting, he made sure everyone knew civilians would be in charge of keeping order during the protest scheduled for that week. Military troops would be pre-positioned and ready if needed. "We need to make sure all our command lines work well, and there are no misunderstandings," Laird told his staff at the meeting. "Requests for troops are to go to the Military Commander and not directly to the troops. Civilians are in charge."[47]

The "March Against Death," began on Thursday and lasted for forty hours leading up to the second Moratorium Day, scheduled for Saturday, November 15. From Arlington National Cemetery to the Capitol, the march was solemn and impressive in the freezing rain. Six drummers beat out a funereal cadence as the march began across the Arlington Memorial Bridge, some twelve hundred marchers passing over the bridge every hour. Each of the forty-five thousand participants carried a placard with the name of one American who had died in Vietnam. As the placard carriers passed the White House, each stopped and, often emotionally, called out the name of the fallen soldier. Participants ended their four-mile procession at the Capitol, where each placard was placed in one of forty black coffins.

Just how big that event was became a matter of dispute. Laird got dragged into the controversy in late December when, at the insistence of journalists, his office released reconnaissance photos taken by an Air Force RF-101 photo plane twenty thousand feet over the event. Air force analysts had determined, in the same way they would systematically analyze a spy photo of a May Day parade in Moscow, that there were 119,000 people at the rally, plus or minus 15 percent. The figure was laughably low; it appeared as if the Pentagon was trying to downplay the moratorium. Laird smelled a big mistake, and ordered a quick review and correction, if necessary. The Pentagon came clean a week later after finding the photos had been taken possibly as late as 4 p.m., when most of the participants had left.[48]

The organizers estimated the size of the rally at about 800,000. Washington's chief of police estimated 250,000, but he admitted that was a conservative guesstimate. Even at that low number, it exceeded the previous record-holder, the 1963 civil rights march, highlighted by Martin Luther King's "I Have A Dream" speech, which peaked at 200,000 marchers. Most likely, there were about 600,000 participants at the moratorium rally, which makes it a record-holder as the largest antigovernment rally ever held in the United States. That figure comes from the National Park Service in charge of the Washington Mall, and that number is officially accepted today.

Laird was at his desk in the Pentagon that Saturday when he had an idea. He was concerned that too many of the military officials and the civilian leaders at the Pentagon were disdainful of Vietnamization and of the need to end the war. They assumed that the "great, silent majority" would continue supporting them year after year, and that the antiwar movement was a mere flash in the pan. Typical of this attitude was Gen. Earle Wheeler, chairman of the Joint Chiefs, who loved to lampoon demonstrators in his speeches. On the day of the first moratorium in October, during a speech to the Association of the U.S. Army, he referred caustically to the peaceful protestors as "groups of interminably vocal youngsters, strangers alike to soap and reason."

The secretary of defense thought there was a pair working in the Pentagon on November 15 who would benefit by rubbing shoulders with the protestors—John Chafee, secretary of the Navy, and his undersecretary, John Warner. Before noon, he called them to his office. "You guys go down to the Mall and give me a report on what's going on," Laird barked at them. He couldn't go himself because he would be recognized by the crowd, but Chafee and Warner could go incognito. The blue-suited pair scared up some old T-shirts they used in the Pentagon gym, khaki slacks, and sneakers. Their chauffeur-driven limousines wouldn't do, so they borrowed a subordinate's old clunker and drove downtown. Warner recalled: "It was a scene that's emblazoned on my mind. Here were hundreds of thousands of young men and young women, in a peaceful sort of way, singing and chanting and holding arms. Yes, we could smell the pot here and there. And occasionally some guy would strip down and dive into the Reflecting Pool to add a little coloration."

While Chafee and Warner were on the mall, Laird spent part of the day with demonstrators, too. He had heard that his niece Jessica and her friend (and future husband) Jim Doyle, fresh from two years with the Peace Corps in Tunisia, would be among the demonstrators that day, so he got word to them to come to his office and bring a dozen friends to talk about the war. "I didn't want people who were professionals"—those who made a profession out of protesting the war and organizing rallies—Laird said of his choice of company that day. "I wanted people who had a very sincere feeling about the American involvement in Southeast Asia." (Jim Doyle later became a three-term Democratic attorney general in Wisconsin and then governor, winning reelection in 2006.)

As for his Mall scouts, Laird had told them he wanted them to judge the mood of the crowd, but his real intent was for Chafee and Warner to get the shine knocked off any lingering prowar sentiments they might be harboring. The assignment had the desired effect. After Chafee died in 1999, Warner emotionally remembered that experience with his Senate colleague as a high point in their long friendship: "I could see John was so terribly upset because it brought back the carnage he had seen in his previous military experience [World War II and Korea] when the whole nation, every American, was solidly behind every person in uniform." In the car on the way back to the Pentagon, Warner remembered Chafee saying to him: "Boy, just put yourself in the shoes of somebody in Nam today, going through all the hell of combat, and the country's not with him. I remember in World War II you knew that everybody in America was just foursquare behind you, and when you faced the dangers that we faced, it wasn't any question in your mind."

Back in Laird's office, when the two men tried to convey what they had felt, the defense secretary was moved. "We've got to figure some way to get our men out of this thing," Laird agreed with them. "Do it with dignity and do it so that the gains and sacrifices aren't lost."

"From that moment on," Warner said, "John Chafee became a very special counselor to the secretary of defense and, indeed, to the president on the need to bring that conflict somehow to a termination."[49]

Laird remembered the day well, too. "They were a little shaken because I don't think they realized the extent of some of the feelings of those young people. That's what I was trying to get them to understand. But I couldn't get the White House to understand that." Indeed, the contrasting Nixon image of the day is unforgettable. The White House was encircled by a protective barricade of fifty-seven city buses parked end-to-end. Sharp-shooting soldiers were stationed behind the balustrade of a tall building nearby, and another three hundred soldiers were in the basement of the White House and the Executive Office Building next door. The president of the United States, by his own choice, was holed up in Fortress White House watching a college football game on television.

13

Ending the Draft

THERE WERE TWO WORDS that had been made the equivalent of expletives in South Vietnam by the end of 1969: *Vietnamization* and *withdrawals*. South Vietnamese president Thieu outlawed the use of both words in the domestic press. He justified the ban by complaining that to use either suggested that "this war has been directed by the Americans and is just turned over to the Vietnamese people's care."[1] For all its promise and for all the money thrown at it, the biggest concern about Vietnamization was that it could only be as good as the support it got from the Vietnamese people. The commander of U.S. forces in Vietnam, Gen. Creighton Abrams, summed it up: "Sooner or later the Vietnamese themselves have got to settle this thing. We can only help, and we can only help so much."[2]

As the man who saw South Vietnam's flaws close up through the magnifying glass of daily disappointment, Abrams had reason to be pessimistic. Out of duty and loyalty to Laird, Abrams gave Vietnamization his best effort, but he was always honest with Laird in assessing how the program was faring. Abrams's reports to Laird were peppered with frustration about the South Vietnamese military, which abided corruption at the highest levels. Thieu filled top positions in his army with political cronies, some of whom Abrams considered grossly incompetent. Laird commiserated with Abrams, but there was little either man could do to force Thieu to fire those commanders. Incompetence and indifference were among the many speed bumps on the road that American troops would take to get home; another was weaning South Vietnam from the dependence on American help, a dependence that the United States had fostered.

Those who saw Laird's Vietnamization as a fraud, a delaying tactic, or a cover for a graceful exit from a hopeless cause did not understand the complexities of disengagement. Gen. Bruce Palmer, for a time the deputy commanding general of U.S. Army forces in Vietnam, wrote years later about possible alternative U.S. strategies. He concluded that the United States should have focused earlier on developing a strong South Vietnam. To that end, the U.S. military should have been training and supporting the South Vietnamese military, rather than fighting the war for them. General Palmer's conclusion was that, given appropriate time and support, such a strategy could have succeeded, but it would have taken time and perseverance by the American people.[3] General Abrams knew that. Unfortunately, by the time Nixon came to office, time was not an ally, and U.S. perseverance was a scarce resource.

Training the South Vietnamese to take over their own war was the only way to avert chaos, as well as American loss of credibility among its allies. The United States could not simply leave South Vietnam overnight, despite demands from the doves in Congress to do just that. To disengage with the haste demanded by those who had lost patience with the war would have caused instant collapse of the South Vietnamese government and economy, and would have meant certain death for thousands of American supporters as the country was overrun by the North Vietnamese army. There was the matter of American POWs who could not be left behind, and the issue of defending the last of the support troops when the majority of the combat units were gone. Not the least of Laird's problems was a president who didn't want to be labeled a quitter and parts of the U.S. military that didn't want to cede authority to the South Vietnamese.

⁓

The fate of Vietnamization never rested solely on Laird's plan. While he could control one aspect—the transitioning of the combat responsibilities from the United States to South Vietnam—there were two more legs to the stool and both were wobbling—the South Vietnamese government, and its economy. Gardiner Tucker, who worked for both Laird and Clark Clifford as a deputy and assistant director of defense in research and engineering, recalled writing a warning report for Clifford: "We haven't done enough to help the South Vietnamese establish a government and an economy that can sustain itself. We thought of [the war] primarily as an opportunity to beat the Communists, not as an opportunity to build something in South Vietnam that can live on its own." Tucker said he made his report and "that was the last I heard about it. I went back to doing research and engineering."[4]

Roger Shields, who later became an assistant secretary to Laird on POW matters, first worked with Laird as an outside contractor studying the economics of Vietnamization. He recalled, "Mel Laird's concern was that you

might win the war militarily and end up with an economy that was in shambles and couldn't hold the peace."[5]

Laird's correspondence and the minutes of his staff meetings show a persistent drumbeat on the economy. It was completely propped up by the United
States from the cost of the war to the stabilizing of the currency. "As part of
the war effort, designed to attract popular support to the cause, we have followed a policy of raising the standard of living for the populace rather than
imposing a regime of austerity," Laird wrote the president in 1970.[6] With $3.6
billion in U.S. nonmilitary aid to South Vietnam already spent over the course
of the war, above and beyond the $105 billion cost of fighting the war to that
point, Congress was tired of doling out money.[7] And Saigon was too comfortable with its unrealistic view of what the United States could continue
to do. "This is a matter to which we and the South Vietnamese must devote
immediate and concerted attention," Laird warned in his memo to Nixon. It
didn't happen, and Laird became a chorus of one on the subject of the South
Vietnamese economy.

Similarly, Laird anguished over corruption in the South Vietnamese government—an attitude that reached into the upper ranks of the military. On
August 12, 1969, General Wheeler warned Laird to go slow on the second
phase of troop withdrawals, the first having been announced at the Midway
conference in June. Nixon was due to announce the second wave in September. Wheeler cited the "serious lack of qualified leaders" in the South Vietnamese army as a drag on Vietnamization and wrote, "Neither the assessment
of the military situation nor the [South Vietnamese] capabilities justifies a
Phase 2 redeployment of more than about twenty-five thousand."[8]

With more than half a million American troops still in Vietnam, removing twenty-five thousand wasn't enough in Laird's mind to show the public
that Nixon was serious about Vietnamization. On September 4 Laird sent
Nixon a memo laying out an update of his big picture for bringing home the
troops. He attached the Joint Chiefs' recommendation, which said the troop
withdrawal should be spaced out over three and a half years—not coincidentally, the exact amount of time left in Nixon's term. Laird gave a bow in the
direction of the chiefs' wisdom, but told the president that two years—not
three and a half—was his preference as a point to aim for on the horizon.[9]

Still unaware of Laird's ultimate goal for complete withdrawal, the chiefs
had also advised that as long as the enemy was still in South Vietnam, at least
267,500 American troops should be left there indefinitely. Laird coyly wrote
to the president, "I see no need to make any firm decision on the size of the
residual force at this time." It wasn't until November 10 that Laird revealed

to the chiefs his real intent. He ordered them to come up with a Vietnamization schedule that would have all U.S. troops, save a small advisory mission, out of the war by July 1973. There was to be no residual force of any size.[10]

On September 16 Nixon announced a second round of troop withdrawals—thirty-five thousand men in the next three months despite Wheeler's plea for no more than twenty-five thousand. The announcement was a piece of broader Nixon strategy to put pressure on Hanoi. In Nixon's mind, as recorded in his memoirs, it was a calculated series of moves to back the enemy into a corner: He sent a letter to Ho Chi Minh with the tone of an ultimatum; he announced that he would give a major policy speech on Vietnam on November 3; and he fixed on November 1, the anniversary of Lyndon Johnson's bombing halt, as the deadline for Hanoi to show some sign of flexibility in the peace talks, or else.

Nixon's tactic to appeal directly to Ho Chi Minh by letter fizzled. Ho responded to Nixon's letter with the usual posturing and demands that the only way to end the war was for the United States to get out of it. Nixon received the reply on August 30, three days before Ho died. The death further diluted Nixon's plans for a November 1 ultimatum and the promised dire consequences; in reality there never were any consequences. Nixon's carrot-and-stick approach had failed. Hanoi didn't go for the carrot, and Nixon had no stick. He was left with just the speech to give on November 3, and in his mind it became a watershed event in his presidency. He closeted himself at Camp David to write the speech, frequently consulting others including Laird, who pressed him to emphasize Vietnamization as the cure.

In the final speech there were no new initiatives and no talk of carrying out threats. Nevertheless, the speech struck home to the silent majority. The cables and letters that flowed into the White House warmed Nixon's heart, even though many of them were churned out by the president's own public relations machine. Even Kissinger recorded that some of the enthusiasm was generated by Haldeman's "indefatigable operatives who had called political supporters all over the country to send in telegrams."[11] Haldeman recorded in his diary that Nixon called him fifteen or twenty times after the speech, checking on the kind of response it was getting and insisting that Laird and Rogers be advised of the volume of mail to "shore them up." As a final plea, Haldeman said, Nixon told him to arrange "100 vicious dirty calls to *New York Times* and *Washington Post* about their editorials," even though, as Haldeman noted, the president did not yet know how those papers would editorialize about his speech the next day. He just assumed the worst.[12]

‿

The Nixon administration's best efforts to peddle their good intentions in Vietnam were frequently undermined by stories from the front—the secret bombing of Cambodia, the growing problems of morale, racial unrest, and drug use among the soldiers. None of those tarnished the reputation of the American military as badly as the horrific stories of GIs run amok. In 1969, Laird coped with the two most damaging of those stories.

The first came to his attention in a phone call from Abrams some time in July. A South Vietnamese spy on the U.S. payroll, suspected of being a double agent for the North, had been executed by American Green Berets—shot in the head and dropped in the South China Sea. Abrams wanted to court martial the Green Berets commander, Col. Robert Rheault, on murder charges. Abrams knew it would be no easy task, because Rheault was a man of no small reputation. Born into a prominent Boston family, he was a highly decorated Korean and Vietnam veteran. He had also done a tour as assistant for special operations to the Joint Chiefs. So when Abrams relieved him of command in July before he was formally charged, it was quite natural that among the three thousand Special Forces troops serving him, many assumed Rheault was just being moved to a general's slot in the Army somewhere, and a promotion would be announced any day.

Seven people under Rheault's command were implicated in the death of the double agent. Two of them claimed that when proof was gathered against the spy, Thai Khac Chuyen, they consulted the CIA and were told that assassination would be the best option, although not one that the government could sanction. The CIA would later deny that assassination was suggested and claim that the Green Berets were specifically told not to get rid of the spy. An investigation by Army secretary Stan Resor put the pieces of the story together. Rheault had ordered the killing, according to his underlings. So on June 20, 1969, three of them took the spy out on a boat, injected him with morphine, shot him twice in the head, filled a canvas bag with tire rims, tied the weight to his body, and threw him overboard in 150 feet of shark-infested water. After the killing, a junior member of Rheault's team, feeling uneasy about what had happened, reported it to the CIA. Rheault initially concocted a cover story, which he tried to float past Abrams, that the man was merely missing while on a dangerous solo mission. But once the facts were out, Rheault admitted he had ordered the assassination but claimed it was with the approval of the CIA.

In a war where body counts were the measure of success or failure, this was just one body. But the alleged double agent had not been killed in battle, nor had he been given the benefit of a trial. He had been interrogated, deemed guilty, and eliminated. Abrams ordered all eight Green Berets put in solitary confinement in the American military prison at Long Binh.

At home, where many already thought the war to be immoral, the Green Beret affair was shaping up as a farce—eight soldiers accused of murder because they killed a suspected enemy agent in wartime. Abrams appreciated that a line had been crossed, and it galled him. But he was not the final authority on the disposition of the charges. That was Secretary Resor, and he went to Laird for advice.[13] First, Laird said, get the arrested soldiers, who had to be presumed innocent, out of the punitive small cells at Long Binh. Resor ordered that move in less than twenty-four hours. Then Laird challenged Resor to think things through. "What's your game plan here?" Laird buttonholed him. Resor offered a few ideas, and together they worked out a strategy. Resor would meet personally with Abrams to go over the evidence and reasons behind the general's decision to court martial, and then come back and report.

Resor flew to Saigon and met Abrams. He recalled that Abrams showed him signed confessions from each man. Resor reported back to Laird that he agreed with Abrams—someone deserved to be charged. But the matter of CIA involvement had to be brought into the trial. The defense would naturally want to call CIA officers to buttress their case. At Resor's direction, Army general counsel Robert Jordan had already checked with the CIA's general counsel and gotten word that the CIA would provide the required witnesses, which would ensure a fair trial.

Laird didn't feel that was enough. With Resor sitting in his office, Laird placed a call to CIA director Richard Helms with whom he had a seasoned relationship of trust. Helms personally assured Laird that the CIA would cooperate. But in the next week, somebody had second thoughts. Most likely it was both Nixon and the CIA coming to the same conclusion independently that the agency would not cooperate. For its part, the CIA saw danger in the person of Rheault's lawyer, Edward Bennett Williams. Williams was at the early stages of honing intimidation into an artful defense. It was a tactic he used in cases involving highly classified intelligence. The prosecution would be scared into retreat after Williams threatened to put unseemly covert operations on public trial. Laird well knew this spooked the CIA.

Resor had no choice but to drop the case. In theory, even though Laird had no statutory authority in the case, he could have pressured Resor to go ahead, but this was not a battle Laird thought was worth the potential end result. Laird was loath to get between the CIA and the Army, even if Abrams was passionate about pursuing the case. As a former military man who had

seen American sailors taking potshots at shipwrecked Japanese sailors floating in the ocean, Laird had witnessed first hand, as he called it, "men that
wanted to kill when people didn't have to be killed." He understood that
lines blurred in times of war. "That's why I tried to support these guys. They
were in an operation where they felt this guy [the double agent] had seriously jeopardized them and almost got them killed. They felt he was out to
execute them."

As the Green Beret murder case was making headlines, Laird was dreading
the day when a far more horrific incident would finally become public. With
this case, Laird was insistent on putting the full weight of military justice
against those responsible. It was the massacre of hundreds of civilians, including women and children, by a company of American soldiers from the
Americal Division. It happened on March 16, 1968—during the Johnson
administration—in a little South Vietnamese village called My Lai.

Remarkably, for nearly a year, the massacre had remained a secret, except
for rumors that circulated among soldiers in Vietnam. Finally in March 1969
one man who heard the rumors during his tour in South Vietnam, Ronald
Ridenhour, wrote letters (after mustering out) to several members of Congress and to General Westmoreland, who was then Army chief of staff, asking for an investigation. It took until about April 1 for one of the letters to
land on Laird's desk. He ordered a quiet investigation, and in September the
twenty-six-year-old platoon leader, Lt. William Calley, was arrested, four days
before he was due to get out of the Army. More arrests among Calley's company quickly followed. Laird braced himself for the expected press onslaught,
but it was surprisingly slow in coming.

The news was kept under wraps until two months later, on November 13,
as Washington was filling with protestors for the Moratorium Day. The horror of the My Lai massacre was then exposed by Seymour Hersh of the Dispatch News Service. His reports, which earned him the 1970 Pulitzer Prize,
precipitated a deluge of front-page stories across the country and extensive
TV coverage. Lieutenant Calley's company had been on a search-and-destroy
mission against the Viet Cong in a small hamlet the GIs had nicknamed
"Pinkville." Because of the reputation the village had as a stronghold for the
Viet Cong, no one was above suspicion. The attack began with an artillery
barrage on the hamlet, then Calley's company moved in, ordered all of the
villagers out of their homes, and began setting fire to the wooden structures
and setting off dynamite charges in the brick buildings. The villagers were
herded into groups and gunned down on Calley's orders. The number who

died that day remains a secret in the Army's files. Initial reports were as high as 567, based not on a body count but on the number of survivors.[14] Later, the Army settled on estimates ranging from 200 to 300, but would not be precise, fearing to prejudice any court martial against the accused killers.

In one of the ironies of Vietnam War history, the majority of public opinion rallied around the soldiers accused in the massacre. Thousands of letters poured into the White House and the Pentagon arguing that a lowly lieutenant and his men should not take the blame for an immoral war perpetrated by generals and politicians. While there may have been public shock and revulsion, there was no sense of surprise. Many folks back home already assumed civilians were being killed indiscriminately, and it looked like the brass had found a scapegoat in Lieutenant Calley.

Laird appointed Lt. Gen. William Peers to head up the My Lai investigation. On Capitol Hill, Laird's old friend Mendel Rivers decided to do his own investigation, and his sympathies were clearly with Calley as a victim of circumstance. Fearing a surge of public sympathy for Calley that could scuttle the court martial, Laird went to Rivers and asked him to call off the congressional hearings. Laird told Rivers that as defense secretary he was already walking a fine line trying not to let public sentiment get in the way of military justice. On the eve of the second hearing, Rivers cancelled it out of respect for Laird.

One option for Laird would have been to blame the Johnson administration for the atrocities that happened on its watch and let the congressional hearings run their course, casting Calley as a martyr in a lost cause. But Laird's preference was to let Calley get due process. For Laird, My Lai was old business that was obstructing the public view of the new agenda, Vietnamization. Again Laird drew on his World War II experiences with fellow sailors who wanted to kill unarmed Japanese sailors out of vengeance, anger, and fear. "I understood why they wanted to do it, but you had to do everything you could to stop them," he said. "An officer in the United States military has certain responsibilities." Laird believed that what Calley had done was appalling, so he told Resor to press ahead with the court martial. Laird took flak from many directions over that decision, including a scathing letter in the *New York Times* signed by a young and unknown Marine lieutenant named Oliver North, who would later have his own spot of fame in the Iran-Contra scandal of the Ronald Reagan administration. Staffers around Laird urged him to give the insubordinate letter writer his comeuppance in public, but Laird refused, saying he didn't want to give the story more legs.

Although Laird and Resor took full credit for the decision to file criminal charges against Calley, a meeting between Nixon and Laird just before that decision was announced cast suspicion on who was calling the shots. *Time* magazine implied in a report on that meeting that Nixon insisted on the court martial. Calley's lawyer was quick to accuse the president of exercising "command influence." If the commander in chief was meddling in a military court procedure, how could the defendant get due process from soldiers who take orders from the president? Laird said it never happened; Nixon never weighed in, and in any case Laird would not have asked his opinion about a court martial.

In 1971 the military court convicted Calley alone of twenty-two counts of premeditated murder. At his sentencing hearing, Calley himself pinpointed the moral dilemma of the war as he pled for leniency: "I've never known a soldier, nor did I ever myself wantonly kill a human being in my entire life. . . . When my troops were getting massacred and mauled by an enemy I couldn't see, I couldn't feel and I couldn't touch—but nobody in the military system ever described them as anything other than Communism. They didn't give it a race, they didn't give it a sex, they didn't give it an age, and they never let me believe it was just philosophy in a man's mind that was my enemy out there."[15] The jury sentenced Calley to life in prison at hard labor.

Many Americans felt it was a just punishment, though not one Calley should serve alone; the lowly lieutenant had indeed taken the blame for a massacre that thousands of Americans believed to be standard operating procedure in Vietnam. An estimated one hundred thousand telegrams flooded into the White House, ninety-nine of every one hundred of them urging the president to intervene and free Calley. Nixon had courted the silent majority, and many of them now demanded by telegram that he listen to them and not let a soldier in the service of his country—a pawn in a larger game—take the rap himself. Some draft boards quit en masse, and Governor George Wallace of Alabama tried to cancel the draft in his state until Calley was pardoned. Calley's appeals continued through military and civilian courts until 1974. Along the way, his sentence was reduced to twenty years, and then ten. At that point Nixon reviewed the case one more time and said he was satisfied with the sentence. Calley finally went to the federal prison in Fort Leavenworth, Kansas, to serve six months before he was paroled.[16]

～

Scandals such as My Lai and the Green Beret murder were side roads that Laird felt diverted the American public from the more important news of Vietnamization. As his first year in office drew to a close, Laird s maneuvered to get as many troops as he could included in Nixon's announcement of the third withdrawal phase. The news release was planned for December 15, 1969. Edgy about a possible North Vietnamese offensive during the coming Tet holiday, the Joint Chiefs advised against taking any more men out. The Tet Offensive of 1968 had taken the American military command by surprise, and each year as the dry season approached, those commanders vowed never to be surprised again. But Laird was not one to be spooked by the past. Where others saw an alarming buildup of enemy strength, Laird saw only the seasonal flux of troop movements in a country where the monsoons determined the battle plans. And he didn't want that to be used as an excuse to slow down his troop withdrawals. "It would be misleading to interpret this seasonal surge as an escalation," Laird wrote to Kissinger on December 2. "I believe it is of overriding importance to remain flexible."[17] Laird was right that year. The North was still reeling from the high price it paid for the 1968 Tet Offensive, and a big escalation was not in the offing.

Still, the Joint Chiefs wanted to move at a more measured pace. If a third round of withdrawal was inevitable, they wanted to send home no more than thirty-five thousand men. And if North Vietnam did escalate the war, the chiefs said the withdrawals should be cancelled, and even reversed, sending more men back into the war. And they said if there was an escalation on the enemy's part, the United States should respond with a new all-out air war against the North, something that hadn't been used since November 1968.

Laird wrote to Kissinger on December 12 asking for the president to announce a fifty-thousand-man withdrawal. In Laird's mind, Vietnamization would go nowhere without taking a few risks. "Progress in Vietnamization begets further progress," he wrote. As for the chiefs' recommendation that the air war resume over the North, Laird showed his typical skepticism about the power of bombs dropped from the skies. "[T]here has been, to my knowledge, no clear relationship demonstrated between a U.S. air/naval campaign against North Vietnam and a reduction in the latter's military capabilities. . . . [T]here is no analysis that I have seen which would demonstrate any decisive results from an air/naval campaign against North Vietnam. To the contrary, for marginal gains we could sustain high and perhaps politically decisive costs."[18]

Kissinger couldn't argue with Laird's political instincts; troop withdrawal was the only thing that would satisfy the voting public back home. But Kissinger privately complained about how Laird was juggling the numbers. From the view in the White House it sometimes seemed that the defense secretary was making unilateral decisions about how many troops were coming home. "Mel Laird is not going to have his own troop withdrawal program,"

Kissinger reportedly snapped once when looking at the numbers of troops coming home.[19] But Laird passed that off as a problem of bookkeeping. Soldiers came in individually for one-year rotations on a regular schedule, but withdrawing troops were taken out in large units. It was a balancing act to keep the exact number of authorized troops in the country, and occasionally that number fell below the official ceiling.

On December 15 Nixon announced the third round of withdrawals at fifty thousand men by April 15, 1970. It was just the figure Laird had asked for and fifteen thousand more than the Joint Chiefs wanted in their worst-case scenario. They could not stop the withdrawal juggernaut that Laird had put in motion. In less than six months, Laird had prevailed over the military establishment and talked the president into bringing home a larger number: 115,500 men.

In tandem with Laird's withdrawal plans was his determination to end the military draft. For four years of the Vietnam buildup the draft had supplied the Army infantry with the soldiers who were most likely to be wounded or die. Avoiding the war became a national preoccupation for many young men. The architect of the inequitable draft system and its chief supervisor was a crusty septuagenarian, Gen. Lewis B. Hershey. He had devised a system that gave deferments to the able and affluent in college or in useful occupations, while those without such options were drafted. Hershey's vision became an exercise in survival of the "fittest" in which the fittest were deemed useful enough to society not to be sacrificed to the war.

With some exceptions, and contrary to previous military policies, the National Guard and Reserves were not called to serve in the Vietnam War. Laird was the defense secretary who changed that for the post-Vietnam military. He established that the Guard and Reserves would be the first called to active duty in the event of major American military action, which occurred in both the 1991 Gulf War and the "War on Terror" in Iraq and Afghanistan.

In his early congressional years Laird had favored the concept of universal service, which was that all young men would serve their country for a set time whether in the military, as a teacher's aide, a hospital assistant, or the like. But the idea never had strong support in Congress, and by the mid-1960s Laird was convinced that an all-volunteer military was the way to go. There were powerful philosophical reasons for Laird to move to an all-volunteer force. He reasoned that if presidents did not have a draft to provide any amount of manpower when needed, they might be less likely to involve the United States in dubious ventures like a land war in Asia. Laird also thought it was important to break the military's unhealthy addiction to the draft. Laird's negative view was fueled by the abysmal treatment of draftees. Their wages were not comparable to private industry and less than voluntary enlistees were getting paid for doing the same jobs. To Congressman Laird, the shameful pay scale had represented a burdensome and hidden taxation of the draftees.

A little more than a week after Nixon's inauguration, he had ordered Laird to develop a "detailed plan" to end the military draft and create an all-volunteer force. Both Nixon and Laird were shrewdly gauging the climate in Congress and at the Pentagon. Nixon thought a presidential commission was needed to prepare Congress to pass the legislation required to create an all-volunteer force. Laird preferred to do the ground work out of the Pentagon, not the White House, but he dutifully went along with Nixon's idea. When Nixon asked for Laird's input on possible presidential commission members, Laird seized the opportunity and weighted the commission with civilians who shared his point of view.[20] Among those recommended by Laird to serve as chairman was former secretary of defense Tom Gates. Thus the president's "Advisory Commission on an All-Volunteer Armed Force" became known as the "Gates Commission."[21] Among those recommended by Laird to serve on the committee were Tom Curtis, a former congressman; Theodore Hesburgh, president of Notre Dame University, economist Dr. Milton Friedman; Allen Wallace, president of Rochester University; and Gen. Alfred Gunther, a former deputy to Eisenhower in Europe.

Laird's first quick-fix idea for the draft was a "random selection" system, but the first roadblock to a lottery was a 1967 law that barred the president from using random selection. In a mid-February 1969 press conference, Laird announced that the administration would send new legislation to Congress to override that law.[22] Standing in the way of that change was House Armed Services Committee chairman Mendel Rivers, who had been opposed to a lottery. Another roadblock was Hershey himself, who considered the lottery idea an affront to his ability to run a fair system. So Laird came up with an ultimatum that he outlined to Nixon in an August 29 memorandum. He said the president should warn Congress that if they did not act by January 1970, Nixon would institute a legally allowed but complex and confusing "moving age group" draft system, which would come a bit closer to a random selection process.[23]

At first Congressman Rivers appeared unmoved, and his subcommittee gave Laird a cool reception. Laird continued to lobby members of Congress, even going to South Carolina with Rivers to be speaker at the Hibernian

Society dinner. Laird flew southern congressmen to the dinner on a military plane, and he used the time to bend their ears about the lottery all the way to Charleston. There was not much help forthcoming from the White House as Kissinger and Alexander Haig were strongly opposed to an all-volunteer force. At one cabinet meeting, Nixon leaned over to tell Laird that his national security staff was afraid he (Laird) was moving too fast, and it might affect negotiations in Paris. The president supported the all-volunteer force but never got too deeply involved in defense manpower issues while Laird was at the Pentagon. (Laird was disappointed when, after leaving office, Nixon opined that the all-volunteer force could have been a mistake. Laird was furious and called the former president, who then publicly corrected himself to again support the all-volunteer concept.) To the shock of Capitol Hill pundits, the House Armed Services Committee unanimously approved the draft bill on October 16, 1969, and sent it on to the full House where it passed 382 to 12, on October 30.[24] Then the full Senate passed the lottery bill by voice vote, and it became law on November 26.

During 1969 Nixon had sent several dozen domestic proposals to Congress. None of the major ones had passed, but the single-sentence draft reform bill, which simply repealed a sentence in an existing law, was declared by the *New York Times* to be "the first major piece of new legislation that the Administration has obtained from Congress during 10 months in power."[25]

The first Vietnam-era draft lottery was held December 1, 1969. While both presidents Wilson and Roosevelt had personally observed the initial draft lottery drawings of World Wars I and II, Nixon declined to be present at the 1969 drawing, which was held in a cramped auditorium of the Selective Service headquarters. At 8 p.m., with a nation tuned in by radio and TV to the almost surreal event, which affected every American male between the ages of nineteen and twenty-six, the lottery opened with a prayer. Then the ranking Republican on the House Armed Services Draft Subcommittee plunged his hand into a glass bowl, picked out the first of 366 blue capsules and twisted it open. He handed it to another official, who called the date: "September 14." The first birth date drawn would identify those men who would be called first in the 1970 draft; the second birth date drawn marking those who would be called next, and so on.

Some of the antiwar youth leaders opined that Laird and Nixon had cleverly decimated their radical ranks. No longer was an entire generation subject to the draft. The two-thirds not likely to go to Vietnam had no personal vested interest in protests, though some of those in the top third likely were radicalized into the antiwar movement. Overall, a Harris poll found three-quarters of Americans approved of the lottery, and three-fifths rated the Nixon-Laird handling of the draft as "good to excellent."[26]

~

Reforming the draft was not the same as ending the draft. It would take Laird three more years to do that. The issue was supposed to have been settled in 1970 by the Gates Commission, but the opposition proved formidable, much of it from inside the highest ranks of the military. At one private hearing of the commission, which Laird was not invited to attend, General Westmoreland declared that he personally would not command an all-volunteer Army because the presumably well-paid men would be nothing more than an "Army of mercenaries." Commission member Milton Friedman angrily interrupted. "General, are you saying you would rather command an Army of slaves?"

Westmoreland took umbrage. "I don't like to hear our patriotic draftees referred to as slaves."

"I don't like to hear our patriotic volunteers referred to as mercenaries," Friedman countered. "If they are mercenaries, then I, sir, am a mercenary professor, and you, sir, are a mercenary general; we are served by mercenary physicians; we use a mercenary lawyer; we get our meat from a mercenary butcher and so on."[27]

After ten months of work, Nixon received a 211-page report from the commission on February 21, 1970. The members had unanimously agreed that "the nation's interests will be better served by an all-volunteer force, supported by an effective standby draft, than by a mixed force of volunteers and conscripts." The committee said the first step should be pay equity.[28] While applauding the commission's general conclusion, Laird was disturbed that it had called for the draft to end when the current authority expired in mid-1971. He needed more time to create a climate where people would want to enlist. Laird felt that the commission's assumption that the way to get a volunteer force was simply to increase pay was wrong. Housing, education, skill training, improving the image of the military, and a host of other initiatives were needed, along with pay increases. These changes would take more time and money than the commission had estimated. Laird had just over one year to figure a way to get Congress to extend the draft one more time when it expired in July 1971.

The strongest, most important ally Laird had was the president himself, but it was not a deeply held view for Nixon that the nation must have an all-volunteer force. Nixon had embraced the goal for political exigency. If the winds of politics had blown another way, he would have been content to keep the draft. The strongest, most important opponent Laird had on the subject was the Army brass who, throughout 1969 and 1970, dragged their heels on the all-volunteer force (AVF), conducting a paper drill to please Laird. Behind closed doors on Capitol Hill, when pressed by members of Congress whom they knew to be AVF opponents, the Army leadership freely expressed their personal opposition to an AVF. Such testimony undercut Laird's initiative, but he was careful about rapping their knuckles at first. He knew Army leaders were gambling that they could outlast him—they had seen presidents and secretaries come and go. Laird was not a man who liked to commit himself to deadlines or timetables, but by mid-1970 he reasoned that the only way to publicly set a deadline to end the draft was with the Joint Chiefs lined up behind him.

Since World War II, Congress had traditionally extended draft induction authority four years at a time. Laird's friends in Congress told him that there was no way he could win a vote for the traditional four-year extension. The easiest victory would be a one-year extension, but Laird didn't think that was enough. He did not want to be fighting for another extension a year later during a presidential election campaign. So he settled on a two-year extension, but Nixon could not make up his mind to support it. In the meantime, Laird moved ahead on his own. Time and again he had proved that if he took unilateral action, the momentum would swing the White House his way.

Laird decided that it was possible to create an AVF by mid-1973. By fall 1970 he was ready to publicly announce that goal. Only one more step was needed before he did that. Laird would have to confront Westmoreland. For almost two years, Laird had allowed the four-star general to speak his mind about the draft in speeches and in congressional testimony, but it was time to shut him down. In late September Laird met with Westmoreland and issued an ultimatum. "I told Westy it was time for him to get on board or get out." Although Laird conveyed it in more courteous terms, Westmoreland knew he was being asked to resign as Army chief of staff if he could not become an active supporter in the development of an all-volunteer force. He told Laird he wanted to keep his job.[29]

Monday, October 12, 1970, was the day Laird set out to announce, with sufficient ceremony, his ambitious mid-1973 time line for the achievement of an all-volunteer force. In a memo to the Joint Chiefs and service secretaries, he informed them that the U.S. military would henceforth be committed to "zero draft calls" by the end of fiscal year 1973. Meanwhile, the services had much to do themselves to make military careers more appealing and competitive with private industry. "This matter should receive your urgent personal attention, and action plans should proceed without delay."[30]

That morning, having already distributed the memo, Laird convened his weekly "Armed Forces Policy Council" staff meeting, which included all senior Pentagon and military officials. He announced the new goal and ticked off events to come: his own press conference to announce the deadline, a speech by Westmoreland on Tuesday, and another press conference by Pentagon manpower chief Roger Kelley on Wednesday. General Westmoreland obligingly chimed in, according to the minutes, with terse support: "Army has been studying this matter for many months. We have several ongoing programs and many are being initiated. Army feels that zero draft calls is a feasible objective."[31]

After a press conference to announce his time line for eliminating the draft, Laird had lunch with Admiral Moorer, who also opposed the AVF but, unlike Westmoreland, had not spoken publicly against it. The lunch was a symbolic opportunity to sign Moorer on for the long haul. As a good soldier, and in Laird's eyes a loyal one, Moorer agreed to follow the Laird line. Then Laird gathered all the Joint Chiefs for an hour-long meeting at which he made sure none of them had any illusions about standing in his way.

At 6:25 p.m. Gen. Alexander Haig arrived for a private meeting with Laird. It was to be the secretary's last hard-sell of the day. As a deputy to Kissinger, Haig had become the most vehement AVF critic at 1600 Pennsylvania Avenue and a powerful influence on Kissinger himself. In the meeting with Laird, the obdurate Army general wouldn't budge, and Laird could not order him to fall in line. Only a month later, Haig was actively pushing for a four-year draft extension, which would buy him the time he needed to thwart the AVF after Laird was gone. Not long after word of Haig's continued opposition got back to Laird, Kissinger found himself required to call Haig on the carpet and direct him to join the all-volunteer team. "I finally got hauled in and told to butt out," Haig recalled. "I was told the president was very unhappy with my opposition." He rightly suspected that it was actually Laird who had outmaneuvered him.[32]

On October 13, Westmoreland dutifully delivered a major address to the annual meeting of the Association of the U.S. Army: "I am announcing today that the Army is committed to an all-out effort in working toward a zero draft—a volunteer force." With this speech, according to one Army historian, "the Army's approach to achieving an all-volunteer force changed. Seemingly overnight, the Army shifted from its wait-and-see attitude to an activist posture."[33]

The final round in Laird's battle to end the draft began when Nixon sent Congress a bill at the end of January 1971 asking for a two-year extension.

The bill included additional requests for draft reforms, as well as a military pay increase and other measures aimed at laying the groundwork for recruitment of an all-volunteer force. The bill embroiled the House and Senate in eight months of stormy debate, taking so long that the draft actually expired for three months in the summer of 1971 because the president's induction authority temporarily expired.

The draft extension bill was close to passage in June when Sen. Mike Mansfield, the majority leader, added an amendment that declared it was U.S. policy to withdraw all American troops from Southeast Asia within nine months of the passage of the bill. The bill, with the nettlesome amendment, passed the Senate, but the president would never have signed it. So Mansfield agreed to soften his amendment language to read that the troops would be withdrawn as soon as was practicable. The House agreed to that, but then the Senate balked.[34]

It was time for Laird to pull out all the stops, which he did on September 14. He wiped his schedule clean for the day and summoned the secretaries of the Army, Navy and Air Force, as well as the four (of five) Joint Chiefs who were in town. After their meeting, five Pentagon limousines roared up to the Capitol, and the magnificent seven of the military trooped down the corridors and into the Senate Armed Services Committee room in what one newspaper called "the most glittering display of brass assembled on Capitol Hill" in the post–World War II era. Then they fanned out to visit the offices of senators from both parties.[35] The next morning, Laird appeared on the NBC *Today* show and expressed concern about the Senate's recalcitrance. Failure to pass the draft bill would mean "utter chaos as far as the [military] manpower problems of the United States are concerned," he said. The next day Nixon held a news conference: "I don't like to speculate as to what would happen if the draft bill is defeated, because I think this would be one of the most irresponsible acts on the part of the United States Senate that I could possibly think of." The Senate approved the bill on September 21.[36]

Besides a two-year draft extension, Laird won most of the serious draft reforms he was after. The final bill was also full of newly funded benefits for military servicemen, the most important of which was a 100 percent pay increase for those with less than two years of service. Laird had been headstrong about that pay raise from his first month on the job. "Too many [military] families suffer financial hardships, some of whom are forced to go on welfare to survive," Laird charged in 1969. He ordered a study, which revealed in early 1970 that more than twelve thousand servicemen were on the nation's welfare rolls. Many more thousands qualified for welfare, but they leaned on family, friends, and their own fiscal restraint to get by without tapping government sources.[37] By the time Laird left in 1973, he had achieved a salary increase for the "under two" servicemen of more than 300 percent, bringing pay closer to what they might receive in civilian life. "They weren't qualified for food stamps when I left," Laird said.[38]

The last draft call was made in December 1972, six months before the president's draft authority expired.

When Laird looked to make the military services more attractive to volunteers, he leaned heavily on the example set by Gen. Bernard W. Rogers who had radically transformed a dismal western post into one with high morale and performance in little more than a year. Just south of Colorado Springs, Colorado, lies the sprawling 140,000-acre Fort Carson. Named after the legendary Christopher "Kit" Carson, the post was created in World War II as both a training facility and prisoner-of-war camp, then evolved into a major Army facility by the late 1960s. As the Vietnam War heated up, it became a year-round training area for units to be deployed to Southeast Asia, prominently including elements of the Fifth Infantry Division (Mechanized), known as the "Red Diamond Division."

By September 1969 when General Rogers arrived as the new commander of Fort Carson's twenty-five thousand men, it was a post in serious trouble, suffering from abysmal morale that came from many sources including racial division, drug-abusing troublemakers, and an overcrowded stockade filled with miscreants, deserters, and those caught AWOL. The division's manpower had a 14 percent turnover every month, which meant that after every seven months, Rogers would effectively be commanding a completely new set of soldiers. More than half of those reported to the post directly from Vietnam combat duty, and many were draftees with only a few months left to go on their two-year hitch. Disenchanted, disgruntled, and not seeing the sense in it, they were in a mood to rebel at any effort to keep them combat-ready. "There was much work to be done," Rogers recalled. His chief of staff, Col. David R. Hughes, a much-decorated combat hero, put it more pithily: "I served in three wars: Korea, Vietnam, and Fort Carson."[39]

General Rogers barely had time to get his boots muddy before Laird came for a five-day visit in October 1969 that included inspections of Fort Carson, the nearby Air Force Academy, and the Cheyenne Mountain NORAD (North American Air Defense Command) complex just west of the post. After morning briefings, Rogers took Laird on a Huey helicopter overview of the sprawling base. Laird's helicopter set down in a remote location to observe a training exercise of the post's Recondo (Reconnaissance and Commando) School. Rogers invited Laird and two friends he had brought along to walk ahead on a trail in the tranquil woods. Suddenly Laird's friends became alarmed as they heard a chorused shout—"Re-*CON*-do!"—and saw a half-dozen black-faced, camouflaged soldiers rushing at them through the bushes, guns pointed. An unruffled Laird eyed the patrol leader and said the pass-word for the day which Rogers had given, "Fort Worth." It was probably the only time during his tenure that American soldiers ever pointed weapons at the secretary of defense.[40]

Laird's primary memory of the visit was his excitement about the new commander, General Rogers, an enlightened Rhodes Scholar and decorated combat veteran who had been commandant of the cadet corps at West Point. After Laird heard a number of complaints during his mess hall lunch with the division's enlisted men, Rogers didn't try to make excuses. "What they need is for someone to give a damn," Rogers said.

"Amen," Laird responded.

He saw in Rogers a kindred spirit. Just two weeks before, Laird had issued a directive that ordered commanders to allow protest within their ranks unless it interfered with morale, discipline, or military "effectiveness." Laird had written: "Dissent in its proper sphere is healthy for the United States [and] the service member's right of expression should be preserved to the maximum extent possible, consistent with good order and discipline and the national security."[41] Both Rogers and Laird believed the soldiers deserved a significant say in troop operations and could be trusted to speak up with-out a loss of discipline. It was the essence of Laird's participatory manage-ment style over the Defense Department.

Both Laird and Rogers had a way of simplifying complicated matters. And both knew that the incoming soldiers—products of the 1960s—were a dif-ferent breed, and that was not such a bad thing. "They want to participate in the policy-making of the Army," Rogers summarized. "They are interested in 'why' we do certain things in certain ways. Answers based on faith, 'just believe me'; or authority, 'it's so because I say it's so'; or custom, 'we've always done it this way,' were not good enough," Rogers said. "These soldiers were prepared to stand up and be counted, to tell it like it is, and they expected the same to be true of their superiors. Intellectually, they were at a higher level at their age than had been my generation, but the challenge was that they didn't have the experience or discipline to balance that intelligence."

Laird felt that if Rogers succeeded in making the Army more attractive and empowering for the men it would be a test case for the all-volunteer force Laird envisioned. When he returned to the Pentagon, he advised Westmoreland to watch for good things to come from Rogers and Fort Carson.

Rogers's successes at Fort Carson were due in large part to an "Enlisted Men's Council" with representatives elected from each unit. Rogers also created "Racial Harmony Councils" so black soldiers could air their concerns. Half a dozen coffee houses had sprung up near military bases in throughout the country, usually run by antagonistic ex-soldiers promoting bitter denunciations of military life and purpose, including antimilitary protest organizing and counseling, which sometimes encouraged desertion. Rogers visited one such spot in Colorado Springs, The Home Front, and thought he should offer a coffee house on the post itself—more convenient for the men and more likely to create the changes they wanted. Thus was born the Inscape Coffee House, which featured coffee, a bathtub full of popcorn, and often a commander on a "hot seat" conducting a give-and-take session.

Rogers's chief of staff, Colonel Hughes, who had been a West Point professor of literature, explained that the command staff applied time-tested principles, and with a heavy dose of true concern for the troops and humility, it worked. "We let the men get it off their chest. We let them do guerrilla theater in the post theater and bring in controversial speakers. At the coffee house and elsewhere, we ordered all the battalion commanders to sit on their butts and keep their mouths shut—and listen. We understood Aristotle's theory of catharsis better than the men did; if they could get it off their chest in a socially approved forum like the coffee house rap session or 'theater,' we could expect them to salute when they walked out the door. And they did."

As a result, many changes were made. Of more than one hundred serious recommendations received from the enlisted men's councils, about 70 percent of them made sense to Rogers and he implemented them. He got rid of make-work projects, the dreaded Saturday inspections, and early-morning reveille. He remodeled barracks to provide more privacy, added recreational options and improved the food in the mess halls. Re-enlistments increased 45 percent, and the retention rate of junior officers doubled. Two-thirds of the non-career GIs rated their own morale as "fair to excellent" in one survey. AWOLs radically declined, as did disciplinary problems and incidents requiring investigation by the provost marshal.[42]

Westmoreland kept close watch on Rogers and Fort Carson from the Pentagon, as Laird had advised him to do. He was impressed enough to ask Rogers to come to Washington and brief the Army commanders' conference.

Some of the commanders openly objected to what Rogers told them. One general groused, "If this is the way the Army's going to be, I'm glad I'm about to retire!"

At that, Westmoreland turned to Rogers and observed: "That's our problem, isn't it, Bernie?"

"Yes sir, that's our problem," Rogers responded. "Old Army folks who won't accept what the future holds for us and what we need to do."[43]

On November 2, 1970, the *New York Times* discovered Rogers and Fort Carson, and hailed their achievement in a major article. Laird was thrilled as a media blitz followed, portraying Fort Carson as the most progressive troop-oriented base in the U.S. military. (Rogers later went on to become Army chief of staff and then supreme commander of NATO.)

Not to be outdone, the Navy stepped up to the plate. After working on a new directive for almost four months, the chief of naval operations Adm. Elmo Zumwalt, on November 10, issued his most famous and controversial directive. (His directives were informally called "Z-grams"). Z-57, originally titled, "Mickey Mouse, Elimination of," ordered liberalization of Navy regulations in twelve areas, including hair and beard styles, where uniforms had to be worn and where they were not necessary, motorcycle use, and so on. The memo itself said its thrust was to eliminate "demeaning and abrasive regulations" in the Navy, which were alternately described in the memo as "Mickey Mouse" or "chicken regs." The message was electrifying, and Zumwalt became a hero to the sailors. At a POW prison in North Vietnam, longtime POW Capt. Jim Stockdale tapped on the walls of a new POW to elicit news: "What's new?" The answer came back: "Got a new CNO, named Zumwalt. No more Mickey Mouse or chickenshit." A silent cheer went up among the American prisoners.[44]

Not to be upstaged, Westmoreland used a commanders' conference on November 30 to issue liberalizing orders that followed Rogers's reforms at Fort Carson almost completely. In one stroke, he abolished daily reveille formations; liberalized pass policies; put beer in the barracks and mess halls; encouraged commanders to establish open-door policies to complaining enlisted men; called for a review to end all "irritants" like "make-work" projects and meaningless rituals; and allowed longer hair.

Still, Westmoreland was the reluctant reformer, never fully on board with an all-volunteer force, as Laird had anticipated. The wily general was willing to go along, gambling that Laird would never accomplish an all-volunteer force. Meanwhile, Westmoreland reckoned the Army could indeed benefit from the improvements. He admitted as much in a private meeting in

January 1971, with Curtis Tarr, the Selective Service chief. "He is going to use the all-volunteer force as a means by which the Army might be improved in ways that otherwise would not be possible. I did not react to this," Tarr wrote in his journal after the conversation. A month later, a *Look* magazine article titled, "The Dump-the-Draft Talk Is Double-Talk," quoted Westmoreland's designated point man on AVF, Lt. Gen. George Forsythe, as saying, "I don't want to get rid of the draft. Neither does General Westmoreland."[45]

14

Objections Overruled

RICHARD NIXON'S PATH TO WATERGATE was littered with friends, aides, and political cronies who were cast aside one-by-one when they disappointed him. All that remained in the end was a phalanx of sycophants who were not prescient enough to stop the president when he crossed the line. Laird was among the first of Nixon's old friends to fall from grace, possibly as early as the EC-121 shoot down in March of 1969. In the immediate aftermath of that event, Laird had taken steps to delay Nixon's orders, avoiding the significant possibility of sparking another war, one with North Korea. William Rogers, Nixon's old friend and secretary of state, was the next to fall out of favor, in large part due to the machinations of Henry Kissinger, who wanted Rogers's job. Kissinger managed to retain the president's confidence much longer.

By 1970, only one year into the new administration, Laird was already out of the inner circle. And that was his preference. In the spring of 1970 when other cabinet members were beginning to mumble that the president was withdrawing himself from his advisors and behaving erratically, Laird had no such complaints. As far as he was concerned, the less meddling he had from the White House, the better. "I liked to run the thing without contact," he said. "I never had any problem getting through to [Nixon], but I always told Kissinger that I didn't want to. I wanted to run my operation. I always tried, however, to keep the president informed."

The Nixon-Laird friendship had unusual aspects. Laird respected Nixon, stuck by him through his early rocky political career, and worked harder than most to see him elected president. In the end, Laird was one of the last of the president's men to believe that Nixon had nothing to do with the Watergate breakin. Yet, in spite of that loyalty, Laird knew Nixon had a penchant for skullduggery, and Laird had installed his own safeguards in anticipation of the moment when he would lose favor in his president's eyes. It began the day Nixon convinced Laird to be defense secretary and signed the cocktail napkin promising Laird full control over all the appointments in the Defense Department. Surrounded by men of his own choosing, Laird was prepared to circumvent any back-channel maneuvers the president might attempt.

That advance work came to Laird's rescue in 1970 when Nixon retreated into himself and his inner circle to plan his most controversial campaign of the Vietnam War—an American ground-force incursion into Cambodia. It was a move that nearly wiped out the public relations gains Laird had accomplished up to that point with his Vietnamization program.

The year had begun optimistically enough with Laird's second trip to Vietnam. He and Joint Chiefs chairman General Wheeler went to the White House on Sunday morning, February 8, 1970, to get marching orders from Nixon for their trip the following day. Wheeler's walk had become markedly slower since the year before, and he showed serious signs of flagging energy. It would be his last trip with Laird. The president wanted the two men to return with a thoroughly honest assessment of Vietnamization as it moved into its second year.

One objective of Vietnamization, albeit a political one, had already been accomplished by early 1970: taking the war off the front pages every day. Nixon was about to change that, but in February when Laird and Wheeler traveled to Vietnam, all the signs pointed toward the fact that Vietnamization was helping to satisfy the American public. In a three-hour meeting with General Abrams in Saigon, Laird got what he later called the "most optimistic" report on Vietnamization to date.

On the way back to the United States Laird stopped over in Hawaii and wrote a fifteen-page report to Nixon. In that report Laird called the mood in Saigon, "cautious optimism," and added, "[W]e now have and can retain sufficient strength to keep the enemy from achieving any kind of military verdict in South Vietnam."[1] Part of the good news in that report was the fact that only about one fourth of the total enemy forces were Viet Cong and three fourths were North Vietnamese regulars. Five years earlier, the ratio had been the reverse. It meant that efforts to neutralize Communist sympathizers in the South were meeting with success. The Tet Offensive had also gone hard on the Viet Cong, significantly reducing their numbers and their commitment to the cause.

Laird reported that Vietnamization had put Hanoi between a rock and a hard place. The Communists were not strong enough to mount a major offensive at that point to test whether Vietnamization was working, or whether the waning of U.S. troops in the region had weakened South Vietnam's ability to defend itself. "The best the enemy can hope for, therefore, is some localized and short-term tactical military success," Laird advised Nixon.[2]

This report to the president included Laird's first strong warnings about the unstable economy in South Vietnam, reflecting his fears that Vietnamization could succeed militarily and still be brought down by the economy. It was a theme Laird would repeat throughout 1970. On April 4 Laird wrote to Nixon warning, "[T]he Vietnamese economy is a major uncertainty and perhaps the weakest link in the Vietnamization program."[3] On May 15, Laird gave Kissinger a report with more dire warnings and a recommendation to focus on building up the Vietnamese private-sector economy: "Unless a sound and expanding economic system can be established in [South Vietnam], as in Korea and Taiwan, the South Vietnamese may not be able to shoulder the major share of their own defense responsibilities for at least a decade to come."[4] On August 13, Kissinger issued the four-page National Security Decision Memorandum 80, titled "Vietnam Economic Policy."[5] It tepidly offered generalized goals such as attempting to tweak sales of imported American rice in South Vietnam. Laird knew the policy was no more effective than spitting in the wind.

Failing to get much response from the White House, Laird began the touchy job of persuading the Saigon government to cut the fat out of its own military budget by reducing the size of its army. In a memo to the Joint Chiefs on June 5, Laird requested that General Abrams begin a review of the South Vietnamese army to see how many soldiers could be cut.[6] It took the chiefs six months to respond to Laird's suggestion, and the answer was "none."[7] Laird was learning that withdrawing U.S. troops was a cakewalk compared to downsizing the South Vietnamese army. The Joint Chiefs were not about to encourage any cutbacks, even in the face of an economic meltdown in Saigon.

At times in 1970, when Laird had to fight for every step in Vietnamization, it seemed his determined optimism about the program was its only asset. It was that year when Nixon showed his own lack of confidence in the plan.

⌒

Nixon's Cambodia incursion—even decades later Laird bristled at the use of the word "invasion" to describe it—had its roots in 1963 when North Vietnam had invaded Laos and at the same time took up residence in several provinces of Cambodia that bordered South Vietnam. The Cambodian chief of state, Prince Norodom Sihanouk, officially ignored their presence, having neither the manpower nor the ideological inclination to rid his country of

Communists. The North Vietnamese ran most of the Cambodians out of those regions and established "sanctuaries"—outposts along the Ho Chi Minh Trail supply line from which main forces staged cross-border attacks into South Vietnam.

Covert U.S. Special Forces teams crossed into Cambodia regularly to harass those sanctuaries. On Laird's first visit to Saigon in 1969 he had authorized overt "protective reaction" raids across the border in an attempt to limit the enemy's ability to wage war from an allegedly neutral country that was just a day's march from Saigon. The secret "Operation Menu" bombing by B-52s begun in 1969 was Nixon's ham-fisted attempt to reduce the value of the sanctuaries, an approach Laird never had much use for.

When Sihanouk left Cambodia in January of 1970 to spend a few months on the French Riviera and shore up friendships in Moscow and Peking, the opportunity arose for Nixon to strike the kind of blow he had been longing for. On March 18, following a series of anti-Communist demonstrations across Cambodia, the country's parliament dismissed the absent Sihanouk and installed Prime Minister Lon Nol as the new head of state. The new government closed the port of Sihanoukville to North Vietnamese supply ships and attempted to blockade the Communists' overland supply routes.

Persuaded that the Lon Nol government would not last long on its own, Nixon asked Laird on March 25 to have the Pentagon come up with a plan for attacks against the border sanctuaries. Laird was delighted. The sanctuaries had long been a threat to U.S. troops in South Vietnam, and Laird saw an operation against them as a way to showcase Vietnamization and the new improved South Vietnamese army. In Laird's mind, the operation could be handled strictly by South Vietnamese troops.

Still, the defense secretary knew, even before Nixon asked, that a South Vietnamese operation wasn't what the president had in mind at all. Nixon did not yet trust the South Vietnamese army to go it alone. The Joint Chiefs fell in line with Nixon. Within a day, they forwarded to Laird a plan for a joint U.S./South Vietnam operation, complete with a list of the American divisions that would cross over the border. Laird slipped into his delay-by-obfuscation mode. On March 26 he sent his own list to the chiefs asking them how much the operation would cost, how it would affect the rest of the Pentagon's budget for Vietnamization, what intelligence they had that an American foray into Cambodia would make any difference, and what the risks were compared with "the marginal benefit which might be derived."[8]

But it was too late for those questions. On the same day, Kissinger sent Laird an order from the president: come up with a proposal for a joint operation into Cambodia within a week.[9] As was Nixon's habit when he knew Laird would not agree, the president didn't admit that he had already made up his mind to send troops into Cambodia no matter what Laird concluded. In this case, he also had to mask his intentions from Rogers who was likely to join Laird's camp. Nixon initially issued orders that the State Department wasn't to be told about the planning. Then on March 27 he said the U.S. ambassador in Saigon, Ellsworth Bunker, could be informed, but he was not to tell his boss Rogers.[10]

By this time, behind the scenes, Rogers was already privately colluding with Laird to slow down Nixon's push on Cambodia. In a letter he hoped the president would never see, Rogers wrote Laird on April 1 that he had some ideas of "steps we might take to influence Cambodia developments." He included his March 31 memorandum to the president, which he confided to Laird was an effort "to highlight our determination to avoid another major involvement in a Southeast Asian country."[11]

Unlike Rogers, Laird didn't stop with memos. He had learned to stay one step ahead of his president. On his trip to Saigon in February Laird had discussed with General Abrams the possibility of a move into Cambodia. Although the topic took up a fair share of their time together, Laird never breathed a word of it in his formal report to Nixon at the end of the trip. The private discussion would later figure prominently in Laird's futile attempt to talk Nixon out of a U.S. operation in Cambodia. Laird's military assistant, Colonel Pursley, sat in on the meeting with Abrams and remembered that the general was confident the South Vietnamese could handle the operation, possibly with some American artillery support from the Vietnamese side of the border in addition to rescue units if needed.[12]

Through his politician's eyes, Laird could see nothing but misery coming out of a U.S. incursion into Cambodia. It would make a mockery of his claims that Vietnamization was going well, and it could be seen by the American public as an expansion of a war that Nixon had promised to end. The president was not oblivious to the possible reaction back home. Also preying on Nixon was the need to decide how many American troops would be withdrawn from Vietnam in the fourth round of redeployments. The Laird plan called for bringing home an average of ten thousand to twelve thousand men every month, but the Joint Chiefs wanted to call off any more withdrawals, especially if Nixon really meant to make a major foray into Cambodia. To further shake the president that month, the Apollo 13 space capsule was crippled in orbit around the Moon, and there was a chance the three astronauts would be stranded in space.

On April 17 Nixon flew to Hawaii on a jubilant mission: to greet the Apollo 13 crew that had managed to limp back to Earth. In Hawaii Nixon huddled with Adm. John McCain, the CINCPAC commander who knew just how to pump the president's aggressive war plans with one of his "big red arrow" briefings. Nixon was so impressed with McCain's take on the Communist menace in Southeast Asia that he invited the admiral back to the Nixon home in San Clemente, California, to give the briefing to Kissinger.

With Nixon planning an invasion of Cambodia and weighing continued troop withdrawals, the last thing Laird wanted him to hear was a McCain pep talk about the winnability of the war. Laird was not invited to San Clemente for the big show. Instead he watched from afar as Nixon went on television in California on April 20 and announced that he would withdraw 150,000 troops from Vietnam over the next year—the number Laird had wanted. He had made up his mind about that possibly as early as April 9, but without telling Laird. Presidential aide H. R. Haldeman recorded in his diary on that day that Nixon had set up a meeting for the following week, ostensibly to get input from Laird and Rogers on the next wave of withdrawals, "But will not tell them the real plan." According to Haldeman, Nixon wanted to leak the news to the *New York Times* and *Washington Post* that he was withdrawing only 40,000 men, and then he planned to surprise everyone with the real figure of 150,000.

Laird was rarely surprised by anything Nixon did. The 150,000 figure sounded good, but Nixon had a way of making less look like more. He ordered Laird to end-load the program by making few withdrawals in the remainder of 1970 and the majority in early 1971. Laird asked for an audience with the president to appeal the decision as soon as Nixon was back in Washington. On April 21 the two men met, and Laird played a card he hoped would resonate with the president. If Nixon didn't take out at least 60,000 men by the November congressional elections, the Republicans could suffer at the polls.[13] Laird recalls telling Nixon that the withdrawal rate had to be steady and that Abrams couldn't function with troops leaving in fits and starts. Nixon disingenuously promised to weigh Laird's advice. The next day Laird got a memo from Nixon ordering that no more than 60,000 of the 150,000 would be sent home before the end of 1970. It marked a significant slowing in the pace of withdrawals to only about 7,500 men a month.

Laird was sure that the slowdown, coupled with an expansion of the war into Cambodia, would be seen by the American public as a betrayal of a promise to end the war, and he wasn't going to let that happen. In August, with the election pressing, Laird persuaded the president to withdraw ninety thousand troops before voters went to the polls. The move was indicative of how Laird managed to have his way throughout the entire withdrawal program by juggling numbers and using his considerable powers of persuasion with the president.

Try as he might, however, Laird could not talk Nixon out of sending American soldiers into Cambodia. On April 22, 1970, Nixon summoned the National Security Council to the White House for a meeting. A decision had to be made about how and when to attack two Communist strongholds in Cambodia—a region called the Parrot's Beak, just thirty-three miles from Saigon, and another area code-named the "Fishhook," which was believed to be the current hideout for COSVN, the mobile headquarters of the North Vietnamese army in Cambodia.

Laird was selective about attending NSC committee meetings, but always had a representative present, preferring to let his subordinates hash out the minutiae at the staff level. But this time he went to stand up for his position. It was time to test Vietnamization, and Cambodia was a perfect test, Laird argued. "You've got to give them a test some time, but if you throw in American support, that isn't much of a test," Laird recalled telling Nixon. His strongest argument was his understanding from Abrams two months earlier that the general was willing to do the operation without putting U.S. troops over the border into Cambodia. Nixon waffled in the face of confrontation and announced to the NSC that he would authorize a South Vietnamese incursion in the Parrot's Beak using only American air support, not ground troops.

Four days later, Nixon called the NSC together again. Since the previous meeting, he had been privately briefed by Adm. Tom Moorer, who was then acting chairman of the Joint Chiefs and in the running to replace the ailing Wheeler. Moorer had explained in detail how U.S. troops could be used to invade the Fishhook while the South Vietnamese were striking in the Parrot's Beak. Nixon had not told Laird about that briefing from Moorer, but Kissinger had informed Laird on the sly. (In his memoirs, Kissinger said he thought it unseemly in that case that the Joint Chiefs should be briefing the president on military operations behind the defense secretary's back.)[14] It was not Laird's only report about the secret briefing. Unknown to the president and Kissinger, the other chiefs regularly informed Laird about any calls or meetings they had with either Nixon or Kissinger.

The NSC gathered on a Sunday evening and Nixon sat there, as if uncommitted, while the rest of them got the same briefing from Moorer. Laird and

Rogers repeated their objections to a joint operation, and both of them added another caution. It looked like the president was once again putting too much stock in wiping out a COSVN headquarters. Laird reminded Nixon that technically there was no such facility in Cambodia, only a scattering of commanders, staff elements, and communications facilities that were constantly on the move. Nixon listened and then adjourned the meeting, confident that he had not shown his cards. Immediately after everyone else left, Nixon told Kissinger to issue the order. U.S. troops would cross into Cambodia.

The next day that order—National Security Decision Memorandum 57—was on Laird's desk, signed and initialed by the president lest anyone question his authority. Perturbed but not surprised, Laird scanned the order for any way he could salvage his position. He found an alarming note in the last paragraph: "The Washington Special Actions Group is designated as the implementing authority for these steps."[15] WSAG was the committee Kissinger had formed to strengthen his and Nixon's authority after the EC-121 crisis when Laird had taken charge of the military response and circumvented Nixon's impulse to attack North Korea. Laird wasn't about to let an NSC committee run an invasion of Cambodia (although he and Deputy Secretary Packard were members of that committee.) He called Kissinger and politely asked to have the memo reworded. Then Laird said he was on his way over to see the president to make one last pitch.

Rogers had the same idea. The two cabinet officers confronted Nixon for an hour that Monday morning. Laird continued to maintain that Abrams didn't think U.S. troops were necessary. To settle the question, Nixon sent a cable behind Laird's back to Abrams asking him once and for all for the "unvarnished truth" on where he stood on the question of American troops in Cambodia. According to Nixon's memoirs, the response from Abrams was unmistakably gung ho: "It is my independent view that these attacks into the enemy's sanctuaries in Cambodia are the military move to make at this time in support of our mission in South Vietnam both in terms of security of our own forces and for advancement of the Vietnamization program."[16]

Laird tells the story with more shades of gray. Yes, Abrams wanted the sanctuaries cleaned out, but as soon as he got the back-channel cable from Nixon asking for the "unvarnished truth," he called Laird. According to Laird's memory of the conversation, Abrams told him the president had asked for a 100 percent guarantee that if American troops were not used, the South Vietnamese army could accomplish the mission on its own. Abrams, not a man to offer guarantees, apologized to Laird that he could not make such a promise to the president. Laird told Abrams he understood.

The next day another memo from Nixon—NSDM 58—arrived in Laird's office. The decision to use U.S. troops was firm. The only change from the prior day's order was in the last paragraph. It now said WSAG would "coordinate" not "implement" the Cambodian incursion.[17] It was only a small victory. Laird was stuck with the operation, but he wasn't stuck with taking the blame. The loyalist in him would carry out the president's orders without any public complaint, but privately he wanted his opinion put in the record. He sent a seven-page memo to Nixon outlining the downside of a U.S. move into Cambodia.[18] Laird's message was tactfully worded but alarming. Things were about to get messy . . . the Congress would not like it . . . the American people would not like it. And Hanoi would capitalize on that dissent and become even more pig-headed in Paris. Laird told Nixon he was risking American public support for Vietnamization and warned that the casualty rate could go up dramatically.

Nixon was undeterred. He was already busy drafting a speech to announce to the American public on April 30 that the Vietnam War was taking a detour into Cambodia. On the day of the speech, Nixon sent William Safire, his conservative speech writer who had polished the text, to the Pentagon with a courtesy copy for Laird to review. "I went right through the wall, in Safire's presence, seated across from my desk," Laird recalled. "I had to call the president." Nixon had loaded the speech with references to the COSVN headquarters and how it was the prime target of the American mission. He was setting the mission up for failure in the public eye because the primary target, announced before the fact, did not exist.

Another line in the speech caught Laird's eye: "For five years, neither the United States nor South Vietnam has moved against these enemy sanctuaries because we did not wish to violate the territory of a neutral nation." Laird's quick call to Nixon included the tactful reminder that American B-52s had been pounding Cambodia for more than a year and, even though the pilots were dummying their flight logs, the bombing was not the best kept secret in Washington. Nixon did not take the line out of his speech.

Sometime during the afternoon, Laird got a note from Haldeman. Laird was disdainful of suggestions from the president's young sycophants, and this one was particularly grating. Haldeman instructed Laird on what kind of spin to put on the Cambodia operation after the president announced it in his speech. Among the things Laird was supposed to tell the press was that without the incursion the American troop withdrawal program would have ended. Laird didn't believe that for a minute and never used the line.[19]

At 9 p.m. on April 30, 1970, Nixon went on camera armed with maps and righteous indignation, and announced that thirty-one thousand U.S. troops were at that moment moving into Cambodia to ferret out the COSVN headquarters. (The original plan was to begin the operation two days earlier, but when Abrams consulted his Vietnamese counterpart about the date he was told that the Vietnamese general's astrologer had advised a delay. Laird agreed to wait until the stars were in a better alignment, but he didn't tell Nixon why. "I just told the White House that the weather and things weren't just right," Laird said.)

The American public's reaction to Nixon's announcement was immediate and virulent. No matter how he dressed up the operation, Americans saw it for what it was: an expansion of a war that they just wanted out of. The fact that the president made the announcement himself on national television contributed to the feeling of escalation. Laird and his public affairs people had urged Nixon to let General Abrams do the briefing in Saigon with as much of a business-as-usual aura as he could muster under the circumstances. But Kissinger advised Laird that the president wanted to look like he was in charge.

When Nixon woke up the next morning, he decided to visit the Pentagon to show just how "in charge" he was. Outside the entrance, at 8:30 a.m., he was heckled by hundreds of antiwar activists protesting the news he had delivered the night before. The president was visibly agitated about the protestors when Laird met him at the entrance. Laird figured that the president probably was caught off guard, unaware that protestors were not barred from the grounds but were allowed to take their demonstrations to the steps of the Pentagon's main entrance. Nixon was first escorted to Laird's office and then to the National Military Command Center where the Cambodia operation was being monitored. Already things were not going as Nixon had hoped; COSVN "headquarters" had not been found, the briefers told the president. Laird stifled the urge to say "I told you so."

The demonstrators who greeted Nixon that morning were just a taste of what was erupting all over the country in response to the Cambodia operation. ROTC buildings were set ablaze on at least five college campuses. A riot at Kent State University on the night of May 1 prompted Ohio governor James Rhodes to call out the National Guard to patrol the campus. On May 3 guardsmen charged students at a sit-in and stabbed some with bayonets. The next day the unthinkable happened. Jumpy guardsmen fired sixty-one shots into a crowd of students, killing four and wounding nine. It was a bloody fulfillment of Laird's warning, which he viewed as a great tragedy. He also saw it as a manifestation of the condition into which the National

Guard had fallen—its budget and training neglected by the Johnson administration while money flowed into the war. In his view, the Ohio guardsmen had too many inexperienced, exhausted young men who simply cracked.

The day after the Kent State killings, Nixon announced to a contingent of congressmen, without consulting his military commanders, that the Cambodia incursion would be over by June 30 and that the American troops would go no more than nineteen miles into Cambodia. The same day Abrams, trying his best to juggle the politics back home with the military objectives in Vietnam, got a memo from General Wheeler, who was serving out his last few days as chairman of the Joint Chiefs. "[I]t would be very much to our advantage to be able to announce . . . the withdrawal of some forces back to Vietnam as soon as this is operationally feasible and desirable. . . . I do not wish to imply that we would want you to prematurely terminate an operation or in any way jeopardize it just to gain a press advantage. However, it would be highly desirable for higher authority to be in a position to exploit fully the termination of an operation or withdrawal of at least some of the forces engaged in Cambodia."[20]

Abrams wrote back that with the sluggish pace of the war of late, "it took some doing to get people back into the offensive spirit," and there was no way he wanted to dampen their enthusiasm now by announcing a withdrawal when the operation had just begun.[21]

～

On May 6 President Nixon opened his *New York Times* to find a story quoting anonymous sources saying Laird and Rogers had "serious misgivings" about the Cambodia incursion. Although Laird was dutifully defending the operation at press conferences and in testimony before hostile congressional committees, the president angrily assumed Laird had leaked the news of his opposition so he could show clean hands, especially after the Kent State tragedy. Laird was adept at leaking, but this one was not his fault, he said later. He would not have provoked the edgy president at that time, nor would he have let news of his doubts leak during the heat of an operation where American lives were at stake. Laird assumed that the leak came from some staffers in Kissinger's office who had resigned from the NSC staff because they could not sanction the Cambodia operation. Within a week of Nixon's decision to invade, four of Kissinger's closest staffers, William Watts, Roger Morris, Larry Lynn, and Anthony Lake (who would later serve as National Security Advisor during the Clinton administration) had resigned in protest. While the four did not openly trumpet their resignations, Laird suspected they were the anonymous sources that planted many of the stories critical of the invasion.

Laird was painted into a corner. He respected the uses that could be made of the press and did not want to ruin his credibility with reporters by lying to them about his misgivings. But he also did not want to be a naysayer at the height of a critical military campaign. He issued a short statement saying he had always supported operations against the sanctuaries. At a press conference on May 6, Laird tiptoed around his opposition to Americans in Cambodia. "I supported the use of Americans as required to carry out this very important mission," Laird said, without adding that he didn't think Americans were required as ground troops in Cambodia. Then he quickly changed the subject to the success of Vietnamization.[22]

Finally on May 14 while speaking to a small group of reporters at the National Press Club, Laird owned up to his opposition, saying that he had initially not wanted to send in U.S. troops but that he had changed his mind when it looked as if the risk to them might be small.[23] It was one of those half-truths that Laird was capable of spinning when he was cornered. Indeed, he had become more comfortable with the U.S. role when he saw the risk would indeed be minimal. But he didn't learn that until the operation was in full swing and the bulk of North Vietnamese troops had abandoned the sanctuaries in advance of the invasion. The enemy opposition was so weak that Laird's original point was proved—the South Vietnamese could have handled it on their own, but Laird could not say that publicly without tipping his hand.

One enduring impression from the Cambodia operation was that Nixon was so angered by Laird's opposition that he tried to cut Laird out of the planning for the invasion. A Defense Department blue ribbon panel, headed by Gilbert Fitzhugh, concluded in July 1970 that the Joint Chiefs bypassed Laird and took some of their recommendations directly to the president knowing he would be more sympathetic. Laird insisted that never happened. Because he opposed the use of American troops, the word spread that Laird was never told about the plan to use them. "That's absolutely false," Laird said. "There was a disagreement and my recommendation was not followed. I was given every opportunity to make my case. The president made his decision after looking over both operational plans, and he insisted on using Americans after I'd had my day in court. I went along. I sent the orders."

As the president had promised, the last American troops were out of Cambodia by the June 30 deadline, one day ahead of a vote by the Senate to ban funding for any future American ground combat forces in Cambodia. The law did not faze Laird. He had already done what he could to make sure there would be no more Cambodian incursions. Two weeks before the operation was over, Laird had his staff draw up rules for future Cambodia operations. "These operations are to be conducted on the ground in Cambodia by indigenous personnel only," the policy said.[24]

~

Scaling down the U.S. operations in Vietnam meant that the Defense Department had to show some sort of "peace dividend"—a budget reduction as the war wound down. Yet Laird needed to hold onto as much money as he could in order to resuscitate U.S. defense operations elsewhere that had suffered from the drag of the war. A frequent target of Laird's budget scissors was the air war in Vietnam—a money-sucking operation that Laird felt yielded too little to justify it.

At one of their regular breakfast meetings in early June 1970, Laird and Kissinger talked about the failings of tactical air operations. On June 5 Laird followed up with a memo hoping to get Kissinger to see the light and perhaps to influence Nixon, who was a big fan of the bombing campaign. Bombing of North Vietnam was not allowed, but bombing of the enemy supply lines through Laos, Cambodia, and South Vietnam had become big business. "Despite the intensity of this interdiction bombing, we have apparently not been able to reduce logistics flows to the point that enemy activity levels in South Vietnam are significantly curtailed," Laird wrote to Kissinger. In the prior year, defense had spent $3.5 billion on aerial bombing—about one fourth of the cost of the war. Yet the enemy rebuilt and resupplied seemingly overnight like an army of ants. If anything was slowing the enemy it was the loss of men in battle, not the loss of trucks and supplies along the Ho Chi Minh Trail, Laird said.[25]

Laird sent the memo and headed off for NATO meetings in Europe. But his deputy, David Packard, kept up the drumbeat while Laird was gone. Packard wrote to Kissinger on June 18 urging a cutback in the bombing budget. "The magnitude of our air operations is unprecedented," Packard said. "Since 1965, we have dropped over 4.5 million tons of bombs on Southeast Asia, which is more than twice the tonnage we dropped in all theaters during World War II and seven times that dropped in the Korean War."[26]

At the same time Adm. Tom Moorer, still acting chairman of the Joint Chiefs and two weeks away from taking over officially, was lobbying for more use of air power. When Laird asked the chiefs in June to come up with other ideas for cutting off the enemy's supply lines, Moorer responded with a pat on the back for the status quo. "The Joint Chiefs of Staff have reviewed the current interdiction strategy and consider the present concept sound," Moorer wrote in a top secret memo to Laird on June 15, the same day Packard was giving Kissinger an earful on the poor results of the air campaign. Moorer added that increased cross-border air raids would help, and he couldn't resist the opportunity to get a dig in about the ban against bombing North Vietnam itself. "The most effective strategy . . . would be to attack the system . . . from the ports of entry in North Vietnam to the individual enemy soldier in the field," Moorer continued. In this war, he added, no bombing is allowed until the supplies cross into Laos.[27]

Once again, Laird was a chorus of one, bucking the president and the Joint Chiefs. Yet he kept singing the same song: building up the South Vietnamese army, not dumping more bombs, was the long-term solution. Laird's personal files on the war are littered with requests from Moorer for permission to bomb more targets in North Vietnam—called "strike authorities"—and to pick up the pace of bombing in Laos and Cambodia. The targets in North Vietnam were frequently surface-to-air missile (SAM) launchers that threatened American reconnaissance planes flying over the North. The SAMs also harassed bombers working over Laos or in the demilitarized zone between North and South Vietnam. Moorer pushed for blanket authority to bomb the SAM sites, while Laird was willing to approve authority only for one-time strikes, as long as the bomber pilots had some proof that a SAM site was actively being used against U.S. reconnaissance flights. Those flights had been allowed to continue after President Johnson had stopped bombing runs over the North in 1968. By 1970 they were the chicken and the egg—an invitation to an attack from the SAMs that then gave the B-52s an excuse to retaliate with more bombs.

On a sweltering morning, July 2, 1970, Laird stood in a hangar at Andrews Air Force Base, surrounded by the top brass of the U.S. military. The whine of a Strategic Air Command tanker jet outside on the tarmac threatened to drown out the festivities. Front and center was General Wheeler, retiring that day after thirty-eight years in the Army and six years as the chairman of the Joint Chiefs of Staff.

Seated near Wheeler was his replacement, Admiral Moorer, whom Nixon had announced two months earlier would be bumped up from chief of Naval Operations to the center seat in the Joint Chiefs' circle. As cunning as he was distinguished, as political as he was military, Moorer would require watching. He would try repeatedly to circumvent Laird's wishes and cut the defense secretary out of the chain of command to the president. Eventually, he would preside over the most bizarre story of intrigue in the history of the

Joint Chiefs—a plot to spy on the White House staff and steal secret documents from Henry Kissinger.

Laird had taken a gamble on Moorer. Although no formal rotation among the services was required in the chairman's seat, the Navy's turn was past due. Laird could have picked any military officer he liked. His top military assistant, Colonel Pursley, had advised Laird that during Robert McNamara's term, Moorer had been "devious," and "was not to be trusted."[28] Moorer ended up with the job because of choices Laird later said he regretted. Nixon was pushing for someone else, and Laird didn't want the president to have his way on the appointment. Also, Laird wanted Moorer out of the chief of Naval Operations slot so he could fill it with a relatively young Navy admiral, Elmo "Bud" Zumwalt Jr. He was one of the Navy's fastest rising, most savvy admirals, and his meteoric ascension had ruffled feathers, including those of Admiral Moorer. In late 1968, Moorer had promoted him to three-star admiral and put him in charge of the riverine forces in South Vietnam, the so-called "brown-water navy." Moorer reckoned that it was a job at which the upstart was doomed to fail. Zumwalt later confirmed, "Moorer's way of getting rid of me: *Promote the son of a bitch and nobody will ever hear from him again.*"[29]

Zumwalt, however, had performed well in the job and, more importantly, had embraced and carried out Laird's Vietnamization program, turning more than 80 percent of all U.S. brown-water combat vessels to the South Vietnamese by mid-1970. He had moved so fast that by year's end, the American inland naval forces could be totally withdrawn. There were many obstacles to the Zumwalt selection. He had never commanded a fleet, and the Navy chiefs traditionally had been aviators or submariners. And there were more than thirty admirals who would have to be passed over to reach down to Zumwalt's rank and seniority.

No one was more surprised at the choice of Zumwalt than Moorer. He "damn near went nuts," Laird recalled. "He spent a lot of time in my office, for two days, concerned that Zumwalt wasn't qualified. He felt that his personality wasn't right to assume command. He had serious questions about Zumwalt's ability." But Zumwalt was the price Moorer would have to pay if he wanted the highest uniformed job in the military. Thus began a contentious relationship between Laird and Moorer that ranged from simple cat-and-mouse games to outright spying by Moorer as each tried to stay one step ahead of the other.

15

Black September

SEPTEMBER 1970 GAVE LAIRD plenty of justification for his fear that Vietnam was sapping the resources of the Defense Department and could leave the United States vulnerable when there were other fires to be put out around the world. What would come to be called "Black September" in the Middle East began as did all their conflagrations—in ancient history. The immediate precedent was the Israeli victory in the 1967 Six Days' War, in which the Jewish state won territory, including Jerusalem and the west bank of the Jordan River. Palestinians fled east in such numbers that, when added to the exodus from previous conflicts going back to 1948, they soon outnumbered the residents of their host country, Jordan.

Jordan's King Hussein, an Arab moderate, was struggling to keep armed raiders from Yasser Arafat's Palestine Liberation Organization from crossing the border from Jordan into Israel to wreak havoc. Sporadic armed battles between the Palestinian guerrillas, known as the *fedayeen,* and the king's troops continued throughout the summer of 1970, particularly after the Palestinians tried twice to assassinate Hussein.

On September 6 hijackers from one of the most extreme groups of the *fedayeen,* the semi-Marxist Popular Front for the Liberation of Palestine (PFLP), hijacked one Swiss and two U.S airliners in Europe.[1] One of the American planes was diverted to Cairo where it was blown up after the passengers had disembarked. The other two planes were forced to land at a remote desert airstrip in Jordan. Palestinian commandos surrounded the planes on the dirt field and wired them with explosives. The PFLP announced that the passengers would be freed only if PFLP terrorists jailed throughout Europe and Israel were released within seventy-two hours. If the demand was not met, the 306 passengers—many of them Americans—would be blown up along with the planes.

Laird quickly began deploying American military resources to the area. The buildup in the next two weeks would eventually include twenty thousand American troops and three aircraft carriers. When Laird convened his weekly staff meeting on Monday, September 8, there was only one piece of good news: the fedayeen had released 127 passengers—all women and children. At that meeting Admiral Moorer revealed that two Pentagon officials and a military enlisted man were among the passengers.[2]

That afternoon, Laird engaged in a lengthy discussion about the crisis with Nixon, Kissinger, Secretary Rogers, Attorney General John Mitchell, and FBI director J. Edgar Hoover at the White House. During that meeting, the only order the president gave Laird was to take the "lead responsibility" in putting armed guards on American airliners and electronic security devices at airports to prevent future hijackings. Otherwise, he listened laconically to Laird's assessment that no successful rescue attempt could likely be made. Unbeknownst to Laird, Nixon had earlier told Kissinger that he wanted to use the hijacking as a pretext to strike back against the Palestinian terrorists in Jordan.[3] Nixon didn't mention that at the meeting, but Laird had known him long enough to discern suppressed rage, dangerously fed by a feeling of impotence.

So Laird was not altogether surprised when he got a call from the president giving him an order so controversial that neither Nixon nor Kissinger decided to include it in their memoirs.[4] The president apparently had had a few drinks, and he ordered Laird to "bomb the bastards."[5] He wanted Navy planes from the aircraft carrier *Independence* in the Mediterranean to bomb at or near the airfield where the hijacked planes were being held and possibly other fedayeen encampments. Laird didn't know what Nixon expected to accomplish. He surmised that the president was obsessed with stemming the tide of Soviet influence in the region, that he suspected the Russians were somehow behind the hijackings, and that he liked to make them think he was a bit crazy and unpredictable.

But Laird knew it would be the height of folly to "bomb the bastards." He chose not to dispute the commander in chief's instructions directly. "I told him we would do the best we could. I didn't have a big argument about it; I just didn't do it." Fearing Nixon's next call would be to the Joint Chiefs, Laird immediately called Moorer. "If you get a call tonight," Laird warned, "just let him know that the weather is bad, because we're not going to make any strike on that airfield in Jordan." The weather remained "bad" for forty-eight hours, until Nixon changed his mind about the bombing.

Was it Laird's place to ignore orders from the president of the United

States? "It's something I don't like to talk about," Laird said carefully in recalling that and other incidents when he felt the president had been rash. "Nixon liked to do things at night. He would call sometimes at very peculiar hours, and you knew probably he was having a couple of snorts with [his friend] Bebe Rebozo or someone like that. I was always very careful about that." Thirty years later, with Nixon dead and the facts relegated to history, Laird still didn't want to say that Nixon had a drinking problem. "I want to allude to the fact that sometimes orders that came at night were not good orders to follow," he demurred.

During the week following Nixon's order to bomb Jordan, Laird's level-headed response was vindicated. The PFLP hijacked a fourth plane, a British airliner, on September 9 and took another 115 hostages. Three days later they blew up the empty planes. Eventually all the hostages were released unharmed, and Nixon began to focus on the emerging threat to Jordan. King Hussein could not allow the belligerent fedayeen to challenge him further without response. He disbanded his civilian government and declared martial law. The fedayeen openly defied the new government, unified themselves under Arafat's PLO banner, and launched a countrywide insurrection on September 17. With the large-scale outbreak of civil war throughout Jordan, Laird ordered the attack aircraft carrier *Saratoga* to join the *Independence* one hundred miles off the coast of Israel. He directed four more destroyers and two attack submarines to the area, and alerted Army units in Europe and the Eighty-second Airborne Division at Fort Bragg to prepare for battle.

On September 19, when it appeared King Hussein was winning without foreign assistance, elements of the Syrian Army, crudely disguised as fedayeen, crossed Jordan's northern border to join the fedayeen. Estimates of the number of tanks that rolled into Jordan over the next two days ranged from several dozen to more than three hundred. King Hussein asked for aerial reconnaissance at one point, and Nixon turned to the Israelis for overflights. But they wanted to do more than just take pictures. On September 22 the Israeli Embassy in Washington sent a message to the White House saying they wanted to strike from the air and possibly send in ground troops.

Laird didn't like the Israeli proposal one bit. He thought King Hussein could hold on by himself, because Laird rightly assumed that the first intelligence reports on the size of the Syrian intervention were grossly inflated. His fear was that the Israeli involvement would tip the delicate Middle East balance into a full-fledged conflagration involving all the other Arab states. Nixon and Kissinger had similar concerns but, in the heat of the crisis, they made costly pledges of aid to the Israelis that threatened to backfire in the future.[6] Within a day, the need for Israeli intervention was moot. On September 23 the Syrians withdrew. The civil war was all but over except for the formal signing of a fourteen-point accord between King Hussein and Arafat on September 27.

⁓

Laird did not let up on his oversight and interest in the Middle East in the months that followed. He believed the war could be won and the peace still lost. The White House was in a mood to give the Israelis whatever they wanted, without regard for their already dominant military superiority in the region. During the previous summer Laird had been almost a lone voice for withholding America's most advanced military technology in the face of increasing demands from the Israelis. At the time, Nixon was trying to induce the Israelis to sign a cease-fire with the Egyptians over disputed Suez Canal territory and troop placements. On June 5, in a top-secret memorandum to Nixon, Laird concluded that Israel's request for more F-4 fighters was counterproductive. "Israel, which already has a very substantial bombing superiority over its combined Arab foes, has no immediate need for such aircraft: against the Arabs they are unnecessary, and against the Soviets they would be insufficient," he wrote. "We must not permit ourselves to be pressured into actions which will weaken our [peace] initiatives. We are looking for long-term solutions, and sleight of hand maneuvers to meet short-term Israeli aircraft requests pose too great a risk to be acceptable."[7] Nixon agreed, for the time being.

In early July the Israelis had urgently reported that the situation along the Suez had worsened. The Soviets had assisted the Egyptians in quickly setting up advanced surface-to-air missile batteries, which threatened Israeli air dominance. Laird repeatedly cautioned the Israelis that there was no surefire protection against the SAMs, as the United States had learned in Vietnam. Israeli planes would be shot down and, in a war of attrition in which the Soviets supplied Arab countries, the Israelis would inevitably lose. The only viable long-term solution was peace.

The Israelis backed off their demands briefly, until an accord was signed with the Egyptians on August 7. After that, their requests increased by quantum leaps. The Pentagon had a program to evaluate the Israeli "orders," and wryly named it "Project Binge." At one point Warren Nutter, head of International Security Affairs at the Pentagon, wrote Laird with alarm, "the list of Israel's 'wants' is limited only by their knowledge, which is extensive, of our latest and most advanced weapons."[8]

After the Jordanian crisis, however, Laird could hardly hold back the flood of Israeli arms requests because an ecstatic Nixon, flush with victory, wanted to show his gratitude to the brave Israelis. In an October 3 private memo to the president, Laird recommended against providing the most advanced equipment Israel had asked for, some of which did not even exist "except in the research and development stage." Supplying Israel, "given present Israeli intentions and in the absence of peace talks, carries with it certain serious risks . . . there is a grave danger here that the Soviets would respond by further escalating the conflict, thus placing Israel in jeopardy and bringing the U.S. closer to a direct confrontation with the Soviets."[9]

At Laird's insistence, Nixon denied the Israelis several specific military items but otherwise the president pledged a $500 million arms package—most of it coming out of the Pentagon's budget. ("There is a tendency by some to feel we can finance almost anything in the Department of Defense," Laird groused in one of his staff meetings.[10]) In December, as Israel's minister of defense Moshe Dayan visited the United States, Laird implored the president in an exceptionally tough memo to resist a rush of arms to the Jewish state. Catering to Israel meant "deferring what I consider to be higher-priority U.S. needs" such as NATO and Vietnam, and "it would further increase Israel's already very considerable advantage in attack aircraft. . . . I am disturbed that what may be our best chance for real peace in the Middle East will be let slip by an Israeli leadership which is too concerned for immediate security advantages to take a reasonable risk for peace."[11]

After the Dayan talks, Laird reported in his Monday staff meeting that the defense minister had indeed been "demanding," and wanted "more goods before Israelis will enter into talks." While Laird told the assembled Pentagon senior officials that "we are working on a sort of acceptable compromise," he opined that the Israelis would likely get more than he wanted them to have. (Nixon soon approved an accelerated delivery of the F-4s to the Israelis.) "The Israelis are smart negotiators," Laird smiled, offering grudging admiration. "We could take lessons from them."[12]

⁓

Less than forty-eight hours after the end of the Syrian invasion of Jordan in September 1970, the United States was frighteningly close to another confrontation—not with a minor Middle Eastern power but with a nuclear superpower, the Soviet Union. It was a possibility that Laird had warned about, and predicted, more than seven years earlier. In February 1963 after the Cuban Missile Crisis, Congressman Laird had told the Associated Press that the real goal of Russian operations in Cuba was establishment of a submarine base there, and that would be more serious than a few missiles.[13] By

1969 the Soviets were intent on demonstrating to the United States that they had a right to sail in any international waters—including America's backyard. In July a flotilla of six surface ships became the first Soviet task force to show their flags in the Caribbean as they sailed to Havana to celebrate Fidel Castro's tenth anniversary in power. Their arrival coincided with what U.S. intelligence determined was the largest-ever deployment of the Soviet Navy out of port, with thirty Russian combat ships in the Mediterranean that summer.[14]

Then in May 1970 a second Soviet naval task force sailed into the Caribbean, coming within forty nautical miles of Louisiana. This time they put in at a deep-water harbor in the Bay of Cienfuegos, on Cuba's southern coast, for a ceremonial welcome. When two of the ships subsequently sailed to Havana, they were given a twenty-one-gun salute as they entered the port. What concerned Laird and the Joint Chiefs was that lurking below the Cienfuegos waters was a Soviet Echo-class nuclear-powered submarine with nuclear missiles.[15] On August 26 a U-2 spy plane overflight of Cienfuegos Bay raised Laird's level of concern. There was new construction on the island of Cayo Alcatraz suggesting the beginnings of a Soviet naval base. When that information was combined with intelligence reports of a third Soviet naval flotilla steaming for Cuba, Laird decided to go public. He chose a morning coffee-klatch with reporters in the secretary's dining room on September 2. "I have a little rundown here on the naval task force of the Soviet Union . . . that has been moving from its usual operating area in the Barents Sea on course toward the Caribbean," he noted. "I think it should be made public," he said, calling it a "significant development." While the size and nature of the force would be unprecedented for the Russians in the Caribbean, he calmly said, "I do not see a crisis."[16]

A week later the Soviet flotilla reached Cienfuegos. Laird ordered a U-2 flyover on September 18 that photographed the makings of a major submarine refueling base well on its way to completion at Cienfuegos. Nixon's first impulse was to sit tight—at least until after his upcoming European trip and the midterm elections two months away. He didn't want a situation as tense as Kennedy's Cuban Missile Crisis.

On September 23 at a National Security Council meeting, Laird made a case for a measured showdown with the Russians before they completed the base. Kissinger, who was of the same mind, wrote that he was "extremely uneasy" about Nixon's go-slow approach during that meeting. "He ordered a very low-key public posture, confined simply to noting that we were aware of what was happening and were watching. Mel Laird pointed out that this would never work; too many people knew what was going on; the story [about the base] would leak."[17] As usual, Laird thought silence would be futile. Kissinger sent press guidance to both the Pentagon and State Department restricting comments about the Cienfuegos facility. But two days later Laird blew the cover off the quiet approach.

New York Times columnist Cyrus L. Sulzberger, in a September 25 editorial page piece titled "Ugly Clouds in the South," warned that the Soviets were building a possible submarine base at Cienfuegos. Laird's deputy press secretary, Jerry Friedheim, knew he would get questions about it that morning. The Pentagon press corps had been asking him daily about the movements of the Soviet flotilla and trailing submarines. Laird opted for public disclosure. He considered it "bad news" to report potentially hostile Soviet activity and knew that Nixon always preferred Laird and his people to give the public the bad news, reserving the "good news," such as troop withdrawals and lower casualties, for presidential announcements.

Friedheim was asked about Cienfuegos by reporters and spelled out in detail what was known about the ongoing construction of a Russian submarine base in Cuba, and it was front-page news. Laird apologized to Kissinger that day—not for disclosing the information but for failing to tell Kissinger in advance. He needn't have. The columnist Sulzberger revealed in his memoirs that it was Kissinger himself who had leaked the story to him. CIA director Helms had filled in more details for Sulzberger, and by the time the columnist had met with Laird to pump him for more information, Laird knew Sulzberger already had the story. And he wasn't the only one. Before Nixon had given the order to be low key about the submarine base, Kissinger had already leaked the details to other journalists and members of Congress.[18]

Instead of the public showdown Kennedy chose, Nixon eventually elected for secret diplomacy, giving the Soviets a graceful exit. That approach also depended on silence from administration officials, and this time Laird wholeheartedly agreed. He knew that if the administration provided the Russians with a painless way out of Cuba they might take it, so Laird maintained a tight hold on information about the negotiations with Moscow. He even had to bite his tongue when his antiwar nemesis, Sen. William Fulbright, taunted him in a Senate hearing, accusing Laird of "hoodwinking" Congress about an alleged base to scare up a bigger defense budget.[19] Laird kept his own counsel, even having his Pentagon briefers imply that the United States was no longer sure that the Soviets had ever intended to bring submarines to Cienfuegos. "That was after we got assurance that they wouldn't," Laird explained later. "We never said we were wrong. We were just cooling off." It worked. Nixon, in his memoirs, said he was pleased that Laird and others had kept "the secret so well that . . . several prominent political leaders and journalists dismissed Cienfuegos as a trumped-up crisis. . . . I did nothing to discourage such mistaken opinions."[20] The Soviet ships sailed home and construction was stopped within a month of public disclosure.

~

With the two latest crises on the wane, Laird accompanied Nixon to Rome for the start of the president's nine-day, five-nation tour of Europe. Laird was deeply religious, and though his upbringing was Presbyterian, he was looking forward to meeting Pope Paul VI when the pontiff gave Nixon an audience. But the U.S. representative to the Vatican, Henry Cabot Lodge, had advised Kissinger that Laird, because of his stewardship over the Vietnam War, should not meet with the papal man of peace.[21] Laird's presence might steer conversation toward the controversial war in Vietnam, and nobody wanted to open that discussion at the Vatican.

Since the president was showing off the U.S. commitment in the Mediterranean, he was to spend the night after the papal audience on the aircraft carrier *Saratoga*, part of the Sixth Fleet.[22] Laird was asked to bring a military helicopter to St. Peter's Square to pick up the president after his visit and transport him to the carrier. Laird arrived on time, but the president was still not at the Vatican. His handlers had ordered his arrival via motorcade through the streets of Rome to set up photo opps that would put the president's European tour in a grander context. But the motorcade was caught in traffic, and so the helicopter that was to take him to the *Saratoga* arrived at the Vatican one hour before the president.

An aide to the pope advised Laird that the president was stuck in traffic and said the pope would like to meet the defense secretary. Thinking it impolite to refuse a papal invitation, Laird allowed himself to be escorted in and spent about thirty minutes talking with the pope about Vietnamization, NATO, and other topics. Thus it was that when Nixon and his entourage, including Kissinger, finally swept into St. Peter's Basilica, they found Laird already ensconced in a papal audience. Kissinger was livid that Laird had violated protocol. "They were shocked to see me sitting there next to the pope," Laird laughed, "but I moved over, you know, so that there would be room for these dignitaries." One of Kissinger's aides, Lawrence Eagleburger, recalled the moment and said Kissinger was humorless. "Henry was convinced that when Mel was told they didn't want the defense secretary with the pope, that Mel did this helicopter exercise purely and simply so he could get Henry. This was an aspect of sort of acute competition between them."[23]

That night on the *Saratoga*, Laird was still flush from his coup over Kissinger and the advance men. At a dinner for Nixon in the officers' wardroom, Laird regaled the assembled dignitaries with details of his papal encounter. The invitation to enter had caught him by surprise, he said, and he quickly had to tuck the cigar he had been puffing on into his suit coat pocket. Then, surrounded by papal functionaries, he noticed his pocket was smoking. Laird said he began slapping at it so hard that others in the company started politely applauding, thinking they had missed something profound from the pope. When Laird told the story to the president and his dinner guests, he swore that the smoke led some to speculate that the College of Cardinals was electing a new pontiff.

Nixon and the others roared with laughter as Laird skillfully blurred the line between fact and fiction. He later insisted that he had couched the whole thing as a joke, but he did not realize he had been taken literally until Kissinger published his memoirs in 1979 and passed the story off as true. Moreover, Kissinger's account suggests he was an eyewitness to the event that never happened—even to the point of claiming he had wisely "urged Laird at least to do away with the cigar while we were in the papal presence."[24]

From the *Saratoga* Laird and Nixon parted company, with Nixon going on to Yugoslavia and Laird, along with admirals Moorer and Zumwalt, making visits to Turkey, Greece. and Malta on NATO business. Between Greece and Turkey, Greece was, at that juncture, the more symbolically important visit. Greece was ruled by a military junta that had wrested power from the elected government three years earlier. It had become known as the "Coup of the Colonels." The primary plotter, Col. Georgios Papadopoulos, became prime minister and also was acting as defense minister at the time of Laird's visit. Attempting to influence the repressive regime, the Johnson administration had instituted a selective arms embargo until the Greeks showed democratic improvement. About a week before Laird arrived in Athens, the arms embargo had been lifted and $56 million worth of U.S. aircraft, tanks, helicopters, and other equipment was to be delivered after his visit. As a crucial member of the southern flank of NATO, Greece had become a friend to openly embrace once again.

Not all Greeks welcomed the embrace. On Saturday October 3, after laying a wreath at Greece's Tomb of the Unknown Soldier, Laird, accompanied by heavy Greek security, went to the premier's office for a discussion. Shortly after they sat down, both were rocked by an explosion about sixty yards away in the national gardens. It was the work of an antigovernment agitator who wanted to assassinate both men. The explosion was heard throughout

Athens, whose residents could also see a pall of smoke rising from among the trees of the park, but neither the prime minister nor Laird was hurt.[25]

~

There was another terrorist bomb that went off during that period that did, in a sense, injure Laird more than the Greek dissident's attempt—even though in this case he was nearly one thousand miles away, safe and secure at Camp David, when it exploded. The University of Wisconsin–Madison was close to Laird's heart. His mother was on the university's Board of Regents, and he had arranged congressional appropriations to fund several research buildings on campus. On the morning of August 24 Laird woke up at Camp David to the news that the Army Mathematics Research Center at UW had been bombed, killing one and injuring four others. Laird took it very personally, even conjecturing that the bomb was a way to get his attention, since he had supported the funding, while in Congress, that had paid for the math center. "I had been responsible for the math center. In the 1950s, I had put in the congressional appropriation for the advanced mathematics facility, one of the first in the country to use computers," he explained. "They thought they were getting even with me now that I was secretary of defense. It was intended to raise hell with me, a sort of retribution. And they killed that young man."

In general, 1970 was a searing year when Laird felt the antiwar protest up close and personal. During the week of the May 4 Kent State shootings, Laird was headed home one evening in Bob Froehlke's chauffeur-driven car; the two men were neighbors and sometimes shared the ride. As the car approached a congested traffic circle near American University in Washington, they could see hundreds of students milling in the circle, reacting to the fresh wound of Kent State. Someone in the crowd spotted Laird and students surrounded the car, shouting, shoving, and rocking the car. "Get the hell out of here!" Laird ordered the driver, but they could only inch through the gridlock of people and traffic.[26]

Speeches by the defense secretary were also a magnet for protestors. Two weeks after the car-rocking incident, on May 23, Laird was invited to the Pick-Congress Hotel in Chicago to speak to the General Assembly of the United Presbyterian Church. He brought along Daniel "Chappie" James, an Air Force general and Pentagon aide for public affairs and POW issues. Imposing in size and military decorations, and noteworthy as one of the Air Force's few black generals, James drew attention when he traveled with Laird. A few among the onlookers that day got unexpectedly rowdy, shouting epithets at Laird. Confident that he was safe among fellow Presbyterians, and aware that

the general himself was a practicing Christian and had a deep baritone singing voice, Laird cranked up the volume on the microphone and announced,
"Ladies and gentlemen, we will now be singing some hymns. And they will
be led by General Chappie James."[27]

James went along with the pacification ploy, which worked. "He could sing
hymns like no one else I've ever heard," Laird recalled. "He was beautiful to
watch." So beautiful was he that when the two men went across the street to
the Conrad Hilton Hotel for a press conference after the speech, Laird prevailed on James to sing a hymn for the jaded reporters, too.

When Laird left Chicago, leaving General James behind, he flew directly
to dedicate the Central Wisconsin Airport in Mosinee, in his former congressional district. He was greeted by more than one hundred demonstrators protesting the Cambodia invasion, among others, and by his mother,
who was quite unsettled by the hostility toward her son. Laird refused to take
personal umbrage at the demonstrators; he ended his talk with these words:
"The chance to hear the viewpoint of young people has always been valuable
to me."[28]

That valued exchange of views was frequently denied to Laird by event
planners. For instance, the annual Madison service clubs dinner held at the
University of Wisconsin campus cancelled Laird as its September 1970 speaker,
fearing disruption by campus dissenters.[29]

No similar rejection caused Laird more hurt than one from his own alma
mater, Carleton College. As Laird recounted it, in the midst of the countrywide protests against the Cambodia invasion, a letter from a Carleton faculty
official arrived at the defense secretary's office and was brought to him by
his aide, Carl Wallace. An incensed Laird read that the faculty was mounting a campaign to have his bachelor's degree revoked to punish him for the
Vietnam War. Though the letter has been lost, Laird remembered that it was
not from Carleton's president, antiwar Quaker John Nason, or from the students, but from a faculty committee. Laird dashed off a response, asking for
a visit and discourse with the faculty to explain Vietnamization. He was sum-
marily turned down. For their part, the college later made attempts at recon-
ciliation, which led to an easing of tensions.[30] Later, research uncovered that
Laird also had been passed over for an honorary degree from Carleton in
the 1980s because he was still considered too controversial.

⌒

While the defense secretary was a reluctant warrior, he was an avid lifesaver.
Laird's first love was his work in the health field, and he found ways to express that passion. The most significant moment came in mid-1970 when he

implemented an idea he had had as a congressman. "One of the brighter spots of our experience in Vietnam has been the effectiveness of helicopter evacuation of the wounded from the front lines," he observed at a national medical conference on trauma in 1968. The previous year, more Americans had died from "the carnage on our highways" than were killed in Korea and Vietnam combined. Many could be saved if helicopters and trained paramedics were available to provide swift treatment and transportation, and the military bases across the country had both in abundance.

Once he was defense secretary, Laird sold Transportation Secretary John Volpe on the idea. In July 1970, they jointly announced the Military Assistance to Safety and Traffic (MAST) pilot program to be conducted in five Western states. Besides traffic accidents, the MAST helicopters also ferried victims of heart attacks and other potentially fatal trauma victims in rural areas. In the first fifteen months, the Air Force and Army flew 681 humanitarian missions and saved untold lives. Two-thirds of the missions took patients from rural and other hospitals safely and swiftly to better-equipped facilities in the state. The pilot program proved such a success that Laird soon approved MAST's expansion to fourteen more states.[31]

As secretary, Laird also dispatched U.S. military relief missions abroad, such as to the Biafrans in Nigeria in 1970 and to Nicaragua when a 1972 earthquake leveled Managua. At home, Hurricane Camille struck Mississippi in August 1969, and Laird ordered more than five thousand military forces to join the state's National Guard in rescue and recovery efforts. Lashing the coast with 160 mile per hour winds, Camille was the second of only three Category Five hurricanes to make landfall in the U.S. during the twentieth century, and 259 people died. Both Nixon and Laird publicly praised the Guard and military for saving lives.[32] Four years later, Hurricane Agnes ravaged the mid-Atlantic region, becoming the most damaging hurricane ever recorded—the worst of it in the central Pennsylvania district of Rep. Daniel Flood, a powerful member of the House Appropriations Committee. When the Susquehanna River roared over its banks, Laird quickly sent Flood his own Pentagon helicopter and forty more to rescue thousands of citizens from roofs and hilltops. The Army Corps of Engineers, 1,500 servicemen, and Laird's own wife, Barbara, vice chairman of the national Red Cross, joined the battle against the floodwaters and saved lives, holding the death toll at 129.[33]

In two famous but failed efforts, Laird's military searchers could not locate the bodies of Pittsburgh Pirate right fielder Roberto Clemente or House Majority Leader Hale Boggs, who died in separate aviation accidents. Clemente was flying on a mercy relief mission to Managua when his plane crashed off the coast of Isla Verde, Puerto Rico.[34] Representative Boggs, a Louisiana Democrat, was flying with another congressman and two others when his plane presumably crashed over a remote section of Alaska's southern coast. After an intensive thirty-nine-day search failed to find the victims, Laird had the sad duty of phoning Boggs's wife, Lindy, to inform her the formal search was being closed. She gratefully responded that she was sure "everything humanly possible" had been done. (Boggs was the father of journalist Cokie Roberts.)[35] More heartening was the successful rescue of famed aviator Charles Lindbergh and forty-seven others on a conservation mission to a remote, densely forested area of southern Philippines.[36]

Among Laird's diverse duties was presiding over the military operation of state funerals. In fact, Secretary Laird had the sad privilege of burying three former presidents on his watch—Dwight D. Eisenhower (March 1969), Harry S Truman (December 1972), and Lyndon Johnson, who died in January 1973 as the war that had broken him was winding down.

Laird also took on one more duty that no other secretary has had to—he became America's Postmaster General for a brief time. In March 1970, U.S. postal workers walked out in the first strike of the federal post office's two-century history. Nixon directed Laird to call up forty thousand reservists who were then trained for postal work. As acting Postmaster General, Laird set up a command postal center in the Pentagon and had the Reserves moving the mail smoothly by the second day. His long-time friend, labor leader George Meany, was furious with him. "Mel, what the hell are you doing?" he demanded on the phone.

"We gotta get the mail through, George, but we'll be real careful," Laird replied. Then he reminded Meany that it was a felony for a federal worker to go on strike. The use of the Reserves spurred a settlement with the postal unions in less than a week.

~

Nineteen seventy was a tumultuous year for Laird on so many fronts, but he ended it well—with the dedication of a room in the Pentagon that filled a personal need for him and, he was sure, for others—a Meditation Room. Not many were aware that the cigar-chewing political animal had a deeply religious side or that he had started a prayer circle in Congress. The surprisingly dovish defense secretary decided that the people at the Pentagon also needed some place to petition God. At a dedication ceremony for the Meditation Room in the A-Ring of the Pentagon on December 15, Laird carefully shared his spiritual side. He told the assembled crowd that the Pentagon had plenty of shops and restaurants to "satisfy the needs of the body."

Now it would have a corner to cater to the needs of the spirit, a place where "the needs of the inner man can find satisfaction. It is a place where men and women can reflect and pray and find guidance and inspiration. . . . This small room is an affirmation that, though we cling to the principle that church and state should be separate, we do not propose to separate man from God. For without Him, who is the source of our being, our wisdom, and our strength, we can do nothing."[37]

16

Friends in High Places

Helmut Schmidt was elected to the West German parliament, the *Bundestag,* in 1953—the same year that Melvin Laird was elected to Congress. Sixteen years later, both men would be defense overseers in the cabinets of their respective countries. And they would become fast friends through a shared respect for the responsibility that comes with military power.

Schmidt had written two books on defense policy and was an expert on military affairs when he became German defense minister in October 1969. Yet when he took the job, he discovered a secret—a NATO plan to bury a chain of nuclear weapons along the Iron Curtain from the Baltic Sea to the Alps. Schmidt was aghast. One of the first meetings on his schedule was the NATO Nuclear Planning Group, to be hosted in November by Laird in Washington, D.C. Schmidt decided he would talk to this American politician privately and see if he was a man who could be reasoned with.[1]

During the Cold War, the United States secretly manufactured hundreds of small nuclear land mines called Atomic Demolition Munitions (ADMs). The smallest of them could be carried in a commando's backpack and had an explosive power of ten tons of TNT. The nuclear wallop of the larger one was a Hiroshima-sized fifteen kilotons, yet it weighed less than four hundred pounds and could be transported easily by boat, helicopter, or jeep. The purpose of ADMs was to blast craters, create landslides, and take out bridges, depots, and dams or underground targets such as pipelines and tunnels. Because friendly troops would be operating in the area of ADM use, the weapons were designed to be as "clean" as possible, giving off minimal (but still deadly) radiation.[2]

The ADMs' best use, in the view of NATO planners, was as nuclear land mines planted along the predictable routes of invasion that Warsaw Pact forces could use to cut through West European countries. To that end, in 1969, when Schmidt and Laird became the defense chiefs of their respective countries, more than two hundred of the American ADMs were stored in West Germany awaiting burial in sunken concrete chambers along the borders. The United States and NATO had not given the green light to actually plant the bombs, nor is it clear whether that would ever have happened, given the need to closely guard any nuclear weaponry. But burial sites had been chosen, and some holes had already been dug in the anticipation that the strategy formed on paper might actually be carried out.

Schmidt pulled no punches at the November 13 meeting with Laird. The German acknowledged the appeal of the smaller-yield ADMs as a defensive weapon but then stated bluntly that pre-positioning ADM's in peacetime along the border would not be possible in his country. Schmidt pounded his fist on his knee to punctuate his questions: Who would control them? Who would be allowed to detonate them? How would the Soviets and the East Germans react when they found out the weapons were buried and waiting?

Laird had been silent but appeared to nod in assent. Finally, he said simply: "Don't worry, Helmut. I realize the problem you raise, so I promise you it will not happen—the ADMs will not be put in place."

The classified record shows that Laird kept his word. Few subjects were more discussed than the issue of ADMs at semiannual meetings of the NATO Nuclear Planning Group (NPG). Between the NPG's founding in the 1960s and a June 1970 gathering of the NATO defense ministers in Venice, Italy, there had been twenty-five different reports on the subject. At the Venice meeting, defense ministers from Italy, Turkey, the Netherlands, Canada, and the United Kingdom all spoke up in favor of the ADMs. Then Schmidt protested, saying none of the proposals for actually planting the ADMs was acceptable to the West German government. When Laird spoke up, he praised all sides for their work on the issue. Schmidt immediately recognized what Laird had *not* said. He had not expressed his own or his country's opinion on chambering the ADMs. "I knew our agreement was in place," Schmidt recalled. It was vintage Laird; he planned to stall the issue while still giving the appearance of progress.[3]

Five months later, on the day before the group met again in Ottawa, Laird and Schmidt had a one-on-one meeting to reaffirm their understanding. Mindful of note takers at the confidential meeting, Laird signaled Schmidt that he was working on getting approval from Nixon on what had been "discussed between our two departments on a secret basis."[4] The next day, the eight NATO ministers agreed to give authority for NATO's military commanders to *plan* for the possible movement of the mines from storage to points closer to where they would be used in the event of war. There was no approval for actually burying of the mines.[5]

During the Cold War, no matter how a military planner looked at it, there was no way for Western Europe to win if the Soviet Union decided to invade. Time and again, the outcome of the highly classified war games was never rosy. Europe would fall unless the United States stepped in with nuclear weapons. After World War II, most West European nations had downsized their military forces, even as the Soviets were building up their own and those of the Warsaw Pact countries. By 1967, in an attempt to motivate the European nations to take more responsibility for their own defense, the U.S. plan for responding to a Soviet invasion had been changed. Instead of an immediate nuclear response, the plan called for a "Flexible Response," which began with conventional forces and contemplated use of nuclear weapons only as a last resort.

This put the NATO nuclear option temporarily on the back bench, or so it seemed. In reality, the nuclear option still remained at the top of the NATO planning pyramid. Since most of Laird's fellow NATO defense ministers were neophytes on nuclear weapons and strategy, he threw himself into using the Nuclear Planning Group for substantive discussion purposes. But Laird worried that even with their limited experience, the NATO partners were getting too heady. For example, smaller European nations were emboldened to push for a U.S. pledge of full consultation with their political leaders if the use of nuclear weapons were imminent. But in a war with the Soviet Union, it was unlikely there would be time, for example, to get Belgium's permission before America reacted.

Now Laird's job was to give the smaller, non-nuclear NATO countries the reassurance that they were being consulted on U.S. nuclear policy, without giving them actual control over decisions. He genuinely felt that in peacetime it was well worth the effort to consult with all of NATO's partners, and he argued with top U.S. military officials that it was time to share a great deal more information. Toward that end, at the NPG meeting in Venice, Laird treated the NATO defense ministers to a highly classified briefing on the U.S.-Soviet strategic balance, using twelve satellite photos of Russian silos, submarine bases, bomber bases, and radar installations. "I must remind you of the extreme sensitivity of this source of intelligence," he began. "Because of the special responsibilities we share in the NPG, President Nixon has agreed with me that you should receive this briefing and see these photographs."[6]

The defense ministers were wowed. And to Laird's surprise, none of them leaked the information.[7] As a result, he was willing to share more secrets at the start of each semiannual NPG meeting. Laird's candor carried the risk of revealing more than he planned about the limitations of U.S. intelligence, and inevitably the NATO defense ministers, particularly Schmidt, began pressing him for more details. Laird had to bob and weave at the meetings to appear cooperative while not spilling sensitive information.

Mike Mansfield, the Democratic senator from Montana, perennially provoked a debate on cutting the number of U.S. troops stationed in Europe. He had begun the effort in 1966, as the Vietnam War caused eroding support for the military and troops abroad. By 1968 it appeared that Mansfield might have enough votes to cut the number of U.S. troops in Western Europe by half—at least that was the way it looked until the Soviets invaded Czechoslovakia, which doomed the Mansfield Amendment that time. Although it was little noted then, the U.S. troop level in Europe had already been substantially cut after reaching a peak (during the 1961–62 Berlin crisis) of 434,000 soldiers. When Laird became defense secretary, the number was 28 percent lower, at 320,000.[8]

Each time Mansfield tried, Western Europeans, and the Germans in particular, reacted vehemently and with some evident fear that the number might be cut. They regarded the level of U.S. troops in Europe as the most important barometer of American concern for the future of NATO and the defense of Western Europe, and they did not feel the need to beef up their own conventional military forces as long as the Americans were there with nuclear weapons. A rational strategy would follow that, having deployed an expensive nuclear deterrent, the United States should be able to decrease the number of American troops stationed in Europe, since their numbers were not great enough anyway to beat back a Soviet attack on the ground. But NATO allies became apoplectic at any suggestion that some of the 320,000 U.S. troops might be sent home.[9]

For himself, Laird was initially opposed to troop cuts as well. But if the Europeans wanted American troops in residence, it followed for Laird that the NATO allies had to share the burden by beefing up their own conventional forces, something those partners resisted. As Laird outlined in his first memorandum to President Nixon regarding NATO: "The United States has for years urged its Allies to provide better conventional forces. [But] there are some Europeans, of course, who continue to believe that the best defense is the *threat* of an immediate nuclear response to almost any aggression.

Having a substantial conventional option makes that threat less credible, in their eyes, and is therefore undesirable."[10]

A critical showdown on this issue occurred as Mansfield once again put forward his amendment in 1971, calling for only 150,000 U.S. troops to be left in Europe by the end of the year. When the vote was finally called just before midnight on May 19, Mansfield lost again, 36 to 61. But neither he nor the issue was finished, as Laird, Nixon, and the Europeans well knew.[11]

At the same time the debate was occurring, the Soviets were making noises that after three years of consideration, they might be willing to sit down and negotiate a mutual force reduction. The propaganda move was well timed to lull Western European governments into thinking that it was unwise to increase their own military forces when levels were likely to be amicably negotiated with the Russians. When Laird met with Schmidt in Garmisch, Germany, five days after the Mansfield Amendment vote, he discovered a despondent defense minister. According to the account from Laird's military assistant, Rear Adm. Daniel Murphy, Schmidt was discouraged about the antimilitary attitude in West Germany and had no hope that the European members of NATO would do more, militarily, for the alliance.[12] The next day, Laird sat down with Peter Carrington, Britain's defense minister, who was feeling equally discouraged. The United Kingdom and Germany were America's two most important NATO partners. The smaller European nations tended to follow the lead of Schmidt and Lord Carrington when it came to defense issues.[13]

When Laird returned to Washington, he tackled the problem of a disintegrating NATO alliance with such energy that the situation was turned entirely around by the end of the year. In November he beat back another challenge from Mansfield, when the senator tried to put a troop-reduction amendment in a budget bill. Then Schmidt and Carrington, with critical assists from Laird at key junctures, won increases in defense spending by their own governments.

The Schmidt-Laird collaboration was an important precursor to the strong cooperation between their two nations when Schmidt served as chancellor of West Germany from 1974 to 1982. Schmidt later explained, "Mel is not too intellectually complicated, but I'm not interested in intellectuals particularly as friends. I'm interested in a dependable human being, and Mel is one of those—a dependable counterpart in international affairs, and a dependable friend."[14] Laird had proven that from the moment of their first meeting when he pledged to Schmidt that the United States would not bury nuclear weapons along the Iron Curtain.

In retrospect, the time Laird invested in shoring up the NATO alliance paid off. According to an internal 1972 Pentagon study, "The visible effect of the Secretary's rapport has been most notable in the cases of some of our largest allies—the United Kingdom, the Federal Republic of Germany [and] France. . . . In each of these cases, we believe Secretary Laird's personal rapport with the allied Minister of Defense . . . was in large part responsible for significant improvements in our relations."[15]

That report added a fourth country with which Laird's relationship with one of its defense ministers had made an historical and positive difference—Japan.

On March 23, 1945, Lieutenant Laird and the sailors on board the USS *Maddox* had joined the American fleet in a series of relentless pre-invasion strikes on the Japanese island of Okinawa, while fending off enemy aircraft attacks. On April 2, the first Marines and Army infantry landed on the island. For nearly three months—from cave-to-cave, and often hand-to-hand—the soldiers had fought for the island. When it was over on June 22, some 7,700 American soldiers had died; the enemy had lost more than fourteen times that number. At sea, the U.S. fleet lost more than 4,900 sailors, making it the bloodiest battle in American naval history. Thirty-two vessels were sunk and 368 damaged, much of it the result of ten major kamikaze attacks using more than 1,500 planes.[16] The peace treaty with Japan gave the United States full jurisdiction over the Ryukyu island chain, including Okinawa. The treaty did not oblige America ever to return the islands to Japan, but the United States subsequently recognized Japanese "residual sovereignty" over the islands.

It is not hard to imagine the depth of feeling that Secretary Laird felt when he was confronted with an insistent demand from the Japanese government that Okinawa be returned to Japan. Not only was there a vivid memory of the sacrifice of his fellow World War II veterans, but also for Laird there was the resistance of Pentagon military chiefs who felt Okinawa was too strategic to relinquish. The island is located within a one-thousand-mile radius of the important areas of all mainland China, most of Japan, the Philippines, Korea, and Taiwan. A quarter-century after the war, Okinawa was a vital link in America's Far East security system and a key staging area for the ongoing war in Vietnam.

When Eisaku Sato became the Japanese prime minister in 1964, the return of Okinawa was one of his primary goals. A first step toward reversion occurred in November 1967 during a summit Sato had with President Johnson in Washington, D.C. They agreed to restore the Bonin Islands and Iwo

Jima to Japan, and stated an "aim of returning administrative rights over [the Ryukyu] islands to Japan." The U.S. ambassador to Japan at the time, career diplomat U. Alexis Johnson, pushed hard for a more substantive promise, and Sato felt he had a private understanding that reversion would take place within two or three years. When Nixon took office, Sato was comforted by the knowledge that the advocate of reversion, Alexis Johnson, was promoted to become undersecretary of state for political affairs.

To send a clear signal to the new president, Premier Sato addressed the Japanese Diet six days after Nixon's inauguration and declared that it was his "firm determination . . . to reach agreement on the date for the return of Okinawa to the homeland." Laird was not happy about Sato's declaration. First, he didn't like the way Lyndon Johnson had agreed to give away critical bases, such as Wheelus Air Base in Libya, without securing congressional approval. Second, the Joint Chiefs were concerned that the State Department was ready to deal away the Pentagon's right to keep pivotal bases on Okinawa if the island reverted to Japanese control.

Laird's dissent carried great weight at the White House. Aside from his normal clout in the administration, a long-standing executive order had designated the defense secretary the sole civil authority over Okinawa. So when Laird, as the administrator of the Ryukyus, voiced a negative view on reversion, Nixon had to pay attention. Laird discerned early that Undersecretary Johnson was playing heavily on Nixon's desire to have a summit with Sato. Japan was America's most important partner in Asia, and Sato had secretly informed Nixon he would not come to Washington unless the president agreed on a fixed date for reversion. Meanwhile, Alexis Johnson pushed through a secret presidential National Security Decision memorandum that chose 1972 as the year for reversion. But before Nixon agreed, Laird added a caveat to the document. Titled "Policy Toward Japan," the May 28 NSDM 13 featured a paragraph stating that "our willingness to agree to reversion in 1972 provided there is agreement . . . on the essential elements governing U.S. military use and provided detailed negotiations are completed by that time." Behind that language was Nixon's private promise to Laird that if the defense department opposed the negotiations over Okinawa at any point, reversion would not happen in 1972.[17]

On June 2 Laird discussed the secret presidential decision at the next top-level Pentagon staff meeting, and sometime later that day, someone leaked NSDM 13 to Hedrick Smith of the *New York Times*. Less than five months into his administration, Nixon reacted furiously to this first major national security leak. He ordered a Justice Department investigation and vowed not to hold another National Security Council meeting. It was over this issue, according to Haldeman's diary, that Kissinger first considered wiretapping his own staff. Nixon suspected either an NSC staffer or a top Pentagon official, and he had Haldeman call Laird several times to demand a Pentagon investigation.[18]

At the same time, Nixon dispatched a handwritten note by messenger to Laird to punctuate his anger. The single sentence read: "That leak on Okinawa was a real blow—as far as our bargaining position with Japan is concerned." Since Laird was well known to have many friends in the press, and it's probable that Nixon suspected him of being unhappy with the reversion and sent the note as a warning. Alexis Johnson also suspected Laird and pressed Secretary of State Rogers to call Laird and ask him point blank if he had done it. Rogers called and Laird assured him that he was not responsible for the leak.

A few weeks after the Okinawa leak, Joint Chiefs chairman General Wheeler unloaded his frustration in a throw-down-the-gauntlet memorandum, which was hand-delivered by messenger to Kissinger at the White House. "Over the years, we have made many concessions to the Japanese," Wheeler began. He included generous trade concessions to Japan that allowed them "to freely market their goods in the U.S." Japan had responded with "restrictions on U.S. trade and capital investment in their country." The United States had gone to enormous lengths and cost to rebuild the conquered Japan into a nation of unprecedented prosperity, and its government had responded by erecting trade barriers that froze out American business. Wheeler argued that he saw no good reason to proceed with such "unnecessary haste" to give them the strategic jewel of Okinawa.[19] Unfortunately for Wheeler and Laird, their go-slow position was unexpectedly undercut by an accident on the island that became public in the summer of 1969.

⌒

A terse message was delivered to the Laird on July 8, 1969: "Rabbit dead at Chibana." Laird bit down on his cigar. It seemed like every day at the Pentagon was two steps forward, one step back. If things went well in one area, they were sure to be catastrophic in another, and that particular Tuesday was no different. He had been looking forward to the day for a historic reason. Solely as a result of Laird's planning and pressure on the president, the first 814 soldiers from a group of twenty-five thousand troops were flown out of South Vietnam that day, marking the first-ever withdrawal of U.S. forces from the conflict. Laird felt like celebrating and was in an ebullient mood as he donned his tuxedo for the evening's White House dinner with the Ethiopian emperor, Haile Selassie. Then came word of the dead rabbit.[20]

The rabbit had been caged near some deadly nerve gas stored in fifty-two earth-covered igloos at the secret Chibana Army Ammunition Depot just off the approach pattern to Kadena (U.S.) Air Force Base on Okinawa. Without the chemical agent detectors that are available today, the Chibana chemical corps relied on animals to alert them to chemical leaks, much as coal miners used caged canaries to alert them to methane gas. The Japanese had never been told that President Kennedy had ordered eleven thousand tons of mustard and nerve gas munitions to be stored on Okinawa for possible use in a Pacific conflict. Since the United States still "owned" the island, such a disclosure to the Japanese government was neither required nor politically wise.[21]

One of the many goals Laird set upon taking office in 1969 was to radically change America's military chemical and biological weapons (CBW) priorities. Laird aimed to persuade Nixon to destroy all U.S. biological weapons and severely reduce the chemical weapons cache. His plan was to destroy most of the World War I mustard gas that made up half of America's total thirty-thousand-ton chemical weapons stockpile. He also planned to detoxify the aging GB and VX nerve gas munitions that made up the other half of the stockpile and replace them with a smaller quantity of new and safer-to-store "binary" chemical weapons, which become lethal only when two or more chemicals were mixed together as a bomb was dropped or as a missile was in flight. A March 1968 VX aerial spraying accident at Utah's Dugway Proving Ground had killed 6,400 sheep and become a major public embarrassment. Laird was determined to move the eleven thousand tons of chemical weapons off of Okinawa before their existence became known. But he instinctively knew when he received the dead rabbit message that secrecy was out the window, and there would be hell to pay.

Within hours, word came to Laird that the rabbit had been felled by a leak of GB nerve gas. The twenty-three Army soldiers and one Army civilian employee who had been near the canisters were taken to a military hospital for observation. They were released and returned to duty with a clean bill of health in less than six hours. Normally, Laird followed a full-disclosure policy regarding accidents, but any mishap involving chemical or nuclear weapons was not disclosed because that would betray the location of the weapons. So Laird waited for the other shoe to drop.

On July 17, *Wall Street Journal* reporter Robert Keatley called Laird's press chief, Dan Henkin, and asked for comment on a story about a nerve gas leak that had put soldiers in the hospital on Okinawa. It was a long night for Henkin, as he reported to Laird the following morning. He negotiated through the night with the *Journal's* editors to "kill publication of this story in the national interest" but to no avail. Laird issued a brief statement saying there had been a minor "mishap" on Okinawa. It was not enough to quench the furor that erupted among Okinawans.[22]

"We could never have imagined that on an island where one million people live, there could be such weapons," editorialized the Okinawa Times. "The flight of B-52s [for Vietnam bombing] made the Okinawan people extremely apprehensive. The port calls of nuclear submarines have also caused uneasiness. But reports about nerve gas have caused a different sort of fear among the people, a more ominous sense of anxiety." A quick connection was made between the Chibana chemical weapons storage facility and the mysterious skin ailment, accompanied by a high fever, that 267 elementary school children suffered one day in August 1968 when they were swimming at a beach less than five miles from Chibana. There were also reports of a strange blight in the pine forest around Chibana, as well as tales of mutant frogs, included a ten-legged one, that had been found nearby. The Okinawan Legislature quickly passed a resolution that demanded removal of the chemical weapons.[23]

Laird confirmed that the chemical agents were there and also revealed that he had requested a CBW study the previous April—in part because he planned to remove the weapons from the island. He publicly pledged to remove the toxic weapons as soon as it was safely possible and a destination was found. At first, the Joint Chiefs resisted Laird's decision to remove the weapons. The chiefs were anxious to have chemical agents at the ready in Asia to deter both the North Koreans and the North Vietnamese from using similar weapons. "But I was secretary of defense, and I never planned to authorize chemical weapons use in Vietnam, so I thought it was crazy that this stuff was in Okinawa," Laird said. "I wanted it moved. Fast." Laird's single vote at the Pentagon was bigger than any other combination of dissenting opinions.[24]

So the Joint Chiefs reshuffled and tried to make a case; first, for an alternate storage site on an island the South Koreans were trying to sell the United States, and second, for moving the deadly gas to Guam. The South Korea option soon fell through, and the residents of Guam protested when they found their small island might be the recipient of the frightening weapons. Next, the Joint Chiefs made a case for moving the materials to the Umatilla Army Depot in a remote part of Oregon, where the townspeople of Hermiston had lived side by side with chemical weapons storage for many years. When that new plan became public in December, the protests were loud and politically damaging to the Republican governors of Oregon and Washington. It hadn't helped the Army's image when another related plan had been revealed to secretly ship twenty-seven thousand tons of aging chemical weapon canisters across the United States and dump them in the Atlantic Ocean near Atlantic City, New Jersey. It had foolishly been dubbed "Operation CHASE," which stood for "Cut Holes and Sink 'Em." The operation was scrapped because of congressional opposition, and the plan to move the Okinawa gas to Oregon was overruled by Nixon in May 1970.[25]

One last straw was grasped when Sen. Ted Stevens of Alaska volunteered to have the chemicals transferred to Kodiak, which he thought would ensure that a local military base there would operate in perpetuity. But the rest of the Alaska delegation, as well as the governor, strenuously objected. The only choice left was to move the stockpile to tiny Johnston Island, 700 miles southwest of Hawaii, where storage facilities and America's first full-scale chemical agent detoxification plant would be built, costing tens of millions of dollars. Under the name "Operation Red Hat," the last of the Chibana toxins were shipped to the island in September 1971.[26] (Johnston Island, where nuclear weapons had been tested in the 1950s and 1960s, remained a CBW dump until final cleanup in 2005.)

Meanwhile Laird had moved so fast and hard on the CBW front that he won a historic, unanimous decision from the National Security Council and the president before his first year in office was over.[27] On November 25, 1969, Nixon personally announced to the press the multifaceted CBW policy, which Laird had crafted. Nixon pledged that the U.S. would never engage in germ warfare and would destroy any remaining lethal biological weapons stocks. The president renounced all but defensive uses of chemical weapons. The key to Laird's success was the change he imposed on the NSC process. Normally, a study group of the NSC looking at an issue would deliberate and make its recommendations. At that point it was usually too late to redirect the focus of the group or even the basic assumptions it had used. Laird insisted that he be able to review the guidelines before the group began its deliberations. His insistence that he be at the head of the parade rather than just on the reviewing stand made all the difference.[28]

Another historic announcement had been made by Nixon with Laird's concurrence four days earlier. Both men had concluded that the only way to win easy approval in Tokyo for the ten-year renewal of the U.S.-Japan Security Treaty in 1970 was to accede to Sato's request for a fixed date on the reversion of Okinawa. At the end of a three-day summit in Washington, Nixon and Sato announced on November 21 that the last major issue of World War II in the Pacific would be resolved when Okinawa was returned to Japan in mid-1972.[29] With the Okinawa issue settled, Laird had an even bigger Japan matter on his plate—weaning the Asian nation from the American military dole.

~

The ink was barely dry on the postwar Japanese constitution when its authors on Gen. Douglas MacArthur's staff came to regret Article 9, the most famous section of the "peace" constitution. It still reads, in part: "The Japanese people forever renounce war as a sovereign right of the nation. . . . Land, sea, and air forces, as well as other war potential, will never be maintained." Many countries in the region were happy to keep Japan toothless, but the Nixon administration was not. Laird felt strongly that Japan should beef up its forces and military spending to become a true partner with the United States in protecting the region's security. It was the primary subject Laird planned to raise with Defense Minister Nakasone when he arrived in the United States for a five-day visit in September 1970.[30]

The two men could not have been better suited to understand one another. Both had come from families whose livelihood was made in lumber. Each served in his Navy as a paymaster. They both had lost brothers in the military—to storms and not combat. (Laird's older brother, Connor, died when his U.S. Navy minesweeper sank during a storm; Nakasone's younger brother Ryosuke died when the plane in which he was flying crashed in a blizzard near the summit of Mount Kyokugatake.)[31] Both Laird and Nakasone were witnesses from afar of the first atom bomb explosions. Nakasone saw the mushroom cloud over Hiroshima from the nearby Takamatsu naval base; Laird was aboard the *Maddox,* close enough to Nagasaki to hear the atomic explosion there three days after Hiroshima.

Both emerged from the war with the resolve to go into politics. Nakasone won a seat in the Japanese Diet in 1947 at the age of twenty-eight, five years before Laird was elected to Congress. Both had their detractors who envied their shrewd, quick ascent in the leadership of their parties. Laird was decried as a "Midwest Machiavelli" whose manipulative ability in pursuit of his political aims was difficult to parry; Nakasone was nicknamed "Mr. Weathervane" because of the way he switched allegiances among various factions of the Liberal Democratic Party to facilitate his rise to power.[32]

When Laird and Nakasone met in Washington in September 1970, each recognized a kindred spirit; they tackled the tough subjects head on. Laird explained that it was time for a genuine mutual security arrangement between the two countries. It was fine that Japan enjoyed the protection of the American umbrella, but that umbrella was costing the United States more than $500 million a year. Nakasone agreed that the Japanese would become involved to a greater extent in sharing the burden of U.S. military costs in Japan. It was the first time that Japan acknowledged it had a responsibility for the cost of its own defense. Nakasone promised to push for a major increase in his defense budget. He was anxious that some of the U.S. bases in Japan, particularly near Tokyo, be turned over to the Japanese. Laird agreed and confided that he already planned to reduce the U.S. force in Japan by ten thousand men, or one fourth of the force.[33]

Perhaps the most sensitive topic dealt with nuclear weapons. Laird knew from American intelligence sources that Nakasone, who had once advocated that the Japanese acquire small defensive nuclear weapons, had earlier in the year ordered a secret study to determine how much it would cost and how long it would take for Japan to become a nuclear power. The study concluded that it would take $555 million and five years, but that it was impractical because of the absence of suitable land for a nuclear test facility.[34]

Laird pointedly asked Nakasone if he still felt the need for a Japanese defensive nuclear force. Nakasone answered no. He was coming to the realization that possession of nuclear weapons would bitterly divide the Japanese, who were the only people in the world to have suffered from the use of the atom bomb. Also, as long as the U.S. nuclear deterrent was in place, there was no need for a separate Japanese atomic force. If Nakasone really believed a Japanese nuclear program was impractical, then Laird said the Japanese shouldn't mind making it easier for the United States to protect them with U.S. nuclear weapons. With evident courage and subtlety, Nakasone agreed, telling Laird that the United States could assume that rules about bringing U.S. nuclear weapons into Japanese territory would be more relaxed in the future. The treaty between the two countries allowed temporary storage and transportation of nuclear weapons in and around Japan without consultation in times of "emergency," and Nakasone said he was willing to be flexible in the definition of "emergency."[35]

Considering the agreements fruitful, Nakasone proposed that the two of them conduct annual consultations. It wasn't as easy as it sounded; no U.S. secretary of defense had ever been invited to Tokyo, for fear of massive demonstrations. Nakasone conceded the problem and said he would think on it further.

After the Washington, D.C., conference, both men were as good as their word. One month later, Nakasone issued the Japanese Defense Agency's first-ever white paper. Previously, defense ministers had been too afraid to put their military priorities in writing. Several months later, Nakasone proposed more than doubling defense spending when he submitted his budget.[36] Also forthcoming was an invitation to Laird to visit Tokyo. The State Department strongly advised against it, but Laird ignored their concerns. He wanted to be the first American secretary of defense to visit Japan.

~

In the spring of 1971, the president's senior military aide, Brig. Gen. James "Don" Hughes, contacted the pilot of Air Force One, Col. Ralph Albertazzie, on a secure phone line and asked him to hurry over to the White House without telling anyone where he was going. Once there, the pilot was taken down to the "shelter," a hardened concrete-and-steel bunker intended for temporary use by the First Family in the event of an attack on the White House. "We've got an interesting one this time," Hughes began, a big grin spreading across his face. "The Boss [Nixon] is sending Kissinger to China. Secretly. You know a way to smuggle him in? And out?"

"You mean Communist China? Good Lord!" Albertazzie exclaimed. Once he was over the shock, the two brainstormed, then Albertazzie headed back to Andrews Air Force Base to mull over the best way to conduct the covert mission.[37]

Of all the secret discussions Kissinger had, those preceding the China opening were regarded by him as the most sensitive. Nixon agreed with Kissinger's request that Laird and Rogers would be kept in the dark until just before the public was informed. But keeping such a secret from Laird was next to impossible, especially when the secret involved military officers, planes, and communications equipment.

The most incontrovertible and detailed information came from the National Security Agency, whose director, Adm. Noel Gayler, was appointed by Laird. Kissinger's communications with the Chinese went through CIA "back channels." The NSA routinely intercepted those international messages, and Gayler personally passed them along to Laird. On May 31, 1971, the Chinese (through Pakistani intermediaries) informed Nixon that they were agreeable to a Nixon visit to Peking, provided Kissinger himself secretly came first to Peking on July 9–11 to make the arrangements. In less than a day after the invitation was issued, Laird was informed by Gayler about it. He smiled to himself and thought he would have some fun with the secretive Kissinger. But first he would give Kissinger a chance to brief him on the mission.

On June 4, Kissinger went to the Pentagon for a routine breakfast. In the course of their wide-ranging discussion, Laird dropped a few questions about the People's Republic of China to give Kissinger an opening, but Kissinger didn't bite. So Laird decided to "throw a hook at Henry," as he put it. Laird was already planning to visit Japan and South Korea in July, which the White

House had approved. A few days after his breakfast with Kissinger, Laird sent the White House an updated itinerary that now included a side trip to Taiwan on precisely the days when Kissinger would be in Peking. It was Laird's playful way of saying he knew what the national security advisor was up to. But Kissinger didn't get the joke. Instead, he was apoplectic. The prospect of a defense secretary in Taipei talking about the U.S.-Taiwan alliance just as Kissinger was in Peking trying to downplay that very alliance was too much for Kissinger. For two days, without giving Laird a good reason, Kissinger frantically pressed Laird to cancel the Taiwan portion of the trip. When Laird had had his fun—which he called "giving Kissinger the needle because he didn't share his trip with me"—Laird let the national security advisor off the hook and dropped the bogus Taiwan plans.

Kissinger never knew it was a setup. In his memoirs, he wrote that "Mel Laird conceived the idea of inspecting defense installations on Taiwan on just the days when I would be in Peking [but he] was a good soldier. Without inquiring into my reasons for asking, he rearranged his schedule."[38] Thirty years after the fact, when the charade was revealed to him, Kissinger took umbrage. "He shouldn't be proud of that," Kissinger said. "That was not something to jerk my chain on." A friend of Kissinger's and Laird's, former secretary of state Larry Eagleburger, thought it was hilarious—and that Kissinger needed to "get over himself. Mel mentioned the whole thing to me as a way of trying to stick it to Henry. I think it's funny under any circumstances."[39]

~

On the Fourth of July 1971 the first American secretary of defense to visit Japan landed in Tokyo to great fanfare. His Japanese counterpart, Nakasone, had arranged for a twenty-one-gun salute and a military band playing the national anthem. "However," Nakasone laughed in recalling the event later, "the staff of Mr. Laird, who got off the ramp of the special plane dressed casually in bell-bottom trousers, surprised the Japanese managing staff who welcomed them. Then there were two teenagers who also got off the plane. One of them was Mr. Laird's son [David] and the other the son's friend. Both of them were sixteen years old and in high school." The proper Japanese were put off because, at the time, "We would never think of allowing children to fly with an official delegate," Nakasone explained.[40]

The following morning, Laird met with Nakasone, who was just minutes from resignation. The week before, Prime Minister Sato had suffered a setback in parliamentary elections, which prompted him to reorganize his cabinet. At Nakasone's request, Sato had kept him on the job long enough to host Laird's visit. The outgoing Nakasone told Laird how much he had enjoyed

their short association. The controversial issue of returning the island of Okinawa to Japan had been settled, and Nakasone also thanked Laird for the
planned removal of chemical weapons from Okinawa and the promise that
the island would also be free of nuclear weapons when it was given back to
Japan a year later (May 15, 1972).[41]

At one point in the Japan trip, Laird experienced an awkward moment.
Nakasone "was vitally interested in U.S. policy toward the People's Republic of China," Laird wrote in his report to Nixon after the trip. "I told Nakasone
we were proceeding cautiously and that, from a military standpoint, I could
see no imminent fundamental changes on either side." While that was true,
the fact that he could not disclose in confidence to this new friend and ally
the visit of Kissinger to Peking four days hence was difficult for Laird. But
he also knew that the Japanese government leaked like a sieve, and such a
public revelation would cause the Chinese to call the whole thing off. So he
kept silent. The meetings with Nakasone had otherwise been very successful.
A top Pentagon official later wrote that it was "as a result of these meetings
[that] Mr. Nakasone swung from being a critic of the [U.S.-Japan] Security
Treaty to the role of an active and staunch supporter." It was this second
visit with Nakasone that firmly established annual consultations between the
U.S. and Japanese defense agencies, which have been conducted since.[42]

Laird had recognized in the dynamic, charismatic Nakasone a present and
future star. "We shall see and hear more of Nakasone over the coming years,"
Laird predicted in his report to Nixon. On July 7 Nakasone hosted a private
dinner for Laird and his group at a Tokyo restaurant. Fueled by saki, the two
World War II veterans slipped back into memories of the engagement in
which they had fought on opposite sides. Nakasone thought his country's surprise attack on Pearl Harbor, objectively viewed, "was a great military coup,
and we should have gone right on to San Francisco and Los Angeles." Laird
courteously disagreed, and then mentioned that he had with him some "medals," which the Japanese had given him during the Pacific conflict.

"I'd like to see those," the curious Nakasone said.

Laird obligingly pulled up his pant leg and showed Nakasone blue-gray
splotches on his leg where pieces of embedded shrapnel were working their
way out. "This is my great remembrance of Japan. I carry a lot of Japanese
metal around with me. I think it's fair to say I've got quite a few Japanese
medals that I've been awarded." Nakasone laughed, and then soberly reflected
on how far the two nations had come. Laird offered a toast. "To be honest,
it will always be difficult for me and many other Americans to forget Pearl
Harbor, but this is a new day." Using a Japanese phrase he had learned for

the occasion, he then held his glass up to toast the "new start" that he and Nakasone had forged between the military leadership of each nation. At his departure press conference, Laird wryly noted that this visit to Tokyo had been more enjoyable than his last one—as a sailor in 1945.[43]

Laird returned to Washington by way of Hawaii, arriving just after midnight on July 14. It was about this time that Kissinger *officially* informed Laird on a secure phone line about his trip to China. Laird did not reveal that he already knew about it, but did request that he be allowed to tell Nakasone six hours in advance of the July 15 public announcement. Kissinger thought it was an unusual request but acceded, in part because Laird had not complained about being kept in the dark. The Laird-Nakasone friendship continued to benefit both the United States and Nakasone later when Nakasone himself was elected prime minister.

The Japanese government as a whole was not as unflappable as Nakasone had been about the U.S.-China opening. The Japanese were not perturbed about the new relationship itself, but were instead very upset that as America's closest ally in Asia, they had not been consulted. It was the first of several "Nixon shocks" that strained the relationship and subsequently contributed to Sato's loss of his post as prime minister less than a year later.[44]

There was other fallout of a more unusual nature from Kissinger's China trip. As it happened, there was a young Navy yeoman aboard the plane who was spying for the Joint Chiefs, rifling through Kissinger's briefcases, and copying documents. But that fact would not be discovered until India and Pakistan went to war at the end of the year.

~

The 1971 skirmish between India and Pakistan was inevitable, given their history. Pakistan was created in 1947 with a partition of India that resulted in two Pakistans—East and West—both under the same government but with the whole of India in between them. Pakistan (East and West) was a nation of Muslims and some Hindus under a military dictatorship ruled by Yahya Khan. India, under the leadership of Indira Gandhi and the world's largest democracy, was predominantly Hindu. In 1971 a strong independence movement was brewing in East Pakistan, but Yahya Khan was not about to let it go. He sent in a sixty-thousand-man army from predominantly Muslim West Pakistan and particularly targeted the Hindus living in East Pakistan for extermination. At least five hundred thousand, and possibly as many as three million, were slaughtered by Yahya's soldiers.

Hindus from East Pakistan fled by the millions into neighboring India.[45] Indira Gandhi decided to weigh in on the side of the independence for East

Pakistan. As superpowers are wont to do, China and Russia took sides, with the Chinese supporting Yahya Khan in his effort to keep East Pakistan under his thumb, and the Soviet Union hinting that it would back India if Gandhi decided to intervene on behalf of East Pakistani independence. On November 23 the Indian Army invaded East Pakistan.

It was inevitable that East Pakistan would and should become an independent country. But Nixon feared Gandhi would use the crisis as a pretext to attack West Pakistan as well. So, the president and Kissinger crafted a secret policy tilt toward Pakistan. Publicly, the White House claimed that the United States was neutral. But those in the secret policy councils chaired by Kissinger in late 1971, primarily the Washington Special Action Group (WSAG), knew better.

At a December 3 WSAG meeting, David Packard and others listened as Kissinger launched into a series of mini-tirades. He sputtered at one point: "I am getting hell every half hour from the president that we are not being tough on India. He has just called me again. He does not believe we are carrying out his wishes. *He wants to tilt in favor of Pakistan.*" After the State Department representative outlined some options that would punish both India and Pakistan, Kissinger complained about having to reproach them equally when he wanted to favor one. "It's hard to tilt toward Pakistan when we have to match every Indian step with a Pakistan step."[46]

It was a cynical deception, and Packard was as disgusted as was Laird, who abhorred Kissinger's penchant for secret maneuvering that was at odds with public pronouncements. Besides, at the Pentagon and in other agencies of the government, many felt that the president and his national security advisor were biased toward Pakistan because they were both obsessed with the China opening—and China was Pakistan's ally.

Nixon suspected Laird was not in accordance with his tilt toward Pakistan and, on December 6 ordered Kissinger to get the defense secretary "to follow the White House line."[47] That same day, military opposition to the tilt toward Pakistan broke out in Laird's top-level staff meeting. Admiral Zumwalt, the chief of Naval Operations, used the meeting to express his doubts. "I am disturbed," he said. "The United States will take a lot of lumps siding with the Pakistanis." He said that inevitably East Pakistan would gain its independence, and the United States would look bad while the Soviets picked the winning side. "In the short term, the military balance in the Indian Ocean area will go against us."[48]

That same day India recognized an independent East Pakistan under the new name of Bangladesh. As the crisis was winding down, however, a leak of the WSAG meeting minutes and other documents to columnist Jack Anderson—proving the Nixon-Kissinger tilt—prompted an investigation that shook the highest levels of government. When the minutes of the heated WSAG meetings on India and Pakistan began appearing in Anderson's column on December 13, the White House scrambled to find out the source of the leak. They found it in the Pentagon. Adm. Robert O. Welander, who was the liaison between the Joint Chiefs and Kissinger, immediately suspected his young stenographer, Navy yeoman first class Charles Radford, who frequented the copy machine and had a soft spot for India where he had once been posted. Radford was hooked to a polygraph machine. Under questioning, his connection to Anderson was left unresolved (and Anderson maintained even until his death in 2006 that Radford was not his source.) Radford did confess that he had been stealing Kissinger's documents, but he did it under orders from Admiral Welander who was then slipping the documents to the chairman of the Joint Chiefs, Admiral Moorer.

Laird's general counsel, Fred Buzhardt, investigated and found a morass of mistrust and spying—the inevitable offspring of Nixon's own secretive and manipulative style that infected every office from the White House on down. Radford's job was to keep Welander informed about what Kissinger was doing, and Welander's job was to keep Moorer informed. Knowing Kissinger's penchant for secrecy, Radford's best option was to pilfer Kissinger's bags. Buzhardt's investigation concluded that while Welander never asked Radford to steal, the admiral knew how the yeoman was getting the documents. Similarly, Moorer never asked Welander to steal, but he also didn't discourage the flow of purloined papers. Buzhardt reported back to Laird that during the investigation, "Admiral Welander acknowledged that he did not believe he would have been given authorized access to much of the materials obtained by Radford on his trips with Dr. Kissinger and General Haig. Admiral Welander stated that he had informed [Moorer] of the method by which Radford obtained the materials."[49]

Zumwalt summed up the bizarre and paranoid environment of the time in his memoir: "Kissinger telling me he distrusted Haig; Haig telling me he and others distrusted Kissinger; Haldeman/Ehrlichman trying to bushwhack Kissinger; Kissinger and the President using Moorer to help them make plans without Laird's knowledge and therefore pretending to keep Moorer fully informed while withholding some information from him, too. . . . What I find hard to believe is that rational men could think that running things like that could have any other result than 'leaks' and 'spying' an all-around paranoia.

Indeed they had created a system in which 'leaks' and 'spying' were everyday and essential elements."[50]

For Laird it was just more justification for his "firewall" between the Pentagon and the White House, and he took steps to reinforce that wall. But he was too sanguine about the atmosphere to be taken by surprise. Kissinger, who had condoned wire-tap spying on the Pentagon, was outraged to be on the other end of espionage. But Laird was as nonplused about the stolen documents as he had been about the wire taps. When Kissinger demanded punishment for Radford, Laird told him to back off. Radford was transferred, and Moorer got a slap on the wrist from Laird. "I called Moorer in and told him that it was the greatest personal disappointment that I'd had," said Laird. "But he said it was all for the good of the Pentagon, 'and for your good too, Mr. Secretary.'" Moorer's excuse was that the White House was too tight with its secrets to the point of blocking the necessary flow of information to the Pentagon. "Well," Laird replied. "I just want it to stop." And the admiral was allowed to go back to work.

Pursley, who called the admiral a "lucky man," said Laird realistically could not have fired Moorer. "The whole idea of a military gone a little berserk was not something, I'm sure, that the Nixon White House contemplated, or wanted to have brought up in an election year," said Pursley. "Having a scandal like the chairman spying on the White House—that makes it really look like nobody's in control." Within a few months, Moorer was back in the good graces of Nixon, who found in him a willing accomplice whenever the president tried to maneuver around Laird.

17

"Management by Walking Around"

IT WAS A WEDNESDAY EVENING in Washington, July 1971, and the joint was jumpin' at the Army-Navy Club, where members of the Piscatorial and Inside Straight Society (PISS for short) were gathered to make some noise. The club of Wisconsinites was started by the dean of the state's political reporters, John Wyngaard, to gather reporters, editors, and politicians who enjoyed fishing and playing cards at lakeside cabins when they were in their home state.[1]

Whenever Melvin Laird convened PISS in Washington, its homeboys roster always included Supreme Court Chief Justice Warren Burger as well as two Democrats—prominent lawyer Tommy "the Cork" Corcoran and Sen. Gaylord Nelson. On this Wednesday evening Tommy the Cork was on the piano, the chief justice was belting out songs, and Laird was picking a fair tune on the garbolene, a country bass fiddle (sometimes called a "gut bucket") made out of string and a large bucket or garbage can.

Some time after midnight, Nelson got into a friendly disagreement with Laird. For years they had been debating one another with healthy mutual respect, since they had served together in the Wisconsin state senate on different sides of the aisle. This particular debate at the PISS gathering turned into a wager—for what stakes, no one remembers.

Senator Nelson insisted that the "hotline" between Moscow and Washington was located at the White House. Laird, who ought to know, maintained that it was at the Pentagon. When Nelson wouldn't concede the point, Laird decided to settle it that very night. He loaded Nelson into a chauffeured car and took him to the Pentagon. Probably the combination of the late hour (3 a.m.), the libations at the PISS affair, and the trust Nelson had in Laird overcame any reluctance the senator might have had to enter the Pentagon.

Nelson was known as a consistent antiwar vote in the Senate, and his legislative interests leaned toward the environment. To have such a man in the
bowels of the Pentagon was a rare event.

Nelson's version of the story suggests what an Alice-in-Wonderland experience it was for him. "I got out of Mel's car and he pulled out the longest
key I ever saw; it must have been four or five or six inches. As he put it into
the [elevator] slot, sparks flew and all that. An elevator came for him and
we were whisked up a couple floors, where we were met by a bird colonel
or a brigadier general." They were then led into a cavernous room two stories tall and full of military personnel at work in the middle of the night. It
was the National Military Command Center, where Laird settled the bet by
triumphantly showing Nelson the hotline, which was similar to a teletype
machine and not a telephone. They spent the whole night there talking.[2]

Laird wooed members of Congress like no other defense secretary before
or since. He probably also set a record for the number of federal legislators
hosted at the Pentagon in a four-year period. In one year he managed to
lure almost all one hundred senators to the Pentagon in groups or individually, often for breakfast or lunch. For many of the lawmakers it was an unexpected and welcome opportunity to explore the inner sanctum.[3]

Not willing to wait for the legislators to come to him, Laird couldn't keep
himself away from Capitol Hill. He would wander the halls of Congress several times a week, his most common excuse being the haircut gambit. Use
of the House barber shop was a perquisite for current and former members
of Congress, and Laird haunted the shop regularly, in spite of his lack of hair
to cut. An internal accounting by a Pentagon intern of Laird's hours spent
on Capitol Hill showed that the secretary's "haircuts" seemed to take anywhere from forty minutes to three and a half hours. "Mr. Laird must have
been especially well-groomed in December [1971], when the record lists three
haircuts in one eight-day period," the study reported.[4]

The wily secretary had discovered an ideal neutral setting in which to
keep up his contacts with individual members of Congress; word would
spread that he was in the barber shop, and people would make their way
there to chat. Laird's legislative affairs chiefs, Rady Johnson and Dick Capen,
were responsible for keeping track of what was happening in Congress. "He
was always a step ahead of us," recalled Johnson. "He'd go up to the Hill and
get—quote—'a haircut' and see fifteen senators I couldn't have seen in a
week." Capen said, "I always knew when he went for this ritual because my
hotline rang the instant he returned; he was calling just to rattle my cage with

information he had gathered and I had not. 'You certainly should have known that!' he'd prod. 'What in the hell are you doing?'"[5]

At one cocktail party, Lt. Col. George Dalferes was asked what it was like working for Laird in legislative affairs. "It's kind of like being the pope's religious advisor," Dalferes quipped drily.[6] All those who worked for Laird could repeat in their sleep his constant reminder to them that Congress is a *co-equal* branch of government. All were told to cooperate as fully as possible with any legitimate request from Congress. Part of that cooperation went beyond the standard fare of protecting bases, military projects, and defense contractors in the congressional districts. On rare occasions Laird could help a member of Congress by arranging a better posting for a soldier. (He recalled doing a favor for Sen. Al Gore Sr. when his son Al Jr. was sent to Vietnam. Laird arranged a desk job at the *Stars and Stripes.* Young Gore never knew what his father had done.) Many requests came from patrons of young men who wanted to avoid the draft, but Laird was unsympathetic. Not once did he keep someone out of the military who didn't otherwise qualify for draft exemption. And only rarely did he hasten a promotion at the request of someone else. A former assistant secretary of the Air Force, Richard Borda, remembered being heavily pressured by one congressman to promote the son of one of his campaign supporters. Knowing Laird's policy generally forbade such special intercession with promotion boards, "I told the congressman 'No,' and he kicked me out of his office."[7]

One of the reasons Capitol Hill leaders liked Laird was because he made himself and his people available for testimony or consultation any time it seemed legitimately necessary. He sometimes used staff meetings to coach his people on how to be model witnesses: Don't hide information just because it looks bad; don't bring too many aides with you because it makes you look like you're not prepared; and *never* get hostile or combative with the legislative inquisitors. Learn how to politely filibuster when time is limited and the questioner seems to be building to a dramatic negative point; in this way you can throw him off his game.[8] (The *Washington Post* once wrote that "when Laird was on Capitol Hill testifying, he was at his best. . . . As a witness, he was clearly better at answering or evading questions than many legislators are at asking them. His ability to make his point, whether it had any relation to the question, was maddening to veteran lawmakers." Sen. William Fulbright once called him "a genius of semantic confusion."[9])

Laird used to his advantage his unique relationship with the General Accounting Office and Elmer Staats, its comptroller general. The GAO is the investigative arm of Congress, and Laird had used it many times to poke around at the Pentagon when he was a congressman. Aware of the damage the GAO could do with a good audit, Laird made a point of helping the auditors tasked to the Defense Department. Because of the personal relationship he cultivated with Staats, Laird was always forewarned about what an audit contained before Congress got it. Thus, he either corrected the problem before the audit became fodder for a legislator, or he had a plan in place that he could immediately announce as a way of correcting the problem.[10]

There is no better measure of Laird's prodigious legislative success than the fact that when he was secretary of defense he never lost a single roll call vote on defense matters in either the House or the Senate. The legislative record confirms that Laird was Nixon's only cabinet official who never suffered a major defeat in Congress. Such a record, by a Republican cabinet officer dealing with a Democratic Congress full of animosity toward the Defense Department, gave Laird standing to ignore or circumvent Nixon and Kissinger if his keener political sense deemed it necessary.

It was not easy for Laird, despite his congressional prowess. It required careful planning, hard work, and shrewd maneuvering. And it required him, by President Nixon's own insistence, to help the administration on Capitol Hill on many nondefense issues, which Laird had originated in Congress when he was ranking member of the HEW Appropriations Committee. These included automatic cost-of-living increases in Social Security payments, the war on cancer, and revenue sharing with the states.

⁓

Laird had an innate ability to anticipate an outcome. CBS newsman Bob Schieffer, who covered the Pentagon in Laird's day, called him "one of those rare guys in Washington who could look at a situation and tell you how it's gonna come out down the road."[11] What Laird saw when he came to the Pentagon was ominous: Lyndon Johnson had robbed men, materiel, and money from every other part of the defense budget—including NATO troop support and weapons research—to feed his Vietnam War machine. Money was needed to produce new weaponry to keep ahead of the Soviets; military pay had to be increased substantially to create an all-volunteer force. The public had to be disabused of any expectation of a "peace dividend," which had been fueled by presidential hopeful Hubert Humphrey in the 1968 campaign and suggested to be anywhere from $8 to $40 billion annually. The man Laird had in the Defense Department on point for this predictably unpopular budget battle was his chief financial officer, assistant secretary Robert Moot.

A week before Lyndon Johnson left office, he had delivered a budget to

Congress that included about $80 billion for defense. Well knowing the mood of many members of Congress as well as the public, Laird feared that Congress would gut his first-year budget by as much as $10 billion, or about 12 percent. Given Laird's plans to increase pay, modernize weapons systems, and restock non-Vietnam supplies in Europe and elsewhere, losing budget dollars was untenable. To Laird it meant that by trying to keep the Soviet Union "contained" through the Vietnam War, that surrogate sideshow might easily have cost America the main show—the Cold War.

Possessing formidable knowledge about every detail of the defense budget, Laird had settled on a bottom-line figure for that first year in office; defense could stand a $5 billion cut. Once he had the number Laird sat down separately with the promilitary chairmen of the four defense-related congressional committees and told them that the military needed $75 billion to survive, and also that he was willing to let Congress take credit for the cuts. One of their number, at the right time, could call for $5 billion in cuts, and, for his part, Laird would publicly grouse about it. At the same time he would progress with a series of moves aimed at meeting the $5 billion figure. Like a shell game, Laird floated several defense budgets at any given time, confiding to only a trusted few which one he really needed.

Congressman George Mahon, Laird's willing co-conspirator in the House, played the role of bad cop in August 1969 and called for serious cuts in the defense budget—"at least $5 billion," he said. Legislators began lining up behind the number, not knowing that Mahon and Laird had already agreed on the figure. In collusion with Kissinger, Laird persuaded Nixon that the military had too many international missions that were not being fully financed by Congress and the taxpayers. Since the end of World War II, Congress had approved mutual-defense treaties with forty-two nations. American troops were deployed to more than two thousand spots around the globe: it was simply too much.

The quickest way to make a change, Laird argued, was to get rid of the U.S. military doctrine that dictated America needed "force levels" capable of fighting two-and-a-half wars simultaneously—such as the Soviets and the Chinese on separate fronts. and a skirmish in the Middle East. When Laird took over the Defense Department, not even the most optimistic military strategists believed the United States could do that. The military was already stretched thin fighting just one war. Laird and Kissinger persuaded the president to change the force-level goal to one and a half wars. On October 11, 1969, Nixon signed the secret National Security Decision Memorandum 27 changing "the approved United States strategy for general purpose forces."

While all this was happening, Mahon and others in Congress were telling Laird that the pressure from colleagues had become so great they weren't sure they could hold the line at the agreed-upon $5 billion in cuts. On October 27 Laird announced that he was going to save $609 million a year by downsizing or closing 307 bases—twenty-seven of them overseas. The 280 domestic bases were spread out over forty-two states, which meant that thousands of jobs would be lost in the districts of eighty-four U.S. senators and a majority of representatives. Even the most ardent defense critics in Congress knew they had been outfoxed. So they declared victory . . . and retreated swiftly back to the safer, compromise $5 billion figure.

Another hurdle unexpectedly arose as Nixon was holed up at Camp David over the Christmas holidays to review the budget one more time. Word was soon passed to Laird that the president wanted to cut another $3 billion or more from defense to balance the budget and pay for increases in popular domestic programs. Rather than confront Nixon directly, Laird called the president's budget officer and said, simply. "Please tell the president that if he wants more cut than the $5 billion, he'll need to look for a new secretary of defense." Nixon immediately capitulated and never again tried to push Laird further than he was reasonably willing to go on the budget.[12]

After the first year's budget battle, Laird went on to close more bases than any defense secretary before or since. "It was political dynamite," recalled his former military assistant Robert Pursley. "For example, his Navy secretary, John Chafee, the former governor of Rhode Island, had to approve shutting down bases in his state right off the bat. Mel made it stick. He made a lot of gutsy calls on that." In four years, Laird closed four hundred unnecessary installations and reduced 1,400 others, saving billions of dollars. By December 1972 he had finished another round that would close or cut back 274 more military bases.[13]

Part of Laird's budget foresight included consideration of the defense budget in reference to the Gross National Product. He believed that the American public would not tolerate more than 7 percent of GNP devoted to national security, so he used that as a rule of thumb, bringing the defense budget from an LBJ high in 1968 of 9.5 percent of the GNP down to 6.4 percent in late 1972, the lowest percentage in twenty-two years.[14]

More significantly, Laird helped Nixon achieve something Democrats had talked about for decades: spending more on human resource programs than defense. The historic turning point came in July 1971, when for the first time the budget of the Department of Health, Education, and Welfare exceeded that of the Defense Department.[15]

In tandem with courting Congress was Laird's mission to win public opinion in the darkest days of the Vietnam War. Within weeks of becoming secretary, Laird lectured his top staff, including the Joint Chiefs, about the need to mingle with the masses on the speakers' circuit.[16] But the order was ignored. So hostile was the American attitude toward the U.S. military that a public speech by any Defense Department representative was likely to be met by obscenities and rotten produce.

At the end of Laird's first year in office, he asked for a statistical summary of speeches and learned that generals and admirals were dodging the lecture circuit. When they did venture out, it was to preach to the choir—to soldiers, veterans, retirees, and friendly Rotarians. Grudgingly, the new Joint Chiefs chairman, Admiral Moorer, scheduled a single college speech, at Princeton University in March 1972. It was a disaster. As Moorer approached the lectern, about one hundred students in the front row stood up and turned their backs to him. Moorer struggled through his thirty-five-minute speech and left despondent, with a memory of one of the large antiwar posters reading: "No Moorer Murder."[17]

General Westmoreland also made a foray or two into academia, with a similar lack of enthusiasm or success. He agreed to give a speech, "The Army's Role in the Search for Peace," at Yale in April 1972. But when he got to the auditorium, it was an out-and-out melee. Demonstrators were overrunning campus police, who told Westmoreland they couldn't guarantee his safety. On the advice of the Defense Department security men with him, Westmoreland left without delivering his speech.[18] David Packard, too, was game, but it was disheartening for him to be spurned at his own Stanford campus— his alma mater, to which he had contributed millions of dollars. It was a place whose administrators, faculty, and students revered him until he agreed to serve his country by becoming deputy secretary of defense during an unpopular war. Admiral Zumwalt commiserated with Packard at a staff meeting after one of his own talks to students. He couldn't even tell the long-haired boys from the girls anymore. "I was talking with one student, saying 'Yes, ma'am,' and I later found out he was a man. Now we have to be careful with these young people when we say 'yes, sir' or 'yes, ma'am' to them."[19]

These were times when, as the new Army secretary Froehlke discovered in 1971, the rank-and-file Army at the Pentagon had to be ordered to wear their uniforms at least once a week. "Particularly the enlisted and the lower-ranking officers didn't want to wear their uniforms when they worked in the Pentagon because people would spit on them and denigrate them," said Froehlke.

He understood why Americans were conflicted, and he sympathized, up to a point. "I want you to know that I'm not sure we're right," Froehlke said in his speeches. "I'm doing what I think is right. But there's one group that I know is wrong, and that's the group that's sure it is right." He didn't always get far enough into his speeches to say that, such as his attempted oration to a crowd of four hundred at Harvard in 1972. "My wife was with me and as I walked in you could see a dozen dirty, disheveled kids right down front. They threw every four-letter word at me," he said. Thinking it would shame them into civility, Froehlke remarked, "I would like you to meet my wife." But the protesters continued to shout and security guards advised the Froehlkes to leave, which they did.[20]

Laird felt it was key to lead by example. He went to speak at almost any college that would have him, but he was sometimes pelted with eggs and had animal blood thrown on him. His speeches tended to be dry, deliberately dull if he chose. His most common way of dodging a question was to launch into a lengthy policy analysis leaving his listeners yawning. Laird didn't mind boring them as long as they forgot what they had asked him in the first place.

By 1970 Laird had become "the talkingest Defense Secretary yet," according to Washington *Star* columnist Orr Kelly. The Pentagon kept audio tapes of speeches and congressional testimony by Laird and his predecessors, and Kelly counted the words. In his first sixteen months in office, Laird had spoken 786,000 words on Defense Department business in public, compared to the 923,000 spoken by Robert McNamara over his seven years in office.[21]

When Laird was defense secretary—and until skyscrapers exceeded one hundred floors—the Pentagon was the world's largest office building, boasting 6.5 million square feet, three times the floor space of the Empire State Building. Laird did a lot of walking in the Pentagon. He believed that the more he was seen by the nearly thirty thousand workers in the building, the greater his success as a manager would be. "Management by walking around" was a much-heralded technique used by David Packard at the Hewlett-Packard company. But no secretary before Laird had used it at the Pentagon. Generally, they holed up in their E-ring offices suite and summoned subordinates to them. Not so with Laird who, as the first professional politician to become secretary, found that walking around suited him as well as walking around the Capitol.

The employees quickly learned that Laird had a sense of humor, shown in the moniker he chose for himself—CINCMINC, "Commander in Chief, Military-Industrial Complex."[22] His public affairs spokesman, Jerry Friedheim, said Laird was fond of popping into offices unannounced to chat with secretaries and enlisted personnel. "Sometimes he'd go to the cafeteria and eat with employees. Somehow, he remembered most of the names of people after meeting them once and would acknowledge them when he saw them again."[23] One of his longest-serving executive assistants, Kathy Weaver, noted that on her first day working for Laird, he came out of his office and surprised her by saying, "Can I get you a cup of coffee?"[24]

Laird's natural way with young people spawned hands-on involvement with the White House Fellows program. President Johnson began the fellowships in 1964. More than a dozen young people at a time were assigned to cabinet-level and other high offices throughout government. When Laird became secretary of defense, he realized how beneficial the fellowships could be for young military officers. He needed to bring up through the ranks people with political savvy and a healthy respect for Congress and the White House. So Laird asked Nixon to bend the rule that said fellows could not come from within government. Laird was given three slots for military officers, all of whom he could personally select.

Laird spread the word among the services and pressured them to send him applications from the best and the brightest young officers they had. Among them was Army Lt. Col. Colin Powell. "There may be one moment in our lives we can look back on later and say that, for good or ill, it was the turning point," Powell wrote in his memoirs, *My American Journey*. "For me, that day came in November 1971" when he received the application to become a White House Fellow. Laird picked him from the list of applicants, and Powell was assigned to the White House's Office of Management and Budget, where OMB director Caspar Weinberger and deputy director Frank Carlucci could mentor him. Both would later become secretaries of defense, and Powell would go on to become chairman of the Joint Chiefs and later secretary of state.[25]

Midway through Laird's term at the end of 1970, the *Armed Forces Journal* recognized that the Defense Department's first politician in chief had become "a good manager," the proof of which was his hiring of Packard and his ability to delegate to the experienced businessman.[26] Explained in shorthand, Packard was "Mr. Inside," and Laird was "Mr. Outside."

Among many qualities, Packard was appreciated for his decisiveness and candor. A favorite memento kept by one of his former military assistants, Lt. Gen. Ray Furlong, is a "buck slip" that reads—in Packard's handwriting— "Tell the S.O.B. no!" It typified his boss's straight-forward, no-nonsense approach. Sometimes Packard's blunt remarks bordered on naïveté. At his first press conference, after he acknowledged he was taking "a helluva cut" to a $30,000-a-year salary, Packard blurted out: "But I don't intend to *live* on $30,000." The press corps, most of whom lived on less than that, nevertheless roared with laughter. They found his lack of pretentiousness refreshing, as did Congress. When the Nixon administration espoused a new nuclear doctrine called "strategic sufficiency"—essentially meaning they could not seek nuclear superiority over the Soviets anymore—someone asked Packard, after congressional testimony on the subject, what "sufficiency" really meant. Packard peered down at the inquirer and said: "It means that it's a good word to use in a speech. Beyond that, it doesn't mean a damned thing."[27]

Since Laird and Packard had never worked together before nor had they been close friends, many expected there would be major differences between them. Much in the way children "test" their parents individually to exploit differences, so too did the military services and Joint Chiefs try to discern Laird-Packard differences to use to their advantage. One of Packard's military assistants, Maj. Gen. James Boatner, said the chiefs viewed Packard as "more of a hawk," so as soon as Laird left town they would come to the deputy's office for approval of more aggressive Vietnam bombing campaigns or other initiatives. Boatner and Furlong made a joke of it. "We'd be sitting there and we'd say, 'Well, Mr. Laird's airplane is about to take off from Andrews. We ought to see the JCS up here shortly." The ploy never worked, Boatner said.[28]

Later efforts to match the Laird-Packard model were less successful. When Dick Cheney was appointed secretary of defense by George H. W. Bush in 1989, Cheney tried to re-create the magic. Emulating Laird, Cheney the politician would be "Mr. Outside" and Donald Atwood, former General Motors vice chairman, would be "Mr. Inside." Cheney conceded their pairing never quite rose to the Laird-Packard standard.[29]

In 1993 when former Rep. Les Aspin—a Wisconsin protégé of Laird's—was appointed defense secretary by President Clinton, Aspin chose technology-oriented William Perry as his deputy. Perry recalled: "When he invited me to be his deputy, he wanted me to do for him what Packard did for Laird. It didn't work out that way, just as it hadn't for Cheney and Atwood. In fact, the Laird-Packard image is so instilled in people's minds that many teams have tried to emulate it. Their explicit goal has been to achieve the same success the Laird-Packard team did."[30]

Laird embraced a new operating philosophy called "participatory management." Robert McNamara had confessed to Laird that one of the greatest mistakes he had made was not truly listening to his employees, particularly the uniformed military men and women. Laird didn't really need to be told that. "Mel liked to get his information by talking to people rather than reading long memoranda," according to the longest-serving Pentagon administrator, David "Doc" Cooke. "Conversely, Bob McNamara would happily read or go through a fifty- or a one-hundred-page memoranda, making notes in a rather unintelligible left-handed scrawl. McNamara was a paper person; Laird was a people person."[31]

Laird made it clear he was not going to micromanage. Since he had personally chosen or endorsed all the top-level political appointees for their jobs, he trusted they would perform at a top level. Trusting his staff was also a matter of self-preservation. At the end of his long days, Laird would often look upon a pile of documents needing his signature. Instead of reading them, he would trust that his staff had prepared them well, take a quick drink, and sign them all. He called it "5 o'clock roulette."[32]

⌢

Laird usually awoke about 5 a.m. daily and swam laps in his pool. His Pentagon driver, William Johnson, would arrive with the morning's important paperwork for Laird's perusal at home and on the way to the Pentagon. Johnson became a beloved Laird family member and was a guest on their holiday vacations. Laird's two sons were somewhat in awe of Johnson, who was a crack pistol shot and provided additional security for Laird. On one family fishing trip, a snake came racing across the water toward one of the Laird canoes. Johnson took out his gun and shot its head off.[33]

The secretary usually arrived at the office about 7:15 a.m. He would either have breakfast alone at his desk or a working breakfast with guests. At least every other Friday, Laird convened an "Intelligence Breakfast," which included CIA director Helms, as well the heads of all the Defense Department intelligence agencies. Air force undersecretary John McLucas also attended because he secretly served as head of the National Reconnaissance Office, the agency that dealt with satellite imagery and was so sensitive that even its name and initials were classified.

Laird's first daily meeting was with the self-dubbed "8:15 Group," which focused on public affairs and legislative issues. This was the meeting Laird used as if he were in an election-year campaign: a way to keep the department "on message," focusing on its primary objectives such as Vietnamization and the All-Volunteer Force, despite whatever crisis might be temporarily distracting them. At the beginning of his term, Laird also met about 9 a.m. every day with the "Vietnam Task Force," made up of military and intelligence representatives—someone from the CIA, Laird's point-men on POW issues, Robert Pursley, someone from ISA, and others. Their job was to make sure Vietnamization was kept on track. Those meetings became less frequent later in his term as U.S. participation in the war lessened.

Laird met with most of his assistant secretaries and discussed their areas of responsibility at least once every two weeks. On the military side, he also met with each one of the chiefs of staff once each week. On Fridays he attended their meeting in "the tank." The chairman separately met with Laird at least twice each day, including one lunch every week. Laird also made sure he had frequent one-on-one meetings with his two personally appointed and loyal heads of the Defense Intelligence Agency and National Security Agency, Gen. Don Bennett and Adm. Noel Gayler, respectively.[34]

Of all the regular meetings Laird held, none was more important than the weekly staff meeting that convened every Monday at 9:30 a.m. in his dining room. Laird sat at one end of the conference table with Packard at his side. Also at the table were the service secretaries and Joint Chiefs in order of seniority. Assistant secretaries of defense and other key staff members sat in chairs around the perimeter of the room. At least twenty and up to thirty of the Defense Department's top officials attended.

"We have to play this game straight if we are to succeed," Laird cautioned at one staff meeting. Because Laird encouraged candor, each meeting was filled with talk of the problems besetting the military. "Some of you have commented that this meeting leaves you with a gloomy attitude for the rest of the week," Laird observed at one meeting. "I don't want to make this 'morbid Monday,' but this is just the meeting we have to have to face up to our problems. Maybe I should start out with a few jokes or stories, but that's not going to help. We have a lot of successes here, too, and we discuss them. But I still want everyone here to speak up about their concerns, even if it's negative. It's the only way we can move toward success."[35]

In his first month as defense secretary, Laird announced at the Monday staff meeting that in March there would be a three-day out-of-town "orientation" conference for staff and spouses. He originally planned to have it at Camp David, but there wasn't enough room, so he settled on busing everyone to a long weekend at the rustic Airlie House conference center in Virginia, forty-five miles southwest of Washington. The first "Laird-Packard Management Conference" in 1969 was a success. Pentagon manpower chief Roger Kelley said, "Relationships grew out of it and we began to function as a team."[36]

The conference's success during the Laird era made it a tradition for Pentagon leadership until James Schlesinger became secretary of defense in 1973.

"My dear friend Jim—whose management style, I often told him, was 'management by intimidation'—didn't think it was worth it," recalled Doc Cooke. Cooke had come to the Pentagon in 1957 as a Judge Advocate naval officer and subsequently held administrative offices in the Office of the Secretary of Defense. Laird recognized that Cooke, by then a civilian, had rare administrative talents and promoted him to be deputy assistant secretary for administration. Long revered by the nickname "Mayor of the Pentagon," Cooke died in 2002, when he was eighty-one, after serving eighteen defense secretaries.

Not long before he died, Cooke recalled with fondness the first Airlie House conference with Laird. "I remember when everybody first gathered for the cocktail party out there that kicked it off. I noticed that the uniformed military was clustering by service in different parts of the room, the civilian staffers in other parts and so on. But by the time we held the fourth [Airlie conference], there had been a merger. Mel had succeeded in creating a healthy give-and-take friendship among a diverse team—the 'Laird-Packard Team.'" The Pentagon never again saw its like, Cooke concluded.[37]

∼

When Laird first went to the Pentagon, he was appalled at how dreary and unwelcoming the building was to employees and visitors. His first improvement was to dedicate the hall in front of his office to the late President Eisenhower, with portraits and commemorative materials on display.[38] The next corridor to be named for a defense luminary was the one in front of the offices of the Joint Chiefs of Staff. General Omar Bradley, the beloved "GI's general," was a natural choice.[39] Following Laird's example, in 1976 Donald Rumsfeld, on his first tour as secretary of defense, named a third corridor for the legendary World War II general and statesman George C. Marshall. After that, there was a controversial groundswell to memorialize Gen. Douglas MacArthur with a hall. President Carter's defense secretary, Harold Brown, refused to so honor the man whose insubordination to President Truman caused his recall from Korea and retirement in 1951. But when Ronald Reagan became president, he chose as his defense secretary a former aide of MacArthur's, Caspar Weinberger, who promptly memorialized MacArthur with a hall in 1981, in the presence of Reagan and MacArthur's widow.[40] Laird thought it was a good idea to have a "Corridor of the Secretaries," which featured portraits of the nine men who had gone before him. At the dedication, he declared with amusement: "This corridor may never rival the Louvre or the National Gallery of Art in popularity, but I am sure that it will never be without visitors—tourists, scholars, military and civilian, the idly curious, and the hopelessly lost."[41]

Some of Laird's beautification effort focused on the Pentagon grounds. He planted new trees, constructed parking lots in a way to protect the greenery and forced the newly burrowing Washington, D.C., Metro subway system to tunnel around some of the older foliage. (In fact, he joked to a Pentagon garden club that he dearly hoped he would be remembered as "the Secretary who saved the trees.")[42]

One particular heartfelt indoor memorial that Laird oversaw was the "Hall of Heroes" that recognized every Medal of Honor recipient beginning with those who fought in the Civil War. While he was secretary, eighty-one servicemen distinguished themselves with "conspicuous gallantry and intrepidity in action at the risk of life, above and beyond the call of duty" during bloody battles in Vietnam. Twenty-five had lived to receive the honor, but fifty-six were awarded posthumously. Laird recalled with deep emotion his participation as the nation's highest honor was presented posthumously to weeping family members in the Pentagon or at the White House.[43]

The final dedication of a corridor by Laird occurred just before Thanksgiving 1972: the "Corridor of Correspondents" as a tribute to the men and women of the media who cover the military through war and peace. At one end of the hall there is a memorial for the thirty-six correspondents who lost their lives in World War II, eight killed in the Korean War, and sixteen correspondents (up to that point) who had died in Vietnam.[44] In that corridor Laird reserved a special place for two glass-framed documents: a replica of the 1967 Freedom of Information Act, which he had supported as a congressman, and a copy of the "Public Information Principles" he had first laid out in a March 1969 memorandum. The aim of those principles was to begin a new day in military-press relations by treating the media "in an open manner, consistent with the need for security." The principles Laird laid out include: "No information will be classified solely because disclosure might result in criticism of the Department of Defense;" and "Propaganda has no place in Department of Defense public information programs."[45]

Laird's relationship with the press was relatively healthy, given the tenor of the times. The preeminent media scourge of the Nixon administration, when it came to uncovering secrets they wanted hidden, was syndicated columnist Jack Anderson, who had taken over Drew Pearson's *Washington Merry-Go-Round* column upon Pearson's death in 1969. Nixon put Anderson at the top of his "enemies list," but Laird seemed to welcome attention from the "muckraker." When Anderson wrote that Laird, "the Pentagon panjandrum," had had the gall to deliver by government limousine his annual Christmas gift (cheddar cheese from Wisconsin) to friends around Washington including members of Congress, administration officials, and journalists, Laird responded with a memorable gag. He picked the most attractive female Marine sergeant he could find and asked her to take a gift-wrapped box of cheese to Anderson's office. She was to deliver it personally to Anderson and take him to the window to point out the fine government limousine in which she had come. The attached note read: "Dear Jack, I'm sorry I forgot you last Christmas." He signed it: "The Big Cheese."[46]

Laird admitted that when he was secretary of defense, he did "leak" stories to some reporters. Having become a practiced planter of unattributed items when he was in Congress, Laird was not about to abandon a useful way to advance his own ambitious goals as secretary. Kissinger—himself a quick study of, and then able practitioner of, the leak—said he had a rule of thumb in dealing with Laird. "If Mel calls you up and complains about a story in today's paper, you know he has put it out."[47]

Most of the time, Laird—or, at his direction, one of his public affairs aides—provided defense-related information to selected journalists in one-on-one background sessions. "If Mel Laird had not foolishly decided to devote his life to public service, he could have actually made something of himself in my business," joked the *Washington Post*'s David Broder, dean of political reporters. "Instead, Mel became one of the—and I capitalize these next two words—Great Sources in Washington, D.C. He scooped up information. He loved to expose plots. When there wasn't a plot to expose, he would invent one."[48]

Broder remembered "a running joke back when he was at the Pentagon, that it was really remarkable that a man with all of those heavy responsibilities that he was carrying could still find time to produce five columns a week under the byline of Evans and Novak." CBS newsman Bob Schieffer recalled using that line in one of his radio commentaries at the time. In fact, Nixon used to rib Laird about his close relationship with syndicated columnists Rowland Evans and Robert Novak. Even at cabinet meetings, Nixon would say, "Well, I read Evans and Novak today, and I enjoyed your column."[49]

With Laird's permission, Novak later acknowledged that Laird was a key source for him and Evans during Laird's congressional days and as secretary of defense. One of the ironies of the times was that by 1970 Kissinger had also become a source for Evans. "So we kind of had competing leaks between them," said Novak. Because the views of Kissinger and Laird were sometimes starkly different on issues, Novak said he and Evans had to be "very careful about it" to keep both as sources.[50] President George H. W. Bush recalled that the "battle of the leaks" between Laird and Kissinger was a source of amusement in Nixon administration inner circles where mid-level aides kept occasional score sheets on who was winning.[51]

By 1970, the *Armed Forces Journal* reported that "Laird has largely erased the Pentagon's credibility gap with Congress and the press."[52] He had two highly capable former newsmen, Dan Henkin and Jerry Friedheim, to help him. Together, they decided that many of the old ways were not good enough. For one thing, the Pentagon was not well served by infrequent press briefings. Laird suggested daily briefings, and Henkin agreed to try it out. The morning Pentagon briefing quickly became an institution and tripled the number of reporters hanging around the Pentagon. Military officers began asking to appear at the briefings, in part because common lore had it that there were two ways to make general or admiral—by fighting or by briefing.[53]

In a short period of time, as Henkin found it necessary to handle the overall Pentagon public affairs efforts, Friedheim became the department's chief spokesman. He won high marks for his coolness under fire, rarely making a mistake and using humor as a disarmament tool. The *New York Times* once castigated him for reaching a "new low in obfuscation." Asked about the editorial during the day's briefing, Friedheim responded: "I don't want to quibble with that. I might have chosen 'high' instead of 'low.'" At a briefing shortly after, Friedheim opened his announcement folder to find a red-white-and-blue banner (placed there by Laird), which urged in large letters: "Eschew Obfuscation."[54]

Henkin's darkest hour at the Pentagon came in February 1971 when CBS aired a documentary called "The Selling of the Pentagon." Narrated by Roger Mudd, the show stated that the military was spending more than $30 million of the taxpayer's money annually to convince those same taxpayers that it was money well spent. To make its case CBS used deceptive editing practices that are no longer allowed today. Henkin had given an interview to the program, but CBS selectively edited his answers to make him appear confused and misleading—even applying answers he had given to one question as responses to another.

On March 21, Henkin, who had been the most maligned by the program, secretly offered his resignation to Laird, who refused it. Three days after that, when CBS re-aired the special, Henkin penned a private tirade to Laird calling the documentary "one of the most vicious, demagogic, arrogant and misleading pieces of television ever seen anywhere."[55]

In public, Henkin's remarks were much more temperate, following Laird's lead. Laird felt the program was unfair, but it had raised a number of legitimate issues about public relations practices that needed to be changed. CBS responded to criticism by airing the program again with fifteen minutes of edited reactions from Laird and others. The chairman of the House Commerce Committee, which had oversight over broadcasting regulations, conducted a full-scale hearing and demanded that the committee be allowed to review all the CBS out-takes and memoranda used in the production of the show. CBS refused, and the House voted down the committee's attempt to cite the network for contempt for its refusal to provide the internal material.[56]

Among those publicly opposed to forcing CBS to provide details of its confidential sources and internal editing methods was Henkin himself. Though personally aggrieved by the program, he publicly stated: "The Pentagon is not for sale, and not for sale either is the right of a free press to criticize the Pentagon."

~

The CBS documentary criticized overt and costly attempts to "sell" the Pentagon's message, which Laird found distasteful. But in truth he had his own way to market the message. Laird's most frequent injunction to his press people was, "Make it a plus!"—try to point out anything positive in the news. If a commonly used word in the media wasn't appropriate or conveyed negativity, Laird told the staff to try to promote a new one. Hence, "body count" was changed to "enemy deaths" or "enemy killed"; U.S. troops were "redeployed" not withdrawn; "cost overrun" became "cost growth;" Staffers were told not to make predictions that might unravel, such as when the war might end; and never answer hypothetical questions because they are traps.

There was no newspaper too menial or backwater for Laird to cultivate. He went to Florida in 1972 at the invitation of a supermarket tabloid, the *National Enquirer,* when the editor in chief asked him to speak at a convention there. At the suggestion of special assistant Carl Wallace, Laird spent part of the afternoon at the *Enquirer*'s headquarters convincing them to support the All-Volunteer Force. As a result the tabloid, with its huge circulation, became one of the strongest supporters of ending the draft.

While he was in Florida, Laird was the keynote speaker at the National Association of Chain Drug Stores in Palm Beach. Miss America 1965 Vonda Van Dyke, an accomplished singer and ventriloquist on the convention circuit, was among the evening performers at the convention. Von Dyke was on edge for that performance because the headliner, legendary comedian Jack Benny, had let her know he might want her to tour with him if she did well, and he was watching from backstage.

The high-risk segment of her show was the ventriloquist act. During her shows, she would select a human "dummy" from the audience to join her on stage. She favored balding men for the show. "I had found that they were more at ease, more comfortable with themselves," she recalled. "If I got someone who was balding, the audience immediately loved them, and they were always more receptive to me."

Among the several men she sang to that night, the audience responded best when she crooned to one man of shiny pate: "You Must Have Been a Beautiful Baby." Vonda did not know she was serenading the secretary of defense. She invited him to join her on stage and, as Laird rose from his seat, half a dozen security men stood up as well and hovered near him, much to Vonda's confusion. Laird dutifully sat on the stool beside her.

"Now, what's your name?" she asked.

"Just call me 'Mel,'" he answered, and the audience roared.

She whispered to him that each time she squeezed the back of his neck, he was to open his mouth as if he was talking. "Are you having a good time?" she asked him. "Oh, my, yes!" he appeared to answer as Van Dyke projected her Betty Boop voice. The audience was soon on its feet clapping and cheering. "I didn't usually get a standing ovation in the middle of the act," Vonda recalled. As she was finishing her "duet" with Laird, Jack Benny came out on stage and interrupted the act. In his patented droll manner, he pleaded: "You've got to stop this. Honey, don't you know who this is?"

"Yes," she said, meekly. "It's Mel."

"That's the secretary of defense," Benny lectured. "You've got to get him off the stage here, because you're ruining my whole act. I cannot follow this!"[57] Those who watched that night got a taste of what it was like when "Mel" was on center stage, which he made a habit of doing regularly with the press. Among his cardinal rules for dealing with the press was, "don't take yourself too seriously."

In four years, Laird averaged one news conference a week, for a total of 194. He never got flustered; he was always in control. In his last month as secretary, the Pentagon press corps presented him with what became one of his most prized possessions: a football with all their signatures on it. It was inscribed, "Laird 194, Press 0," a recognition that Laird had gone away undefeated. Even *Sports Illustrated* was moved to report on the unusual tribute, adding a quip: "Now, that's *dee*fense."[58]

18

Minority Report

THE DECISION WAS NOT EASY for Robert Froehlke when his old friend "Bom" asked him to come work at the Pentagon. During their many years together—commiserating over Mel's fifth grade punishment by Miss Semrau with a rubber hose, debating, shooting hoops in high school, living as duplex neighbors in college with their brides, or campaigning around the Seventh District for nine congressional elections—neither imagined they would work together at the top of the U.S. military hierarchy. But once he was there, Bom couldn't imagine doing it without Bob.

While Laird was in the Pacific on a destroyer, Froehlke was in Europe rising to the rank of captain in the Army. After the war, Laird went into politics, Froehlke went into law. Within a few days after Laird accepted Nixon's arm-twisting offer to be secretary of defense, he knew he needed his lifelong friend, first as an assistant defense secretary and then as secretary of the Army.

Froehlke learned early that the more success he achieved on the job, the more assignments Laird would give him. In May 1969 he accepted an unusual new task from Laird—to evaluate the performance of the military's various intelligence agencies. Laird had an ingrained distrust of intelligence bureaucracies. In his first days as secretary, he moved quickly to grab the reins of the intelligence services. He ordered the ultrasecret National Reconnaissance Office (NRO), run by the Air Force, to turn over satellite photos to him first. Previously, the photos went to the CIA, which then sent them to the White House and the Defense Intelligence Agency. The DIA would forward them to the Joint Chiefs and, maybe, to the defense secretary. Laird changed the pattern so *he* saw the photos first, but he ordered that his practice be kept secret. He didn't look at every picture and wasted no time in approving transmission to the CIA, which then shared them with the White House and DIA.

Laird had been in Washington long enough to know that information is the ultimate power, and getting your own agency's information first was essential to effective control.

Still, he knew that intercepting his own department's intelligence was not enough to control it. The DIA had more than six thousand employees, and the larger National Security Agency, which dealt with electronic intelligence such as communications intercepts, had another ten thousand military and civilian staff members. Many were career employees who had seen defense secretaries come and go, and did not readily spill their agency's secrets to someone who was only going to be around for four years. So Laird decided to impose a strong hand. He had several concerns: that the services were exceeding their charters, conducting potentially embarrassing clandestine operations; that they were wasting millions of dollars in duplicative espionage activities; and that they were being limited in their productivity by questionable management processes and organizational structure.

Among Froehlke's first recommendations was that Laird should put his own men over the DIA and NSA. So Laird put Froehlke in charge of finding those loyalists. Second, Froehlke advised Laird he needed to take a deeper look. In mid-August 1969, Laird gave Froehlke an additional title—special assistant to the secretary for intelligence. With a fourteen-member staff to assist him over the next two years, he shook up the intelligence community, improved communication between the intelligence services, and eliminated waste by uncovering excessive duplication.

Froehlke's staff also found some espionage abuses by the military agencies and corrected them. But one big problem, which Froehlke and Laird thought they had arrested, continued to run on, silent and deep, until its exposure became a major controversy in 1970–71: spying and massive information collection by the U. S. Army on American civilians who were engaged in perfectly legal political activities.

In early 1965 the Army Intelligence Command had been formed and headquartered at Fort Holabird, Maryland. One of its purposes was to conduct security checks on Army personnel and those seeking clearances for Army operations. But civil unrest and race riots prompted the military to expand its mandate to include dossiers on Americans likely to cause civil disturbances. By 1968 when the CONUS (Continental United States) Intelligence operation peaked, there were more than one thousand military intelligence agents in three hundred field offices across the nation gathering "intelligence" on at least eighteen thousand civilians who were thought to be planning potentially violent demonstrations.[1]

By the time Nixon took office in 1969, at least three large Army data banks held thousands of dossiers on Americans. When Laird first inquired about the program, he was told not to worry, that it was mostly a collection of newspaper articles, not wiretapping or the like. He was informed that among the files were the names of people who had made threats against him. But Laird had a rule when it came to intelligence: Never trust the first incident report, or even the second. And he didn't completely trust the assurances he got from Army intelligence, so he directed Froehlke to shut down any surveillance of civilians, such as political activists if they had not threatened Laird personally or the military in general.[2]

Unknown to either Froehlke or Laird, data continued to be collected and operations continued. The first alarm bell was sounded by a small publication, the *Washington Monthly*, in January 1970. In an authoritative article by a former Army intelligence officer, the entire operation was laid out factually and critically, using as the source an Army captain who had been a part of "CONUS Intelligence."[3] Froehlke went back to the service intelligence officials to make sure there was no misunderstanding and that spying on law-abiding Americans must end. Laird then ordered the Army to destroy all "inappropriate" files on civilians.[4]

Sen. Sam Ervin took up the crusade and began an investigation, some details of which leaked to the press. Former Army lieutenant Joseph Levan, who was attached to the 108th Military Intelligence Group, said his Manhattan field office ordered him to spy on campus activities at the city's colleges and on welfare mothers protesting outside City Hall. The unit even paid tuition to register a black agent in college who was then tasked to spy on the black studies program.[5] In September 1969 when military agencies heard there would be a large antiwar demonstration outside Fort Carson, Colorado, spies were dispatched to pose as demonstrators. One sergeant involved said there were 119 people at the rally, 53 of whom were either Army spies or reporters.[6]

A whistle-blower from an Army intelligence unit in Chicago charged that his group had targeted eight hundred civilians in Illinois including newspaper reporters, religious leaders, political contributors, and politicians—among them, Sen. Adlai Stevenson III when he was Illinois state treasurer.[7] Army secretary Stanley Resor investigated and said the allegation against Stevenson was "without foundation in fact."[8] But Laird asked Froehlke to take a closer look, and he found the file on Stevenson. Froehlke had to go to Capitol Hill to apologize and confess that there was indeed a file on the senator. But he said it was only a collection of newspaper clippings, and that the Army had never done actual surveillance on the senator.[9]

On December 23, 1970, given the level of concern on Capitol Hill and his own concern, Laird issued a directive aimed at shaking up the military intelligence services. In it, he shifted control of all military intelligence activities to a civilian, Froehlke, and out of the hands of the Joint Chiefs. In addition, the Defense Intelligence Agency and the National Security Agency were to report directly to Laird. The news rolled through the Pentagon brass like a shock wave; Laird not only ignored the outrage of the Joint Chiefs, he included in the memo to them a warning against setting up their own ad hoc intelligence networks to bypass the DIA and NSA.[10]

The more Froehlke dug into the matter, the more he found that the Johnson White House was mostly responsible for foisting the spying duties on the military. Although Froehlke mentioned no names, he told Ervin's Senate panel that he found "high civilian authorities" had ordered a "reluctant" military to conduct investigations on civilians.[11] In closed-door testimony at the same time in a House appropriations hearing, Laird echoed Froehlke's account that the trail led to the Johnson Oval Office. "This operation was completely known to the highest authorities within our government," he stated emphatically, providing no names or further details.[12]

The Ervin hearings unearthed little news that had not already been leaked, and it soon became clear that the Pentagon and Froehlke had weathered the storm.

～

Laird had a gift for choosing loyal friends such as Froehlke who could be trusted to follow his lead. Daniel "Chappie" James, was one of them. At six feet nine inches and 235 pounds, with a deep, rich voice to match his physical frame, James was a commanding presence. As an Air Force colonel, he was just the man Mel Laird needed to handle a tense crisis in Libya, during which James faced down Muammar Qaddafi, pistols at the ready. Later, James was precisely the person Laird needed at the Pentagon to be the department's compassionate liaison with the wives of POWs and MIAs. He also delivered dozens of flag-waving speeches on the college campuses of the nation, where he spread the word that despite racial divisions erupting in the armed services, the Defense Department was serious about equal opportunity—that the military was one of the best places for African Americans like himself to be.

Because he believed what he said and believed in Laird, James earned Laird's gratitude, loyalty, and patronage, which became pivotal on his path to becoming the first black four-star general in the U.S. Air Force. As he was growing up in the ghetto section of Pensacola, Florida, his mother had told him, "Don't stand there banging on the door of opportunity and then when

someone opens it, you say, 'Wait a minute, I got to get my bags.' You be prepared with your bags of knowledge, your patriotism, your honor so that when
somebody opens that door, you charge in." With World War II raging, James
became one of the now-famous "Tuskegee Airmen," an Army aviation "experiment" to see if Negroes could learn to fly complex airplanes. In the late 1960s
Colonel James served heroically in Vietnam. With five rows of medals on his
chest, his next assignment in 1969 was to the relatively sedate Wheelus Air
Base in Libya, where he became the new commander.[13]

Wheelus, near the Libyan capital of Tripoli, was the largest American air
base in the world at the time. On September 1, 1969, while the seventy-nine-
year-old Libyan king Idris was undergoing medical treatment in Turkey, a
group of Libyan army leaders led by the twenty-seven-year-old Muammar
Qaddafi, overthrew the throne, and created the Libyan Arab Republic. At first
the revolutionaries said the Americans could stay at Wheelus, but by the time
Colonel James assumed command of the base on September 22, Qaddafi's
nationalist zealots were making threats about kicking the Americans out.
Laird made a series of phone calls to James, telling him that there was an
"urgent need" for the United States to hang on to Wheelus. James agreed,
but that meant he would have to stand up to Qaddafi.

A defining moment occurred on October 18 when Colonel Qaddafi himself stormed onto the base with a column of halftracks driving at full speed
through the housing area and then out again. When Colonel James rushed
to put up a barrier at the front gate and faced the menacing Qaddafi and his
nationalist firebrands, it looked like a scene out of *High Noon*. James relayed
an account of the incident excitedly to Laird on the phone that evening: "I
met Qaddafi a few yards outside the gate. We were both standing. He had a
fancy gun and holster and kept his hand on it. I had my .45 in my belt. I told
him to move his hand away. He finally did. If he had pulled that gun, he never
would have cleared his holster!"

Qaddafi left and never came back, and he didn't send any more halftracks
for a repeat show of force, but James operated the base for weeks in a crisis mode. American oil companies, fearful Qaddafi might nationalize their
Libyan operations, had pressured the State Department to mollify him by
abandoning the base. To the great disappointment of Laird and James, the
diplomats during the last days of the Johnson administration had agreed that
the United States would voluntarily abandon Wheelus by July 1970. But when
Qaddafi insisted the United States leave millions of dollars worth of equipment behind, Laird was furious and knew he was within legal rights to refuse.
He issued a direct order to Colonel James: "Take it all out. Fly everything to

Germany at night, if you have to. Don't you leave so much as a damned type-writer there!"

It was not an easy order for James to carry out. As the base began pack-ing up, several Libyan "delegations" descended on James to protest. One of the first such groups demanded that the valuable U.S. radar systems must stay. James invited them into his house to talk, but when their driver joined them, resting a submachine gun in his lap, James was furious. "I told the senior officer in charge that I was going to count to three and if that S.O.B. was not out of my living room by that time, I would physically throw him out," James recounted to Laird on the phone that evening. "The man left, and was pretty quick about it."

The final agreement for evacuation was signed in Tripoli on December 23. Over the next few nights, per Laird's instructions, U.S. military cargo jets flew much of the most valuable equipment out under cover of darkness. James managed to remove everything that wasn't nailed down, and a lot of things that were.[14]

As James was winding up his Libya command in 1970, Laird called him back to the Pentagon for a conference. Greatly impressed with James, Laird told the colonel he needed him in the Public Affairs section of the secretary's office. "But you know I'm a fighter pilot," James responded.

"Listen, Chappie," Laird said, "you *were* a fighter pilot. Now you're going to fight different battles on the ground and over the airwaves. Some of them will be tougher than combat. You're going to be promoted to general for this position, and your uniform won't be blue anymore. It will be purple, because you'll be representing *all* the services, not just the Air Force. I need you."[15] James wasn't sure he was up to it, but true to his mother's advice, his bags were packed when the door of opportunity opened.

The new deputy assistant secretary of defense for public affairs was a larger-than-life figure, the kind of person Laird wanted to front for the mil-itary on college campuses, so he asked James to join him for several speaking engagements. And when Laird—the son of a minister—learned the general had a fine baritone voice for singing spirituals, he couldn't help but turn some of their appearances into revivals. Laird would sermonize and James would sing.[16]

Often the subject of race came up during the Q&A after James's speeches. A white youth heckled him at one university: "How can a black man like you defend the racist, fascist establishment?" James retorted: "Look friend, I've been black fifty years, which is more than you will ever be, and I know what I believe in."[17]

One of the most emotional moments for him came during a speech at an all-black university where hundreds of students had previously watched with approval as an arsonist burned the ROTC building to the ground. James began his talk quietly, but his anger built as he thought of the arson. He vented to the antimilitary students in the crowd: "You didn't have the right to do that. You didn't have the right to destroy what you didn't build! You didn't build that; I did! I built it with sweat and blood and to prove that black men could be responsible pilots in the United States Air Force, and they deserve ROTC establishments on black campuses to produce these black officers, because that's where most of us came from."

One of the things James was most proud of was the way Laird's Defense Department was leading other government agencies and segments of private business in the equal opportunity arena. At a talk on the topic of "racism in the military" to the Air Command and Staff College in Alabama, the general said he was tired of "wild charges of institutionalized racism in the services." What James had personally seen was a defense secretary who was devoted to solving race problems. "If we catch any practicing bigot, he is dead professionally in [the military]. We do not have any place for a commander who cannot be concerned about racism and have a commitment against it. Mr. Laird has stated there will be no more of that. And if we find them out, they will not command a latrine detail in this service, anymore, anywhere, I can promise you."[18]

⌇

Laird's private actions demonstrated his inner beliefs about racial equality. As a congressman, he had joined the Kenwood Golf and Country Club because it was within walking distance of his home, and had a swimming pool for his children. But in 1968, when the waiters refused to serve his luncheon guest, Walter Washington, the black mayor of Washington, D.C., Laird was furious. He held his temper, though, but insisted and got service. Later, the club president took him aside and told him he couldn't do that again. Laird didn't storm out; he did decide that if the policy didn't change, he would resign from the club. Others, led by Senator Frank Church, started a petition drive in late 1968 to force the club to open up to blacks. In 1970, as the petitioners pursued a court case, it was revealed in court documents that two prominent Republicans, Laird and Secretary of State Rogers, had already resigned in protest of the club's discriminatory membership practices.[19]

As the new defense secretary, Laird came out fast and hard for equal opportunity throughout the department. His point man for this initiative was Roger Kelley, the assistant secretary of defense for manpower and reserve affairs.

Kelley thought something more than memos and directives was needed—perhaps a charter. One was written around a table with Packard, the Joint Chiefs and all the service secretaries, lest anyone miss the message.[20] The "Human Goals Charter" was issued in August 1969, signed by the department's highest-ranking civilian and military leaders. It stated, in part, "We [will] strive . . . to make Military and Civilian service in the Department of Defense a model of equal opportunity for all regardless of race, sex, creed, or national origin." The eight-paragraph charter was rapidly mass produced on parchment and prominently placed in glass frames throughout the Pentagon and at Defense Department facilities around the globe. The charter was also reproduced in full on the back of Laird's annual defense reports.[21]

Laird well knew the lessons of American history regarding race. A high-minded charter was just words unless it was followed up with action, such as promoting more black officers to flag rank. But he had to force the uniformed military to comply, and that meant tabling promotion lists until qualified blacks (and, later, women) were on those lists. When Laird became secretary, only two blacks held the rank of general. By the end of his term, the armed services had promoted another thirteen.[22] While the Air Force and Army appointed black generals, the Navy was slow to appoint a black admiral. Laird leaned on Navy secretary John Chafee in early 1969 to make sure the service moved quickly to promote a black captain to admiral. Laird suggested the first candidate, Capt. Samuel L. Gravely Jr., a frigate commander who in 1962 had become the first black to command a U.S. warship. So conservative had the Navy been that Gravely was the only possible choice for admiral; he was the only one of three black Navy captains who had had a sea command. (The other two were a chaplain and a medical doctor.) With the help of Chafee and the innovative Admiral Zumwalt, Laird was able to announce in April 1971 that Gravely would become the first black admiral in American history. "I will not be the last," Gravely said in a radio message from aboard the USS *Jouett* in the Pacific.[23]

While the Army had promoted blacks as generals, none had a division command until Laird's tenure at the Pentagon. At that time, the Army had about two hundred major generals (two-star), but only thirteen divisions, so most of the generals wound up in desk jobs. Maj. Gen. Frederic Ellis Davison became the first black to command an Army division when he was tapped in April 1972 to head the Eighth Infantry Division in Europe.[24]

As for the Air Force, Laird saw it as a personal mission to push the career of Chappie James, who was then serving as the number three man in the Defense Department's public affairs division. Normally, it is difficult for anyone to be promoted in such a noncommand position, but Laird felt James was so valuable to the military that the secretary made sure he was given his second star in 1972 and his third in 1973 (after Laird had resigned but at his recommendation). Laird's influence on behalf of this protégé continued into the Ford administration, when Laird helped engineer James's appointment to general of the North American Air Defense Command in Colorado. When receiving the honor that made him the first black four-star in American history, James quoted his late mother: "My mother told me a long time ago that there are two Negroes we can do without: That *first* one and the *only* one; the *first* one to do this and the *only* one to do that. She said, 'I'm looking forward to the day when so many black people will be doing so many things that are noteworthy that it will no longer be newsworthy.'"[25]

~

When it came to insisting that American and foreign businesses deal with minority troops on an equal basis, the primary tool Laird used was the threat to cut them off. For example, an investigation of 4,100 German establishments during Laird's term found 123 of them had discriminated against U.S. servicemen, 50 of them specifically against black servicemen. Laird declared 35 of the worst offenders—German hotels, nightclubs and restaurants—to be "off limits" to all U.S. troops regardless of color, stationed in or traveling in Germany.[26]

The problem was not confined to foreign postings. In the same month he was promoted to general, Chappie James was refused service in a bar in his hometown because he was black. (He had returned to Pensacola to accept an award from the Kiwanis Club as the "Man of the Year.") The bar was soon declared off limits to Defense Department personnel, which deprived the club of a major source of its revenue.[27] The same action was taken against apartment buildings that refused to rent to minority servicemen.[28]

Prior to the Nixon administration, a series of equal employment laws imposed nondiscrimination policies on any company that wanted to do business with the federal government. Laird looked for a case to show he was serious about enforcing those rules. He found it in early 1970 with the huge contract award for the Air Force's F-15 fighter. Notre Dame's president, the Reverend Theodore Hesburgh, was appointed by Nixon in March 1969 to serve as the chairman of the United States Civil Rights Commission, and in January 1970 he learned that the contractor of the multibillion dollar F-15 fighter plane, McDonnell Douglas Corporation, was not following the rules. Fr. Hesburgh wrote to Laird that the Defense Department compliance office had not yet made the required inspection of McDonnell Douglas employment policies.[29] When Laird found out that Hesburgh was correct, he promised quick action.

Laird called Air Force secretary Robert Seamans's office, but Seamans was at a Strategic Air Command (SAC) conference in Puerto Rico and Undersecretary John McLucas was in charge. Laird let McLucas know that Seamans better get to St. Louis and solve the problem *that very day*.[30] Seamans was enjoying a Caribbean respite at the conference, planning afterwards to spend the weekend in the Virgin Islands with his wife and her mother, when he got the phone message. His undersecretary told him that Laird was threatening to re-bid the whole F-15 aircraft contract if the Air Force didn't handle this satisfactorily and promptly. Seamans ordered McLucas to handle it, but McLucas responded, "Mel insists *you* go to St. Louis *this afternoon.*"

Seamans was shaken. He informed the SAC commanders he had to be in St. Louis "in the shortest possible time." He recalled, "I was soon taken by SAC police, sirens screaming, to the flight line where a tanker was off-loading fuel as we approached." Seamans and aides clambered up a ladder into the nose of the tanker and by midafternoon arrived in St. Louis. Hearing in advance of Seamans's unusual unplanned flight, reporters from Washington had scrambled to St. Louis to meet him. His plane taxied onto the ramp at the McDonnell Douglas plant. Awaiting them were James McDonnell, the CEO of the company, and a bevy of journalists including TV news crews. "After shaking hands all around, I vented my pique about the lack of an affirmative action plan, in front of the TV, and we then headed for the negotiation table," Seamans remembered. "The contract was appropriately amended in a few hours. Mel Laird was appeased, and I returned to Puerto Rico."[31]

⁓

Dramatically overshadowing equal opportunity was the racial tension that existed in the military. In the late 1960s and early 1970s, black and white soldiers alike jockeyed for position, chafed at integration, and often chose violence as a response. It was the war within the war, and Laird felt responsible to negotiate peace. In Vietnam, the treatment of minorities was mixed. Out on patrol, when lives depended on cooperation, black and white soldiers found camaraderie fighting a collective enemy. But as more troops withdrew, and the majority of the American force was no longer in combat, latent racial tension and resentment erupted sporadically, sometimes in murders known as "fragging" because of the use of the fragmentation grenade in some of the assaults. In Germany, where racial tension was also at violent levels, a white noncommissioned officer confided anonymously to a reporter: "*Race* is my problem—not the Russians, not Vietnam, [not] maneuvers. I just worry about keeping my troops—black and white—from getting at one another."[32]

At various times during Laird's term, a variety of groups—his own civil rights experts, teams from the services, NAACP fact-finders, and members of the Congressional Black Caucus (CBC)—took the temperature of the armed forces worldwide and found trouble. For Secretary Laird, the battle against racism was as complex and frustrating as it has been for America generally. As General James had pointed out in one speech, Laird made sure that "practicing bigots," especially among the officer corps, were reeducated or court-martialed out. At least a dozen officers, including an Army captain who refused to shake hands with a fellow black officer, were discharged from the services.[33] Yet, for every racial issue Laird solved, two more cropped up to take its place. Laird figured that among the best solutions were increased communication and education. So Laird encouraged formation of "human relations" or "racial harmony" councils that would bring black activists in contact with white senior officers to air differences. He directed that a crash course in race relations and sensitivity become a standard part of basic training. He applauded "black festivals" put on by black soldiers, such as one at the Air Force Academy that introduced the predominately white cadet corps to soul food, soul books, soul singers, and soul thought.[34]

Together with Roger Kelley, Laird created the Defense Race Relations Institute at Patrick Air Force Base in Florida, to which thousands of equal opportunity officers were sent for training. In time, gender sensitivity was added to the training, and the institute became the "Defense Equal Opportunities Management Institute" and is still in operation.[35]

～

The history of women in the military reads less like a Cinderella story and more like a war of attrition. By posing as men, women first maneuvered their way into military service during the Revolutionary War. They were also present behind the scenes in the Civil War. Women did not officially join the armed forces until the turn of the century. The U.S. Army and Navy Nurse Corps were formed in 1901 and 1908 respectively, and during World War I the number of women in uniform reached approximately thirty-six thousand. Servicewomen performed such tasks as fingerprinting, administration, and munitions work.[36] The Women's Army Auxiliary Corps was created in 1942 by Congress and President Roosevelt. (Its name was soon shortened to Women's Army Corps, or WAC). Women also served in the Army air forces, the forerunner of the U.S. Air Force.

After World War II, the 1948 Armed Forces Integration Act granted both regular and reserve status to women in all four services, but with significant restrictions. One was an enlistment cap stipulating that women could make up only 2 percent of the total enlisted strength in each service. There was also a promotions cap at lieutenant colonel for the Army and Air Force and commander for the Navy. In 1967 President Johnson lifted many of those restrictions, but his administration paid lip service to the law. Jeanne Holm, a female pioneer in the Air Force, observed that secretaries McNamara and Clifford didn't promote the cause of women in the armed forces. "It was almost as if we didn't exist," she said. "Women were then treated kind of as separated categories of people in the military, though that was typical of our society at the time."

That all changed when Laird came along. "I'll never forget the day he walked in as the new secretary of defense at the Pentagon," Holm, then a colonel, recalled. It was January 23, 1969, and many Pentagon civilians and uniformed employees had been invited to the fifth floor Pentagon auditorium to hear a welcoming address from President Nixon. But Holm's memory was of Laird. "Mel Laird came in there like he owned the place and like he just loved every bit of being with us. He was just wallowing in the event." She found this first impression was correct. "He went around the halls and met people, and he always remembered you."[37]

Like Holm, Laird remembered the day Nixon visited the Pentagon in January 1969. The new secretary recalled searching in vain for any women among the honor guards carrying flags and the ceremonial military bands on hand for the auspicious occasion. It was symptomatic of an exclusion of the gender that had to end, not only because it was unfair but because Laird knew the all-volunteer force could come into being only if a significant number of women were attracted to join. That day would be the first time, but not the last, that Laird would express his disappointment to organizers of such events. Public affairs aide Jerry Friedheim said, "Mel would look around and say at some point during or after the ceremony to the officer in charge, 'You have this really nice-looking honor guard. They're wonderful young men; they're spit-and-polish; they're the very best. But, you have some women in the Navy, don't you? I didn't see any of them out there today at the ceremony. You know, I think the next time that you have a Navy ceremony out here, I think I'm going to come down to the front door, and look out, particularly at the honor guard, and if I don't see a woman in there, I may not come out the door. You wouldn't want me to do that, would you?'"[38]

Far more important to Laird than pushing for a smattering of women among the public relations units was the need to promote qualified woman to flag rank in the services. That was more difficult to accomplish because each service had its own promotion board, and they prized their independence. Civilians had, in effect, a veto power over promotion lists that first went to Laird, then Nixon, and then Congress. At any point in the chain of command, the list could be sent back. But in practice that had happened only rarely, which meant the boards had come to believe that promotions were one area where the civilians would not meddle. Laird changed that.

At times, he used the same ploy he had used to advance blacks—refusing to accept a promotion list unless there was a woman on it. The requirement was not put in a memo, nor was it explicitly stated; Laird hoped to get there by implicit persuasion. When Navy secretary John Warner handed him an all-male promotion list, Laird responded: "John, I'm not going to accept this, and you know why. It is incomplete. You haven't done your homework, so take this damn thing back."

The implicit method didn't always work, so there were times Laird had to issue explicit orders to the services in the form of deadlines to promote a certain number of women to specific ranks. Either the uniformed military leaders complied or they were disregarding an order from their superior. The net result was the first-time promotion of women to flag rank in the three primary services. The first service iceberg to move was the Army. On June 11, 1970, Anna Mae Hays, director of the Army Nurse Corps, and Elizabeth Hoisington, director of the Women's Army Corps, became America's first female brigadier generals.[39] A year later Jeanne Holm became the first female brigadier general in the Air Force. Later, just before he left the Pentagon, Laird made sure Holm was promoted to major general, becoming the first female two-star.[40]

The conservative Navy was not moving full speed ahead toward eliminating the gender barrier, so in 1972 Laird began applying pressure to John Warner. First, he repeatedly returned Warner's promotion list as incomplete. Then Laird began mentioning in every public speech that he fully intended to name the Navy's first woman admiral before he left as secretary. Finally, the admirals shook off the barnacles and nominated Capt. Alene B. Duerk, chief of the Navy Nurse Corps, to rear admiral rank.[41]

The pace of change began to accelerate until the various services were subtly vying for firsts: first woman on a warship, first woman in a combat-ready cockpit, first woman in command of a major unit, and so on. In August 1972 the Navy announced it would begin sending women to sea on warships, a move many saw as a harbinger to women in combat. The Air Force answered a few days later with the announcement that it had become the first service to place a woman in command of a major unit composed of both men and women.[42] By the time Laird left office, there were seven female admirals and generals. On one of his last days on the job, Laird invited all of them to his office for a farewell coffee. By way of appreciation, they presented Laird with a framed group picture, on which was irreverently written: *The women Mel Laird made while he was at the Pentagon.*

~

Among Laird's most urgent problems was the rampant drug abuse among U.S. soldiers in Vietnam. The troops were demoralized by the unpopular war, far away from home and in a country where drugs were cheap and readily available. The drugs flowed into South Vietnam from Cambodia along a supply line eerily similar to the Ho Chi Minh Trail. Because drugs were so cheap on the streets, Laird suspected North Vietnam of subsidizing the market to hook American soldiers and then funneling the money back to the Viet Cong.

Laird also suspected that Nguyen Van Thieu's government didn't care much about the drug problem. Laird knew that Ambassador Bunker had a secret list of Thieu's own government officials who were reputed to be narcotics traffickers.[43] So the frustrated Laird went public with a blunt accusation that Thieu and his government were "not doing enough" to cut off the drug flow into South Vietnam. He was the first senior U.S. official to make the charge.[44] The Thieu administration got the message and began a crackdown, tacitly admitting that drug abuse in Vietnam was no longer solely an American problem.

The American military drug problem reflected the growing civilian drug subculture. The majority of those using drugs in Vietnam had begun that use in the United States.[45] Contrary to popular belief, "the volunteers were twice as likely to abuse drugs as the draftees were, which was counterintuitive," recalled Dr. Richard Wilbur, the former assistant secretary of defense for Health whom Laird assigned to concentrate on the military drug problem. "You would have thought the draftees, having been dragged over there, would use the drugs."

Laird and those addressing the problem at the Pentagon were frustrated by the lack of reliable statistics regarding users in the ranks. After a preliminary congressional inquiry into the problem in early 1970, Sen. Thomas Dodd concluded, "We find that up to 80 percent of our service personnel in Vietnam may be abusing drugs to one extent or another."[46] Contemporary press reports seemed to settle on a figure of more than 50 percent. Laird called these estimates "a gross exaggeration." He authorized issuance of a fact sheet disputing the notion that a majority of service men and women in Vietnam were drug abusers. "The unique environment of military life, characterized by close personal association . . . make it altogether unlikely that any great number of persistent drug or marijuana users would go undetected for any protracted period of time." Nevertheless, "no military establishment, where security is always vitally critical and relies on the team concept, can risk having any member of the team mentally unbalanced, even if only for a moment, through the voluntary use of drugs."[47]

Laird initiated a massive urinalysis testing program for all troops leaving Vietnam, which the soldiers called "Operation Golden Flow." Laird felt that the military had a responsibility to find and treat its drug addicts before they were discharged. The program marked the first wide-scale drug-testing ever undertaken by the U.S. government or a civilian entity.[48] In a private note to President Nixon in May 1972, Laird said the Pentagon's pioneering urinalysis testing also offered "hope for success in the civilian sector."[49]

The military urinalysis program was quickly expanded to test not just those leaving Vietnam but all service personnel still there. Next it was moved to the troops in Europe, and then random testing was instituted. Another new aspect of the Laird drug-detection program was to offer amnesty from court-martial to those addicts who voluntarily came forward to accept treatment. The number of drug treatment centers run by the military and the Veterans Administration expanded rapidly. Ironically, the Nixon administration, which was the first to declare a "war on drugs," is the only one to have authorized more money for education and treatment than for law enforcement.[50]

By mid-1972, the heroin drug crisis was well under control. "You did an outstanding job last year in responding to the heroin abuse crisis in Vietnam," Nixon told Laird in a May 3 memo. "You can rightly take pride in your success in creating an effective program to deter, detect, and treat military drug abuse."[51] Laird appreciated the note, but he was under no illusions. As he had drily observed in a staff meeting the year before, the best way to handle the drug problem in Vietnam was to get the troops out of Vietnam.

19

The Secret War

O N NEW YEAR S DAY 1971, the halfway point in Laird's term at the Pentagon, fresh fighting broke out when the North Vietnamese once again violated a holiday truce. One American soldier was killed, becoming the first casualty in the second decade of the Vietnam War. During the Johnson administration, the Vietnam War had already become America's longest war. For the purpose of keeping statistics, the Pentagon dated the U.S. entry into the war at January 1, 1961. A decade later, despite two years of troop withdrawals under Vietnamization, the casualty statistics were grim—44,900 Americans dead and 293,225 wounded. The South Vietnamese had lost 117,900 men. The count of enemy dead was just a guess but hovered around 690,400 North Vietnamese and Viet Cong.[1]

Laird set out for Saigon the morning of January 5, 1971, for his third official visit there and another chance to take the pulse of Vietnamization. One day earlier, the last of the U.S. Green Beret camps in Vietnam had been turned over to the locals, marking the end of the official Special Forces role in the war.[2] There were still 335,800 Americans in Vietnam, down from more than half a million when Laird took command, and President Nixon had tried to put a gag order on any public pronouncements about more withdrawals until Laird returned with a report. Kissinger had forwarded that order in a memo to secretaries Laird and Rogers and CIA director Helms: "The President has directed that there will be no speculation either on or off the record or in any forum."[3]

Laird never felt the directive applied to him. He went on with business as usual, arriving in Paris on the way to Saigon and telling the press corps there that the U.S. combat role in Vietnam would end by mid-year, marking the end of "Phase 1" of Vietnamization. Laird said the United States could then move into "Phase 2"—providing logistics and air support for the South and security for the remaining U.S. support troops.[4] Back in Washington, reporters asked presidential spokesman Ron Ziegler if what Laird said was true, that U.S. combat troops would be out by summer. "[W]e are not prepared to say." Ziegler demurred.[5]

Laird had deliberately overstepped his bounds, publicly committing the administration to a goal that had been his alone. And he did not stop there. In Saigon Laird used his favorite phrase to describe the pace of troop withdrawals, saying the Pentagon would "meet or beat the announced troop authorization strength of 284,000 as of May 1, just as we have met or beaten every troop reduction announcement made by the President since redeployment started in mid-1969."[6] Each time Laird said he would "meet or beat" the deadlines, he infuriated the Joint Chiefs and Kissinger, all of whom had to meet the deadlines but were not eager to "beat" them. Laird paid lip service to Nixon's original conditions for withdrawal, repeating that the pace of withdrawal would always be tied to progress at the Paris peace talks and the strength of the enemy. But then, as always, those standards were honored more in the breach than in the observance.

One of Laird's prime objectives in Saigon, in addition to assessing the progress of Vietnamization, was to talk Gen. Creighton Abrams out of leaving. Abrams, who was fifty-six, had been in Saigon for more than four years, and speculation was rampant in the press that he would be reassigned and replaced by his deputy, Gen. Frederick Weyand. Abrams's health in the previous year hadn't been the best, but it wasn't health that had him down. It was the crushing impact of being too long in charge of an unpopular war. Laird knew that Abrams wanted to return to the United States and get another assignment that would wash the stain of Vietnam off him before he retired.

Laird, however, wasn't ready to part with him, so he promised that if Abrams would stay, Laird would make him chief of staff of the Army when Westmoreland retired. The top job in the Army was appealing to Abrams, but probably more persuasive was Laird's call to duty; the secretary told him his country needed him.

In a day-long briefing with Abrams, Laird got an earful of the general's fears that the South Vietnamese, and particularly President Nguyen Van Thieu, were not taking Vietnamization seriously. The meeting the next day between Thieu and Laird was a cat-and-mouse game.[7] Laird shared tentative numbers for the next withdrawal—150,000 more American troops out between May 1971 and May 1972. Thieu wanted the number end-loaded after 1971 because he was running for reelection that fall.

Laird's publicly stated reason for going to Saigon that January was to assess Vietnamization, but his secret agenda was to plan a test of Vietnamization—an invasion of Laos using South Vietnamese troops. In principle, it made sense; in practice it would become as dicey as the U.S. incursion into Cambodia in 1970 and not nearly as successful.

The geography of the small kingdom of Laos, about the size of Idaho, doomed it to a history of conflict. Laos bordered six other nations, including the People's Republic of China (from which its people primarily migrated in the thirteenth century). Both North and South Vietnam were on its eastern border. Throughout the 1950s, Laos strove mightily to resist being drawn into the maelstrom of the Vietnam conflict. Finally, the 1962 Geneva Convention, at least in theory, guaranteed Laotian neutrality and independence. All signers, including North Vietnam and the United States, agreed to keep their troops out. But the North Vietnamese ignored the agreement after signing it and conducted seasonal wars with the Lao government forces. Each dry season since 1964, the North Vietnamese—with assistance from nearly fifty thousand indigenous Communist Pathet Lao forces—had successfully attacked government strongholds. And each wet season that followed, when Communist supply lines slowed down in the mud, the Royal Lao government forces generally retrieved their territory.

The United States could hardly let the Communist incursions go unchallenged. In 1961 the CIA had recruited a Laotian Hmong tribal leader, Vang Pao, to raise an army, and they put at his disposal "Air America." This fleet of planes was ostensibly contracted to the U.S. Agency for International Development (USAID) to deliver food to Laos, but it was bought and paid for by the CIA, and carried as much weaponry as it did rice. Vang Pao controlled the weapons and gave the rice only to those villages that had contributed men to his army.[8] On return flights, Vang Pao's army often carried crates of opium from the Golden Triangle area; the profits from drug sales helped keep Vang Pao and his top officers happily in line.

In his first year, Secretary Laird had more to worry about with Vietnamization and massive troop withdrawals than the problems in Laos. He had loosely followed the issue as a congressman, so he wasn't particularly alarmed when he got a mid-September 1969 top secret "Eyes Only" note from Kissinger passing on Nixon's directive that more M-16s and airplanes be given to the Laotian forces. "If more pay and allowances would make the Lao fight better, this, too, should be provided," Kissinger wrote.[9]

It was no secret to Laird that U.S. military planes regularly bombed the

Ho Chi Minh Trail as it ran through Laos. But most Americans—and many
in Congress—were unaware that there were hundreds of air strikes being
called in to support the Royal Laotian forces and their allies in their civil war
against the Communist Pathet Lao. In fact, when bombing of North Vietnam had stopped in November 1968, the Pentagon had simply moved the air
war to Laos. From time to time, there were more American planes peppering the skies over Laos than over South Vietnam. Losses of American planes
over Laos were not publicly acknowledged because the Johnson and then
Nixon administrations did not admit to the flights in the first place.

Laird began to engage fully in the Laos question in October 1969 when a
Senate subcommittee held closed hearings on the subject. When details of
the classified testimony leaked to the press, Sen. William Fulbright obligingly confirmed the story, saying the United States was spending more than
$150 million a year to supply, arm, train, and transport a clandestine army
of thirty-six thousand men in Laos. Fulbright offered a commentary: "I knew
that we were doing a little of this and a little of that in Laos, but I had no
idea it was a major operation of this kind."[10]

The White House forced Laird to respond with one hand tied behind his
back. Nixon, with the secretive Kissinger urging him on, was adamant: neither Laird nor his people were to confirm CIA and State Department activity in Laos, on or off-the-record.

Laird later regretted not raising a greater objection to the secrecy and the
untenable position his department had been put in of paying the bills in
Laos while the CIA and the State Department controlled the operation, the
"commander" being a diplomat in pinstripes—G. McMurtrie Godley, the
U.S. ambassador to Laos, whom Laird referred to as the "field marshal."[11]
Laird wasn't happy with his role as banker to the field marshal without any
say over how the money was spent. While he didn't personally want to preside over a war in Laos, covert or overt, Laird did want to exercise enough
control to keep operations there from escalating. So, in the fall of 1969, he
had his staff review the way things were being handled and sent a report to
Secretary of State Rogers on December 1, warning of the "political impact"
the covert war could have. Laird suggested more input from the Joint Chiefs.[12]

Meanwhile, by early December, Senator Fulbright and his supporters were
in full throttle. The Laos operation, in their view, was perfect evidence that
Nixon was expanding instead of contracting the war. (This predated the more
widely condemned Cambodia operation of the following spring.) Behind
closed doors, the Senate voted 73 to 17 to order that none of the $69.3 bil-
lion in defense appropriations could be spent "to finance the introduction

of American ground combat troops into Laos or Thailand." The measure was called the Church Amendment, for its sponsor, Sen. Frank Church. Under it, ground troops were banned, but the State Department and CIA could still use air cover to continue their secret war.

In February 1970 the North Vietnamese picked up the pace of fighting in Laos and Nixon ordered the financing of two Thai battalions to go to the aid of the Laotians. He added American B-52s to the mix of fighter bombers and helicopter gun ships already active in Laos. The daily sortie rate was approaching six hundred flights, which was a little too noisy to be a secret. Three Western reporters hitchhiked to an air base in Laos and saw Americans, in civilian garb, directing operations there.[13] The day after they broke the news, Laird testified before a House Appropriations Subcommittee saying, "We have no American ground combat forces stationed in Laos. Ground combat activities are carried on by Laotian forces. We have a small military advisory and training group there. We are interdicting supplies on the Ho Chi Minh Trail with B-52s and tactical aircraft."[14]

When the members of Congress pressed Laird for more details, he went off the record, and the official transcript doesn't include his response. "I told them off the record in the classified briefing that it was a CIA operation," Laird recalled of that hearing.[15] Two days later he was called back to Capitol Hill, this time to explain Laos to the House Armed Services Committee. He told them there were 220 American military people in Laos, and he quibbled with the legislators over what to call them, if they were not combat troops. Laird said they were attachés with the embassy, military advisors, and training personnel, but he refused to call them a formal Military Assistance Advisory Group (MAAG), because such military advisors were banned under the Geneva neutrality treaty regarding Laos. What about the fact that the Americans wore civilian clothes, the committee wanted to know?

"Well, they are often out of uniform," Laird hedged, and then turned to Gen. Earle Wheeler to elaborate.

"I have never been to Laos," Wheeler said.

The obfuscation about the U.S. presence in Laos was not fooling anyone. Finally Nixon himself decided to make a speech on the Laotian war. Laird tried to coach the president on what to say: Nixon should stress that North Vietnam was the repeat offender when it came to Laotian neutrality; the president should restate that there were no U.S. ground combat troops in Laos, and no plans to send any. Laird included a short list of what Nixon should *not* talk about including the cost of the Laos operations, the extent of the CIA involvement, and whether the Americans there constituted an official MAAG.[16] The return interoffice mail on March 4 brought a draft from Kissinger of the statement Nixon wanted to make. It ignored Laird's cautious approach and, in Nixon's aggressive style, defended the obligation of the United States to do all it could to help Laos in its fight against Communism.[17]

That cut too close to the original rationale for entering the Vietnam War, and Laird wrote back immediately: "[T]his is not the kind of statement the President should make." There was too little about why and what the U.S. was doing in the present and too many promises about what it could deliver in the future. Nixon made no mention of the B-52s, even though the press was clamoring for an explanation about what they were doing in Laos. "The tone of the statement is alarming," Laird wrote. Nixon used terms such as "massive presence," "blatant moves," and "deliberate and open onslaught" to describe the enemy presence in Laos. And then he promised the United States would do something to stop that enemy. "This appears to be an open-ended commitment rather than minimal activity," Laird warned.[18] Laird rightly assumed that a magnanimous pledge to protect yet another country in Southeast Asia from the Red Menace would not sit well with the American public.

Nixon paid some heed to Laird's warning, toning down the speech which he delivered from Key Biscayne on March 6, 1969. He promised that no U.S. ground troops would be sent to Laos. And then Nixon made a statement that strained credulity. He said: "No American stationed in Laos has ever been killed in ground combat." Laird almost jumped out of his seat when he heard that. From his congressional days, he knew of two Americans who had died in ground combat several years before. In fact, in his first memo to Nixon about the speech he specifically listed "casualty data" among the items he "should not discuss." The *Los Angeles Times* was the first to put the lie to the statement. Within hours of the president's speech, they reported that Army Capt. Joseph Bush had been killed during a Communist attack at the western edge of the Plain of Jars only a month before; he had even earned a posthumous medal for heroism.

The White House then had to acknowledge the death of Captain Bush and twenty-six American civilians, but failed to mention the two hundred Americans dead and 183 missing in air operations, which the press was also quick to point out. The fudging of those numbers and the failure of Nixon to say anything about the B-52s in Laos continued to raise more questions than answers. The president's attempt to explain the Laos operations wound up looking more like a cover-up.[19]

～

All of the attention to Laos in early 1970 made the State Department uneasy. It was their own joint operation with the CIA that came closest to violating the Senate ban on funding ground operations in Laos—the Church Amendment. But the diplomats privately pointed the finger at what they said was a bigger offender, and that was operation "Prairie Fire." That was the code name for shallow cross-border raids by South Vietnamese soldiers taking place about forty times a month with the help of American air cover and directed by the U.S. Army. Those raids, controlled by the Defense Department, were to gather intelligence and to harass the flow of enemy supplies along the Ho Chi Minh Trail.

On May 29 Elliot Richardson, then undersecretary of state, sent a top secret memo to David Packard, saying that Prairie Fire constituted American ground combat in Laos, no doubt about it. "We therefore consider that the language of the Church Amendment and the President's statement require us to terminate U.S. involvement in this type of operation," Richardson wrote. "In addition, we are concerned about the possible political cost should these operations become generally known."[20]

Packard asked the Joint Chiefs to rethink the need for operation Prairie Fire. "I am convinced that there is sufficient uncertainty now with respect to the congressional attitude toward this type of program to see if less politically sensitive alternatives are feasible," Packard told the chiefs in his written order.[21]

On July 17 the State Department sent Packard the written opinion of its legal advisor—that Prairie Fire was a violation of the Church Amendment and that the American soldiers who accompanied South Vietnamese raids into Laos did not track with Nixon's promise on March 6 that "There are no American ground combat troops in Laos."[22] Undersecretary of State for Political Affairs U. Alexis Johnson added his own opinion to that of the lawyer: "It has been almost four months since the President's statement on Laos in which he stated categorically that 'there are no American ground troops in Laos' and that the Administration 'had no plans for introducing ground combat forces in Laos.' In light of these strong statements from the President, I believe it would be extremely embarrassing for us to have to explain an apparent failure to comply with the President's stated policy."[23]

The president himself was not pressing the Pentagon to live up to his "stated policy." In fact, he was caught in the middle of the debate between Laird and the State Department. In Laird's mind, the president had simply misspoken. As far as Laird was concerned, the small Prairie Fire missions did not add up to all-out ground combat and did not violate the Church Amendment. He put the raids in the bushel basket he called "protective reaction."

Nixon solved the problem with a compromise. In October 1970 he secretly endorsed the Prairie Fire operations for a ninety-day period (back-dated to September 18) to give the Pentagon time to come up with a way to replace the American soldiers with South Vietnamese troops.[24] Laird let the president's deadline slide while working without much success to get the South Vietnamese to take over. The ninety-day order expired in mid-December and Laird formally asked Nixon for a sixty-day extension.[25] He never received a response. After that, there was no more word from Nixon on the matter, and Laird stopped asking for permission.

~

For American military planners, the Ho Chi Minh Trail had become the prime target of opportunity to foil the enemy. In the 1960s Ho Chi Minh had piggybacked on the ancient trade routes between Southeast Asian capitals to build a network of trails over which his soldiers could transport supplies to within shooting distance of South Vietnam. The main north-south trail, dubbed "Route 92" by the U.S. military, traveled through Laos parallel to its border with South Vietnam and down through Cambodia. In some places it was as narrow as a footpath and others as wide as thirty miles. And all along it were trails branching off east and west. The U.S. military eventually mapped 3,500 miles of the trail and its many tributaries, but it may have been less than half of the system.[26]

Down this road came hundreds of thousands of tons of food and supplies on the backs of men, on bicycles, in oxcarts and, where the trail was widened, in trucks. Supply depots, rest areas, truck parks, and telephone lines needed constant tending, and as many as fifty thousand boys and women worked on the road repair gangs, called the "Youth Shock Brigades Against the Americans for National Salvation."[27] During the dry season, usually from November to March, the trail teemed with thousands of Viet Cong guerrillas, North Vietnamese regulars, and their support forces—all hidden under a jungle canopy.

Beginning in mid-October 1970, Laird directed an unprecedented bombing campaign against the trail and its trucks. The Air Force claimed that twenty-five thousand trucks were destroyed between October 1970 and May 1971. Sometimes as many as five hundred bombing sorties were flown in a day. (From 1965 to 1971, along this single battlefront of the Vietnam War, more bomb tonnage was dropped over the Ho Chi Minh Trail than was used in all theaters in all of World War II.[28]) But it was not enough. As the dry season in late fall of 1970 approached, Laird knew the enemy would be engaged in the largest overland supply effort of the Vietnam War. In less than six months they had to bring enough food to supply four hundred thousand

soldiers for a full year. Laird also determined from intelligence reports that
the enemy was planning to greatly increase its shipments down the trail in
preparation for a 1971 offensive not just to disrupt South Vietnamese elections but also stockpile for a major offensive to discredit Nixon before the
U.S. presidential election in 1972. At Laird's request, plans were prepared by
the Joint Chiefs for a ground operation against the trail. Laird was appalled
at the chiefs' first suggestion—to use American ground forces, along with
South Vietnamese troops, in direct violation of the Church Amendment.
Laird quickly discerned that Westmoreland and Haig were behind the idea
to use American soldiers.

Whether Nixon would have considered such a plan if Laird had proposed
it will never be known. Instead, Laird sent word to Abrams to devise a pre-
emptive plan against the trail using *only* South Vietnamese soldiers backed
by U.S. air power. Abrams suggested a three-month cross-border operation
into the Laotian panhandle. Two days before Christmas 1970, Nixon convened a meeting to discuss the plan. All present—Laird, Moorer, Kissinger,
and Haig—agreed to it in principle.[29]

The president authorized Laird to discuss the plan further during his January 1971 trip to Saigon. The South Vietnamese leadership needed no convincing, although, according to Laird's record of the conversation, Thieu was
concerned about "political repercussions. Some would say we had widened
the war. He suggested our reply should be that we are widening the peace,"
Laird wrote.[30]

On January 27 Nixon signed off on Phase 1 of the Laotian invasion. The
South Vietnamese code named it Lam Son 719 after an ancient Vietnamese
victory over the Chinese in 1427.[31] They named the three key helicopter landing zones for the operation, "Liz," "Sophia," and "Lolo," after three movie
stars—Elizabeth Taylor, Sophia Loren, and Gina Lollobrigida.

At 10 a.m. on February 8, 1971, the First Armored Brigade of the South
Vietnamese Army (ARVN) rolled across the border into Laos. They went
alone; not a single American soldier or advisor accompanied their advance.
American troops were not allowed across the border, a fact pointedly made
by a sign erected just short of the border that read:

"Warning, No U.S. Personnel Beyond This Point."

On the reverse side, a GI had defiantly added another message:

"No North Vietnamese Troops Permitted Beyond This Point."[32]

The plan was for the South Vietnamese solders, with air and cross-border
artillery support from the Americans, to move into Laos on Highway 9 toward
the hub of Tchepone on the Ho Chi Minh Trail. In the first week, the South

Vietnamese located and destroyed huge caches of enemy food, ammunition, and supplies. American air support demolished additional caches and enemy troop concentrations. When White House briefers explained the operation to the public, they strayed from the cautionary script Laird had provided, implying that the final objective was Tchepone and that the operation would last a couple of months—neither of which was true. The objective was to destroy the caches all along the way to Tchepone, and there was no time limit.[33]

Laird and U.S. commanders were both surprised and unhappy when the South Vietnamese halted their advance about ten miles short of Tchepone on February 12, although they were virtually unopposed. A month later American commanders heard reports that the field commanders had halted on secret orders from President Thieu. Unbeknownst to U.S. commanders, Thieu had allegedly ordered his generals to halt the Laos operation once they had sustained three thousand casualties, dead and wounded. Thieu, who was up for reelection that year, was all for invading Laos as long as it didn't affect his numbers at the polls. Thieu himself denied that he gave such an order. And there was no reason for stopping because, at that point, there were few casualties. It was more likely Thieu stopped the advance to better assess what the enemy reaction might be, but it was a serious mistake. It allowed the North Vietnamese to mass the largest force they had ever assembled for a single battle, which had been significantly underestimated in the Lam Son planning. According to a North Vietnamese history of the war, sixty thousand troops were sent into the area.[34]

The press began to smell disaster, pinning their judgment on the idea that the South Vietnamese army was "bogged down," unable to move to Tchepone. The reality was that the pause had allowed the enemy to join the battle in massive numbers, and the South Vietnamese found themselves overwhelmed. Still, they inflicted greater casualties (with American air support) than they suffered.

On February 24 Laird thought it was time to hold a press briefing to remind the media what the real objectives of the operation were. He brought with him Lt. Gen. John Vogt, head of the Joint Staff. "Tchepone is not a city," Vogt informed them. "Tchepone is not an objective in itself. Tchepone is a deserted village [with] a few bombed-out buildings. It presents, by itself, no worthwhile military objective." Tchepone "has never been an objective [of] this operation," Laird agreed.[35] The objective, Laird iterated in the ninety-minute Q&A session, was "to slow up, to disrupt, the logistics supplies, to cut off and to downgrade the capability of the North Vietnamese to wage any type of warfare in South Vietnam."[36]

That briefing temporarily marred Laird's record of candor with the press when a misleading impression was left regarding a visual aid—a three-foot section of Russian pipe. At one point, Laird stepped aside to let Vogt tell about a major achievement of the South Vietnamese two days before in cutting 1,500 feet of a 150-mile gasoline pipeline ,which began in North Vietnam, and which was used to supply gas to the trucks all along the Ho Chi Minh Trail. "I would like to show you what that pipeline looks like. I have a segment of that pipeline," Vogt continued, unveiling the example.

The reporters didn't ask, and Vogt didn't say, *when* this particular section of the pipe had been cut, and *who* did the cutting. But the reporters were left with the impression that the pipe had come straight from the battlefield of the Lam Son operation and that it had been cut by South Vietnamese soldiers. Vogt probably felt he could not reveal the true provenance of the piece because it had been retrieved several months before in a cross-border intelligence-gathering raid by South Vietnamese and U.S. Special Forces troops who weren't supposed to be there.

Whether Laird himself knew the truth about the pipe is in question. In later years he used the story as an example of how important it had been for him to be straight with the press. Laird's memory is that General Abrams called him after the press conference and told him the implication about the pipe was inaccurate. At that point, Laird said he immediately called another press conference to clear up the record. But during questioning by Congress in 1971, Laird testified that he *knew* that the pipe had not been collected during the Lam Son operation.[37] In his congressional testimony Laird said, "I do not hold General Vogt in any way responsible—I support him. It was probably an oversight on my part. . . . If anything happens in the Department of Defense, I take the heat for it. Don't feel sorry for me in that regard."

The press had a field day with the pipe story. Humor columnist Art Buchwald wrote an imaginative story in which Laird, "wearing his usual ebullient smile," unveils rifles from Custer's Last Stand, chickens from a World War I engagement, sandbags from the battle for Iwo Jima and, finally, Chinese tanks captured at the Korean War battle of Inchon.[38] Laird saw the minor flap as symptomatic of a much greater problem—intense press frustration with the administration over the Lam Son operation, which would seriously taint their stories about its success. They had bridled at a news embargo during the first few days of the operation and had been prevented by the South Vietnamese from going into Laos and reporting on the battles. Laird explained the seriousness of this problem at the March 1 staff meeting: "We can't bar this kind of reporting. There are 150 newsmen in the area and they don't have anything better to do."

But the long-term ramification was the risk that the media could turn military victory into a defeat, Laird reminded his top Pentagon officials. "We must bear in mind that we don't want to make these operations into either a victory or defeat at the present time. We don't want the psychology in the country to end up like it did after the enemy's Tet Offensive of 1968. Here an allied victory was turned into a defeat. The TV and newspaper assessments that Tet was a defeat could never be turned around."[39]

⌒

During the initial weeks of the Lam Son operation, Kissinger was on the defensive, and taking heat from Congress. He knew there was nothing like success to silence critics. And, to him, only by reaching Tchepone could Lam Son be qualified as a military victory. He demanded explanations and action from Laird, who was quick to remind him that the South Vietnamese were calling the shots: "I'm not the secretary of defense for the South Vietnamese, and President Nixon isn't their commander in chief. It's *their* operation," Laird recalled telling Kissinger.

At that point, in Laird's view, the operation had already been quite successful in capturing supplies and foiling traffic on the trail. But Kissinger, through Abrams, had pushed Thieu into mounting an offensive against the desolate town of Tchepone. Thieu ordered his troops back into the fray and sent in reinforcements.[40] He decided that if he leapfrogged an airborne assault near the village he could declare victory and depart—a "touching base" maneuver. No one expected him to hold Tchepone, since Lam Son was supposed to be an in-and-out operation.

So on March 6, the U.S. forces at Khe Sanh mounted the largest, longest-ranging helicopter assault of the Vietnam War. Making three round trips each that day, 276 Huey helicopters took two South Vietnamese infantry battalions forty-eight miles to a landing zone next to Tchepone. There, they held on long enough to destroy substantial caches of supplies and equipment. Two days after the landing, General Abrams pronounced Lam Son a success. They had seized enough rice to feed 159 battalions for thirty days; enough rifles, small arms, machine guns, mortars and artillery pieces to equip seventeen infantry battalions; and 714 tons of ammunition.[41]

Four days after arriving in Tchepone, the South Vietnamese began to pull out, against the wishes of Laird and others who had hoped Thieu would capitalize on the success a little longer. The retreat quickly took on the look of a rout. Route 9 was a tangle of disabled tanks and other vehicles that had run out of gas—and not a few corpses. Most of the South Vietnamese troops had to either hike or be helicoptered out. Given the high helicopter losses sustained by the U.S. force from the antiaircraft artillery along the trail, pilots were ordered to fully pack their choppers with retreating soldiers to cut down on the number of round trips. A small number of panicky soldiers interpreted the situation as a shortage of room and jumped onto the helicopter skids, creating unforgettable photographic images when they landed in Khe Sanh where the American news media waited.

As the South Vietnamese numbers in Laos diminished, the enemy attacked in greater force, and the situation became desperate. Instead of an orderly retreat, the final days left the impression of a desperate scramble to safety inside South Vietnam. Laird publicly defended the performance of the South Vietnamese soldiers and praised their success. Behind closed doors, he expressed disappointment during the March 29 staff meeting that they had not stayed longer.[42]

While the military leaders were relatively sanguine, Nixon and Kissinger were not—and the object of their anger was the dutiful soldier, Creighton Abrams. Nixon was so angry that, according to Haig's memoirs, the president ordered Haig to take over for General Abrams: "Go home and pack your bag. Then get on the first available plane and fly to Saigon. You're taking command." Haig said he replied, "Good God, Mr. President, you can't do that." The next day Nixon changed his mind; Haig was dispatched, instead, on a fact-finding mission to Saigon.[43] Nixon may have changed his mind because of a phone conversation with Laird that same night. Laird remembered getting a call from Nixon late at night saying that Haig was going to Saigon to replace Abrams. "Mr. President, that's alright," Laird responded, "but I want you to know I'll be walking out of the front door of the Pentagon tomorrow morning." The implication was that Laird wouldn't be coming back. The details of Nixon's order are not recorded anywhere but in Haig's memoir. And the only part of it that Laird was skeptical about was the claim by the ambitious Haig's that he had refused the assignment.

Abrams died several years after the war without penning his own memoirs, but Lewis Sorley published transcripts of tape recordings Abrams made of his meetings in his office in Saigon. In August 1971 Abrams had conducted a review of Lam Son, calculating the damage done to enemy supply lines and the reduced ability of Hanoi to mount a major offensive that year. "I'm beginning to have a conviction about Lam Son 719 that that was really a death blow," Abrams is quoted on one tape as saying.[44] Laird himself believed similarly, that the operation diverted the North for a period of time to reconstruct that portion of the supply route. An independent review of the operation, including assessment of action reports that came into Laird's office, suggests that Lam Son 719, while not pretty, was a qualified success. U.S. intelligence concluded that more than thirteen thousand enemy troops were killed, and probably twice that number wounded, suggesting a casualty rate as high as 70 percent. United States air power was pivotal in achieving that result.[45]

Lam Son seriously disrupted the Ho Chi Minh Trail. The CIA's Office of Economic Research sent a report to Laird that spring concluding that "large-scale enemy military operations in South Vietnam for the remainder of 1971 were probably impossible and that Hanoi would have to undertake a major resupply campaign before any offensive could be launched in 1972."[46] Documentary evidence suggests that it took more than a year for North Vietnam to recover from the loss of men, supplies, and equipment. North Vietnam declared a great victory, but Laird knew Hanoi was reeling because intercepted messages demonstrated that the usual chest-thumping propaganda from the field was more subdued.[47]

A final positive point for Laird was the relatively muted student unrest over Lam Son—far less in number and intensity than the Cambodia opposition of the previous spring. Still, Laird was the target of protests. For example, he had agreed to deliver a speech at the University of Wisconsin before Lam Son but had to cancel during the ongoing operation. General "Chappie" James went in his place and received an antiwar reprimand from the chancellor and a thirty-name petition protesting the war from the students serving the luncheon. Out in the cold were about two thousand antiwar protesters led by Rennie Davis, who had been convicted in the "Chicago Seven" trial of crossing state lines to incite a riot at the 1968 Democratic National Convention. He shouted to the demonstrators in Wisconsin, "If the government doesn't stop the war, we are going to stop the government." And he chided Laird for not showing up: "Laird is not all fool. If he would have come here today, we would have really kicked some ass!" On February 10, several hundred students at the University of Illinois in Champaign burned Laird in effigy.[48]

~

Lam Son had caused Laird to focus more closely not just on the Ho Chi Minh Trail interdiction but also on the secret war in Laos which the Pentagon was required to support. In 1971 he became fed up with standing on the side lines while the CIA and the State Department ran the covert war in Laos, using his budget. He decided he wanted a man he could trust to take a closer look and ride herd over it. The man he chose would eventually become chairman of the Joint Chiefs of Staff during the Reagan administration—Gen.

John W. "Jack" Vessey. In late 1971 he was a new brigadier general running support operations out of Thailand for the effort in Laos.

Laird visited Thailand in person and told Vessey to pack his bags and go to Laos. Vessey presented himself at the U.S. Embassy in Vientiane to report to Ambassador Godley. Godley's assistant, Monte Sterns, waylaid him and said, "The ambassador is pretty busy today and won't be able to see you. Why don't you get a room and look around and make contact with the other agencies?" Vessey made the rounds of the CIA and the Agency for International Development, which had a role in the war and provided cover for the CIA. In two days Vessey was back at the embassy. Sterns again came to the waiting room. "Well, the ambassador's still not ready," he said. But Vessey wasn't leaving. "I've been ordered to report to the ambassador. It seems to me I ought to see him."

At that point, having overheard the conversation, Godley stormed out of his office and confronted Vessey. "I didn't ask for you and I don't want you here!" he bellowed.

"Well, Mr. Ambassador, I didn't ask to come here, and I really don't want to be here," Vessey retorted, "but I've been ordered to be here and it seems to me we ought to figure out how to make this work."

Godley calmed down, but he set one ground rule: "The first thing I want to tell you is you can't send any back-channels to your military superiors." Vessey fell back on good military order and said he couldn't cut off any means of communicating with his superiors, but he promised he would never send anything to Washington without showing it to Godley. Then he added, "Maybe we can work out the same arrangement." To his surprise, Godley agreed that the channel of communications would be open on both sides.

While neither ever conceded that the other was the boss, Vessey was firmly in charge of the purse strings. The constraints imposed by Congress and the Geneva Convention meant that Vessey had to do much of his strategizing on the sly. His own presence in Laos was known only to a few insiders. He kept a low profile, and on the few occasions when he went to social events he wore civilian clothes. "I think the only people who knew I was there were the Russians and the Chinese," he recalled. They would follow him with cameras on his rare public outings. Vessey was one of the few American soldiers who actually lived in Laos during the war.

Under his cloak of secrecy, Vessey managed to impose Laird's stamp on the Laos operations. He stayed within the budgetary limits that Congress had set for aid to Laos and forged tight relationships with the CIA and State

Department bosses there. "By the time the cease fire came around [in 1973], we had almost all the rice-growing land under the control of the [Lao] government. We had about 80 percent of the people [under] control of the government, and it was a relatively successful strategy," Vessey said.[49]

Successful indeed in a nation where the United States never officially fought a war.

With South Vietnamese General Ngo Quang Truong, February 1970. Distinguishing himself in South Vietnam's response to the Tet Offensive of 1968, and playing the leading role in the defense against the Easter Offensive of 1972, Truong earned widespread respect among the U.S. military leadership. General H. Norman Schwarzkopf, a Vietnam veteran, would later call Truong "the most brilliant tactical commander I'd ever known."

With Army General Creighton Abrams, February 1970.

Nixon, Laird, and Packard at the Pentagon, May 1, 1970.

Lunching with troops aboard the USS *Little Rock*, 1970.

With mother, Helen Connor Laird, on the occasion of the dedication of the Central Wisconsin Regional Airport, May 1970. Wisconsin Governor Warren P. Knowles descends the steps behind them.

Japanese Defense Minister Yasuhiro Nakasone meets with Laird at the Pentagon in September 1970. This meeting and immediate friendship led to the first-ever visit to Japan by a U.S. secretary of defense the following summer, when Laird and Nakasone agreed to a new burden-sharing arrangement. Nakasone became prime minister in 1982.

Laird, Air Force General Daniel "Chappie" James Jr., and Hal Short, owner of the Washington Senators, look on as Army Master Sergeant Daniel L. Pitzer, who spent four years as a POW, throws out the first ball of the 1971 baseball season at Kennedy Stadium in Washington, D.C.

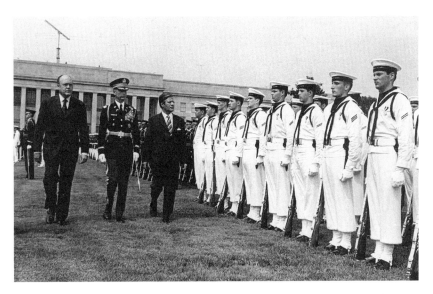

Laird, with his friend German Defense Minister Helmut Schmidt, reviews the honor guard at the Pentagon's River Entrance, July 1971. Schmidt became chancellor in 1974.

With fellow Congressmen Gerald R. Ford (R-MI) and Bob Michel (R-IL) at Burning Tree Club in Bethesda, Maryland, discussing their favorite subject—politics—prior to a Saturday afternoon tee-off, November 1971.

Morning staff meeting in Secretary Laird's office, June 1972.

With General Omar Bradley at the dedication of the Pentagon corridor named in his honor, June 1972.

Illustrating final Vietnam troop withdrawals at a press conference, October 1972.

Having the last of the regularly arranged breakfasts with National Security Advisor Henry A. Kissinger, January 1973.

With the women who made flag rank during his tenure as secretary of defense, 1973. Prior to Laird's new initiative on women in the military, women had never been promoted to flag rank (general or admiral).

During the energy crisis of 1973–74, in his role as counselor for domestic affairs, Laird urged Americans to turn down their thermostats and start wearing sweaters—advice that was promptly spoofed in this *New York Times* cartoon. (Reproduced with permission of Zenowij Onyshkewyeh.)

"DON'T THINK IT WASN'T GREAT WORKING FOR YOU, DICK"

TO MEL LAIRD — GOOD LUCK AND BEST WISHES ON YOUR NEW ADVENTURES — GENE BASSET

Laird resigned from his position in the Nixon White House in February 1974. At the press conference where he made the announcement, he encouraged the House Judiciary Committee to undertake its constitutional obligation to consider impeaching the president. (Reprinted with permission of Scripps Howard News Service).

With Kissinger, Ford, and wife Carole at the Laird Center dedication.

With Kissinger and Ford at the dedication of the Melvin R. Laird Center for Medical Research at Wisconsin's Marshfield Clinic, September 1997.

Laird informally advised Secretary of Defense Donald H. Rumsfeld throughout his six-year tenure in the George W. Bush administration. Meeting with Rumsfeld in February 2001, Laird reminded his successor that "it's a helluva lot easier to get into a war than it is to get out of one." In this meeting they were joined by author Dale Van Atta, left.

The Laird family in front of the Marshfield, Wisconsin, home where Melvin Laird spent his childhood.

20

The Hawks Have Flown

O N THE BRISK SPRING EVENING of April 5, 1971, the secretary of defense left the Pentagon shortly after 8 p.m. and was driven to the Watergate apartment complex in Georgetown. He looked forward to the private dinner for ten senators and Laird, hosted by Sen. Jacob Javits. The secretary expected a companionable evening, with a wide-ranging discussion on administration policy. But not long after sitting down to eat, Laird realized that he was to be the main course. The Republican leadership at the table were sick of Laos, sick of Vietnam, and disenchanted with the president's exit plan, and they took it out on Laird.

"The president must think in terms of finality," declared Hugh Scott, the Senate minority leader. Knowing that Nixon was scheduled to make his next major troop withdrawal announcement two nights later, Scott lamented that these withdrawal increments were no longer enough. "He must make public some formula that clearly indicates the end of American participation of the war." It was an untenable position to Laird, who knew that giving a certain date of departure would rob the United States of negotiating power with the North Vietnamese.

Adjourning for cognac and cigars in the living room, the senators continued their assessment of the war and its impact on the American people. Sen. Marlow Cook asked directly: if the president announced that the war was over tomorrow, how long would it take to get the troops and equipment home? Laird reckoned nine months. Time and again, the senators came back to their central theme: they would not be able to hold their party together on war issues if Nixon did not announce an end date. Alaska's Ted Stevens told Laird, "I come from the most hawkish state in the union. I ran in '70 as a hawk. I couldn't do it in '72." Scott soberly added: "You don't see any hawks around here. The hawks are all ex-hawks."[1]

The next morning, Laird composed a memo to Nixon, whom he was sure would be feeling the lack of patience in his party as he looked to reelection in 1972. Titled "Tempo of the War," Laird's memo began with heartening words: "The attention given to operations in Laos tends to obscure the fact that U.S. involvement in the war is declining rapidly." Laird reminded Nixon of some of their war-related achievements, which the president could use in his scheduled address to the nation the following night: The enemy had been able to launch only two large attacks in the previous nine months, compared to eight in the same period the previous year; U.S. troop numbers were 44 percent below their high point; combat deaths were down 55 percent from the prior year; the cost of the war had fallen by $4 billion in 1970 and would fall another $5 billion in 1971.[2]

The president was cheered by the memo and summoned Laird at noon the next day to his hideaway office at the Old Executive Office Building to go over the speech. In it, Nixon announced the fifth round of troop withdrawals from Vietnam. As with the prior four, the behind-the-scenes maneuvering had been intense. The Joint Chiefs and General Abrams were emphatic about slowing down the rate of withdrawal to only 8,500 a month, instead of 12,500.[3] Laird tactfully reminded Nixon that the president had promised publicly in two speeches that the withdrawal would "continue at its present level," so the Joint Chiefs' recommendation was unacceptable for that reason alone. He advised Nixon to consider a faster withdrawal rate for three reasons. First, the president should understand that "congressional and popular U.S. support for our programs in Southeast Asia are now more tenuous than ever."

The second and third reasons Laird raised had to do with the terrible human and financial costs of the war. Even though casualties were far fewer than under the Johnson administration, more than fifteen thousand Americans had died in the war since Nixon took office. Only by increasing the rate of withdrawal would combat deaths continue to come down.

Though rarely mentioned in public up to that time, Laird made a powerful point in his private memo to Nixon about the second great cost of the Vietnam War—that of falling behind the main enemy, the Soviet Union. The impact of the war's financial drain on the defense budget "is one of the major reasons the Soviet Union has been able to make such marked military strides relative to the United States during the past few years," Laird wrote. But Laird had made a persuasive argument and Nixon announced in his speech that another 100,000 troops would be withdrawn by December 1, leaving about 184,000 Americans in Vietnam.

Most congressional leaders were not satisfied, however, including those who had attended Javits's party. Still, as they began to add up the numbers, it was undeniable that such a continued withdrawal rate meant that only twenty-five thousand troops would be left in Vietnam when voters went to the polls in November 1972 to reelect or bounce Nixon.

Media prognosticators wondered whether a reelected Nixon would leave that many troops in the war indefinitely as a "residual force." In his speech, the president had promised "total withdrawal," provided peace negotiations were concluded, but Laird had spoken earlier of a minimal residual force, if for nothing else to stay until the last American POW had been released. The president didn't want any mention of "residual forces" after his speech, and he thought that Laird might stoke the issue in the press. Nixon's fury was captured on the secret taping system in his office on April 9 as he conferred with Kissinger. "We don't want a residual force; our goal is total withdrawal!" Nixon insisted. "Why can't Laird shut up?" Kissinger promised to have a talk with Laird at a private Pentagon luncheon the following Tuesday. "I'm going to try to shape him up."[4]

Kissinger left, but Nixon continued to fume. He decided he couldn't wait until Kissinger had a private word with Laird. Instead, Nixon issued a highly unusual gag order, classified it "Secret/Eyes Only," and had it delivered to Laird, Rogers, Helms, and the Joint Chiefs: "Until further notice, I want no discussions by Government officials with the media concerning U.S. troop withdrawal plans or U.S. plans for maintaining a residual force in South Vietnam. This applies to discussions with the press, either on or off the record, background briefings and informal speculation."[5]

Laird received copy number one, and he knew it was a slap on the wrist. The order would be easy for the others to keep because they rarely talked even in background briefings about Vietnam plans. By default, this made Laird the front man on Capitol Hill and with the media. When Laird could not be informative at a news conference a few days later, the correspondents were frustrated and detected a strain. The *Washington Post*'s experienced Pentagon correspondent, George Wilson, wrote: "Laird appeared defensive and jumpy—his hands visibly shaking at times."[6] Laird was suffering from a double hernia and was anticipating surgery, but his shaky performance probably had less to do with physical pain than the veteran politician's discomfiture at working under a gag order.

One of the subjects raised at that press conference was a new type of antiwar demonstration slated for the following week—a march by antiwar veterans. Never before had American veterans marched on Washington to protest a war that was still being fought. Worse, the Pentagon and press had been told that many of the disenchanted Vietnam vets planned to return, en masse, their service medals. At the heart of this movement was a persuasive young Navy officer, John Kerry.

On April 22, Kerry appeared as a witness before the Senate Foreign Relations Committee and asked the searing questions that would echo in Senator Kerry's run for the presidency more than thirty years later: "How do you ask a man to be the last man to die in Vietnam? How do you ask a man to be the last man to die for a mistake?" The twenty-seven-year old Kerry was no hippie. He was a decorated veteran who had commanded "swift boats" in Vietnam, been awarded three Purple Hearts, a Silver Star, and a Bronze Star. He had joined a small, moribund protest group—the Vietnam Veterans Against the War—and was instrumental in inflating its influence beyond its numbers. The group's performance became the opening act of the spring 1971 protest season in the nation's capital.

Kerry's public statements rankled many at the Pentagon; although no longer on active duty, he was still in the Navy Reserves. Chief of Naval Operations Admiral Zumwalt, and Navy Secretary Chafee urged Laird to agree to court-martial proceedings against Kerry, but Laird turned them down flat. His view then was that Kerry would enjoy a few minutes in the spotlight and never be heard from again.

For several months, the Pentagon geared up for the expected spring 1971 demonstrations. From a potential pool of more than two million veterans, about two thousand Vietnam veterans answered the call for a variety of demonstrations beginning on April 19. They called it "Operation Dewey Canyon III, a limited incursion into the country of Congress." The first few days were inauspicious and ad hoc: a demonstration at Arlington Cemetery and the Supreme Court; a day lobbying Congress; and a march of about fifty veterans to the Pentagon to turn themselves in as "war criminals." Gen. Daniel "Chappie" James met with three of them and concluded: "I'm sorry, but we don't accept American prisoners of war here—why don't you try the Justice Department."

Kerry's moving testimony on April 22 was followed the next day by the final scene of the protest, a wrenching return of medals and honors to the government. Over a wire fence hastily erected in front of the west entrance of the Capitol, about six hundred veterans lobbed ribbons and medals (the highest being a Silver Star), all of which landed in a pile at the feet of the statue of Chief Justice John Marshall.[7] (Kerry admitted in 1984, during his first successful run for the Senate, that he had tossed someone else's medals for them that day because he was proud of his own service and medals.[8] For

the same reason, others at the demonstration chose to keep their more valued ribbons or medals.)

The protest culminated on April 24 with the seventh mass march in
Washington against the Vietnam War. More than double the number of the
expected protesters came—two hundred thousand plus—the largest mass
rally ever to be held on the West Lawn of the Capitol grounds, and the most
peaceful antiwar march yet. The next day, the goodwill began to erode as
about one thousand homeward-bound New England demonstrators stopped
their cars on the New Jersey Turnpike and built a bonfire, which blocked
traffic for four hours, and resulted in one hundred arrests. Another group
of protestors made a special trip to Maryland to Laird's home. His children
were at school, and he was at the Pentagon. His security man, Joe Zaice, had
been forewarned and was inside the house with Barbara Laird. Zaice and
his men watched as a dozen or so demonstrators in "costume" conducted a
mock battle on Laird's lawn, spilling a red liquid, shouting oaths, and hanging a Viet Cong flag from his front porch.[9] Laird himself appeared unruffled
about it the next day at a press conference. "My wife was home, but I'm sure
people know where I am most of the time. I was here trying to do my job."

In an ebullient mood, Laird told the assembled correspondents that he
had called the press conference in part to report that he would check into
Walter Reed Army Hospital the next day to take care of his double hernia.
He said the problem was minor, and he would soon be back to work. "I'll
be around until the change of the guard [in 1973]," Laird said. "I've always
said that Secretary McNamara served too long. I think that four years is long
enough to serve in this particular job. So when you ask me how long, it'll be
that long and no longer." With that, Laird publicly restated his initial one-
term pledge, making him the first member of the Nixon cabinet to state unequivocally that he was leaving.

The correspondents asked if he would consider going back to Congress,
to which Laird responded, "I don't think I want to go back and start all over
again." He did confirm, however, that he believed the Republican Party would
return his seniority to him if he were elected to the Congress again. The
remarks prompted a flurry of speculation on his political future. *Time* magazine concluded that Laird had presidential ambitions and might run for
the Senate from Wisconsin as a step to the White House.[10] Laird quickly put
that rumor to rest. But other theories circulated that he would take a different cabinet post, or that Nixon would dump Agnew and choose Laird as his
running mate in 1972. No one could believe at that point the career politician would simply walk away from it all at the top of his game.

~

Laird had had a ticking time bomb in the walk-in safe of his office since the day he moved in, and in the spring of 1971, it was about to explode. Shelved there among other top secret documents was a seven-thousand-page history of how the United States had stumbled its way into the Vietnam War. The existence of the forty-seven-volume set was known to few in or out of government; only fifteen copies had been distributed. The public revelation of portions of the study, which became known as the "Pentagon Papers," would prompt one of the most dramatic confrontations between the press and government in American history. From that conflict would emerge a more emboldened, cynical, and hostile press, as well as a more paranoid president determined to protect his Oval Office by any means necessary, legal or illegal.

The Vietnam War history project was conceived quietly and conducted on a need-to-know basis by Robert McNamara. When finished, the weight of its research analyses inevitably proved the Johnson administration's tragic Americanization of the war. The study also uncovered the deception that Johnson and McNamara knowingly or unknowingly engaged in to justify the war.

One of the few individuals with insight into the project's genesis was the man who began it at Secretary McNamara's request, Col. Robert E. Pursley. As military assistant to McNamara, Pursley was taken aside privately by his boss in May 1967 and given the assignment. He conferred with the chief of the Pentagon's International Security Affairs (ISA) section, John McNaughton, and they settled on one of his "whiz kids," Leslie H. Gelb, to head up the "Vietnam History Task Force." (Gelb later became a top State Department official, *New York Times* reporter, and then headed the influential Council on Foreign Relations.) He assembled an all-star team of nearly forty people for the project.[11] After the most important documents were assembled, sections of the study were apportioned out to at least thirty-six people who wrote analyses to introduce the documents. Few of these authors or additional consultants, such as Harvard professor Henry Kissinger, knew of the big picture. Fewer still were ever cleared to read the study, other than their own portions.

The project was so comprehensive that it was not completed until after McNamara resigned as defense secretary. The final study was not distributed until June 1969—five months into Laird's term.[12] The study, titled "History of U.S. Decision-Making Process on Vietnam Policy,"[13] comprised 2.5 million words. Laird put his copy on the top shelf of his large vault, without reading it first. He referred to the books from time to time but never read all seven thousand pages.

Team members Leslie Gelb and Mortin Halperin, who both resigned from the Nixon administration to work at the Brookings Institution, decided to put their copies in the vaults of another private think tank, the Rand Corporation.[14] Rand's success had been built on a series of lucrative defense contracts under McNamara, who considered Rand's analysts worth ten times what he paid them. One of those analysts was Dr. Daniel Ellsberg, a former Marine, who took an assignment in Vietnam to work on the CIA's "pacification" program to neutralize the Viet Cong. He came back from Vietnam with his prowar opinions tempered. When he was assigned by Rand to work on a portion of the Pentagon Papers, Ellsberg soon evolved into a full-blown antiwar convert, although he kept his conversion a secret in Washington.

Ellsberg's first leak of a portion of the Pentagon Papers occurred on November 6, 1969, when he met with Sen. William Fulbright and several staffers for the Senate Foreign Relations Committee. Ellsberg gave him a section of the study that proved the Gulf of Tonkin incident was deliberately overblown so that President Johnson could escalate U.S. involvement in Vietnam. Fulbright asked Laird for the full study, and Laird took six weeks to say no. The release of the papers would have shifted blame for the war away from Nixon and back to the Johnson administration, but Laird worried that the uproar it might cause would interfere with Vietnamization and an orderly exit from the war.

In February 1970 Ellsberg secretly delivered another three thousand photocopied pages of the study to Fulbright's staff. When Fulbright wrote Laird again in April, the senator was already in possession of about half the documents he was requesting from Laird. Laird stonewalled Fulbright, turning down the senator's fourth and final request on July 21, 1970. After six months of fruitless attempts, Fulbright took to the Senate floor on August 7 and denounced Laird's decision. He warned Laird, "[A]s the old saw goes, 'Nothing is secret for long in Washington.' I hope that the first enterprising reporter who obtains a copy of this history will share it with the Committee." Ellsberg got the message. By late March 1971, he had found just such an "enterprising reporter": Neil Sheehan of the *New York Times*.

～

On Saturday afternoon, June 12, 1971, Laird was enjoying a game of golf at the Burning Tree Country Club. The game wasn't as leisurely as he usually liked because he had an appointment at 4 p.m.—the White House Rose Garden wedding of the president's oldest daughter, Tricia, to Harvard University law student Edward Cox.[15] Laird was on the sixteenth hole when a club employee rushed out to tell him Kissinger was calling, urgently. Laird told the messenger he would be along to the clubhouse soon to return the call.

So many top Nixon officials enjoyed playing on Burning Tree's links that a secure phone to the White House had been installed in the clubhouse. Laird used it to call Kissinger after the game. "Henry started right out raising hell—telling me the president of the United States was very upset with me for leaking the papers" to the *Times,* Laird recalled. It was a repeat of Kissinger's call to Laird a year before accusing him of leaking the Cambodia bombing to the *Times.* So Laird had little patience for yet another false accusation and, when he could get a word in, responded angrily: "Henry this is *absolute bullshit!*" Then he hung up the phone.

The next morning, Sunday, the *New York Times* landed on doorsteps across America. In the top left-hand corner, under the headline, "Tricia Nixon Takes Vows," was a picture of the bride and her proud father standing in the Rose Garden. Next to the picture was another headline, "Vietnam Archive: Pentagon Study Traces 3 Decades of Growing U.S. Involvement." The front-page story continued inside the paper on six full pages of mind-numbing detail from the secret study that, likely, only the editors themselves would read from start to finish. But alarm bells went off all across Washington who knew what they were holding in their hands that morning.

Laird was scheduled to appear on the CBS talk show *Face the Nation* that morning. To prepare for the worst, he met top aides for a major "DQ" (dirty questions) session over breakfast at the Mayflower Hotel. Thus loaded for bear, Laird walked over to the CBS studio. Incredibly, no one asked a single question about the Pentagon Papers. In retrospect, Laird later wished he had raised the topic himself. He said he would have talked freely and in dismissive terms about the Pentagon Papers, emphasizing how little of the collection was really newsworthy, and characterizing it as a Johnson administration problem. And, he would have stressed that there were few if any real secrets worth hiding in the papers. "I could have set the tone for the whole administration that day," he said, speculating that Nixon might never have gone so far as to condone multiple burglaries to get to the source of the leak.

Nixon, indeed, was immediately unnerved by the story. In public, he waved the flag of national security concerns, but in private, as the White House tapes indicate, he was deeply affronted because what should have been one of the happiest days in his life had been ruined by an antiwar story using purloined state secrets.

Nixon let Attorney General John Mitchell know on Sunday that he wanted action, strong and quick—prosecute the leakers to the full extent of the law and shut down further publication of the documents. In a phone call the same day with Mitchell, Laird formally requested that the Justice Department investigate the breach of national security. He supported the pursuit of leakers but did not favor a Nixon court challenge of the *Times'* right to publish the information. The Constitution's guarantee against prior restraint of the press was likely unassailable, in Laird's view. Besides, Laird believed that if the issue were kept out of the courts, the story would probably die quickly of its own voluminous, scholarly weight. He privately told his general counsel, J. Fred Buzhardt, to cooperate fully on the leak investigation but to "go easy" on the press challenge.

Nixon focused his suspicions on Gelb, Halperin, the Brookings Institution, Rand Corporation, and a new suspect whom Haig moved near the top of the list, Daniel Ellsberg.[16] Not the least of Nixon's targets was the *New York Times.* On the president's instructions late Monday, Mitchell sent the editors an "or-else" cable. If they did not voluntarily suspend publication of the Vietnam War history in Tuesday's editions, the government would take legal action. The *Times* editors refused to stop the presses. Tuesday morning, the *Times* published the third installment of the ten-part series, which by then already totaled eighteen full pages of newsprint.

The Justice Department filed a civil suit in the U.S. District Court in New York, and Judge Murray I. Gurfein issued a temporary injunction against publication while the courts sorted out the issues. For the first time in America's two-hundred-year history, a newspaper had been restrained in advance by a U.S. court from publishing a specific article.

~

One of Laird's frustrations with the Pentagon Papers was not being able to give them a better name that would stick. At the June 21 top-level staff meeting, Laird expressed his "concern about them being called the Pentagon Papers," because it suggested an overlap into the Nixon administration. "I would like you all to refer to them as the 'McNamara Papers," Laird told the staff.[17] Press aide Jerry Friedheim tried out the new moniker at a Pentagon press briefing that day, and reporters noticed immediately. Friedheim pointed out, with some of his usual wit, that if Laird had done a similar study of his own administration, it would have been called "How We Got the U.S. Out of Vietnam."[18]

No matter what the report was called, Laird was not unhappy that it had leaked. The study proved what he had been saying for years, that the war had been Americanized. Still, he was surprised at the magnitude of interest in it. Nixon had inflated the scoop exponentially by seeking a restraining order against the *Times*, transforming a retrospective story about the sins of his predecessors into a mammoth scoop about how the government was trying to cover up the history of the war. Laird had tried to talk him out of it. Failing to sway Nixon, Laird tried working on Kissinger, but his advice went unheeded again.

True to form, Laird didn't stop when he failed to influence Nixon or Kissinger on the *Times* case. In a back-door maneuver not even known to his colleagues at the Pentagon, Laird went to the man who would matter most in the fray, a longtime Sunday morning golfing buddy, U.S. Solicitor General Erwin Griswold. He would prosecute the government's case against the *Times* if it got as far as the Supreme Court, which it did after the Justice Department got restraining orders against *Washington Post*, and the *Boston Globe*, also beneficiaries of Ellsberg's distribution.

It was a classic constitutional confrontation that was decided more by Griswold and Laird than historians have hitherto realized. As the government's lawyer, Griswold had to prove further publication would pose grave and imminent danger to national security. To do that, he would need Pentagon security experts familiar with the 2.5 million words in the Papers, to tell him what secrets in the report were worth protecting. Laird assigned the work to be done, but he privately told Griswold that there were only "six or seven paragraphs in the whole thing that were a little dangerous"—and they had already been published. Laird said the national security claim was flimsy, and he made it clear that he personally would not join in the government's challenge. There would be no affidavit from the secretary of defense about national security secrets. He didn't believe in the rightness of the cause.

Armed with Laird's warning, Griswold put the screws to the Pentagon's security experts, forcing them to whittle down their voluminous list of items in the Pentagon Papers that were allegedly too sensitive to publish.[19] They came up with thirty-three items that fit the description. Laird's personal view, again shared with Griswold, was that not even those thirty-three would hold up in court, since the most sensitive of them had indeed already been published. Before the Supreme Court, Griswold undercut his own case when he disavowed the list as "much too broad." The justices ruled for the press, 6 to 3, on June 30, and the *New York Times, Washington Post, Boston Globe*, and other newspapers began on July 1 to publish the rest of the papers that had been leaked.

Laird felt that the public deserved to know what the papers revealed. Nixon appeared to view the same episode as an assault on the sanctity and prerogatives of the Oval Office. Before it was over, the stink of Watergate would

disgrace, and even send to jail, officials from different executive branch depart-
ments who had been caught by the many tentacles reaching out from the
Oval Office. But those tentacles never penetrated the Defense Department.
Laird's natural instincts had already built a formidable barricade around the
Pentagon, which Nixon and his White House cronies found unassailable.

If there was a single day that could be pinpointed when the Nixon presidency began to unravel, it was June 30—the day of the Supreme Court decision. Nixon was embittered that the press had lionized the leaker Ellsberg,
and the president told his closest associates that everything must be done
to paint Ellsberg as a criminal, instead of a patriot. Nixon began peppering
all his private conversations with the word "conspiracy" and the growing conviction that Ellsberg had not acted alone. He was, simply, the most visible
culprit in a broad-based leftist conspiracy against Nixon personally.

Laird had gone to the White House on the afternoon of June 30 for a
National Security Council meeting. While they met, the Supreme Court's decision against the government was handed down. Directly following the NSC
meeting, Nixon gathered a brainstorming session in the Oval Office, which
included Laird, Mitchell, Kissinger, and Haldeman. According to Haldeman's
diary, the conversation turned to the conspiracy theory: "There's a general
agreement that there is very definitely a conspiracy here, on these papers,
and Laird alluded to some intelligence they had that he didn't get into detail
on." On the tape of the Oval Office conversation, though somewhat garbled,
Laird can be heard using the word, "conspiracy" and saying that he had "several hundred people" at the Pentagon working on an investigation and declas-
sification of the papers.[20] Having used the word "conspiracy" with Nixon,
Laird had unwittingly stoked the president's growing paranoia. It was a veritable red flag, but Laird later contended that Nixon had misunderstood his
meaning.

It had become evident to both Pentagon and FBI investigators that there
was, indeed, a limited family-and-friends plot to leak the Pentagon Papers.
Ellsberg had not acted alone. Others were already known to have assisted
him in the voluminous photocopying of the documents. That was the conspiracy Laird said he had spoken about, not the one Nixon was imagining.
Nixon believed that the "unauthorized disclosure" of the Pentagon Papers
had been part of a concerted leftist campaign by former liberal NSC staffers
and their cohorts to end the war.

By the next morning after his meeting with Laird et al., Nixon was on a
tear. The White House taping system recorded the details. Nixon told Haldeman and White House aide Charles Colson that they needed to prosecute

Ellsberg and his co-conspirators in the press, because the courts would take too long. "Convict the son of a bitch in the press! That's the way it's done," he insisted. Nixon said he needed someone who could "run this," a first-class political operator who didn't mind dirtying his hands. Among all the names discussed, Laird was mentioned as someone to whom the appointed cloak-and-dagger man could go for information. "Laird's got lots [of people on this]," Nixon observed. And Laird had "said there's a conspiracy." The most promising prospect to do the President's dirty work was suggested by Colson—the name was E. Howard Hunt who had just left the CIA.[21]

In a meeting the next morning, July 2, with Haldeman and Ehrlichman, Nixon opined about Laird being the best disseminator of a countercampaign: "Now Laird—this is one place where we can take a guy who's a . . . sonofabitch—and maybe Laird just might want to make a hero out of himself. I want you two to have a talk with Laird." Ehrlichman knew that would be fruitless—Laird wouldn't even take his calls. So he dismissed the idea, reminding the president that Laird was away on a foreign trip for three weeks.[22]

Amid the many meetings Nixon had with White House intimates hatching plots that summer of 1971, Laird's name came up at least once more. Laird and his general counsel, Fred Buzhardt, had become aware that Nixon had misunderstood Laird, thinking the Pentagon was on the verge of proving a broad-based conspiracy. On July 1, Laird dispatched Buzhardt to the Justice Department for a meeting with Mitchell to douse the conspiracy talk. Mitchell reported that to the president on July 6. In the middle of a lengthy conversation about the Ellsberg investigation, Nixon reminded Mitchell: "Laird sat in here, as you recall, and said he had all this thing—that he thought it was a conspiracy and so forth."

"But I want to tell you, Mr. President," Mitchell finally had to correct, "after Mel Laird said that that day, I asked Buzhardt over the next day—and they weren't even close to it [proving a widespread conspiracy.]"

"Is that right?" Nixon asked, surprised. "They [were] just bulling?"

Mitchell didn't respond.

"But they've got a much bigger outfit working on this than Edgar Hoover has," Nixon pressed.

"I know they have," Mitchell conceded, explaining that they weren't finding proof that any of Nixon's suspects were part of a conspiracy.[23]

Laird had started to sense that White House aides, particularly Haldeman and Ehrlichman, were getting a little wild, so it was imperative for him to control the information. J. Edgar Hoover had helped by refusing to bring the FBI in on the hunt for conspirators. That allowed Laird to control the information uncovered by a Pentagon investigation. Buzhardt confirmed that important victory at the July 12 staff meeting: "We are doing this ourselves, rather than having outsiders do it."[24]

~

Laird's final security response to the Pentagon Papers was to clamp down on loose practices at the Rand Corporation, now that it had been confirmed it was Rand copies that were leaked. He ordered Air Force guards to take over security of all classified documents in Rand's possession—an amazing collection of 173,000 documents, according to an Air Force survey.[25] President Nixon was of the same mind regarding Rand, but in his mind there was a bigger think tank ripe for a clampdown: the Brookings Institution where Gelb and Halperin worked. He saw it as a house of enemies. Breaking into the Brookings safe became a Nixon obsession.

The first meeting at which the president uttered this thought out loud was the same June 30 evening meeting, which followed the Supreme Court decision and included Laird, Mitchell, Kissinger, Haldeman, and Ehrlichman. While the National Archives log of the White House tapes suggest they were all in the room from 5:14 to 6:23 p.m., for many minutes while the Brookings break-in was postulated by the president, Laird's voice was not heard. "I wasn't in the room," Laird recalled emphatically. "I know I was not present for anything like that. I was not in that room at that particular time."[26] Nixon hammered on the break-in idea for three days in private meetings. Laird was recorded as being in only the first meeting.[27] From those three days of increasingly insistent presidential orders, the infamous "Plumbers unit" was born.

Gerald Ford pondered for many years the reasons Nixon went awry after his promising beginnings. In a 1997 interview with the author, Ford concluded, "He made one serious mistake. He put Haldeman, Ehrlichman, and Colson in his inner circle. They were an evil influence on Dick Nixon." But had Laird been part of that White House inner circle at the same time, Ford said Watergate would never have happened, because Laird would have put a stop to it in its earliest stages—"absolutely! Mel Laird had absolute political integrity."

A tip-off regarding the trio's influence came from Ford's examination of Nixon's White House tapes. When Haldeman, Ehrlichman, or Colson were in the room or on the phone, the president used coarse language that neither Ford nor Laird ever heard him use in their presence. Ford said, "I'll bet you that 90-something percent of the bad language he uses on the tapes is when those three people are there. He appointed them, and they poisoned him."[28] Ford's conclusion was that the trio brought out the worst in Nixon, and they were willing to serve his darkest desires.

Ehrlichman created the "Special Investigative Unit," which called themselves the "Plumbers." Their initial plan was to portray Ellsberg as eccentric and unstable, so in September 1971 they broke into the Beverly Hills office of Ellsberg's psychiatrist looking for the doctor's notes on Ellsberg, but couldn't find them. That same month, they were unsuccessful in breaching the Pentagon fortress; Plumber Gordon Liddy showed up at one of the Pentagon's entrances, flashing his White House pass. Laird had firmly established a rule that White House staffers could not approach the Pentagon in person or by phone without going through his personal assistant, Carl Wallace. Now, Wallace was called by the Pentagon guards. Liddy said he wanted to look at some files in connection with the ongoing Pentagon Papers investigation. Wallace and Buzhardt had Liddy escorted out of the building immediately.

In September Howard Hunt also tried to get some documents from the Pentagon that Nixon wanted to smear the previous Democratic administrations. The president wanted the Plumbers to get as much classified material as possible that would embarrass Johnson over Vietnam or Kennedy on either the Bay of Pigs fiasco or collusion in the 1963 assassination of South Vietnamese president Ngo Dinh Diem. Over a week's time, Hunt made several cursory contacts and at least one visit to the Pentagon hunting for incriminating assassination-related material. Each time, he was stopped short by Laird and Wallace.

At about the same time, having failed to breach the Pentagon's defenses, the Plumbers tried to go around Laird by asking one of his top intelligence chiefs over to the White House for a schmooz and strong-arm. National Security Agency chief Adm. Noel Gayler dutifully showed up, thinking he was going to an NSC meeting. He found himself in an unusual meeting with Attorney General Mitchell and some White House aides (later identified with the Plumbers), who asked for any wiretap or other information about anti-administration Americans who hadn't been identified as part of the Pentagon Papers investigation. Knowing Laird would be upset if he had even gone to the White House without clearing it first, Gayler made a quick exit without offering any help. He headed straight for Laird's office, where he was chewed out for accepting the invitation. Laird then called Mitchell. "Listen," Laird began, "I'm willing to share some of this NSA or DIA material with Justice and the FBI when there's something criminal involved. But I'm not sharing any of this information EVER on civilians."

⌇

Of all the instructions Laird's subordinates ever received, the "liaison law" was the most repeated and most enforced: "My office deals with the White House; you don't." Wallace handled the White House staff, and Pursley dealt with the National Security Council. Otherwise, only Laird himself and Packard were authorized to talk to anyone at 1600 Pennsylvania Avenue.[29] Assistant Secretary Barry Shillito, who had served in earlier Democratic administrations, said he and others who worked at the Pentagon were "fortunate" that Laird put the firewall in place "so quickly and so early in the administration" before the White House staff realized what Laird was doing. Dr. Johnny Foster, who served as director of research and engineering for McNamara and Laird, called it a "very clever move. I don't know any other secretary that has done that. . . . Hell, if he hadn't done that, I would have been making mistakes which he thus arranged for me to avoid."[30]

Nixon-era scholar and author Stanley I. Kutler thought Laird "wasn't out to protect people. He was out to cement his own power."[31] Certainly keeping others' noses out of his Pentagon business was a real motivation for Laird. "White House staffs back to Eisenhower's days had become harder and harder to handle," explained Shillito. "They'd grown like mad, taken on a power base of their own. And Mel saw that Nixon's White House staff tried to move into his decision-making process almost immediately."

Another reason Laird established the rules was that he knew many Pentagon officials could get themselves into trouble because of the "holy cow" factor. Shillito said it's hard for outsiders to "appreciate the impact it can have on a fairly sound-thinking person who comes into government and gets a call from the White House. Even really mature people are over-awed by this crap . . .—some Mr. XYZ, almost a nonentity, asking for a favor. But somehow they get this weird idea that the president is calling them for some kind of a fireside chat."[32] At one staff meeting in 1970, according to the minutes, Laird pointed out that there were some three hundred people working at the White House and "each of these . . . people has a telephone. Many of them think they are speaking for the president, but usually they are not. We have to protect the president himself from these types of requests."[33]

Air Force Secretary Seamans once made the mistake of complying with a request that came from the White House one weekend in the early months of his appointment. He agreed to loan the White House one of his public affairs officers for a while, so he was surprised to see the man still in the Pentagon on Monday. "I didn't think I was going to see you this morning. I thought you were going over to the White House," Seamans said.

"I never heard anything about that," the staffer responded.

Puzzled, Seamans hurried over to Laird's office for the regular Monday staff meeting. At one point in the meeting, Laird said, "Now, I've told all of you that you're not to communicate with the White House. You're not to respond to any requests from the White House."

"Mel, I guess you're talking about me," Seamans sheepishly owned up.

"I am," Laird said, "and I mean it, and don't do it again."

Seamans called it "a good lesson" that stuck. He never did it again, he said, which "saved me a lot of trouble." For example, a White House functionary called him on behalf of the First Lady asking if a tiger could be slipped aboard a National Guard training flight from St. Louis for delivery to the San Diego Zoo. Seamans responded, "Well, you know, a decision like that is not really one for me to make. You need to talk to Carl Wallace."

"Oh *shit!*" the White House aide muttered. "I've already talked to him, and he turned me down."[34]

So that there was no misunderstanding, Laird reiterated the liaison law each time it was ignored. "I am not exaggerating when I say that he reiterated his rule maybe a hundred times in the four years," Bob Froehlke recalled. This is how the lecture would go: "Don't take a call from the White House. If someone says, 'The White House is calling—', you say, 'A building can't talk.' If they say, 'The president wants ——', you tell them, 'Whatever the president wants, he will tell Mel Laird.'"[35]

Laird's top-level staffers were uniform in their gratitude for his liaison policy. "There wasn't anybody who got into any trouble. Nobody was within five jillion miles of Watergate," said Capen.[36] Two men who served Laird as successive Navy secretaries, John Chafee and John Warner, understood that Laird's instincts had preserved their reputations in such a way that they were both able to become influential, respected members of the Senate. Two days before Chafee died unexpectedly in 1999, he reviewed his personal debt to Laird and became emotional. There was no way to thank his friend Mel Laird enough for what he had done other than to say that, in retrospect, "what made my respect for Mel go up even more" was the prescience of funneling all White House contacts through Laird's assistant. "I've recommended to every secretary of defense since then that they adopt this, that they use exactly the same system that Mel had." None, he found, took the advice.[37]

Alone among all of the top Pentagon officials, Warner had worked closely with Haldeman, Ehrlichman and others as part of Nixon's 1960 and 1968 presidential campaigns. Warner recalled that he had only been at the Pentagon a couple of weeks in 1969 as Navy undersecretary when Haldeman and Ehrlichman began calling. Laird heard about it and ordered Warner to come to his office.

"I hear you're seeing your old buddies," Laird began sternly. He got up from his desk, and went over to the window, motioning Warner to follow. "What's that over there?"

Warner didn't know what he was pointing to and made a couple of wrong guesses.

"It's the Potomac River!" Laird finally said, exasperated. "I want you to hear this and remember it well: DON'T YOU CROSS THAT RIVER AND GO TO THE WHITE HOUSE! IF I EVER SEE YOU CROSSING THAT RIVER TO GO TO THE WHITE HOUSE, YOU'LL GO HOME IN A TAXI AND NOT COME BACK!"

In imitation of Laird, Warner paced around his room, shouting as Laird had. But then, Warner laughed softly. The message had been received loud and clear. "So I stiffed old Haldeman and Ehrlichman and everybody else. If I hadn't done that because of Mel, I might have done something in the whole Watergate thing. And that would have been the end of me."[38]

21

Withdrawal Symptoms

THE 173RD AIRBORNE BRIGADE, called the "Sky Soldiers" had been the first Army line unit deployed to Vietnam. In August of 1971 the unit finally packed up its gear and came home. Laird went to Fort Campbell, Kentucky, on September 2 to personally welcome the unit home. The return of the first Army unit to go to Vietnam was major evidence that American involvement in the war was ending, and there were other signals—large and small—throughout 1971. For example, in a Fort Campbell press conference, Laird noted that when he first came into office, some twenty-seven million cases of soft drinks and "good Wisconsin beer" were shipped annually to Vietnam, but that had dropped to a yearly rate of seven million cases.[1]

The year also saw the departure from Vietnam of the Fifth Special Forces Group, the First Cavalry Division (Airmobile), the Twenty-fifth Infantry Division, the last U.S. Marine command unit, and the Twenty-third Infantry Division, known as the "Americal Division." By the end of the year only one full U.S. division—the 101st Airborne—was still operating in Vietnam. For Laird, the best news from the war in Vietnam in 1971 was that the American casualty rate was declining rapidly, from an average of below fifty a week in the early part of the year to less than ten a week by year's end. In one week in late December, only one American was killed—and that compared to as many as five hundred dead in the weeks before Laird became secretary of defense.[2]

The departure of ground combat troops at the rate of twelve thousand a month in 1971 prompted Admiral Moorer to intensify his requests for more air strikes. On April 6 General Abrams asked for at least ten thousand tactical air flights, or "sorties," and one thousand B-52 sorties each month extending into 1973. "The maintenance of these sortie levels is essential to the progress of Vietnamization and vital to the orderly and secure redeployment of US Forces," Abrams wrote. "Anything less than this proposed sortie level significantly increases the risk of achieving US objectives in [South Vietnam.]"[3] Moorer and Abrams found receptive ears at the White House, but not at the office of the secretary of defense.

Laird was not a booster of the air war and in fact had begun to suspect that the Air Force and Navy were flying more missions than necessary, just to preserve their funding for the air war and to make it appear as though the high numbers were needed.[4] He was also skeptical about the success they claimed for the sorties. As the White House prepared to approve Moorer's request for increased air sorties, Laird weighed in with several critical points, which revolved around expected congressional opposition. "As far as Congress is concerned, support for our air operations is the lowest it has ever been," he wrote Kissinger in May. Laird offered an example of why Congress would balk. Two months before, in March, with the B-52s alone, "we dropped more than twenty-three thousand tons of ordnance in a twenty-by-thirty-mile area of South Laos. That equates to more tonnage . . . than the less-than-20 kiloton impact on Hiroshima in 1945."[5] He knew that would set Congress off. Indeed, the following November Laird told his staff to "stay away from precise tonnage figures" because "they are large in relative and absolute terms." Then he dropped an incredible, secret statistic: "Probably more than six million tons have been dropped in all of Southeast Asia during this war, which is roughly three times the amount dropped by the U.S. in all theaters during all of World War II."[6] And the war was not over yet.

Laird's objections fell on deaf ears at the White House. Nixon was a big fan of air power, and in early August 1971 he approved the sortie levels Abrams and Moorer wanted.[7] Laird told the military chiefs, now that they had gotten what they asked for, they were going to have to eat the increased costs from the current budget—which his staff estimated to be as high as $720 million.[8] The cost will have to "come out of your hides," he wrote the Joint Chiefs in a memo.[9]

As 1971 progressed, the Joint Chiefs pressed for an expansion of their target list to include North Vietnamese surface-to-air missile sites and MiG fighters striking below the twentieth parallel. Admiral Moorer related in one staff meeting that "the North Vietnamese have deployed the heaviest antiaircraft defense against us so far in the war."[10] So they pushed Laird hard for authority to hit off-limits targets in North Vietnam itself. Typical of the dance between Laird and Moorer on this subject was an exchange in late February and early March of 1971. Moorer had asked for permission to hit SAM sites in North Vietnam in the name of "protective reaction"—the term

Laird had used in 1969 when authorizing cross-border raids into Cambodia. He didn't do it often, but this time Laird passed the request on to Nixon with this warning: "I feel that there is military value to this proposal. . . . On the other hand, from a political point of view, I believe that this is not the proper time for such action by the U.S. government."[11]

Nixon approved the request, and on March 6 Laird informed Moorer that U.S. planes could make a one-day strike against the SAM sites. Laird's language was testy. He reminded Moorer that in 1969 and 1970 he had approved general operating orders for air strikes in North Vietnam when needed under very limited conditions, and he wanted to know why those orders weren't adequate. Laird tried to give Moorer a lesson in political vs. military reality. "If we continue strikes into North Vietnam, particularly on a frequent basis, we encounter certain risks. On the one hand, unless we strike repeatedly and on a sustained basis, we risk not achieving any substantial durable military benefits. . . . On the other hand, if we do strike repeatedly and with enough frequency to have any significant or long-term military value, we will have clearly abrogated the November 1968 bombing-halt understandings. As you appreciate, there are military ramifications to such actions, as well as impacts that transcend the military."[12] Laird was not willing to nickel-and-dime his way around the bombing ban, nor was he ready to ignore it completely. As much as it was violated, it still had the effect of keeping the North from building up troops in the demilitarized zone. That was the deal Hanoi made when Johnson halted the bombing.

Moorer's response bristled with sarcasm. He expressed "regret" that Laird was under the impression that the old operating orders should be adequate, because they never were. And he said he agreed with Laird that anything less than sustained strikes against the SAM sites could be a waste of time. Had his pilots been given freer rein over the North all along, things would have been different, Moorer said. As it was, they were hamstrung by decisions made in Washington instead of in the field. "[I]t is imperative that this strike authority be held by the field commander rather than requiring him to process a time-consuming request to higher authority," Moorer wrote. It was his oft-repeated refrain, but Laird was not about to grant that authority.[13]

Laird's files are replete with such correspondence between him and Moorer. Sometimes Laird said yes to the strikes, sometimes he said no. "I just don't understand their request," he puzzled in one Vietnam Task Force meeting in July 1971. "I don't see why the Joint Chiefs are suggesting increased bombing and use of the B-52s in North Vietnam at this point in time. It's just an impossible thing to do, given the current low level of combat activity, and the political situation here."[14] Laird consistently refused to transfer blanket authority to the field.

In the fall of 1971, North Vietnamese MiGs intensified their harassment of American bombers and fighters headed for missions over Laos. Hanoi was pressing its advantage along the DMZ, sensing that the United States was hobbled by the top-down chain of command for bombing and by the 1968 bombing halt. They were partly right. In late October Moorer asked Laird for permission to blow up a North Vietnamese airfield from which many of the MiGs took off, but Laird turned him down. Three weeks later, Moorer came back with another plan to hit the same airfield, and Laird said no again Finally, after a near miss between a MiG and a B-52 over Laos on November 30, Moorer asked again—and Laird took a harder look.[15] Moorer's request was ambitious. Instead of a one-time strike against the offending airfield, as first proposed, Moorer wanted at least forty-eight hours of sustained strikes against several targets in North Vietnam.

Two days after making the request, while Laird was still considering, Moorer stormed into Laird's office clutching a cable that he wanted to send to Saigon. A jittery Air Force general in the field, without consulting Washington, had halted all B-52 raids over Laos in reaction to the MiG attacks. Laird wasn't in the office, but David Packard told Moorer to send the cable immediately, ordering the resumption of bombing. The loss of a B-52 would be terrible, Moorer acknowledged in the cable, "However, a precipitous termination of B-52 operations in this vital interdiction area also has considerable military and political significance. Consequently, it would have been helpful at the Washington level if the JCS could have had some prior warning that you contemplated such unilateral action."[16]

Moorer's frustration, and that of the pilots, fairly shouts between the lines of memos that made their way around the Pentagon that December as the MiG activity heightened. "Protective reaction" attacks on the MiGs were allowed, but the American pilots who were fired on had to get permission before shooting back, and delays frequently hampered their hot pursuit. On December 3 MiG radar locked on four F-4 fighters escorting B-52s on a bombing raid over Laos. The fighter pilots received permission to defend themselves, but within minutes permission was rescinded because the hot pursuit was taking the F-4s too far into North Vietnam. Chief of Naval Operations Elmo Zumwalt described the on-again–off-again dogfight to Packard in a memo the next day. Packard scribbled a note and clipped it to the memo, apparently reflecting a conversation with Moorer: "Tom Moorer. Why don't we let these fellows shoot? DP"[17]

Why, indeed? Because Lyndon Johnson had set the rules in November 1968 by ending bombing missions over the North in exchange for certain expectations of good behavior from the enemy. It was a deal that Hanoi never acknowledged but that Washington stuck to. On December 9, 1971, Laird decided it was time to bend the rules. On that day he sent a memo to Nixon proposing the first sustained bombing raids over North Vietnam since 1968. Laird offered Moorer's suggestion for a forty-eight-hour campaign code-named "Proud Deep" against four enemy airfields and other targets. "It would have the best chance among the options available to signal our concern caused by their violating the bombing halt understandings and possibly to deter further MiG aggressiveness," Laird wrote.[18] Nixon agreed, and on December 19, one day after MiGs shot down four U.S. fighter-bombers over Laos, Moorer sent the cable to Admiral McCain in Hawaii authorizing the execution of Proud Deep. It was to begin as soon as possible, and end before the already-planned Christmas cease fire.[19]

Bad weather moved in, pushing off the operation until after the Christmas truce (which the enemy violated at least nineteen times in twenty-four hours).[20] Finally as midnight approached in Washington on December 25, B-52s took off in Southeast Asia to begin the pounding of North Vietnam. The original forty-eight-hour mission was extended until December 30 when, after nearly eight hundred bombing runs over the targets, Moorer cabled McCain to terminate Proud Deep. The mission cost Nixon in heavy criticism at home, most of it from the Democrats who were shaping up to oppose his second run for the presidency. But Nixon saw it as a setback he could overcome before the election. His five-day display of air power that December was designed to show Hanoi that the air war could go on even as American foot soldiers withdrew.

～

Throughout 1971, the prospect of a one-candidate election in South Vietnam threatened the progress of Vietnamization. President Nguyen Van Thieu had taken office in 1967 with the support of only 35 percent of the voters. He wanted a clear mandate for the second election and wasn't above skulduggery to get it. After Laird's trip to Saigon in January, he advised Nixon that it was in the United States' best interest to have Thieu remain in office. On the trip, Laird met with the only other likely candidates—Vice President Nguyen Cao Ky and Gen. Duong Van Minh (known as "Big Minh"). Laird concluded that Thieu was better qualified to carry out his program of Vietnamization. Laird suggested that the Nixon administration should do all it could, quietly, to support Thieu. "I recommend an explicit but discreet program to support

Thieu's reelection," Laird wrote the president, while "assiduously avoiding public or official intervention in the South Vietnamese election process." That translated to "sensitivity" about election day when choosing the timing and numbers of U.S. troop withdrawals; it helped stabilize the South Vietnamese economy; and it put out the word that the Thieu regime was cooperating in the Paris peace talks. Actually, Thieu had little interest in the Paris talks. When Laird visited Paris on the way to Saigon in January, he learned that Thieu's representatives at those talks got little or no guidance from Saigon. "They rely for preparation, mainly on the U.S. team in Paris," Laird reported to Nixon. "When I mentioned to President Thieu that I had met with his representatives in Paris, he showed little interest."[21]

It was pivotal for the American involvement in the war that South Vietnam have a multicandidate election. As early as February, Laird personally reminded Thieu that the world needed to see an open and fair process in a country that was supposed to be championing democracy over communism. In April, Laird's nervousness was compounded when some members of Congress threatened to cut off all funding to Vietnam if it looked like the Nixon administration was trying to pull a fast one in the election.

In retrospect, however, Thieu's reelection was all but guaranteed five months before the May vote as a result of his wily legal maneuvering and the CIA's substantial political war chest, which was made available to Thieu. The CIA bankrolled him to the tune of millions of dollars, which he carefully dispensed to ensure political support across the spectrum. It assisted him in privately receiving promises of endorsements from the majority of those in both houses of the South Vietnam National Assembly, and most of the five hundred-plus provincial councilmen. Once he had those pledges in his pocket, Thieu shrewdly proposed a new election law saying presidential candidates had to "qualify" to run by obtaining the endorsements of at least forty of the national legislators or one hundred of the provincial councilmen. After some bribery by the CIA among National Assembly legislators, the law was passed in early June.[22] Thieu had the numbers sewn up, and the other candidates dropped out.

Thieu won the October 3 election with 94.3 percent of the vote. The embarrassment of the landslide was compounded by his government's dubious claim that 88 percent of Vietnam's 7.2 million registered voters were civic-minded enough to turn out for an uncontested election.[23] The message to Americans was that they were spilling their own blood to keep the Communists out of a "democratic" nation that couldn't even mount a fair election, and whose leader behaved more like a banana republic dictator.

In public Laird plied the U.S. government line: While he had hoped for a race with more than one candidate, America could not dictate to South Vietnam. The United States cannot be "the political policeman of the world" and cannot force other nations to choose their governments in an American manner.[24] In private, Laird felt it had been a serious blow to Vietnamization. And there was no way he would sit, smiling, next to Thieu at his October 31 inauguration. So when the White House tried to push him to represent the administration, he openly squelched it at a mid-October cabinet meeting. "I am not going to go," he emphatically stated at the meeting. Treasury Secretary John Connally went instead.[25]

~

As U.S. troops turned the reins over to South Vietnam, Laird became increasingly concerned about the will of the South Vietnamese to fight. He lectured at the June 21, 1971, staff meeting: "The North Vietnamese either have to fight or be killed. There is no return for them. The South Vietnamese soldier has a choice of fighting or going home. These two sets of choices make the leadership and motivation of the South Vietnamese very important."[26] Two days later, he wrote a memo to Moorer ordering a substantive review of South Vietnamese leadership—including a listing of the seventy-five best and seventy-five worst South Vietnamese commanders. "In many cases, the reason for poor performance has been poor morale and leadership, not insufficient equipment or [U.S.] support."[27] The Joint Chiefs and General Abrams responded in November that "only one senior [South Vietnamese] military commander needs changing."[28]

Dan Henkin carefully tracked the behavior of the Saigon-based U.S. media and predicted increasingly negative news reports—even as Laird was doing exactly what the majority of the American public wanted—bringing the boys home. "Vietnam continues to be of lesser interest" to the better correspondents, Henkin said at a September staff meeting, noting that the number of correspondents had dropped from 450 to 335 and would continue to decrease rapidly.[29] Observing the replacement of first-string journalists by second- and third-stringers, Henkin concluded at a November meeting that, "as far as the present stories coming out of Vietnam, we have not the best talent assigned to the area to begin with and it is getting worse."[30]

Another unusual trend Laird detected in 1971 as the war wound down was the increasing number of official visitors who wanted to go to Vietnam. They were taking up too much of General Abrams's time and taxing his ability to protect them. When Sen. George McGovern arrived in September, he had given the State Department only two days' notice. He declined any official briefings, opting to look independent of the Nixon war machine. (At the time he was the only announced Democratic presidential candidate for the 1972 race.) Once in Saigon, McGovern also turned down military security, which led to a terrifying incident. Outside a meeting in a Catholic school with South Vietnamese antiwar leaders, a mob quickly gathered and erupted into violence. McGovern was trapped for twenty minutes inside as the mob threw firebombs and stones at the building, and burned vehicles. American military police and U.S. Embassy security had to ride to his rescue.[31]

Laird declared after the McGovern mishap that all official visits to Vietnam must be cleared with the Pentagon's International Security Affairs division. He remained tough on that point. In an early October Vietnam Task Force meeting, he angrily reported that he had learned via "a back-channel message" that Westmoreland, still the Army chief of staff, was planning a late October visit just before Laird's own scheduled visit to Saigon. "I thought I made it clear that I wanted no one to visit Vietnam during the weeks before my visit or after," Laird reiterated. The ISA lamely noted that they knew nothing about it because Westmoreland hadn't cleared it with them, so Laird "turned that trip off myself."[32]

A few days later, the State Department approved a Vietnam visit for former Joint Chiefs chairman Gen. Maxwell Taylor, who had served as ambassador to South Vietnam for two years. Laird cancelled it over the "strong opposition" of the State Department, and he had to talk to President Nixon to do it. Nixon accepted Laird's logic that any other officials visiting Vietnam in the October-November time period would dilute the president's upcoming troop withdrawal and Vietnamization message.[33]

Soon after President Thieu's reelection and inauguration, Laird made his fourth and final trip to Vietnam, leaving on November 2, 1971. Just before boarding his plane at Andrews Air Force Base outside Washington, Laird reminded the press corps of his first visit in March of 1969 when there were more than half a million Americans fighting in Vietnam. Now the number was 196,000 and dropping. Laird had come directly from the White House where he and the president had discussed how many more troops would be brought out in the tenth withdrawal phase, the details of which Nixon was supposed to announce in mid-November. Laird told Nixon that he would like to speed up the rate of withdrawals to at least eighteen thousand a month, with a goal of having only sixty thousand Americans in Vietnam by June of 1972. In late August he also instructed the reluctant Joint Chiefs to plan on that as the bottom line.[34]

Previously Nixon had agonized over the figures, but this time it was different. He didn't tell Laird before the trip, but the president was aiming for an
even higher figure than Laird wanted. Nixon's interest in having more troops
on the homebound planes was growing in direct proportion to the proxim-
ity of the 1972 presidential election. Laird had expected that would happen.
"I knew that from the day I became secretary of defense," he said. "Early on,
I had to put the pressure on, but the last two years, the president was all for
it. The first two years he was a little reluctant because Kissinger was always
telling him, 'Don't withdraw until we get an agreement [in the Paris peace
talks].' My position was, we'll never get an agreement." Laird thought Kissinger's reluctance about troop withdrawals was fueled in part by his military
assistant Al Haig. "Haig had no political feel for anything," said Laird.

Laird spent four days in South Vietnam, much of it in the company of
General Abrams, who was optimistic about the progress of Vietnamization.
"I think actually we may have hoped they would step up to the plate the
way they have," he told Laird, "but there certainly wasn't anybody that could
guarantee it. But I think the truth of the matter is the Vietnamese have stepped
to the plate."[35]

Laird left Saigon bound for Honolulu where he spent the weekend com-
posing his report to Nixon. These Hawaii stopovers had become welcome
respite for Laird between the war zone in Vietnam and the political battles
back in Washington. This time the memo to Nixon was carefully crafted to
keep the president on the fast track to total withdrawal. "The view of U.S.
civilian and military leaders in Vietnam and of the [South Vietnamese] leadership is that we now have and can maintain sufficient military strength to
preclude the enemy from achieving any kind of military verdict in South Vietnam," Laird wrote. "The United States can continue its force redeployments.
In fact, the redeployments can safely be accelerated."

Laird buttressed his optimism with statistics: Nixon had brought home
nearly 360,000 troops; American combat deaths were less than 10 percent
of what they were in Johnson's last year in office; the Vietnamese economy
was more stable; the cost of the war, in 1972 dollars, had dropped from $25
billion to $8 billion during the Nixon term; and tactical bombing flights
were down from thirty-five thousand a month at the height of the Johnson
years to six thousand a month. (Acutely aware of Nixon's fondness for air
power, Laird noted that "We are maintaining, of course, the capability to fly
sorties at higher rates, as you have specified.")

Laird never liked body counts as a way of gauging the success of the war,
but he couldn't pass up the chance to tell Nixon that enemy combat deaths

were running at about one hundred thousand a year. For a country the size of North Vietnam, that was the equivalent of the United States losing a million men a year. The willingness of Hanoi to sacrifice men in such astounding numbers meant that even though a big enemy offensive was unwise in the coming year, Hanoi might try one anyway, in an attempt to show that Vietnamization was not working.

Laird's report concluded with three options for the next withdrawal phase: 12,500 a month, which was the Joint Chiefs' preference; 18,000 a month, which was Laird's preference; and 25,000 a month, which neither wanted.[36] On November 12, two days after receiving Laird's options, Nixon announced his own plan, a hybrid of Laird's three. He said 45,000 more Americans would be called home in December and January, a rate of 22,500 a month. It was the shortest withdrawal increment the president had used to that point, and he explained it was necessary to maintain leverage in the peace talks. Unlike past announcements, which had been made in televised speeches, Nixon made this one without warning at a press conference. Thus, Nixon could take credit for a big drawdown, without the drum roll and flourishes that gave Hanoi an excuse for grandstanding at the peace talks.

Americans were getting wise to Nixon's reelection agenda, and the following Sunday on NBC's *Meet the Press* Laird was asked to make the connection between the pace of withdrawals and the coming election. Robert Goralski of NBC said, "It does strike many as perhaps a remarkable coincidence that perhaps the troop withdrawal timetable will reach a denouement just about the time that Americans are considering who to vote for for president next year. Are you saying that domestic politics have nothing to do with the withdrawal timetable from Vietnam?"

"That is correct," said Laird, for whom domestic politics was reason enough to bring the military home.[37]

The next day Laird sent orders to Moorer to keep a tight lid on speculation about any troop withdrawal numbers after January. But, for planning purposes, Laird said, "[Y]ou are authorized to look towards a U.S. force goal in the Republic of Vietnam of sixty thousand by 30 June 1972." Moorer wanted off the roller coaster of shifting monthly withdrawal mandates from the president. On December 30 he wrote to Laird asking for a bit more flexibility in the next round. General Abrams and Admiral McCain had both complained that the short-term announcements "could generate severe problems in personnel turbulence, logistics, base closures and force structuring." If sixty thousand was the bottom line for June, then Moorer hoped the president would announce that and give the chiefs six months to get there at a monthly pace of their own choosing based on the needs in the field.[38] It was a reminder that getting out of a war of this size was not just a matter of loading up the troops and flying them home, as some in Congress assumed. It was a delicate dance that involved the safety of the remaining troops and the interplay of their various responsibilities for keeping one another alive.

~

The year ended with a touch of sadness for Laird. His right-hand man, David Packard, resigned as expected to go back to his company, Hewlett-Packard. At a press conference in mid-December, Packard offered an ode to Laird. "I did not really know Mel Laird when I came out here three years ago, but I do know him now." He called him "a great secretary of defense with fine administrative ability combined with a great compassion for people. I also know him as one of the great politicians on the contemporary scene. And I know him also as a very good friend." Packard said, he could "recall no major issue in which he and I have had a fundamental disagreement. In fact, I guess, Mel, I can think of hardly any minor ones either."[39]

Packard pledged to "do whatever I can to help the president win the election next year." But the Laird-Packard team had already been instrumental in securing Nixon's reelection. Thanks to Laird's persistence, by the time Americans went to the polls one year later, Vietnam was barely a campaign issue for Nixon. Even at the end of 1971, it was slipping from the top of the national priority list. A Gallup Poll in mid-December found only 15 percent of Americans felt that the war was the biggest problem facing the nation. Their bigger worry was the economy.[40]

On January 6, 1972, Laird wrote an "Eyes Only" memo to the president expressing his frustration at finding a suitable replacement for Packard. He had been conducting "an extensive talent search" since the previous spring, personally interviewing thirty people and reviewing the qualifications of another sixty. His greatest disappointment was not finding a single acceptable candidate outside government who wanted the job. He lamented to Nixon that "it seems everyone I talk to from the outside would love to work at the State Department or be an ambassador to some country, but when it comes down to this building [the Pentagon], the tendency is to run like scared rabbits." Privately, Laird had one hands-down favorite for the spot—Robert Froehlke. But Laird had agreed with Nixon that Packard's successor needed to be someone who could either continue as deputy secretary for another two years or assume the secretary's position should Laird keep his promise and leave after one term. Froehlke did not want to stay at the Pentagon after his friend Laird departed, so he had taken himself out of the running. In the January memo to Nixon, Laird proposed some other names.[41]

Nixon sent back word by the next morning that he wanted Texas business-man William Clements.[42] Laird was aware that whoever replaced Packard might well become secretary when Laird left, and he was wary of Clements's chummy relationship with some in Nixon's inner circle, including Halde-man, Ehrlichman, and Attorney General John Mitchell. Laird knew he could insist on his own nominee for deputy, but he reckoned this would look like impractical pique. If the person were to stay on, or have any hope of suc-ceeding Laird, he had to have Nixon's full approval and confidence. So, re-couping quickly, less than a day after he had submitted his memo to Nixon, Laird put in an early evening call to Kenneth Rush, the U.S. ambassador to West Germany, asking him to come to the Pentagon at his earliest conven-ience for a discussion of some urgency.

Rush had been an assistant law professor at Duke University where he taught a bright student, Richard Nixon, with whom he had forged a lifelong bond. Instead of staying at Duke, in 1936 he took an executive position at the Union Carbide Corporation, where he rose to become president. In mid-1969, Nixon had chosen him to be the ambassador to West Germany.

When Ambassador Rush arrived at Laird's office on January 11, he sat down for a tough two hours of arm-twisting. The two had met on several occa-sions, even golfed together, and enjoyed each other's company. But Rush did not want to be deputy secretary of defense. "I want to be secretary of state," he kept telling Laird.

"If you want to be secretary of state," Laird argued, "coming over here as deputy will be great preparation—and you might even want to stay here as secretary of defense."

"No, I want to be secretary of state," Rush maintained.

By the end of the session, Laird felt he had won, but Rush didn't give him a decision right then. Laird informed Nixon that his old friend and profes-sor had been offered the job, and the president was relatively pleased with the compromise candidate. What Laird didn't know then was that Nixon, through outgoing Attorney General John Mitchell, had secretly promised Rush that if he took the less-desirable job of deputy secretary to Laird, the president would guarantee his ascension to secretary of state in 1973. (Nixon didn't keep that promise.) Rush came aboard in late February. Laird had nothing negative to say about his performance, but Rush was no savvy star like Packard, and his heart was always across the Potomac River at the State Department.

～

In 1972, as Laird began his fourth and final year in the grueling job, the fissures began to show. He was not one to whine, but when Laird was closely questioned by the press between February and April 1972, he offered brief acknowledgments of the pressure and spoke about looking forward to a long vacation after his resignation. At a Milwaukee press conference in late March, Laird said: "After I have completed this particular term, I hope to take six or seven months off, and then I will consider some very attractive offers which have been made to me. I will not consider them until I have had at least six months off from this job, which has required twenty-four-hours-a-day duty, 365 days a year."[43] In April, at a breakfast with TV correspondents in New York, one asked him if he "agonized" about the job. Laird conceded, "[I]t should be no surprise, it is rather difficult. I am not overjoyed with being Secretary of Defense."[44]

In what became almost a mantra at that time, Laird noted that seven of the previous nine defense secretaries had averaged less than two years in the position before resigning. As to the prominent exception, McNamara, Laird implied that McNamara had privately admitted it was a mistake for him to stay longer than four years. "I have a great deal of respect and admiration for Secretary McNamara, and we get together quite often [to] discuss some of our problems," Laird began. "But I think that he would be the first to state that he stayed too long in the office of secretary of defense."[45]

The idea of a man with his level of competency leaving a job no one else wanted was unsettling even to critics and political opponents in Washington. On February 15, 1972, when Laird appeared before the Senate Armed Services Committee for a budget hearing, senators from both parties pressured him to reconsider his one-term pledge. The normally taciturn chairman from the opposing party, Sen. John Stennis, began his plea in a stumbling manner: "I want to make it clear to Secretary Laird that I am not here flattering him; I am not given to flattery—I hope I am not. I think he has done an outstanding job as secretary of defense. He has had more than his share of the problems. Whatever limitation you have made that you are planning to leave, I hope you will reconsider and stay with us."[46] As he did with the senators, Laird noted to reporters outside the hearing room that, though flattered, he still planned "to serve out my term" and then leave.

One of Laird's greatest supporters during the time—though also an intermittent scolding critic—was his mother, Helen Connor Laird. She peppered him with letters of advice, and he was always willing to listen. The two had an undeniable connection; one's unhappiness invariably precipitated sadness in the other. Secretary of Defense Rumsfeld told a favorite story about his

friend and mentor. A news magazine had described Laird as "clever." Rumsfeld remembers Mrs. Laird "called him, and she was dadburned upset about
the fact that her dear, loveable, sweet, warm, fuzzy son, Melvie, had actually
been called 'clever.' That is NOT a nice word for someone to call him, she
felt. So Mel was ranting and raving and saying to me, 'People should stop
using that word.' I remember it as the time I saw Mel the most excited, unhappy, concerned, anguished and irritated."[47]

The converse was also true—that one's joy could easily uplift the other.
Jerry Friedheim remembers a high-level staff meeting that was interrupted
by a call from Mother Laird. Early in his term, Laird had given his mother
a private phone line into his office after too many confused receptionists had
fumbled calls from an older woman asking for "Bom." That line lit up on his
console one morning in the middle of a somber national security discussion
with top staff and military leaders. As Friedheim remembers, Laird punched
the button, and his mother was on the speaker-phone.

"Hi, Bom," they could hear Mrs. Laird say.

"Oh, hi, Mom!" the secretary effused.

"I just wanted to tell you that the most beautiful cardinal has just landed
on my bird feeder. And it's just lovely. I thought you'd like to know about that."

Friedheim recounted, "He talked to her for about fifteen minutes about
the cardinal on the bird feeder. Everybody sat there while he talked to her,
and then he said, 'It was very nice talking to you this morning, Mom. I'm
glad it's a nice day out there in Marshfield.'" Friedheim said it was a "Lairdism"
that helped explain why his staff was so loyal to him.[48]

Such bucolic moments were too few and far between, especially when vit-
riolic protests hit home. In a revealing private letter, President Nixon acknowledged that the stress of those events was much greater on Laird, whose
Bethesda home area was occasionally "invaded." Unlike Laird, Nixon closeted
himself in the fortress he made of the White House during the protest years,
with a phalanx of sycophants to keep the hordes and critics at bay. Laird
waded among the protesters and took the worst they had to offer, defending their right to speak out unless a law was broken in the process. Still, it
inevitably had a deleterious, disheartening effect, which Nixon recognized.

In addition to the ordinary burdens you have had as Secretary of Defense, you
and your family [have been] subjected to the brutal brunt of the anti-defense,
peace at any price establishment. I had not realized until we spoke, of how
personally difficult that must have been for Barbara and for your children,
not to mention yourself. After my speech of November 3, 1969, the decision on

Cambodia, and May 8, 1972, not to mention Laos and ABM, all of the violent protesters with their obscene words and acts, descended on Washington. But, Pat, Tricia, Julie and I, at least had the haven of the White House. If the air-conditioning were turned up high enough, we could not hear them chanting outside as they marched by the thousands past the gates. On the other hand, you had no such protection. When I heard of some of the things they did right in your front yard, my heart went out to your family and to you. What really matters is that you didn't let it get to you. You continued to do your job with your usual splendid, unruffled spirit.[49]

Laird could look back and laugh on some of the indignities. He recalled the day one famous antiwar poet, Allen Ginsberg, urinated on the front of his house, with television cameras duly recording the protest.[50] Another protester threw a brick through his den window. To take the pressure off, sometimes, Laird would take the family for a Camp David retreat when the president was not there.

The greatest difference for the family was that he was much busier than he had been as a congressman. His oldest son, John, who lived in Wisconsin during Laird's Pentagon years, said, "He had so many things on his mind that he was just kind of *not there* sometimes when we were together. When we sat down to watch TV at Christmas time, within five minutes he was sound asleep because he just needed to relax and rest."[51]

With John in Wisconsin, and his daughter Alison off to college in 1969, David was left at home to be most impacted by a more-absent father. He did not complain about it, however. A fond and frequent memory was that nearly every time his father would join David and his friends to watch a football game on TV, his dad would be snoring within a few minutes. "Then a huge snore would jostle him up and he'd have five little faces looking at him. 'Great game, eh boys?' And he would know exactly what was going on in the game!"[52]

On the Vietnam front, early 1972 was the calm before a major storm. The North Vietnamese were planning a multipronged military action that, according to captured enemy documents and other intelligence, appeared to be scheduled around the mid-February lunar Tet holiday. Laird was determined that, this time, the enemy would not win politically in an American election year, as they had in 1968, while clearly suffering a military loss. His aim, beginning the previous November, was to prepare the American public for the expected offensive, and thus project a win for the South and a sure victory for Vietnamization.

In Laird's view, there was no reason to slow the American troop withdrawal even though the enemy was massing to strike. Neither General Abrams nor Admiral Moorer agreed with him. As Nixon prepared to announce new withdrawal numbers in mid-January, Abrams and Moorer argued that in view of the looming invasion, the withdrawal rate should be drastically reduced to 15,800 men per month between February and July. Laird presented the Abrams-Moorer point of view in his memorandum of recommendations to the president on January 11. But he argued that going along with the military meant that Nixon would have to go back on his public statement of nine days before that "our withdrawal will continue on schedule, at least at the present rate," which was then averaging 22,500 a month. Laird wrote that Nixon would have to offer a "major explanation to the U.S. public" on why he was reversing himself so quickly, when there had been no actual change in the situation. Instead, Laird suggested increasing the rate to 24,000 a month.[53] Nixon leaned to Laird's counsel, deciding on a rate of 23,300 a month for three months. At a joint White House news conference with Laird two days later, the president announced that 70,000 more Americans would be withdrawn from Vietnam by May 1, 1972, leaving only 69,000 in South Vietnam on that date.

After announcing the numbers, Nixon turned the microphone over to Laird who seized the moment to make his points about the coming offensive in the most high-profile forum he had:

> On my return from Vietnam in November, I had the opportunity to brief many of you in this room and I made the point at that time that the enemy during the dry period would be able to stage what I referred to as two or three spectaculars with the kinds of force which they had. I had confidence—and General Abrams had confidence—in the capabilities of the South Vietnamese military forces to handle their combat and security responsibilities during this period. That does not mean that the South Vietnamese will win every battle during this period, but I can assure you that the vast majority of the battles will be won by the South Vietnamese forces. They have the capability, they have the equipment, they have the training through this Vietnamization program to do this job.[54]

At the first Monday morning high-level staff meeting, Laird reminded those present that the American military had been given three full years to train the South Vietnamese to take over their own war. While the Pentagon had done its best and the South appeared ready, he stated that "we are not in a position to guarantee the will and desire of any military force anywhere in the world except our own." Laird continued, with a verbal nod to the Joint

Chiefs: "there will be some who say we need another eighteen months, another two years, another three years" to train the South Vietnamese, but time had run out. "We have done the best we could and we should take pride in the job that has been done, particularly by General Abrams and his people. We are now nearing the cut-off date. We have to be strong."[55]

Intelligence indicators continued to point to a mid-February launch date for the enemy offensive, but the February 15 Tet holiday came and went without incident. Intelligence reports were recalculated to suggest that the offensive would start on or before Nixon arrived in Peking a week later for his historic summit. Still, it didn't come. Admiral Moorer reported on March 6 to Laird and assembled Pentagon officials that "it is quite clear the enemy is in a position to attack in South Vietnam. We just don't know why he has not done so, except that he may have been significantly hurt by our air strikes."[56] Later evidence suggests that a combination of the early 1971 Lam Son operation in Laos, bad weather, and other factors had delayed the launch date.

The president had a gambit in mind that might blunt the invasion. On January 26 he broke the news that Kissinger had been secretly negotiating with Hanoi in a shadow effort to the formal Paris talks. Nixon's purpose, in part, was to silence critics who said the United States was being intransigent in Paris. At the same time, Nixon offered a cease-fire and a complete withdrawal of American troops within six months if Hanoi agreed to his terms. If North Vietnam was going to continue with plans for an invasion, then the president was doing his best to make them look like the warmongers.

Behind the window dressing of peace proposals, however, Nixon was actually preparing to escalate the war. On February 4, National Security Decision Memorandum 149, signed by Kissinger, landed on Laird's desk. The president had ordered that a fourth aircraft carrier be made ready for Vietnam duty and that additional B-52s and fighters be sent to Guam and Thailand to be ready for the offensive.[57]

On March 9 Moorer sent Laird an "Urgent Request for Air Authorities," which looked to Laird like an all-out resumption of the bombing of the North.[58] Laird passed the request on to Nixon, emphatically stating he didn't agree with Moorer. Laird believed the 150,000 tons of bombs the United States had already dropped on key targets in Southeast Asia since January 1 under the "protective reaction" premise had hampered Hanoi's ability to mount a major offensive. But "there has been no flagrant provocation for renewed air attacks," Laird added, and thus no defensible public reason for abandoning the 1968 bombing halt understandings. He advised the president to wait until the invasion was launched.[59]

For the time being, Nixon, who was leery of renewed congressional and public protest in an election year, agreed. He wrote Laird on March 18, "The request for additional air and naval gunfire authorities are not approved at this time. [They] will be reassessed should the anticipated major enemy assault begin." To give it greater chain-of-command authority, the order was signed not by Kissinger, as was the norm, but by Nixon himself.[60]

A disturbing subtext to the military push for expanded bombing was the discovery by Laird in March that his top Air Force commander in South Vietnam, Gen. John D. Lavelle, was deliberately defying his commander in chief and ordering unauthorized missions. Lavelle, the commander of the U.S. Seventh Air Force in Vietnam, was a highly respected officer by the time he was posted to take charge of air operations in the war. By November 1971 he had become alarmed at an enemy buildup of air defenses north of the Demilitarized Zone—more sophisticated ground control radar and surface-to-air missile sites, which were threatening his reconnaissance and attack flights. It also began to look like the enemy might be putting anti-air sites in the DMZ itself and was gearing up to add more MiG fighters to the mix. So, when Laird visited Vietnam at that time, Lavelle asked for a private meeting with him at Ambassador Ellsworth Bunker's home to plead for more bombing authority. Laird was sympathetic but told the general he must do the best he could under the current rules.(Lavelle would later defend his actions based on that conversation, claiming that Laird had implied the general had permission to bend the rules.)

The day after Laird left Saigon, Lavelle made a decision to stretch the existing "rules of engagement" to the breaking point; he sent planes on a mission unauthorized by the president, the secretary of defense, or even the field commander General Abrams. Under the McNamara authorities, before Laird instituted "protective reaction," various targets were allowed only if the enemy had fired upon American planes. Laird's "protective reaction" permitted a more liberal interpretation, hitting enemy antiaircraft sites if enemy radar tracked an American plane or had been activated on previous missions to the same area. Lavelle took it one step farther, authorizing a policy of "planned protective reaction." The pilots were to assume that they would be fired on for every mission. In Lavelle's mind, his orders were within the "protective reaction" authority, but he was not sure his bosses would see it that way, so he mandated falsification of the pilot reports, on both target coordinates and enemy reaction. It began the first time one mission came back after dropping bombs on North Vietnam, truthfully reporting "no reaction," meaning the enemy had not fired upon them. An angry General Lavelle told his next in command, Gen. Alton Slay, that the pilots should never report "no reaction" on any mission. Lavelle later said he never intended to order his pilots to file false reports of enemy fire or give false coordinates of where the flights went. But Slay and the pilots took it to mean that they could file false reports.

Laird's first hint that something was amiss came in December 1971 when he noticed an uptick in the number of "reaction" incidents being reported. He sent Admiral Moorer a memo questioning the numbers. Moorer came back to him with a report in January concluding that there was nothing inappropriate about the figures. Laird asked him to keep an eye on the statistics but heard nothing more from him about it. The Lavelle subterfuge went on for three months before the first whistle was blown in late February 1972 by a lowly intelligence analyst who wrote to his senator, Harold Hughes, a member of the Armed Services Committee. By a quirk of fate, Senator Hughes received the letter on March 3 just before a lunch appointment with Air Force chief of staff Gen. John Ryan. The senator shared the contents of the letter, and Ryan was immediately concerned, but he could not imagine General Lavelle was involved.[61]

Ryan hurriedly sent an inspector general team to Southeast Asia to investigate. Lavelle denied the charges, but the Air Force inspectors soon uncovered at least seventeen unauthorized missions and accompanying false reports. Ryan ordered Lavelle back to Washington and confronted him on the weekend of March 24. On Monday morning Ryan took his findings to Laird.[62] While he admired Lavelle's military record and considered him to be a "fine officer," Laird was not surprised that the general would aggressively stretch and break the rules in the belief he was better protecting his men and aircraft. Laird was surprised, however, that Lavelle would lie about it when caught and that he would have ordered his men to lie on their mission reports. Ryan and Laird agreed that no senior officer should condone lying.

The day after his meeting with Ryan, Laird wrote a stern memo to Admiral Moorer stating that "the authorized rules of engagement must . . . be adhered to strictly." The secretary wanted an immediate check "throughout the command channels to insure strict compliance with the authorized rules of engagement." The Lavelle incident was not specifically mentioned.[63] When Ryan recommended that Lavelle be relieved of his post, Laird agreed, and on March 30 he wrote another memo to Admiral Moorer: "(I)t is in the best interests of the United States and all concerned to remove the incumbent Seventh Air Force Commander from his existing post and place him in a different status." This should "be handled on an urgent and discreet basis."[64]

In deference to Lavelle's previously distinguished career, Ryan told him he could stay in the Air Force and receive a lesser assignment, or he could retire quietly. Lavelle chose the latter, retiring on an emphysema disability. The day before it was publicly announced, Laird informed the appropriate senators about it.[65] The "disability" excuse did not hold up, and soon Laird had to issue a statement that Lavelle had been relieved "because of irregularities in the conduct of his responsibilities."[66]

Both Ryan and Lavelle were called before a closed door hearing of a House Armed Services investigative subcommittee on June 12, 1972. "I'm the commander and the buck stops here," Lavelle admitted. But he added: "I think General Abrams knew what I was doing." That was enough to prompt a three-week inquiry by the Senate Armed Services Committee that ultimately cleared Abrams, who neither knew about nor would have approved the missions.

The immediate upshot of the scandal was that the veteran air chief in Southeast Asia had been relieved on the very day that the North Vietnamese finally began their long-anticipated offensive.

22

Easter Offensive

I T WAS RELATIVELY TRANQUIL at noon on March 30, 1972, just south of the Demilitarized Zone—the forty-mile-wide strip that separated North and South Vietnam. The South Vietnamese soldiers in the fire bases in northern Quang Tri Province were getting ready for lunch when the first shell came screaming south across the DMZ. It was followed by an artillery barrage the likes of which few had experienced—a total of twelve thousand rockets and mortars throughout the Easter weekend. On March 31 whole divisions of the North Vietnamese army came out of the DMZ with tanks and new Soviet 130mm guns, which had a range of eighteen miles. Over the next two days, the North Vietnamese also invaded through Laos and Cambodia, attacking the South Vietnamese in the Central Highlands and farther south, headed for Saigon. The invasion force would eventually grow to number about 350,000 men from fourteen of Hanoi's fifteen regular Army divisions. Along with hundreds of artillery pieces and armored personnel carriers, nearly four hundred tanks led the soldiers in the multipronged offensive intended by the North to be the last battle of the war.

Depleted by the Tet Offensive of 1968 and hammered by U.S. and South Vietnamese forays against the Ho Chi Minh Trail, the North Vietnamese took four years to get to the point where they could mount such an attack. This was not stealthy jungle guerrilla warfare or hit-and-run skirmishing from the sanctuaries in Laos and Cambodia. This was tank and artillery battering of cities, and massive movement of troops taking territory inch by inch the old-fashioned way. It was just the kind of conventional warfare Americans excelled at, but the Americans were essentially gone from the ground war. Only ninety-five thousand U.S. troops remained, and few of them, other than the advisors, were in ground "combat" roles. So, by dint of circumstances and timing, this was to be the bloody "acid test" for Melvin Laird's Vietnamization strategy, and it came in the last year of his leadership at the Pentagon. Hanoi named the campaign "Nguyen Hue," after an eighteenth-century Vietnamese emperor who had repelled an invading Chinese army. The Americans simply called it the "Easter Offensive."

On Good Friday, March 31, Laird advised President Nixon that the artillery barrage and first indications of an invasion force in Quang Tri province were not just another battle but were likely the beginning of the major offensive the allies had been waiting for. South Vietnamese president Nguyen Van Thieu told his people grimly that night in a ten-minute TV speech: "This is the final battle to decide the survival of the people."[1]

Nixon waited a few days to see how the South Vietnamese would handle the challenge. A debate about the use of American air support raged behind the scenes, with Nixon and Kissinger leaning toward an all-out bombing campaign over the North, and Laird—backing the judgment of General Abrams—wanting to concentrate the bombs on the battlegrounds as direct assistance to the South Vietnamese troops. Laird's vision of Vietnamization had always been to prepare South Vietnam to defend itself on its home turf, not to take the battle across borders.

Against the massive North Vietnamese assault on the ground, the South Vietnamese army gave way in less than a week, abandoning seventeen fire bases and falling back behind the Cua Viet River. On Easter Sunday, April 2, after the North Vietnamese had succeeded in overrunning the northern half of Quang Tri province, President Nixon, against Laird's advice, ordered full-scale bombing of the North, including the use of B-52 bombers stationed at Guam. Before the offensive was over, the number of B-52s involved had increased from 42 to 148, shutting down an entire runway on Guam for use as a parking lot. Four more aircraft carriers were also brought into the seas off Vietnam, along with five cruisers and forty-four destroyers. In all, the number of airplanes assigned to the war went from 549 to 1,240.[2]

Laird and Nixon had decided that it was best that the president not speak publicly about the invasion for awhile, lest he contribute to an atmosphere of crisis. So Laird himself became the point man in defense of the increased American air power. An April 18 hearing before the hostile Senate Foreign Relations Committee and its antiwar chairman, William Fulbright, was full of fireworks. Laird dominated the hearing so strongly that, at one point, Fulbright jumped in to silence him. "If I could say one word or two before you interfere," Fulbright bristled. "This is supposed to be a hearing, not a monologue."

"I would like to testify as to those points," Laird countered, unabashed. "I would like to make an observation," Fulbright interrupted and then filibustered his views for several minutes.

"You are excellent as a witness," Laird smiled at the senator, with only the barest hint of sarcasm.

"I am not as professional as you are," Fulbright allowed.

When Laird was questioned about the buildup of U.S. naval and air forces while the combat troops were marching out the back door, he acknowledged that Navy presence in the seas off Vietnam had nearly doubled. "But this isn't an increase in the number of people in the Navy, it is a change of their operational area for a given period of time, and that is what naval power is all about," Laird said. The added B-52s and tactical air squadrons were not technically stationed in Vietnam, Laird went on. And half the air sorties were being flown by South Vietnamese pilots, although Laird had to admit that they were not doing the flying in the raids over North Vietnam. "We have not given them the ability to penetrate and attack outside of their country. One part of our program is to give them defensive capability to maintain their own in-country security."

Fulbright tried to shut down Laird's pep talk on the success of Vietnamization: "You have sold us all and I am sure you have sold everybody here on the idea that you are making progress in Vietnamization, but you haven't sold me that that is worth what it is costing the United States . . . I am strongly of the view that, granted everything you have said, it is a wrong policy and is not in the interest of the United States to continue this war."[3]

Laird wrote to Kissinger privately a few days later, suggesting it was time to tone down the air support. Laird argued that "the sum total of these additions [the added naval and air forces] to friendly forces exceeds, in my judgment, that which is needed for military purposes. It is doubtful that sending additional elements would have much positive political visibility." Shortly after, Kissinger notified Laird that "the president agrees that for the present we should not proceed with further air or naval augmentation." But Nixon did not want to curtail the bombing of the North.[4] Laird saw it as misdirected bloodshed in the North that would not stop or slow the invasion in the South.

On April 28 Nixon sent a "flash message" to Laird through Kissinger that synthesized his own philosophy about the bombing of the North and hinted that he knew Laird did not agree. Nixon ordered the "absolute maximum number of sorties must be flown" to have the "maximum psychological effect." He also demanded an immediate report on how his orders were to be carried out, and he closed with, "There are to be no excuses and there is no appeal."[5]

From years of working with Nixon, Laird knew there was always an avenue of appeal, using political grounds, especially in an election year as was 1972. That is how he succeeded in persuading Nixon to continue with American troop withdrawals even as the North Vietnamese invasion of the South was peaking. Nixon had publicly announced in January 1972 that he would take 22,500 men out of Vietnam every month until May 1. As that date approached, the pressure mounted for Nixon to announce the next withdrawal phase. On April 16 Abrams had sent a request through channels that the troop withdrawals be stopped until July 1, given the fact that the Easter Offensive looked like it would stretch into the summer.[6]

Laird reported the request to Nixon but sent two of his own reports to the president within three days of each other asking that the withdrawals continue at a slower pace of about 6,700 a month with the long-range goal of having only 15,000 men in Vietnam by December 31. The first memo to Nixon spelled out Laird's rationale, but four days later he had reason to think the president might not pay attention to him. General Haig had made a fact-finding trip to Vietnam, and Laird feared that Haig's gung-ho attitude about the war might prevail, persuading Nixon to suspend any more withdrawals.

"The denigration of Vietnamization is one of Hanoi's key goals in its current offensive," Laird warned Nixon in writing on April 24. "An announcement of redeployment suspension would lend credibility to Hanoi's charge that Vietnamization is a defunct concept. Of equal importance, an announcement of redeployment suspension would have, in my judgment, a dramatic adverse political impact domestically." To this memorandum General Pursley appended a note for his boss: "Hope this does the job." It did.[7] Nixon not only continued the withdrawals, but announced a higher monthly rate than Laird had recommended, and over a shorter term—sending twenty thousand more men home by the end of June, a rate of ten thousand a month.

Laird felt confident about continuing the troop withdrawal program in part because he was receiving glowing reports from General Abrams (which he forwarded to the president) about the success of Vietnamization in the face of the Easter Offensive. "The clear purpose of this invasion is to destroy the Armed Forces of South Vietnam," Abrams began in a cable sent on April 26, the day of Nixon's announcement on new withdrawals. "In this battle so far, U.S. air power and advisory support have been of tremendous value. This invasion could not have been held at this point without U.S. air support. However, ten times the air power could not have done the job if the Armed Forces of South Vietnam had not stood and fought."[8]

⌒

The news was not all good. The provincial capital of Quang Tri City withstood punishing artillery assaults for a full month when the offensive began, but lackluster South Vietnamese leadership finally spelled its doom. Late on April 30, all the top generals and military leaders in Quang Tri City "bugged out" by helicopters, and middle-ranking officers commandeered trucks, after loading up refrigerators and other booty to take with them. The demoralized troops panicked and fled, causing the fall of Quang Tri on May 1—the first provincial capital the North Vietnamese were able to capture. Abrams cabled Laird: "This is a battle to the death. The Communists have planned it that way and will not quit until they have been totally exhausted." Abrams ordered his field commanders to stop airlifting jittery South Vietnamese commanders out of the heat of battle unless they had orders from higher up.[9]

The offensive brought into stark relief the weaknesses in the South Vietnamese military leadership, which had long reflected the corruption and nepotism in Thieu's government. That corruption was one of the enemies of Vietnamization that Laird had not been able to defeat. Now, in the heat of battle, he tried again. On May 1 Laird forwarded Abrams's assessment of the situation to Nixon: "I must report that as the pressure has mounted and the battle has become brutal, the senior leadership has begun to bend and in some cases to break."[10] The next day Abrams met with Thieu and told him some of his field commanders were not up to the job. "I told the president [Thieu] that it was my conviction that all that had been accomplished over the last four years was now at stake, and, at this stage, it was the effectiveness of his field commanders that would determine the outcome—either winning all or losing all." Thieu responded by recalling all his top commanders to Saigon for a meeting.[11] Within a week, Thieu had fired several generals and replaced them with more reliable men.[12]

In the days after Quang Tri City fell, some media critics badgered Laird about the failure of Vietnamization and the imminent collapse of South Vietnam. Laird was nonplused; he had always thought some territory would be lost in the initial stage of an enemy invasion, only to be regained later. While Laird was able to allay panic throughout the department and uniformed military, his calming influence was not enough of a tonic for the commander in chief. Nixon was at this point a skittish president who feared he might be presiding over America's first war loss at precisely the time he was running for reelection. Now, in the fervid milieu of those early May days, Nixon made a decision to do something Laird had advocated seven years before— mine the harbors of North Vietnam.

When he was a congressman in 1965, Laird began strongly and repeatedly urging Lyndon Johnson to mine the harbor at Haiphong as a way of preventing huge shiploads of Soviet military hardware from entering enemy territory.[13] Laird saw mining as a cheap, relatively safe, and extremely threatening way to attack North Vietnam's supply lines. It made more sense to interdict at that point without risking American servicemen than to rain bombs on the Ho Chi Minh Trail when supplies were already in the pipeline. As defense secretary Laird made the same argument, but Nixon and Kissinger didn't initially favor mining. Laird said that Nixon feared a Russian ship might be blown up in the process, and Kissinger feared mining might "queer the negotiations" with Hanoi on the war and Moscow on arms control.

Once the Easter Offensive began, Laird was inclined to think that it was too late for the mining, since the horse was already out of the barn. In early April when the joint chiefs submitted a plan for mining Haiphong harbor, Laird sent it along to Kissinger with a recommendation that it be rejected. Laird's note to Kissinger at the end of the typed memo said: "Henry—The political impact of these plans may be what is wanted by the President. The military impact would be minor and the impact on the present battle would be even less."[14]

The political argument finally won out in May. Kissinger, who was paving the way for Nixon to attend a summit meeting in Moscow, thought he had received some assurances from the Soviets that they could make North Vietnam be more flexible in the peace talks. Kissinger hung his hopes on a negotiating session May 2 with his North Vietnamese counterpart in Paris, Le Duc Tho. But the meeting went nowhere, and it was apparent that the Soviets, the major suppliers of war materiel to North Vietnam, either could not or would not twist arms in Hanoi to bring the war to an end. Kissinger returned to Washington convinced that it was time to take off the gloves with the North Vietnamese. He said as much to Nixon.[15]

Precisely at 9 a.m. on May 12, all of the mines switched on. As Laird had been predicting for seven years, it was a "fail safe" operation: no men or planes were lost.[16] There was, however, loss of face in Saigon where General Abrams was not told about preparatory Navy ship movements toward the harbors before the presidential decision. Laird had dispatched Barry Shillito in early May to assess the needs of the South Vietnamese army. At a meeting the first week of May, Abrams complained to Shillito about ongoing Navy exercises that he had not known about. He raged that, as usual, the Navy was fighting its own war without a word to him about it.

Shillito instantly realized that the exercises were a runup to the mining operation and that Abrams was completely in the dark about the deployment.

Abrams had known that the mining was being considered, but the command to move the ships in preparation had gone to Abrams's boss, Adm. John McCain, who had not told Abrams. Shillito cabled the news to Laird, who was embarrassed and angry. He knew that McCain and Abrams were barely on speaking terms at the time. Laird called McCain on the phone and chewed him out. Then Laird cabled an apology to Abrams, who took it in stride.[17]

According to the polls, the majority of Americans supported Nixon's mining decision. However, the mining and intensified bombing had the effect of rousing the sleeping antiwar movement in the United States, triggering one protest that hit home for the secretary of defense.

～

May 19, 1972, was Ho Chi Minh's birthday, and a radical antiwar group called the "Weathermen" decided that a bomb in the Pentagon would be the perfect gift. "Everything was absolutely ideal on the day I bombed the Pentagon," wrote one of their unrepentant leaders, Bill Ayers, in his 2001 confessional memoir. "The sky was blue. The birds were singing. And the bastards were finally going to get what was coming to them."[18] It exploded at one minute before 1 a.m. on Ho's birthday. The blast on the fourth floor of the Pentagon's E-ring shook that section of the building, including the offices of Air Force Secretary Robert Seamans and Air Force Chief of Staff John Ryan. Windows and a lavatory brick wall were blown out, and thousands of gallons of water poured through a gaping hole in the floor.[19] While security sweeps for other possible bombs began, a transatlantic call was placed to Laird in Copenhagen where it was after 7 a.m. He was already up, dressing for a morning meeting of the NATO Nuclear Planning Group. Assured that no one had been hurt, Laird ordered Dan Henkin to downplay the incident with the press. He did not want to give the terrorists the satisfaction of extensive attention.[20]

May 22, 1972, was the day thousands of protestors were supposed to march to the Pentagon and shut down the morning traffic. In preparation, several hundred Pentagon employees holding critical middle-level positions slept overnight at the building. Many others arrived at work in the predawn hours to avoid the expected "blockade." (Laird was on a NATO-related visit to Spain.) With some apparent disappointment, the media reported that the protest "fizzled," drawing only one thousand marchers. Still, the group was a boisterous and noisy lot, chanting "You kill people! You kill people!"[21]

The protest movement found another rallying point that year when some of North Vietnam's dikes suffered ancillary damage during bombing runs. The system of dikes held back the Red River—both the giver of life, and the destroyer when it floods.[22] The worst flood in decades had occurred in 1971.

Aerial photography and intercepts of North Vietnamese cables sent to its embassies confirmed that the flooding had exceeded normal flood stage by as much as sixty feet in places. Raging water had broken through sections of major dikes, leaving two million people homeless and destroying much of the autumn rice crop. Rail and highway traffic between Hanoi and China was stopped for most of September. Even in November 1971, huge areas of the delta east of Hanoi were still under water. Given the North Vietnamese propensity for hard work, Western intelligence analysts were surprised that so many of the dikes still needed repair by the following March. When the Easter Offensive started, it was evident that North Vietnam had chosen to siphon much of its manpower into the military invasion instead of dike maintenance.[23]

Given the widespread nature of the dike-and-dam system and the intensified bombing, it was inevitable some of the dikes would be hit. The North Vietnamese realized they had a major propaganda issue, especially in an election year. On May 9 they tentatively tested it by charging over Hanoi Radio that the United States had deliberately hit several dikes. The story was false and did not draw too much attention. But, at the same time, Nixon was musing about authorizing dike bombing beginning in early May as he was egged on by his new confidant, the hawkish treasury secretary John Connally. In a May 4 Oval Office chat recorded on the taping system, Connally goaded Nixon. "Bomb for seriousness, not just as a signal," he said, "and don't worry about killing civilians. Go ahead and kill them. . . . People think you are now [killing civilians anyway]. So go ahead and give them some."

"That's right," Nixon responded.

"There's pictures on the news of dead bodies every night," Haldeman chimed in. "A dead body is a dead body. Nobody knows whose bodies they are or who killed them."

No dike-bombing order was ever given by Nixon, who frequently engaged in such braggadocio with his pals that never went beyond the Oval Office. However, the Pentagon had looked at the possible military value of dike-bombing and decided it was a bad idea. "The extensive dike system of the Red River delta offers a potential target whose destruction during the wet season would flood some 10,500 square kilometers of the most densely populated area in the country," one DIA appraisal summarized for the Joint Chiefs. But "because of the massiveness of the earthen dikes (some of which are 80 to 100 feet at their base), a large expenditure of ordnance would be necessary to breach them." The U.S. Air Force was already stretched thin bombing high-value military targets in North Vietnam, and it simply wasn't worth it—especially considering the political fallout of such an action.[24]

The North Vietnamese continued to claim the United States was deliberately targeting dikes. On July 6 Laird issued the first authoritative denial during a press conference. He said, extemporaneously, "We have never targeted
a dam or a dike in our targeting system as far as North Vietnam is concerned." He added that the enemy sometimes put antiaircraft weapons on
dikes and dams, and then they became fair game. But the real damage to the
dikes had been done by flooding. "I believe that the North Vietnamese with
their people are carrying on this [propaganda] campaign in order [to] relieve
themselves from the responsibility with their own people for their failure to
adequately repair this system since the major flooding of last year.[25]

The rumors of dike bombing festered into August, helped by "fact-finding"
teams of American civilians touring North Vietnam.[26] The most notorious
of those tourists was a lone woman—actress Jane Fonda . She became prominent as an antiwar critic by touring U.S. bases and nearby neighborhoods
with a counterculture show. She saw the dike issue as tailor-made for an election year. When the North Vietnamese invited her to visit Hanoi in mid-July
1972 and see for herself, she jumped at the chance. As she got off the plane,
Fonda breathlessly issued an opening statement of support for the enemy:
"Your struggle, courage and culture has forced us to recognize certain truths
about our country . . . I come to Vietnam as a comrade."[27]

For two weeks, occasionally ducking U.S. air raids, Fonda was led through
museums and outdoor exhibits that purported to illustrate American war
crimes, including dike bombings. Fonda made at least ten broadcasts over
Hanoi Radio pleading with American pilots to stop their bombing campaign.
Those broadcasts earned her the sobriquet "Hanoi Jane," a reference to World
War II's "Tokyo Rose."[28] On the last day of her visit, Fonda, clad in black Viet
Cong–type pajama pants, allowed herself to be photographed and filmed in
the gunner's seat of an enemy antiaircraft battery being used to shoot down
American planes. In her 2005 memoirs, *My Life So Far,* Fonda wrote that the
pose was a "lapse" of judgment, and the only one on the whole Hanoi trip
for which she felt "regret."[29]

In her final Hanoi press conference at the time, Fonda aimed her enmity
at Nixon and Laird. "Melvin Laird the other day said that bombing of the
dikes may be taking place, but that it is accidental, and it only happens if
there is a military target on top of the dikes," she said. "Does he really think
the Vietnamese would be foolish enough to put a military installation on top
of an earth dike?" At that press conference, and another when Fonda stopped
in Paris, some reporters pointed out that if there hadn't first been an invasion by the North Vietnamese of the South, the Americans would not be

bombing. She was unmoved. "Vietnam is one country," she argued. "How can the Vietnamese invade Vietnam?"[30]

Fonda's actions prompted charges of treason on the floor of the House and Senate. When Laird was asked on July 17 by a reporter whether her broadcasts "constitute treason or grounds for prosecution under our laws," he answered yes, but said it ultimately was for the Justice Department to determine, not the secretary of defense. The primary question was whether her Hanoi Radio broadcasts—which were played repeatedly over North Vietnamese radio stations and into the cells of American prisoners of war—rose to the level of a violation of the law intended to punish anyone who foments "insubordination, disloyalty, mutiny, or refusal of duty by any member of the military or naval forces of the United States." While Fonda never urged the men to defect, the clear intent of the messages to the American pilots and sailors was that they should disobey orders. However, the Justice Department declined to prosecute, a decision Laird supported.[31]

In 1972 Laird's personal inclination—and his direction to the top military leaders—was to ignore Fonda. Publicly he was careful to say she was not "helpful," but privately his views were stronger: "She was there to demoralize the troops who were in the Hanoi Hilton and South Vietnam, to demoralize all the men and women serving us in that war, and to demoralize public opinion." At the July 31, 1972, staff meeting, Laird was quoted in the minutes as saying: "Jane Fonda's visit was worth millions of dollars to Hanoi for propaganda. When Hanoi does this kind of propaganda campaign, and we spend all our time answering, we will lose. A response to Fonda's visit would only increase the momentum of their campaign. We just cannot win on the dikes and dams."

At that point, Admiral Zumwalt interjected: "Why wasn't Jane Fonda invited to South Vietnam to view the damage *there?*"

"Well, she was invited to talk to the South Vietnamese representatives in Paris, but she refused," Laird reported.[32] Laird felt that Fonda and others were being both illogical and hypocritical while remaining silent about the more egregious war crimes committed by Hanoi as they eagerly indicted the United States. As for the dike issue, it finally washed away in late August 1972 when, during the normal flood season, it was plainly evident to the world that no flooding occurred as a result of damaged dikes.[33]

～

The anti-Vietnam sentiment hung over the 1972 presidential elections, even though U.S. troop numbers were obviously dwindling. Inveterate campaigner Laird was loath to sit on the sidelines, but tradition held that a secretary of defense did not become involved in the partisan battle. At a press conference in December 1970 Laird had been asked if he would take part in Nixon's reelection campaign. "It's very difficult for me to remain inactive politically," he had responded. "But I have followed the instructions of the commander in chief, and I have stayed away from partisan politics ever since I have been in this position."[34]

Laird was almost constitutionally incapable of keeping such a pledge. It was Nixon's opponents themselves who let Laird into the campaign when they began poking a stick at Vietnamization. In January, two of Nixon's potential Democratic challengers, Hubert Humphrey and Edmund Muskie, said Nixon was too slow to get out of Vietnam. This was too much for Laird. Although he also wanted to accelerate the pace of withdrawal, he could not keep silent while the party that had escalated the war was criticizing the party that was winding it down. Without naming names, Laird said, "Strangely enough, some of those individuals that are going around the country today criticizing programs to withdraw Americans from Vietnam were silent in 1968 and before when we were on the escalator going up and up and up."[35]

The unpopularity of the war seemed to change some old campaigning truisms—such as the one that mandated that no presidential candidate during a war could appear to be soft on defense. During Nixon's first run at the presidency, John F. Kennedy made big points charging that the Eisenhower-Nixon administration had allowed the United States to fall behind the Soviet Union militarily (the so-called "missile gap" issue). This time around, the leading Democratic contender, Sen. George McGovern, attacked Nixon for spending too much on defense.

McGovern unveiled his "alternative defense posture" on January 19, 1972. He advocated a $30 billion cut in the Pentagon's budget, which he said could be accomplished through cutting the Navy's fleet of aircraft carriers from fifteen to six, canceling the F-14 and F-15 fighter projects, withdrawing all forces from Southeast Asia and South Korea, and reducing the American troops in Western Europe from 300,000 to 130,0000. As aghast as Laird was over McGovern's alternate defense plan, he might not have found a way to speak out about it if he had not been asked his opinion during congressional hearings on June 5. Senator William Proxmire, a conservative defense critic, asked Laird to evaluate the McGovern proposal. Laird's answer made the next day's headlines: "I would say that the thing to do if you go the $30 billion reduction route is to direct the Department of Defense to spend at least a billion dollars in white flags so that they could run them up all over because it means surrender." Thereafter, Laird continued to refer to McGovern's plan

as the "white flag-surrender budget," sometimes amplifying the point by saying that the Pentagon would have to buy out all the white sheets in stores
across the country and hang them out of the windows if McGovern became
president.[36]

In Laird's mind, there was no question about using political pressure during the campaign to end the war. He had played the politics card repeatedly
to keep Nixon on track with troop withdrawals. In June 1972, when the Easter
invasion was in its twelfth week and the Joint Chiefs were calling for an end
to troop withdrawals, Laird got Nixon to hold to the schedule. Admiral
Moorer wrote to Laird on June 21 asking to temper the next round of withdrawals unless "overriding considerations at the national level dictate continued redeployment increments." The overriding consideration, of course,
was the reelection of Richard Nixon.[37]

Laird suggested that Nixon announce a withdrawal rate that would put
the total number of U.S. troops in Vietnam at fifteen thousand by the end of
the year.[38] On June 28 the White House announced that ten thousand more
troops would return home before September 1, bringing the total remaining down to thirty-nine thousand. It was a more conservative option than
the one Laird recommended, and it slowed the pace of downsizing, but it was
still a surprise to many who thought the United States would halt withdrawals. The biggest news in Nixon's June 28 announcement about the new withdrawal numbers was that no more draftees would be sent to Vietnam unless
they volunteered to go. The president had pushed Laird hard for more than
three years to be allowed to make that announcement.

In 1970 Nixon first became enamored of the idea of not forcing draftees
to go to Vietnam. He wanted to use it then to boost the electoral chances of
some Republican congressional candidates. But Laird, the Joint Chiefs, and
all the military services were opposed to giving Vietnam service any special
draft-free status, fearing the effect on the morale and quality of the troops,
so Nixon backed down.[39] Six months later, with the midterm election heating up, Nixon was again ready to make the announcement, but Laird talked
him out of it again.[40] Nixon revisited the topic yet again in October 1971, and
Laird again objected. But 1972 was a different year, and Laird knew it. That
year, it was not just a congressional election on the line, but Nixon's own
reelection. When Nixon pressed more than once during the spring, Laird forwarded the Army's primary objection: "We believe that the all-volunteers-for-
Vietnam concept is quantitatively possible [but] philosophically extremely
dangerous. . . . It is a Pandora's box, and would give official sanction to those
who contend that a soldier should be allowed to decide when he does or

doesn't want to follow his country's policy."[41] But Laird knew he had pushed Nixon as far as possible. He provided some carefully chosen words to the president "if you wish to make a statement."[42] With that green light from Laird, Nixon announced that no more draftees would go to Vietnam, but by then, the draft was almost history.

~

William Westmoreland was a man whom many colleagues felt was more style than substance, a prima donna like Patton or MacArthur but without their brilliance. "He was not a bad person, but he was overly consumed with appearance and not too deep," Robert Froehlke carefully recalled. Froehlke's predecessor as Army secretary, Stan Resor, agreed that Westmoreland "concentrated on what he looked like, and on style. . . . And he was quite a stuffy fellow."[43] Laird was wary of Westmoreland but preferred to focus on his positive traits—competence, loyalty to the civilian leadership, and his unique ability to support the careers of promising men such as Abrams.

Westmoreland looked as distinguished as ever on the evening of June 30, 1972, when he stood for his last parade in the gymnasium at Fort Myer, Virginia. Rain had forced the retirement ceremony inside, somewhat dampening the pomp and circumstance to which he was entitled after a thirty-six-year career that spanned three wars.[44] Laird was on hand to praise the departing Westmoreland generously, for commanding with "boldness, valor and great professional skill" through his last assignment as chief of staff of the Army. The words were heartfelt, but privately Laird was relieved to see the general go. The two men had disagreed fundamentally on the Vietnam War—Westmoreland convinced it could be won with enough U.S. troops, equipment, and money, and Laird equally convinced that it wasn't America's fight anymore. Westmoreland's four years on the Joint Chiefs had been frustrating for both men as Laird listened to and then dismissed the general's suggestions for a more aggressive approach to the war.

Westmoreland was disappointed that he was not asked to stay with the Joint Chiefs another term, as General Wheeler had been. He had political ambitions and may well have thought he might run for president in 1976. Instead, he ran for governor in his native state of South Carolina and lost. Creighton Abrams stood in sharp contrast to Westmoreland, being all substance and little style. Abrams loathed ostentation and pomp. When he took over from Westmoreland in Saigon in 1968, Abrams had ordered the lavishly decorated office to be redone, using only standard Army issue equipment. When a visiting politician advised him that surely someone of his rank deserved something better than his metal green desk, Abrams shot back: "As long is I've got men fighting and dying out there, I will not sit behind a damn mahogany desk."

In private, however, few enjoyed life's luxuries as much as Abrams. When the occasion allowed, he loved fine wines and gourmet food. He was also a prodigious cigar smoker, having four to six of them lined up like soldiers next to his dinner plate. He also loved classical music, of which he had an encyclopedic knowledge and with which he laced his briefings at times. He explained while delivering one battle plan that "a great conductor will rehearse his orchestra until all the members are skilled enough to do a perfect job. That's the way a military operation should be regarded. An air strike or a round of artillery must come at an exact moment, just as in a symphony one stroke of a drum must come at an exact millisecond of time."[45]

Unvarying honesty touched everything Abrams did. He never once predicted stability for Vietnam without the essential qualifiers, and he stubbornly refused to offer quick assessments of events, even if the president was demanding them. He constantly admonished those around him, "Bad news does not improve with age." Once Laird asked him why he had recommended the severest of penalties for an errant commander. Abrams's face flushed with anger and he growled, "I could have forgiven his mistakes, but I will not tolerate a man who lies." It was often said in Saigon that this general, who had been Patton's favorite tank commander in World War II, "deserved a better war" to oversee than Vietnam. Laird always felt that Abrams deserved more recognition than he got. "Because of the turmoil surrounding our final years in Vietnam—and Abe's steadfast refusal to allow others to trumpet his actions to the press—the American people largely missed the style that he brought to his command. It should never be forgotten," Laird wrote in a 1976 *Reader's Digest* profile.[46]

When he became defense secretary, Laird gave Abrams the difficult task of Vietnamizing the conflict while simultaneously withdrawing U.S. troops under his command. That Abrams did this with loyalty, equanimity, and a minimum of complaints earned him Laird's highest praise and promotion. In a March 1972 Laird called Abrams in Saigon to test his feelings about becoming Army chief of staff upon Westmoreland's retirement. "Well," the fifty-seven-year-old general replied, "my goal throughout my career has been to become Army chief of staff. I don't believe I'm too old for this." But, as Laird recalled the conversation, Abrams only wanted to serve half of the standard four-year term. Laird was pleased at Abrams's acceptance but cautioned that confirmation might be difficult because some senators were hot about the Lavelle bombing episode, which had happened on Abrams's watch. Abrams understood that. As he explained to one of his own aides: "Just remember this, the higher you get up the greasy pole, the more your ass shows."[47]

What Abrams didn't know was that within the administration, Laird stood almost alone in his support of Abrams for the post. President Nixon, who had a personal dislike of Abrams, favored Alexander Haig to replace Westmoreland. Even Laird's closest friend, Froehlke, argued that Abrams was not the best choice; Froehlke wanted to appoint a younger four-star or even three-star general to shake up the Army, as Zumwalt had done for the Navy. Laird went ahead anyway, metaphorically waving his cocktail-napkin promise from the president. A "highly placed source" told the New York Times that "Laird feels obligated to Abrams because Abrams has gone along with Vietnamization even when the Joint Chiefs of Staff objected."[48]

So the only barrier standing in the way was Congress. The Lavelle debacle was still winding its way through congressional investigations, and Laird realized it would be months before Abrams's skirts would be cleared of any responsibility. Two weeks before Abrams left Saigon, Laird sent Nixon a memo advising him that Abrams would not be able to assume his new duties for awhile. In the meantime, Laird told Nixon, Gen. Bruce Palmer would be acting Army chief. To soften the news for Nixon, Laird said he would propose promoting Haig as the new vice chief of staff once Abrams was approved by Congress.[49]

When General Abrams had arrived in Saigon as Westmoreland's deputy five years earlier, the United States had more than half a million troops in Vietnam. When Abrams left, there were only forty-nine thousand troops (mostly airmen and advisors). Westmoreland's strategies for the war had been up-ended by Abrams. Under Laird's policy of Vietnamization, the general had reversed the roles of the Americans and Vietnamese, even in the face of a full-scale North Vietnamese invasion. The New York Times summarized the job as "one of the most difficult ever given to a military man—withdrawing his troops from a country continuously engaged in combat with a well-equipped and highly-motivated enemy without allowing a catastrophe to befall them."[50]

Abrams slipped out of Saigon in June without the usual fanfare or the speeches of a formal change-of-command ceremony. His deputy, Gen. Fred Weyand, moved into his office as the new commander of diminishing U.S. forces in Vietnam, downgraded to an "advisory group."[51] Laird had not even considered going to Saigon to give Abrams a big sendoff. "Abe felt that getting the men and the military bands out and going through all those reviews was kind of a waste of time," he explained.

The change of command in June 1972 coincided with Laird's realization that the enemy's Easter Offensive was stalling out. The high-water mark of the North Vietnamese invasion had been the capture of Quang Tri on May 1. On that day, Laird had warned his staff not to be unduly alarmed. "The South Vietnamese have stood up well in most cases," he said.[52] A week later, Laird's logistics man on the scene sent back gloomy reports about the performance of America's ally at various locations. Too many of its commanders panicked too quickly and called for a helicopter airlift out or requested unnecessary heavy air support. "One general told me that they tend to call for air support every time they go to the bathroom," Barry Shillito cabled Laird. "It is a physical impossibility for anyone to meet all their demands." He added, "The greatest single problem is unwillingness of some elements to get in the fight."[53]

George McGovern's presidential campaign, as well as antiwar members of Congress, capitalized on the growing media reports that hinted of an impending defeat for South Vietnam. Some within the Nixon administration itself feared the South might not hold. But not Laird. In response to badgering questions and criticism about South Vietnamese losses, he said at a press conference, "The American people always have supported our president when Americans are endangered and the cause of freedom has been threatened. This is no time for quitters or for a lot of talk about instant surrender. I don't think the American people want to clamber aboard some sort of a bug-out shuttle."

By early June, Laird's optimism was looking more like realism. After sixty days the enemy had failed to achieve any one of its goals: the collapse of the South Vietnamese army; taking meaningful territory; or generating a popular uprising in the South in favor of the communists. When the South retook Quang Tri in mid-September, the enemy offensive was officially over. South Vietnamese ground forces and U.S. air power had turned the enemy back. But Laird knew all this did not mean that the South had won. He rightly expected North Vietnam would try again.

By late July, Laird felt confident enough about the South Vietnamese military that he publicly stated it would be possible to withdraw even more U.S. troops than already announced. An NBC *Today* show interviewer complained to Laird when he appeared on July 20 that the United States was unilaterally withdrawing while the North Vietnamese were doing nothing to decrease their effort. How was that sensible? "We're withdrawing on the basis of the improved strength of our partner," Laird patiently explained. "That's what the Vietnamization program is all about."[54]

The last American ground unit in Vietnam—the Army's 1,043-strong Third

Battalion, Twenty-first Infantry, which guarded the huge U.S. air base at Da Nang—was withdrawn on August 11, 1972. A week later, at a press conference held at California's McClellan Air Force Base, Laird noted: "It was only three and a half years ago that there were eleven American divisions that had the total and complete ground combat responsibility in South Vietnam. Only one South Vietnamese division was capable of handling a ground combat responsibility. Today, the situation is reversed. There is not a single American division having a ground combat responsibility." Even better, by mid-September, the weekly casualty report listed not a single American killed in action, the first time that had happened in seven years.[55]

23

No Time for Quitters

THROUGHOUT 1972 THE REELECTION OF NIXON was never far from
Laird's mind. Ever the canny politician, Laird offered to address both
Republican and Democratic platform committees before each of the party
nominating conventions.[1] The Democrats didn't proffer an invitation to their
convention in Miami in July. George McGovern gave his acceptance speech
around 3 a.m. on July 13, after the prime-time audience had gone to bed. His
oratorical theme was "come home, America"—from war, waste, privilege,
and prejudice. In a sideswipe at Nixon from the 1968 campaign, he added:
"I have no secret plan for peace. I have a public plan. As one whose heart
has ached for ten years over the agony of Vietnam, I will halt the senseless
bombing of Indochina on Inauguration Day."[2]

The speech and McGovern's campaigning suggested that he expected to
win election on the war issue. But Laird's persistent push for troop withdrawals and Vietnamization of the war had robbed McGovern of any hope
for the high ground. A Harris Survey taken several days after the Democratic Convention showed 52 percent of Americans supported the Vietnamization plan for "ending U.S. involvement in Vietnam," while only 33 percent
supported McGovern's war-ending proposals.

During the week before the Republican National Convention began in
Miami in August, Laird was the first administration official to appear before
the GOP Platform Committee. He urged the platform writers to "reject policies of planned weakness, of white-flag waving, of begging and of abandonment of the nation's role in helping to maintain peace."[3]

On the road, Laird was a formidable noncampaigner for Nixon. He targeted cities that relied heavily on defense employers and traveled there for
speeches in which he warned how decimated their local economies would be

if McGovern were president and implemented his severe defense cuts. McGovern took to calling Laird the chief "fright-monger" for the Nixon campaign, a "lackey" who was "do[ing] Nixon's dirty work."[4]

Just before the election, and over David Packard's objections, Laird ordered four new electromagnetic pulse (EMP)-protected 747 planes from Boeing for presidential airborne command posts. The planes were needed for use against the newly identified EMP threat—but not urgently. By ordering early, Laird propped up Boeing and insured Republican support in the Seattle area where the jobs would go. The same thing was true when he bought trucks in Detroit, and toilet paper in Wisconsin and elsewhere.[5]

As a subtext of the Vietnam War issue, the cause célèbre of the 1972 election season was the prisoners of war and missing in action in Southeast Asia. Actress Jane Fonda was among the more prominent people who went to Hanoi, visiting with seven POWs during a July 1972 trip. She was followed by former U.S. Attorney General Ramsey Clark, who declared that Hanoi's treatment of POWs "could not be better." As a matter of fact, the health of the POWs with whom he met was "better than mine, and I am a healthy man," Clark said.[6]

In March, McGovern campaigned with three POW wives at his side, and he chose a POW wife to second his nomination to be the Democratic presidential candidate. On June 28, meeting with South Carolina delegates in advance of the national convention, he was cornered by one delegate, upset by what appeared to be McGovern capitulation to Hanoi: "You want us to do all they demand and then beg them to give back our boys?" McGovern replied, "I'll accept that. Begging is better than bombing. I would go to Hanoi and beg if I thought that would release the boys one day earlier." It was a negotiate-from-weakness comment McGovern never lived down. Laird immediately began calling it a "surrender now, beg later" policy.[7]

Laird's outrage about McGovern's approach to the POW issue peaked in September after Hanoi released three American pilots into the hands of an antiwar group that flew them home via Beijing and Moscow. When U.S. military officials attempted unsuccessfully to get the POWs to go home on a military transport instead, McGovern accused the Nixon administration of delaying the release of the three men and "playing politics" with them. Laird lashed out at McGovern: "Senator McGovern apparently is willing to act as an agent for Hanoi in undermining the rights of American prisoners of war under the Geneva Conventions. It is a despicable act of a presidential candidate to make himself a spokesman for the enemy." One wire service report called it "the harshest rhetoric of the 1972 presidential campaign."[8]

Throughout the year, Kissinger had been feverishly negotiating a peace treaty with Hanoi in hopes of settling the war before voters went to the polls in November. His efforts to strike a deal with Hanoi in the Paris peace talks boiled down to three demands: (1) American POWs would be returned; (2) South Vietnamese would be allowed to determine their own form of government; and (3) there would be a cease-fire "in place," meaning the enemy troops could hold their positions in South Vietnam.

Thinking this might be a workable deal, both the Soviet Union and the United States began pouring supplies into the field, assuming at some point a peace treaty would require each of them to back away from helping their surrogates and turn the battle into a true civil war between North and South. Under Laird's direction, nine squadrons of planes were handed over to South Vietnamese pilots along with one hundred thousand tons of equipment.[9]

As a show of support for the peace talks, on October 14 Laird ordered Admiral Moorer to gradually reduce the number of bombing runs over North Vietnam. Although Laird was uncomfortable using bombing strategy as a bargaining chip in Paris—and not confident that it would make any difference—he bowed to Kissinger's request. At the same time, Laird let Kissinger know that if Hanoi didn't come around quickly, the bombing would be intensified.[10]

Contemporary press accounts hinted that Nixon and Kissinger had taken over direct command of the bombing raids, picking targets, and dictating how many raids would be flown, just as Lyndon Johnson had done in his effort to micromanage the war from Washington. Laird insisted that was never the case with all the bombing targets. But he began sending the most sensitive targets, such as power plants, to the White House for approval, acknowledging the delicate juncture in the peace talks. He recalled sending Nixon and Kissinger a sampling of about seventy-five targets in the few weeks before the November election. The cautious Nixon, mindful of his own reelection campaign and Kissinger's challenge in Paris, approved only about one third of them. And on October 24, Nixon halted all bombing above the Twentieth Parallel in North Vietnam, which included the cities of Hanoi and Haiphong.

Two days later, Kissinger uttered a phrase at a press conference that would haunt him: "We believe that peace is at hand." Nixon was not pleased with the off-the-cuff remark, Laird recalled. It made the president look like he was trying to manipulate the minds of voters two weeks before the election, with a promise of peace but no treaty signed. Laird himself never believed Kissinger was close to a deal with Hanoi at that point. He based his opinion on lukewarm communications that the National Security Agency intercepted between

Hanoi and its delegation at the talks in Paris. But Laird also didn't think that Kissinger was playing politics, other than an attempt to do the president a favor by settling as quickly as possible. Laird believed Kissinger sincerely thought peace was at hand.

The November 7 election came and went without a peace treaty. Nixon won 61 percent of the vote. If there had been manipulation of the war to win the election, the moves that had mattered were Laird's four years of behind-the-scenes maneuvers, which had succeeded in pressuring Nixon and Kissinger to withdraw American troops at a rapid rate and end the draft. "Nixon was elected in 1968 on the Vietnam War issue, and he was elected again on the war issue in 1972," Laird said. "By the time 1972 rolled around, Nixon realized that the troop withdrawals and ending of the draft were his biggest victories on which to campaign. He wound up with a huge majority in one of the greatest reelection victories any president has ever had." Laird considered that an endorsement of his Vietnamization program.

~

There was no time for the worker bees in the Nixon administration to revel in his election victory. The president himself made sure of that by firing them all on the morning after the election. He called an 11 a.m. White House staff meeting and explained that he was going to shake up the administration. Without sitting down, he perfunctorily thanked those present for their work. Then, by Haldeman's account, he asked for all their resignations immediately and for a list of documents in their possession that should be added to his own papers.[11]

Even Laird was surprised by the Nixon he saw at the cabinet meeting that followed the White House staff meeting that morning. Nixon was thankful for their efforts, but he was surprisingly withdrawn, as if so many defeats in the past had been easier to handle than an all-out victory. Laird was not disturbed for himself but rather for his people who might want to stay on into the second term. Laird had already submitted his resignation letter that morning, noting that all of his goals had been achieved or were within sight. "As we discussed four years ago, I have felt strongly that no individual should serve as Secretary of Defense for more than four years," Laird wrote to Nixon. "Therefore, I respectfully request that you allow me to submit, and that you accept, my resignation [effective] January 20, 1973."[12]

That afternoon, Carl Wallace received a packet of letters from the White House, individually addressed to each political appointee in the Defense Department. Inside was an unsigned White House memorandum, instructing them to resign, form letters for resignations, and a job application to be filled out if they wanted to stay.[13] Laird was furious at the tactless move; he told Wallace not to deliver the letters and to call a special staff meeting for the next morning, Thursday, November 9, at 10 a.m.

Laird backed into the painful purpose of the meeting with a pep talk about the election victory and goals achieved, most of which had been possible because of the team's hard work. "No cabinet officer or the president has received greater loyalty exhibited by the presidential appointees and noncareer executives than I have had at this department during the last four years," he declared. But the term was not complete, and Laird needed their continued focus and help. "The next sixty days will be very important to the success or failure of the Vietnamization program," he said. "We are at the make-or-break stage." Laird said he hoped no one saw him "as deserting the ship. I simply feel that this ship will be better run if someone new comes in."

Then to the matter at hand: the packet of letters and job application forms from the White House. Laird said the White House was handling things in an "unfortunate" manner. Froehlke was asked to read aloud the unsigned White House memorandum they received. Laughter rolled through the room. The pro forma letters of resignation were standard practice, but Laird said he would refuse to submit them to the White House. "Your letters will not leave this Department," he said. "And there will be no applications and no job descriptions filled out by any of you. . . . We have a great team, and I apologize for the way the White House has done this. I will speak to the President about it. Otherwise, I advise you to let Carl toss these packets in the trash." (One of the appointees recalled that several of them ceremoniously dropped their unopened packets in Wallace's waste basket.)[14]

The election year had already seen personnel moves of historic importance—among them Westmoreland's retirement and Abrams's promotion to Army chief of staff. For the new vice chief, Laird had to keep a promise to Nixon that Al Haig could have the number two job if Abrams were number one. Haig's elevation to vice chief of staff, the second highest position in the Army, was meteoric. He had been a major general (two stars) for only six months—so short a time that on the day of the announcement of his nomination, the release of an official photograph was delayed because no picture could be found of Haig with more than one star. Vaulting him from two-star to four-star rank also meant that Laird had to jump him over 243 more senior generals. He was given the high post without ever having commanded a division or even a brigade in the Army.[15]

Probably the second most serious loss to the Laird team—after the December 1971 resignation of David Packard—was the departure of Laird's right-hand man, Air Force Major General Pursley. For six years, Pursley had been putting in grueling sixteen- to eighteen-hour days as the military assistant to three successive secretaries of defense. Clark Clifford called him "one of the most intelligent and broad-gauged military officers I have ever known." Laird said of Pursley, "He would not only take on the chief of staff of the Air Force, but would also take on the chief of staff of every service, and the chairman of the Joint Chiefs on my behalf. He took on Al Haig over at the White House, too, almost every day. And he took them all on tough." It was one of those many encounters that pushed Pursley beyond his limits.

Laird was in Europe at a NATO meeting in May 1972 when Pursley paid a call on Haig at the White House, hoping to talk about ways they might improve relations between their offices. Instead, Haig turned to a credenza behind his desk and produced a large black notebook in which he said he had been collecting a list of grievances against Pursley since early in the Nixon administration. (Pursley didn't know then the most egregious of the collection techniques—the tapping of Pursley's phones for extended periods.) The black book was the last straw. When Laird returned from NATO, Pursley told him that he didn't think he could continue to work for the Nixon administration; he wanted to retire. But Laird could not let him go altogether, so he persuaded Pursley to take on a new assignment. In December he became commander of the Fifth Air Force as well as U.S. forces in Japan. A third star came with the assignment, making Pursley the youngest lieutenant general in the Air Force at the time.

Another major departure in 1972 was Navy secretary John Chafee. Laird had persuaded him to take the job after Chafee had lost his bid in 1968 for a fourth term as a rare Republican governor in the predominantly Democratic state of Rhode Island. The Defense Department job so rejuvenated Chafee that by early 1972, with Laird's support, he decided he would go back to Rhode Island and run for the Senate. Chafee lost because, in a fervently antiwar state where Democrats outnumbered Republicans two to one, he could not overcome his three-year association with the Vietnam War. Four years later, however, Chafee won a Senate seat, which he held until the day he died in 1999.[16] With Chafee gone from the Pentagon, John Warner finally got the job of navy secretary, for which he had waited three years.

Shortly after Nixon's reelection victory, he retreated to Camp David to cogitate and seek inspiration on second-term appointments. On Friday afternoon, November 17, Nixon invited Laird to the presidential retreat in the western Maryland mountains, for a bittersweet, three-hour chat. The president's first order of business was to determine if Laird would reconsider resigning, or would accept another post, such as an ambassadorship, or U.S.

representative to the United Nations. Laird politely turned Nixon down.[17] The next matter of business was to ask Laird for his recommendation on a successor for the Defense Department. Nixon already had plans to make the deputy defense secretary Kenneth Rush the undersecretary of state, with the promise that he would move up when William Rogers retired.

Nixon asked Laird what he thought of making HEW secretary Elliot Richardson the new defense secretary. Laird respected Richardson and considered him a friend. Laird's only "knock" on him was that he never seemed to hold a job more than two years. "He seems to always want to move to something else," Laird warned Nixon. True to Laird's prediction, Richardson would be the shortest-serving defense secretary ever. He lasted only four months on the job before accepting Nixon's request to become attorney general in May 1973.

Most of Laird's session with Nixon was warm and nostalgic as both men realized their service together was ending. Nixon confided that he felt he had won reelection on the very issues that Laird had spearheaded for him, such as the Vietnamization policy, the impending end of the draft, and the creation of an all-volunteer force. That evening, after Laird left, Nixon wrote him a four-page letter expressing a "profound sense of sadness" at losing Laird, the administration's "indispensable man—the right man for the right place, at the right time." Nixon praised Laird for the part he played in winding down the war. "To have bugged out the day after we got into office would have been easy—and some say—good politics," Nixon wrote. "It would have won us a few good headlines and a great deal of public support in the short run—for a few days, weeks or even months. It would, of course, as we both know have been disastrous for America in the long run, and for the cause of peace and freedom in the world. We saw it through and although our contemporaries may not praise us, historians will record we did the right thing."[18]

⁓

During the three months between the election and Laird's resignation, he did not have the luxury of being a lame duck. He had to shepherd the 1973 fiscal year budget and form up the next budget, which Richardson would inherit. Lingering business included the next phase of submarine modernization, the Undersea Long-Range Missile System (ULMS).

The need for ULMS was great, Laird felt. The Soviets' accelerated submarine-building program meant that by 1978 they would have about ninety modern nuclear missile submarines while the U.S. would have only forty-one aging Polaris and Poseidon subs. The ULMS, with more missiles, and each of them with multiple independently targeted warheads, would more than match the Soviet sub missile power. Because of their longer range, the ULMS submarines did not need foreign bases close to Russia, nor did they need to patrol so close to Soviet naval bases.

In January 1972 Laird had recommended that Nixon immediately request from Congress more than $900 million for the program, and Nixon complied. Laird's next step was to get the submarine a better name than ULMS. John Warner suggested "Trident" and it stuck. Laird understood the value of a name. He had already broken the Navy's pattern of naming new cruisers after cities; Laird changed it to states, thus ensuring a larger fan base for the ships. Breaking with a seventy-year Navy tradition, Laird also mandated in his first year in office that attack submarines would no longer be named after fish, but after pro-defense legislators who had died. "I had a bitchy time with Adm. Hyman Rickover when I told him we would quit naming submarines after fish," Laird recalled. Rickover, who headed the nuclear propulsion division at the Pentagon, was a cranky, often-arrogant power in his own right. After a two-hour showdown between the two men over ship names, Laird finally convinced the politically-savvy Rickover with three words: "Fish don't vote!" Rickover capitulated. The first new attack submarine was named *William H. Bates* for a Laird friend who had been ranking member of the House Armed Services Committee. Three more followed, named after late friends of the Pentagon in Congress, *L. Mendel Rivers, Richard B. Russell,* and *Glenard P. Lipscomb.*

Shortly after Nixon's reelection, Laird urged him to give the Trident program an official designation as being of the "Highest National Priority," which made it a "crash" program that had first call on the nation's industrial capacity. Nixon concurred in December, but in the post-Laird era, his successors had difficulty obtaining continuing funds for the $1 billion-a-sub program. As a result, the first Trident sub, the USS *Ohio,* was not deployed until 1981. Within about twenty years, eighteen Trident submarines were deployed in the Atlantic and Pacific fleets, carrying about half of all U.S. strategic nuclear warheads. As much as anyone else, Laird was the father of the Trident.[19]

Laird similarly "fathered" a dozen other key weapons systems, many of which remained in use three decades later. On that list are the cruise missiles, whose tactical use was formidable in both wars with Iraq and in Afghanistan. Nuclear missiles were first "MIRVed"—given multiple warheads—under Laird. The B-1 strategic bomber program also began during his term. While that expensive bomber was rarely deployed, some of its advanced technology was incorporated into the B-2 stealth bomber. Among other Laird-sponsored standouts are the Air Force's F-15 and F-16 fighters, the A-10 close air support aircraft, and the radar-packed E-3 Airborne Warning and Control System (AWACS); the Navy's F-14 and F-18 fighters, S-3 carrier-based sub-hunting aircraft, DD-963 class destroyers, SSN-688 *Los Angeles* class attack submarines as well as the strategic Trident; and the Army's antitank TOW missile system and main battle tank, the M1. After Laird left public life, he successfully lobbied to name that tank the *Abrams*.

With his resignation letter in the president's hands, Laird still had to put the draft to bed. The fourth and last draft lottery had been held in February 1972. Three months later, Laird had announced that no more than fifty thousand men would be called up for military service in 1972—the lowest number since 1949. It was a major achievement for Laird and Nixon; the year before they came into office, draft calls had peaked at nearly three hundred thousand.[20] In a secret July report to the president, Laird wrote that the "dramatic decline in draft calls" was made possible partly by attracting more voluntary enlistees. Laird had also reduced the overall size of the active forces by more than a third from a Vietnam War peak of 3.5 million to 2.3 million, which helped reduce the need for draftees. As a result, Nixon and Laird were able to announce in March 1972 that if Congress passed a pay increase for the military, the draft could officially end on June 30, 1973, when the two-year draft law extension expired.[21]

Laird knew. however, that there were still changes to make toward that goal before he left office. The 1971 draft extension bill had not included something Laird thought was needed: enough money to end KP ("kitchen police") and janitorial duties for soldiers. The Air Force and Navy had already contracted those duties to civilians for the most part. But the Army still inflicted the despised chores on its rookies. In trying to finally end KP, Laird ran into trouble with an old friend in Congress, George Mahon, the House Appropriations Committee chairman, who felt that it was good for a GI to peel potatoes, just as Mahon himself had once done in the service. Besides, contracting out the work would cost $100 million. Nevertheless, Laird still won the short-lived KP debate in Congress. Wisconsin congressman William Steiger persuasively argued that it made as much sense to have trained soldiers do KP as it did to have members of Congress "clean the latrines in the Rayburn (House offices) Building."[22]

As the draft wound down to a close, Laird faced a new problem of dwindling medical personnel. Enough doctors and nurses had joined the services during the height of the war so they could avoid the draft and get better assignments.[23] The end of the draft would eliminate that incentive. Laird

eventually solved the medical shortage with more medical school scholarships, higher enlistment bonuses, and pay increases. The most innovative
solution was Laird's creation of a special military medical academy, the Uniformed Services University of the Health Sciences (USUHS). Nixon opposed
the idea, but that didn't stop Laird from joining forces with Rep. Edward
Hebert to persuade Congress to fund the university. When White House aide
John Ehrlichman called to suggest that Laird not testify on Capitol Hill in
favor of the idea, Laird responded, "If the president doesn't want me to testify, he'll tell me."[24]

The USUHS, adjacent to the naval hospital in Bethesda, Maryland, enrolled its first thirty-two students in 1976. On Laird's recommendation, its
first president was Dr. Tony Curreri, a noted Wisconsin physician, and its
first chairman of the board of regents was David Packard. President Jimmy
Carter tried to kill the university by cutting off funding, but Laird mounted
a formidable defense. "Mel kept calling me, saying, 'Don't do it!'" recalled
Harold Brown, who was Carter's secretary of defense. "Then he went around
to his friends in Congress and insisted it be funded—so it was." When the
Clinton administration attempted to close USUHS in the late 1990s as part
of Vice President Al Gore's "reinventing government" initiative, once again
Laird succeeded in rallying opposition to what he felt was a misguided, short-
sighted move. When the school was again put on the chopping block during
the George W. Bush administration, Laird called Defense Secretary Rumsfeld
and said if the school was cut, "I'll never speak to you again." USUHS escaped
the budget axe.

Opposition to the government-owned university came consistently from
those who wanted the military medical students farmed out to other public
and private medical schools. But Laird believed that a military medical school
fostered more loyalty and long-term commitment from the doctors and
resulted in more specialty training for the demands of combat medicine. In
its first three decades USUHS graduated more than twenty-five hundred
physicians. The majority of health professionals in both Gulf Wars were military medical school graduates—including 78 percent of the doctors serving in Iraq in the War on Terror.[25]

The final piece of Laird's plan to end the draft on schedule was increasing
the benefits, training, and missions of the nation's Reserve Forces and the
National Guard. Almost seven hundred thousand reservists and guardsmen
were called up during the Korean War, but the political fallout had been
severe. Because most units were filled with men from the same local area of
a state, if they suffered high casualties, it had a devastating impact on those

communities. During the 1961 Berlin crisis, President Kennedy had called up the Reserves, which also had unwelcome political repercussions. When Lyndon Johnson decided to escalate U.S. participation in Vietnam, he avoided using the Reserves. Johnson found it easier to draft the men he needed, so the Reserves and National Guard became a haven from the draft.

Congressman Laird thought that was all wrong. He felt the primary value of the Reserves and National Guard was to provide trained backup forces to supplement the active forces in time of national emergency or war. As secretary of defense, he issued a historic memorandum on August 21, 1970, mandating that the Reserves and National Guard would be called upon *first* in such times. He called it the "Total Force Concept," and it necessarily stipulated beefing up those Reserve forces that had been cannibalized by Johnson. When Laird entered office, the Reserve budget was $2.1 billion. By the time he left, it was $4.1 billion to fund much-needed new equipment, training, and modernization.[26] Laird's 1970 decision regarding the "total force" concept became an integral and institutional part of military planning for thirty-five years. Both presidents Bush used the Reserves and National Guard for the two Gulf wars in precisely the way Laird had envisioned.

For the last draft induction of the Vietnam War, three hundred men were ordered to report to their local induction centers on December 28, 1972. But former president Harry Truman died and that day was pronounced a national day of mourning. Some potential inductees reported anyway and were sent home to await further instructions that never came. The draft was dead, except for the formal expiration of the law, even though the war in Vietnam was still not over.

Although Laird lacked total faith in the peace negotiations as they dragged on, he nevertheless sent Kissinger a memorandum in mid-November listing negotiating terms Laird felt were essential. The most prominent among his points was the return of the POWs and an accounting of the missing—to include American inspections of crash sites in North Vietnam. A month later, and still with no treaty finalized, Laird took his case for the POWs directly to Nixon.[27]

The nation was weary of the yo-yo peace talks and promises of an accord. South Vietnamese president Thieu was digging in his heels for more concessions, and the Hanoi government kept changing the terms. While Nixon and Kissinger seemed to aim for an airtight treaty, Laird's solution was to sign whatever marginally acceptable agreement Hanoi had offered, get the POWs home, and worry about compliance later. The North Vietnamese "appear to be stiffening by reopening issues once considered settled," Laird wrote the president on December 12. Kissinger had "encouraged the U.S. people and the rest of the world to believe that peace is at hand and that our POWs would be home momentarily," and congressional leaders "do not understand why we are delaying the signing of the agreement. . . . I am concerned that you are putting in jeopardy your reputation as a world leader and your future effectiveness on the world scene. I believe the far better course of action is to sign the agreement now, get all our POWs home and get an accounting of our MIAs, and then test the sincerity of the North Vietnamese. If the test proves that the North Vietnamese have deceived us, then is the time to take action to help the [Saigon government]."[28] (The emphasis on "putting in jeopardy your reputation as a world leader" was new language for Laird, who could no longer use reelection as a lever to move Nixon.)

Nixon didn't choose the sign-now-pay-later route. He had suspended bombing over North Vietnam on October 22 as a negotiations incentive, but it didn't work. So Nixon leaned toward one last massive bombing campaign by B-52s to bring the enemy swiftly to its knees. At Nixon's request, Laird sent him a plan on for a bombing attack "designed to produce a mass shock effect in a psychological context." Laird submitted a list of thirty-seven targets, from railroad yards and shipping docks to power plants and bridges. They could be taken out in seven days, if the weather cooperated. Tangentially, he also recommended re-seeding the harbors with mines, although he never believed the tactic had much short-term military impact.[29] (According to one analysis for Laird after the initial mines were planted in May, it appeared that Hanoi had taken only three months to reroute its formerly seaborne supplies to road and rail supply lines.[30])

When Kissinger reported to Nixon on December 16 that the peace talks were at an impasse, Nixon ordered the bombing of North Vietnam to resume again the following day (after a two-month hiatus). Anticipating the president's decision, Laird had already advised the Joint Chiefs to prepare for massive B-52 strikes beginning on the seventeenth, but it wasn't until the eighteenth that conditions were suitable, and the twelve-day campaign began. It was officially known as "Operation Linebacker II," but it came to be called the "Christmas Bombing." It was brutal and costly. By Laird's count, 121 American pilots and crewmen were killed or taken prisoner. The United States lost 10 B-52s in the first three days. Through private and public signals, Laird made sure Nixon and Kissinger were informed that the campaign had no military value. It was strictly an attempt to bring Hanoi back to the negotiating table.[31]

After four days of bombing, Nixon cabled North Vietnamese leaders to say that the assault could end if they came back to the negotiations. Getting no response, Nixon directed Laird to let the pilots take Christmas Day off and then ordered the heaviest bombing attacks of the war, beginning on December 26. More than 1,300 bombing sorties were flown, dumping twenty thousand tons of bombs, more than the total nuclear equivalent dropped on Hiroshima. Within a day, Hanoi said it was ready to talk, but it took three more days of negotiating the terms of the next meeting before Nixon finally halted the bombing on December 29. In the end there were virtually no more military targets worth hitting in North Vietnam. They had all been destroyed.

~

While Nixon and Kissinger dickered with Hanoi about restarting the peace talks in January, Laird began cleaning out his desk. He had promised four years earlier that he would leave on the inaugural day of January 20, 1973, whoever was president, and he had reserved a taxi for that purpose in advance. In mid-December, Laird had hosted a going-away party for his team in the elegant reception rooms of the State Department. David Packard came from California, and retired Gen. Earle Wheeler joined the party to give it the air of a family reunion. The party stands out as one of Laird's fondest memories from his four years at the Pentagon. He didn't prepare a speech, but he stood to tell the small group that he was proud of them and proud of their families for what they had sacrificed. Froehlke looked over the group of friends and said it was more than a party. "When you look at all these people, you realize there's more than a facade of a party here; it goes deeper ... [I]t shows Mel Laird put together an amazing team. Some day the American public will appreciate what this team did—not today, but some day."[32]

On January 8 Laird testified before the House Armed Services Committee for the last time and declared that Vietnamization was essentially, and successfully, completed.[33] The South Vietnamese had in hand more than $5.3 billion in equipment provided by the United States in the last year of the war, and they knew how to use it to keep the enemy at bay. When Kissinger reopened the peace talks that same week, he began putting in place the rules for continuing resupply of Saigon by the United States and of Hanoi by the Soviet Union. Each of the superpowers was going to be allowed to keep their surrogates resupplied with replacement parts, but not to escalate the level of aid.

Laird held his last press conference on January 19, and reporters tried to get him to come clean on some of his disagreements with Nixon: How did he *really* feel about the invasions of Cambodia and Laos and the last massive bombing of North Vietnam? Discreet to the end, Laird responded: "I am not going to discuss matters of privileged communications between the President of the United States, the Secretary of Defense . . . and the Joint Chiefs in connection with on-going operations or previous operations. I can only state to you that I supported the actions which we have taken and I have always supported those actions, and I continue to support those actions."

Laird expressed disappointment that the Senate had not yet confirmed Elliot Richardson as his successor, which meant Laird could "not leave this building unattended." He explained, "I left the Congress because I felt I had a duty to serve my country. I did that as a favor to the President, and a duty to my country. You can discount it all you want, but that is the reason that I am here. . . . I have fulfilled my commitment, but you cannot leave this building without a Secretary of Defense."[34]

In the next few days, Laird made some phone calls to senators asking them to speed up the process so he could get on with his new life. However, the nine-day postponement of his taxi ride did allow him to leave on a high note. On Monday, January 22, Laird talked with Kissinger before he left on his final flight to Paris where both of them knew he would initial a secretly-concluded agreement with Hanoi. "If it hadn't been for your work, I would not be leaving this morning to initial this agreement," Kissinger said emotionally in sincere tribute to Laird. The peace accord was initialed by Kissinger and North Vietnamese negotiator Le Duc Tho in a public Paris ceremony on January 23 and was formally signed four days later by the respective foreign ministers.[35]

For the United States, the Vietnam War was over. (Former president Lyndon Johnson died at the age of sixty-four of a heart attack the evening before the treaty was initialed.) The United States and Hanoi both agreed to put no more troops into South Vietnam; the POWs would be returned within sixty days; and the war would continue with each side replacing lost equipment but adding no more to the conflict—all terms proposed by Laird to Kissinger in his previous advisory memoranda. Laird genuinely believed that under those terms Vietnamization of the war had been and would continue to be a success. The United States had agreed to bankroll the war in Vietnam but not send any more of its young men to die there, as 45,933 of them already had, according to the best estimate at that time.

In a defense secretary's staff meeting, General Abrams echoed Laird's feelings about the treaty and reminded the group that it hinged on more than just the military transformation brought about by Vietnamization: "[A]s far as an agreement, it does not make much difference what it says. We have either gotten the job done or we haven't. This we will find out over the next three to five years. . . . The question is whether what we have done in the south is enough to have provided them a durable defense for the future. The biggest factor will be whether the South Vietnamese have had time to develop political as well as economic strength. This factor may be even more important—certainly it is just as critical."[36]

Before Nixon went on television to address the nation at 10 p.m. on Tuesday, January 23, he held a special 8:30 p.m. cabinet meeting. During the meeting, Nixon confidentially reported on how the agreement was reached and singled out Laird for praise. "Without Vietnamization," he said, "there would have been no settlement, and this night would not have been possible."[37]

Four days later, Secretary Laird accomplished his final major goal by declaring an end to the draft five months ahead of schedule. In an official order transmitted to the three service secretaries and the Joint Chiefs on January 27, Laird declared: "I wish to inform you that the Armed Forces henceforth will depend exclusively on volunteer soldiers, sailors, airmen, and Marines. Use of the draft has ended."[38]

"I don't think at the time the public appreciated the significance [of Laird's order], but in retrospect it was a major accomplishment," reflected former president Gerald Ford, who added that Laird deserved to be called the "father" of the modern volunteer armed forces. Many prominent Democrats have agreed. "The volunteer Army was a huge achievement by Laird," noted Clinton administration ambassador Richard Holbrooke, who co-authored Clark Clifford's memoirs. "Ending the draft was one of the most important pieces of social legislation that the United States has had. And it was Laird, who was the only guy in the Nixon administration who understood politics as well as policy, who brought us to an outcome that has served the nation very well."[39]

Among Laird's most treasured memorabilia is a handwritten note dated the same day the draft ended and the Vietnam cease-fire began. "My warmest congratulations on your successful efforts in dealing with the war in South Viet Nam," wrote a White House official by the name of Donald Rumsfeld, who considered himself a Laird protégé. "It has been a privilege to see the intellect, wisdom and courage you and your associates have brought to bear on this thorniest of problems." Without any foreknowledge that he himself would serve as secretary of defense under two future presidents, and oversee the next unpopular war, Rumsfeld concluded: "You are one hell of a guy and my candidate for 'The best Secretary of Defense in history.'"[40]

On February 1, 1973, Laird closed his office door for the last time and left

without any fanfare. Eleven days later, on February 12 at 3:20 p.m. Washington time, the first of the American POWs came off an airplane at Clark Air
Force Base in the Philippines. Laird watched it on television, as the rest of
the nation did, and uncharacteristically shed a few tears. A week later a letter
arrived at Laird's home from President Nixon: "As I saw our POWs come off
the plane at Clark Field, I was never so proud to be an American. . . . I just
wanted you to know how much I personally appreciate all you have done
to help achieve the honorable peace we fought for."[41]

24

Watergate

"MEL AND MOM DO THE TOWN," read the headline of one Wisconsin newspaper a week after Laird resigned as secretary of defense. With his eighty-five-year-old mother, Helen, on his arm, Laird walked the streets of Madison shopping for a coat for her and then taking her for a medical checkup. When Laird stopped at a private club for lunch, he was hailed in the lobby by old friends who called out, "What are your plans now?"

"I'm going to rest for three months," Laird said.[1]

"You deserve a rest and change of environment—God knows you've earned it!," an old friend, Interior Secretary Rogers Morton, said in a letter. Morton's missive was one of hundreds of accolades Laird received upon his retirement in the form of newspaper articles and editorials, television and radio commentaries, and private letters. One of those praising him was James Schlesinger, chairman of the Atomic Energy Commission, who wrote: "This has been a difficult period to lead the Department, as you well know, in view of the disenchantment both on the Hill and in the public at large. In these troubled circumstances, I can think of no one who could have handled the problem more skillfully than you have done." (Schlesinger himself would have to take on the role of defense secretary a few months later.)[2]

Laird had promised his wife that he would go to work in private business so they could settle down out of the limelight. Offers poured in. At least one major airline company and one large aluminum firm wanted Laird to come aboard as the chief executive officer. While Laird acknowledged that he would like to serve on the boards of several major companies (twenty-two had offered seats), he did not want to be a CEO . He also turned down an invitation to become the chairman of the New York Stock Exchange.[3]

Laird was only fifty and at the top of his game. Few could believe that he would abandon politics altogether. *Washington Star* military correspondent Orr Kelly, wrote that one clue to Laird's future was the fact that "he is one of this nation's relatively few true professional politicians. He is not one of those successful lawyers, businessmen or labor leaders who turn to politics. He began in politics when he was barely old enough to vote and legislative politics has been his life's work except for the last four years." Although Laird himself had considered the Pentagon a "political graveyard," Kelly observed that "he probably is coming out with a better reputation than he had expected. Since his resignation was announced . . . editorials in newspapers throughout the country have been almost uniformly complimentary and some have praised him lavishly." So a political future was not unthinkable.[4]

Many reports quoted friends saying that Laird was being urged by Wisconsin Republicans to consider running for governor, senator, or even congressman again from his home state.[5] There was also a spate of stories pushing the proposition that Laird would almost certainly run for the presidency in 1976. "It can be flatly stated that Laird believes Spiro Agnew should not be the next President of the United States after Nixon. Less flatly, it can be said he wants the job," opined the *Chicago Tribune*. David Broder of the *Washington Post* reported that Laird indeed considered himself "and ought to be considered" as a "potential contender" for the presidency. Broder quoted an anonymous Laird "associate" as saying, "Laird may not be well-loved by liberals, but if he goes into the primaries battling Spiro Agnew, it would do wonders for his middle-of-the-road image. And Mel knows the middle of the road is where the payoff is." The *Christian Science Monitor* editorialized that there was no harder job in the federal government than the one Laird had just left, so he would have no trouble being president next. "When Republicans start thinking seriously about their ticket for 1976 they will be thankful for a Melvin Laird in their spectrum."[6] Nixon privately told Ehrlichman that he thought his friend Mel wanted to run for the Senate, having already been in the House.[7] In a November 1972 letter to Laird, Nixon urged him to get back into politics:

> When you told me today that you were "only" fifty years of age I thought back to the fact that I was 50 in 1963 right after I had lost the race for Governor of California and when the odds makers in Las Vegas, not to mention myself, wouldn't have given me a million-to-one shot to come back and be elected President in 1968 and win by an overwhelming landslide in 1972.
>
> You are taking your *sabbatical from political life* at the same age, but you are going out not in defeat but on top . . .

I wish you the best in whatever you undertake in the future. But as I told you in our meeting today, the Defense Department's gain was politics' loss. You are one of the most astute politicians that America has produced in this century . . . a fact that is recognized by most political observers across the country today.

The Nation needs you. After you and your family have a well deserved period of relief from the enormous burdens you have carried over these past four years I hope you will re-enter the political arena. Whatever you decide to do you have my best wishes.[8]

Laird got his short vacation, but no more than that. He would be working in the White House sooner than any prognosticator had forecast. And while there, Laird would find himself in the unique position of being the only man in history to almost single-handedly choose a president of the United States—the only president ever to hold the job without anyone outside his home state electing him to any public office.

$\sim$

The day after Laird left the Pentagon he played golf at Burning Tree Club with Jack Mills. On the second hole, Laird putted to within three feet of the cup. Although it's possible to miss such a short putt, courtesy often induces an opponent to declare it done. But Mills said nothing, and Laird peered up at him. "Is this good?" he asked Mills.

"Would have been good yesterday," Mills said dryly. "Yesterday I would have given you the putt."

"You son of a bitch!" Laird growled as he sank the simple putt.

"Oh, how the mighty hath fallen!" Mills laughed. Courtesy would have demanded he give the defense secretary the putt. "But you don't have to give a three-foot putt to a guy who's not important anymore!"

Mills had not wrung everything he could out of the joke. Back in the clubhouse, Laird held up his finger and beckoned Mills, who was talking to other club members. Loudly, so all could hear, Mills said, "Mr. Secretary, let me tell you something. When you lost your private helicopter and your private plane, and your limousine, you lost all your personality. As far as I'm concerned, I don't want to see you put that finger up again and order me around. You are nobody now."[9]

Laird loved it. He was getting back to the life he once had, and began to enjoy being home without crisis phone calls at all hours of the day and night. In March, the Lairds spent two weeks together on a beach in Mexico. Barbara had prepared a list of 150 books she knew Laird would enjoy now that he had time to read for pleasure. He got a good start on the list in Mexico.

By the time he returned to Wisconsin in late March for a meeting of the Laird Youth Leadership Foundation in Stevens Point, he was tanned, rested and ready—but for what? Local reporters asked about his political future, and he artfully dodged the question. He was also pointedly silent about the news of Watergate that had percolated in his absence. He had been out of touch in Mexico, he demurred.[10]

It is unlikely that Laird, the political animal, had missed anything, even while tanning on that Mexican beach. The scandal called Watergate had begun in June of 1972 with the break-in at the Democratic National Committee headquarters in the Washington, D.C., Watergate Hotel. Seven men were arrested in the act of planting bugs in the office at the behest of Nixon's Committee to Re-elect the President. The news dribbled out at such a slow pace that by election time in November, only the seven hired burglars and their immediate handlers were implicated, leaving the president and the upper echelons of his campaign organization clear of any charges of wrongdoing. It was not a significant campaign issue.

In January 1973, as Nixon prepared for his second inauguration, five of the seven pleaded guilty to burglary and wire-tapping charges. Then the culpability began to spread like a blood stain. The Justice Department charged that Nixon's reelection committee was playing fast and loose with its money, some of which had gotten into the hands of G. Gordon Liddy, one of the remaining defendants who was also the lawyer for Nixon's campaign finance committee. There were implications in the press that some of the money went to the burglars, even after they were arrested, as inducements to take the fall for higher-ups in the campaign organization. Liddy and the other remaining burglar, James McCord, were convicted on January 30. But the president's skirts apparently remained clean.

While Laird was shopping with his mother in Madison in early February, the Senate was voting to start its own Watergate investigation, chaired by the irascible Democrat from North Carolina, Sam Ervin. While Laird was vacationing in Mexico, the Watergate mystery crossed paths with the nomination of Patrick Gray to be Nixon's new FBI director. As acting director of the FBI, Gray had been in charge of a Watergate probe and had fed information about the case to Nixon's White House counsel John Dean. Gray told the Senate committee voting on his confirmation as FBI director that Dean had probably lied to Watergate investigators, but Gray continued to send Dean confidential FBI reports on the investigation. Then Gray clammed up at his confirmation hearing, saying he was under new orders from the attorney general Richard Kleindienst not to talk to Congress about Watergate anymore.

Within a month, Gray's nomination had been withdrawn. Then he resigned as acting FBI director when it was reported that he had burned some FBI files related to Watergate because John Dean told him they "should never see the light of day." On April 30 Dean resigned over the blossoming Watergate affair, along with Kleindienst, Haldeman, and Ehrlichman. Laird's replacement at the Pentagon, Elliot Richardson, was quickly pressed into service to be the new attorney general, confirming Laird's complaint that Richardson never camped very long in any job.

A few days earlier, Laird had been visiting his mother again in Marshfield, still trying to maintain the aura of being on a hiatus as he watched from a distance while the White House crumbled. A local reporter asked him if the rumors were true that Laird would be taking Haldeman's job as chief of staff. "I was drafted four years ago to end our involvement in South Vietnam and to end the draft, and I cannot be drafted again," Laird responded, smiling broadly. "We are now on a basis of all-volunteer service."[11]

Laird had a few more days in late April to pretend Watergate was not his concern. On May 1, he acknowledged that two cabinet members, Secretary of State Rogers and Treasury Secretary Shultz, had asked him if he would consider working at the White House to straighten out the havoc Watergate was wreaking on day-to-day business there. But Laird insisted he wasn't interested. And, he added ominously, if it was discovered that Nixon himself was involved in the scandal, it would be better if the country never found out. "From the standpoint of getting into a trial of the presidency, that would be a terrible mistake," Laird said. "I am confident from knowing the president that he just would not be involved in any way in this kind of operation. If he were, it would be very bad for the country."[12]

At the same time, Laird said he had no plans to get back into politics. He had already secretly accepted an offer from DeWitt Wallace, publisher of the *Readers' Digest*, to join the magazine as a senior counselor for national and international affairs, which meant retiring from public life.

In the game of musical chairs that was to become the *modus operandi* for the Nixon administration's second term, Nixon found a new chief of staff in Alexander Haig, who thus served only four months as Army vice chief of staff. But the domestic policy advisor post remained empty, and Laird began to hear alarming reports from his old friends on Capitol Hill not only that the business of running the country had ground to a halt because of Watergate but also that Nixon had withdrawn into a cocoon. Laird knew that the president needed help but rightly guessed that Nixon didn't necessarily want it from someone as strong-willed as his old defense secretary, so Laird continued to mind his own business.

He was more distressed by the thoughts of a Pentagon adrift without leadership; Richardson was gone after only eighty-seven days, and Bob Froehlke was going through with his long-planned resignation as secretary of the Army. Laird made a call to David Packard to see if he would return as defense secretary. For a few days the offer hung in the balance, then Packard declined, as he did not think it would be possible to work out the same blind trust arrangement that Laird had engineered through the Senate for him in 1968. The president finally settled on CIA director James Schlesinger to take over the Pentagon.[13]

~

Within days of the April 30 resignations of Haldeman and Ehrlichman, House minority leader Gerald Ford and other senior Republicans saw that the White House was floundering. Vital government business was being sidelined as Nixon wallowed in the Watergate morass. At this point everyone knew that something had to be done. They needed to find some old hands the bipartisan leadership could trust and then persuade them to shore up the sinking ship at 1600 Pennsylvania Avenue—and persuade Nixon to accept their help. The first name that came to them was Melvin Laird. The second name was Bryce Harlow, the presidential counselor who had advised both Eisenhower and Nixon.

The party leaders agreed on a full-court press. Harlow made an appointment for them with Laird at his Bethesda house, and they descended on him en masse in early May. The group was led by two Democrats, Senate majority leader Mike Mansfield and House Speaker Carl Albert, who were backed by Senate minority leader Hugh Scott and House minority leader Gerald Ford. Another dozen legislators of both parties, including future Speaker Tip O'Neill and future House minority leader Bob Michel, crowded into Laird's basement for the secret conference.

Their message was stark. The president's domestic agenda was in shambles. No one was putting together the next fiscal year's budget, no legislation was getting through Congress, and the president was incommunicado. Would Laird and Harlow come back to the White House as a team to avert a calamity and get the administration back on track? Ford later remembered, "I made a pitch on a very patriotic level, frankly, that if they didn't do this, it would be a catastrophe for the new administration . . . and that it was in the obvious best interests of the United States." Harlow was willing, but he stated that "Mel was very reluctant to go. He had all these new connections in the outside, nonpolitical world. He wondered if going down there wouldn't aggravate these new business relationships. He wasn't very happy about going down there and working in '*that jungle*,' I think he called it."

Harlow lingered behind after the others left. The two old friends and veterans of many a political battle were both poised on the brink of normal life; Laird had promised Barbara that things were going to be different for them with the appointment at *Readers' Digest*. Harlow was already settling into a job as government liaison for Procter & Gamble. The two men agreed then that they would go either as a team or not at all.[14]

Laird's former aide Bill Baroody and Defense Department general counsel Fred Buzhardt had gone to work at the White House and were enlisted to lean on their former boss to roll his sleeves up and join them. Spiro Agnew also pressured him to accept. As part of the lobbying effort, some friends tried to get Barbara Laird's endorsement. But Laird's wife was unmoved. "She thought President Nixon was lying about the Watergate cover-up, that he was involved," Laird explained. "She thought I should get the hell out of town for a while."

As naive as it sounds with Watergate and Nixon's undisputed culpability being taught in U.S. history books now, Laird believed in May 1973 that the president was innocent. It wasn't that Laird didn't think Nixon capable of deceit; it was simply that Laird thought he had measured the president enough times to know when he was lying. But he had to know for sure, if only to reassure his wife. So when Nixon summoned him and Harlow to Camp David for a face-to-face job tender, Laird was determined to raise the delicate issue as directly as he could.

At one point in the hours-long discussion, Laird approached the question naturally but indirectly at first. "I told him how my wife felt, and then I put it to him: 'Mr. President, did you have anything to do with the break-in or the cover-up?'"

"Absolutely not," Nixon replied.[15]

Laird recalled Nixon was "vehement" in his denial—that he "had nothing to do" with Watergate in any way. "I believed him; I really did."

Eventually, and only after Harlow had signed on, Laird let Nixon know he was willing to be the president's new counselor for domestic affairs. Then he had to tell his wife. Laird met her at Washington National Airport, which he thought was useful as public and neutral ground. Barbara was a Red Cross official heading disaster relief efforts, and she had just been in Mississippi, where tornadoes, accompanied by heavy rains and flash floods, had killed at least forty-seven people in ten states over the Memorial Day holiday weekend.

"I told her I was going over to the White House." Laird said. "She damned near walked away from me; she was really mad. She had loved the Congress, and she never liked Nixon."

Nor was Nixon himself likely any happier that Laird had accepted. He respected Laird enough to run the Pentagon, but didn't trust him with White House secrets, and there were secrets aplenty. Nixon had been talked into hiring Laird by the congressional leadership and by Haig. At one point the secret White House taping system in Nixon's office recorded an exchange between Nixon and Haig on Laird's appointment:

HAIG: "We made a helluva move and I think Laird's gonna be a big asset around
    here. We need—"
NIXON: "Somebody to go out and leak everything."
HAIG: "That's right."
NIXON: "He loves to do that."
HAIG: "That's right." (Laughter)

Haig then reminded Nixon that Laird was a "tough political in-fighter" who would be a "big asset" in their ongoing battle with Congress. In a later interview, Haig remembered lobbying Laird, and the gratitude he felt for Laird's sacrifice in coming to work at the crippled White House. "When I got there, it was no-man's land," Haig recalled. "We had ninety vacancies, including cabinet positions, agency chiefs, independent agency chiefs, assistant secretaries. In all our departments, we had ninety vacancies to fill in an America in which it became almost the kiss of death to join the administration. You had to risk your whole life, your reputation and career. I asked five major financial leaders to be secretary of the treasury, and they all turned me down." Although Haig and Laird had butted heads, Haig knew that Laird was the one Nixon needed to shepherd his domestic legislative package through Congress. "If Mel was any single thing, he was a mirror of the legislature. Mel Laird knew the body from which he came, and in an incredibly astute way," Haig said.[16]

White House chronicler John Osborne of the *New Republic* described the day of the announcement of Laird's appointment—as well as Haig's retirement from the Army for his civilian White House job—as a "weird" one. Without acknowledging the prearranged presence of one hundred reporters and photographers, Nixon, Laird, and Haig stepped out of the Oval Office and into the Rose Garden, smiling and chatting. As if they weren't being watched and photographed, the trio walked the full length of the garden, wheeled around, and walked back into the Oval Office. "On the porch steps, Mr. Nixon reached up and patted General Haig's right shoulder," Osborne wrote in a column. "It was done in total silence. Something about the scene, perhaps nothing more than its staged artificiality, made the watching reporters nervous. One of them said in a shaken tone, 'I guess it's to show that Nixon is up and taking nourishment.' Another said, 'I don't believe it. It didn't happen.' Why we felt that way, I don't know and probably never will."[17]

In a few moments, Laird brought the surreal moment back down to earth when he paid a visit to the White House press room. He was introduced by White House press aide Gerald Warren, who announced that—unlike Ehrlichman, whose job Laird was filling—the former defense secretary would hold cabinet rank and sit in on National Security Council meetings because of his expertise on defense matters. Then, for thirty minutes, Laird answered questions. Osborne thought he looked "distraught and somehow embarrassed" to be there. But a *New York Times* White House correspondent reported that Laird "in his relaxed and easy manner submitted to questions."[18]

Laird was pressed with Watergate-related queries. He said he personally had "great confidence in the president of the United States. I have been assured of his noninvolvement, and I accept that." A reporter followed up: "Did you personally ask the president for his assurance that he was not involved?" Laird confirmed that he had received "personal" assurance of Nixon's innocence.

Laird told the reporters he had accepted the White House job in part because "the government, in some quarters, is at a standstill, and this cannot be allowed to continue." He had been promised twenty-four-hour access to Nixon, but he didn't want the press to get the wrong idea. "I am not much of a night man," he laughed. A reporter asked if he had "any intention of running for office at any future period?" Laird emphatically stated: "No, I do not." But then he added, "I didn't have any intention of coming here," either.[19]

As the tentacles of Watergate reached into the White House, the news media uniformly praised the placement of Laird in the West Wing. But at home, the reaction was not so positive. Barbara made plans to move to North Carolina to be near their daughter in the hope that her husband wouldn't be at the White House more than six months. She didn't believe Nixon was innocent, and she wasn't going to wait any longer for her husband to find out and extricate himself from politics. Laird called the choice to go back to work for Nixon perhaps "the biggest mistake I made. It wasn't good for my relationships with my wife or my family."

⌒

As the incoming secretary of defense in 1969, Laird had known that President Lyndon Johnson had a system for taping phone calls and meetings in the

Oval Office. The system had been operated by the Army Signal Corps from the White House basement, but Laird had ordered all the equipment pulled out. Laird assumed that Nixon had put in another system, without the help of the Defense Department. Toward the end of his term, Laird discovered that Nixon had had the Secret Service install and operate the Oval Office system. Laird was, in fact, never worried about anyone hearing his own voice on the White House tapes that were later released; for the four years that he was in the cabinet, he took it for granted that every conversation he had with Nixon or a White House official was being recorded and might be leaked. "I always assumed that anything I said in any conversation could possibly appear in the *Washington Post* the next day," he said.

Laird also was pretty sure in 1973 that Ehrlichman had done the same with his office. So before Laird moved into that office on June 14, 1973, he ordered an electronic sweep. The federal inspectors discovered two concealed microphones—one of them in the ceiling—which were tied to tape recorders hidden in a cabinet behind Ehrlichman's desk. Laird had them all removed before his first day on the job.[20]

About the same time, Fred Buzhardt, Nixon's lead special counsel, was listening with increasing horror to some of the secret Oval Office recordings from the time of the June 1972 Watergate break-in through the spring of 1973. Because of Fred's particular position, he was the only one allowed past the Secret Service guards and into the basement room in the Executive Office Building where the tapes were kept.[21] A former South Carolina lawyer, Buzhardt had spent eight years as a top aide to Sen. Strom Thurmond before Laird recruited him to be general counsel for the Defense Department. Then on May 10, 1973, Nixon named him as the president's special counsel on Watergate. Immersing himself in the defense of the president, Buzhardt had helped persuade Laird to accept the White House job with assurances that Nixon was innocent.[22]

After a month on the job, Buzhardt found out by listening to the tapes that his client, the president of the United States, was guilty, at a minimum, of criminal obstruction of justice. Buzhardt agonized over the information, which, because of attorney-client privilege he was bound by professional ethics not to share with anyone. He couldn't tell Haig or any of the other White House officials who seemed convinced of Nixon's innocence and were actively defending the president. Buzhardt decided to share the news with the one man he felt he owed more to than the commander in chief—his old boss, Mel Laird.

So it was, in late June or the first week of July, that a distraught Buzhardt dropped by Laird's home late one evening. They went to the basement room for a confidential conference. This is how Laird remembered the conversation:

"I've misled you, Mel," Buzhardt began apologetically. "The president was involved in the cover-up."

"How do you know?" Laird asked.

"I've listened to some of the tapes," Buzhardt responded, "and he was in the cover-up right up to his eyeballs from the beginning."

Laird was dumbstruck. After Buzhardt's visit, Laird brooded through the night on what he had to do. When he was a boy, he had learned a hard lesson about lying. The house rule was that he couldn't have breakfast until he made his bed. One morning he told his mother he had made his bed when he hadn't, and he was severely disciplined for the lie. Even though he had been in politics most of his life, Laird always presumed that those with whom he dealt would tell the truth.

But as a congressman who interrogated witnesses with finesse, Laird had found there were many who would shade the truth to their advantage. While he liked to believe on first meeting that a person would not lie to him, Laird also had a healthy skepticism. In the more than two decades that he had been friends with Nixon, while Nixon may have hedged, dodged, and kept secrets, Laird believed the president had never outright lied to him. The depth of his disappointment with Nixon over the Watergate lie was hard for Laird to discuss, even years later. It was only the second time he felt he had been misled in a major way, the first being Defense Secretary McNamara's account of the August 1964 Gulf of Tonkin incident as a witness before Laird's Defense Appropriations Subcommittee. "Those two lies—Nixon's and McNamara's— were two very big disappointments," Laird said.

The morning after Buzhardt informed Laird of Nixon's guilt, Laird went to the White House determined to confront the president on the matter. He waited all day for the opportune moment. Finally, it came on the walk back to the White House from an early evening meeting with Nixon and others in the president's hideaway office in the Executive Office Building. Laird maneuvered himself into position next to Nixon, out of earshot of others, as they strolled back to the West Wing. "That's when I confronted Nixon," said Laird. "I can remember it as if it were yesterday: I told him that I had been advised that he had not leveled with me on his involvement in the Watergate cover-up, and it was hard for me to stay and work there. I said at the time, 'I would have come here probably anyway, if you'd have told me the truth. I was here to help because my friends on the Hill wanted me to be here to help. But having not been told the truth, it's very hard to help somebody.

I just can't stay.'" Nixon was quiet; his silence confirmed his guilt as far as Laird was concerned. The only response the president finally offered was a single sentence: "Well, I hope you don't leave."

After another night to think it over, Laird notified two friends—Harlow and Buzhardt—that he would be leaving. Both contacted key members of Congress to warn them that it looked like a despondent Laird was going to jump ship. Within two hours, congressional leaders including Jerry Ford were on the phone to Laird. Without divulging what he knew about the tapes from his confidential source, Laird explained to them: "I've got a problem over here, and I told the president it was very difficult for me to work any further for him." Unanimously, they told him that he couldn't leave because the country needed his work on the budget and other legislation that Nixon was neglecting. Reluctantly, Laird was persuaded to stay through the preparation of the 1974 budget.

It wasn't until two weeks after the dramatic Buzhardt revelation to Laird and subsequent confrontation with the president that the American people learned of the existence of Nixon's tapes. On July 16 Alexander Butterfield, a former Haldeman aide, testified before the Watergate committee about the extensive taping system Nixon had used since 1971. For the next year the nation would be embroiled in a constitutional crisis as Nixon resisted congressional and court-ordered demands for access to the tapes. During that time, Laird was one of the few individuals who absolutely knew their release would sink the president.

Laird's knowledge of the president's guilt had "poisoned" their relationship. Nixon had not apologized for his dishonesty; and Laird could not forgive him. A review of Laird's public remarks and press conferences in late July and early August offers hints of what life was like for him as he continued to work for the sake of the country but not for the president. "The longer I'm here, the more the President will like Haig and dislike me," Laird bluntly told a reporter on July 22, in what appeared to be an overt reference to Haig's tendency to kowtow to Nixon.[23] By then, Washington was awash with rumors that Laird, after only a month on the job, was leaving. Probably some inkling of the earlier lobbying by congressional leaders had finally leaked. But it also had become clear that Laird was no longer part of the "inner circle," based on an analysis of the time he was spending with the president versus the amount of time Nixon gave Haig and press secretary Ron Ziegler. So on July 26 Laird called a press conference primarily to deny the rumors that he was leaving. "The word 'quit' is a good word for headline writers, but

I would like to see the word 'stay' used. I am a 'stayer' and I will be staying as long as I can make a contribution," he declared.[24]

Laird wrestled for weeks with his decision. What constituted the greater good? If he left, he could hold his head high, his family would be happy, and he could look forward to less stress with a much larger salary. If he stayed, he risked his reputation and his marriage, and staying would add nothing to his future financial security. On the other hand, he would be performing a public service by steering needed legislation through Congress while others (including the president) were obsessed with Watergate. By August 10 he seemed to have settled the inner conflict. In a Chicago speech before the National Legislative Conference, Laird used words that, between the lines, read like a personal resolution of his private dilemma:

"I have faith in America. I have faith in Americans. I don't believe that we're going to become a nation of quitters and nay-sayers just because we happen to be living—as in the days of Tom Paine—in 'times that try men's souls.'" In the same talk Laird was optimistically prescient: "This is the most exciting time imaginable to be alive and to be active in politics in America," he added. "We are on the brink of something very big and very basic. The faith of the Founding Fathers in the ability of free men to govern themselves is going to be vindicated once again."[25]

～

Laird had an office in the West Wing and was a member of the Nixon cabinet, but that did not make him a member of the president's inner circle. That circle was defined by access. As the besieged Nixon hunkered down in mid-1973, journalists adopted a rule of thumb: Those who spent the most time with Nixon were the most powerful. During Nixon's first term and into his second, it was apparent that he had shown a penchant for operating in a solitary manner. When he reached out, it was no further than to a palace guard of political amateurs. Even as Watergate was unraveling, the distrustful Nixon walled himself off behind protective yes men. In the first term, Nixon had an inner phalanx of three—Haldeman, Ehrlichman, and Kissinger—none of whom had professional political experience. After the first two were fired in April 1973, the new trio in the second term became Haig, Kissinger, and Ron Ziegler—again, none of whom had a professional political background.

From late July on, Laird was pestered repeatedly with questions about his "access" to the president or the lack of it. "I have no problems as far as access is concerned," he said at one press conference. For him, the more time he spent with the president, the less real work he could get done. "I am not going to go to all the social functions in the White House," he added. "The president has told me that I don't have to go to all of them." That was why, he explained, he had declined an invitation to a state dinner for the Shah of Iran and was home mowing his lawn instead.[26]

At another point he affirmed that he visited with Nixon "every day that he is in town, and I am in town." The closest any reporter got to what was really happening was when one journalist on the NBC *Today Show* asked Laird: "Do you have the access to the president you would like to have?"

"Yes, I do," Laird answered.[27]

He could see Nixon any time he wanted to, but he simply didn't want to—for several reasons. One was that the wound of betrayal was too fresh. Another was that Nixon felt Laird had been forced upon him, and their working relationship suffered because of that. Finally, it was a waste of time to visit with the president. "I could go in and see him any damn time I wanted," Laird recalled, "but Nixon really had withdrawn from active participation in anything. I didn't really find out until I got over there that the only thing the president was concerned about was Watergate. Otherwise, he was completely withdrawn. He didn't want to make decisions about anything else, so there was no sense in meeting with him."

One promise Laird had won from Nixon before accepting the White House job was that he would not be required to be involved with Watergate-related problems. Instead, his job was to jump-start stalled domestic projects and legislation, which meant specifically not getting pulled into the Watergate maelstrom. After Laird confronted the president about his culpability and Nixon knew that Laird knew the truth, the president was even more determined to keep Laird out of the Watergate loop. Nixon told Haig on July 12 that regarding participation in any Watergate defense, "you can't get Mel in it at all."[28]

Four days after that Oval Office conversation, on July 16, the world was officially informed via a televised Senate Watergate hearing that Nixon had a collection of secret tapes that might establish his innocence or guilt. Immediately, the Senate Watergate Committee—officially, the Senate Select Committee on Presidential Campaign Activities—demanded Nixon release tapes from June 1972 and other conversations that might have involved Watergate-related discussions. Even though he knew the action might sink the president, Laird privately but strongly urged Nixon: "Release the tapes!" Instead, Nixon denied the committee's request.

Even as the specter of Watergate hovered over the Capitol, Laird plied his agenda through the halls of Congress as if the credibility of the republic was not on trial around him. He spread his message quickly by meeting in the first two weeks with each cabinet secretary. He found them hamstrung by Watergate and unwilling to make decisions. One contemporary column called the cabinet secretaries "obsequious yes men . . . who were turned into limousine puppets by the Ehrlichman-Haldeman White House."[29]

But after Laird's visits, there were almost immediate signs of a reinvigorated cabinet, ready to get their message to Congress. "The heavy hand of the White House was lifted, and we were able to do very much the kinds of things that we thought we should do with very little direction or dictation from the White House," recalled Caspar Weinberger, who was then Secretary of Health, Education, and Welfare. Even after pumping up the cabinet, Laird still saw it primarily as his responsibility to break the logjam of White House domestic bills on Capitol Hill.[30] Sometimes he ruffled cabinet feathers by stepping between other cabinet members and Congress.

One of the most turf-conscious among the second-term cabinet members was George Shultz, secretary of the treasury. He was happy to have a "heavyweight" in the White House, but that didn't mean Shultz enjoyed it when Laird poached upon his territory. Shultz was attending an international trade conference in Tokyo when Laird made front-page news with the announcement that Nixon was "considering" tax changes to curb inflation. A Reuters correspondent caught up with the fuming Shultz who complained: "He [Laird] always gives press conferences on economic subjects when I'm away. . . . I think the President's advisor on domestic affairs can keep his cotton-picking hands off economic policy."

Shultz's deputy, Bill Simon, rushed to the White House to head off reports of internecine domestic policy warfare and to make it clear there was "no disagreement" between his boss and Laird. On the way into the White House, Simon borrowed a pair of white cotton gloves from a Marine guard standing outside and presented them ceremoniously to an amused Laird—a reference to his "cotton-picking hands." When Shultz returned from Tokyo and they met, Laird carefully explained to Shultz that he (Laird) had been working on economic tax policy in Wisconsin "before you were even in government," and he would continue to keep his hands on *every* aspect of domestic policy.[31]

At other times, Shultz was grateful for Laird's legislative meddling on his behalf, including a time when "he traded a body for a vote," as his former Pentagon legislative aide Rady Johnson recalled the tale. In September 1973, Sen. Russell Long asked Laird to help him arrange a burial in Arlington National Cemetery for a friend whose military background didn't meet all the criteria for an Arlington plot. Laird was moved by compassion, and by the fact that Senator Long was pivotal to passing important economic and tax legislation. Laird got President Nixon to sign a waiver allowing the burial.[32]

The Department of Health, Education, and Welfare was also a special interest and focus for Laird because of his prior work in Congress. In the previous two years, Nixon had vetoed three different HEW appropriations bills as being too high. Laird broke that old impasse. He negotiated a compromise that meant HEW—for the first time in three years—could operate on a budget passed by Congress and signed by the president. Laird engineered a similar compromise for the large Defense Department appropriations bill, whose secretary, James Schlesinger, didn't get along well with Congress.[33]

Among the other major bills Laird engineered and steered through Congress were a manpower retraining bill, the creation of the first health maintenance organizations or HMOs, a reorganization of volunteer agencies such as the Peace Corps into a single department, a four-year highway program that allowed localities to use federal funds creatively for developing mass transit systems, and programs needed to meet a growing national energy crisis without resorting to gas rationing.[34]

Laird spent little time discussing these measures with the president. In fact, there were many signatures on presidential documents in those days that Laird later admitted came from Nixon's auto-pen. Sometimes when he was in doubt as to what Nixon might want, Laird asked Vice President Agnew for permission before using the pen. Not once did Nixon overrule Laird on any of his recommendations to sign or veto domestic legislation.

～

Amidst the malaise of Watergate in the summer of 1973, according to Laird, Kissinger was lobbying hard for Nixon to make him secretary of state. Kissinger maintained in his memoirs that he had "not sought Cabinet office," but Laird said that was false modesty. "Henry was always pushing Nixon to become secretary of state. He kept pushing him—pushing him awfully hard." A widespread rumor in July that Secretary Rogers would soon resign brought an angry response from a top "State Department official," according to columnist Joseph Kraft. The official said, "the source of the rumors about Rogers stepping down was Dr. Kissinger. [He further] said that Kissinger wanted the State Department job to get out from under Watergate and did not have the guts to ask the President directly."[35]

In his memoirs, Kissinger said Laird had advised him the previous spring "that my position as [White House] Assistant would soon become untenable. I would be ground down between Congress and the increasingly assertive bureaucracy. I would have to become Secretary of State or resign." In August,

Nixon asked Rogers to resign and finally named Kissinger to the post, a popular move he thought might draw attention away from Watergate. Nixon also
asked Kissinger to continue as National Security Advisor. (The president thus
reneged on his promise to promote Deputy Secretary of State Kenneth Rush
to secretary when Rogers left.)[36]

In the fall of 1973, the White House was the choke point for a series of
foreign policy crises for the new secretary of state. Indochina military issues
had been resolved to a certain extent, but the Middle East was shaping up
to be the next most likely hot spot for a surrogate U.S.-Soviet military clash.
The Arab-Israeli conflict had already spilled over into increasing incidents
of terrorism. In one such incident, a Syrian-operated spy ring tried to mail
letter bombs to Nixon, Laird, and Rogers, but alert Israeli security officials
intercepted them. In another case, Laird personally conveyed a tip from U.S.
intelligence sources that saved Israeli Prime Minister Golda Meir from a
planned car bomb.[37]

Arab provocations and tough Israeli reprisals finally culminated in full-
scale war on October 6, 1973—Yom Kippur, the holiest day of the Jewish cal-
endar. On that day, Egypt and Syria attacked Israel simultaneously on its
northeastern and southwestern borders. Israel had so dominated the Arabs in
previous wars that it came as a shock to its leaders and its American ally that
they desperately needed equipment and ammunition resupply in less than a
week. At first, Kissinger tried to avoid using a U.S. military airlift, for fear of
aggravating the Soviets. Laird jumped in to get a military airlift going. He first
had to overcome Defense Secretary Schlesinger's foot-dragging. Schlesinger
was planning to send only three of the huge new C-5A Galaxy transport
planes, but Laird argued for more and Nixon agreed. So began a thirty-three-
day airlift code-named "Nickle Grass."[38] Kissinger negotiated a cease-fire in
the conflict on October 22.

The United States paid a high price for its lone support of Israel. Before
the cease-fire was in place, several Arab countries, including Saudi Arabia,
instituted a total oil embargo against the United States. As that expanded to
include oil from all Arab countries, America found itself in the midst of
a full-scale energy crisis. Laird oversaw efforts to combat the shortages, including the appointment of an "energy czar" (former Colorado governor
John Love). As November began, Laird urged Americans to turn down their
thermostats and wear sweaters, which became a rich source of editorial car-
toons about Laird, as well as much ribbing from all quarters. ("Where's your
sweater?" Nixon needled Laird in late November as they posed for photographs prior to a televised presidential address on energy conservation.)[39]

As if a war in the Middle East and Watergate were not enough to handle, the news broke that Vice President Agnew had accepted cash bribes of thousands of dollars in unmarked envelopes handed to him in his White House office. The stage was set for a top-level shuffle, and Laird intended to manipulate it his way.

25

Picking a President

PRIOR TO 1973, the vice presidential office had been vacant a total of thirty-seven years in American history. Seven vice presidents had died in office and another had resigned. A few, including Harry Truman and Lyndon Johnson, had succeeded to the presidency upon the death of a president. (Truman was president almost a full term with no vice president.) In all those instances, the Republic survived without vice presidents because the presidents did not die or resign. But practicality compelled Congress in 1967 to ratify the Twenty-fifth Amendment to the Constitution, which provided that the president could appoint a new vice president, subject to approval by a majority of both houses of Congress, without a national election.[1]

When the amendment got its first test in October 1973, the choice should have been Nixon's. In reality, because the president was crippled by the Watergate scandal, the decision came down to the most powerful man in the White House who was still functioning—domestic counselor Melvin Laird.

Spiro Agnew had never been a favorite of Nixon's, and Agnew began to suspect in mid-July that an ongoing secret grand jury investigation into contractor bribes in Baltimore County, Maryland, might just be a White House–instigated effort to get rid of him. Attorney General Elliot Richardson talked with Laird about the seriousness of the evidence being gathered and provided some details about the witnesses and the testimony they were prepared to give at the grand jury. Two key witnesses had admitted they had been paying kickbacks to Agnew for state contracts he had funneled to their companies when he was Baltimore County's chief executive in the mid-1960s. Both said they had delivered payments to Agnew in the White House to settle old debts.[2]

Laird urged Richardson to vigorously continue the investigation regardless of Agnew's high office. Laird's first opportunity to warn members of Congress came on August 4 as he flew to Groton, Connecticut, for the launching of a new nuclear submarine. Ford and Laird sat next to each other on the ride back to Washington aboard an Air Force plane. They conversed about Nixon, the White House, Watergate, and the "rumors" of an Agnew investigation. "You think things are bad now," Laird hinted. "They're going to get worse." "Tell me about it," Ford pressed him.

Laird said that the Agnew matter was serious and that Ford should be careful about aligning himself with Agnew and should "be prepared for some major changes."[3]

Laird felt an Agnew resignation was the best resolution of the crisis, and he made that argument to Attorney General Richardson. Then Laird and Harlow sent an intermediary, Fred Buzhardt, to broach the subject with Agnew, who wanted a guarantee he would not go to jail. "He indicated that if we could get Richardson to agree not to go forward with the prosecution, he would resign," Laird said. "It was somewhat difficult to get Elliot to go along with that sort of an arrangement. But over a period of a couple of days, quite rightly, he saw the merit in the proposal. Some people said it was a mistake not to prosecute him; others said it was the best way to handle it. I feel it was the best way to handle it."[4]

Agnew finally capitulated. On October 10, 1973, he became the first vice president of the United States to resign in disgrace. Minutes after the formal letter was tendered to Kissinger, Agnew pleaded "no contest" in the U.S. District Court in Baltimore to one count of income tax evasion. He was fined $10,000 and given three years' probation.

On the morning after the Agnew resignation, the *Wall Street Journal* placed Laird as the second strongest vice presidential possibility, after John Connally. On all the TV network newscasts, as well as in the *New York Times, Washington Post,* and other newspapers, Laird was listed in the top three or five candidates. None of the pundits had talked to Laird himself, however. He had already decided to mount a campaign to pressure Nixon to select Jerry Ford.[5] Laird felt because Connally had changed parties, his confirmation process would be a partisan bloodbath. More ominously, Laird was looking ahead to possible impeachment and resignation of the president. He felt Ford was the one with enough good will in Congress to ride out the storm, and he had the trust and integrity the nation needed in a crisis.

Bryce Harlow was pushing Laird to seek the position himself, as was a congressional group led by John Byrnes. But Laird never varied, despite the flattering blandishments. He thought he was the only one who could talk Nixon

out of Connally, and he could not do that if Nixon suspected he was promoting himself. Never before had Laird concentrated so intensely on a task,
in part because he knew the time was short. Between the time Agnew resigned
on Wednesday, October 10, 1973, and when the new vice president was announced late Friday, October 12, Laird talked with Nixon almost a dozen
times. In at least two face-to-face meetings, Harlow had accompanied Laird
to provide extra support. In one of those meetings, Nixon firmly told them
that Connally was going to be his choice. (He had already promised the job
to him four days earlier.)

"Mr. President," Laird said firmly, "we cannot get Connally confirmed. It
will be a disaster."

"Well, I disagree with you," the president said. "Connally is the best qualified, and he is my choice."

Laird agreed that Connally was qualified and a capable politician. "I have
nothing against him," he added. "But he has antagonized many Democrats
by converting to the Republican Party, and many Republicans don't really
accept him as a true Republican. They regard him as an opportunist. It would
be a long, hard struggle to confirm Connally."

Harlow added a few carefully chosen words, concurring with Laird's dismal assessment of Connally's confirmation prospects. On a different tack,
he added: "Why don't you look at it from John Connally's perspective? If he
is rejected by Congress in the confirmation process, it would end his political
career."

Laird chimed in again: "We cannot help. It is an impossible assignment to
get Connally confirmed."

Laird had one last gambit left with Nixon, and it was a strong one. "Mr.
President, would you at least talk to the leaders of the Senate and House—
both parties—before you make your decision? We'll get them in here to talk
to you." Nixon agreed.[6] When the members of Congress arrived and were
asked to weigh the choices, their message was unmistakable—Ford was acceptable; Connally was not. Nixon instructed Haig to call Connally and tell him
that it was becoming evident that Ford might have to be the choice in the
interest of a speedy confirmation. Nixon still had made no final decision,
so he was not yet reneging on his commitment, but Connally immediately
conceded.[7]

On the night of October 12, 1973, Jerry and Betty Ford were home watching the television news about 10 p.m. when the phone rang. It was Laird. He
made small talk for a few minutes, a habit that Ford recognized in his old

friend as a prelude to something big. Then Laird got to the point: "Jerry, if you were asked, would you accept the vice presidential nomination?"

This was a very serious matter. "I knew Mel well enough to realize that his question hadn't come just like that," Ford said. "*Someone* had told him to call." So Ford asked for some time to talk with his wife before he would call Laird back with an answer.

Jerry had already promised Betty that he would be finished with politics in January 1977. Since there was little chance as a Republican that he might achieve his ambition to become Speaker of the House, he would not run for congressional reelection in 1976. They debated the pluses and minuses of the vice presidency as opposed to continuing his Republican leadership in the House. In the end, both saw it as a "splendid cap" to Ford's political career. Ford called Laird back before midnight and said: "We've talked about it and agreed that, if I were asked, I'd accept. But I won't do anything to stimulate a campaign. I'm not promoting myself."

"I understand," Laird responded. "I don't know what's going to happen. I just wanted to check. But if the president *does* call, don't hedge! Just say, 'Yes.'" Ford agreed.

Laird called Nixon to relay Ford's willingness but shrewdly emphasized that "Jerry has promised Betty he will get out of politics in January 1977." The point was not lost on Nixon, who now knew he had a vice presidential option who would leave the 1976 Republican field open for Connally.[8]

As Thursday, October 11, dawned, Nixon had sent surveys to about four hundred Republican Party leaders from all over the nation and in Congress asking them for their top picks for vice president. Representative Barber Conable, who was policy chair of the House Republican Research and Policy Committee (and later president of the World Bank), thought Ford was being overlooked in the polling and in the press. "I was concerned that Nixon liked Connally so much," Conable said. So he called Ford's best friend at the White House, Mel Laird. Unaware of Laird's aggressive campaign, Conable said he wanted to sponsor a congressional resolution backing Ford as the best choice and was sure he could get it passed in the House. Laird was aghast. "Barber, I'd appreciate if you didn't do that," Laird quickly responded. "It would be the worst thing we could do during this difficult period over here at the White House because that kind of resolution will get Nixon's back up. He might harden on a Connally choice instead of Ford."

Conable dropped the idea immediately and asked what he could do instead. Laird told him it might be helpful if he got some Democrats in Congress to write Nixon a letter suggesting Ford—but not too many, or the president would get suspicious. Also, make sure Republicans filling out the president's survey rank Ford as their first choice. "Consider it done," Conable said.[9]

～

In one of Laird's meetings with the president on October 12, Nixon asked if he would be interested in the job himself. "Absolutely not." By the end of the day Wednesday, Nixon had hundreds of surveys to consider, and he took them to Camp David. As he tallied the results, according to his memoirs, Nelson Rockefeller and Ronald Reagan were the top choices, but he reckoned either of those two political polar opposites would split the Republican Party.[10] Ford was near the bottom of the list. Nixon returned to the White House by helicopter at 8:30 Friday morning. He told Haig he had decided on Ford and asked him to contact both Ford and Sen. Hugh Scott (a possible candidate because he was Senate minority leader) for a meeting. Laird slipped in to see Nixon in the Oval Office before leaving for a West Virginia engagement because he wanted to make sure Nixon was still leaning to Ford; the president confirmed that Ford was indeed his first choice. Then Nixon summoned Ford to the White House and confirmed that he wanted him for vice president. Nixon asked for assurances that Ford didn't have any political ambitions beyond that because Nixon wanted to leave the field open for Connally in 1976. "That's no problem for me," Ford replied, and the deal was sealed.[11]

The official announcement, broadcast live across the nation, was made by Nixon at 9 p.m. in the White House before an East Room audience of cabinet members, congressional, and other federal leaders. Laird himself was in West Virginia at the Homestead resort speaking at a Business Council dinner at the request of David Packard. But he was pleased at a distance with the conclusion of his production. "*That* was a really successful operation," he said to himself.

In various interviews Laird usually hedged claims of credit for other achievements with extensive qualifiers or a list of others who deserved credit. But, with the single exception of gratitude for Harlow's support as a White House ally, Laird was unequivocal about his historic role in this particular gambit: "I know—as much as I can know anything in politics—that if I had not been in the White House, Jerry Ford would never have been president, because he would never have become vice president first. If I hadn't been at the White House, John Connally would have been selected. I *know* that; he [Ford] knows that." Over the years, a curious Ford listened to every account from every witness he could find in the Nixon White House about how he was selected. He wound up concluding that Laird's claim was true: Laird had been the most responsible. In a 1997 interview he said, "I'm sure Mel was the one who convinced Nixon that I should be the nominee; he was the coalescent who saw all the realities and convinced Nixon."[12]

⁓

Throughout the fall of 1973, Nixon resisted legal efforts by Watergate special prosecutor Archibald Cox to obtain nine Oval Office tapes. On August 29, U.S. District Judge John Sirica ordered the president to release the tapes to him so he could listen and determine whether the claim of executive privilege should prevent the tapes from becoming public. Nixon appealed to the U.S. Court of Appeals, which, on October 12 (the same day Ford was nominated as vice president), upheld Sirica in a 5 to 2 decision. Instead of an immediate appeal to the Supreme Court, Nixon came up with a compromise. He would allow a Democrat, the respected seventy-two-year-old Sen. John Stennis of Mississippi, to listen to the tapes and verify the accuracy of the White House summaries Nixon was willing to release.

With Nixon's concurrence, Attorney General Richardson had named Cox, his former law professor at Harvard, to the special prosecutor post the previous May. The two were old friends, but Cox also skewed toward the Democrats. Nixon felt Cox was out to "get" him. The president told Richardson he would have to fire Cox if he refused to accept the Stennis compromise.[13]

On Friday afternoon, October 19, Richardson privately conferred with Laird and told him he was willing to fire Cox only if Cox proved obdurate. Several hours later, however, as Laird was preparing to go to a charity ball, he was called to the phone and heard an anxious Richardson say that everything had come apart. "When I went back to the Justice Department after I talked with you earlier, there was an outright rebellion among my people over this whole thing," Richardson said wearily. "I've changed my mind. Cox has refused the compromise, and I just can't fire him. I can't do it. I'll have to resign." The conversation was short, and Laird tried to calm Richardson, telling him not to do anything hasty. They would talk the next day, and Bryce Harlow would be with him. Richardson accepted that, then hung up.

Laird went ahead to the charity ball but was interrupted when he was called by Haig to go back to the White House. Once Laird arrived, he found Harlow already there. Haig told them that Nixon was determined to fire Cox, but it would actually be Attorney General Richardson who would do it. Haig asked Laird to call the members of the cabinet to give them advance warning. Laird was in a quandary. He wasn't going to tell Haig about his conversations with Richardson, but he also thought Nixon was fooling himself if he thought

Richardson would fire Cox. "I'll be glad to call them, but I have to know first, are you sure Elliot's on board?" Laird said.

Haig missed the hint that Laird had inside information. Instead, Haig confidently replied "Yes"—Richardson was ready to follow Nixon's orders.

"Well, you'd better call and make sure," Laird advised. Haig agreed, and asked Harlow to do it. "No, I'm not really on board," Richardson cautiously told Harlow. This was news to Haig, who said he would have to talk with the president, and they should wait until the next day to warn cabinet members and others.

Laird went back to the ball. A lot was on his mind, and he decided to confide in a good friend at the table, Fred Vinson, and ask for recommendations to replace Cox. Vinson was a politically connected Washington attorney, a Democrat, and the son of a former chief justice of the Supreme Court. As Laird remembered the conversation, he whispered to Vinson, "I could use your help, Freddy. We have to have a real good Democrat to appoint as the replacement for Cox. Elliot is refusing to fire him and will probably resign. But *someone* in the Justice Department will fire him then, and we'll have to clean up the mess by finding, fast, a very good Democrat to be special prosecutor." Vinson asked for time to think.

"You gotta give me one now, Freddy," Laird pressed.

"Okay, here's the best one: Leon Jaworski," Vinson responded. "I know him well. He's a Democrat and he lives in Houston. He was president of the American Bar Association and has an absolutely flawless reputation. If he would take it, he would be the best." Laird didn't need time to think about it. He knew of Jaworski through one of Laird's uncles, Dick Modrall of Albuquerque, New Mexico, who was a good friend of Jaworski's. *He's perfect,* thought Laird.

The next morning, Saturday, October 20, Laird and Harlow had a private meeting with Richardson, who once again let them know that he would not fire Cox, even if the president ordered it. In the early afternoon, Cox held a news conference that deliberately baited Nixon. Cox said he refused to accept Nixon's idea to have Stennis vouch for the content of the tapes, and was going to pursue his lawsuit for access to them. Shortly after 2 p.m., Nixon transmitted the order through Haig to Richardson to fire Cox. Richardson refused and told Haig he wanted to see the president so he could tender his resignation. Nixon and Haig met with him at 4:30 p.m., but they could not talk Richardson out of resigning. His deputy, William Ruckelshaus, also refused to fire Cox and resigned instead. The third man in the Justice Department line of authority was Solicitor General Robert Bork. Later a controversial Supreme Court nominee, Bork didn't necessarily agree with Nixon's decision to remove Cox, but he felt the president had the authority to order it. So Bork gave Cox his walking papers. A firestorm of criticism erupted, and the event was soon dubbed the "Saturday Night Massacre."

On Sunday morning, NBC news producer Lawrence Spivak knew he had scored a coup for his network talk show, *Meet the Press*. Laird was already scheduled for an appearance, and now they had a white-hot subject to grill him about. That morning also marked the first appearance of a nervous young NBC correspondent named Tom Brokaw. Just before the show began, Brokaw recalled that Spivak told him, "Listen this is going to be the most important program all year, and tradition has it that the NBC correspondent gets to ask the first question, so it better damn well be a good question." As the cameras rolled, Spivak introduced the distinguished guest, and then said: "We will have the first questions now from Tom Brokaw of NBC News." A little nervous, Brokaw began:

"Mr. Laird, let me briefly summarize all that has happened this weekend. The president has ignored an order from the federal Appeals Court; he has fired the special Watergate prosecutor, Archibald Cox; he has accepted the resignation of Attorney General Elliot Richardson, and he has forced the resignation of Deputy Attorney General William Ruckelshaus. In view of all that, don't you expect now that impeachment proceedings against the president will begin in the House of Representatives?"

Laird was too much of a political pro to be caught by Brokaw's question, and immediately deflected it. "First, with all due apologies to you, Tom, I can't accept the premise of your question." He instead repeated Nixon's compromise, which had at its core the respect and trust of Congress for one of its own, the venerable Senator Stennis. But Brokaw didn't let Laird off the hook and continued to question whether having Stennis review the tapes would be enough to satisfy the court. Laird said he was no lawyer and gamely continued to defend the compromise. "I believe that the compromise that has been worked out should have been accepted by the special prosecutor," he added. Congress might see it that way, too, and decide not to initiate impeachment action against the president, he suggested.[14]

Over the weekend, Nixon had confided to Laird that there would be no more special prosecutors; he would dissolve the office, and assign the investigation to Justice Department regulars. But Laird knew the decision could not pass public muster. So, two weeks after his successful "operation" to win Nixon's acceptance of Ford as vice president, Laird felt it was his duty to mount a new campaign for another candidate that required Nixon's appointment—Leon Jaworski as special prosecutor. Toward that end, manna fell from heaven into Laird's lap. He received a call on a Sunday afternoon from a respected Republican congressman from Texas, Bill Archer, one of many of Laird's congressional protégés.

Archer told Laird there was only one candidate to be the new special prosecutor, a friend of his by the name of Leon Jaworski. Laird didn't let on that Jaworski was already his choice. Instead, he listened as Archer made his case: Jaworski was at the sunset of an illustrious career. He had been a prosecutor at the Nazi war crimes trials in Germany. A Democrat, Jaworski became a respected Texas trial lawyer with influential friends including Lyndon Johnson, who had offered him an appointment as attorney general or a seat on the Supreme Court, but Jaworski had turned both down. During the 1972 presidential campaign, he had headed Texas Democrats for Nixon. In spring 1973 Jaworski had been approached by Richardson to be the special prosecutor before Cox was chosen. Jaworski threw cold water on the idea, feeling that there would not be enough independence from the White House to do the job right. The Jaworskis were next-door neighbors to the Archers. "He is the most honorable man I know," Archer averred.

"Then, how could we get him to accept that job now?" Laird asked.

Archer had already sounded Jaworski out and found that he might be willing to accept the position under the right conditions. Archer had appealed to Jaworski's sense of duty, and Jaworski had responded, "I think I may be able to be of service to my country, but I would need to be guaranteed total independence."[15] Laird suggested Archer make two calls to White House officials—Haig and fellow Texan Anne Armstrong, who was at the time a counselor to Nixon. Laird cautioned Archer not to mention Laird's name.

It was at this point, Sunday, October 21, that Laird's campaign for Jaworski kicked into high gear. The plan was to funnel Jaworski's name to Haig from as many sources as possible. Haig, who had important military contacts, was a political neophyte with no civilian network to tap—either for recommendations for a vice president two weeks earlier or a special prosecutor now. In the White House, Haig depended on Laird and Harlow for the highest level political contacts and prodigious Rolodexes. But President Nixon had many political connections, and Laird worked hard to make sure the name he got from them was Jaworski.

At first, Nixon wasn't interested in *anyone* for the office. He tried to stick with his plan of disbanding the special prosecutor's office, but the response to the weekend "massacre" was too withering. In the press and in Congress he was called "reckless," "desperate," "Gestapo," and without "respect for law." By Tuesday there were twenty-one resolutions calling for his impeachment, and six formerly pro-Nixon newspapers had called for his resignation.[16] On November 1 acting Attorney General Bork announced Nixon's nomination of Jaworski as the new special prosecutor. To win Jaworski's assent—as well as head off a congressional move to name a special prosecutor themselves— Nixon promised Jaworski that he could not be fired without the approval of at least six of eight designated congressional leaders.[17]

Because of Jaworski's integrity, and because of Nixon's guilt, the appointment was a serious setback for the president. "Jaworski's political and professional reputation denied the President the chance to portray him as a partisan or ideological enemy. The Texas lawyer had enormous prestige, with currency in a world apart, even alien, from that of Cox," wrote Wisconsin professor Stanley Kutler, a Watergate historian. Jaworski was professionally head and shoulders above Cox. Even though Cox has "always remained the hero to most members of the Watergate Special Prosecution Force and to much of the media," Kutler avowed that it was Jaworski's appointment that "truly was a disaster for Richard Nixon."[18]

~

Four days before the Saturday Night Massacre, Laird had said something that rocked the capital on its heels. At a breakfast meeting with reporters on October 16, Laird confirmed rumors that he had privately advised Nixon that he would face impeachment if he dared to defy any Supreme Court decision to turn over the White House tapes to the Watergate grand jury. That made Laird the first White House official to publicly utter the word "impeachment."[19] Privately, Laird was likely the only White House official hoping that the House of Representatives would begin impeachment proceedings as soon as possible. He had looked down the road and reasoned that impeachment hearings were inevitable, and the sooner they happened, the better for the country. On the basis of cold analysis by Laird, it was better to force the issue at that time, *before* the 1974 congressional elections. This partly explains why it was Laird from within the White House who pushed the president to turn over the tapes, even though Laird had knowledge that they would likely be very damaging. He was ready to sacrifice Nixon for the good of the party.[20]

The pressure for impeachment took a quantum leap following the Saturday Night Massacre. Three days later, Nixon publicly vowed to release the nine subpoenaed tapes. Ten days after the "massacre," the House Judiciary Committee, on a party-line vote, gave itself subpoena power. On November 15 the House of Representatives appropriated $1 million for the Judiciary Committee, chaired by Peter Rodino, to begin the process of impeachment. For any special committee investigation, the most important person is not so much the congressional chair as the chief counsel who stage-manages the investigation. Rodino began his search in earnest on October 22, the first workday after the Saturday Night Massacre. Over the next two months, he screened more than one hundred candidates. Toward the end of that process, he got word from Laird that there was an excellent prospect named John Doar. Rodino had already looked at Doar, but Laird's call let him know that Doar would be accepted by Republicans.

Doar was from a solid Wisconsin Republican family; his father was a law partner with Warren Knowles, a popular governor. Laird was a good friend of the Knowles and Doar families. In 1960, toward the end of the Eisenhower administration, Congressman Laird's recommendation had placed Doar in the Civil Rights Division of the Justice Department. In 1965 Doar was named head of the division. He was on the front lines in the cause of civil rights. He was on hand for most of the key civil rights marches and events of the first half of the 1960s, whether personally marching at Selma, Alabama, riding buses with the freedom riders, or representing the federal legal position on civil rights in Southern courts. Doar was at black student James Meredith's side when Meredith was turned away by the governor at the doors of the University of Mississippi. He was back again in September 1962 when Meredith was finally admitted, which touched off a riot. Doar slept in Meredith's dormitory room that night to give him official protection. In 1963 Doar's presence and reputation prevented a riot in Jackson, Mississippi, after the head of that state's NAACP, Medgar Evers, was assassinated. Five thousand black mourners came to the funeral and were confronted at one point by two solid lines of police. Some of the angry mourners started throwing bottles at the police. Doar stepped between the two camps and shouted: "My name is Doar, D-O-A-R. I'm from the Justice Department and anybody around here knows I stand for what is right." He then circulated through the crowd, helping to quell the threat of violence.

When Doar left the Justice Department in 1967, Laird tried to talk him into running for Congress or some state position in Wisconsin. But by then, Doar was a committed apostle of civil rights, and he decided to head up Bobby Kennedy's self-help organization, the Bedford-Stuyvesant Development and Services Corporation. Nobody could accuse the Democrat Rodino of partisanship if his chief counsel was Doar. On December 20 Rodino announced his choice for chief counsel, and Doar was introduced to a national television audience.

~

When he first agreed to accept the domestic counselor position, Laird had pledged to Nixon that he would stay "six months to a year" and no longer. That disinterest in keeping the job imbued Laird with a special authority. But there was much that he could not control; the situation at the White House was deteriorating rapidly. Around the time Jaworski was chosen as special prosecutor, Buzhardt appeared in court and revealed that two of the nine subpoenaed tapes no longer existed. The "missing tapes" revelation, on top of the Saturday Night Massacre, prompted the *New York Times* to editorialize for the first time that Nixon should resign. In its first editorial in fifty years, *Time* magazine also called for Nixon's resignation. Sen. Edward Brooke of Massachusetts became the first Republican in Congress to publicly urge Nixon to step down. Then, on November 21, Buzhardt disclosed to Judge Sirica that one of the subpoenaed tapes had been partially erased—a tape that recorded conversations three days after the Watergate break-in, and the first workday on which Nixon had the opportunity for discussions with Haldeman, Ehrlichman, and others in the Oval Office.

Buzhardt explained that, as near as could be determined, the president's secretary, Rose Mary Woods, had "accidentally" erased it. On the day she was transcribing that tape, she got a phone call and left the recorder running while "accidentally" hitting the "record" button. She testified that action only accounted for "four or five minutes" of the eighteen-and-a-half-minute erasure, because she had not been on the phone that long. Just who caused the infamous gap will probably remain Watergate's lingering mystery. A panel of experts chosen by Jaworski and the White House unanimously concluded it was no "accident." Watergate investigators tended to believe that either Woods or Nixon himself had done it, although his defenders maintained the president was too mechanically inept to erase the tape. Nixon pointed the finger at others, including his own lawyer, Buzhardt."[21]

None of those disclosures helped Laird do his job as domestic counselor. Because he had always been straight with the press, he naturally was pummeled with questions about Watergate when he gave interviews on the defense appropriations bill or other domestic issues. Asking him a question about the scandal risked getting a "filibuster in response," *Newsday*'s Martin Schram wrote. When Laird was asked about a brewing influence-peddling scandal involving the nation's milk producers, his response dwelled "on the modern economic history of cheese producers in Laird's home state, Wisconsin."[22]

When Laird met with a group of reporters gathered by Sarah McClendon in the White House's Roosevelt Room on the morning of November 29, the first questions were about whether the erased tape had hurt Nixon's public relations efforts with Republican members of Congress. Laird responded directly: "Yes, it has hurt; it has not helped." But he explained that he had always been an accurate vote-counter in the House and, based on his survey the previous day, there would currently be "a substantial vote" *against* impeachment.

Then Laird told the reporters that as soon as Ford's nomination for vice president was confirmed by Congress, Laird would leave the White House. Until Ford came along, Laird was considered the only White House official with enough influence in Congress to push through the president's legislative agenda and budget. As Laird explained it: "I think the work I am doing and my responsibilities can be better done by Jerry Ford as vice president than by me."[23] Laird was heavily lobbying his former colleagues in Congress to speed up the Ford confirmation process. His anxiety had much to do with his knowledge from Buzhardt that release of the tapes would prove Nixon was guilty.

The Senate finally confirmed Ford on November 27, by a 92 to 3 vote. The House followed on December 6 with a 387 to 35 vote. Laird was invited to be present as Ford was sworn in that same day in the House chamber, the site of so many years of Ford-Laird service as Republican leaders. Included in the media's speculation that day was that if and when Ford needed his own vice president, it would be his loyal friend Melvin Laird.[24]

On the same day as Ford was confirmed, Laird gave written notice to Nixon that he would be resigning at the end of the year—only a month away. At first, Nixon refused to accept it. He told Laird he didn't think Ford could do everything that Laird had been doing. Laird maintained that Ford was "eminently qualified," but that Nixon would need to give him extended authority as vice president to do it; a domestic counselor would not be necessary. Nixon finally agreed, but with one stipulation: Laird must not leave until the end of January—after he had helped prepare the 1974 State of the Union message and the budget. "I will be pleased to postpone my departure from the White House staff for thirty days in order to help," Laird wrote in a formal December 17 letter of resignation that he presented to Nixon in an hour-long Oval Office meeting that afternoon.[25]

Two days later, a press conference was held to announce that the president had accepted Laird's resignation, effective February 1, 1974, as well as to report Laird's new job as senior counselor for national and international affairs for *Reader's Digest*. After three decades of public service, Laird told the assembled journalists: "I would like to encourage people that are interested in seeking a very rewarding career to not turn aside from politics." One definition called politics "the art and science of government," Laird continued, and he strongly felt that, just as other scientists have done much for "the well-being of people through their work, [so] I think the science of politics is very rewarding." Considering the friends he had made and the good they had done together, "political service has been very rewarding to me," Laird continued. "I have been treated very well as a politician."

What made news from the press conference was Laird's unusual encouragement of the House Judiciary Committee to undertake its constitutional obligation of considering impeachment of the president. But he urged that a House vote on impeachment be taken no later than March 15. "I think a vote would be healthy and I do not believe it would serve this country well to postpone that vote just to have it closer to the 1974 congressional election," he said cautiously. Laird was demonstrating his independence to the end, as well as highlighting some of his differences with the president.[26]

At that juncture, however, Nixon wasn't taking offense at anything Laird said or did. The president who had yanked Laird from a comfortable seat in Congress; who had lied to him about Watergate; who had shut him out of the Oval Office; and who had failed to heed his advice, now sent Laird a kind letter. "More than anything else, I have valued your loyal friendship during this difficult period. It has been a constant source of reassurance to me and words cannot adequately convey how much I appreciated your steadfastness."[27]

The news of Laird's resignation plans was received with editorial lament. For the second time in less than a year, newspapers across the country mourned the passing of Melvin Laird from government. Laird himself wasted no time grieving. He had accomplished the domestic agenda he set for himself and had served without compromise under a president whom he no longer respected. The one thing Laird could not do was to get Nixon to listen to his advice on healing the wounds created by Watergate and reestablishing a relationship with his party and with Congress. But Laird felt confident that he was leaving that job in the capable hands of Gerald Ford.

26

Kitchen Cabinet

The last thing Laird expected a year after American soldiers and POWs came home from Vietnam was an antiwar demonstration. Yet there it was, as he arrived at Providence College on January 27, 1974, one year and a day after the peace agreement had been signed in Paris. When Laird's friend John Fogarty had died in 1967, the family had set up a foundation to honor those who made significant contributions to the field of mental retardation. Laird considered his work on health issues with Fogarty in Congress to be one of his finest contributions as a politician. When Laird was chosen to receive the foundation's 1974 award, Jerry Ford offered him a ride on Air Force Two to the college in Rhode Island—and to have the new vice president personally present the award.

As Ford and Laird stepped out of their limousine at the campus, their ears were assaulted with shouts from about 150 protestors : "Humanitarian we say no, Melvin Laird has to go!" "Melvin Laird, you can't hide, we charge you with genocide!" "Ford, Laird, better start shakin', today's pigs are tomorrow's bacon!" The demonstrators also burned an effigy of Laird.[1] He was unflustered, but the irony was not lost on him. He felt he had been as much responsible for "peace" in Vietnam as Kissinger. Yet Kissinger received the Nobel Peace Prize, and Laird was still having eggs thrown at him.

What irked Laird the most was not lack of credit for helping to achieve "peace," but the propensity of Nixon and Kissinger to characterize the Paris accord in any form as "peace." Laird never saw it as peace, only as turning the war over to an improved South Vietnamese military. Two weeks before the Paris accord was signed, Laird had confided to his senior staff: "I am concerned that many people will be carried away with any agreement and oversell it. The war may quiet down a bit for a few months, but it will resume.

The more any accord is sold as a peace agreement, the more difficult it will be to get the U.S. support needed to help the South Vietnamese repel further attacks."[2] Throughout 1973, Nixon and Kissinger had left the American public with the impression that peace had been achieved.

In his last month as presidential counselor, Laird vented some of his frustration with the overblown peace rhetoric. Without naming either the president or Kissinger, he gave several interviews in January 1974 disparaging their persistent pronouncements of peace, and noting that about sixty thousand North and South Vietnamese had been killed since the declaration of "peace." "The war in Southeast Asia has gone on for thirty years and will go on, perhaps, for another twenty years," Laird predicted. When he referred to the Paris accords, Laird said he "always talked about *United States involvement* . . . I never thought [it] would bring peace, and I never sold it as a peace program."[3]

Private life gave Laird more freedom to speak his mind publicly, and he did so January 29 at his last press conference before leaving the White House. After making several candid comments about Nixon administration missteps, Laird waved off other probing questions with the remark that he was about to be one of the media, and he needed to save some of his choice editorial observations for publication in *Reader's Digest,* his new employer. When the press conference was over, and a few exclusive interviews had been given to favorite journalists, Laird had effectively unloaded on Nixon for failure to clear up the Watergate mess, on Kissinger for his handling of NATO allies, and on new Defense Secretary Schlesinger for changing the U.S. nuclear weapons strategy. He publicly advised Ford not to get involved with Nixon's Watergate defense. He also spelled out, in stark relief, his differences with Nixon on the subject of amnesty for draft resisters who were in prison or exile. Nixon was adamantly against amnesty but Laird saw shades of gray in the argument. In 1972 he had directed Secretary of the Army Froehlke to secretly work out a postwar amnesty plan.[4] Both Froehlke and Laird acknowledged the existence of that plan when they were out of office.[5]

Nixon did not let Laird's parting criticism cloud his view of the personal and political debt he and the country owed Laird. At a White House dinner in Laird's honor on March 26, Nixon presented him with the Medal of Freedom, the nation's highest civilian honor. Any evidence of a rift between the two was put aside as Nixon hosted the East Room gala attended by more than one hundred government and military luminaries as well as Laird friends and family. "Few men have served America better," Nixon said. Laird was effusive in return: "No other President could have given a Secretary of Defense any stronger support than you gave me."[6]

As the Watergate investigation proceeded, admiration for the president was in short supply, especially in the office of the Watergate prosecutor. Nixon had been led to believe by Laird and John Connally that Leon Jaworski would be far more favorable to the president's interests than Archibald Cox had been. Laird's primary belief, however, was that Jaworski would impartially weigh the merits of the prosecution. Jaworski had come to the job as a Nixon admirer, but that admiration had evaporated as he listened to the White House tapes.[7]

On April 11 John Doar secured a 33 to 3 House Judiciary Committee vote to send subpoenas to the White House demanding the tapes and related documents. Nixon agreed to turn over some heavily edited transcripts, and even those contained explosive revelations. For many Americans, the most interesting of those revelations was the president's salty vocabulary. (So much of the language was edited out that the transcripts became famous for bringing the words "expletive deleted" into the American lexicon.)[8] The House Committee was not satisfied, nor was Jaworski; both demanded more complete transcripts. By mid-July, even the chief of the White House military office, Bill Gulley, could see that the president knew he was doomed. He recorded that three signs of Nixon's imminent demise were: (1) Kissinger was beginning to speak in the singular form, abandoning the "we" that previously included Nixon; (2) Haig granted more White House perks to Vice President Ford; and (3) Laird was a more frequent visitor to the White House and was telling journalists that Nixon couldn't hold on much longer.[9]

In mid-February Laird began urging Ford to think about who he would want in his cabinet. For a month, the vice president demurred. Behind the scenes, Laird had already become part of an informal group of Ford friends plotting the presidential transition. By July he was inundated with phone calls from Nixon cabinet secretaries who wanted to know what Ford thought of them. Laird told each person what he could about what might happen in a transition, but publicly Laird continued to maintain that the House would not impeach Nixon, and Nixon would not resign.

All that changed overnight on July 24 when the Supreme Court unanimously ruled that Nixon must turn over all subpoenaed tapes. Nixon knew that on one of those tapes, he had incontrovertibly schemed to thwart an FBI investigation by falsely claiming that the CIA had national security concerns. Once Nixon relinquished the tape, he suspected impeachment in the House of Representatives was a sure thing.[10] The same day as the historic Supreme Court ruling, the House Judiciary Committee began its impeachment hearings. By July 30 they had passed three articles of impeachment regarding obstruction of justice and abuse of power. The articles were forwarded to the full House for a vote. By that time, Jaworski had secured a sealed judgment from the Watergate grand jury that Nixon was considered an "unindicted co-conspirator" in the various Watergate-related crimes.

At 11:30 a.m. on August 7, 1974, four men bowed their heads in prayer in the office of House minority leader John Rhodes. It was the regular Wednesday morning prayer meeting for this group, which had first come together for spiritual fellowship in the 1960s when they all served in Congress together. Rhodes was there, along with Minnesota congressman Albert Quie, Vice President Ford, and Laird. As was their habit, they each took a turn saying a prayer and then recited the Lord's Prayer together. They didn't mention the president's troubles. Quie remembered that toward the end of the prayers, Rhodes's secretary came into the room and said, "I know I'm never supposed to interrupt this meeting, but considering the circumstances I think I should. The White House just called and said Jerry Ford should come down to the White House right away." No one needed to ask why.

Quie had one question for Ford: "Just before you leave, Jerry, you always have said you never wore your religion on your sleeve. But what if, when you have a press conference, somebody should ask you, 'Where were you and what were you doing when you found out that you were going to be the president?'"

"Nobody's going to say that," said Ford over his shoulder as he left the office. "Well, on the way down there, think about it," Quie called after him.[11]

Ford went to the White House for a meeting with Nixon, who said he was close to making a decision about resigning. For his part, Laird could take satisfaction from having saved the nation from one additional trauma. While Nixon was pondering resignation, John Connally, the man Laird talked Nixon out of choosing as his vice president, became embroiled in a bribery scandal. In August 1974 the nation's largest dairy cooperative pleaded guilty to bribing Connally to increase federal milk supports when he was treasury secretary. Connally himself was indicted on two counts of accepting an illegal payment, one count of conspiracy to commit perjury and two counts of making a false statement to a grand jury. (He later was found not guilty on the bribery charges, and the other counts were dropped.)[12]

On Thursday evening, August 8, Nixon announced over national television at 9 p.m. that he would resign on the following day, at noon. He was the first U.S. president ever to do so. Nixon was neither contrite or apologetic; instead he suggested that he was only resigning because his congressional support had abandoned him. At 12:03 p.m. the next day, in the East Room of the White House, with Laird looking on, Ford was sworn in by Chief Justice Warren

Burger as the thirty-eighth U.S. president—the only unelected chief executive in American history.

A few days later Ford, having not yet moved into the White House, gave a small party at his modest home in Alexandria, Virginia. Present were the Fords, their four children, and a few intimate friends, including Mel and Barbara Laird. "Some of us sat on the floor of the small living room and Betty served snacks as we talked," Laird recalled. "Having taken off his coat and tie, Jerry helped in the kitchen and made sure everyone felt at home. He paid as much attention to the opinions of his children as those voiced by his friends. His questions showed me, and them, just how intently he was listening. I had seen Jerry in his shirt sleeves listening to others countless times. Now I realized I was no longer looking at Jerry but at the President." Sitting cross-legged on the floor, Laird smiled and savored the moment.[13]

~

The man at the top of Ford's list for vice president was Melvin Laird. As the old friends had played a round of golf in the summer of 1974, Ford confided to Laird that he wanted to name Laird as his vice presidential successor if Nixon resigned. "That's a terrible idea," Laird laughed. "I'm from Wisconsin and you're from Michigan. We're too close to each other. You'll need someone who's not from the Midwest to balance the ticket in 1976 when you run for reelection."

"Now, Mel," Ford responded, "you know I've promised Betty—and the Congress—that I will not be a presidential candidate in 1976, no matter what happens with President Nixon."

Laird paused at the hole they were playing on the Burning Tree Club course. Then he looked Ford squarely in the eye: "Jerry, if you do become president this year, you *can't* rule out running in 1976. If you do, you'll be a lame duck from the minute you take the oath, and you won't be able to get anything done!"

Ford was taken aback by Laird's vehemence, but finally smiled. "Okay, Mel," he said, noncommittally, to end the conversation.

Laird's best defense against a job offer he didn't want was the one he had often used in the past—to come up with someone he could argue was a better candidate, in this case Nelson Rockefeller. The conservative wing of the Republican party did not like Rockefeller's "liberalism," but Laird appreciated his breadth and depth of knowledge and ideas. So well known was Laird's affinity for Rocky that it was rumored in early 1974 that he would be campaign manager for Rockefeller's 1976 presidential bid. Rockefeller, however, was suspicious of Laird's motives. When word spread among insiders that

Laird was thinking about backing Rockefeller for vice president, he and some of his aides were convinced Laird had floated the name to create a firestorm of conservative protest, forcing Ford to reach for the best compromise candidate—Laird himself. "Mel has many friends . . . *all wary*," groused one Rockefeller aide to the *Wall Street Journal*, which added that Laird could be characterized as "a man whose playful deviousness is his most enduring feature . . . a kind of unguided missile within the Washington establishment, leaving intrigues, strategies and inside information in his wake."[14] This time, however, there was no hidden agenda.

After Ford became president, he told Congress he would announce his vice presidential choice in about ten days. Just as Nixon had done, he requested that Republican leaders submit suggestions. On the next Sunday, he scheduled meetings with a dozen close friends to hear their advice; first up would be Laird and Bryce Harlow. Before mounting a full-court press for his candidate, Laird had wanted a firm commitment from Rockefeller, who was notorious for vacillating on political opportunities. Laird reached him on Saturday, August 10, at his summer home in Seal Harbor, Maine. "I have recommended to the president that *you* should be the vice president," Laird informed him.

"No, Mel, *you* are the man who ought to be the one," responded Rockefeller, still wary that he was being set up. Laird immediately parried the suggestion with the same arguments he had made to Ford more than once, the most important of which was that he really didn't want the job. Then he continued with his pitch: "Now, Rocky, I want to make sure you're on board with this thing because I'm not going to go to a lot of trouble and find out that you're going to play games."

Rockefeller took a breath. At the age of sixty-six, after several failed presidential bids, he was ready and very much willing to become vice president. So he responded, "Mel, I'm not playing any games. I'll do it; I *want* to do it."

"That's all I want to know," Laird said.[15]

The next day Ford asked Laird once again if he would consider being vice president. And once again Laird declined, and made another pitch for Rockefeller. Until the president named his choice, Laird was consistently named in the press as high on the "A list" of possibilities. (One political cartoonist whimsically assembled the ideal vice president for Ford by cutting out parts of each of the potential candidates; Laird's donation was his brain.)

When Ford golfed with Laird at Burning Tree again on Sunday, August 18, Laird raised the subject, and Ford confided that he had already decided on Rockefeller. President Ford announced his choice on August 20, and the decision was hailed by opinion makers in politics and the media. The following day, the president authorized his spokesperson to announce that Ford would "probably" run for the presidency in 1976.

~

On the day he became president, Ford's immediate choice to head a rapid transition team was Donald Rumsfeld, then the U.S. ambassador to NATO. The team completed its work in two weeks, and Rumsfeld returned to Europe. But in late September, he was asked to be Ford's chief of staff, and he quickly drafted as his deputy Richard Cheney, a former subordinate and Laird protégé.

One of Rumsfeld's most insistent suggestions to Ford in his first week on the job was that, since he was going to keep a majority of the Nixon cabinet in place, he also needed a group of trusted outside advisors. The use of "wise men" from outside government had been a hallmark of the Roosevelt, Truman, Eisenhower, and Kennedy administrations. Rumsfeld explained the advantages: "People are generally reluctant to tell a president what they think. As chief of staff, they'd come to me and say, 'Oh my God, President Ford is messing up this or that. I've gotta see him.' Fine, I'd say, and take him in. As soon as he walks in, the guy kisses the president's ring, slobbers all over his hand, tells him how wonderful he is and then comes out and says: 'Well, I really told him!' So I felt Ford needed guys who knew him so dad-burned well that they would tell him what they thought—with the bark off."[16]

The group informally advising Ford came to be known as another "kitchen cabinet." While as many as a dozen names were included in various listings of the kitchen cabinet, Ford identified in his memoirs a core group of six— Laird, Harlow, former congressman John Byrnes of Wisconsin, David Packard, former Pennsylvania governor William Scranton, and William Whyte, vice president of U.S. Steel. The shadow cabinet met with Ford at least once a month. The group's primary function was to tell Ford the unvarnished truth, a job which, Cheney recalled, Laird excelled at.[17]

Aside from the kitchen cabinet and the frequent private meetings and phone calls, there were many other opportunities for Laird to associate with his political and social friend of two decades. The prayer meetings continued, although not weekly. About once a month the group would gather at the White House to pray with Ford. Both Ford and Laird kept their membership in the Chowder and Marching Club, too. And in the informality of that setting, the new president occasionally took a beating. Former congressman Clarence "Bud" Brown of Ohio remembered one session where the society members aired their complaints about Kissinger and implied that he was running roughshod over the president. Brown recalled that Ford followed him out of the meeting and gave him an order: "'Bud, you get back and tell those so-and-sos that I AM the president of the United States, in spite of the way they treated me at this meeting. I DO make policy."[18]

Laird also golfed almost every weekend with Ford at Burning Tree, something the friends had started doing together in the early 1950s when they were seatmates on the House Defense Appropriations Subcommittee. Two earlier presidents, Nixon and Eisenhower, had moved their lockers upstairs to a special private room dubbed "Fairyland" by the members, but Ford kept his regular locker. Jack Mills recalled that Ford was changing clothes there one day when the locker-room phone near him rang. "It kept ringing, so President Ford picked it up and said, 'Burning Tree.'" The caller was looking for another club member who was in the card room. Ford, who happened to be naked, told the caller to hold on for a minute. "He's bare ass, except for a towel around his hips, and he pokes his head in the card room and says, 'You've got a phone call.' That's what kind of guy Jerry was," recounted Mills. He answered the telephone and went into the card room without any clothes on. Nixon never would have done that."[19]

Laird's influence on Ford was so pervasive that he was profiled as "The Man of the Ear" by *New York* magazine in September 1974. The cover featured a caricature of Laird whispering into the enormous left ear of a befuddled-looking Ford. The article, written by friends of both men, Rowland Evans and Robert Novak, stated that Laird's prominence as an advisor was a good thing: "In an age of specialization, he is the political Renaissance Man, whose flexibility and adaptability vividly clash with the self-destructive stolidity typifying the Republican party's congressional wing. What may obstruct Ford from fully partaking of this cornucopia of good sense is the highly unusual manner of doing business, often bordering on the obstreperous or even obnoxious, that has made Laird something less than the most beloved man in Washington. . . . Laird is that rare figure who has made his way in this town by force of will and knowledge, not amiability."[20]

~

While Laird was still in the Nixon White House as domestic counselor, he had talked to Vice President Ford about a conditional amnesty for draft evaders. With Ford as president, Laird was convinced that conditional amnesty would be an ideal program for Ford to announce early in his administration. Prodded by Laird, Ford raised the idea of amnesty with Secretary of Defense James Schlesinger, who expressed his approval. Ford chose a speech before the Veterans of Foreign Wars in Chicago on August 19 as the venue to announce his plans for something he called "earned reentry" for draft evaders.[21]

It was a fair plan that won praise from most quarters, but the warm feelings Ford earned quickly faded in September with the single act of clemency he granted to a lone exile in California—the ill-timed pardon of Richard Nixon.

If Ford had been a complex man like Nixon, commentators might have thought the pardon reflected a deep-seated desire for self-destruction. But Jerry Ford was not a man full of such deep crosscurrents; he was not a layered thinker. He lacked the strategic political view that Laird had in abundance and simply failed to foresee the folly of issuing a pardon to Nixon so soon. Laird could have provided him with that foresight, but Ford did not ask, nor did he even inform Laird before he made the pardon public on national television. The reasons he did not confide in Laird can be deduced from Ford's autobiography and knowledge of both men. First, Ford was worried that his decision might be leaked in advance of his announcement. If Laird had received early warning, he might have instigated a media and congressional backlash to stop Ford. Also, the new president knew that Laird was quite capable of talking him out of the precipitous action—and Ford didn't want to be talked out of it.

During the first two weeks of Ford's presidency, Laird had learned that Haig and Kissinger were planning to lobby Ford for a swift pardon of their old boss. Laird never felt that pardoning Nixon was wrong, but in politics timing is everything, and the time for a pardon was months away. So Laird called Phil Buchen, who was then acting as Ford's White House counsel, and said, "Now is not the time for this." Buchen agreed.[22]

During those same two weeks, Laird also talked briefly with Ford about the possibility of a pardon, only to find the new president wasn't interested in discussing it. Laird advised him that if he did plan to pardon Nixon at some point, it was best if it looked like the idea came from Congress. Laird had already put out some feelers; he was convinced that he could line up an impressive coterie of House and Senate leaders to take credit for it. Ford gave Laird the impression that the prospect of a presidential pardon in the near future was nonexistent. Then Ford underwent an unexpected turnaround on the subject almost as a knee-jerk reaction to his first press conference on August 28.

The first question came from UPI White House correspondent Helen Thomas who asked if Ford would pardon Nixon. Ford tried to dodge the question, but as reporters pressed him, he acknowledged that he was not "ruling out" the pardon option.[23] Ford was furious as he walked back to the Oval Office from the press conference. In an interview years later, Ford recalled what was going through his head. "Goddamn it! I am not going to put up with this. Every press conference from now on [will] degenerate into a Q&A on: 'Am I going to pardon Mr. Nixon?' . . . I had to get the monkey off my back."[24]

Laird was wholly in agreement with Ford's primary reason for granting a pardon: the need to move beyond Watergate as quickly as possible. But Ford's method and timing were all wrong. Laird was a great believer in allies and coalitions. "I was convinced that I could get thirty of the top people in the Congress to visit with Ford and urge him to pardon Nixon for the good of the country," Laird explained later. There is little reason to doubt that Laird could have accomplished the feat, but only after the November 1974 congressional elections. Before that time, both parties would be posturing for maximum political advantage. During the Thanksgiving and Christmas holiday season, after the election, was the ideal time for a pardon.

Ten days after the pivotal press conference, on Saturday, September 7, Ford and Laird were partners in a two-day golf tournament at Burning Tree. Ford was in a good mood and invited Laird to join him at an afternoon crab fest he was hosting for Soviet cosmonauts. Laird declined the invitation. Ford never told Laird that he had more planned for the weekend than a crab fest. He was going to pardon Nixon.

On Sunday morning, before resuming the golf tournament with Ford, Laird gave a speech to an association of women journalists at the Kennedy Center for the Performing Arts. As he was leaving, one of the women approached him with the news: "Ford has pardoned Nixon." He had gone on television that morning and granted a "full, free and absolute pardon . . . for all offenses against the United States." A stunned Laird managed to express his agreement with the decision to the reporter and then headed for Burning Tree to finish the golf tournament.

The two partners met on the first tee; Laird was uncharacteristically quiet. Ford broke the silence and said, as Laird recalled the conversation, "Mel, I went ahead and did it. I just wanted to get it out of the way. I signed the papers this morning. What did you think of that?"

"Mr. President," said Laird, "we're on the first tee. We can win this tournament. We'll talk about that after our golf game, not now." They lost the tournament by two strokes. Afterwards, Laird gave Ford an earful about what should have been done and just how costly his lone decision was going to be. Ford was taken aback. "Mel's reaction was a harbinger of the public outcry that was developing," Ford recalled in his memoirs. Laird pitched in quickly to try to get as many statements of support as he could, but it was too little too late.[25]

Instead of administering a healing balm, Ford had poured salt into the Watergate wounds. Many Americans were outraged by what appeared to be a sense of dual justice—Nixon free and his aides facing prison. Others were angered at the hypocrisy of offering draft evaders a "conditional" amnesty while Nixon was forgiven outright. Republican congressional leaders were privately aghast that Ford would expose his own party to criticism just eight weeks before the election in which every House seat and a third of the Senate seats were being contested. (Republicans lost forty House seats and four Senate seats, disproving Ford's rationale that his pardon would make it easier for him to govern.) His popularity dropped twenty-one points overnight. "The President's going to have to be unpopular for a while," Laird flatly told the *New York Times*.[26]

A final irony of Ford's mortal mistake was that if he had waited just a few weeks a pardon would not have been necessary; Watergate Special Prosecutor Leon Jaworski had already decided not to indict Richard Nixon for any crime. This was something Jaworski did not admit even in his 1976 best seller, *The Right and the Power*. In the memoir, Jaworski details his disgust with Nixon and his belief that Nixon had committed a series of crimes. "I had no doubt but that the grand jury wanted to indict him," Jaworski wrote. "But to be valid, an indictment required the signature of the Special Prosecutor so, in the last analysis, the decision of whether to indict the President was my responsibility." Jaworski never publicly admitted that he was on the verge of recommending that the grand jury not indict Nixon when Ford's pardon preempted him.

He did, however, tell the two men most responsible for his appointment as special prosecutor—Laird and Rep. William Archer. In a 2000 interview conducted simultaneously with both men, the secret came out. Discussing how the two had engineered Jaworski's selection, Laird lamented to Archer that Nixon never understood how principled Jaworski was, and how that would have benefited Nixon in the end. Both men said Jaworski had confided separately to them that he was ready to recommend against an indictment. Jaworski had personally concluded that while Nixon deserved censure by Congress, he should not have been removed from office.[27]

        ~

Despite the enduring friendship of Ford and Laird, there was one thing that Laird could not forgive—the abandonment of South Vietnam during the Ford administration, more than two years after the withdrawal of the last U.S. troops. The deep sense of personal betrayal Laird felt after the fall of South Vietnam in 1975 continued for decades. Vietnamization, for him, was never a cover for retreat or a face-saving "decent interval" before South Vietnam was overrun. It was a plan that Laird firmly believed would have worked if the United States had not reneged on the promises it had made at the signing of the Paris peace accords.

When Congress voted in 1975 to cut off funding to South Vietnam, it spelled the end for that nation. But Laird personally blamed three men: Henry Kissinger, who lacked the will and ability to persuade Congress to honor the treaty that had won him the Nobel Prize; Defense Secretary James Schlesinger, who was, by personality and intellectual arrogance, incapable of engendering enough good will in Congress to effectively lobby for defense programs; and President Gerald Ford, who failed to use the weight of his office to uphold the treaty. "There's *no* president that should be defeated on an issue like this if they choose to really exert full presidential authority and commit to fulfill a firm commitment of our country," Laird said.

At the Paris accord signing in January 1973, the North Vietnamese pledged to respect South Vietnam's right to determine its own political future. They also pledged not to send more troops and arms into South Vietnam. Both pledges were promptly broken. After the cease fire, the Russians and Chinese poured arms and aid into North Vietnam conservatively valued at $2.5 billion.[28] Throughout the same period, the Nixon and Ford administrations did just the reverse for their ally, progressively reducing the amount of support far below what was allowed by the treaty. When the first major North Vietnamese treaty violations occurred in 1973, Nixon failed to respond with American air support as he had promised. Then in August 1973, Congress took away Nixon's options for a renewed air war by banning any further U.S. military combat activities in Southeast Asia.

While Congress still allowed some funds to flow to Saigon for the replacement equipment, parts, and ammunition promised in the treaty, that pipeline began to be squeezed in 1974 when Congress cut deeply into the appropriation for South Vietnam. The North Vietnamese had closely watched the American retreat from the Paris agreement and viewed the new president as someone who would be unable to hold the line. Prime Minister Pham Van Dong privately expressed to his comrades his view that Ford was "the weakest president in U.S. history." Hanoi tested Ford by capturing the capital of Phuoc Long province of South Vietnam. "When Ford kept American B-52s in their hangars, our leadership decided on a big offensive against South Vietnam," recalled North Vietnamese Col. Bui Tin.[29] Within weeks, the North Vietnamese began pouring a massive force into South Vietnam. By late March 1975 they had captured thirteen more provinces. In the meantime, the

Communist guerrillas in Cambodia achieved major victories and surrounded the capital of Phnom Penh, preparing for the kill. Ford requested an emergency $222 million supplemental appropriation for Cambodia, but Congress denied the funds. Schlesinger's lobbying was inadequate; Kissinger was away on diplomatic junkets. At several stops along one of those trips in March, U.S. and foreign diplomats asked Kissinger if the trip was going to be cut short because of the desperate situation in Cambodia and Vietnam. Kissinger appeared surprised at the questions. "What more can I do?" was his usual response."[30]

In 2006, documents came to light that hinted Kissinger might have given up on a democratic South Vietnam as early as June 1972. George Washington University's National Security Archive made public some of his papers, including notes from his trip to China that month to meet Premier Chou Enlai. At the time, Nixon had ordered bombing of North Vietnam to resume to counter the Easter Offensive, and Kissinger was trying to finesse the situation with Chou. Kissinger indicated then that he was open to the possibility of a Communist takeover of the region, "if, as a result of historical evolution it should happen over a period of time, if we can live with a Communist government in China, we ought to be able to accept it in Indochina." He cautioned Chou that, if the Communists moved in too soon after the U.S. withdrawal, then Nixon might have to send American troops back in. Appearing to allow for some attempt at a truce followed by renewed fighting, Kissinger told Chou, "If the North Vietnamese, on the other hand, engage in serious negotiation with the South Vietnamese, and if after a longer period it starts again after we were all disengaged, my personal judgment is that it is much less likely that we will go back again, much less likely."

When his words were dredged up in 2006, Kissinger said he was trying to get "Chinese acquiescence in our policy," and cautioned against judging that in hindsight.[31] But for Laird it was further proof that Kissinger was predisposed to take a passive role in 1975, a time when he should have been defending the Paris accords and demanding ongoing congressional aid to an ally.

On March 25, 1975, President Ford dispatched Gen. Frederick C. Weyand, then Army chief of staff, on an urgent mission to Saigon to assess the situation. Weyand reported back to Ford that the South was about to lose because it was running out of ammunition. Ford appeared before a joint session of Congress on April 10 to ask for $722 million in military aid and $250 million for economic and humanitarian assistance. "We cannot . . . abandon our friends while our adversaries support and encourage theirs," he argued. There was little applause, and two freshmen Democrats walked out on Ford.

Congressional leaders told the president they would take up the request after the Easter recess, but by then it was too late.[32]

On April 17, 1975, Phnom Penh finally fell to the Khmer Rouge forces, who quickly demonstrated the face of monumental evil that was to become their hallmark. The bloodbath that Americans leaders feared would occur if Southeast Asian allies were abandoned unfolded with appalling rapidity. Every resident of the city of nearly three million was ordered to leave immediately. Many Cambodians who were pushed out of the hospitals died in the first hours. In less than a day, everyone who was mobile was on congested roads going out of the city. Those who fell behind on the slow march, including children, were executed on the spot. As many as three hundred thousand were killed by the Khmer Rouge in the first week's forced marches. Pushed into the rural areas that became Pol Pot's infamous "killing fields," as many as three million Cambodians were slaughtered at the hands of the Khmer Rouge over the next four years.[33]

Four days after Phnom Penh fell, South Vietnam's President Thieu resigned and fled the country as Communist forces moved closer to Saigon. In Washington there was an eerie anxiousness to have the end come swiftly. On April 25 Communist forces surrounded Saigon and began the final siege of the city. Four days later American Armed Forces Radio played "White Christmas" and announced: "It's 105 degrees in Saigon and rising." This was the pre-arranged code for all Americans and key South Vietnamese employees to go to their evacuation locations. In eighteen hours, seventy helicopters and 865 U.S. marines flew 630 round-trips from Saigon to safety, carrying about seven thousand Americans, South Vietnamese, and "third country nationals" out of the war.[34]

Melvin Laird went to the White House to join the Ford staff monitoring and mourning the death throes of Saigon on April 30.

The North Vietnamese Communists were perhaps not as methodically savage in victory as the neighboring Khmer Rouge, but much blood did flow. As many as 250,000 South Vietnamese died in brutal "reeducation" prison camps; another 65,000 were executed outright. Two million became refugees, with an unknown number of "boat people" lost at sea. During the war itself, 275,000 South Vietnamese soldiers had been killed in action, while another 365,000 civilians had died during the shelling of cities or were assassinated by terrorist infiltrators. Hanoi had also paid a high price for the war. According to its own estimates, the North counted at least 1.1 million dead and 300,000 missing.[35]

In the years since, many voices have been heard about how South Vietnam was lost—some blaming Congress, others citing South Vietnamese ineptitude. In Laird's view, it was lost not because the South Vietnamese people proved unequal to the task, but because the Ford administration lacked the will and wherewithal to continue the arms lifeline in the face of congressional opposition. "I hold Ford, Kissinger, and Schlesinger responsible for not putting on a full-court press to meet our commitment," Laird said. "Kissinger was the one who made those commitments in Paris, yet he didn't spend a day in Congress—*not one day*—in support of the agreement in those last months. I tried to help a little, but there was no support from the State Department, very minimal support from defense, and hardly any support from the White House. They lost that vote and that broke the back of the Vietnamese." Laird was convinced that the outcome would have been different had he been walking the halls of Congress lobbying for continued support of South Vietnam.

His Vietnamization program was chalked up in the history books as a failure, but Laird never saw it as such. The Left blamed Laird for being too slow to withdraw from a losing situation; the Right said he had used Vietnamization to sabotage a just war. In that camp was General Haig who considered that Vietnamization had been a "contrivance," to back away from a confrontation with the Soviet Union.[36] Spiro Agnew thought Laird used Vietnamization to manipulate a political agenda, not to save South Vietnam. In his memoirs, Agnew wrote: "It was a sad thing for me to see Nixon at the National Security Council sessions, seated across the massive conference table with a dove at each elbow—Bill Rogers on the right hand and Mel Laird on the left." Agnew said he believed Secretary of State Rogers was a "genuine ideological dove" who was manipulated by the "eastern liberal establishment." But, Agnew concluded, "Laird was a different kettle of fish. Pragmatic, evasive, with ice water in his veins, he was the ultimate professional politician. He feared that the aggressive action needed to win the war would enrage the Congress and split the country. He asked only, 'What is politically expedient.'"[37]

Columnists Rowland Evans and Robert Novak saw Laird as a pragmatist who understood politics and the democratic system better than most:

What the public never did understand was Laird's crucial role in forcing the policy of unilateral withdrawal of U.S. troops from Vietnam (against the inclinations of a seemingly uncomprehending Nixon) at a rate faster than Henry A. Kissinger wanted and slower than Laird would have preferred. Laird's orchestration of the American troop pullout in Vietnam is probably one of his greatest achievements and his most audacious exercise of power. It is clear now that

in 1969, Nixon had no plan for Vietnamese disengagement and was rather
inclined to re-escalation; that Kissinger was still unsure of himself in Washington, taking no firm stands; and that the Pentagon brass and the U.S. high
command were flatly opposed to unilateral withdrawal. Laird coped with his
opposition by pretending it did not exist. When Nixon still had not approved
the plan, Laird began leaking its essence to newsmen; when it was still in its
most tentative stages, Laird was telling newsmen that the pullout of troops was
irrevocable.[38]

Laird's legacy, and that of everyone who believed in Vietnamization, was
forever tainted on April 30, 1975, as the world watched televised images of
the evacuation of Americans and South Vietnamese allies from the roof of
the U.S. Embassy in Saigon. Those pictures remain the freeze-frame of the
"end" of the Vietnam War for the United States, even though U.S. military
involvement had really ended in an orderly withdrawal and a treaty more
than two years before. In 1975, only about fifty Americans remained in Saigon
to be lifted off that roof.

Laird never believed the United States lost the war. Instead, he believed
Ford, Kissinger, and Congress doomed the South Vietnamese by breaking
the promises made to them in the Paris accords.

27

A Second Career

IN THE FALL OF 1975, citizen Laird, by then an accomplished coach from the sidelines of power, got a call from New York governor Hugh Carey. New York City was on the verge of declaring bankruptcy, and Carey was getting nowhere with President Ford. Did Laird have any suggestions? Characteristically, Laird invited the governor to Washington to play a round of golf at Burning Tree.

Laird already had a good idea of what it would take to save New York City. In May 1975 Mayor Beame and Governor Carey had asked for an urgent meeting with Ford. The city had overspent and undertaxed, and needed $1 billion in credit to prevent imminent bankruptcy. But the federal government was already subsidizing 25 percent of the city's budget through welfare and other programs, and Ford said he wasn't willing to spend a penny more. Then when Carey turned to Congress for help in October, Ford promised to veto any congressional bail-out legislation.

In desperation, Carey turned to Laird for help. This is Carey's memory of how his appeal to Laird went: "I'm getting nowhere with Jerry," Carey said. "I thought I had a good relationship with Jerry. He knows I walked into the middle of this New York City mess when I came in as governor. It's been cold water all around. Can you help me? What should I do?"

"I can't tell you over the phone what you should do," Laird said. "Have you got an airplane?"

"Yeah, I've got an airplane, a state airplane."

"Well, get in the airplane and make believe you're going to New York [City] and turn south and come to Dulles [airport, outside of Washington] and meet me," said Laird. "Bring your golf clubs and we'll talk this over."

"I haven't got any time to play golf," sputtered Carey.

"If you don't come down, I can't tell you," replied Laird. "I'll pull up near your airplane. I'll have a long, sleek, silver car. You'll find me in the back, and see how I live," Laird said, enjoying every minute of the game he was playing.

Carey said Laird indeed showed up in a limo with his golf clubs and a fully stocked bar in the back. "So what am I going to do about this?" Carey pressed him.

"No, no, be patient," replied Laird. "You brought your sticks? We're going to Burning Tree. We're going to play eighteen holes of golf and I'm going to play you for money. Then, when we've played the eighteen holes, if you settle up—then, *maybe,* I can give you some help."

They played, and Laird won a $100 wager. He made Carey pay up on the eighteenth fairway in full view of the picture window of the clubhouse. Carey looked up and realized Laird had filled the "gallery" with political cronies to see him skunk the governor at golf. "I looked up at all our colleagues. Everybody I could think of was looking through the window. Mel had advertised he was going to play me, that the governor of New York was going to give him $100 when he beat me in golf," Carey laughed.

Laird took the money. "You've done your part of the bargain," he said, then led Carey to a quiet corner of the clubhouse for a drink.

"I'll tell you what your problem is," Laird said. "Jerry's been told by *somebody* that when New York collapses, the financial center of the United States may move west to Chicago. Your friend Daley [Chicago Democratic mayor Richard Daley] heard that, and that's why you're not getting votes out of Chicago or Illinois."

"Who's doing this?" Carey asked.

Laird paused for a moment, leaned closer and lowered his voice. "Well, Rummy comes from Illinois," Laird hinted, his eyebrows arching. "Rummy" was Donald Rumsfeld, Ford's chief of staff who had once been a congressman from Illinois. "Rummy is not averse to making friends with Mayor Daley. *Rummy* is your problem for the time being." Carey was surprised. Was there indeed a conspiracy afoot?

"I know Don," Carey responded in slight disbelief. "We weren't enemies. I'll go see him."

"No," said Laird. "You won't change Rummy's mind. He's having some fun with you on this. Go visit with Daley in Chicago instead."

So Carey did, and learned that Daley had indeed been influenced by the siren song of some Chicago bankers who saw golden opportunity in the collapse of New York. Carey appealed to his sense of fair play and turned Daley around.

Laird himself followed up with a dizzying array of telephone calls and visits with key players, including Rumsfeld. "I said, 'Rummy, you're making a helluva mistake here. We can't let New York go down the drain!'" Rumsfeld finally gave in to Laird's argument. He hadn't been deeply opposed in the first place but had simply seen little benefit for the White House to help out the city—and he had seen the up-side for Chicago if New York City belly flopped.

Laird also bent Vice President Rockefeller's ear. The stumbling block there was both personal and political: Rockefeller didn't like Carey and had no interest in helping either him or Beame, both Democrats. But Laird brought Rockefeller up short by reminding him that when he had been governor of New York, he had personally contributed to the problem that Carey inherited. Rockefeller sheepishly agreed. "Yeah," he laughed, "I drank the champagne and Carey's got the hangover." He said he would set aside party differences and help the city.

In addition to some back-patting on Capitol Hill, Laird added other touches. As a board member of Metropolitan Life of New York, Laird encouraged its president, Richard Shinn, to step up to the plate. Shinn was named chairman of the city's new management council, and MetLife became a major purchaser of New York City bonds. Laird even asked his friend Helmut Schmidt for help. During a subsequent conversation with President Ford, the West German chancellor found a perfect moment to make his point. While speaking with Schmidt about the European economy, Ford asked, "How's the Bundesbank? How's the mark?"

""Mr. President, never mind the Bundesbank or the mark!" Schmidt responded bluntly. "If you let New York go broke, the dollar is worth shit!"

Laird moved in for the coup de grace: an arm-twisting session with Ford himself. Laird complimented the president for holding tough, which had forced Beame and Carey to come up with rigorous fiscal reforms. "You've got to do this right away before this falls through the cracks," Laird said. "We can't have this happening in New York City when it is being worked out in a way that will satisfy most of the issues."

Ford was impressed and agreed to meet with Governor Carey again. Carey outlined further reforms and pledges New York City and the state were prepared to make in return for federal aid. Ford made the deal immediately. On November 26, in a nationally televised address, the president asked Congress to approve legislation making up to $2.3 billion available to the city annually—which would be repaid at 1 percent higher than the prevailing interest rate. The process had been painful, and the Big Apple had to make do with reduced services, but in the end both the city and state kept up their ends of the bargain. Carey gave substantial credit to the advice and hard work of citizen Laird. "It would never have happened without Mel. He saved New York City."[1]

~

Laird was the one man President Ford wanted to oversee his 1976 campaign, but Laird declined, thinking he could not expect his new employers at the *Reader's Digest* to understand any more detours from private life. However, in typical Laird fashion, he was full of advice.[2] The biggest challenge, Laird said, would come from Ronald Reagan. There was a growing group of conservatives around Reagan rallying and urging him to run. Vice President Rockefeller was a lightning rod for the Republican right wing, which could use him as a reason to reject Ford. But Laird firmly believed Ford should not dump Rockefeller from the ticket because it would make Ford look disloyal and reactionary.[3] Rockefeller finally became frustrated by the mixed signals of support from Ford. As a test of sorts, during Rockefeller's weekly meeting with the president on October 28, the vice president offered to remove himself from the 1976 campaign, and Ford eagerly accepted.

On October 16 five charter members of the "kitchen cabinet" had met with Ford for what turned out to be a rough session. Bryce Harlow cited criticisms the outside advisors had identified about the Ford White House. The most serious was the appearance of "internal anarchy" and feuding at the top. Laird agreed that something had to be done to get the White House in order, but he also knew that wholesale firings were not the solution at that point in the campaign. Ford had already been forming a plan to reorganize his administration's leadership, and the Harlow lecture sped up his implementation of that plan.[4]

Ford was particularly unsettled by his relationship with Defense Secretary James Schlesinger. The two men routinely butted heads on defense issues, with Schlesinger showing little deference to the office of president. Ford decided he would offer the contentious Schlesinger another job in government and make Donald Rumsfeld the new secretary of defense. Dick Cheney would be promoted to White House chief of staff to replace Rumsfeld. Knowing that the Schlesinger dismissal would anger conservatives, Ford planned to mollify them by removing Kissinger from his second job as national security advisor and promoting his conservative deputy, Brent Scowcroft, to the post. To round out the reorganization, Ford wanted to replace CIA director William Colby with George H. W. Bush, who was in China serving as America's chief liaison officer. The prickly part of the equation was Schlesinger, who would not go willingly. On October 28, when Rockefeller unexpectedly offered to announce he would not run for the vice presidency, Ford considered it a political gift that would "appease" Reaganites even more than the Kissinger demotion.

On Halloween, October 31, Ford called Laird in Paris and wanted to run the plan by Laird. The president informed him of Rockefeller's offer to bow out and the plan to fire Schlesinger. Laird told the president the whole thing was a "stupid" idea. "I can understand that you want to dump Schlesinger tonight. But *don't dump Rockefeller*—and, if you do, you must *absolutely* not do it at the same time as Schlesinger!" said Laird.

Laird recalled later that he understood why Ford wanted to drop Schlesinger. "Ford was a smart guy, but Schlesinger was always kind of speaking down to him. He had such a superior attitude that Ford just couldn't stand it. Ford knew defense better than Schlesinger. He'd been on the House Defense Appropriations Committee for twenty years while Schlesinger was down there teaching economics at the University of Virginia." It was a budget issue that was the final straw for Ford. Schlesinger was balking at Ford's proposed defense budget, refusing to take what the president offered, and complaining publicly about the "deep, savage and arbitrary cuts" he was asked to accept.

"I can't have a secretary of defense that won't support the budget," Ford raged over the phone to Laird. "My mind is made up. I just can't get along with him."

Laird gave up on Schlesinger and tried to save Rockefeller. He told Ford that "dumping Rockefeller isn't going to get Reagan to pull out of the convention."

"I tell you," Ford countered, "the Reagan group will crucify me if I don't make that announcement soon."

"Jerry, they're going to oppose you whether you dump Rockefeller or not."

Laird's bottom line was that no matter what Ford decided, he should not blurt out the news without greasing the political machine first. "Can't you wait until I get back there?" Laird pled. "We need to talk more about it, because this is a very bad political mistake. It's almost as bad as the way you handled the [Nixon] pardon." The two men argued over the phone for more than an hour. The president agreed only to think it over again and perhaps delay the sequence of events.[5]

However, the following day Ford learned that *Newsweek* had the scoop on part of his plans and was going to press on Monday with the story. The president wanted to break the news himself, so he sped up the timetable, firing Schlesinger that morning.

On Monday, November 3, Ford announced the sweeping personnel shifts and that Rockefeller would not be his running mate in 1976. Once again, as with the Nixon pardon, it had the opposite effect to what Ford had intended. "I am not appeased," said Reagan, who formally announced his challenge of Ford for the nomination two weeks later. Opinion-makers wrote that the "Halloween Massacre" was reminiscent of Nixon and had demonstrated Ford's weakness. Reagan jumped ahead of Ford in the polls.[6]

Many suspected at the time that an ambitious Rumsfeld, who had been critical of Rockefeller, was the hidden hand behind the whole imbroglio. While Rumsfeld denied playing any puppet-master role, Laird put some of the responsibility on him for allowing Ford to do something "stupid."[7] Ford never regretted firing Schlesinger, but the Rockefeller abandonment was an entirely different matter. "It was the biggest political mistake of my life," he later concluded. "And it was one of the few cowardly things I did in my life."[8]

~

Starting in late 1975, Kissinger became a juicy target for Reaganites and a campaign liability. He offered to resign as secretary of state at one point, but Ford refused to accept. Laird wholeheartedly agreed that Kissinger should stay on through the rest of Ford's term. When rumors surfaced that Kissinger might be fired, Laird was also rumored as his replacement. The magazine publisher Malcolm S. Forbes sat down with both men and inquired of Kissinger "how it felt to fall from Deity to Devil." Kissinger laughed and poked Laird, asking: "Mel, why were you in my office the other day with that interior decorator?"[9]

Ford narrowly beat back the Reagan challenge at the Republican National Convention held in Kansas City in August. During the convention, Laird stumped hard to get Ford to announce he was keeping Rockefeller on the ticket, but the president chose Kansas Sen. Robert Dole instead.[10] In the end, Ford could not overcome all the baggage he had collected in his brief term in office, the heaviest of which was the Nixon pardon. Jimmy Carter was elected president on November 2, 1976, by a mere 2 percent margin of the popular vote. The electoral vote for Carter was the narrowest presidential victory in sixty years.

On January 18, 1977, the Fords were preparing to leave the White House and the president arranged one last gift for his wife. He lured her away from the White House to a private dinner party, and while they were gone, the Marine Band slipped into the White House along with some surprise guests. Betty Ford had known the band would be there that night for a photo session, so their presence at the foot of the grand staircase was not unexpected when she and Jerry arrived home.

With the guests in hiding, the president said, "So long as we're here, why don't we have a last dance?" She smiled and asked the band to play, "Thanks for the Memories." As the two twirled around the floor, from the hallway emerged other couples gliding onto the floor, including the Lairds, the Harlows, and the Kissingers—more than one hundred friends in all, dancing around the First Couple. Betty Ford gasped in surprise and began crying, hugging, and kissing friends as the dance drew to a close.[11]

It was the end of an era of sorts for Melvin Laird, too. His party was out of power, and he was free to jump completely into private life.

DeWitt Wallace, the most successful magazine publisher in American history, had courted Laird for nearly two decades. Founded by DeWitt and Lila Wallace in 1922, *Reader's Digest* quickly made its mark with a mixture of stories and anecdotes full of humor and drama, as well as flag-waving patriotism, praise for self-reliance, faith in God and capitalism, and muckraking reports on the evils of Communism and excessive American government spending.

On its thirtieth anniversary in 1952, the same year Laird first ran for Congress, *Reader's Digest* circulation had soared to nine and a half million in the United States and six million abroad. Two years later, after the Republicans had taken a bath in the midterm election, the conservative DeWitt Wallace sat down and studied a directory of the Eighty-fourth Congress looking for surviving conservatives he ought to get to know. The biography of Melvin Robert Laird impressed him, not just because of his whiz-kid style or his party affiliation, but also because he was the son of a Presbyterian minister in Wisconsin. Both DeWitt's father and Lila's father had been Presbyterian ministers in the neighboring state of Minnesota. DeWitt invited Laird to New York for lunch, and the two hit it off immediately.[12]

During Laird's final days as secretary of defense in late 1972, Wallace made him promise that he would accept no other job offer before *Reader's Digest* was able to put together an attractive employment package. When Laird was quickly drawn back into the Nixon administration, Wallace had to wait. In November 1973 Laird found himself and Barbara being wined and dined in unforgettable fashion. They were flown by private plane to the Wallaces' 105-acre wooded estate in Mount Kisko, New York, overlooking Lake Byram. On the walls of the twenty-two-room mansion were some of the most valuable privately held paintings in the world. What Laird remembered most from the evening was the gold cup from which Lila Wallace drank. Laird asked about it, and with an "oh-this-little-thing" expression, Lila reported that it was a golden chalice from King Tut's tomb. As a sponsor of the traveling

Tutankhamen exhibit in the United States, she had "borrowed" the cup for a little while. (Considering that the Wallaces' arts and museum donations went into the hundreds of millions of dollars, no curators were likely to complain.) Wallace made Laird an offer he couldn't refuse. He wouldn't have to move to the *Reader's Digest*'s Pleasantville, New York, office. Instead, he could have a Washington office, secretarial assistance (longtime secretary Laurie Hawley and newcomer Kathy Weaver), a chauffeured car, and an expense account. Wallace had left two spaces blank on the contract—the amount of Laird's salary and the length of employment. Laird was invited to fill in the blanks, so he added a six-figure salary and an initial ten-year term.[13] And that's how Melvin Laird, one of the most powerful politicians of the day, went to work for a magazine.

He had not been bluffing all those months when he said he would not run for president or any other office. Laird the politician, who was then only fifty-one, would be Laird the editor, writer, and advisor for nearly twice as long as he spent in Congress or at the Pentagon. In the next few years, as Laird traveled the world visiting the outposts of *Reader's Digest,* his picture appeared in newspapers around the world, and he used the bully pulpit provided overseas to speak out on politics at home and abroad. He was an international celebrity who never failed to draw the press wherever he went.

When Laird joined the *Reader's Digest* in 1974, U.S. circulation was eighteen million, and other millions of readers around the globe were able to read the magazine in their own languages. During Laird's tenure, the *Digest* continued to grow, reaching a peak worldwide-readership of one hundred million with forty-eight editions in nineteen languages. This made the "international" portion of Laird's job description pivotal. Besides glad-handing and pep-talking the local *Digest* leadership during on-site visits, Laird also enmeshed himself in solving critical labor, postal, and other issues for those foreign editions

At first Laird also wrote two or three articles a year for the magazine, which often made headlines and had an impact on the policies of the Ford and Carter administrations. There were also news scoops along the way. In a 1976 article, "Let's Stop Undermining the CIA," Laird reported one of the CIA's secret successes. Israel's premier Golda Meir had been targeted for a terrorist attack while visiting New York City on March 4, 1973. Police, following a tip, found two cars on a street Meir would pass, "with enough Soviet-made explosives to kill everyone within a 100-yard radius."[14]

To protect intelligence sources and methods, Laird did not reveal in that article he had saved Meir's life on another occasion when he had been secretary of defense. (He could not recall the date of the event.) Shortly after

Meir became Israel's first female prime minister in 1969, Laird received urgent intelligence from the National Security Agency that indicated a car bomb was set to go off on a Jerusalem street as Prime Minister Meir was driving by. Laird conveyed the intelligence to Meir. The threat proved real, and a grateful Meir later personally presented Laird with fourteenth- and seventeenth-century BC bronze artifacts including two arrowheads, a spearhead, dagger, and war axe in a framed case.[15] "This is for saving my life," she explained.

DeWitt "Wally" Wallace wanted to put Laird on the *Reader's Digest* board when he joined the privately held company in 1974, but he also recognized that it might not be politic to install Laird as an "inside" director when he had had no previous history as a *Digest* employee. After the childless Wallaces died, leaving no heirs, 72 percent of the voting shares reverted to two charitable foundations. In 1990, when the *Digest* went public, Laird went on the board and helped drive up operating earnings from $240 to $353 million in the first three years.[16] The magazine's CEO figured out early that the best way to use Laird was not on the editorial side but on the business side. Considering the revenue he raised and the money he saved the company, his strictly financial value for the *Digest* added up to tens of millions of dollars.

One way Laird accomplished that feat was as an ad salesman. He traveled from one end of the country to another and abroad at the request of many *Digest* advertising account executives. He attended numerous industry conventions and made community appearances at the request of advertisers. Successive *Digest* publishers called his entertainment of advertisers "legendary."

Laird's work with the *Digest* on postal and regulatory issues began when he was a congressman. At that time, Congress had the responsibility for establishing postal rates—an issue of critical interest to the magazine. The *Digest*'s business manager for decades, Al Cole, the man who turned the magazine into an international powerhouse, met Laird at a luncheon at the Wallace's house and the two men became friends. In time, Congressman Laird came to believe in the axiom: "What is good for *Reader's Digest* is good for the country."

When Laird became an employee of the company, his missionary fervor accelerated. Nobody schmoozed with America's postmasters general like Laird did. His appointment books beginning in 1974 were filled with golf outings, lunches, and dinner meetings with "PMGs." Since *Reader's Digest* mails out millions of pieces of literature every month, and is one of the postal service's largest customers, Laird didn't think it uppity when he first asked PMG Bill Bolger (1978–84) for a monthly meeting to discuss business issues. Bolger agreed, and the PMGs who followed him continued the practice.

The 1970 Postal Reorganization Act took the responsibility for setting postal rates out of the hands of Congress and gave it to the independent Postal Rate Commission, whose members are appointed to staggered six-year terms by the president. That commission and the Postal Service are often at odds, and Laird acted as an intermediary. It also didn't hurt that he knew all the commissioners. The fact that Laird was respected and considered a close friend by disparate powers in the postal nexus paid off in big dollars for *Reader's Digest.* One example is Laird's successful negotiation for a *Digest* discount on the first class rate in late 1977 because the magazine was presorted before it got to the post office. The discount saved the *Digest* $14 million in the first year alone.

The hardest thing Laird ever did in his three-plus decades with the *Digest* was getting the Postal Service to issue a stamp honoring DeWitt and Lila Wallace. No *Digest*-related mission was more heartfelt for Laird, whose gratitude for the Wallaces did not diminish with the years. Laird's stamp quest took more than ten years of frustration and bureaucracy. When the Wallaces were finally honored with a first class stamp in July 1998, Laird's elation was tempered by the realization that it had been easier for him to make Gerald Ford the president than it had been to get a stamp printed.

∽

The Wallaces never minded that Laird kept his fingers in many pies while the *Reader's Digest* was his day job. Laird's favorite pet project was the Laird Center at the Marshfield Clinic. He wasn't fond of people naming things after themselves, and during his time in Congress he had routinely voted against naming projects after living people. Then, in 1994, Bob Froehlke had come to him with a proposition. The Marshfield Clinic was literally bursting at the seams. A new medical center was needed, and Froehlke, who had become a prodigious fund-raiser in private life, knew there was only one way to do it— talk Laird into letting it be named after him.[17] Laird quickly agreed. In October 1994 Health and Human Services secretary Donna Shalala announced the Laird Center project. Having once been chancellor of the University of Wisconsin at Madison, Shalala was a longtime Laird friend and booster.[18] Once Laird had agreed to put his name on the center's marquee, raising the needed $12.6 million from Laird's many friends and fans had been a snap for Froehlke. In the first two months, two *Reader's Digest* charities pledged $2 million, and David Packard pledged $1 million.

The long-awaited dedication of the Laird Center in September 1997 started with an accident. Central Wisconsin dairy farmer Meldon Maguire was driving home at night when, in his headlights, he spotted a white stretch limo on the side of the road with its hood up, steam hissing from the radiator. The cause was obvious—a newly dead deer in the middle of the road. Maguire steered his pickup truck to the shoulder of the road and offered to help. One of the men from the limo approached and introduced himself as Reed Hall, director of the Marshfield Clinic, and his wife, Ellie. Then Hall turned to the portly gentleman near him and said, "This is Dr. Henry Kissinger." Maguire chuckled, thinking how interesting it was that a doctor at the Marshfield Clinic had the same name as a former government bigwig.

Maguire dragged the deer off the road and offered to drive the group to Marshfield in his extended-cab truck. He pushed aside some fast-food refuse to make room for the Halls in the back, with Nobel laureate Kissinger riding shotgun. It was only after they were well down the road that it began to occur to Maguire that this was *the* Henry Kissinger. The tipoff was some small talk about Kissinger's attendance just five days earlier at the funeral of Princess Diana, and his anxiousness about keeping President Ford waiting in Marshfield. "I almost asked him a couple times what he did for a living before it dawned on me who he really was," Maguire recalled.[19]

Kissinger and Ford and a host of other luminaries descended on Marshfield for the dedication of the Melvin R. Laird Center for Medical Research at Marshfield Clinic. On September 12, 1997, Laird sat on a stage surrounded by political movers and shakers. After decades in politics and private life, he had returned to his first doctor's office and to the first love that he found in Congress—the promotion of health care. The day was a particularly heartwarming one for Laird as he sat beside his second lease on love, Carole Howard Laird, whom he married in 1993 after Barbara died of cancer in January 1992. Children and grandchildren were there to swap stories.

The keynote speaker, President Ford, said, "Long before today's talk of a health care crisis in America, Mel Laird was legislating in hopes of averting a crisis." Former colleagues from Congress were there, such as Bob Michel, John Rhodes, and Gaylord Nelson. Representative David Obey and Governor Tommy Thompson, who would later serve George W. Bush as Health and Human Services secretary, were also on hand. Kissinger praised the man who had frequently been his sparring partner in the White House. He speculated aloud that Laird had probably arranged the encounter with the deer the night before. "He trained the deer for weeks and he had it on the side of the road," Kissinger opined as Laird erupted into laughter. It was a roundabout salute from America's Machiavelli to the man from Marshfield who had been more than his equal in the halls of power.

The two-story, 52,000-square-foot Melvin R. Laird Center helped to make the Marshfield Clinic one of the ten largest medical research complexes in the United States. Congressman Laird had secured the clinic's first federal research grant in the 1950s. Within four decades, and with the addition of the Laird Center, the clinic boasted more than 750 scientists and physicians leading five hundred studies involving more than thirty-six thousand patients. These researchers publish hundreds of scientific papers each year in scientific books and journals, which focus on pioneering applications of molecular genetics combined with preventive medicine, as well as rural health and safety research. The Laird Center itself houses the National Farm Medicine Center, the Center for Medical Genetics, and the Marshfield Epidemiology Center.[20] In 2008 the Laird Center more than tripled in size with the addition of a 129,000-square-foot building. Funding for the $40 million building began with a $10 million federal grant that Dave Obey attached to a House Health Appropriations Subcommittee bill. It secured easy passage because the language stated that in addition to the research this would fund, it was also a way to honor one of the subcommittee's most distinguished members.

The path leading from the halls of government to the corporate board room is a well-worn one, and Laird didn't feel he was selling out to follow it. When he left the White House as domestic counselor in 1974, he had invitations from twenty corporate boards looking for the prestige and insider knowledge of the former defense secretary. At first, DeWitt Wallace agreed that Laird could serve on just six boards. The first six Laird accepted were Northwest Airlines (1974–94), Chicago Pneumatic Tool (1974–86), Metropolitan Life Insurance Company (1974–94), IDS Mutual Funds Group (1974–97), Communications Satellite Corporation (1974–96), and Purolator Inc. (1975–81). Eventually Laird added more corporate boards to his schedule, some of which landed him in the middle of the most infamous hostile takeover bids of the twentieth century.

The decade of rapacious corporate cannibalism began on August 25, 1982, the day the chairman of Bendix Corporation, William Agee, announced his hostile intention to acquire America's twelfth largest defense contractor, Martin Marietta, led by Thomas Pownall. In Bendix's court was a distinguished member of its board, former Ford defense secretary Donald Rumsfeld. Martin Marietta had its own former defense secretary on the board, Mel Laird.

The takeover bid was foiled when Laird and the Martin Marietta board turned the tables and tried to buy Bendix instead in what was called their "Pac Man" defense. They succeeded in intimidating Agee into surrender. In the process, Rumsfeld resigned from Bendix. When the dust cleared, Martin

Marietta had paid a heavy price to keep its independence. The company accumulated a $1.3 billion debt primarily as a result of its takeover defense. To reduce the debt as quickly as possible, the board authorized a radical restructuring and within just one year had recovered.[21] Laird eventually helped promote a strong successor to Pownall in 1988, Norman Augustine, who had been Laird's deputy director of research and engineering at the Pentagon. Augustine called one side of the Martin Marietta board table "Power Alley," for Laird, former attorney general Griffin Bell, Jack Byrne (chairman of Geico Corporation), and Jack Vessey (former chairman of the Joint Chiefs of Staff).

Big oil also had come courting Laird as a potential board member during his last days in the White House in 1973, but he was in no hurry to choose. He was inclined toward Oklahoma-based Phillips Petroleum, the country's ninth largest oil company, but did not join the Phillips board until 1976 when he was ordered to do so by a federal judge to help clean up the company in the wake of a major political slush fund scandal involving the company.

As part of the investigation of Nixon and his reelection campaign, Watergate special prosecutor Archibald Cox had found that some American companies had made illegal contributions to Nixon, including Phillips. The company's chairman resigned, and Phillips was fined $5,000. Then a class action suit on behalf of Phillips's shareholders resulted in an order from Federal district judge Jesse Curtis to restructure the company whose board had allowed itself to be controlled by company managers. He mandated that six new "outside" directors be added to the eleven-member board. One of the new members was Laird. Although there is no record of who first raised his name during the court negotiations, it is likely that it was Clark Clifford, Phillips's lawyer in Washington.[22]

Laird had always liked Phillips because it was an oil company that had a "family" feel to it. Phillips research had been pivotal in the production of high-octane aviation gasoline and artificial rubber during World War II. In 1951 the company invented polyethylene plastic and, later, the first all-season motor oil. The first to drill for oil in Alaska, Phillips also drilled the first commercial oil well in the North Sea, which led to the discovery of the West Europe's first large oil field. Much of that innovation had occurred under the direction of Phillips president, K. S. "Boots" Adams. On Adams's sixty-sixth birthday in 1965, schools closed in the Phillips company town of Bartlesville, Oklahoma, so families could attend a parade. The guest of honor was Adams's golfing buddy, Dwight D. Eisenhower. Also in the parade was an important Republican House leader, Melvin Laird.

Laird felt his primary role on the board was to keep Phillips "cleaner than a hound's tooth." He did that in part by stocking the board with friends, including Carol Laise, the retired director general of the U.S. Foreign Service. Laise had been U.S. ambassador to Nepal when her husband, Ellsworth Bunker, was U.S. ambassador in Saigon. In April 1984 Laird brought the chairman of the Equitable Life Assurance Society onto the Phillips board—Bob Froehlke.

By December 1984 Laird and the others were ready when they faced the biggest corporate war in the history of Phillips. Their opponent was a former employee who became the most famous American raider of them all, T. Boone Pickens. He had left Phillips in 1954 and struck out on his own, founding Mesa Petroleum. Then he began buying up other companies and set his sights on Phillips. As he had on the Martin Marietta board, Laird urged Phillips's chairman to fight to the death. Laird was pivotal in directing a public relations strategy that turned Pickens almost overnight from a folk hero into a villain in the mold of TV's J. R. Ewing. The people of Bartlesville rallied in impressive fashion. "Boone Buster" logos appeared everywhere on T-shirts, buttons, and coffee cups. Local churches held twenty-four-hour prayer vigils.[23] The TV networks obligingly covered the battle of the small town against the evil corporate raider. Pickens capitulated and cut a deal, which still allowed him to walk away with an $89 million profit. Meanwhile, another corporate raider, Carl Icahn, was buying Phillips stock and made a run at the wounded company several weeks later. He also failed.

On the list of people Laird admired most from his service on boards was Sandy Weill, the president of American Express. Something of a perpetual motion machine, Weill was always on the lookout for the next big deal, and in July 1983 he decided Amex could acquire Minneapolis-based Investors Diversified Services (IDS) for $1 billion. Laird had been on the board of the IDS mutual funds group for almost a decade, and continued on the board after the companies merged. When Weill bought Commercial Credit Company, he invited Laird to join the board of directors. Laird agreed and recruited another member, former president Gerald Ford.

⸺

For Laird, board positions were more than an easy paycheck or the honor of being asked. He could anticipate issues emanating from Washington that might affect the companies. He could be window dressing for a building dedication or a ribbon cutting one day, and the next be a savvy advisor who didn't mince words. Accustomed to having people carry out his orders without delay, Laird had little patience for board meetings that meandered off the topic. He snapped many meetings back on track with pointed humor or a firm course correction. David Heebner, who served with Laird in the Pentagon and later on the board of Science Applications International Corporation (SAIC), recalled a meeting where an executive promotion was being discussed.

"Do you intend for that fellow to report to so-and-so?" Laird asked. The chairman said, "Yes."

"That'll never work," said Laird.

"Why?"

"Those guys can't stand one another," Laird observed.

"Well, how do you know that?" asked the chairman.

"Look," said Laird, "I come to your pre-board dinners, and I watch how your people interact with one another. I make my life understanding how people relate to one another. And let me tell you, I will guarantee that those guys can't get along."

Laird was "right on the money," Heebner recalled.[24]

In 1974 Laird was persuaded to join the board of Communications Satellite Corporation (Comsat) by another board member, labor leader George Meany, also a Laird golfing partner. Comsat was formed in 1962 as a quasi-public enterprise to pursue satellite technology. Laird quickly became one of the most influential Comsat board members, according to Joseph H. Charyk, the founding Comsat president. Not only were his ideas useful but Laird was willing to expend his considerable political capital on behalf of Comsat. It also gave him another spot to exercise his penchant for mentoring. When Lt. Gen. Colin Powell was national security advisor to President Reagan, in early 1988 he was paired at a dinner function with Laird. Powell made some small talk at the dinner about an article in the *Wall Street Journal*, which stated that black generals were having trouble breaking into the business world when they retired from the military. "That's astonishing!" Laird said, genuinely surprised by the news. "This is ridiculous—these guys would bring such talents to any board."

Sensing an opportunity, Powell offered his prime example: after a distinguished thirty-four-year career, the first black four-star in the Army, Gen. Roscoe Robinson had been retired for more than two years and hadn't been able to land a seat on a major corporate board. Laird was offended at the news. General Robinson had served him well in Japan during the reversion of Okinawa when a more senior commander had been dragging his feet. Powell recounted, "Before I knew it, Mel had called Roscoe and put him on a board." That May 1988 board appointment was at Comsat. The following January, Laird got Robinson on the Northwest Airlines board and, in 1991, paved the way for appointment to the MetLife board. When Robinson died in 1993, Laird set up a perpetual Comsat scholarship in Robinson's name for black students from Washington, D.C.[25]

Robinson wasn't the only beneficiary of Laird's "placement service." After Lynne Cheney left her post as Reagan's chairman at the National Endowment for Humanities, Laird was anxious to help the talented wife of his long-time protégé, Dick Cheney.[26] Laird made sure she was appointed to the boards of American Express/IDS, Lockheed Martin, and *Reader's Digest.* When Hubert Humphrey died leaving his wife Muriel only a Senate pension, Laird saw to it that she was appointed to the American Express/IDS board. When Sen. Barry Goldwater retired on his Senate pension without benefit of a family fortune, Laird saw an opportunity to help him, too, and got President Reagan to appoint Goldwater to the Comsat board.

⌒

Under his original agreement with DeWitt Wallace, Laird was not limited in the number of nonprofit public service boards he could join. Wallace specifically wanted Laird on the board of the World Rehabilitation Fund headed by Wallace's friend, Dr. Harold Rusk. In short order, Laird added public service board memberships, among them the Kennedy Center for the Performing Arts, George Washington University, the American Film Institute, Airlie Foundation, Rep. John Fogarty's Research Foundation, the Sen. Henry M. Jackson Foundation for Medical Research, the Boys Clubs of America, and as chairman of the Wolf Trap Foundation, the arts center in Virginia. Over time, Laird served on twenty-seven nonprofit boards.

No nonprofit service carried more financial responsibility than Laird's work with the eight trusts and two foundations that DeWitt and Lila Wallace left in place after their deaths. Laird felt a very personal responsibility in handling the Wallace money. He served as chairman of the investment committee for their funds, which exceeded $5 billion in value.

The time Mel Laird spent in Washington on nonprofit boards, and personal financial donations he offered, did not usually have as much emotional resonance as the special charities he set up closer to his family roots. For example, Laird made contributions of more than $454,000 to the "Laird Endowment for the Arts," which funds programs in the Helen C. Laird Fine Arts Building and Theater of the University of Wisconsin–Wood County. The building was dedicated in 1984 in loving tribute to his mother, who was committed to education and the arts. It houses two practice theaters and a state-of-the-art library. Laird additionally designated the fine arts program as the beneficiary of one of his life insurance policies. He also directed a $100,000

Lila Wallace grant to support the arts programs, for a total of more than $1 million.[27]

"My greatest *personal* pride and joy with the nonprofit work is with the Laird Youth Leadership Foundation," Laird said. He established it when he was serving in Congress to honor his father and to mentor bright young people. The funding first came from honorariums he received while in Congress and expanded through his personal donations of more than $1 million after he left government. (The program is also the beneficiary of a life insurance policy and other personal endowments upon Laird's death.) Beginning in 1954, the foundation awarded scholarships to students, ranging from $1,000 to $5,000. As of 2008, it had awarded 385 such scholarships and had established an award of five scholarships per year of $2,000 each. The foundation later added a biennial cash award for "Leadership in Art." The foundation, chaired by Laird's son John, continues to support the Laird Youth Leadership Day hosted by the University of Wisconsin–Stevens Point. Keynote speakers for affair have included former presidents, cabinet members, and every Wisconsin governor since its inception.

28

War and Peace and War

THE APACHE HELICOPTERS of the 101st Aviation Brigade crossed the border into Iraq on a clear night, with a new moon giving advantage to their night vision capability. They had been chosen to spearhead the biggest air assault in world history—and to fire the first shots of Operation Desert Storm on January 17, 1991. Many miles to the south in Riyadh, Saudi Arabia, Gen. Norman Schwarzkopf assembled his staff in the War Room and asked a chaplain to pray for the troops. But the United States had more than a prayer going for it because of the groundwork Melvin Laird had laid two decades before. Most of the equipment at Schwarzkopf's disposal, and even the nature of the U.S. fighting force, were directly traceable to the Laird era.

Shortly after Saddam Hussein's army invaded Kuwait on August 2, 1990, the massive C-5As and other cargo planes built during the Laird administration began lifting American personnel and equipment to bases in Saudi Arabia, beginning an operation to free Kuwait. On August 22, when President George H. W. Bush called up forty thousand Reserve troops, his ability to do so came because of Laird's "Total Force" concept. Twenty years earlier, to the month, Laird had ordered that the Reserves, rather than the draft, would provide manpower for future troop buildups.

During the four decades between World War II and Desert Storm the Reserves had been called up eleven times—the Korean War, the Berlin airlift, the Cuban missile crisis, after the Tet Offensive, and for various civil disturbances at home. President Nixon used the Reserves once—to handle mail during the 1970 postal strike. Both Nixon and Johnson had been loath to use the Reserves and National Guard for the Vietnam War, so those outfits had become a haven for young men who wanted to avoid combat. The derisive term "weekend warriors" came into the lexicon, and these units were considered second- or third-string until Laird mandated the Total Force Policy at the end of his term. During the next twenty years the Army, Navy, and Air Force became dependent on the Reserves. Roughly 70 percent of the Army's combat support functions, such as those performed by medical and logistical units, were being filled by the Reserves by the dawn of Desert Storm. They comprised two-thirds of the water supply units, and half the ammunition and fuel-handling units. Reserves accounted for 93 percent of the Navy's cargo-handling battalions and 59 percent of the Air Force's tactical airlift capability.[1] Schwarzkopf eventually tapped more than two hundred thousand reservists during the conflict for a wide variety of needs, including combat; seventy-one of them lost their lives in that first Gulf War. There was no more snickering about "summer soldiers."

While the Apache helicopters were striking Iraqi antiaircraft missile batteries in the early hours of January 17, the navy was firing its first shots, primarily from the USS *Wisconsin,* marking the first use of Tomahawk cruise missiles in battle. Laird had started the cruise missile program over the objections of the Air Force and Navy. Those forces were pilot-oriented, and the cruise missile could be seen as making pilots obsolete. Laird's successors also had to overcome fierce opposition to keep the missiles in the defense budget.

The subsonic missiles rocketed away from the *Wisconsin* at speeds up to 550 miles per hour, hugging the ground at altitudes as low as fifty feet (well below radar range) through the use of preprogrammed photographic terrain data. Fired from more than eight hundred miles away, the Tomahawks were able to strike targets within a few feet of the bull's-eye. Some of them easily penetrated concrete-reinforced Iraqi bunkers by bursting through doors. More than 85 percent of the first 150 Tomahawks launched in the war struck their intended targets. As praise was heaped upon him during Desert Storm, the missile's designer, Robert Lynch, publicly affirmed that "the only thing that kept cruise missiles alive was the determination of Defense Secretaries [beginning with] Melvin Laird."[2]

When Secretary Laird took over in 1969, the military procurement situation was a colossal mess. "Many major weapons systems were in serious trouble," Pentagon comptroller Robert Moot wrote in a 1972 summary report. The reasons were varied—daily demands of the Vietnam War, inflation, procurement procedures instituted by McNamara, and some questionable weapons choices. "Whatever the causes," Moot wrote, "the Department had a great amount of expensive dirty linen to wash at a particularly inopportune time"— just as Laird was taking the job.[3]

Laird felt the first way to tackle the problem was to identify just how bad

things had become on his predecessors' watches, then candidly hang out that
"dirty linen" in front of the Congress. The first time Laird appeared before
a congressional committee on the defense budget, he delivered the bad news
all at once. In a review of current defense contracts, he had found a total of
$16.2 billion in cost overruns on thirty-four major defense weapons systems.
He told the committee it was important "to set forth all of the overruns
which we uncovered when we took over this new watch. . . . The only reason these reports haven't been put in the record before is that they contain
classified information on these weapons systems." Laird declared he wasn't
going to hide behind the secrecy stamp as other secretaries had done. He
pledged to disclose even the most embarrassing facts about weapons procurement as he learned of them.[4]

Laird explained at a press conference, "In the weapons acquisition area,
[it] is far easier to identify the troubles in a timely fashion than it is to devise
practical, immediately-effective solutions," especially when that included serious interservice rivalries competing for dollars. Time and again, at his Monday top-level staff meetings, he would urge: "Please, we need to keep the
hustling of service weapons programs to a minimum. We have to show unity
in our requests to the Hill rather than pulling against each other—or we all
will lose."[5]

One of the most nettlesome service vs. service procurement issues that
Laird inherited was the bitter "close air support" debate. Three aircraft—
the Air Force A-X, the Army Cheyenne helicopter, and the Marine Harrier—
were all being developed for roughly the same mission: supporting American
ground forces in a battle by knocking out enemy tanks, guns, and troops from
the air. Altogether the services were trying to buy about one thousand aircraft
at a cost of $4–5 billion. Laird, who had monitored the requests when he was
in Congress, immediately put David Packard to work on a compromise.[6]

Within weeks, Packard knew what the solution was: The trouble-plagued
Cheyenne helicopter program needed to be canceled; purchase of the Har-
riers from the British had to be scaled back; and the Air Force should get
the go-ahead for the A-X. As sharp and deft as Packard was, however, it took
him three years to get the feuding services to come to the same conclusion.
It was an emotional issue, particularly for the Army, which didn't feel that
the Air Force in wartime supported Army troops as willingly as they performed other, more glamorous Air Force missions. The Army didn't seem
to want to have to rely on the Air Force to come to the rescue in a timely
manner with the A-X when an Army Cheyenne could do the same job, with
the added bonus of always being dependably on call.

Packard's first move in May 1969 was to cancel the production contract for the Cheyenne, declaring Lockheed was in "default" for having failed to solve serious rotor stability problems. Next, in January 1970, Packard ordered that the Army and the Air Force come up with "a unified Department of Defense position."[7] The result two months later was a document so rare that the Pentagon didn't have stationery to accommodate it. "Departments of the Army and Air Force" had to be typed in at the top of the joint memorandum signed by Army secretary Stan Resor and Air Force secretary Robert Seamans. Between the lines was the mutual opinion of the civilian secretaries that the A-X should move to production while the Cheyenne would be stopped at the prototype stage.[8]

Seamans wrote in his memoirs that the uniformed military was uniformly furious. Air force chief of staff Gen. John Ryan berated his service secretary, Seamans, for allowing continued work on the Cheyenne in any form. Army chief of staff Westmoreland similarly pounded on his secretary, Resor, for "giving away the store." Resor later remarked: "Bob [Seamans] and I must have done something right. Both of our staffs told us that we sold them down the river."[9]

Packard wasn't finished. Common sense said that the Cheyenne helicopter should be terminated, but the Army was not ready to give it up. After more than a year of additional contentious meetings, David Heebner, a Pentagon research and development official who worked on the issue, privately approached Packard with a draft of an order to kill the Cheyenne, which he urged Packard to sign.

"Have you ever herded cattle?" Packard, the working ranch owner, asked Heebner.

"No," Heebner answered, wondering where Packard was going.

"When you herd cattle, you spend a lot of time going over the range rounding them up. After a lot of work, you get them alongside the corral fence. Then, acting real cool, you have somebody open the gate kind of slowly. Pretty soon, one of those doggies walks into the corral, and then the rest of 'em follow in. And you're done. But, sure as hell, if you try to push them, they'll scatter all over the range and you have to do it again. I think we have them alongside the corral fence. Just wait a little longer."[10]

Sure enough, Heebner recalled, within a few weeks the Army brass told Packard they were ready to *consider* giving up on the Cheyenne. The program was finally killed in August 1972, having cost $400 million. (The research was not completely wasted, however; years later, the R&D for the Cheyenne was rolled into the Army's Apache attack helicopter.) Meanwhile the Marines were limited to purchasing 60 Harriers from the British instead of the 112 they wanted.[11]

The A-X became the Fairchild-Hiller A-10; more than seven hundred of these awkward-looking aircraft (nicknamed "Warthogs") were produced. Although Air Force commanders were never fond of the ungainly plane, the Army was grateful they had been built. The A-10s and their Air Force pilots performed heroically and with efficiency during the 1991 Gulf War. The A-10 carried Maverick missiles, five-hundred-pound bombs, and anti-armor cluster bombs, but its chief armament was a 30mm, seven-barrel Gatling gun the size of a Volkswagen, which fired dense depleted-uranium ammunition at 4,200 rounds a minute. Besides supporting ground troops, the Warthogs in that war also knocked out Scud missile sites, artillery supply points, radar installations, and surface-to-air missile sites. One even rescued a downed Navy pilot, while another won a dogfight with an Iraqi helicopter. Not one of the Warthogs was downed by antiaircraft fire. One that was hit had a gaping hole in its right wing, a destroyed landing gear pod, and one of its hydraulic systems taken out, but the plane made it back to its base and flew again.[12]

~

In the run-up to the first Gulf War, Laird was not one of those who was anxious to see his procurement and manpower decisions ratified in the heat of real battle and loss of life. In October 1990, three months before the first shots were fired, Laird met with President George H. W. Bush for a Sunday brainstorming session in the upstairs White House sitting room. He urged continued caution, including the imperative that war—if it came—should be a United Nations operation, just as Korea had been. "This is a test, not only for the charter and purpose of the United Nations, but also a test even for the *name* United Nations," he explained to a Marshfield audience. "We cannot go it alone."[13]

Bush successfully pushed for UN support and, on November 29, won U.N. Resolution 678, which authorized the use of force against Iraq if it did not withdraw its forces from Kuwait by January 15, 1991. It marked only the second time in the UN's forty-five-year history that it had affirmatively provided authority for member states to wage war against another country. (The first was in 1950, at the outset of the Korean War.) The day after the UN resolution, Laird and six other former defense secretaries were gathered in Atlanta for a PBS forum sponsored by the Southern Center for International Studies. All seven were in agreement that Bush should pursue a peaceful end to the Kuwait crisis, counseling patience to give economic sanctions more time to work. Laird added, however, that it would be a mistake to send a signal to Saddam Hussein that the United States would be unlikely to use force. "The important thing here is that we have until the fifteenth of January to get down to some very serious business with Saddam Hussein," he added. "It would be a very grave error to send a direct message about what we will or will not do." Laird qualified his own view with the observation that the United States only has "one Secretary of Defense at a time," and he would support Secretary Dick Cheney in upcoming Senate testimony.

Only one of the former defense secretaries was singled out by the press as being particularly hawkish. Donald Rumsfeld "stressed the merits of an attack on Iraq," the *New York Times* summarized. He said American superiority could be used to destroy Iraqi weapons of mass destruction, ending Western and Saudi concerns about them. "I am not the slightest bit uncomfortable with military action, particularly if it goes to degrade the unconventional weapon capability of Saddam Hussein." Rumsfeld additionally observed that Saddam "is not going to be persuaded by diplomatic niceties. He [only] understands force."[14]

In the end, Saddam would not capitulate, which prompted forty days and forty nights of war. The final test of the war came for the ground-combat component of Laird's most important legacy, the All-Volunteer Force. At 4 a.m. on Saturday, February 24, Armed Forces Radio played Elton John's "Saturday Night's Alright (For Fighting)," and the ground war was on. One hundred hours later, it was over. Iraqi forces were evicted from Kuwait and thoroughly routed. The All-Volunteer Force had proved its mettle and wisdom at every level. While reflecting on the All-Volunteer Force six years after the war, George H. W. Bush noted that, "Desert Storm was clearly the first major, all-out war since the volunteer Army began. I'm a strong supporter of that. Anybody who saw the dedication and the commitment of these forces would agree that this was the finest fighting force the United States had ever put together. Everybody was there because they wanted to be. 'Let's get on with it. Let's get on with this mission. Get the job done and come home.' I heard that time and time again. To the degree that it was an all-volunteer effort, it vindicated Mel Laird's commitment to having that kind of force. We *did* call up the Reserves and the National Guard. But still they were there because they wanted to be there."[15]

Colin Powell felt the same when he later served as George W. Bush's secretary of state. Powell said Laird was owed a debt of gratitude for the All-Volunteer Force—which Powell and many other senior military officers had opposed when Laird pushed it. "But over time, we all became the greatest champions of the All-Volunteer Force, especially after President Reagan came in and funded it properly," Powell recounted. He added, with emphasis: "You won't find anybody in active duty—well, you might find one, but I doubt it—who, at a senior level, would want to go back to a draftee force. I would never again serve with people who didn't want to be in the service."[16]

~

Laird publicly and privately advised every administration, whether Democrat or Republican, over the three decades after he retired from government. President Carter considered his association with Laird to be a fond one, despite the differences in their political parties. His respect for Laird increased when Laird supported Carter's attempt to withdraw all U.S. ground troops from South Korea. The controversy erupted in May 1977 when Carter announced—without careful political preparation of his own military and allies—that he was going to pull U.S. troops out. The chief of staff of the American military command in Seoul, Maj. Gen. Jack Singlaub, was quoted by a reporter as criticizing his commander in chief; he was promptly ordered home and fired by the president.

Carter tried to regain the initiative, in part, by personally asking Laird for a supportive statement that Carter could use at a May 26 press conference. Laird was more than willing to oblige since his own plan, when he was secretary, had been to remove those ground troops. He had begun the first phase by removing twenty thousand U.S. troops from Korea. Just as he had with Vietnamization, it was Laird's plan to Koreanize Korea—provide enough funds and training so Korea could defend itself in ground combat. In his statement to support Carter, Laird said, "I have always questioned . . . a ground combat role for our forces in Asia" when the allies in question can provide it themselves. "Our Asian allies should rely primarily on air and sea support from the United States and must accept under these mutual defense treaties the primary responsibility in providing the ground combat deterrent. This was my position during the Eisenhower, Kennedy, Johnson, Nixon, Ford, and Carter administrations. It has not changed."

President Carter used the statement to some effect at his press conference, but the opposition to his plan was already too strong in Congress. Laird said he would have helped more if Carter had included *all* of Laird's plan—which had as its key element a seven-year modernization program of Republic of Korea ground, air, and sea forces, funded by the United States. "Carter forgot that part of the plan so his effort failed," Laird concluded.[17]

Carter enlisted Laird again regarding the Panama Canal treaty. Returning the canal to Panama was an implicit promise made by a number of administrations. Panamanian president Omar Torrijos insisted that the time had come to finalize a treaty. Carter asked Jerry Ford and Laird to round up moderate Republicans to come out in support of a treaty. The conservative Republican opposition, led by Ronald Reagan, was intense and emotional in the counterattack, charging a "giveaway" of the canal. In the end, Carter and Torrijos signed treaties providing for the return of the canal to Panama twenty-three years hence, on January 1, 2000. The bitter politics of that battle so tainted Carter that, twenty years later he explained, "in my own life, I kind of divide people into two parts—the ones who helped me with the Panama Canal treaties, and the other ones who tried to stab me in the back. . . . And Melvin Laird was one of those who knew the importance of keeping the canal open, and he was a good supporter of those treaties, which I really appreciated."[18]

On occasion, Laird had some fun with the earnest and intense Carter. In 1978, while Laird was on a Phillips Petroleum trip with his two sons, John and David, he included a stopover in Hamburg to visit his old friend, West German chancellor Helmut Schmidt. Schmidt had just completed a four-day summit with Soviet premier Leonid Brezhnev and had tried to call Carter to personally brief him on the talks, but Carter was teaching his Sunday School class and wouldn't take a phone call unless it was an emergency. Laird and his sons arrived soon after, at 5 p.m. that Sunday. "Let's have a drink," Schmidt pronounced, unwinding after the four-day summit. Then Schmidt asked Laird why Carter wouldn't come out of church to talk with the chancellor. Laird understood Carter's priorities and did his best to explain. Carter finally returned the call while Schmidt was drinking and chatting with Laird.

Schmidt and Carter talked for about twenty minutes about the summit and other issues, arguing heatedly at least once. More than a little irritated with Carter, and just for fun, Schmidt finally said, "I have a good friend who's here with me, and I'm going to let him talk to you."

"So I get on the phone," Laird recalled. "Carter didn't know who I was so I said, 'This is Mel Laird,' which drove Carter a little nuts because he thought I was there somehow for the Brezhnev meeting."

After a short exchange between Laird and Carter, Schmidt came back on the phone and ended the conversation. As soon as Schmidt hung up, he groused to Laird: "That son of a bitch. I was doing something nice to call him at all, and he started arguing with me . . . raising hell about the things I *didn't* talk with Brezhnev about!" Schmidt was never a fan of Carter, who waffled on three important occasions when Schmidt took an unpopular stand on behalf of Carter (including support of the neutron bomb), only to have Carter reverse his position. "Carter was always asking his moral conscience,

'Is it right what I said yesterday? Is it right what I decided yesterday?' And then, under the influence of his wife, Rosalyn, he would come to another conclusion the next morning. But I had relied on his decision yesterday, and taken action on the basis of that decision. Then, a couple of days later, he comes up with a new insight. This happened several times."[19]

The morning after drinks with Schmidt, Laird got a frantic call from the CIA's top man in Berlin, George Carver. Laird knew Carver well, since he had been one of his CIA briefers on Vietnam when Laird was defense secretary. "I have to see you right away," Carver urged.

"The boys and I are not going to be in Berlin until Tuesday or Wednesday," Laird responded.

"I HAVE to see you," Carver reiterated. "The president is all upset with us that we didn't know what you were up to regarding Schmidt and Brezhnev."

Laird's son John remembered that his father responded, "I'm here with my two boys, so we'll have to go out to dinner when we get to Berlin. What's the best restaurant in town?" Carver grudgingly agreed to pick up the tab, only to find that Laird had been on a harmless visit with an old friend instead of being part of some massive right-wing conspiracy with Schmidt to undercut Carter's initiatives with Russia.[20]

Perhaps Laird's biggest impact on the Carter administration was his role as a burr under Carter's saddle on the SALT II strategic arms limitation talks. Laird was a proponent of arms control but only if the United States kept up its strategic strength with robust defense spending. In August 1977, after the Russians rejected a radical arms-reduction proposal by Carter, Laird offered a plan to get the talks moving again. The plan meant that Carter would have to promise to increase defense spending, which was a commitment he would not make at the time. In December Laird used the *Reader's Digest* to air his opinion in a story titled: "Arms Control: The Russians Are Cheating!" Laird deplored the fact that even as the Soviets were increasing their own defense spending, the United States was decreasing its budgets.[21] After the article appeared, Defense Secretary Harold Brown began consulting more regularly with Laird, anxious to enlist him on the side of SALT II. But Laird continued to express displeasure with some of the cruise missile limitations being proposed, as well as other issues.

Carter and Brezhnev signed the SALT II agreement in Vienna on June 18, 1979. Three months later Laird published another *Reader's Digest* article that questioned the value of the treaty. Although Laird was disparaging about aspects of the treaty, he did not come right out and oppose Senate ratification. Brown said that was the result of a deal he had made with Laird: "In return for an increase in defense spending, Mel agreed to at least keep quiet about it—*not* oppose it."[22] It was the Soviets who killed any possibility of ratification when they invaded Afghanistan in December 1979. Though it remained unratified, both sides generally abided by the signed accord for seven years.

Laird and Carter never became bosom buddies, but they shared a healthy mutual respect. At a minimum, Carter respected Laird's network of friends. When the former president ran into a zoning problem regarding an access road to his presidential library in Atlanta, Laird called a childhood friend from Marshfield who was a city councilwoman in Atlanta. He prevailed upon her to rule in Carter's favor. One thing Carter never knew: Laird wrote a private letter in the mid-1990s to the Nobel Prize committee arguing, as a Republican, that Jimmy Carter, the Democratic former president, deserved the Peace Prize. When Carter was finally awarded the coveted honor, Laird heartily congratulated him without mentioning the letter.

~

The intellectual foundation of what became the "Reagan Revolution" was laid most prominently by the American Enterprise Institute for Public Policy Research (AEI). Congressman Laird was one of its original founders and kept his hand in it. After he resigned as defense secretary, Laird became more intimately involved in buttressing and growing the AEI. The failure of Gerald Ford to win his first election for the presidency in 1976 proved a particular boon to AEI, which became a virtual Republican government-in-exile during the Carter years as nearly two dozen former top Ford and Nixon officials collaborated with the organization. By 1977 AEI's budget had ballooned to $10 million, and the following year, Laird spearheaded a three-year campaign to raise a $60 million endowment. Laird used it as a launch pad for some of his strongest ideas during the Carter administration, particularly on military matters. Laird coauthored a study on military personnel costs with former Pentagon official Lawrence Korb and was credited with framing the debate on that subject and getting the military a much-needed pay raise. (On Laird's recommendation, Korb was later appointed assistant secretary of defense for manpower in the Reagan administration.) In 1978 Laird's former assistant, Bill Baroody Jr., succeeded his father as president of AEI.

Presidential aspirant Ronald Reagan and his advisors kept in close touch with AEI to utilize its expertise while preparing his presidential run.[23] Meanwhile, to Laird's surprise, Jerry Ford was showing signs that he might like to try for the presidency again in 1980. "Jerry is bitten with running again," Laird told the *Washington Post* in September 1978. "I think it's a mistake,

and I've told him that. But he thinks lightning can strike twice." In March
1980 Ford voiced his thoughts about possibly running, and there was Laird,
acting in the role of an honest friend, dousing the sparks again. While it would
be "very easy" to find Republicans eager to have Ford run, Laird told the *Post's*
David Broder, it would require every one of Reagan's opponents, including
George H. W. Bush, to drop their races and back Ford to wrest the nomination from Reagan. "I don't want to see Jerry hurt," Laird told another reporter.
"I just don't think the numbers are there now," and he was right.[24]

After Reagan won the nomination, Ford angled for the vice presidency.
Reagan aides and Ford's emissary, Kissinger, determined that what Ford really
wanted was power that would make him a co-president of sorts. Laird did
nothing to help. Instead, he quietly advised Reagan in the strongest terms that
there was only one possible choice as his vice presidential nominee—George
H. W. Bush. "I thought that would be the best way to bring the party together. As a moderate, George was the best candidate and could do more for
Reagan than any other candidate." Although he had not been forceful publicly about it, Laird had actually been pro-Bush, not Reagan, during the presidential primary cycle—in part, out of loyalty to Ford. "Jerry was never really
able to recover from Reagan's challenge in 1976, and I always held Reagan
responsible for that loss," Laird explained. "Maybe I should forgive and forget, but I am blessed or cursed with a long memory."

When Reagan won the nomination, Laird put those feelings aside and
jumped into the campaign on Reagan's behalf. He authored editorials, made
speeches, and otherwise stumped for the Reagan-Bush ticket.[25] It was enough
to earn him a seat at the table when Reagan began choosing his cabinet. Laird
flew to California and gave a hard pitch to make George Shultz secretary of
state. Laird had promoted Shultz's career, suggesting him for Nixon's first
secretary of labor, then later secretary of the treasury. Working against Shultz
was Caspar Weinberger, a longtime rival. Shultz was president of Bechtel Corporation, and Weinberger was its vice president. Weinberger whispered in
Reagan's ear that Shultz didn't want to leave Bechtel. Laird learned of this
deception but couldn't warn Shultz in time. Meanwhile, Weinberger and
Reagan advisors were pushing hard for Alexander Haig as secretary of state.
Laird's take on Haig was, "Hell, you can appoint him, but you'll be sorry
because he has no feel for the political situation. You have to have someone
in the State Department who has some good political instincts." He said as
much to Reagan's advisors, but the they overrode him. Haig was appointed
secretary of state, and Weinberger became defense secretary.[26] Nine months
later Laird was at a White House reception when an exasperated Reagan took

him aside: "Mel, you sure were right. I wished I'd have followed your advice in the first place." Haig lasted only eighteen months on the job before he was replaced by Shultz.

Laird despaired of Weinberger's long reign at the Pentagon. Weinberger had been called "Cap the Knife" when he was chief of Nixon's Office of Management and Budget, regularly trying to slash Laird's defense budgets. But once he became secretary himself, Cap the Knife became Cap the Ladle, pouring out money and capitulating to the services. In a November 1980 *Washington Post* op-ed essay, Laird warned the incoming Reagan administration of the course Weinberger would take: "The worst thing that can happen is to go on a defense spending binge that will create economic havoc at home and confusion abroad and that cannot be dealt with wisely by the Pentagon." He urged a moderate buildup, not a binge, now that the defense-minded Reagan was in control. What disturbed Laird the most—other than the record deficits that began to accrue with increased defense spending—was *what* Weinberger was choosing to spend it on: nuclear weapons. In two *Washington Post* essays in 1982 and 1983 Laird urged the administration to focus on quality manpower, not the bells and whistles of costly new hardware.[27]

By the second Reagan administration, with Weinberger still in place and pushing the expensive Strategic Defense Initiative (SDI, or "Star Wars"), Laird raised the volume of his criticism. Not only was the complicated technology not workable, but it was also burning up money that would be better spent on the men and women of the military. While not abandoning his pursuit of nuclear missilery, Weinberger did lobby successfully for better funding for personnel. "The volunteer system was breaking down and they always kept asking me *when* we were going to start the draft again. Not *whether*," Weinberger recalled. With Laird's help, he acknowledged, "we ultimately turned the whole thing around. By the time I left, we had waiting lists of people who wanted to get in the military. We didn't have enough slots for them."[28]

Laird's loyalty to the men and women serving in the military was matched privately by his loyalty to veterans who had worked for him. When his long-time aide Carl Wallace died of cancer in 1982, Laird prevailed on Reagan's Army secretary Jack Marsh to waive the strict requirements and allow Army veteran Wallace to be buried in Arlington National Cemetery. Five years later, though, Marsh turned him down when Laird wanted the same favor for his former public affairs chief, Dan Henkin, who had been in the Merchant Marine. Henkin's widow, who was herself dying, had begged Laird to bury her husband in Arlington, so Laird couldn't quit after Marsh's rejection. Time was running out because Henkin was Jewish and had to be buried within twenty-four hours. Laird picked up the phone and went over Marsh's head to get approval from President Reagan himself.[29]

~

During the Reagan administration, Laird was continually plied with requests to serve in government again. He rejected some entreaties but accepted others. The first came from president-elect Reagan, who asked him to serve as chairman of the Foreign Intelligence Advisory Board. Because of Mel's position as senior counselor for national and international affairs at the Reader's Digest Association, the association considered it a conflict of interest, so Laird turned it down.

In early 1982 Laird accepted a co-chair position (along with former senator Adlai Stevenson) on the Commission on the Presidential Nominating Process under the auspices of the White Burkett Miller Center for Public Affairs at the University of Virginia. The ten-member bipartisan panel concluded something that Laird already knew before the commission was formed—that the presidential primary system was a mess. But the panelists put it more politely in their final report, saying the whole process had become "cumbersome, complex, and confusing."

In the 1960s most delegates to party conventions were chosen in state party caucuses and could exercise an independent choice about their party's nominee. Presidential primaries played an important, but secondary, role, with many of the delegates still retaining the right at the convention to choose the candidate they wanted, no matter who had won the state primary. By 1980, however, some thirty-seven states held primaries, and nearly three-quarters of the delegates were bound in their convention to follow the popular vote. The problem was that the early primaries knocked out some candidates, leaving voters in the later primaries without a full slate of choices.

The Laird-Stevenson panel recommended a reduction in the number of primaries to no more than sixteen, which proved impossible to achieve. Among other recommendations, they urged that more ex officio delegates— drawn from among members of Congress, governors, and high party officials—be included in the nominating conventions because they would not be bound by the results of state delegate selection contests. The Democratic National Committee, which was already considering changes, adopted several of the reforms, including the participation of a specified number of elected officials at their national conventions.[30]

The following October, in the wake of a terrorist bombing that killed 241 Marines in their Beirut, Lebanon, barracks, Reagan and Shultz leaned on Laird to take over for Robert McFarlane as the administration's roving Middle East envoy. (McFarlane had been appointed the new national security advisor.) "My non-acceptance was not easy to communicate to these two friends," recalled Laird, who felt he was too busy at the *Digest* and on corporate boards fending off raiders to accept such a no-win assignment. Columnists Evans and Novak noted that Laird had long been frustrated that the Reagan administration (and others preceding) had put the United States in the role of "playing 'Israel's attorney' and thus alienating the Arabs." That one-sidedness invited future disaster, he warned. Reagan and Shultz went to their second choice, Donald Rumsfeld, who agreed to take on the difficult task.[31]

That same year, John McCloy invited Laird to a luncheon at the River Club in New York. Among other things, McCloy had been undersecretary of war in World War II, high commissioner to Germany following the war, and chairman of Chase Manhattan Bank. McCloy explained that he would soon be stepping down as chairman of the Public Oversight Board (POB) and wanted Laird to take his seat as a member. The autonomous body of five members was established in 1977 by the American Institute of Certified Public Accountants' to oversee the self-regulation of accounting firms. Laird accepted and served from 1984 to 2001.[32]

In February 1985 the Center for Strategic and International Studies (CSIS) at Georgetown University announced that Laird had agreed to co-chair a forty-one-member Commission on National Elections with former Democratic party chairman Robert Strauss. The commission heard from thirty-seven witnesses at five public hearings before issuing its report on November 26, 1985. Its chief contribution was the creation of the Commission on Presidential Debates to institutionalize quadrennial debates. Prior to that time, the League of Women Voters had sponsored the debates. The two-party commission has run the presidential and vice presidential debates for the last two decades, while the league has continued to sponsor presidential primary debates.

~

As interesting as some of the panels and commissions were, none of them could hold a candle for sheer intrigue to the outfit President Reagan got Laird to chair in 1987—a panel to assess serious problems at the old and new U.S. embassy buildings in Moscow. Since 1952 the U.S. mission had been housed "temporarily" at an old apartment building on Tchaikovsky Street in Moscow. During those years, the Soviets had managed to bug it in every possible manner. In 1987 American electronic experts discovered a tiny microphone in the middle of a hand-carved replica of the Great Seal of the United States, which had been presented as a gift from the Russians and had likely heard every conversation near it since 1945. From 1953 on, the Russians bombarded the embassy with microwaves in an attempt to pick up emanations from other bugs in the embassy. In May 1964 Americans found fifty-two microphones that had been cleverly hidden in bamboo tubes built into the embassy walls. In one of the more infamous episodes, from 1976 to 1984 the Russians managed to place bugs in thirteen electric typewriters used at the embassy. The bugs transmitted the movements of the rotational typing element to nearby listening devices, allowing the Russians to re-create the secret memos, reports, and correspondence typed on those machines.[33]

Two embarrassments finally caused Reagan to convene the Laird panel in April 1987. Marines had been arrested in sensational espionage cases, which portrayed them as having been compromised by KGB-controlled Russian girlfriends. And, the new chancery at the U.S. embassy under construction in Moscow had been found to be so infested with electronic bugs that many thought it should be torn down and reconstructed under tighter security measures. It was an intelligence disaster, and Laird felt a patriotic call to arms to correct the problem. He chose as his fellow panelists Gen. John Vessey, former chairman of the Joint Chiefs of Staff; Richard Helms, former CIA director and ambassador to Iran; and Diego Asencio, former ambassador to Brazil and Colombia. Gen. Robert Pursley, by then retired from the Air Force, served as special assistant.[34]

In June the panel traveled to Moscow, where the Russians accommodated them in a thoroughly bugged guest house. Vessey's room had twin beds, while two women—counterintelligence experts assigned to the panel—had to share a double bed in an otherwise similar room. One day, when Laird and Vessey were walking down a Moscow street near the embassy, the general suggested he switch rooms with the women. By the time they got back to the guest house, their belongings had already been moved to the new rooms. Somehow the conversation between Laird and Vessey had been picked up on the street by the KGB, and orders had been given to make the move.[35]

The Moscow Assessment Review Panel's final report was classified and never publicly released. The panel made fifty-three recommendations, the majority of which were enacted, according to a subsequent (also classified) State Department report.[36] Laird placed ultimate blame for lax security on U.S. ambassador Arthur Hartman, although he was not actually named in the report. "The Ambassador, as the senior official present, is responsible for all that the Embassy staff does or fails to do. . . . He employed a management style that remained aloof until a specific event occurred that required his attention. This was clearly inadequate," the report read. Hartman once ordered

a metal detector removed from a Marine post because he found it inconvenient. He also advocated continued use of Russians in clerical positions
even though he knew that many of them were KGB agents. His attitude about
counterintelligence needs left the building and its American employees wide
open to Soviet surveillance.[37]

Laird's report urged a clearer policy regarding embassy personnel and frat-
ernization with the Russians, as well as a downsizing of personnel while vital
repairs were made to the old embassy, which the report described as "seedy"
and "disgraceful."[38] In the wake of the report, President Reagan made the
decision to tear down the new, unoccupied embassy and rebuild it from
scratch with only American workers and materials. The Bush administration
agreed with the decision, but experts during the Clinton administration felt
it could be saved as long as they put a four story "top hat" of secure offices
on the top of the building. In 1976 the new embassy had been projected to
cost from $75 to $100 million. After construction, deconstruction and recon-
struction, when the new building finally opened in May 2000, it had cost
$370 million, making it the most expensive diplomatic building project in
U.S. history.[39]

꙾

Bill Clinton and Mel Laird were never pals. "I attended briefings at the White
House, some receptions and a couple of lunches," he recalled. "But I don't
have a great personal relationship. I'm not his greatest admirer." Nevertheless, successive Clinton defense secretaries counseled with Laird, just as their
predecessors had done. The first was a close friend of Laird's, former Wisconsin representative Les Aspin. His tenure was short, and he was replaced
by William Perry, a longtime Laird fan who listened carefully to what Laird
had to say. A key reason for that respect was Laird's "Founding Father" role
for the All-Volunteer Force. Perry said, "To qualify my view, I'd say I was
somewhere between skeptical and negative about instituting the volunteer
Army, when it began. I knew Mel had quite a lot of resistance from other
sources on that, but he bulled it through anyway. By the time I became
deputy secretary [in 1993], I came to believe that it was one of the great successes in reorganization of defense in decades. It's a magnificent success story
now, and Mel doesn't get full credit for it. He gets the credit for instituting
it, though it took a lot of other people after him to actually implement it."[40]

While Laird was fond of Perry, he was less enamored of his successor, former Maine senator William Cohen. Laird got so frustrated with Cohen's inability to manage the Pentagon and hold off the White House's demands that
he wrote a letter of complaint in 1998 to Sen. John Warner, chairman of the

Senate Armed Services Committee. "Over the past several months, I have con-
tinued to get reports that the Administration is using the Defense Department as a dumping ground for non-performers in other parts of government,"
Laird wrote. A former Clinton White House deputy chief of staff had related:
"We use the Pentagon to take our underperformers from the White House."
Having learned by his own experience, as Warner well knew, Laird asked
Warner to remind his former Senate colleague to resist such manipulation by
the White House. "I have failed to get this message to our friend Cohen. He
is headed for real trouble if he does not get the message."[41]

Perhaps the most intriguing aspect of Laird and the Clinton era was his
relationship with his former intern, Hillary Rodham Clinton. She considered
him an important mentor, and the friendship endured, mostly carried on
behind the scenes through a mutual friend, Health and Human Services secretary Donna Shalala. Once chancellor of the University of Wisconsin, which
brought her into Laird's circle of friends, Shalala secured his help for her confirmation process. "He's my favorite wise man," she said. "He just knew more
than anybody how to survive in Washington." Early in 1998, Laird correctly
predicted to Shalala and other friends that Hillary would run and be elected
to the Senate from New York.[42]

But Laird could never bring himself to admire her husband. When a dis-
graced President Clinton, post-impeachment hearings, was invited in 2000 to
speak and receive an honorary degree at Laird's alma mater, Carleton College,
Laird was not pleased. He said of Clinton, "This is the greatest actor we've ever
had in the White House; he could give acting lessons to Ronald Reagan." Laird
was "at a loss to understand why Bill Clinton is so admired and respected."

⁓

Laird considered George W. Bush's electoral victory over Al Gore in November 2000 *prima facie* evidence that "Bush is the luckiest presidential candidate
in my lifetime—because everything was against him. Gore had everything
going for him, and he just lost the election. Gore was a little too polished,
and he made everybody think he was brighter than them. What you want
to do is make people always feel that they're brighter than you." The *second
best* piece of advice Laird gave Bush during the campaign was to debate Gore.
"Bush didn't want to debate, and his father agreed with him. His father
didn't like debating in the House or as a candidate, so that colored his thinking. So I leaned real hard on (George W.) Bush to debate." Laird solicited
Bob Strauss, his partner in establishing the Presidential Debate Commission,
to urge Bush's participation in the debate. Laird was confident that Bush
would come across as more approachable than the stiff Gore.

Laird maintained that the *best* advice he gave candidate Bush was to select Dick Cheney as his running mate. With the election over, Laird regularly called and visited Cheney during the transition. "I made certain recommendations, among them that Rummy [Rumsfeld] be secretary of defense. I went through all kinds of hell doing that. But that's another story," and one Laird was not willing to detail. Cheney leaned toward Paul Wolfowitz in defense, but finally recommended that Rumsfeld would be secretary and Wolfowitz would be deputy secretary. (That was not ideal, in Laird's view, since it meant that Rumsfeld had to take Cheney's recommendation and could not pick his own man as his deputy.) That was the package recommended to Bush, who signed off on the appointments.

Laird's advice, while never totally predictable, was always interesting. When President Reagan died in June 2004, Laird was recovering from knee replacement surgery and could not travel to Washington for the funeral. But he rallied to stop a move by Senate majority leader Bill Frist to name the Pentagon after Reagan. He called John Warner and recounted how, in the emotional aftermath of Eisenhower's death, Senators Goldwater and Tower and others had called on Laird to support naming the Pentagon after Ike. The late five-star general was a soldier-hero of the first order, yet Laird thought it was a mistake to name the Pentagon after anyone. Warner agreed with Laird and opposed renaming the Pentagon. The Senate was appeased by naming National Airport after Reagan. "Mel, my valued advisor: Your input on this naming issue was critical," Senator Warner wrote by hand after the debate. "The 'Pentagon' will, I am confident, remain!"[43]

29

Another Vietnam?

AMERICA'S TENTH SECRETARY OF DEFENSE arrived at the Pentagon for a wide-ranging private conference with the newly installed twenty-first secretary of defense on a brisk February afternoon in 2001. The escort whom Secretary Donald Rumsfeld had sent to meet his friend Mel Laird at the River Entrance offered to give Laird the standard VIP tour. "Sure," Laird said with a smile. But soon he took over the tour himself, providing the escort with an insider's view of history.

When they reached the defense secretary's complex, Rumsfeld emerged and greeted Laird warmly. It was a fine time for the military, they agreed. The eight-year era of Bill Clinton's strained relationship with the Defense Department was over, the peacetime demands on the U.S. military were manageable, and Rumsfeld, a Navy veteran, had time to work on a transformation of the Pentagon.

Over the course of the visit the two secretaries, past and present, naturally turned to topics of abiding national interest. Remembering the Watergate era, when Nixon had closed his ears to the honest counsel of those he should have trusted most, Laird warned that the new administration must not closet itself with a cadre of yes-men. "Don't worry," Rumsfeld said, "you're preaching to the choir." Rumsfeld rehearsed how he, as White House chief of staff, had advised President Ford of the same thing. It was at Rumsfeld's own urging, he pointed out, that Ford had created the "Kitchen Cabinet" of which Laird became a prominent member.

As they went on to discuss some of the key lessons of Vietnam, Rumsfeld praised Laird's program of Vietnamization. While grateful for the remark, Laird reminded the younger secretary that it was in 1975, when Rumsfeld served as Ford's chief of staff, that Vietnamization had collapsed and Saigon had fallen. A weak White House lobbying effort had failed to prevent Congress from cutting off military supplies and financial aid. Rumsfeld took the veiled criticism well, and the conversation continued to other topics.

The most memorable moment came as Laird was leaving. The two were standing in the hall, looking at some of Rumsfeld's photos and talking about past wars that had left thousands of U.S. troops still stationed around the world in a protective capacity—Germany, Japan, South Korea, Bosnia, and elsewhere. Laird got up close to his old friend and pointedly said, "Remember this, Rummy: *It's a helluva lot easier to get into a war than it is to get out of one!*"

"I will, I will," an amused Rumsfeld agreed, happy that he had inherited a first-class volunteer military that was not engaged in any war.[1]

Laird's first reaction to the events of September 11, 2001, was similar to that of other Americans—profound shock and deep sorrow. But like many veterans of battle, he quickly turned to the practical and strategic question—how to respond. It was the kind of training ingrained into the young Ensign Laird and other Navy men in the Pacific in 1945 as they fended off kamikaze attacks by the Japanese. Memories of that shared experience had not faded, and the day before 9/11, some of the men of the *Maddox* had coincidentally been sharing those memories. It was an eerie backdrop for Laird and his former shipmates as they watched suicide pilots of another ilk crash planes into the World Trade Center and Pentagon. "Today's events are shockers—even for vets," observed a shaken *Maddox* shipmate of Laird's, Mel Cunningham.[2]

In the wake of 9/11, many retired defense experts and officers aired their views on television and radio shows, in magazine and newspaper columns. As they freely dispensed advice to President Bush and Secretary Rumsfeld about how to respond, Laird remained silent. When the *Washingtonian* magazine rushed out an article identifying the "71 People the President Should Listen To," prominently naming Laird among them, still he offered no public comment.[3]

Three weeks after 9/11, a friend pressed Laird on why he wasn't in the thick of it.

"What makes you think I'm not?" he responded.

Laird had learned that the most useful advice is given privately, when the advisor seeks no attention or credit for it. Although Rumsfeld had called him soon after 9/11, Laird had declined to join the host of self-proclaimed experts. Early on, he went to the Pentagon several times, at Rumsfeld's request, to review the intelligence and offer ideas. In the new war against terrorists, Laird stressed, "fast solutions are not possible." But he chose not to go public with this or any other advice.

Laird's only visible contribution in the aftermath of 9/11 took a very different form, one inspired by sympathy for its victims. In 2002 he was asked by Rumsfeld to serve on an eleven-member committee to determine the appropriate memorial for the 184 service personnel and civilians who died when American Airlines Flight 77 struck the Pentagon on 9/11. Together with the others on the committee, Laird consulted with the families of those killed and pored over almost twenty-five hundred design entries. The winning design, "Light Benches," featured 184 illuminated aluminum benches, each engraved with the name of a victim. The resulting memorial, which includes clusters of shade trees, now stands on two acres of Pentagon lawn, within three hundred feet of the crash site.[4]

In the run-up to the March 2003 invasion of Iraq, behind the scenes Laird firmly opposed the timing of the action and the claims to its necessity. Only an occasional hint of his feelings showed in public. For instance, almost a year before, at the fourteenth annual Conference of the Secretaries of Defense, Laird had opined that the key issue with Iraq was not whether a war could be won. "The question is what we do afterwards," Laird said. Frank Carlucci chimed in with agreement. "If we thought [nation-building in] Afghanistan was tough, try Iraq!" Added Harold Brown: "If you put American troops in an urban setting where there are terrorists, the Americans are going to end up being the target."[5]

Perhaps most distressing to Laird in early 2003 was that the top officials of the Bush administration did not seem to want to listen to anyone who was not bent on war. Laird and his friends Brent Scowcroft and Larry Eagleburger (who served, respectively, as national security advisor and secretary of state to the first President Bush) spoke about this frustration among themselves. Only the usually cautious Scowcroft had gone public with his opposition, and he was now paying the price for it. His authorship of an August 2002 *Wall Street Journal* column criticizing Bush's Iraq policy had made him persona non grata at the White House. Polling their respective sources within the George W. Bush administration, each of the three men found an inflexible determination to bring down Saddam Hussein. President Bush and Vice President Cheney had become absolutely committed to the course. Scowcroft was surprised to discover that his own protégé, National Security Advisor Condoleezza Rice, was just as evangelical as Bush and Cheney about changing the face of the Middle East.

Rumsfeld, too, was "gung ho" on the idea of a challenge in Iraq. As Deputy Secretary Paul Wolfowitz and close Pentagon advisor Richard Perle stoked Rumsfeld's enthusiasm, Laird advised waiting for more reliable intelligence reports about weapons of mass destruction in Iraq. He reminded Rumsfeld of the intelligence failures leading to the U.S. escalation of the Vietnam War— the assassination in 1963 of President Bui Diem and the nonexistent second "attack" in 1964 in the Gulf of Tonkin.

Laird pinned his hopes for restraint on Secretary of State Colin Powell, the man whose illustrious career Laird had helped launch by sending him over to the White House as a young officer. Again he was let down. "A war cannot be fought by this country without the support of both the State Department and the Department of Defense—any president knows that would be folly," Laird said. "But Colin did not question the intelligence in a more adequate and firm way, so he acquiesced when I believe he shouldn't have." Powell's acceptance of the intelligence on weapons of mass destruction in Iraq was a disappointment to Laird.

The unlikely trio of "antiwar" conspirators had one last move. Scowcroft would ask his friend, former president George H. W. Bush, to get Scowcroft and a few others into the Oval Office for a confidential sit-down. But the men then learned from another veteran of the first Bush administration that the younger Bush's mind was made up, and "he wasn't listening to the old man." "The president's circle of friends had become very small. He just didn't want to talk to anyone who cautioned patience, who suggested he should wait a few weeks more to build up support," Laird said. The backstage lobbying of the three had failed, and once the invasion was on, they felt they had little choice but to publicly support America's new war effort.[6]

Rumsfeld would occasionally ask Laird for his opinion, and get it in spades. With Laird's candor, the distance between them grew. For a time he attended the periodic briefings offered at the Pentagon to former defense secretaries to keep them up to date on the war. On one such occasion, frustrated by the lack of genuine exchange, he walked out in the middle—introducing a fissure in his relations with Rumsfeld.

In early 2004, with the presidential election heating up, Rumsfeld reached out again and asked for Laird's opinion. "You asked me to be frank on how things are going," Laird began in a February 11 note. "You were somewhat upset with me for walking out of the briefing last year on the Middle East situation. I hope you have gotten over it. The briefing was so formalized there was no opportunity to raise questions or make suggestions, only listen. No one is required to follow anything we old timers say, but sometimes it doesn't hurt to listen." Laird reminded Rumsfeld of Laird's own policy about intelligence—never believe the first and second reports. "As I told you in your first week in office," he said, "you can believe the third assessment report on any operation if they concur with the first two—and even then you can be disappointed." The administration was making a serious mistake, he warned, in thinking that stabilizing Iraq would be "a cakewalk."

The four-page letter covered a variety of subjects. Laird urged Rumsfeld to release Bush's entire National Guard record because of the presidential election-year controversy then swirling around about whether Bush had avoided Vietnam service. The same advice about openness held for their mutual friend, Vice President Cheney. "Cheney's unwillingness to divulge the names of individuals meeting with him on energy policy continues to be a mistake. Because of his background after leaving government, transparency and full disclosure should have been his number one concern," Laird wrote.

"Anyway, Rummy, I have rambled around in this note—[but] you asked for it," he concluded. "Tear it up after you have read it, but remember I do love you and [Rumsfeld's wife] Joyce. Your plate is full, but by putting on an extra full-court press, we may be saved and win in November."[7]

The temporary rift was repaired. Rumsfeld found the recommendations useful and prescriptive. "I just once again reread your February 11th memo and found it helpful," he wrote back on June 6. "If you have other thoughts and suggestions as we go along, please do let me have them. Thanks, my friend."[8]

~

In May 2004 the first photos and reports came out revealing the American torture of Iraqi prisoners at Abu Ghraib prison, twenty miles west of Baghdad. The notorious building that once served Saddam Hussein for the torture of dissidents and innocents now served American interrogators in their extraction of information from alleged insurgents. In a striking parallel with an earlier era, it was Seymour Hersh, the same reporter who had exposed the My Lai massacre in Vietnam in 1968, who now disclosed the Army's own damning fifty-three-page investigation of Abu Ghraib in *The New Yorker*. Laird, who during the Vietnam War had spoken up so often and eloquently against the North Vietnamese torture of American prisoners of war, found the practices at Abu Ghraib abhorrent.

Memories of My Lai surfaced again that same month in a different new story—this one featuring Laird himself, cast in an unfamiliar and unwelcome role. On May 26, the National Archives made public twenty thousand pages of private Kissinger documents, the release of which Kissinger had

unsuccessfully contested. Reporters quickly unearthed many tantalizing tid-
bits, especially in the notes of telephone conversations taken by Kissinger's
secretary. Laird had seen some of the notes before and had considered the
source to be questionable. He knew Kissinger had a habit of doctoring the
notes to make himself look better.

Among the conversations reporters latched on to was a November 21, 1969,
discussion between Kissinger and Laird about the unfolding scandal of the
My Lai massacre, an event that had happened during the Johnson administration but had only recently come to light. Laird remembered being most
upset that the previous defense secretary, Clark Clifford, had not acted against
the soldiers involved in the massacre of hundreds of men, women, and children after the incident had occurred in March 1968. More than a year later,
it was up to Laird to respond to the public outcry voicing a grief and rage
he shared.

"K[issinger] was calling about the atrocity case," the secretary's notes began.
"The President wants to make sure L[aird] [has] got a game plan. K said it
was going to be a terrible mess." Laird asked if Kissinger wanted to see the
photos, which were "pretty terrible," but Kissinger declined. "L said about a
game plan, he'd like to sweep the whole thing under the rug, but you can't
do that."[9] On the contrary, he planned to confirm the story by releasing the
results of an investigation he had begun the previous March.

When the notes taken by Kissinger's secretary decades earlier were finally
published in May 2004, Laird was surprised to see attributed to him a phrase
uncharacteristic of his approach in general and incommensurate with his
actions in this specific case. Far from sweeping My Lai under the rug, he
had been the one to launch the investigation and insist that military justice
take its course to address a wrongdoing that had not even happened on his
watch. As he tried to reconstruct that long-ago conversation, Laird remembered telling Kissinger that the investigative report on My Lai would have
to be released as soon as military lawyers gave the okay.[10] It was ironic that
Laird, always an advocate of openness, should now find himself parrying
accusations of concealment.

But it was an irony on which Laird could not dwell for long. During the
past year he had become increasingly concerned about the handling of another
war, one whose far-flung fronts and elusive enemies had led to a uniquely
ominous-sounding appellation—the "War on Terror." Although a frank man
by nature, as a retired government official Laird had always hesitated to speak
out publicly. Gradually, he would begin to break that silence.

～

By 2004, with Iraq now becoming a "quagmire" in its own right, commentators and politicians had begun making more frequent comparisons to Vietnam. This talk, resurrecting old recriminations about the war, roiled Laird's sense of pride in Vietnamization and fanned his long-smoldering resentments about how Ford, Kissinger, and Congress had abandoned South Vietnam in 1975, throwing away the work of Vietnamization. Vietnamization, as he envisioned it from the outset, meant a very gradual ceding of responsibility to the South Vietnamese. While constantly pushing for an accelerated withdrawal of American troops, in his role as secretary of defense Laird had depended on other branches of government to provide South Vietnam with the economic and political support that he viewed as essential to the success of the program. And he trusted those others to follow through as well on their guarantees of continuing military assistance in the form of equipment and strategy.

Renewing the debate with his old friend and frequent sparring partner, Laird wrote Kissinger a private letter in January 2002 after reading an incomplete account by the former secretary of state about the fall of Vietnam. Laird felt Kissinger was distancing himself from the Paris Accords negotiated, as he wrote, "under your skillful leadership." "I sold Vietnamization to the President, you, the Congress, [General Creighton] Abrams, [Ambassador Ellsworth] Bunker, and the Joint Chiefs in 1969, clearly stating that our personnel withdrawals would be based on our longer-term military aid to the South until the South and North could themselves negotiate a settlement," Laird wrote to Kissinger. "We welshed on our promises as a nation, thus assuring that no peaceful agreement between the North and South would ever be reached. We invited, by our actions, the complete takeover by the North." For this failure he blamed the Ford administration. "I never lost a vote on Vietnamization and the support of military aid to the South Vietnamese forces upon our withdrawal," he wrote. But after Laird left office, "the ball was dropped . . . by the White House, Defense, and State [Kissinger himself] in marshaling the support for the promises of the Paris Agreement and the Vietnamization program. . . . It takes hard work to get the right numbers to obtain a majority vote, but any Secretary of Defense or State who can't get that vote just hasn't tried hard enough."

Although candid in his criticisms, Laird signed off "with best wishes" and assured Kissinger that the very real difference of opinion about the historical moment they shared in no way lessened Laird's respect and admiration for the accomplishments of his fellow statesman.[11]

Meanwhile, throughout 2004 and into 2005, talk escalated in Congress and around the nation about how the United States should get out of Iraq before it became "another Vietnam." For the octogenarian Laird, it was time to start speaking up. In an effort to set the record straight, Laird wrote a lengthy analytical cover article for the November 2005 issue of the influential journal *Foreign Affairs*, published by the Council on Foreign Relations. Entitled "Iraq: Learning the Lessons of Vietnam," Laird wrote that he feared a shorthand version of history had left America "timorous about war, deeply averse to intervening in even a just cause, and dubious of its ability to get out of a war once it is in one." The article compared and contrasted the Vietnam and Iraq wars and said that the only way the Iraq War could become "another Vietnam" would be if the United States ignored the lessons of history and pulled out of Iraq precipitously. Echoing his early advice to Rumsfeld, he added in a much-quoted sentence: "Getting out of a war is still dicier than getting into one, as President George W. Bush can attest."

The lesson of Vietnamization, Laird wrote, was that the Bush administration "must adhere to a standard of competence for the Iraqi security forces, and when that standard is met, U.S. troops should be withdrawn in corresponding numbers." It had worked in Vietnam, and similarly in Iraq, "the United States should not let too many more weeks pass before it shows its confidence in the training of the Iraqi armed forces by withdrawing a few thousands U.S. troops from the country. We owe it to the restive people back home to let them know there is an exit strategy, and, more important, we owe it to the Iraqi people. The readiness of the Iraqi forces need not be 100 percent, nor must the new democracy be perfect before we begin our withdrawal."

As to the treatment of detainees, there was no excuse. "To stop abuses and mistakes by the rank and file, whether in the prisons or on the streets, heads must roll at much higher levels than they have thus far," Laird wrote. "For me, the alleged prison scandals reported to have occurred in Iraq, in Afghanistan, and at Guantanamo Bay have been a disturbing reminder of the mistreatment of our own POWs by North Vietnam. The conditions in our current prison camps are nowhere near as horrific as they were at the 'Hanoi Hilton,' but that is no reason to pat ourselves on the back. The minute we begin to deport prisoners to other nations where they can legally be tortured, when we hold people without charges or trial, when we move prisoners around to avoid the prying inspections of the Red Cross, when prisoners die inexplicably on our watch, we are on a slippery slope toward the inhumanity that we deplore."

Regarding Secretary Rumsfeld, Laird's friend of more than forty years whose appointment he had personally urged on President Bush, it was time for a make-over. "[H]is overconfident and self-assured style on every issue, while initially endearing him to the media, did not play well with Congress during his first term." It was also a mistake for Rumsfeld to think he had to appear "much smarter than the elected officials" to whom he reported on the Hill. Laird said he had been heartened that Rumsfeld seemed to be modifying his style to become "more collegial."

Laird implied that Bush, meanwhile, had become the Great Uncommunicator. "His west Texas cowboy approach—shoot first and answer questions later, or do the job first and let the results speak for themselves—is not working." Laird publicly advised the president to more forcefully and candidly explain to the public the purpose of the mission in Iraq. "When troops are dying, the commander-in-chief cannot be coy, vague, or secretive. We learned that in Vietnam, too."[12]

The article, with equal parts criticism and support, attracted national attention. As the *New York Times* observed, the piece had been "heavily read." Senators John Kerry and Russell Feingold quoted from it as they grilled Secretary of State Condoleeza Rice at an October 19, 2005, hearing of the Senate Foreign Relations Committee. Laird, anxious that his advice should reach those best positioned to implement it, made sure copies of the *Foreign Affairs* article were delivered in advance to both Rumsfeld and Bush. Prodded, it would seem, by Laird's recommendations, Bush soon began a series of prime-time television speeches to educate the public on the Iraq mission.

On January 5, 2006, the president convened a bipartisan meeting of thirteen former secretaries of defense and state. It was a lost opportunity: rather than an authentic exchange of opinions, the event turned out to be a dog-and-pony show, with military briefers on video feed from Iraq monopolizing the discussion. Only Laird and former secretary of state Madeline Albright forcefully spoke their minds. As the group stood for a photo opportunity, Bush told reporters that "not everybody around this table agreed with my decision to go into Iraq, and I fully understand that. And I am most grateful for the suggestions that have been given. We take to heart the advice."

The *New York Times* called it singular that Bush "had waited more than 1,000 days into the war in Iraq—and after many mistakes had been made—to gather together the men and one woman who once held their own skull sessions in that [the Roosevelt] room, and who once used the West Wing as a backdrop for arguments over Vietnam and Somalia, the Balkans and the 1991 Gulf War." *Times* columnist Maureen Dowd found it "disturbing . . . that with several hundreds of years' worth of foreign policy at his elbows, and a bloody, thorny mess in Iraq, Mr. Bush would devote mere moments to letting some fresh air into his House of Pain."[13]

Privately Laird felt similarly; less than fifteen minutes had been allotted for any or all of the thirteen to speak. But he was heartened in the following days to see Bush personally escalate his public relations campaign about the war and Rumsfeld become a bit more respectful of Congress. Then on May 12, Laird returned with nine of the other secretaries for a second meeting, at which Bush acknowledged there had been little time for them to talk during the first round. "This time he really did want to listen, and it was a much better meeting," Laird said.[14]

The War on Terror also gave Laird occasion to come to the defense of his "Total Force" concept. In an essay for the *Washington Post* on February 6, Laird praised the work of the National Guard and Reserves during the war and criticized moves by the Bush administration to downsize the Guard and to scrimp on equipment.[15]

Laird had not been timid about tutoring or criticizing Rumsfeld, but he was equally quick to defend "Rummy" against what Laird saw as unwarranted criticism. In the spring of 2006, several retired generals went public with their complaints about how Rumsfeld was handling the war, accusing him of sidelining those in the military who disagreed with him. Laird took up his pen again, this time with former military assistant Bob Pursley as coauthor on another *Washington Post* essay. The two men wrote that the carping generals had passed up plenty of chances to speak when they were on active duty. Armchair quarterbacking was divisive and would be perceived by the enemy as a sign of weakness. Laird valued and defended civilian control of the military. "Rumsfeld respects the delicate balance between military and civilian control, but in the end, the decisions are his to make," Laird and Pursley wrote.[16]

Laird gave no quarter to increasing calls for Rumsfeld's resignation. But in June, at the annual conference of former defense secretaries, Laird reiterated his belief that no defense secretary should serve more than one term. "I told that to Rummy—that he should stay only four years," Laird said. "But he didn't pay any attention to me." In September Laird again noted to a *USA Today* reporter that "I've cautioned everybody that four years is enough in that particular job. You kind of wear yourself out."[17]

Rumsfeld, the two-time defense secretary, had been both the youngest and oldest man to serve in the post. He resigned in December 2006, only a few days short of being the longest-serving secretary; Robert McNamara still holds that title.

～

"Let's face it, the war was the top issue," Laird bluntly told the *Los Angeles Times* as the reason for the Republican loss of Congress to the Democrats in November 2006. "It's easy to get into a war, but it's hard to get out—that's what voters are telling the president and Congress, and now they have to get it right."[18] But Bush did not seem to get the message. Without reelection of his own to worry about, the president became increasingly intractable, and his approval numbers plunged. The openness and public dialogue that Laird saw as key to public support for the War on Terror fell victim to Bush's determination to justify his agenda in Iraq. Congress saw an opportunity to excoriate Bush, and piled it on.

Without defending Bush's performance or leadership, Laird instead argued in early 2007 that this was no time for Congress to cut off funding for the war. In Vietnam "it would have been devastating if Congress had cut the purse strings before our troops were withdrawn and before the South Vietnamese had learned to stand on their own," Laird wrote in the *Washington Post*. "Democrats are positioned to offer a plan for Iraq, but cutting off funding is not a plan."[19] He urged an increase in the defense budget to assure better pay and equipment—essentials for the all-volunteer Army to thrive.

Parenthetically, he praised his former intern, Sen. Hillary Clinton, as a model of probity in thoughtfully addressing the issue. He called her "the best hope for leadership" from the Democratic majority, and said other presidential candidates "would do well to follow her example." Though Senator Clinton's views on the war evolved after Laird wrote that in January 2007, Laird's point was valid: "In 1972, the Democratic presidential nominee, George McGovern, carried only two states because he had no plan for the war; he only criticized the Vietnamization withdrawal plan." Any presidential candidate in 2008 who simply slammed Bush without proposing his or her own well-reasoned exit strategy for Iraq was not likely to win, in Laird's view.

The "lessons learned" from Vietnam continued to percolate in Laird's thinking. He wrote in the *Washington Post* again on June 29, 2007, recalling his tough talk with the South Vietnamese leadership in early 1969. "The South Vietnamese finally realized that they had the ball in their court: There would be no more 'surges' in American military personnel—only reductions. . . . The schedule of withdrawal should never be telegraphed to the enemy, nor should the ebb and flow of the enemy attacks dictate the pace of withdrawal. That pace should be based on the improvement of the Iraqi defense forces. But Iraq might need some straight talk and threats to make those improvements, just as Saigon needed to see the first American combat units walking out the door."

He concluded: "The same kind of well-devised plan for withdrawal over time is needed for Iraq as it takes over the military security job that belongs to the Iraqi government." The executive and legislative branches, he argued, cannot simply "walk away from their responsibilities and promises as they did in 1975. We have an obligation to carry through in Iraq. Many Americans did not agree on the reasons for going to Iraq in the first place, but the Middle East, with its political, economic, social and cultural issues, is of greater long-term interest to our national security than was Vietnam. Wars are very easy to start but very hard to get out of, as we are finding today in Iraq."[20]

In August 2007 President Bush began making his own comparisons between Iraq and Vietnam. "Three decades later, there is legitimate debate about how we got into the Vietnam War and how we left," Bush said in a speech before the Veterans of Foreign Wars convention in Kansas City, Missouri. "Whatever your position is on that debate, one unmistakable legacy of Vietnam is that the price of America's withdrawal was paid by millions of innocent citizens whose agonies would add to our vocabulary new terms like 'boat people' [and] 're-education camps,'" and the United States must not similarly "abandon" Iraqis struggling to build a democracy.[21]

At the time of the president's speech, U.S. troops had been in Iraq for more than four years, and the taxpayers had spent more than $600 billion on the War on Terror, roughly equal to the inflation-adjusted $614 billion spent on the Vietnam War, according to the nonpartisan Congressional Research Service. During that time, more than 3,700 U.S. soldiers and hundreds of thousands of Iraqis had been killed.[22]

Finally, in September 2007, Bush accepted a recommendation from his commander in Iraq, Gen. David Petraeus, and announced plans to begin bringing home a few U.S. troops. For Laird, Petraeus's recommendations were an echo of reports from Gen. Creighton Abrams in Vietnam. "Training the Iraqi troops is a difficult job indeed, but it can be done if the Iraqi government really wants security," Laird said. His own assessment was a reminder of his Vietnam drumbeat—that if the people of South Vietnam really wanted their democracy, they were capable of taking over the war to win that democracy.

~

Melvin Laird turned eighty-five in September 2007. Although his two knee-replacement surgeries in 2004 had limited his air travel, age had not dulled his political or military instincts. Powerful friends in and out of government continued to give him a bully pulpit whenever he had something to say. As long as his mind was clear, his pen sharp, and his phones and computer in good working order, quitting was not an option. "I plan to be active until the day I die," he said. For a man who was involved in public service, one way or another, for more than sixty years, the reason is the same as the young Ensign Laird proffered to his shipmates coming home from World War II: He felt there was some good he could do.

Epilogue

POLITICIANS LIKE MEL LAIRD don't come along often. In his second life, the one after politics, he did not have to remake himself. He moved through the years with the confidence of one who did not need to make excuses for himself. To observe him is a lesson in how politics ought to work—with civility and integrity, across party lines, compromising for the greater good, and keeping a close ear to the rumble of public opinion and the sound of democracy. Reading the speeches made about him at the 1997 dedication of the Laird Center for Medical Research is like hearing a clarion call for what is needed in politics today.

"Wouldn't it be great if our politics today could also reflect Mel's blend of principle and pragmatism?" Gerald Ford asked.

To many voters, and even more non-voters, parties today are suspected of being decidedly unrepresentative. At worst they appear as little more than conduits for huge amounts of special interest money. But fund-raising abuses are by no means the only cancer eating away at our democracy. Today we look with horror upon the smoke-filled rooms of legend. Over the years, I've sat in more than my share of smoke-filled rooms. So has Mel. I think it's sort of fair to say, both of us, we've even inhaled from time to time. I ask you, who is more accountable to the voters? Those in the smoke-filled room whose jobs depended on keeping their word and who gave us Lincoln, both Roosevelts, Truman and Eisenhower? Or the professional hired guns of today, whose services are for sale, whose convictions are located in focus groups, and whose loyalty may not outlast election day?[1]

For Laird, the nation as a whole was the only focus group that counted, and politics was the art of answering to that focus group with a rare and successful blend of integrity and pragmatism. It wasn't always just about doing good but about having fun as well. David Broder, who was also on hand at the Laird Center dedication, drove home that point in a short speech. He cited three reasons why Laird got along so well with journalists when so many politicians don't.

> Mel Laird was a great source for us in Washington because he scooped up information from his network of pals. He was a reliable source on everything from the latest political gossip to the most arcane and important international strategy.
>
> The second thing that made him [unique] was that he loved to expose plots. And when there wasn't a plot to expose, he would invent one! And sometimes, as when he maneuvered President Ford into the Oval Office, those plots actually worked! And he usually got someone else to carry them out.
>
> Most beguilingly for me and many others, Mel Laird always did his business with that twinkle in his eye that told you that he knew, as well as you did, that politics was really the only game that was worth a grownup's time.[2]

NOTES

Rather than citing each of the hundreds of quotations drawn from interviews the author conducted with Melvin Laird between 1997 and 2008, the following notes cite interviews with Laird only when the date is important to the context of the quotation.

Prologue

1. Laurie Hawley, Laird's longtime executive assistant, interview, 8/12/99; Sen. John Warner, interview, 11/10/99; Richard Capen, former assistant secretary of defense (Legislative Affairs), interview, 8/8/00; Rady Johnson, former assistant secretary of defense (Legislative Affairs), interview, 8/22/00; Herb Klein, former White House director of communications, interview, 7/30/01.

2. "Energetic Laird's Success No Surprise to Followers," *La Crosse Leader-Tribune,* 12/12/68.

3. Richard M. Nixon to MRL, 11/17/72.

4. In interviews with Melvin Laird and former president Ford, variations of the timetable for the conversation and events were offered. The accepted timeline comported with what each of them said most consistently, made the most sense given the *Palm Springs Desert Sun*'s accounts of the governors' conference, and followed the timeline reported in the contemporary *New York Times* account on the selection. "The choice of Rep. Laird . . . was agreed upon by Mr. Nixon and the Wisconsin legislator in a conversation aboard an Air Force jet between Los Angeles and Palm Springs, Calif., on Friday. Mr. Laird talked again with the President-elect on the way from Palm Springs to New York on Saturday." "Laird Reported Choice of Nixon to Head Defense," *New York Times,* 12/9/68.

5. MRL, statement, distributed by Carl S. Wallace, administrative assistant, 12/11/68.

Chapter 1. The Man from Marshfield

1. World War II veterans of the *Maddox,* interviews: Joseph Fanelli, 7/1/01; Marshall (Zeke) A. Monsell, Jr., 8/14/01; Mel Cunningham, 8/30/01; Bill Haldane, 9/8/01; Dr. Malcolm Burris 8/30/01; J. P. Truesdell, Lieutenant, USNR, *Deck Log,* Log Book of the USS *Maddox* (DD731) entry for 1/21/45; James S. Willis, Commander, U.S. Navy, USS *Maddox,* War Diary, USS *Maddox* (DD731), entry for 1/21/45; *War Damage Report,* "Report

of damage from suicide plane crash aboard at 1310 (I) 21 January 1945 while on picket duty in Task Group 38.1 during air strike on Formosa," 1/28/45; (*Maddox*) War Communique No. 2, March 1945; Morison, *Liberation of the Philippines* vol. 13, *History,* 180–81; MRL, "Interview with David Frost," *David Frost Show,* 12/2/70; Capt. Paul Arbo (Ret.), *Howgoesit,* USS *Maddox* veterans newsletter, 3/94; Harlan Laws, GM3/c, notes from the personal diary of Harlan Laws 1944/45, *Howgoesit,* 5/95; Bill Jordan, *Howgoesit,* 9/96; Mel Cunningham, *Howgoesit,* 11/98.

2. Robert Froehlke, interview, 9/10/97. MRL, "Sidelight," *Your Washington Office Report,* 4/26/61; MRL "Interview with David Frost," *David Frost Show,* 12/2/70; Sen. Gaylord Nelson speech, 9/12/97; Marshfield History Project, *Marshfield Story,* 20, 23–24, 27–32, 34, 36–37, 42, 51–54, 72, 167, 188–89, 229, 237, 360–63, 421–22.

3. Froehlke, interview, 9/10/97; Ambassador Tom Graham, former acting director of Arms Control and Disarmament Agency, interview, 10/26/99; Kleiman, interview, 9/27/01. MRL, "Certificate of Registration of Birth," Omaha, NE, 9/1/22; *Marshfield News Herald,* 3/19/46; program, "Melvin Laird Appreciation Night," 11/12/59; *Marshfield News Herald,* 12/9/68; *Marshfield Story,* 8–9, 12–16, 22–23, 31, 118, 184, 190, 361–63.

4. MRL, "Why I Chose a Liberal Arts College," personal essay, ca. 1941.

5. MRL appearance on "Interview with David Frost," *David Frost Show,* 12/2/70.

6. David Laird, MRL's son, interview 2/27/01; Jack McDonald, interview, 9/29/01.

7. James A. Gibbs, author and shipwreck expert, interview, 9/28/01; Coast Guard cables on relevant dates; John L. Reynolds, commander, USN, director, Welfare Division, memorandum for the director of special activities, 2/27/43; Gibbs, *Shipwrecks,* 155–56; Marshall, *Oregon Shipwrecks;* "Oregon Coast Proves a Veritable Graveyard for Ships," *Oregonian,* 2/14/99.

8. MRL transcript, St. Mary's College, Winona, MN, 11/11/43.

9. The number and names of all those aboard the *Maddox* are in the ship's Deck Log for Friday, June 2, 1944. All the Deck Logs, the War Diary, and the Action Reports cited in this chapter have been preserved by the National Archives.

10. Captain Arbo, *Howgoesit,* 3/94 and 5/96; Captain Cunningham, *Howgoesit,* 9/96.

11. Capt. C. Raymond Calhoun, USN (Ret.), 8/24/01; Cunningham, 8/30/01; Calhoun, *Typhoon,* 29; Cunningham, *Howgoesit,* 6/97.

12. *Maddox* War Diary and Deck Logs for relevant time period; Calhoun, *Typhoon,* 20, 32–38; Morison, *Liberation of the Philippines,* vol. 13, *History,* 63–65; Arbo, *Howgoesit,* 3/94 and 5/96; Cunningham, *Howgoesit,* 6/97 and 12/97.

13. Joseph Fanelli, interview, 7/1/01; Burris, *Howgoesit,* 1/93 and 12/97; Cunningham, *Howgoesit,* 12/95 and 12/97.

14. Calhoun, *Typhoon,* 161–62. A Court of Inquiry found that "Admiral Halsey was at fault in not broadcasting warnings to all vessels early in the morning of the eighteenth. The aerological talent assisting was inadequate." Calhoun, *Typhoon,* 161.

15. Morison, *Liberation of the Philippines,* vol. 13, *History,* 82–87; Adamson and Kosco, *Halsey's Typhoons.*

16. USS *Maddox* War Diary and Deck Logs for relevant dates; *Maddox,* "War Communique No. 2," 3/45; Morison, *Liberation of the Philippines,* vol. 13, *History,* 91–92, 157–58, 164–75; Lott, *Brave Ship, Brave Men,* 65–66; Arbo, *Howgoesit,* 3/94 and 5/96; Harlan Laws, GM3/c, "Notes from the Personal Diary of Harlan Laws 1944/45," *Howgoesit,* 5/95; Cunningham, *Howgoesit,* 11/98.

17. The men of Destroyer Squadron 61 never received the commendation they should have for this mission, but some veterans of the operation are attempting to secure appropriate recognition. Owen Gault, with the key help of *Maddox* shipmate Joseph Fanelli, wrote a detailed article on the raid, which appeared in the April 1996 issue of *Sea Classics* magazine. Joseph Fanelli, interview, 7/1/01; Selby Santmyers, interview, 7/5/01; Marshall Monsell, interview, 8/14/01; Bill Haldane, interview, 9/8/01; Mel Cunningham, interview, 9/11, 10/3, and 10/4/01; War Diary and Deck Logs on relevant dates; Morison, *Victory in the Pacific,* vol. 14, *History,* 330–31; Cunningham, *Howgoesit,* 12/92; Arbo, *Howgoesit,* 6/94; Monsell, *Howgoesit,* 12/95; Arbo, *Howgoesit,* 5/96; Burris, *Howgoesit,* 1/93.

18. Dorsey O. Thomas Jr. to MRL, 1/3/73.

19. MRL, "Release to inactive duty—request for/by Melvin R. Laird, Lt. (j.g.), (SC), USNR, 331064," to Chief of Naval Personnel via Chief of Field Branch, Bureau of Supplies and Accounts, 3/19/46.

20. John Wyngaard's June 1943 column suggesting Laird Sr. for governor was published in the *Marshfield News-Herald* and was quoted in a profile of Melvin Robert Laird Sr. in the paper on 12/9/68, on the occasion of his son's selection as secretary of defense.

21. Froehlke, interview, 9/10/97.

22. A smaller group had met with Bovay a month before, on February 28, for the same purpose, but adjourned without forming a new party. The meeting in March is considered the "birth" of the Republican Party by many because the fifty-four present did form a new party and called it "Republican." The National Register of Historic Sites designated the Ripon schoolhouse, which still stands, as the birthplace of the Republican Party, as has the Republican National Committee, because of the March 20, 1854, meeting led by Bovay. However, there are several dozen other claimants to this title. In fact, during that same time period, many similar meetings were held by Northerners in a variety of cities, although only a few used the term "Republican" at their anti-Democrat protest gatherings. For example, Iowans believe the Republican Party started at Crawfordsville during a February 23, 1854, meeting at the Seceder Church. The former governor of New Hampshire, Hugh Gregg, had campaigned by letter and book, to have Exeter, New Hampshire, designated the birthplace. A meeting of anti-Democrat political leaders held by Congressman Amos Tuck at the Blake Hotel on October 12, 1853, not only preceded by months the Ripon meeting but also heard a suggestion by Tuck to use "Republican" as the name for their new party. But three other claimants say that these small local meetings cannot truly be the birth of the party. Michigan Republicans say the first Republican *statewide* convention held there, in Jackson, on July 6, 1854, should be the birth date. But those in Pittsburgh state that the real beginning is in their city, when the Republican Association, forerunner to the Republican National Committee, held its fist meeting there in February 1856. Not so, say Philadelphians. The real birth of Republicans was in their city, some months after the Pittsburgh meeting, when they had their first national Republican convention in 1856. "Paternity Disputes Over Birth of a Party," *Washington Post,* 11/30/86; Frank Baker, "Former Gov. Says GOP Started in New Hampshire, Not Wisconsin," AP, 10/14/93; "Grand Old Dispute: Where Were the Republicans Born?" *Chicago Tribune,* 10/19/93; AP, "Candidates Ignore Crawfordsville, Republican Birthplace Claims," *Dubuque (IA) Telegraph Herald,* 1/28/96; "Exeter Is Birthplace of Republican Party, Britannica Says," *Manchester*

(NH)Union Leader, 10/9/97; "N.H. Historians Not Relinquishing Claims Exeter Was Birthplace of GOP," AP, 8/10/99; "Disputed Birthplace of the GOP in Iowa," AP, 1/21/00.

23. See also AP, "GOP Birthplace Needs New Owner," Chicago Tribune, 3/31/87; "Ripon Traces GOP's Roots to a Schoolhouse," Chicago Tribune, 4/14/88; "Ripon's Grand Old Party Ties; Town Claims Mantle as Site of Meeting That Led to Creation of Republican Party," Milwaukee Journal Sentinel, 7/2/98.

24. Additionally, a University of Wisconsin economics professor, Edwin Witte, has sometimes been dubbed the "father of Social Security" for his role in crafting that program.

25. Thomas Reeves, Life and Times of Joe McCarthy, 71.

26. Six years after he left the Senate, in March 1953, Robert La Follette Jr. committed suicide.

27. Another of "Fighting Bob's" sons, Philip, served two terms as Wisconsin's governor, 1931–33, 1935–39. He was the author of several of the social reforms that are key credits of the Progressive movement.

28. From Craig Gilbert's comprehensive articles on Wisconsin political history in the 8/8/99 edition of the Milwaukee Journal Sentinel. Shalala was once chancellor of the University of Wisconsin–Madison.

29. Jack Mills, interviews, 11/12/99 and 6/2/00.

30. "Senator Laird Speaks to Rotary," Greenwood Gleaner, 4/22/48.

31. Untitled speech, Laird documents, University of Wisconsin collection, ca. 1948.

32. Senator Nelson's quotes are from an interview of 2/7/01 and a speech he gave at the dedication of the Laird Center in Marshfield, WI, 9/12/97.

33. "Kohler to Attend Recommissioning of USS Wisconsin," Wisconsin State Journal, 2/19/51; "Weather Nearly Torpedoes States Battleship Delegation," Milwaukee Journal, 3/4/51.

CHAPTER 2. GUNS AND BUTTER

1. "On the morning of Monday, January 26, less than a week after the inauguration, I entered the Cabinet Room of the White House for the first such meeting with the Republican leaders of the Senate and the House. . . . Among the senators I knew Bob Taft best . . . on the House side, I knew Charlie Halleck best." Eisenhower, Mandate, 194.

2. Representative David Obey, speech at dedication of Laird Center, Marshfield, WI, 9/12/97.

3. "Laird Speaks Up," Marshfield News Herald, 2/19/53.

4. "Claim Benson Killed Dairy Setup Ike OK'd," Sheboygan Press, 3/31/54.

5. Congressional Quarterly, "1985 Guide to U.S. Elections."

6. Samuel Walker, In Defense of American Liberties; "ACLU Celebrates Its Veterans," Washington Post, 11/17/78; "Founder of the A.C.L.U. Reflects on His 97 Years," New York Times, 1/22/81; "Roger Baldwin, 97, Is Dead; Crusader for Civil Rights Founded the A.C.L.U.," New York Times, 8/27/81; "Roger Baldwin, a Founder of ACLU, Dies," Washington Post, 8/27/81; "Roger Baldwin," Washington Post, 8/28/81; "Roger Baldwin's Feisty Legacy," Legal Times, 5/7/90.

7. Bellamy was then on the staff of the popular Boston magazine The Youth's Companion, which first published the pledge on September 8, 1892. About half of America's schoolchildren first recited the pledge on October 12, 1892, when urged to do so by

President Benjamin Harrison to commemorate the four hundredth anniversary of Columbus's voyage. "Socialist Wrote Pledge of Allegiance," AP, 10/17/88; "'I Pledge Allegiance . . .' Nears Century Mark," AP, 9/2/92; Harry Wessel, "Pledge of Allegiance Rolls into 2nd Century," *Orlando Sentinel,* 10/21/92; Arthur Schlesinger, Jr., "When Patriotism Wasn't Religious," *New York Times,* 7/7/02.

8. "Big Issue in D.C.: The Oath of Allegiance," *New York Times,* 5/23/54

9. "Include God in Pledge, Lawmakers to Be Urged," *Milwaukee Sentinel,* 5/5/54; MRL, press release, 5/6/54; "Laird Asks Flag Pledge Revision," *Wisconsin Rapids Tribune,* 5/6/54; "God in Pledge of Allegiance," *Two Rivers Reporter,* 5/6/54; "God in Pledge of Allegiance," *Chippewa Falls Herald,* 5/10/54; "Congressman Laird Sponsors Change in Pledge to Flag," *Adams Times,* 5/13/54.

10. MRL, "Religious Note," *Your Washington Office Report,* 5/19/54.

11. "Motto on Coins Remains at Odds with Ruling against Pledge," *Dallas Morning News,* 7/6/02.

12. MRL, speech, "A Christian's Place in Politics," 2/19/58.

13. Laird was on the Department of Commerce and Related Agencies Appropriations Subcommittee for only one term, 1957–58. He was first assigned to the Department of Defense and the Military Construction Appropriations Subcommittees in 1958, and he was already on the Departments of Labor, Health, Education, and Welfare Appropriations Subcommittee. Only in 1958 was Laird on four appropriations subcommittees. However, he served on the other three major appropriations subcommittees simultaneously from 1958 to 1962.

14. MRL to Wisconsin journalist John Wyngaard, 3/3/58.

15. AP, "Laird Reveals One of His Disappointments," *Stevens Point Daily Journal,* 3/27/53.

16. *1953 Congressional Quarterly Almanac,* 131; MRL, "Tax Reduction," *Your Washington Office Report,* 7/22/53.

17. Phrase "birth of affluent society" from Brendon, *Ike,* 261.

18. Nixon, *Memoirs* , 167; Ambrose, *Eisenhower: The President,* 285.

19. Ford, interview, 8/28/97. Three unpublished manuscript histories distributed to C&M members: "The Chowder and Marching Club, 1949–1955," 1955; "The History," part of program and menu for Twentieth Anniversary Celebration of the Chowder and Marching Club, 3/20/69; "A History of the Chowder and Marching Club," 1/84.

20. Charles E. Potter of Michigan, who was later elected a senator. Besides Jackson, Davis, Nixon, Ford, and Potter, the other ten original charter members of C&M were: Johnny Byrnes (WI), John J. Allen Jr. (CA), Caleb Boggs (DE), Norris Cotton (NH), Kenneth Keating (NY), John Lodge (CT), Harold O. Lovre (SD), Thruston B. Morton (KY), Charles P. Nelson (ME), and Walter Norblad (OR).

21. Brodie, *Richard Nixon,* 190; Volkan, Itzkowitz, and Dod, *Richard Nixon,* 53; Gellman, *Contender,* 268.

22. "G.O.P. Success Recipe Often Includes Chowder," *New York Times,* 3/15/82.

23. Ford, interview, 8/28/97.

24. Manuscript history of Chowder and Marching Club, 1955; John Wyngaard, "Rep. Laird Member of Exclusive 'Chowder and Marching Society,'" *Marshfield News Herald,* 4/17/54; *Appleton Post-Crescent,* 5/19/54; "Rep. Davis Guest Breakfast Meet at White House," *Beaver Dam Citizen,* 5/22/54.

25. In two interviews, Jack Mills estimated the money they raised for this one-night affair to be anywhere from $5,000 to $20,000 (Mills, 11/12/99 and 6/2/00). Laird thought the cost was roughly $30 a head, which, with 500 attendees, put the total at about $15,000, a healthy sum for a party in 1956.

26. Nixon to MRL, 1/12/56.

27. MRL, "National Convention," *Your Washington Office Report*, 8/1/56.

28. Kenneth Anderson died of a heart attack at the age of forty-seven, just five days before the Wisconsin Democratic primary. His widow, Margaret, was drafted to run. "Democrat Files For Congress," *Wausau Record-Herald*, 7/14/56; "Anderson, Upstate Democrat, Congress Candidate, Dies," unidentified Wisconsin newspaper, 9/7/56; "Mrs. Anderson Would Accept Nominee Post," *Stevens Point Daily Journal*, 9/24/56.

29. "Contest in 7th District like Script for Movie," *Milwaukee Journal*, 10/27/56.

30. In 1848, Zachary Taylor won the presidency while his party lost the House and Senate. *1956 Congressional Quarterly Almanac*, 752; Martin and Donovan, *My First Fifty Years in Politics*, 222.

31. Eisenhower to Harry Bullis, 1953, OF 99-R, Eisenhower Papers at the Kansas presidential library.

32. *Marshfield Story*, 75–76.

33. MRL, "Communists in Government," *Your Washington Office Report*, 5/5/54.

34. "Laird Terms Row Hearing 3-Ring Circus," *Wisconsin Rapids Tribune*, 5/8/54. In his 5/19/54 newsletter (*Your Washington Office Report*), under the heading "Trip to the District," Laird explained his view further: "My criticism was not directed at the news media in our District but at the situation as it exists in Washington. There are many measures which are being considered in this session of Congress which are of great importance to our future. The working press here is so involved with this Senate circus that the attention of our entire nation has been diverted from many important problems and decisions. I do have to personally admit that this is one of the greatest disappointments which I have encountered in my political life."

35. "Laird and McCarthy . . . ," *Wausau Daily Record-Herald*, 5/11/54.

36. "McCarthy Assailed As 'Cruel, Reckless' in Attack by Welch," *Washington Post*, 6/10/54.

37. "Time Never Lags for Congressman: Representative Laird Likes Job although It Pays No Overtime and Lacks Security," *Milwaukee Journal*, 12/6/53. Laird recorded in his newsletter *Your Washington Office Report*, 5/15/57: "This past week I missed the first roll call in the House of Representatives while attending the funeral ceremonies of the late Senator Joseph R. McCarthy. I have been proud of my record in answering every roll call but it certainly was necessary that I be in Wisconsin." On the other hand, Laird missed the birth of his third and last child, David, on July 16, 1954, because, unlike congressional votes, births are not as well scheduled. In "Stork Doesn't Wait, Laird Gets Home Late," the July 20 *Stevens Point Daily Journal* had some fun with Laird over David's early arrival and his dad's tardiness: "Congressmen are supposed to know what's going on in their districts, and Laird usually does, but sometimes things happen a little before they are expected. That was the case Friday when a new constituent arrived in (Laird's) district. Laird had planned to be on hand when the newcomer arrived, but the exact time of arrival was an uncertainty. So Mr. Laird hastened to board a plane at Washington

and, although he took 'the high road' instead of 'the low road' (an auto), David Malcolm Laird was in Marshfield before him."

38. See Robert A. Caro's account of the potential Senate split in Caro, *Years of Lyndon Johnson*, 955, 1000–1001.

39. Of the thirty-five Midwestern Republicans from farm districts who voted with Benson, ten had been defeated by Democrats. One who retired, and one who died, had both been replaced by Democrats. "On Farm Voting: Benson Loses Midwest Farm Support in House," Fact Sheet, *Congressional Quarterly Almanac*, 1958, 737–38.

40. The meeting occurred on 6/25/53. Laird also presented him with a leather-bound state tourism book, *This Is Wisconsin*, which included pictures of Ike fishing in Wisconsin after a postwar European tour. MRL, *Your Washington Office Report*, 6/24/53; "Laird Chats with Eisenhower; Gives Him State Cheese," *Green Bay Press-Gazette*, 6/26/53; "Laird Fishes for a Wisconsin Vacationer," *Wisconsin State Journal*, 6/26/58.

41. MRL, "Dairy Imports Create Emergency Situation," weekly column, 9/25/68; MRL, "Emergency Restriction on Dairy Imports Welcome," weekly column, 10/2/68.

42. MRL, *Your Washington Office Report*, 3/4/53; AP, "Rep. Laird in Tussle with VA over Butter, Oleo," Wausau *Daily Record Herald*, 7/16/53; "Congressman Wins Battle to Have Butter Served by VA," *Appleton Post-Crescent*, 1/20/54; "New Contract Will Give Vets Butter," *Clintonville Tribune-Gazette*, 1/21/54; *1954 Congressional Quarterly Almanac*, 101.

43. MRL, press release, 3/5/55.

44. Laird's cosponsor, Rep. August Andresen (R-MN), was his senior, but Andresen's death in 1958 left it to Laird to carry the milk pail for the program into the last Eisenhower years and successive Democratic administrations.

45. Eisenhower also had a story about how *he* had gotten lost in the Pentagon when he was the new Army chief of staff during World War II. He cited an oft-told tale of "an Army Air Corps captain" who got so lost that by the time he got back to his office "he discovered that he had been promoted to full colonel." MRL, "Sidelights," *Your Washington Office Report*, 2/18/53; D. D. Eisenhower, *At Ease*, 315–16.

46. MRL, "Defense Department," *Your Washington Office Report*, 2/10/54.

47. "Laird Charges Duplication Wasting Funds; Defense Department Policies Blasted by Badger Lawmaker," *Appleton Post-Crescent*, 8/10/59.

48. The Fords referred to Laird as their "adopted" child after a July fourth weekend getaway at the Tides Inn on the Chesapeake Bay with the Chowder and Marching Club. Barbara Laird was in Wisconsin, and the inn was fully booked, so Jerry and Betty Ford put up Laird in a little "nursery" room in their hotel suite.

49. Ford interview with Trevor Armbrister, undated, ca. 1978.

50. MRL, "Interview with David Frost," *David Frost Show*, 12/2/70.

51. Max Elbin, interview, 1/11/02.

52. For a more thorough recitation of Johnson's accumulation of wealth see Caro, *Years of Lyndon Johnson: Means of Ascent* , 80–118.

53. Nixon to MRL, 11/7/58.

54. In a 1959 AP account, Laird is quoted as saying, "there were more who favored either Byrnes or Ford for leader than Halleck." However, in 1978 and 1979 interviews, Laird stated that Ford polled last, not Halleck. In all accounts, Laird consistently said that Byrnes received the most votes. "Badgers in Wisconsin: Tell Laird, Byrnes Role in Defeat of Rep. Martin," AP, 1/16/59.

55. MRL, "Not Needed," *Your Washington Office Report*, 9/12/62; MRL, press release, "Rubber Stamp Congress Not Needed," Mel Laird Testimonial Dinner, Shawano, Wisconsin, 10/10/62.

56. Ford, *Time to Heal* , 71; Cannon, *Time and Chance*, 65.

57. Froehlke, interview, 9/10/97.

58. Lyon, *Eisenhower*, 851.

59. Ambrose, *Eisenhower: The President*, 175.

60. "Competition, Restrictions, Top Threats to Dairymen, Laird Asserts at Athens," *Milwaukee Journal*, 5/8/54.

CHAPTER 3. A HOUSE DIVIDED

1. Robert Froehlke, interview, 9/29/00.

2. Lieberman and Kwon, *Facts versus Fears*, 6–7.

3. Burns, *Cranberries*, 10–12, 43.

4. "Case of Confusion: Work Starts to Clear Innocent State Berry," *Appleton Post-Crescent*, 11/11/59; AP, "FDA Team to Check on State Crop," *Eau Claire Leader*, 11/11/59; "U.S. Widens Taint Check for Cranberries" and "Cranberry Crop Facing Huge Loss," *New York Times*, 11/11/59.

5. Herbert Klein, interview, 9/29/00. "Nixon-Kennedy Cranberry Duel Ends in Dead Heat," *Madison Capital-Times*, 11/13/59; "Kennedy Tells Throng of Communist Danger," *Milwaukee Journal*, 11/13/59; Nixon photo caption, "Yes, He Likes Cranberries," *Wisconsin Rapids-Tribune*, 11/13/59.

6. Eisenhower's appointments log, 7/29/53. According to *Newsweek*, "Update; Polish Defector: Making It Big," 11/5/79, Jarecki, who changed his first name to Frank, married an American woman, had four children, and became a millionaire by making precision valves through his own Jarecki Industries in Erie, Pennsylvania.

7. "Laird Gets Important GOP Convention Role; 'Highly Honored' with Resolutions Committee Office," *Green Bay Press-Gazette*, 5/12/60.

8. Front page and accompanying stories in the 7/24/60 *New York Times*: "Secret Nixon-Rockefeller Talks Draft a Basic Platform Accord; Rule Out Governor for 2d Place"; "Rockefeller Gains as Well as Nixon"; "Pact Opens Way for Party Amity"; UPI, "One Party Line Failed Nixon and Rockefeller"; "Chicago: The Truce of Fifth Avenue, or Morningside Revisited." Also, "11th-Hour Encounter," *Newsweek*, 8/1/60; T. White, *Making of the President, 1960*, 191–98; Nixon, *Six Crises*, 313–16; Nixon, *Memoirs*, 215; *National Party Conventions, 1831–2000*, 119.

9. This account comes from Laird, who recounted the phone call in several interviews. David Abshire, who was in the hotel room when Ike called and overheard the call, remembered it slightly differently. He recalled Eisenhower as saying, sarcastically: "Tell Dick Nixon he doesn't really need my support in the campaign. He can get along without me." David Abshire, interview, 4/5/2001.

10. After word leaked out about Ike's mood, his aides denied to journalists that he was angry about the compact or meddled with the platform. For example, a Newport-datelined *New York Times* story quoted White House sources as saying that "the President does not intend to influence in any way the preparation of platform pledges." "President Shuns Goldwater View; Doesn't Consider Agreement by Rockefeller and Nixon a Republican 'Munich,'" *New York Times*, 7/25/60. During an August 10, 1960,

press conference, Eisenhower also disingenuously denied expressing displeasure about the Fifth Avenue Compact. Chalmers M. Roberts of the *Washington Post* asked: "(On) the Nixon-Rockefeller agreement, it was reported in Chicago at the time of the convention that you were personally upset at what that agreement had to say about defense on the grounds that it was implicitly critical of your Administration. Were you upset and did you try to get the platform language changed at Chicago?" Eisenhower: "No. I don't remember that I was upset. . . . Now, there were many calls as to what I thought would be a good thing to put in—in the planks of the platform—that had to do with defense, and I conferred by telephone with a good many people and for a good many hours." Press conference, *New York Times*, 8/11/60.

11. "G.O.P. to Present Its Platform in a $25,000 TV Spectacular," *New York Times*, 7/9/60.

12. A later *New York Times* profile put it this way: "In 1960, Mr. Laird, as vice chairman of the GOP platform committee, took command from the chairman, Charles H. Percy, a businessman, to break a committee stalemate over civil rights through his grasp of practical politics." "Professional Politician: Melvin Robert Laird," *New York Times*, 7/7/64. The *Chicago Tribune* noted: "In 1960, he was made vice-chairman of the platform committee. The policy disputes of that convention were memorable. Insiders said Laird should be credited with the bringing of order out of chaos and the drafting of party principles on which dissident elements could unite." "Rep. Laird: Bright G.O.P. Star; Chose His Career as Wisconsin Lad of 17," *Chicago Tribune*, 6/23/63. Equally telling was the note Eisenhower's secretary made of a phone call between Bryce N. Harlow and the former president on September 3, 1963. The first matter discussed was whether Eisenhower should support businessman Charles Percy in a Republican primary bid for the governorship of Illinois. "BNH says no," the note reads. One of the primary reasons he gave Ike for not backing Percy was his lack of political skill as demonstrated when the "1960 convention platform operation of Percy's failed—Laird had to help out." Eisenhower appointments log, 9/3/63.

13. Charles Percy, interview, 4/18/01.

14. "Mention Laird's Name as Defense Secretary," *Green Bay Press-Gazette*, 9/7/60.

15. Eisenhower press conference, 8/24/60. Nixon later interpreted the remark as an unintentional verbal stumble by the president, who really meant that he wanted time to make an accurate list. According to Nixon's memoirs, Eisenhower apologized and said, "Dick, I could kick myself every time some jackass brings up that goddamn 'give me a week' business." Nixon, *Memoirs*, 276.

16. Cannon, *Time and Chance*, 68.

17. Nixon to MRL, 4/11/61.

18. MRL to Nixon, 5/1/61.

19. In his 4/26/61 *Your Washington Office Report*, Laird wrote: "This past week I had visits with President Kennedy at the White House, Chancellor Adenauer at lunch, and many other leaders in and out of government." The Kennedy meeting was the Bay of Pigs briefing to seek congressional support.

20. MRL, "Back Door Diplomacy," *Your Washington Office Report*, 6/14/61.

21. Laird, *House Divided*, 64, 117–20.

22. Nixon to MRL, 1/16/61.

23. Dwight D. Eisenhower to MRL, 3/29/62.

24. MRL, *House Divided,* 33 and 43.

25. Abshire, interview, 4/5/01; J. A. Smith, *Strategic Calling;* "Abshire to Aid Reagan Team," *Washington Post,* 11/9/80; "Right's New Weapon—Think Tanks," *Christian Science Monitor,* 2/10/81; "Revolving Door to Power Gives GU New Pride," *Washington Star,* 7/5/81; "Thick & Think Tank; David Abshire's CSIS Ponder Policy with Kissinger & Fred Flintstone," *Washington Post,* 9/21/82; "Abshire: 'Pragmatic Republican,'" *Washington Post,* 11/30/86; "For Abshire, New Step in Career as Counselor," *New York Times,* 12/27/86; J. A. Smith, *Idea Brokers,* 4, 13, 208–12.

26. Edwin Feulner, interview, 7/30/01; John Dressendorfer, interview, 7/20/00; "Issue-Oriented Heritage Foundation Hitches Its Wagon to Reagan's Star," *National Journal,* 3/20/82; "Heritage Led by a True Believer; Foundation Chief's Resume Impeccably Conservative," *Washington Post,* 9/24/85; J. A. Smith, *Idea Brokers,* 194–202; Edwards, *Power of Ideas,* 3–11, 23, 41–49, 185–91.

27. MRL quoted in "Laird Asks Americans to 'Back Kennedy,'" *Manawa (WI) Advocate,* 10/25/62.

28. MRL, press release, "Laird Renews Call For Peace Blockade of Cuba," 9/25/62.

29. MRL, *House Divided,* 74.

30. "Melvin Laird—Man of Judgment," *Wausau Record-Herald,* 11/1/62.

31. *1962 Congressional Quarterly Almanac,* 63 and 1029–30.

32. Nixon to MRL, 11/16/62, congratulating Laird on his sixth congressional campaign victory.

33. Rep. David Obey, speech at dedication of Laird Center, Marshfield, WI, 9/12/97.

34. Percentages averaged from the *Congressional Quarterly Almanac* annual reports 1961–63.

35. Laird wrote contemporaneously: "A Member of Congress should not be a rubber stamp for the Executive Department. Research organizations studying voting records show that when President Eisenhower was in office, I supported his legislative requests 68 percent of the time. During the 87th Congress, I have supported President Kennedy's legislative requests 63 percent of the time. Some write complaining I support President Kennedy's programs, others that I oppose them. The fact is I support some and oppose others. It's my feeling you regard me as your Congressman, not the President's—and want me to study the issues, then vote 'aye' or 'nay' according to what seems best for the U.S.A., for Wisconsin and for our area." MRL, "Not Needed," *Your Washington Office Report,* 9/12/62.

36. D. D. Eisenhower, *Waging Peace,* 614–16.

37. Because commentators focused on only the warning paragraph of Eisenhower's January 17, 1961, farewell address, Laird always felt the speech was frequently misinterpreted as a screed against defense spending. "I talked to Ike about that quite a bit," and the former president agreed, Laird said. In the speech itself, Eisenhower stressed the vital need for a strong military posture. MRL, "Eisenhower Farewell," *Your Washington Office Report,* 1/25/61.

38. "Missile Gap Issues Fizzles," *1961 Congressional Quarterly Almanac,* 144; MRL appearance on *Washington Viewpoint,* 6/18/62.

39. MRL, *House Divided,* 48.

40. MRL, "Remarks on the Floor of the House," press release, 1/25/61; speech before the Women's Forum on National Security, Presidential Ballroom, Statler Hotel, 1/27/61.

41. MRL appearance on *Washington Viewpoint*, 6/1/62.

42. Karnow, *Vietnam*, 252.

43. MRL, *House Divided*, 111.

44. O'Donnell and Powers, *"Johnny, We Hardly Knew Ye,"* 16. After an excerpt of the book appeared in *Life* magazine, Senator Mansfield confirmed that Kennedy had told him he would pull out the troops after the 1964 election. "JFK Decided in '63 to Order Viet Pullout After Election," *Washington Post*, 8/1/70.

CHAPTER 4. LAIRD ALSO RISES

1. MRL, "For Immediate Release," statement, 11/22/63.

2. MRL, undated draft of remarks for Gridiron dinner, which was cancelled after the assassination out of respect for Kennedy.

3. Eisenhower was often asked to name Republicans who would be good presidential candidates. Prior to the European trip, in a June 30, 1963, letter, he named ten: generals Lucius Clay, Alfred Guenther, and Lauris Norstad; senators Thruston Morton and Barry Goldwater; governors Nelson Rockefeller, George Romney, and William Scranton; and two perennial favorites, his brother Dr. Milton Eisenhower and Robert Anderson, the ex-secretary of the treasury. Eisenhower, "Personal and Confidential" letter to Chauncey Weaver, 6/30/63. At a fifteen-minute press conference on August 15, 1963, in the USS *United States*'s promenade lounge, Eisenhower gave a more public list of ten names, including only five from his confidential letters of six weeks before—Clay, Goldwater, Norstad, Rockefeller, and Romney. The new five were governors John Anderson Jr., Mark O. Hatfield, and John A. Love; Gerald Ford, and banker Gabriel Hauge. "Eisenhower Hints He Backs Treaty," *New York Times*, 8/16/63. That Laird was an eleventh name Ike added was confirmed by an Eisenhower spokesperson in an AP story, and by later accounts in the *New York Times* and other newspapers. For the next six years, when the issue was raised periodically by journalists writing about Laird, Eisenhower never denied that he had named Laird as one of the eleven Republican men "well-qualified" to be president. AP, "Laird Is Presidential Timber: Ike," *Wausau Record-Herald*, 8/17/63; "Professional Politician: Melvin Robert Laird," 7/7/64; "After the Pentagon, What? Melvin Laird Looks Ahead," *Baltimore Sun*, 8/7/72. During the ship's press conference, Eisenhower explained why Nixon wasn't on his list, saying that Nixon "told me frankly and positively he just cannot be considered."

4. Ford, *Time to Heal*, 73–74; Cannon, *Time and Chance*, 75.

5. Robert Novak, interview, 10/2/00.

6. The eight congressmen who joined Laird on the project were Gerald R. Ford (R-MI.), Thomas B. Curtis (R-MO), Peter Frelinghuysen (R-NJ), Charles E. Goodell (R-NY), Glenard P. Lipscomb (R-CA.), Clark MacGregor (R-MN), John J. Rhodes (R-AZ), and Robert Taft Jr. (R-OH).

7. Mary McGrory, "Melvin Laird Relishes Job as G.O.P. Umpire," *Louisville Courier-Journal*, 6/30/64.

8. MRL, chairman of the Republican Platform Committee, "Statement," 6/64.

9. "Surprisingly, there were only three areas in which any criticism to this document was raised," Laird wrote in his newsletter. MRL, "The Republican Platform Committee Chairmanship," *Your Washington Office Report*, 8/12/64; MRL, press release, 10/5/64.

10. Edwards, *Goldwater*, 207 and 302.

11. AP, "Platform Should Name John Birch Society, He Says," *Rhinelander News,* 7/7/64; AP, 7/11/64.

12. MRL, draft of remarks for Gridiron dinner, 11/63.

13. Republican Platform 1964, "For The People," presented to the Republican National Convention, San Francisco, 7/14/64.

14. "Cactus Jacobins Ready for Revolt on Bastille Day," *New York Times,* 7/15/64.

15. "G.O.P. Caucus Will Test Halleck's House Strength," *New York Times,* 12/14/64.

16. Richard Reeves, *Ford, not A Lincoln,* 5–9.

17. MRL, speech, "Tax-Sharing with the States—A Way Out," National Conference of State Legislative Leaders, Shoreham Hilton, Washington, D.C., 11/17/66; MRL, House Floor speech, "Strengthening the Federal System—The Case for Revenue Sharing," *Congressional Record,* 2/15/67.

18. Among the observations regarding Laird's revenue sharing authorship as the Heller Plan was being touted were these: "The 'Heller Plan' is not really the creature of former Presidential Advisor Walter Heller. That key Republican legislative proposal—federal sharing of tax revenues with the states—is the brainchild of Rep. Melvin Laird, chairman of the Republican Conference Committee." Vera Glaser, *Washington Star,* "That 'New' Heller Plan Is Really Melvin Laird's," *Berkshire Eagle,* 11/23/66; "Laird has been pushing this idea since 1958." *Business Week,* "GOP Congressmen Get Early Start on '68," 9/2/67; "Although Heller was responsible for generating widespread interest in the proposal, many persons who studied the issue gave Rep. Melvin R. Laird (R-WI) the credit for having introduced in 1958 the first bill which embodied many of what later were considered the essential principles of revenue sharing. The Laird bill provided for the automatic return of a portion of federal revenues to the states with relatively few conditions attached." "Tax Policy—1967 Chronology," *Congress and the Nation, 1965–1968,* 164; "He was the first Congressman in either party to introduce revenue sharing legislation." "Viet Picture Pleases Laird," *Philadelphia Bulletin,* 11/14/71; "He had made his mark in diverse fields: revenue sharing, of which he was a pioneer advocate; medical care, which brought him the Albert Lasker Award in 1964." "After the Pentagon, What? Melvin Laird Looks Ahead," *Baltimore Sun,* 8/7/72; "The father of modern revenue-sharing is generally acknowledged to be Walter Heller, the economist, yet the concept claims a spectrum of champions. Among them were the former Representative Melvin Laird, who advocated revenue-sharing in 1958; Senator Barry Goldwater, the Republican Presidential nominee in 1964, and two Democratic Presidential candidates, Edmund S. Muskie and Hubert H. Humphrey. Howard Baker, later Republican majority leader, was first elected to the Senate in 1966 by advocating revenue-sharing." James A. Cannon, "Federal Revenue-Sharing: Born 1972. Died 1986. R.I.P.," *New York Times,* 10/10/86.

19. Evans and Novak, "Inside Report: Walter Heller's Boomerang," *Washington Post,* 11/18/66.

20. MRL, question-answer period following remarks to AP editors, Kansas City, MO, 11/16/72.

21. Ehrlichman, *Witness to Power,* 208–10.

22. Bob Harlan, president and CEO, Green Bay Packers, 1/25/02; Harrington, *Pro Football Hall of Fame,* 125–27; "America's Small-Town Team: Packers Play for Touchdown not for Profits," *New York Times,* 1/13/96.

23. "CBS Gets Rights to Pro Football," *New York Times,* 4/27/61.

24. "TV Football Pact Voided by Court; National League-CBS Deal Held Antitrust Violation," *New York Times,* 7/21/61; AP, "National Football League Denied Plea to Delay Voiding TV Pact," *New York Times,* 7/29/61.

25. *NFL's Official Encyclopedic History of Professional Football,* 32; Harris, *League,* 14–15.

26. Tex Schramm, interview, 1/25/02.

27. Harris, *League,* 17; Mann, *Legacy to Power,* 272–75.

28. Brock and Eldridge, *25 Year;* LaBlanc, *Professional Sports Team Histories,* 471–72.

29. C. Robert Barnett, interview, 1/25/02; Joe Horrigan, interview, 1/25/02.

30. Sen. David Boren, interview, 5/14/02; Burke and Thompson, *Bryce Harlow,* 75, 139–40.

31. MRL to sixty-four high school principals, 10/28/65; MRL, news release, 11/3/65; MRL, weekly column, "Youth Leadership Workshop," 11/24/65; MRL, "Remarks before the Student Body, Wayland Academy," 1/14/66.

32. Lee Dreyfus, who was UW–Stevens Point chancellor from 1967–79 (resigning to become governor of Wisconsin), also said Laird's program powerfully elevated the quality of the university, the only one in Laird's congressional district. "My own belief is that the quality of the university is determined by the quality of the students, not the professors so much. The students will push the professors and make them better," Dreyfus observed. "So here was Mel inviting the top two juniors and seniors of every high school to my campus every other year—a first-class recruiting opportunity for us." Dreyfus, interview, 1/29/02.

33. David S. Broder, "Two Good Choices," *Washington Post,* 1/9/83.

34. Although technically a sovereign nation, the Menominee were located in Laird's Seventh Congressional District and were actively seeking his representation in Congress. Moreover, the Menominee were eligible to vote in local and national elections.

35. James F. Frechette Jr., interview, 12/17/01; "'Melvin R. Laird Day' Sunday on Menominee Reservation," *Shawano Evening Leader,* 8/15/53.

36. MRL, statement, "A Plea for Justice for the Menominee Indian People," 5/9/61.

37. Peroff, *Menominee DRUMS,* 129; "For 12 Long Years, Reservation Struggled to Make It as a County," *Milwaukee Journal Sentinel,* 5/21/98; "Income Data Make Poverty Painfully Obvious," *Green Bay Press-Gazette,* 8/15/65.

38. Ada Deer, interview, 1/18/02; Patricia Raymer, "Wisconsin's Menominees: Indians on a Seesaw," *National Geographic,* August 1974, 247–49; "The Indian," *Newsweek,* 7/4/76.

39. Deer, interview, 1/18/02.

40. Peroff, *Menominee DRUMS,* 215–16.

41. "Senate Panel Signs Off on Bill to Pay Menominee Tribe," *Milwaukee Journal Sentinel,* 6/11/99.

CHAPTER 5. CLOUD RIDERS

1. MRL, speech on the floor of the House of Representatives, *Congressional Record,* 5/25/67.

2. Dick Cheney to MRL, 8/15/02.

3. Jimmy Carter, interview, 10/23/97.

4. "Marshfield Clinic: A Special Place," brochure produced by the Marshfield Clinic, 1989.

5. G. Stanley Custer, MD, Marshfield Clinic historian, "The Making of Stephan Epstein, M.D." and "The Epsteins Come to America," both published in 1991 issues of *Pulse*, the clinic's staff newsletter.

6. MRL, "Medicine and Politics," speech before State Officers' Conference of the American Academy of General Practice, 4/20/68.

7. MRL, speech, Detroit, 11/12/68.

8. "Representative John Fogarty Dies at 53," *New York Times*, 1/11/67.

9. Strickland, *Politics, Science, and Dread Disease*, 80.

10. At one point, Fogarty won passage of an appropriations bill amendment that, while not naming Great Britain, effectively banned foreign aid to them until their partition of Ireland ended. Waking up "the morning after" to Fogarty's clever move, the House reversed itself two days later. He had made his point.

11. Mary Fogarty McAndrew, interview, 9/30/03.

12. Hugh Carey, interview, 10/24/01.

13. Strickland, *Politics*, 91–96; Regis, *Virus Ground Zero*, 50–52.

14. In a private thank you letter for Fogarty's election eve Wisconsin visit, Laird wrote that he was very well aware the visit was "a very great personal favor." "Hospital and Foundation," *Marshfield News Herald*, 9/28/64; MRL to Rep. John R. Fogarty, 10/1/64.

15. John Chafee, interview, 10/22/99.

16. D. D. Eisenhower, *Mandate for Change*, 494–97; "Public Health," *Congressional Quarterly, Congress and the Nation: 1945–1964*, 1136–37; Brendon, *Ike*, 232 and 311; Shorter, *Health Century*, 64–70; Etheridge, *Sentinel for Health*, 71–80.

17. Dr. Carl Baker, interview, 1/16/02.

18. Rettig, *Cancer Crusade*, 25–26.

19. *NIH Almanac 2000*, 254–58; MRL, weekly column, "Health Needs Deserve High Priority," 4/10/68; MRL, speech before State Officers' Conference of the American Academy of General Practice, "Medicine and Politics," 4/20/68; MRL, press release, 4/26/68; MRL, "Interview with Hugh Downs on Irving Kupcinet Show," Chicago, 3/24/72; MRL, "Remarks and Question-Answer Session at TV Correspondents' Breakfast," Harvard Club, New York City, 4/26/72.

20. The seven National Institutes that existed when Laird came to office were: Cancer (1937), Heart (1948), Dental Research (1948), Microbiological (1948), Mental Health (1949), Arthritis and Metabolic Diseases (1950), and Neurological Diseases and Blindness (1950).

21. Eisenhower to MRL (draft), 7/27/59.

22. Dr. David Laird, MRL's brother, remarks at a Wisconsin dinner in his brother's honor, 9/11/97.

23. MRL, *Your Washington Office Report*, 9/28/66.

24. HEW then had the following "ecological" entities: National Air Pollution Control Administration, Bureau of Solid Waste Management, Bureau of Water Hygiene, Bureau of Radiological Health, and the Food and Drug Administration (which restricted pesticide use).

25. *1963 Congressional Quarterly Almanac*, "Labor-H.E.W. Funds," 156–57; *1964 Congressional Quarterly Almanac*, "Labor-H.E.W. Funds," 186; "Public Health," *Congress and the Nation: 1945–1964, Congressional Quarterly*, 1145, 1148–50.

26. MRL, remarks before the Wisconsin Chapter of the American College of Surgeons, Marshfield, WI, 10/27/73.

27. Carla Garnett, "Surgeon General Visits, Touts Oral Health," NIH *Record*, 4/17/01; Michael Housman, "Smoking and Health: The 1964 U.S. Surgeon General's Report as a Turning Point in the Anti-Smoking Movement," Harvard *Health Policy Review*, Spring 2001.

28. Alison Laird-Large, interview 3/2/01.

29. Strickland, *Politics*, 118–19.

30. Rusch, *Something Attempted*, 119–22.

31. Dr. Ilse Riegel, historian, McArdle Laboratory for Cancer Research, interview, 9/21/01; Rusch, *Something Attempted*.

32. CDC, "Bioterrorism-Related Anthrax: Inhalational Anthrax Outbreak among Postal Workers, Washington, D.C., 2001," *Emerging Infectious Diseases*, 10/02.

33. Cheney to MRL, 8/15/02.

34. Etheridge, *Sentinel for Health*, xvii.

35. Dr. Elizabeth Etheridge, interview, 1/12/04; Etheridge, *Sentinel*, 107.

36. Fiscal Year 1953 CDC figure from *The Budget of the United States Government for the Fiscal Year Ending June 30, 1955;* FY 1969 amount from *The Budget of the United States Government, 1971.*

37. Etheridge, *Sentinel for Health*, 104–5; Regis, *Virus Ground Zero*, 49–52.

38. Regis, *Virus Ground Zero*, 62–69.

39. MRL, weekly column, "The 18th World Health Assembly," 5/19/65.

40. Fogarty had suffered his first heart attack in 1953 and used Eisenhower's heart specialist, Paul Dudley White, and NIH Director Dr. James Shannon as personal doctors. Dr. James P. Crowley, "Paul Dudley White, MD and John E. Fogarty," *Rhode Island Medicine*, 12/92.

41. Howard A. Rusk, MD, "Mr. Public Health: Death Ends Efforts by Representative Laird to Give United States Freedom from Disease," *New York Times*, 1/15/67.

42. MRL, eulogy, included in the *Congressional Record*, 1/18/67.

43. "Coveted on Capitol Hill: The Hideaway," *New York Times*, 3/7/83.

44. "Laird's Transfer to Defense Dept. May Be Felt Most on Medical Front," *Janesville Gazette*, 12/19/68.

CHAPTER 6. INTO THE QUAGMIRE

1. Robert Pursley, interview, 7/17, 10/3, 11/6, and 11/28/00; Alexander Haig, interview, 1/21/02; "Interview with Melvin Laird," *David Frost Show*, 12/2/70; "Gulf of Tonkin 'Attack' Doubted by Many," *Christian Science Monitor*, 6/28/71; "Ellsberg Says Tonkin Tapes Show Congress Was Misled," *Washington Post*, 7/10/71; Orr Kelly, "A Book for Today: Tonkin Gulf Incident Recalled," *Washington Star*, 9/28/71; *U.S. News and World Report*, 7/23/84; "Debris from the Tonkin Resolution," *New York Times*, 8/5/84; "The Tonkin Chronology," *Los Angeles Times*, 4/29/85; J. Norville Jones, former Senate Foreign Relations Committee staffer, 1964–77, Letter to the Editor, "Robert McNamara's Bad Information," *Washington Post*, 11/23/95.

2. *U.S. News and World Report*, 7/23/84; McNamara, *In Retrospect*, 133.

3. MRL, House floor speech, *Congressional Record*, 8/7/64; "Laird Reminds House

Viet War 'Still Goes On,'" *Appleton Post-Crescent*, 8/8/64; AP, "Congressmen Say Attacks Deliberate," *Stevens Point Daily Journal*, 8/5/64.

4. AP, "Grim Viet Decision Ahead, Laird Warns," *La Crosse Leader-Tribune*, 3/3/64; AP, "Laird Denies Congress at Fault for Viet Nam," *La Crosse Leader-Tribune*, 3/9/64.

5. White House Tape, 5/21/64, section beginning at 12:42 p.m. transcribed at Lyndon Baines Johnson Library, Austin, Texas.

6. Radio Press International, "From the People," 5/31/64; AP, "U.S. Preparations for Blow at North Vietnam Reported," *New York Times*, 6/1/64.

7. President Johnson Press Conference, 6/2/64.

8. Tape transcripts by Michael R. Beschloss, *Taking Charge*, 379–83.

9. *Public Papers of the Presidents, Lyndon B. Johnson, 1963–64*, vol. 2, 1126, 1164, and 1391.

10. Alison Laird-Large, interview, 3/2/01.

11. "Laird Boycotts Policy Briefings, Says GOP Is Used For Publicity," *Milwaukee Journal*, 4/18/65.

12. MRL, "Republican Opportunity and Responsibility in the 89th Congress," remarks on floor of the House of Representatives, 3/1/65.

13. Gaylord Nelson, interview, 2/7/01; Lawrence F. O'Brien, special assistant to the president, to MRL, 5/13/65; "Viet Nam Defense Funds," *1965 Congressional Quarterly Almanac*, 74; Vandiver, *Shadows of Vietnam*, 112–14.

14. MRL, statement, 6/14/65.

15. "Portions of 3 U.S. Divisions Reported Going to Vietnam," *New York Times*, 6/15/65.

16. Beschloss, *Reaching for Glory*, 360–62.

17. MRL, *Your Washington Office Report*, 6/30/65.

18. Beschloss, *Reaching for Glory*, 403–5.

19. Clifford with Holbrooke, *Counsel to the President*, 422.

20. Evans and Novak, "Johnson's Home Front," *Washington Post*, 7/30/65.

21. "President Scores a Leader of G.O.P. for 'Untrue' Talk," *New York Times*, 8/2/65; Tom Wicker, "Misunderstanding, Ford Says in Reply to Johnson Attack," *New York Times*, 8/3/65; "Ford Declines to Argue Over LBJ's Charge," *Washington Post*, 8/3/65.

22. "Laird Seen behind Row between Johnson, Ford," *Los Angeles Times*, 8/8/65.

23. "News Conference," *New York Times*, 8/26/65.

24. "Viet Critics Brushed Off by Johnson; But GOP Leaders Fire New Rounds at Own News Parley," *Washington Post*, 8/27/65; "GOP on Viet-Nam; Looking Both Ways," *Washington Post*, 8/27/65; "The One-Two Punch," *Time*, 9/3/65.

25. "GOP Leader Urges War Declaration; Idea Not Aimed at Demonstrators, Laird Tells UROC," *Los Angeles Times*, 11/21/65; "Laird Would Support War Declaration," AP, 11/22/65.

26. David Broder, "Ford and Laird View Vietnam as Major '66 Issue," *New York Times*, 11/25/65.

27. Lt. Gen. Charles G. Cooper, U.S. Marine Corps (Ret.), "The Day It Became the Longest War," *Proceedings of the U.S. Naval Institute*, May 1996, 77–80.

CHAPTER 7. FIGHT NOW, PAY LATER

1. "Laird Reported to Be Nixon's Pentagon Choice," *Washington Post*, 12/9/68; "Rep. Laird Knows Navy; New Defense Boss Served on Destroyer in War," *San Diego Union*, 12/12/68; "Laird Tough McNamara Critic," Scripps-Howard, 12/10/68.

2. There is no transcript of this session available. At the time, intemperate remarks were often excised before the final hearing record was published. However, Laird's words to McNamara were later quoted in a contemporary account by a Wisconsin journalist, who placed the incident in March 1966. "The Vast Empire of U.S. Defense May Get Vaster under Laird," *Milwaukee Journal*, 12/15/68.

3. "Window on Washington: Mel's Prediction Comes True," *Madison Capital Times*, 3/13/67.

4. MRL, "The Costs of War," weekly column, 10/5/66.

5. "Window on Washington: Mel's Prediction Comes True," *Madison Capital Times*, 3/13/67; Laird appearance on "From the Capital," ABC radio news, 7/18/66.

6. MRL, *Your Washington Office Report*, 1/26/66.

7. MRL, "Guns or Butter?" weekly column, 8/11/65; Tom Wicker, "'Guns or Butter'; Republicans Pressing the Issue," *New York Times*, 8/15/65; "'Guns or Butter' Haunting Laird," unidentified Wisconsin newspaper clipping, 1/26/66; "It's 'Rifles or Ruffles' to a Butter Booster," *Milwaukee Journal*, 1/26/66.

8. MRL, "Memorial Day 1967," weekly column, 5/24/67.

9. Gaylord Nelson, interview, 2/7/01; "Congress Races Start to Hum," *Madison Capital Times*, 9/26/66; "Laird's Foe Better Bet for Postmaster," *Milwaukee Sentinel*, 10/25/66; "Myhra Runs Hard in Race with Laird," *Milwaukee Journal*, 10/31/66.

10. Paul Hassett, former executive secretary to Gov. Knowles, interview, 12/29/01; "Cheney Began Career in Badger State," *Milwaukee Journal Sentinel*, 7/26/00.

11. Cheney, interview, 2/20/01.

12. Republican Conference of the House of Representatives, MRL, Chairman, "The United States and the War In Vietnam," 19–21, 9/20/66.

13. "G.O.P. Chiefs Say War Is Johnson's; 3 House Leaders Assert He Must Bear Responsibility," *New York Times*, 9/20/66; AP, "G.O.P. Says Johnson Deceives on War," *New York Times*, 9/21/66; Laird appearance on NBC's *Today Show*, 9/22/66.

14. MRL, press release on Rockton, Illinois, speech, 3/5/66.

15. MRL, "The Elections of 1966," weekly column, 11/23/66. This was the largest Republican House membership in ten years, and the net gain of eight Republican governors meant that their party had a chief executive in half of the fifty states, including five of the nation's seven largest. "Republicans Score Net Gain of 47 House Seats" and "Coattail Effects," *1966 Congressional Quarterly Almanac*, 1398.

16. White House, "Text of the Joint Communique Issued at the Manila Summit Conference, Manila, The Philippines," press release, 10/25/66.

17. Ted Lewis, "Ford, Laird Seek Top GOP Spot in House," 1/5/67.

18. In an interview as defense secretary, Laird was asked by David Frost whether he considered "as a compliment or an attack" the phrase "our Lyndon Johnson," which one Republican had used to describe Laird. "I have heard that term used," Laird smiled, before moving on to the next subject without characterizing his view. MRL appearance on "Interview with David Frost," *David Frost Show*, 12/2/70.

19. John H. Averill, "Both Parties Watching as Laird Stirs Again; GOP's Gray Eminence Steps up Criticism of Johnson's Policies on Vietnam, Taxes," *Los Angeles Times*, 9/18/67.

20. "Melvin Laird's Platform Caper," *New York Herald-Tribune*, 3/26/66; "Mel Laird: The Complete GOPolitician," *Milwaukee Journal*, 1/21/68.

21. Gerald Ford, interview, 8/28/97.

22. Ibid.

23. "House Republicans—They're Out to Win," *Wall Street Journal*, 3/14/67.

24. Ford, interview, 8/28/97; Albert H. Quie, interview, 4/5/01; Ford, *Time to Heal*, 25–27; Cannon, *Time and Chance*, 267 and 275; Quie, *Riding the Divide*, 273–76.

25. McNamara, *In Retrospect*, 269.

26. Ibid., 307.

27. Robert McNamara, interview, 12/13/01.

28. MRL and David Packard, press conference, 12/30/68.

29. Former Wisconsin governor Lee Dreyfus, interview, 1/29/02; AP, "Report Lists 3 Casualties from State," *Fond du Lac Commonwealth Reporter*, 3/24/67; "'Couldn't Say No,' Said Albertson of Mission," *Stevens Point Daily Journal*, 3/24/67; "Dr. James Albertson and Team of Educators Killed in a Plane Crash in Vietnam," press release, Wisconsin State University–Stevens Point, 3/24/67.

30. MRL, "The Late James A. Albertson, President, Wisconsin State University, Stevens Point," House floor speech, *Congressional Record*, 5/4/67.

31. Paul Johnson, "Charles Leo Johnson, Native of Marshfield, KIA Vietnam," and "Herb and Adele Johnson," *Marshfield Story*, 403–6.

32. MRL to President Lyndon B. Johnson, 2/9/67; AP, "Laird Calls Goal in Vietnam Vague," *New York Times*, 2/28/67.

33. William J. Jorden, White House memo, 2/17/67.

34. Douglass Cater, White House, memorandum for the president, 2/1/67. In a February 8 news column, Laird elaborated on his dinner conversation points. "For every dollar the Soviet Union spends in support of North Vietnam, the United States spends $18 to $20. In addition, the impact on their economy is in no way as damaging as the impact of the Vietnam War on our own economy. Most importantly, the loss in life and limb to America is high whereas to the Soviet Union and its satellites, it is minimal." MRL, "U.S. Trade Policies Prolong Vietnam War," weekly column, 2/8/67.

35. MRL, press release, 3/23/67; "Laird Demands Red Trade Ban," *New York Times*, 3/24/67; Richard L. Strout, "U.S. Urged to Apply Soviet Trade Lever," *Christian Science Monitor*, 3/28/67.

36. The Dirksen statement was part of "Press Release Issued Following a Leadership Meeting," the Republican Leadership of Congress, 5/25/67. The press release listed the leadership as: For the Senate—Everett M. Dirksen (IL), Thomas H. Kuchel (CA), Bourke B. Hickenlooper (IA), Margaret Chase Smith (ME), George Murphy (CA), Milton R. Young (ND), Hugh Scott (PA). For the House of Representatives—Gerald R. Ford (MI), Leslie C. Arends (IL), Melvin R. Laird (WI), John J. Rhodes (AZ), R. Allen Smith (CA), Bob Wilson (CA), Charles E. Goodell (NY), Richard H. Poff (VA), William C. Cramer (FL). Presiding—the National Chairman, Ray C. Bliss.

37. "Laird Sees No Hope of Real Vietnam Win," *Marshfield News Herald*, 3/30/67.

38. MRL, "U.S. Trade Policies Prolong Vietnam War," weekly column, 2/8/67.

39. George H. W. Bush, interview, 10/14/97.

40. George H. W. Bush with Vic Gold, *Looking Forward*, 94–95.

41. Bush, interview, 10/14/97.

42. "Cheney Began Career in Badger State," *Milwaukee Journal Sentinel*, 7/26/00;

Nicholas Lemann, "The Quiet Man: Dick Cheney's Discreet Rise to Unprecedented Power," *New Yorker*, 5/7/01.

43. Cheney to MRL, 8/15/02.

44. Bush, interview, 10/14/97.

45. MRL to Bill Moyers, assistant to the president, 2/19/66.

46. Robert S. McNamara, memorandum for the president, 2/23/66.

47. Gulley and Reese, *Breaking Cover*, 22–23.

48. Ibid., 30.

49. MRL, news release, 4/18/64; MRL, "The Defense Appropriations Committee," *Your Washington Office Report*, 5/6/64.

50. "Window on Washington: Mel's Prediction Comes True," *Madison Capital Times*, 3/13/67.

51. AP, "Laird Censored," *Manitowoc (WI) Herald-Times*, 5/4/67.

52. "Absurd Action," *Milwaukee Sentinel*, 5/6/67.

53. MRL, "Remarks before the Lion's International Convention," Chicago Stadium, 7/8/67.

54. MRL, press release, "Keynote Address at Welcoming Luncheon of American Mining Congress' 70th Annual Convention," Denver Hilton ballroom, 9/11/67; "Laird Ends Viet Policy Support," *Denver Post*, 9/11/67; AP, "Rep. Laird Withdraws Johnson Policy Backing," *Washington Star*, 9/11/67; "Laird Ends GOP Support of Vietnam War," *Waukesha Daily Freeman*, 9/12/67; "Mr. Laird Changes Course," *Christian Science Monitor*, 9/16/67; John H. Averill, "Both Parties Watching as Laird Stirs Again; GOP's Gray Eminence Steps Up Criticism of Johnson's Policies on Vietnam, Taxes," *Los Angeles Times*, 9/18/67; Barry Goldwater, column, *Los Angeles Times* Syndicate, 9/20/67.

55. Evans and Novak, "Dirksen Seen as Too Near LBJ," *Marshfield News Herald*, 12/22/67.

56. "Laird Would Accept Coalition in Vietnam," *Milwaukee Journal*, 1/20/68; "Laird Proposes Direct Talks with Viet Cong," UPI, 1/20/68; Mary McGrory, "Laird, Nixon and Rocky," *New York Post*, 1/23/68; MRL, Chairman, HRC, "As the Other Side Sees It," *U.S. News and World Report*, 1/29/68; MRL, weekly column, "Vietnam," 1/31/68.

57. Oberdorfer, *Tet*; Karnow, *Vietnam*, 515–66; Adam Land, "Tet Offensive," in *Encyclopedia of the Vietnam War*, 536–41.

Chapter 8. The Resurrection of Richard Nixon

1. John Culver, interview, 10/5/00.

2. "Laird Refutes Charges in Ripon Society Book," *Milwaukee Journal*, 10/9/66.

3. Daniel P. Moynihan, contributor, "Where Liberals Went Wrong," *Republican Papers*, 131.

4. MRL, statement before the full Committee on Resolutions (Platform Committee), Fontainebleau Hotel, Miami, Florida, 7/29/68.

5. The figure for the dead at the time of the Republican Convention is from White, *Making of the President, 1968*, 287. The total casualty figures and "$1 million spent every twenty minutes" are from the convention keynote address by Washington governor Dan Evans, August 5, 1968, referring to a war that "we have not won in Saigon, cannot negotiate in Paris, and will not explain to the American people."

6. "GOP Platform Debate Backs Anti-War Plank," *Baltimore Sun*, 7/30/68.

7. AP, "Laird Eyes Rock as No. 2 Man," *Marshfield News Herald*, 8/5/68; "Laird Stays Offstage, but Tries to Play Influential Role," *Milwaukee Journal*, 8/7/68.

8. Ambrose, *Nixon: The Triumph*, 162–63.

9. "Badgers Angered by Choice of Agnew," *Madison Capital Times*, 8/9/68; "Agnew Splits State's Vote," *Green Bay Press-Gazette*, 8/9/68.

10. Cohen and Witcover, *Heartbeat Away*, 3–16, 91–96.

11. Clinton, interview, 1/20/98. Also interviews with other classmates of the Maine South High School Class of 1965: Mike Andrews, who later became a math teacher at Maine South High School, 5/3/99; Ellen Press Murdock, the LBJ-supporter who debated Goldwater-supporter Rodham, 6/7/99; Penny Pullen, later a Republican state legislator, 6/7/99.

12. Dr. Alan Schechter, interview, 6/7/99.

13. Clinton, interview, 1/20/98.

14. Ibid.

15. Clinton, *Living History*, 34–35; "In '68, Hillary's Convention Time Was with GOP," *Chicago Tribune*, 9/18/95; "Good Old Days," *Washington Times*, 9/20/95.

16. Clinton, interview, 1/20/98.

17. Robert Pursley, interview, 10/28/97.

18. "Laird Reports Troop Cut Plan; Campaigning with Nixon, He Foresees 90,000 Reduction—Officials Voice Doubt," *New York Times*, 9/25/68; Don Oberdorfer, *Washington Post*, 9/25/68; White, *Making of the President, 1968*, 389–91.

19. MRL, "Statement in answer to a question concerning Humphrey's troop withdrawals (and) Vietnam question directed to Representative Mel Laird by *New York Times, Washington Post* and *Los Angeles Times*," 9/24/68; AP, "Nixon Supports Laird on Troop Withdrawal Forecast," *Wisconsin Rapids Tribune*, 9/25/68; Orr Kelly, "2 Pullout Versions Offered by Laird," *Washington Star*, 12/1/71; Ambrose, *Nixon: The Triumph*, 196–97.

20. *Washington Post*, 9/25/68.

21. "Clifford Denies Vietnam Cutback; Clarifies Rebuttal to Laird on Reducing Troop Level," *New York Times*, 9/26/68.

22. Transcript, Clark Clifford on *Meet the Press*, NBC News, 9/29/68; "Clifford Doubts Early Cutback; Chides Those Who Forecast Day Troops Will Return," *New York Times*, 9/30/68; "Clifford Raps Guess on GI Withdrawal," *Milwaukee Journal*, 9/30/68; Clark Clifford, secretary of defense, memorandum for the president, 10/3/68; "Laird Affirms Forecast of Troop Withdrawals," *Wisconsin State Journal*, 10/5/68.

23. "Nixon Vows to End War with a 'New Leadership,'" *New York Times*, 3/5/68; William Safire, "The Secret of Mr. Nixon's 'Secret Plan,'" *New York Times*, 9/12/72.

24. Godfrey Sperling, "Nixon's 'Secret Plan' That Never Was," *Christian Science Monitor*, 12/9/97.

25. "Humphrey Vows Halt in Bombing if Hanoi Reacts," *New York Times*, 10/1/68; White, *Making of the President, 1968*, 412–16; Nixon, *Memoirs*, 318–19.

26. Barefoot Sanders, "Memorandum for the President," Monday, 9 p.m., 9/30/68, Lyndon Baines Johnson Library, Austin, Texas.

27. Sister Francis Louviere, Daughters of Charity of St. Vincent de Paul, Carville, LA, interview, 5/8/03; Betsy Bensen, Iberville Parish Library, interview, 5/12/03; "Carville Hospital Celebrates 40th Anniversary," *Baton Rouge Advocate*, 2/6/71; "The Only World They Know," *Newsweek*, 3/29/99; "Last Days at the Leprosarium," *Life*, 4/99. After he

returned to Washington, Laird put through an emergency appropriation for much-needed maintenance work at Carville. In 1994, when the hospital campus celebrated its centennial, the keynote speaker was Bill Clinton's chief political strategist, James Carville, whose family gave the town its name. Carville himself had spent evenings at the facility watching movies in the hospital theater. One of his father's best friends was a patient there. "James Carville will be speaker at celebration," *Baton Rouge Advocate*, 11/20/94. In 1999 the facility was transferred to the Louisiana National Guard and has been partially used as a boot camp for high school dropouts who want to earn a diploma. About fifty residents were allowed to continue living in their longtime homes at Carville, driving for treatment elsewhere.

28. "Live Nixon Show Climaxes Cabinet Search," *Washington Post*, 12/12/68; "Getting to Know Them," *Time*, 12/20/68; "The Great Presentation: Day Starts Out Calmly," *New York Times*, 12/12/68.

29. Kissinger said it was "very possible" that Laird was, indeed, the key man who promoted his candidacy, but "I have no idea." Kissinger, interview, 1/10/01. Occasional news reports suggested Laird's behind-the-scenes role. *Los Angeles Times* reporter Rudy Abramson wrote in early 1972 that "it is widely believed that Laird . . . is largely responsible for bringing Henry A. Kissinger into the Administration as the President's national security affairs advisor." Abramson, "Even Pentagon Fails to Ruin Laird's Career," *Los Angeles Times*, 2/20/72. Laird would occasionally drop hints that his relationship with Kissinger predated that of the president. For example, in a March 1972 interview when he was secretary of defense and was asked about his relationship with Kissinger, Laird told a defense correspondent in his Pentagon office: "Henry and I sat right at that table this morning and had breakfast. I've known Henry longer than the President has." Orr Kelley, "Laird May Aid Nixon Drive," *Washington Star*, 3/4/72.

30. "Pentagon Heir Apparent: Melvin Robert Laird," *New York Times*, 12/10/68.

31. The conversation with Eisenhower is reconstructed from Laird's memory of the visit. No presidential diaries or stenographer's notes exist of the hospital visits during this period. The author consulted with the following Eisenhower specialists in regard to these events: Barbara Constable, archivist, Eisenhower Library, National Archives, 8/1/01; Carol Hegeman, supervisory historian, Eisenhower National Historic Site (Gettysburg, PA), 12/18/01; Lillian (Rusty) Brown Black, Eisenhower's longtime secretary, 1/11/02.

32. Clifford with Holbrooke, *Counsel to the President*, 603–4.

33. Herb Klein, interview, 7/30/01; MRL, secretary of defense-designate, "News Conference at Pentagon,"12/13/68; "Laird Plans Visit to the War Zone after He's Sworn," *New York Times*, 12/14/68; "Laird Vows Arms Policy Reappraisal; Blue-Ribbon Committee Is Planned," *Washington Post*, 12/14/68; "A New Administration Takes Shape," *Time*, 12/20/68.

34. Gulley with Reese, *Breaking Cover*, 95; "White House Kiss and Tell," *Newsweek*, 5/26/80.

35. President Lyndon B. Johnson daily diary, entry for Monday, 12/23/68. Mike Parrish, researcher, Lyndon B. Johnson Library, Austin, TX, interview, 7/25/01; "Rogers Joins Johnson for Report on Talks," *Washington Post*, 12/24/68.

36. In one of his first meetings with top-level staff at the Pentagon, Laird referred to this counsel: "President Johnson went out of his way to stress this point to Mr. Laird. He said that every effort would soon be made to divide the State Department and the

White House, the State Department and Defense, and the White House and Defense. It was one of the biggest problems of his Administration. We would have to go out of our way to knock these efforts down." Senior staff meeting minutes 2/10/69. At the end of his second year in office, Laird recounted the LBJ advice in an interview with David Frost: "President Johnson . . . recommended that we [Rogers and Laird] play golf once a week. We have played perhaps twenty times . . . this has been most worthwhile, I think, because the Department of State and the Department of Defense, in this administration, are closer together and working for common goals as those two Departments never had. I think this is the best record. They never have been as close as they are today." "Interview with Melvin Laird," *David Frost Show*, 12/2/70.

37. Clifford with Holbrooke, *Counsel*, 603.

38. The 12/23/68 conversation between Laird and Johnson was reconstructed from Laird's memory. At a future date, the actual transcript may be available from the Lyndon B. Johnson Library, which is slowly, and chronologically, releasing the Johnson tapes.

39. Beschloss, *Taking Charge*, 547–50.

40. Robert Seamans, interview, 10/12/00; Dick Capen, interview, 8/8/00.

41. John Warner, interview, 11/10/99.

42. Paul Warnke, interview, 7/25/01.

43. Richard V. Allen, director of foreign policy research, Nixon-Agnew Campaign Committee, memorandum, "Confidential Verbal Comment of the Joint Chiefs via Gen. McConnell," delivered to MRL after his appointment on 12/11/68.

44. Moot, having voted for Eisenhower as well, said he "switched back to Republicans" when Laird reappointed him, "and have been a Republican ever since." Robert Moot, interview, 2/6/01.

45. At first, Seamans said he couldn't serve as Air Force secretary until June 1969, but he became available sooner. Harold Brown served Laird only one month into the Nixon administration, until February 15. Robert Seamans, interview, 10/12/00; Harold Brown, interview, 2/20/01.

46. Warner, interview, 11/10/99.

47. Frosch, interview, 7/31/01.

48. The document referenced was a "current status report covering all Presidential, Non-Career Executive, and Schedule C professional appointments within the Department of Defense," Froehlke wrote in the memorandum. "As requested . . . we have indicated political affiliations." Probably because he found it repugnant and an invasion of privacy, in the seven-page chart that followed, Froehlke did not type in the political affiliation. He penned them in (D, R, I, Unknown) next to the names, which meant it would not be disseminated widely—only the typewritten "current status report" would be distributed. Robert F. Froehlke, "Memorandum for John C. Whitaker, Secretary to the Cabinet, The White House," 9/5/69.

49. Packard, *The HP Way*, 174–75.

50. John Gardner, interview, 4/30/01.

51. There was a precedent, which Laird cited: In 1967, the Senate Armed Services Committee had approved a similar trust arrangement involving oil stocks and leases held by former governor Price Daniel of Texas so that he could take the post of director of the Office of Emergency Planning.

52. Laird and Packard, press conference, 12/30/68.

CHAPTER 9. LOOKING FOR AN EXIT

1. Sorley, *Better War*, 94.

2. Robert Pursley, interviews, 7/17, 11/6, and 11/10/00; Jerry Friedheim, interview, 7/19/00; Thelma Stubbs Smith, interview, 4/23/01; Ann Waisbrot, New Visions Gallery, Marshfield, WI, interview, 8/2/01. Jack Anderson, "Secretary of Defense Mel Laird's Pentagon Hideaway," *Parade*, 7/13/69; Vera Glaser and Malvina Stephenson, *Philadelphia Inquirer*, 5/23/71; UPI, 4/13/72; MRL, Question-Answer Period Following Remarks to AP Editors, Kansas City, MO, 11/16/72.

3. Westmoreland, *Soldier Reports*, 467–73; Palmer, *25-Year War*, 80; Perry, *Four Stars*, 184ff.; Clifford with Holbrooke, *Counsel*, 479–501.

4. Sorley, *Thunderbolt*, 222.

5. U.S. Army, Office of Chief of Information, "Biography: General Earle G. Wheeler," ca. 1/69; MRL, "Remarks at Special Retirement Review for Gen. Earle G. Wheeler," Andrews AFB, 7/2/70; Korb, *Joint Chiefs of Staff*, 42; Perry, *Four Stars*, 121, 134.

6. Robert Pursley, interview, 10/9/00; "Masterful Bureaucrat," *Newsweek*, 2/23/70; Perry, *Four Stars*, 132–35, 167–68; Clifford with Holbrooke, *Counsel*, 479–80.

7. "Wheeler Reappointment," *Congressional Quarterly 1965–1968*, 858, 860.

8. Robert Pursley, interviews, 10/9 and 11/10/00; minutes, "Extension of General Wheeler's Term," senior staff meeting, 4/21/69; Perry, *Four Stars*, 201–3.

9. U.S. Air Force, "Biography: General John P. McConnell," 9/15/68; "Former Air Force Chief of Staff: Retired Gen. John Paul McConnell Dies," *Los Angeles Times*, 11/29/86; Perry, *Four Stars*, 132, 164, 166.

10. Perry, *Four Stars*, 212–17.

11. Zumwalt wrote that at the beginning of 1973, "I was sorry to see Mel Laird go. . . . The last two paragraphs of the farewell letter I wrote Mel were from the heart: 'Because of your loyalty up and down the chain of command and your evident concern for people, today's Navy man and woman are better trained, better housed, better paid, and more motivated than any of their predecessors. You have been a fair and inspiring boss and a loyal and faithful friend, both to me and to the Navy. I believe the legacy of achievement which you will pass on to your successors is the stuff of which greatness is made.'" Zumwalt, *On Watch*, 267, 309–10.

12. Robert Pursley, interview, 12/19/00.

13. "Nixon Meets His Top Aides and Orders Vietnam Study," *New York Times*, 12/29/68.

14. Henry Kissinger, interview, 1/10/01. Kissinger also wrote about the visit he and Gen. Goodpaster made to Eisenhower in his memoirs. Kissinger, *White House Years*, 41–43.

15. Lawrence Eagleburger, interview, 2/7/01.

16. Kissinger, *White House Years*, 44.

17. Robert Pursley, interviews, 8/7/97, 6/15/00, 1/21/02.

18. John Warner, interview 11/10/99.

19. Robert Pursley, interview, 10/12/00; Paul Warnke, interview, 7/25/01. "Nixon Meets His Top Aides and Orders Vietnam Study," *New York Times*, 12/29/68; "'69 Report' to Nixon Was Split on War," *Washington Post*, 4/25/72; MRL, "Remarks and Question-Answer Session at TV Correspondents' Breakfast," Harvard Club, New York City, 4/26/72; Kissinger, *White House Years*, 237–38; Hersh, *Price of Power*, 46–50.

20. Paul Warnke, memorandum to MRL, 2/13/69.

21. Clifford with Holbrooke, *Counsel,* 539.

CHAPTER 10. OFF THE MENU

1. Paul Warnke, memorandum to MRL, 1/25/69.

2. "Nixon Cabinet Will Be Named Tomorrow," *Wall Street Journal,* 12/10/68; "Pentagon Gets a Tough Pragmatist," *Business Week,* 12/14/68.

3. Joint Chiefs of Staff, "Operations in SVN Involving Laos," cable to CINCPAC, part of memorandum to MRL, 8/13/73.

4. Hammond, *Military and the Media,* 61.

5. Sorley, *Better War,* 115.

6. Hammond, *Military and the Media,* 74.

7. U.S. Senate hearing, 3/19 to 3/20/69.

8. *Meet the Press,* NBC, 3/23/69.

9. "Secret Laird Plan Will Allow Early Troop Pullout," *Washington Post,* 3/24/69.

10. Nixon, *Memoirs,* 392, emphasis added.

11. Lawrence Eagleburger, interview, 2/7/01; Kissinger, "Our Present Course on Vietnam," memo for the president, 9/10/69.

12. Robert Pursley, interview, 9/11/97. In early 1969, among America's national security hierarchy, only Secretary of State Bill Rogers and CIA Director Richard Helms supported Laird's Vietnamization program. "The Nixon administration wasn't going any place (until Laird's plan was proposed)," Helms recalled in a 7/24/01 interview. "We had to find some way out of Vietnam and out of all the choices we had, Vietnamization was a pretty good choice."

13. Nixon to MRL, 3/26/69; MRL, memorandum to chairman, JCS, 3/31/69.

14. Nixon, *Memoirs,* 375.

15. Secretary of State Bill Rogers, memorandum to American Embassy in Moscow, 4/15/69.

16. Pursley, memorandum to Kissinger, 4/15/69.

17. Department of Defense, Options Paper prepared for National Security Council Meeting, 4/16/69.

18. Perry, *Four Stars,* 221.

19. Kissinger, *White House Years,* 320.

20. Perry, *Four Stars,* 221.

21. MRL, interview, 11/13/07.

22. MRL, testimony before House Committee on Armed Services, 4/15/69.

23. MRL, memorandum to Kissinger, 6/24/69.

24. MRL, "Amendments to FY 1970 Defense Budget," memorandum to Kissinger, 3/1/69.

25. The official renaming of the modified Sentinel program to "Safeguard" dates first to a March 19, 1969, memo in which deputy defense secretary David Packard wrote Army secretary Stan Resor: "As I am sure you have noted, the public and the press increasingly are identifying the modified Sentinel system as the Safeguard Program. I believe that in order to avoid confusion and to increase public understanding of this matter we should refer to it, as the Safeguard Program." The next day, the administration publicly announced it would officially be "Safeguard" henceforth.

26. MRL, "Statement Before the Subcommittee on International Organization and Disarmament Affairs of the Senate Foreign Relations Committee on the Ballistic Missile Defense System," 3/21/69; Hearings, United States Senate, Foreign Relations Subcommittee on International Organization and Disarmament Affairs, "Strategic and Foreign Policy Implications of ABM Systems," 3/21/69, 165, 173, 175, 177–78, 187, 204–7, 213; *1969 Congressional Quarterly Almanac,* 260–61.

27. One of those sticking to the old intelligence estimates that the Soviets were not interested in a first-strike capability was Air Force General Joseph Carroll, whom Laird had inherited as the head of the Defense Intelligence Agency. Carroll was a McNamara loyalist who had served in the post for nearly eight years and whom Laird had planned to replace with someone whose loyalties would be with the new defense secretary. It was part of Laird's strategy to control the flow of intelligence information. General Carroll was reassigned in July 1969 in the middle of the ABM debate and opted to retire instead, after back surgery. His son, antiwar activist James Carroll, charged that General Carroll had been "fired" because he dared to differ with Laird on the "first-strike capability" issue. James Carroll even implied that his father's health was permanently damaged because his spirit had been "broken" by Laird. (The general died in 1991 at the age of eighty.) When those accusations were published in Carroll's book, a surprised Laird said he had no recollection of such a heated conflict with General Carroll. "I told both Dick Helms (CIA director) and General Carroll that their assessment was wrong based on my information which was later shared with them," Laird said. Carroll, *House of War,* 331–37, 439.

28. Laird did not remember his mother saying specifically, "You're scaring everybody," although he confirmed that she called and said she didn't like hearing the frightening things he was saying in the hearing. The specific remark was first reported in the *New York Times,* which no doubt got the story from a Laird aide paraphrasing what his boss had told him about the phone call. Laird later told David Frost that it seems to have become "a true story because it has been repeated so many times," and because it did summarize what Mrs. Laird said. MRL, "Interview with David Frost," *David Frost Show,* 12/2/70.

29. "Laird-Helms Confrontation on ABM Is Being Sanitized," *Washington Post,* 7/9/69.

30. At the time, the longest debate in Senate history had been the 1964 debate over the Civil Rights Act, which lasted eighty-two days. The ABM debate ranked as the sixth longest debate in the Senate since the end of World War II. *Congressional Quarterly,* "Longest Military Debate," 1434, 8/8/69.

31. Dick Capen, interview, 8/8/00; James Lawrence, interview, 7/31/01.

32. Minutes, senior staff meeting, 8/4/69.

33. *Congressional Record,* U.S. Senate, 22453, 8/6/69.

34. Nixon, *Memoirs,* 418.

35. Kissinger, *White House Years,* 212, 208. John Newhouse, in his book on SALT, reached the same conclusion. "Safeguard did help to promote the May [1972] agreement limiting ABMs because the Russians wanted to avoid a competition in modern ABMs and sought to discourage America's program by making a deal." And, "Almost certainly, the misdirected ABM program has been a useful bargaining instrument at SALT." Newhouse, *Cold Dawn,* 30–31, 78.

36. Nixon, *Memoirs*, 615.

37. Henry Kissinger, speech at dedication of Laird Center, Marshfield, WI, 9/12/97.

38. Newhouse, *Cold Dawn*, 68.

39. Smith, *Doubletalk*, 29.

40. Robert Pursley, interview, 10/3/00.

41. Chalmers M. Roberts, "Nitze: Right Man for Geneva?" *Washington Post*, 1/12/82; "Paul Nitze, 97: Key Player in U.S. Foreign Policy during Cold War," *Los Angeles Times*, 10/21/04; "Paul H. Nitze, Missile Treaty Negotiator and Cold War Strategist, Dies at 97," *New York Times*, 10/21/04; "Architect of Cold War Had Role in Ending It," *Washington Post*, 10/21/04.

42. Newhouse, *Cold Dawn*, 48.

43. Harold Brown, interview, 2/20/01.

44. Kissinger, *White House Years*, 147.

45. MRL, "Control of the SALT Delegation," memorandum for Secretary of State (Rogers), cc Kissinger, 6/1/70; William P. Rogers to MRL, cc Kissinger, 6/2/70; MRL, "SALT," letter and memorandum for Secretary of State (Rogers), 6/5/70; MRL, memorandum for the president, 6/5/70; MRL, "Breakfast Meeting with US SALT Delegation in Brussels on 11 June," cable to Deputy Secretary of Defense Packard, 6/11/70; Rogers to MRL, 6/16/70; Ambassador Gerard Smith to MRL, 6/17/70.

46. Harold Brown, interview, 2/20/01.

47. Newhouse, *Cold Dawn*, 265.

48. MRL, "Implications of New Intelligence for SALT," memorandum for the president, 3/9/71.

49. Nixon, *Memoirs*, 522–25.

50. MRL, "SALT—Next Steps," memorandum for national security adviser (Kissinger), 9/4/71.

51. MRL, "SALT," memorandum for national security advisor (Kissinger), 10/29/71.

52. Kissinger, *White House Years*, 1131, 1149.

53. MRL, memorandum for the president, 1/18/72; Kissinger, *White House Years*, 1129–31, 1149–50.

54. Nitze, *From Hiroshima to Glasnost*, 295, 298–99.

55. The acronym SALT was invented by a member of the Brussels-based U.S. NATO mission in 1968. In a public statement immediately after the 1972 signing, Laird first referred to the interim agreement as "SALT I" and said he looked forward to SALT II. The administration and press quickly accepted the roman numeral procedural pattern Laird had invoked. "What Went Wrong with Arms Control?" *Foreign Affairs*, November–December 1985.

56. Smith, *Doubletalk*, 135–36, 180, and 188.

57. Kissinger, *White House Years*, 535.

58. Hersh, *Price of Power*, 535.

59. Gardiner L. Tucker, assistant secretary of defense (Systems Analysis), "Taking Stock," memorandum for MRL, 1/30/73. Tucker's analyses and draft documents, as well as his participation in Washington inter-agency SALT meetings, was invaluable in helping Laird form his positions and plan his own SALT strategy.

60. The ABM Treaty limited each country to two sites, one to guard the capital city and the other to guard a portion of the nation's offensive missile force; the U.S. chose

Grand Forks, North Dakota, for the second site. Presidents Ford and Brezhnev signed a protocol in 1974 that limited each side to only one site. Russia has an active ABM system around Moscow, while the U.S. chose not to build an ABM system at any site. This treaty was the more significant of the two accords. As Nixon put it: "The ABM treaty stopped what inevitably would have become a defensive arms race, with untold billions of dollars being spent on each side for more and more ABM coverage." Nixon, *Memoirs*, 617–18. Under SALT I, the total number of land-based intercontinental and submarine-launched ballistic missile launchers allowed was 1,710 for the U.S. and 2,238 for the Soviet Union. The numerical superiority accorded the Russians was partly offset by the American lead in inter-continental bombers, not covered by the treaties, by the superior accuracy of American missiles, and its MIRV technology.

61. SALT II was signed in June 1979 by President Carter and Brezhnev, but withdrawn by the former from Senate ratification after the Soviets invaded Afghanistan. Signed by Presidents Reagan and Gorbachev in December 1987, the Intermediate-Range Nuclear Forces Treaty eliminated a whole class of nuclear weapons, requiring more than 1,500 to be destroyed. Each country was limited to a total of six thousand warheads when START I (Strategic Arms Reduction Talks) took effect in July 1994, having been signed by presidents George H. W. Bush and Gorbachev in July 1991. In January 1993 the same pair signed START II, which limited each country to 3,500 or fewer warheads. Though it was ratified by the governing bodies of both countries by 2000, it has not yet gone into effect. START III was signed by presidents Clinton and Boris Yeltsin in 1997, and would have limited each country to 2,500 or fewer nuclear warheads, but it has not been ratified by either country. Presidents George W. Bush and Vladimir Putin signed the Strategic Offensive Reductions Treaty (SORT) on May 24, 2002, which limits each country to 2,200 nuclear warheads or fewer, but this has not been ratified either.

62. In 2001, Laird worked energetically to try and persuade Bush and defense secretary Donald Rumsfeld not to withdraw from the ABM Treaty. Laird understood the two wanted to build a small-scale missile defense against a possible future nuclear missile launched by a rogue nation or terrorists. But he felt that could be done by amending the ABM Treaty, and said so in a *Washington Post* editorial on August 23. The treaty had worked for thirty years and was "key to maintaining stability" between the United States and Russia. "Deep-sixing the treaty instead of negotiating amendments would only create a less stable and less predictable deterrent relationship," he continued. "There is no substitute for the predictability, transparency, and irreversibility that come with formal arms reduction agreements." MRL, "Why Scrap the ABM Treaty?" *Washington Post*, 8/23/01. At a press briefing the same day, Rumsfeld confirmed he had read the editorial. "Mel is a smart man," he said, but the president was determined to live up to his campaign pledge to pursue a national missile defense. The *St. Louis Post-Dispatch* found it wonderful that a former defense secretary whose conservative politics and bald head had once been caricatured as "a human nuclear bomb" would now find himself in the twenty-first century "to the left of a Republican president on the issue of arms control." "Listen to Mr. Laird," *St. Louis Post-Dispatch*, 8/25/01. President Bush did listen to Laird, as well as many other strong opponents of treaty withdrawal. He knew he had not won a solid election mandate on the anti-Treaty issue—or on many other issues—so he was well advised to proceed carefully. But the 9/11 terrorist attacks, which came less than three weeks later, changed the world and prompted the president to move

ahead and abandon the ABM Treaty for a yet-to-be-completed national missile defense that might not even work. In mid-December, he notified the Russians that the U.S. would withdraw the following June 2002.

63. Robert Pursley, interview, 8/27/07.

CHAPTER 11. GOING PUBLIC

1. Gen. Earle Wheeler, chairman, JCS, memorandum to MRL, 5/31/69.

2. Kissinger, interview, 1/10/01. In fact, three months after the Midway conference, Kissinger wrote in an "Eyes Only" memo to the president: "Withdrawal of U.S. troops will become like salted peanuts to the American public: The more U.S. troops come home, the more will be demanded. This could eventually result, in effect, in demands for unilateral withdrawal—perhaps within a year." Kissinger, "Our Present Course on Vietnam," memo for the president, 9/10/69.

3. *Washington Star*, 6/9/69.

4. Clark M. Clifford, "A Viet Nam Appraisal," *Foreign Affairs*, July 1969, 601–22

5. Hammond, *Military and the Media*, 92–93.

6. Dick Capen, interview, 8/8/00.

7. V. E. Davis, *Long Road Home*, 201–3.

8. Ibid., 206–9.

9. U.S. Embassy, Vientiane, Laos, cable to State Department, 7/18/69.

10. MRL, memorandum to Kissinger, 8/23/69; Kissinger, memorandum to MRL, 10/22/69.

11. "What You Can Do for American Prisoners in Vietnam," *Reader's Digest*, November 1969.

12. Davis, *Long Road Home*, 222ff.

13. White House, press release, 12/12/69, attached to MRL, memorandum to Vice President Agnew, 12/22/69.

14. Handwritten note from the president in MRL personal files.

15. Office of Assistant Secretary of Defense Public Affairs, news release no. 949-70 and press conference, 11/23/70.

16. Senate Foreign Relations Committee, "Hearing on Bombing Operations and the Prisoner-of-War Rescue Mission in North Vietnam," 11/24/70.

CHAPTER 12. DUELING MACHIAVELLIS

1. Kissinger, *White House Years*, 32–33.

2. Kissinger speech at dedication of Laird Center, Marshfield, WI, 9/12/97; Kissinger, interview, 1/10/01.

3. "Pentagon Heir Apparent: Melvin Robert Laird," *New York Times*, 12/10/68.

4. George Shultz, interview, 2/6/01.

5. James Schlesinger, interview, 7/27/01.

6. Ivan Selin, interview, 2/19/01.

7. Entries for October 11 and 15, 1969, Haldeman, *Haldeman Diaries*, 98–100.

8. Jack Mills, interview, 6/2/00.

9. Nixon, *Memoirs*, 289. Although he knows others described him as "devious," Laird does not believe that Eisenhower ever did so. As a man personally aware of Nixon's penchant for lying, Laird maintains that this is one more Nixon fabrication.

10. Ehrlichman, *Witness to Power,* 95.

11. Caspar Weinberger, interview, 1/25/01.

12. Kissinger speech at dedication of Laird Center, Marshfield, WI, 9/12/97.

13. Kissinger, *White House Years,* 32.

14. Ibid., 32–33.

15. Robert Pursley, interviews, 8/7/97 and 10/12/00.

16. Lawrence Eagleburger, interview, 2/7/01.

17. Kissinger, *White House Years,* 32–33; Kissinger speech at dedication of Laird Center, Marshfield, WI, 9/12/97.

18. Barry Shillito, interview, 8/8/00.

19. Robert Pursley, interview, 10/12/00.

20. Ehrlichman, *Witness to Power,* 96–97.

21. Kissinger implied that the Nixon Doctrine was an outgrowth of his discussions with the president. Kissinger, *White House Years,* 222–25. Biographer Walter Isaacson suggested that the doctrine was a derivative of Kissinger's long fascination with the "doctrine of limits," which directs policy makers to recognize real-time boundaries that cannot be crossed in strategy development. Isaacson, *Kissinger,* 239–42.

22. Laird gave several aides credit for Nixon Doctrine ideas, including Col. Robert Pursley, speechwriters William Baroody and William Prendergast, public affairs chief Dan Henkin, assistant secretary of defense (International Security Affairs) Warren Nutter, and Paul Warnke, the high-level Clark Clifford aide who stayed on for a few months at Laird's request.

23. MRL, "Remarks at the 'Salute to Mel Laird' Dinner,'" Milwaukee, WI, 3/23/72; UPI, 3/23/72; "Laird Has Quiet Visit at Home," *Marshfield News Herald,* 3/27/72.

24. Mel Cunningham, 12/93 and 12/95 issues of *Howgoesit,* the *Maddox* veterans' newsletter.

25. Haldeman, *Haldeman Diaries,* 86.

26. Ehrlichman, *Witness to Power,* 95–97.

27. Col. Ralph Albertazzie, interviews, 4/2 and 4/22/01; Lt. Gen. James D. (Don) Hughes, interview, 4/22/01; terHorst and Albertazzie, *Flying White House,* 275–95.

28. All quotes in this chapter from John Laird and Alison Laird-Large are from interviews with them 2/27/01 and 3/2/01, respectively.

29. "Interview with David Frost," *David Frost Show,* 12/2/70.

30. "'Dove Kids' on Garde," *Washington News,* 1/26/70.

31. MRL, speech upon receiving Demolay Honorary Legion of Honor, New York City Masonic Temple, 4/15/71.

32. Joe Zaice, interview, 7/16/01.

33. Julian Levine, interview, 8/1/01.

34. Zaice, interview, 7/16/01.

35. Articles in the *Tampa Times* and *St. Petersburg Times,* 4/28/69. The news accounts were based on details provided by officials at MacDill Air Force Base.

36. Zaice, interviews, 7/16 and 7/24/01.

37. "Laird Hails Nixon's Peace Bid; Labor Gives Support," *New York Times,* 10/8/69; "Laird Says Anti-War Forces Press for Capitulation to Hanoi," *Washington Post,* 10/8/69.

38. Nixon, memorandum to MRL, 10/8/69.

39. Eau Claire political science professor Karl Andresen said in a 1/3/02 interview:

"I'm not sure who made that call. I can't remember whether I did or not." But he may have, he conceded, because he was "in the thick of the antiwar movement in Eau Claire" from the beginning. "I was in the very first antiwar demonstration [in 1965] when there were only about twenty-five of us. John Laird was here later, and became an important figure because of his father's position in the cabinet."

40. *Janesville Gazette*, 10/9/69; AP, "'Dad's Doing His Best'—Laird's Son to Protest War," *Washington Star*, 10/11/69.

41. In the same interview, John Laird confessed to having some fun with a stuffed shirt in the Pentagon's Public Affairs office, who had been assigned—though not by Secretary Laird—to monitor John's media-related activities. "He was going crazy because I was out here in Wisconsin, on my own, and I didn't have any handlers. So I appointed one of my friends as my press secretary. Every time (the Pentagon officer) would call, I would say, 'I can't talk to you. You'll have to talk to my press secretary.' So this friend of mine was my press secretary." *Washington Post*, 10/15/69.

42. "Agnew's Comment Stirs Debate, *Facts on File*, 10/16–22/69, 674–75

43. "Forum Unique: Laird Plans to Face Wisconsin Students," *Washington Star*, 10/11/69. "Mr. Laird Confronts the Students," *Wall Street Journal*, 11/3/69.

44. *Washington Post*, 10/28/69.

45. Agnew had used the "silent majority" phrase several times in May. White House speechwriter William Safire, later a noted *New York Times* columnist and expert on language, says he coined the phrase, having gotten the general idea from a former senator's speech. Interestingly, Nixon must also have read as well the *Washington Star*'s October 15 editorial on the Moratorium, which concluded: "Despite the tumult and the shouting on this Moratorium day, we think the *great, silent majority* of the American people want their President to stand firm for what he knows is right" (emphasis added).

46. "Gallup Finds 77% Support Nixon View," *New York Times*, 11/5/69.

47. Minutes, senior staff meeting, 11/10/69.

48. "Laird Puts Protest Crowd at 119,000," *Washington Post*, 12/20/69; "Laird Erred on Antiwar Crowd Photo," 12/31/69; "Pentagon: Holes in the Head-Count," *Newsweek*, 1/5/70.

49. Senator Warner's account of that day came from an 11/10/99 interview and from a memorial remembrance of Chafee, which Warner offered on 10/25/99, *Congressional Record*, S13079.

CHAPTER 13. ENDING THE DRAFT

1. "Thieu Doesn't Like the Word: 'Vietnamization' a No-No," *Christian Science Monitor*, 11/21/69.

2. Quoted by *Los Angeles Times*, 2/26/70.

3. Palmer, *25-Year War*, 178–79.

4. Gardiner Tucker, interview, 4/23/01.

5. Roger Shields, interview, 4/18/01.

6. MRL, "Trip to Vietnam and CINCPAC, February 10–14, 1970," memorandum for the president, 2/17/70.

7. "Fighting Slows Down, but Saigon's Woes Increase," *U.S. News and World Report*, 8/17/70.

8. Gen. Earle G. Wheeler, chairman JCS, "Force Planning," memorandum for MRL, 8/12/69.

9. MRL, "Vietnamizing the War" (NSSM 36), memorandum for the president, 9/4/69.

10. MRL, "Vietnamization—RVNAF Improvement and Modernization Aspects and Related U.S. Planning," memorandum for the chairman, JCS, 11/10/69.

11. Kissinger, *White House Years*, 307.

12. Haldeman, *Haldeman Diaries*, 104–5.

13. An incident related to the Green Beret murder case made Nixon and his top White House aides even more paranoid about their inability to outmaneuver Laird and keep him in the dark. At a Camp David dinner on September 12, 1969, Nixon asked an aide to quietly find out what Adm. John McCain in Hawaii thought about court-martialing the Green Berets involved. "Less than an hour later, Secretary Laird called [me] to ask why the White House was trying to call McCain," Ehrlichman wrote in his memoir. "At that time Camp David's telephones went through an Army Signal Corps switchboard [whose operators] were all Army enlisted men and their supervisors were Army officers. The only question was: how closely did Mel Laird monitor the President and the rest of us at Camp David when we called someone on his Army telephone system? Did he just keep track of whom we called, or did he also know what was said?" H. R. Haldeman confirmed the dinner-table paranoia in his memoirs as well: "Tried to call Admiral McCain to get his view, and Laird found out, and called K[issinger], very upset that we hadn't gone to him instead. The fact that Laird apparently knew immediately of our attempt to call McCain from Camp David gave us something new to worry out. Were the Camp David phones tapped for the Defense Department?" Representing a rich historic irony, only a few years later Nixon's reelection committee would attempt to bug the Democrat's national headquarters at the Watergate, and these two men—Ehrlichman and Haldeman—would be jailed for their attempts to cover it up. Ehrlichman, *Witness to Power*, 95–97; Haldeman, *The Haldeman Diaries*, 86.

14. *New York Times*, 11/17/69.

15. *Newsweek*, 4/12/71.

16. Hammond, *Military and the Media*, 258.

17. MRL to Henry Kissinger, 12/2/69.

18. MRL, "Force Planning," memorandum for assistant to the president for National Security Affairs, 12/12/69.

19. *Detroit Free Press*, 12/15/69.

20. MRL, memorandum for the president, 2/7/69; minutes, senior staff meeting, 2/24/69; minutes, "All Volunteer Force," senior staff meeting, 3/10/69; "Nixon Names Advisory Panel to End the Draft," *Washington Post*, 3/28/69; minutes, "Defense Studies," senior staff meeting, 4/14/69; M. Anderson, *Making of the All-Volunteer Armed Force*, 4–5; Witherspoon, "The Military Draft and the All-Volunteer Force," 331–32, 336–41, 461.

21. Besides former defense secretary Gates, the panel included two former supreme allied commanders in Europe, the retired generals Alfred Gruenther and Lauris Norstad.

22. Transcript, "Department of Defense Briefing on Manpower," 2/18/69.

23. MRL, "Draft Reform," memorandum for the president, 8/20/69; minutes, senior staff meeting, 9/8/69.

24. Roger Kelley, interview, 7/27/01; MRL, "Press Conference Following Appearance before House Armed Services Committee," 9/30/69; "House Group Cool to Draft Changes," *New York Times*, 10/1/69; "Draft Evasion in High Places," *New York Times*,

10/10/69; MRL, "Press Conference," Pentagon, 10/16/69; "Nixon's Draft Lottery Plan Approved by House Panel," *New York Times*, 10/17/69.

25. "Draft Reformers Clear a Lottery for Senate Vote," *New York Times*, 11/12/69; "Senate Passage of Draft Bill Seen Certain," *Washington Post*, 11/12/69; "Congress Clears Bill Permitting a Draft Lottery," *New York Times*, 11/20/69; "Senate Approves Lottery Draft Plan, Sends It to Nixon," *Washington Star*, 11/20/69.

26. "Lottery Is No. 1 Topic Among the Nation's Youths," *New York Times*, 12/3/69.

27. John Chafee, interview, 10/22/99; Milton Friedman, interview, 5/7/02; Witherspoon, "The Military Draft," 358–60; Friedman and Friedman, *Two Lucky People*, 380.

28. "How Much for a Volunteer Army?" *New York Times*, 1/4/70; "Nixon Panel Asks Volunteer Army by Middle of '71," *New York Times*, 2/22/70; "1971 End to Draft Is Urged," *Washington Post*, 2/23/70; "Panel Says Draft Could End in 1971," *Washington Star*, 2/23/70; Witherspoon, "The Military Draft," 360–65.

29. Martin Anderson, interview, 5/6/02; Witherspoon, "The Military Draft," 385–86.

30. MRL, "Zero Draft Calls by July 1, 1973," memorandum for secretaries of the military departments, and chairman, JCS, 10/12/70. Four days earlier, Laird had excitedly confided to an audience in Duluth, Minnesota, that the administration now "hope to reach the goal of zero draft in 1973." Only veteran correspondent Charles Corddry caught it. Corddry, "Laird Says 1973 Is Target For End to Draft System," *Baltimore Sun*, 10/9/70. The key memorandum was originally dated October 8, the same day Laird mentioned the administration "hopes" in that speech. Also, his manpower chief, Roger Kelley, told a confidant on October 10 that Laird had already "signed a memorandum to each of the service secretaries requiring them to move ahead" on the new schedule. Curtis Tarr journal, 10/10/70. Apparently, the secretary realized that Monday, October 12, was a better launch date for the new goal, and he could schedule related actions that day and week, which explains why a handwritten "12" was inserted over the typewritten "8" in the date.

31. Minutes, senior staff meeting, "Zero Draft Calls," 10/12/70.

32. James Schlesinger, interview, 7/27/01; Roger Kelley, interview, 7/72/01; Alexander Haig, interview, 1/21/02; Robert Pursley, interview, 1/21/02; Curtis Tarr journal, 11/18/70.

33. Robert K. Griffith Jr. PhD, U.S. Army Center of Military History, unpublished paper, "Moving Mountains: The Army and the Transition from the Draft to the All Volunteer Force; A Preliminary Historical Inquiry," 6/83.

34. "Draft Halts as Congress Snags on Bill," *Washington Post*, 7/1/71; "Tarr Keeps Draft Going," *Baltimore Sun*, 7/2/71; "Draft Lottery Is Scheduled for Aug. 5 as Deadlock in Congress Is Maintained on Extension of the Law," *New York Times*, 7/21/71; UPI, "Laird Fears Harm from Draft Delay," *New York Times*, 7/23/71. Also, minutes, senior staff meeting, "Legislative Affairs," 7/6, 7/12, and 7/19/71.

35. MRL, "Memorandum for Correspondents Regarding Secretary of Defense Views on Draft Legislation," 9/14/71; "Laird Runs Lobby Blitz on Draft," *Washington Star*, 9/14/71; "Stennis Warns of a Crisis if Draft Bill Isn't Passed," *New York Times*, 9/15/71; "Draft Act Battle Shaping Up," *Washington Post*, 9/15/71; "Pentagon Presses Drive to Save the Draft," *Baltimore Sun*, 9/15/71; "Laird Plans Big Push on Draft Bill," *Chicago Tribune*, 9/15/71; "Pentagon Brass Comes to the Aid of Draft Bill," *Washington Star*, 9/15/71.

36. "Service Chiefs Press Senators for Draft," *New York Times*, 9/16/71; "Laird Says Draft Delay Signals U.S. Weakness," *Washington News*, 9/16/71; transcript of Richard

Nixon news conference published in *New York Times,* 9/17/71; "Antidraft Coalition in Senate Is Broken by Nixon Pressure," *New York Times,* 9/17/71; "Nixon Pay Pledge Revives Draft Bill," *Washington Post,* 9/17/71; AP, "Vermont Gets New Senator in Draft Fight," *Washington Post,* 9/17/71; "Senate Rejects a Delay on Draft by 47-to-36 Vote," *New York Times,* 9/18/71; "Draft Bill Survives in Senate," *Washington Post,* 9/18/71; "Doubts on Ending Draft," *Washington Post,* 9/18/71; "Senate Approves Draft Bill, 55–30; President to Sign," *New York Times,* 9/22/71; "Senate Votes Cloture, Passes Draft Measure," *Washington Post,* 9/22/71; "Nixon May Delay Military Raises," *New York Times,* 9/23/71; "President Signs Draft Extension, Delays Pay Increase for Military," *Washington Post,* 9/29/71.

37. AP, "Army Pay Forces Thousands onto Welfare," *Detroit News,* 10/13/69; Jack Anderson, *Parade,* 9/7/69; MRL, "Civilian and Military Pay Increases in 1970 and 1971," memorandum for the president, 12/11/69; "Thousands of Military on Relief," *Air Force Times,* 2/4/70; AP, "Service Families on Welfare Lists," *New York Times,* 2/7/70.

38. "House Unit Votes a Sharp Pay Rise for Servicemen," *New York Times,* 3/23/71; "Senate Votes $2.7 Billion GI Pay Boost," *Washington Post,* 6/9/71; MRL appearance on *Issues and Answers,* 1/30/72; MRL "Press Conference," Milwaukee, WI, 3/23/72; MRL, interview with newsmen before address to National Association of Supervisors, Pensacola, FL, 10/13/72; Robert C. Moot, comptroller, "Taking Stock: Financial Management," memorandum for the secretary of defense, 12/12/72.

39. Bernard W. Rogers, interview, 1/22/05; David R. Hughes, interview, 1/22/05; also, by permission, Rogers's unpublished memoir, ch. 18, *Ft. Carson, Colorado, 1969–1970.*

40. Jack Mills, interview, 6/2/00; Paul Martin, Fort Carson historian, interview, 7/25/01; Bernard Rogers, interview, 1/22/05; David Hughes, interview, 1/22/05; also, *Red Diamond Brand and Mountaineer* (Fort Carson post newspaper) articles, "Secretary Laird Here Today," 10/3/69, and "Defense Secretary Laird Finds Carson Outstanding," 10/10/69.

41. UPI, "Pentagon to Allow Protest in Services," *New York Times,* 9/16/69; UPI, "Allow Protests within Limits, Military Told," *Washington Post,* 9/16/69; AP, "Laird Releases Guide about Post Protest Activity," *Baltimore Sun,* 9/16/69; UPI, "Politics," 10/1/69.

42. Bernard Rogers, interview, 1/22/05; David Hughes, interview, 1/22/05; "Humanizing the U.S. Military," *Time,* 12/21/70.

43. Bernard Rogers, 1/22/05; Rogers unpublished memoir.

44. Zumwalt, *On Watch,* 182–96.

45. Tarr journal, 1/7/71; "The Dump-the-Draft Talk Is Double-Talk," *Look,* 2/23/71.

CHAPTER 14. OBJECTIONS OVERRULED

1. MRL, "Trip to Vietnam and CINCPAC, February 10–14, 1970," memorandum for the president, 2/17/70.

2. That may have sounded like wishful thinking, but Laird turned out to be right. The South Vietnamese army held its own with dwindling U.S. combat support. What it could not live without, however, was U.S. money, equipment, and supplies, and the loss of those would eventually prove its downfall two years after the troops were gone. It came as no surprise after many warnings from Laird.

3. MRL, "Vietnam," memorandum for the president, 4/4/70.

4. MRL, "Economic Aspects of Southeast Asia Conflict," memorandum to assistant to the president for National Security Affairs (Henry Kissinger), 5/15/70.

5. Kissinger, "Vietnam Economic Policy," NSDM 80, 8/13/70.

6. MRL, "Military Strategy in Southeast Asia," memorandum for chairman, JCS, 6/5/70.

7. Mason Freeman, vice director, Joint Staff, JCS, "RVNAF Force Structure," memorandum for MRL. 12/1/70

8. MRL, "Contingency Plan for Attacks on North Vietnamese/VC Cambodian Sanctuaries," memorandum for the chairman, JCS, 3/26/70.

9. Kissinger, "Operation against Enemy Base Camps in Cambodia," memorandum for MRL, 3/26/70.

10. Hammond, *Military and the Media*, 287.

11. Rogers stamped his memo to the president "Secret." But he had his memo to Laird classified even higher, "Top Secret/Sensitive," adding "Exdis," so that only Rogers could say who could see it. William Rogers to MRL, 4/2/70; Rogers, "The Cambodian Situation and U.S. Initiative," memorandum for the president, 3/31/70.

12. Robert Pursley, interview, 11/17/00.

13. Kissinger, *White House Years*, 481.

14. Ibid., 496. Kissinger never wearied of game-playing. He never told Nixon he had kept Laird in the loop and implied otherwise at the time. In an "Eyes Only" memo to prepare the president for the April 26 meeting, Kissinger hypocritically cautioned: "Care should be exercised at today's meeting not to surface the fact that General Wheeler has been conducting intensified planning to implement the attacks on (Cambodian sanctuaries) *without the full knowledge of the Secretary of Defense.*" Kissinger, "Meeting on Cambodia," memorandum for the president, 4/26/70, emphasis added.

15. Nixon, "Actions to Protect U.S. Forces in South Vietnam," NSDM 57, 4/26/70.

16. Nixon, *Memoirs*, 450.

17. Nixon, "Actions to Protect U.S. Forces in South Vietnam," NSDM 58, 4/28/70.

18. MRL, "NSDM 57—Actions to Protect U.S. Forces in South Vietnam," memorandum for the president, 4/27/70.

19. Haldeman, memorandum for MRL, William P. Rogers, and Henry Kissinger, 4/30/70.

20. Gen. Earle Wheeler, chairman, JCS, "Completion of Individual Operations," message to Admiral McCain and General Abrams, 5/4/70.

21. Gen. Creighton Abrams, "Completion of Individual Operations," message to Gen. Earle Wheeler, Chairman, JCS, 5/5/70.

22. MRL, "Press Conference," Pentagon, 5/6/70.

23. The Godfrey Sperling "group" were influential journalists that the respected *Christian Science Monitor* reporter put together, usually, for background-only breakfasts and briefings. MRL, "Press Briefing at [National] Press Club for Godfrey Sperling Group," 5/14/70.

24. G. Warren Nutter, ASD for International Security Affairs, "Plan for SALEM HOUSE Operations after 30 June 1970," memorandum for MRL, 5/21/70.

25. MRL, "Tactical Air Operations in Southeast Asia," memorandum for the assistant to the president for National Security Affairs, 6/5/70.

26. David Packard, "Air Operations in Southeast Asia," memorandum for the president, 6/18/70.

27. Adm. T. H. Moorer, acting chairman, JCS, "Interdiction of North Vietnamese Supplies," memorandum for MRL, 6/15/70.

28. Robert Pursley, interview, 11/22/00.

29. Zumwalt Jr. and Zumwalt III with John Pekkanen, *My Father, My Son,* 41.

CHAPTER 15. BLACK SEPTEMBER

1. The hijacking of a fourth plane on September 6, an El Al Airlines plane bound from Amsterdam, ended when security guards shot and killed one hijacker and wounded another. The dead commando was a twenty-seven-year-old American citizen who lived in Los Angeles. The wounded hijacker was Leila Khaled, twenty-four, who had been involved in hijacking a TWA plane in August 29. She was jailed in London and released as part of an exchange with the Popular Front for the Liberation of Palestine during the September 1970 crisis.

2. Minutes, senior staff meeting, 9/8/70.

3. Kissinger, *White House Years,* 602.

4. Laird could not recall the exact date on which Nixon issued this order, but close analysis of the sequence of events, accounts of the crisis in various memoirs, and review of classified military histories place it on the evening of September 8, one day before a fourth airliner was hijacked.

5. A young National Security Council aide who was in and out of the Oval Office during this crisis told the author Seymour Hersh, "I'd walk in and begin to give a specific listing of what'd happened overnight and Nixon would interject, 'Bomb the bastards,' or some other wild remark." Referenced in Hersh's *Price of Power,* 243–44.

6. Hersh, *Price of Power,* 245–47.

7. MRL, "Proposed US Peace Initiative in the Middle East," memorandum for the president, 6/5/70.

8. G. Warren Nutter, ISA director, memorandum to MRL, 7/9/70.

9. MRL, "Follow-up Actions with Israel," memorandum for the president, 10/3/70.

10. Minutes, seniors staff meeting, 8/24/70.

11. MRL, "Visit of Israeli MOD Moshe Dayan," memorandum for the president, 12/10/70.

12. Minutes, senior staff meeting, 12/14/70.

13. AP, "Held Greater Threat: Laird Says Sub Base Russian Goal in Cuba," *Monroe (WI)Evening Times,* 2/2/63.

14. According to the minutes of the 8/18/69 senior staff meeting—presided over by David Packard in Laird's absence—Adm. Thomas Moorer "commented that the Soviets have the largest number of ships out of area to date. There are 30 combatants in the Mediterranean. There are more subs out and more . . . intelligence collectors. . . . Packard said we should possibly get information out to the press on the Soviet threat problems."

15. Chief of Naval Operations Moorer briefed the senior staff meeting on 6/8/70, according to the minutes, on "Russian Naval Forces in the Gulf of Mexico." He noted that the naval task force, which had "been off of New Orleans and Miami," was "heading home." He added: "Noteworthy is the fact that an Echo Class Soviet nuclear-powered submarine put into Cienfuegos. This is the first time that the Soviets have found fit to send a nuclear powered submarine into a foreign port."

16. Transcript, "Press Conference," Pentagon, 9/2/70; Laird further issued a two-page press release, "Memorandum for Correspondents from Secretary Laird," 9/2/70.

17. Kissinger, *White House Years,* 643.

18. Sulzberger, *Age of Mediocrity,* 655, 660.

19. "Fulbright Warns on Cuba," *Washington Post,* 9/28/70; UPI, "Fulbright Hits Sub Base Talk as 'Hoodwink,'" *Washington Star,* 10/5/70.

20. Nixon, *Memoirs,* 488.

21. Ironically, Lodge himself was a key architect of the war in Vietnam, having served as U.S. ambassador in Saigon during the Johnson administration.

22. The press made a minor flap out of speculation that Laird had had to shuffle the three carriers in the Mediterranean so that Nixon would not be forced to spend time on the USS *John F. Kennedy,* named after his political enemy. But the Pentagon press office denied this report.

23. Lawrence Eagleburger, interview, 2/7/01.

24. Kissinger, *White House Years,* 924–25.

25. "Laird Meets Athens Leaders; Blast Shakes Downtown Area," *New York Times,* 10/4/70; Reuters, "Bomb Explodes Near Laird," *Washington Post,* 10/4/70.

26. Robert Froehlke, interview, 9/10/97.

27. "Laird Advocates Religious Values," *New York Times,* 5/24/70; transcript, "Remarks by MRL at the Presbyterian General Assembly," Chicago, IL, 7:15 a.m., 5/23/70; transcript, "Question-Answer Period Following Address To Presbyterian General Assembly," 5/23/70.

28. Transcript, "Address by MRL at the Dedication of Central Wisconsin Airport," Mosinee, WI, 11:30 a.m., 5/23/70.

29. "Censoring Agnew and Laird," *Milwaukee Journal,* 9/5/70.

30. During and after a summer 2001 research visit by the author, Carleton College archivist Eric Hillemann and his staff made efforts to uncover records confirming the serious slight, but failed. Laird knew the search would be futile, he said, because a college official once confided to him that all references to the faculty's threatened action had been destroyed. (Details about the college's efforts to "repair some of the breech created decades ago" are included in a letter from Carleton College president Robert A. Oden Jr. to William P. Wuehrmann, a Laird friend and a college supporter. Letter in the personal files of MRL, 12/16/06.)

31. MAST had three rules: their assistance had to be requested, it had to be within one hundred miles of a military base, and assistance could be declined if the helicopters and paramedics were already busy with mandated national security tasks. MRL, press statement, 4/30/68; "Military Invades Civil Domain with MAST," *Armed Forces Journal,* 11/71; "MAST," AP, 2/4/72.

32. Minutes, senior staff meeting, "Hurricane Camille," 8/18, 8/25, and 9/8/69.

33. Minutes, senior staff meeting, "Department of Defense Participation in Disaster Relief," 6/26/72; "Watch Out for Flood," *Newsweek,* 2/13/78.

34. "Clemente," UPI, 1/9/73.

35. "Boggs Search Is Halted," *Washington Post,* 11/25/72.

36. "Lindbergh," UPI, 4/1/72.

37. Transcript, "Remarks of MRL at the Dedication Ceremonies for the Meditation Room," Pentagon, 12/15/70.

CHAPTER 16. FRIENDS IN HIGH PLACES

1. Helmut Schmidt, interview, 2/4/01; Col. J. E. Stannard, DoD, "Meeting with German MOD Schmidt," memorandum for MRL, 11/4/69; "Leading from Strength," *Time*, 6/11/79; "Schmidt vs. Strauss: They're Using Bare Knuckles," *New York Times*, 7/27/80; "The Schmidt Factor," *New York Times*, 9/21/80; "A Talk," *New York Times*, 9/16/84; MRL, "My Friend Helmut Schmidt," unpublished article for *Reader's Digest*, 1990.

2. Headquarters, Department of the Army, "Employment of Atomic Demolition Munitions (ADM)," Field Manual, 8/71; Jack Anderson and Dale Van Atta, "Little Weapons with a Big Bang," *Washington Post*, 6/3/84.

3. Schmidt, interview, 2/4/01; State Department, "Seventh Meeting of the Nuclear Planning Group," memorandum of conversation, 6/8/70.

4. G. Warren Nutter, ASD (ISA), "German/U.S. Bilateral," memorandum of 10/28/70 Ottawa Conversation, 11/9/70.

5. State Department, "Eighth Meeting of the Nuclear Planning Group," Ottawa, 10/29/70; "NATO Officials Draft Guidelines for Use of Nuclear Land Mines," *Washington Post*, 10/31/70.

6. Minutes, senior staff meeting, "NATO," 5/25/70; MRL, "Secretary of Defense Presentation to NATO NPG, 8–9 June 1970," 6/8/70; State Department, "Seventh Meeting of the Nuclear Planning Group," memorandum of conversation, 6/8/70.

7. Minutes, senior staff meeting, "NATO Meetings," 6/15/70.

8. Robert Pursley, interview, 1/31/01; Frederick S. Wyle, deputy assistant secretary (ISA), "US/FRG (West German) Meeting (of 10/12/68)," memorandum of conversation, 10/23/68; *1968 Congressional Quarterly Almanac*, "National Security," 82; MRL, "NATO Defense Issues," memorandum for the president, 2/20/69.

9. George Shultz, interview, 2/6/01; Lawrence Eagleburger, interview, 2/7/01; Donald Rumsfeld, interview, 2/28/01; G. Warren Nutter, ASD (ISA), "Secretary Laird/Secretary General Brosio Meeting (Cape Kennedy, 3/18) during the NATO SATCOM Launch Program," memorandum of conversation, 3/30/70.

10. G. Warren Nutter, ASD (ISA), "Meeting of Mr. Laird with Minister Schroeder, February 1, 1969," memorandum of conversation, 2/4/69; MRL, "NATO Defense Issues," memorandum for the president, 2/20/69.

11. Kaplan, *NATO and the United States*, 131–32; Hoff, *Nixon Reconsidered*, 191–94.

12. Rear Adm. Daniel Murphy, military assistant to MRL, memorandum of (5/24) conversation, 5/26/71.

13. Murphy, memorandum of (5/25) conversation, 5/26/71.

14. Schmidt, interview, 2/4/01.

15. Armistead I. Selden, "Summary Paper for the Record—Effect of Personal Rapport Among MODs on Relations Between US and Its Allies," 12/4/72.

16. Mason, *Pacific War Remembered*, 333; Humble, *World War II Aircraft Carriers*, 26.

17. Kissinger, "Policy Toward Japan," NSDM 13, 5/28/69.

18. Haldeman, *Haldeman Diaries*, 62–63.

19. Gen. Earle G. Wheeler, chairman, JCS, "Okinawa Negotiating Strategy," memorandum for deputy secretary of defense David Packard and MRL, 7/24/69.

20. Dick Capen, interview, 8/89/00; "Trip Report of Chemical Munition Safety Survey

(of) Chibana Army Ammunition Depot," delivered to MRL and secretary of the Army Stan Resor, 5/8/70.

21. Kennedy approved a total of sixteen thousand tons of chemical weapons for shipment to Okinawa, but the last five thousand tons was held in the United States awaiting presidential approval for shipment from Kennedy's successors (Johnson and Nixon), which never came. Ivan Selin, ASD, "Storage of Chemical Warfare Weapons on Okinawa," memorandum for MRL, 7/19/69; Gen. Earle Wheeler, chairman, JCS, "Chemical Weapons on Okinawa," memorandum for MRL, 9/12/69; MRL, "Chemical Weapons on Okinawa," memorandum for General Wheeler, chairman, JCS, 10/24/69.)

22. Dan Henkin memorandum to MRL, "News Items of Special Interest," 7/18/69; "24 Felled, Nerve Gas Is Blamed," *Washington Star,* 7/18/69.

23. "Okinawa Gas Leak Report Perils Sato's Treaty Plan," *Washington Post,* 7/20/69; "Okinawa Report on Gas Provides Windfall for Opposition in Japan," *New York Times,* 7/23/69; minutes, senior staff meeting, "CBW," 7/28/69.

24. Gen. Earle Wheeler, chairman, JCS, "Overseas Storage of Toxic Chemical Agents/ Munitions," memorandum for MRL, 8/28/69; MRL, "Chemical Weapons on Okinawa," memorandum for Army secretary and ASD (I&L), 10/24/69.

25. Glenn V. Gibson, acting ASD (I&L), "Chemical Weapons on Okinawa," memorandum for MRL, 11/7/69; Gov. Tom McCall (OR) to Richard Nixon, 12/5/69; MRL to McCall, 1/8/70; MRL, "Removal of Chemical Munitions from Okinawa," memorandum for Kissinger, 4/2/70; Gov. McCall (OR) and Dan Evans (WA) telegram to MRL, 4/18/70; MRL to McCall, 5/9/70; Kissinger, "Delay of Chemical Weapons Removal from Okinawa," memorandum for MRL, 6/8/70; Thaddeus R. Beal, undersecretary of the Army, "Relocation of Chemical Munitions from Okinawa (RED HAT)," memorandum for Deputy Secretary of Defense Packard, 6/16/70; minutes, secretary of defense staff meetings, "Operation RED HAT," 9/8 and 9/14/70.

26. The Johnston Atoll Chemical Agent Disposal System (JACADS) facility finished its mission in November 2000 after destroying nearly 7 percent of America's chemical weapons, including those previously based on Okinawa. "Possible Alternate Location (Alaska) for RED HAT Munitions," MRL talking paper, 5/13/70; Admiral Flanagan, "Operation RED HAT," office memorandum to Warren Nutter, ASD (ISA), 5/13/70; AP, "U.S. to Start Moving War Gas on Okinawa to Atoll in January," *New York Times,* 12/5/70; "More Okinawa Turbulence Seen Despite Token Gas Removal," *Washington Post,* 1/14/71; minutes, senior staff meeting, "Operation RED HAT," 2/1/71; UPI, "U.S. Moving Okinawa Gas to Island in Mid-Pacific," *Washington Star,* 7/15/71.

27. MRL, memorandum for Kissinger, 4/30/69; Kissinger, "CBW Study," memorandum for MRL, 5/9/69; Kissinger, "U.S. Policy on Chemical and Biological Warfare and Agents," NSSM 59, 5/28/69; MRL, "NSSM 59," memorandum for Warren Nutter, ASD (ISA), 8/6/69; "Laird Backs Senate Curb on Chemical War Agents," *New York Times,* 8/10/69; minutes, senior staff meeting, "Chemical Warfare/Biological Research," 8/11/69; "Summary Report on Chemical Warfare Programs and Biological Research Programs," MRL submission to NSC in response to NSSM 59, 10/8/69; minutes, senior staff meeting, "Chemical Warfare," 11/17/69.

28. "United States Policy on Chemical Warfare Program and Bacteriological/Biological Research Program," NSDM 35, 11/25/69; transcript, "Remarks of the President on Announcing the Chemical and Biological Defense Policies and Programs," Roosevelt

Room, White House, 11/25/69; *New York Times*, 11/26/69; "Joint Chiefs Lost Battle Over Chemical Warfare," *Washington Star*, 11/27/69; minutes, senior staff meeting, "Chemical/ Biological Warfare Resolution," 12/1/69; MRL, "Press Conference," Pentagon, 12/1/69.

29. Minutes, senior staff meeting, "Okinawa," 11/3/69; MRL, "Okinawa Reversion," memorandum for Kissinger, 11/18/69.

30. "U.S. Says Japanese Bear Responsibility for Defense," *New York Times*, 8/24/70; "Japanese Seeking U.S. Nuclear Data," *New York Times*, 9/11/70.

31. Nakasone, *Making of the New Japan*, 26–41, 47–50.

32. Ibid., 159.

33. Minutes, senior staff meeting, "Visit of Japanese Director General for Defense Nakasone," 9/14/70; transcript, MRL interview with *Asahi Shimbun*, 9/24/70; minutes, senior staff meeting, "Base Closure/Reduction Package," 11/16/70; UPI, "Japan Says U.S. Will Pull Out 15,000 of 40,000 GIs by June," *Washington Star*, 11/29/70; "U.S. Cutbacks Spur Move in Japan for Defense Buildup," *Washington Post*, 11/30/70; minutes, senior staff meeting, "Base Closures," 11/30/70; Nakasone, *Making of the New Japan*, 159.

34. "Nakasone Says Japan Considered Going Nuclear," *Japan Economic Newswire*, 6/18/04; "Ex-Japanese Premier Once Challenged Japan's Non-nuclear Taboo: Report," *Agence France Presse*, 6/18/04; "Japan Considered Developing Nukes: Nakasone," *Japan Times*, 6/19/04.

35. "Japan Won't Go Nuclear, Official Says," *Washington Post*, 10/12/71; *Asahai* News Service, "Ex-prime Minister Nakasone Ok'd Nukes for Japan," 12/20/00.

36. "Japan Endorses Limited-Defense Concept," *Baltimore Sun*, 10/21/70; Reuters, "Japan's Military Forces Winning Public Approval," *New York Times*, 11/15/70; Reuters, "Japanese Defense Plan Doubles Expenditures," *Washington Post*, 4/28/71.

37. TerHorst and Albertazzie, *Flying White House*, 299–301.

38. Kissinger, *White House Years*, 729.

39. Kissinger, interview, 1/10/01; Lawrence Eagleburger, interview, 2/7/01.

40. Yosuhiro Nakasone, interview, 10/9/01; Daniel Henkin, ASD, "News Release," 6/30/71; "Secretary Laird Arrives in Tokyo," *New York Times*, 7/5/71.

41. MRL, "Trip to Japan," memorandum for the president, 7/19/71.

42. Armistead I. Selden, Jr., acting ASD, "Summary Paper for the Record—Effect of Personal Rapport among MODs on Relations between US and Its Allies," memorandum for MRL, 12/4/72; "Exemplary Envoy: Japanese Ambassador to U.S. Wins Friends, Helps Put Out Fires," *Wall Street Journal*, 1/2/85.

43. MRL, "Interview with Newsmen on Departing Japan," Tokyo, 7/11/71.

44. In September 1972, Sato's successor, Kakuei Tanaka, conducted summit talks in Peking at which it was agreed Japan and the PRC would establish diplomatic relations. "Japan's Pro-U.S. Posture: Automatic no Longer," *Christian Science Monitor*, 7/30/71; "Japan: Sato Role on China Assailed," *New York Times*, 10/27/71; William J. Baroody, Jr., assistant to MRL, "Far East Trip Report," memorandum for MRL, 11/9/71.

45. Minutes, senior staff meeting, "South Asia," 5/24/71; minutes, senior staff meeting, "India/Pakistan," 7/12/71. (The number of East Pakistan refugees would eventually peak at 9.5 million.)

46. Minutes quoted by columnist Jack Anderson, "U.S. Soviet Vessels in Bay of Bengal," *Washington Post*, 12/14/71.

47. Kissinger, *White House Years*, 900.

48. Minutes, senior staff meeting, "India-Pakistan," 12/6/71.

49. J. Fred Buzhardt, "Interim Report of Investigation of Recent Unauthorized Disclosure of Classified Material to Columnist Jack Anderson and the use of Unauthorized Communications Channels between the Nation Security Council Staff and the Office of the Joint Chiefs of Staff," memorandum for the secretary of defense, 1/10/72.

50. Zumwalt, *On Watch*, 375–76.

CHAPTER 17. "MANAGEMENT BY WALKING AROUND"

1. Wisconsin governors Warren Knowles and Walter Kohler prided themselves in being members of this distinguished group.

2. Robert Pursley, interview, 10/12/00; Gaylord Nelson, interview, 2/7/01; secretary's schedule, entry for July 28–29, 1971; "The Liberal Wilderness: Roasting Gaylord Nelson," *Washington Post*, 4/20/90; "Man Behind Earth Day Says Individual Action Can Turn Environmental Tide," *Los Angeles Times*, 4/17/90; "Another Gala for Gaylord," *Madison Capital Times*, 4/17/00; "Significance of Earth Day," *Milwaukee Journal Sentinel*, 4/22/00.

3. Dick Capen, interview, 8/8/00; minutes, senior staff meeting, 3/23, 4/13, and 11/16/70, and 3/8/71; "Laird Clears Way for Bigger Budgets by Patching Pentagon Links with Congress," *National Journal*, 7/31/71; Seamans, *Aiming at Target*, 168–69.

4. David Cooke, interview, 7/18/01; D. Douglas Blanke, "Secretary Laird's Impact on Defense-Congressional Relations," memorandum for Dr. Prendergast, 8/28/72.

5. Rady Johnson, interview, 8/22/00; Dick Capen, interview, 8/22/00; Capen to MRL, 8/12/02.

6. George Dalferes, interview, 7/19/00.

7. Robert Pursley, interview, 7/17/00; Rady Johnson, interview, 8/22/00; Richard Borda, interview, 4/2/01.

8. Dick Capen, interview, 8/8/00; Rady Johnson, interview, 8/22/00; minutes, senior staff meetings: 4/20/70; "Inconsistent Testimony Before Congress," 5/10/71; "Legislative Affairs," 3/6/72.

9. "Laird's Years: The Big Price for Keeping the Brass Off His Back," *Washington Post*, 1/22/73.

10. Elmer Staats, interview, 1/29/02.

11. Bob Schieffer, interview, 7/25/01.

12. "Tough Decisions for a New Decade," *Newsweek*, 1/5/70.

13. Robert Pursley, interview, 10/30/00; "Pentagon Planning $1 Billion Bases Cut," *Baltimore Sun*, 11/14/72; Barry J. Shillito, assistant secretary of defense (I&L), "Taking Stock," memorandum for MRL, 12/19/72; "Richardson Faces a Storm Over Plan to Close Bases," *New York Times*, 4/14/73; MRL, appearance on CBS's *Face the Nation*, 10/10/76.

14. Minutes, senior staff meetings: "Budget," 1/5/70, "Defense Budget," 2/2/70, "FY 1972 Budget Briefing," 1/28/71, "Beyond Vietnam," 4/26/71; "B-1 Essential to U.S. Security, Laird Says after Touring Plant" [includes Laird's rule-of-thumb quote], *Los Angeles Times*, 8/25/72; MRL, "Interview with Newsmen before Remarks to Civic Clubs," Oklahoma City, OK, 9/27/72.

15. Minutes, senior staff meetings: "Budget," 1/5/70, "Budget Matters," 7/6/70, "Budget Matters," 12/28/70; "House Passes Money Bill for HEW; With Trust Funds It Tops $77 Billion," *Washington Post*, 7/28/71; MRL, "Interview with Newsmen," Oklahoma City, OK, 9/27/72.

16. Minutes, senior staff meetings, 4/7 and 4/21/69.

17. AP, "Students Razz Moorer," *Washington Star*, 3/15/72; UPI, 3/15/72.

18. AP, 4/5/72; "Yale Melee Cancels Talk by Westmoreland," *New York Times*, 4/6/72.

19. Minutes, senior staff meeting, 11/1/71.

20. Froehlke, interview, 9/10/97; "Army Chief Seeks, Finds Boston Fight," *Boston Globe*, 12/3/72; Dan Henkin, "News Items of Special Interest," memorandum for MRL, 12/9/72.

21. Orr Kelly, "Laird Leads as Talkingest Defense Secretary," *Washington Star*, 5/31/70.

22. Laird's press chief, Dan Henkin, used the title in September 1969 after the *Washington Post* reported that "unsympathetic State Department wits have thought up" the derisive nomenclature, CINCMINC, for him. In a note to his boss, Henkin acknowledged that Laird was the original source of the title. "I have always preferred CINCMIC, but you have always used CINCMINC. Obviously, you have leaked (your version) to the State Department and they have been leaking to the press." "Laird Is Given New 'Title,'" *Washington Post*, 9/15/69; Dan Henkin, "News Items of Special Interest," memorandum for MRL, 9/15/69.

23. Jerry Friedheim, interview, 7/19/00.

24. Kathy Weaver, interview, 7/11/02.

25. Secretary of State Colin Powell, interview, 12/18/01; Powell with Persico, *My American Journey*, 161–78.

26. "DoD after Two Years of Laird," *Armed Forces Journal*, 12/21/70.

27. Furlong, interview, 8/23/00; transcript, MRL and David Packard, "Press Conference," 12/30/68; "Mr. Packard Would Rather Listen," *Washington News*, 9/18/69; "Pentagon May See Return of Management by Politician-Industrialist Team," *Washington Post*, 3/11/89; MRL, "David Packard, 1912–1996," *Proceedings of the American Philosophical Society*, 147, 3/98.

28. Furlong, interview, 8/23/00; James Boatner, interview, 10/4/00; minutes, senior staff meeting, 12/13/71.

29. Atwood was actually president-elect Bush's choice for the number-two Pentagon position when he put forward Sen. John Tower as his secretary of defense nominee. After Tower failed to win Senate confirmation, Bush asked Cheney to serve as defense secretary. Cheney thus "inherited" Atwood as his number two. Dick Cheney, interview, 2/20/01; "Choice for Pentagon Deputy Seems to Be G.M. Executive," *New York Times*, 1/15/89; "GM Official Seen Headed for Senior Pentagon Post," *Washington Post*, 1/17/89; "Manager for Pentagon: Donald Jesse Atwood," *Washington Post*, 1/26/89; "Pentagon May See Return of Management by Politician-Industrialist Team," *Washington Post*, 3/11/89.

30. Perry, who had been under secretary of defense for research and engineering during the Carter administration, performed well as deputy, but Secretary Aspin didn't. Clinton forced Aspin to resign after only a year on the job, then selected Adm. Bobby Inman to replace him. Shortly into the Senate confirmation process, Inman removed himself from consideration. Clinton then asked Perry to accept the position. Perry was easily confirmed by the Senate to become the nineteenth secretary of defense, and he served from 1994 to 1997. William Perry, interview, 1/18/02; Stuart Rochester, Historical Office of the Office of Secretary of Defense, interview, 1/25/01; "Perry Moves to Erase Aspin's Marks Upon Pentagon Organization," *Washington Post*, 2/17/94; "Perrypatetic," *Economist*, 4/9/94.

31. Cooke, interview, 7/18/01.

32. "The Inspector," *Washington Post*, 6/21/87.
33. David Laird, MRL son, interview, 2/27/01.
34. Noel Gayler, interview, 1/16/01.
35. Minutes, senior staff meeting, "Meetings during the Week," 8/17/70.
36. Dick Capen, interview, 8/8/00; Roger Kelley, interview, 7/27/01.
37. Cooke, interview, 7/18/01.
38. Cooke, interview, 7/18/01; minutes, senior staff meeting, 2/24/70; MRL, "Keel Laying Ceremony of USS *Eisenhower*," Newport News, VA, 8/15/70.
39. George Blanchard, interview, 10/24/01; "Omar Bradley Honored," *Washington Star*, 6/14/72; "Corridor for Bradley," *Baltimore Sun*, 6/15/72; "Salute to an Old Soldier," *Washington Post*, 6/15/72.
40. Col. Lane VanderSteeg, interview, 10/25/01; "Penetrating the Pentagon," *New York Times*, 4/18/82; "The Pentagon at 50," AP, 5/11/93.
41. "Pentagon," 1/18/72; *Newsweek*, 1/31/72.
42. Excerpts from a luncheon speech to the Office of Secretary of Defense Garden Club, as printed in "Notable & Quotable," *Wall Street Journal*, 12/1/72.
42. *New York Times*, 4/18/82.
43. MRL, "Remarks by the Honorable Melvin R. Laird at the Dedication of the Correspondents Corridor, The Pentagon," 10 a.m., 11/21/72.
44. MRL, "Public Information Principles," memorandum for secretaries of military departments; chairman, Joint Chiefs of Staff; director of Defense Research and Engineering; assistant secretaries of defense; assistants to the secretary of defense; directors of the Defense Agencies; 3/4/69; Dan Henkin, "Memorandum for Correspondents," news release, 3/5/69.
46. Jack Anderson, "AF Staff Car Used for Columnist," *Washington Post*, 4/18/72; "Tower Ticker," *Chicago Tribune*, 5/18/72.
47. Henry Kissinger, speech at dedication of Laird Center, Marshfield, WI, 9/12/97.
48. David Broder, speech at dedication of Laird Center, Marshfield, WI, 9/12/97.
49. Bob Schieffer, interview, 7/25/01.
50. Robert Novak, interview, 10/2/00; Henry Kissinger, interview, 1/10/01.
51. George H. W. Bush, interview, 10/14/97.
52. "DoD after Two Years of Laird," *Armed Forces Journal*, 12/21/70.
53. Jerry Friedheim, interview, 7/19/00; minutes, senior staff meetings 4/21, 4/28, and 7/7/69, and 9/27/72; Orr Kelly, "A New Era for Pentagon Press?" *Washington Star*, 5/13/69; "Briefings: A Ritual of Noncommunication," *Time*, 10/10/69.
54. "The Voice of the Pentagon: Jerry Warden Friedheim," *New York Times*, 1/5/73; "Friedheim," UPI, 1/8/73; "Obfuscation Revisited," *Aerospace Daily*, 1/8/73.
55. Henkin, "News Items of Special Interest," 3/3/71.
56. "House Vote Kills Move to Cite C.B.S. on Pentagon Film," *New York Times*, 7/14/71.
57. Joe Zaice, interview, 8/31/01; Vonda Van Dyke Scoates, interview, 5/8/05. Also, information from Miss America Pageant officials and web page; Program/Annual Meeting, "The Challenge of Change," National Association of Chain Drug Stores, Palm Beach, FL, 5/7 to 5/11/72; "Miss America Alumnae: Checking In with an Exclusive Sisterhood," AP, 9/18/83; "Eight Decades of Miss Americas," *People*, 10/16/00.
58. "Ball," UPI, 1/9/73; *New York Times*, 1/10/73; "People," *Sports Illustrated*, 1/73.

CHAPTER 18. MINORITY REPORT

1. "Army Spied on 18,000 Civilians in Two-Year Operation," *New York Times,* 1/18/71.

2. MRL, "News Conference at the Pentagon," 12/28/70.

3. *Washington Monthly,* 1/70.

4. "Army Spy Shakeup Ordered," *Washington Post,* 12/24/70.

5. "Ex-Army Officer Says Unit Spied on Campuses in City," *New York Times,* 12/23/70.

6. "Ex-Agents Tell of Duplication and Competition in Army 'Watch' on Civilians," *New York Times,* 2/26/71; "Military Spying Overkill Described to Senate Panel," *Washington Post,* 2/26/71.

7. "Army Spied on Politicians, Ex-GI Says," *Washington Star,* 12/16/70; AP, "Ervin Says Army's Agents Spied on Illinois Politicians," *New York Times,* 12/17/70.

8. UPI, "Illinois Spying Denied by Army," *New York Times,* 12/18/70.

9. UPI, "Army Admits Snooping on Stevenson," *Washington News,* 3/3/71; "Senators Told Johnson Officials Began Army Check on Civilians," 3/3/71; "Army Admits Spying on Civilians," *Chicago Tribune,* 3/3/71.

10. MRL, "Department of Defense Intelligence and Counterintelligence," memorandum for secretaries of the military departments, JCS chairman, directors of the defense agencies, 12/23/70; minutes, senior staff meeting, 12/28/70; "Laird Acts to Tighten Rule over Military Intelligence," *New York Times,* 12/24/70; "Army Spy Shakeup Ordered," *Washington Post,* 12/24/70.

11. "Laird Picks Panel to Curb American Spying on Civilians," *New York Times,* 2/19/71; AP, "Johnson Men Did Not Mean Army Spies to Cover Riots," *Baltimore Sun,* 2/20/71; "Ervin Views Army Spying as Illegal," *Washington Post,* 3/3/71; "Senators Told Johnson Officials Began Army Check on Civilians," *New York Times,* 3/3/71.

12. UPI, reporting on Laird's closed-door session the previous March 4, "Laird Parries Spy Blame," *Washington News,* 6/21/71.

13. "General-to-Be Is a Black Panther," *Washington Post,* 2/1/70 (the term "black panther" was a reference to an insignia he wore in Vietnam and Korea, not to the militant group.); "Chappie James' Life Dedicated to Tenet 'Thou Shall Not Quit' an American Success Story," *Washington Post,* 7/21/75; "Gen. Daniel (Chappie) James, Former NORAD Chief, Dies," *Washington Post,* 2/26/78; "'Chappie' James, 1st Black 4-Star General, Dies," *Washington Star,* 2/26/78.

14. "U.S. to Abandon Wheelus by July," *Baltimore Sun,* 12/24/69; "Libyans Invite France to Wheelus," *Washington News,* 3/5/70; McGovern, *Black Eagle,* 109–16; Phelps, *Chappie,* 255–66; McLucas and Benson, *Confessions of a Technocrat.*

15. "Pentagon Deputy," UPI, 2/3/70; AP, "Negro Pilot to Be PIO for Laird," *Washington Post,* 2/4/70; "Negro Gets Key Post at Pentagon," *Washington Star,* 2/4/70.

16. Phelps, *Chappie,* 277–78.

17. *Washington Post,* 7/21/75.

18. For quotes from James's speeches, see McGovern, *Black Eagle,* 109–10, 269–78; Phelps, *Chappie,* 255–66, 279–88.

19. Laird said he shouldn't get "too much credit" for resigning from Kenwood because he preferred to golf at Burning Tree anyway—and, by 1968, he had built a swimming pool behind his house for the family. Alison Laird-Large, interview, 3/2/01; "Laird Opposes Club Race Bar," *Washington Post,* 12/21/68; "Laird Will Resign from Country

Club," *Milwaukee Sentinel,* 12/21/68; "Laird Has Stayed Out of Club's Racial Rift," *Milwaukee Journal,* 12/23/68; "Rogers, Laird Quit Kenwood Country Club," *Washington Post,* 4/16/70.

20. Roger Kelley, interview, 7/27/01; MRL, "Address and Question-Answer Period," Fort Leavenworth, Kansas, 11/23/71.

21. MRL, "Press Conference," Pentagon, 11/17/71; MRL, interview on NBC's *Today Show,* 11/30/72; minutes, senior staff meeting, 12/4/72.

22. "Racial Climate Improving in Military," *Washington Star,* 6/15/71; Carl S. Wallace, special assistant, "Information Regarding Accomplishments by the Department of Defense in the Area of Equal Opportunity During the Nixon Administration," memorandum for Brig. James D. Hughes, USAF, military assistant to the president, 6/17/71.

23. "Richmond Man Selected as First Black Admiral," *Washington Post,* 4/28/71; "Blacks Named to Navy Posts," *Washington Star,* 4/29/71; "1st Black Admiral 'Won't Be the Last,'" *Chicago Tribune,* 4/29/71; "Rear Admiral, USN," *Christian Science Monitor,* 4/30/71.

24. "General," UPI, 4/19/72; "Black Generals," UPI, 7/27/72; "Black General Named to Command Ft. Carson," *Jet,* 9/21/72.

25. "'Chappie' James, 1st Black 4-Star General, Dies," *Washington Star,* 2/26/78.

26. "Bias in Germany," *Parade,* 9/10/72.

27. AP, "James," 2/5/70; McGovern, *Black Eagle,* 133.

28. MRL, "Equal Opportunity within the Department of Defense," Department of Defense directive no. 1100.15, 12/14/70; "Anti-discrimination," AP, 12/17/70; "Pentagon Widens Rules to Prevent Racial Inequities," *New York Times,* 12/18/70; minutes, senior staff meeting, "Equal Employment Opportunity," 12/21/70.

29. United States Civil Rights Commission to MRL, 1/24/70; signed by Rev. Theodore M. Hesburgh, C.S.C., chairman; Stephen Horn, vice chairman; Frankie M. Freeman, Maurice B. Mitchell, Robert S. Rankin, and Manuel Ruiz, commissioners.

30. "Negroes an Issue in F-15 Contract; Air Force Prods Company to Comply on Hiring," *New York Tines,* 1/31/70; "U.S. Pressing F-15 Contractor on Job Policy," *Washington Post,* 1/31/70; AP, "Laird Orders Close Checks on Job Bias by Contractors," *Washington Star,* 2/1/70.

31. Seamans, *Aiming at Targets,* 172; David Packard also reviewed what happened that Friday when he conducted a subsequent staff meeting in February 1970 when Laird was out of town. Minutes, senior staff meeting, "Equal Employment Opportunity and Contract Compliance," 2/9/70.

32. "'I'll Bleed for Myself,' Says Black U.S. Soldier in Europe," *New York Times,* 10/11/70.

33. "Captain Shifted after Snub," *Washington Post,* 2/12/71; "7 Officers Said to Lost Posts in Rights Cases," *Washington Post,* 7/28/71; "Military Has Enforced Bias Rule, Aide Says," *Washington Star,* 7/29/71.

34. John H. Chafee, secretary of the Navy, "Improved Communications with the Department of the Navy," memorandum for MRL, 3/25/70; minutes, senior staff meeting, "Minority Groups," 10/19/70; "200 Trainees at Ft. Dix Get Course in Race Relations," *New York Times,* 2/5/71; "Minorities Study Is Military 'Must' Now," *Chicago Tribune,* 3/3/71; "The Air Force Academy Blows Its Mind," *Ebony,* 3/72.

35. Roger Kelley, interview, 7/27/01; Frank Render, former assistant secretary of

defense for civil rights, interview, 1/18/02; "Pentagon to Train 1,400 to Teach Race Relations," *Washington Star,* 3/5/71; "Secretary of Defense Laird Establishes Equal Opportunity Education Program," DoD news release, 3/5/71; "Classes on Race Ordered for All in Armed Forces," *New York Times,* 3/6/71; "U.S. Struggles to Make Equality Work," *Washington Post,* 3/6/90.

36. Segal, *Recruiting for Uncle Sam,* 114.

37. Jeanne Holm, interview, 10/26/01.

38. Jerry Friedheim, interview, 7/19/00.

39. Holm, interview, 10/26/01; Elizabeth P. Hoisington, interview, 10/28/01; Stan Resor, interview, 10/30/01; "First 2 Women Generals in U.S. Chosen by Nixon," *New York Times,* 5/16/70; MRL, "Making Greater Use of Women's Skills in High Level Positions," memorandum for the president, 6/6/71.

40. Holm, interview, 10/26/01; "Women's Rights," AP, 3/31/70; "Lady General," AP, 1/22/73; "Lady General," UPI, 1/22/73; McLucas and Benson, *Confessions.*

41. Jerry Friedheim, interview, 7/19/00; Dick Capen, interview, 8/8/00; "Navy Set to Select a Female Admiral," *Washington Post,* 3/23/72; minutes, senior staff meeting, "DACOWITS," 4/10/72; "Woman Selected to Be 1st Admiral," *Washington Star,* 4/27/72; "First Woman Admiral: Alene Bertha Duerk," *New York Times,* 4/28/72; AP, "Navy Names First Woman Admiral," *Washington Post,* 4/28/72.

42. "Navy Would Put Gals Aboard Men o' War," *New York Daily News,* 8/9/72; Dan Henkin, "New Items of Special Interest," memorandum to MRL, 8/12/72.

43. During a June 1971 session of a special subcommittee of the Senate Government Operations Committee, Attorney General John Mitchell revealed the existence of this list.

44. Vera Glaser and Malvina Stephenson, "Secretary Laird's Future," *Washington Sunday Star,* 5/23/71.

45. Lewis Sorley noted that in one unit alone, the 173rd Airborne Brigade, "a study of about one thousand men showed that 84 percent of drug users began use in the United States." Sorley, *Better War,* 296–98.

46. UPI, 3/24/70.

47. "Fact Sheet," Department of Defense Drug Abuse Control Committee, 1/5/70.

48. PBS, "Thirty Years of America's Drug War: A Chronology," *Frontline,* 2000.

49. MRL, "DoD Drug Abuse Control Program," memorandum for the president, 5/12/72.

50. PBS, "Thirty Years of America's Drug War."

51. Richard Nixon, "Increased DoD Support for International Narcotics Control," memorandum for the secretary of defense, 5/3/72.

CHAPTER 19. THE SECRET WAR

1. AP, "U.S. Enters Second Decade of Viet War," *Baltimore Sun,* 1/2/71.

2. AP, "Last U.S. Green Beret Camps Turned Over to S. Vietnamese," *Washington Post,* 1/5/71.

3. Kissinger, "Discussion of Troop Withdrawals and Vietnamization," memorandum for secretaries of defense and state, CIA director, 1/6/71.

4. MRL, "Press Conference," Paris, France, 1/6/71.

5. "Laird Sets Date, but . . . : White House Wary on Viet Phase-out," *Christian Science Monitor,* 1/8/71.

6. MRL, "Interview with Newsmen on Departure from Vietnam," Saigon, Vietnam, 1/11/71.

7. MRL, memorandum of conversation, 1/11/71, included as part of MRL, memorandum for the president, 1/16/71.

8. Kutler, *Encyclopedia of the Vietnam War*, 561–62; Castle, *War in the Shadow of Vietnam*,; Hamilton-Merritt, *Tragic Mountains*.

9. Kissinger, memorandum for MRL, 9/15/69.

10. "Fulbright Attacks U.S. Role in Laos," *Washington Post*, 10/29/69.

11. During the Johnson administration, the "field marshal" was U.S. ambassador William Sullivan.

12. MRL, "Operational Control Procedures, Laos," letter with attachment to secretary of state William P. Rogers, 12/1/69.

13. AP, "Senators Ask Facts on Role of U.S. in Laos," *Washington Star*, 2/26/70.

14. "Department of Defense Appropriations for 1971," Hearings before a Subcommittee of the Committee on Appropriations, House of Representatives, 2/26/70, 359.

15. MRL, "Interview with Newsmen Following Appearance before House Committee on Appropriations," 2/26/70.

16. MRL, memorandum for the president, with two attachments, "Draft Statement on Laos" and "Check List," 3/3/70.

17. Kissinger, "Presidential Statement on Laos," memorandum for secretaries of defense and state, and CIA director, 3/4/70.

18. MRL, "Presidential Statement on Laos," memorandum for assistant to the president for National Security Affairs (Kissinger), 3/5/70.

19. A number of Air Force deaths in Laos remained a secret even after the fallout from the president's speech. Laird told Kissinger about those belatedly in a top secret memo on March 13 (MRL, memorandum for Kissinger, 3/13/70). Those deaths occurred in 1967 and 1968, and the airmen were voluntarily working under cover as civilians at the time. The Pentagon needed to install radar sites in Laos, and the best people to do it were Air Force personnel. The men were mustered out of the Air Force and put on the Lockheed corporate payroll as contractors. Fourteen of them were killed in two separate raids on radar sites; thirteen were posthumously reinstated in the Air Force so their widows could get their military benefits, and that made them military ground combat casualties; one of them, Sgt. Richard L. Etchberger, had even been awarded the Air Force Cross for heroism. The fourteenth man, a sergeant, was not posthumously reinstated to the Air Force because, according to Laird's report, his "wife was not a U.S. citizen, and, therefore, not considered clearable. She was not briefed regarding the project on her husband's status vis-à-vis the U.S. Air Force. Therefore, his status remains that of a civilian." Sgt. Etchberger's citation was for "extraordinary heroism in military operations against an opposing armed force on 11 March 1968." On that date he was manning a defensive position when the rest of the northern Lao base was overrun by the enemy. "The enemy was able to deliver sustained and withering fire directly upon this position from higher ground. His entire crew dead or wounded, Sgt. Etchberger managed to return the enemy's fire thus denying them access to his position. During this entire period, Sgt. Etchberger continued to direct air strikes and call for air rescue . . . enabling the air evacuation force to locate the surrounded friendly element. When air rescue arrived, Sgt. Etchberger deliberately exposed himself to enemy fire in

order to place his three surviving wounded comrades in the rescue slings, permitting them to be airlifted to safety. As Sgt. Etchberger was finally being rescued, he was fatally wounded by enemy ground fire. His fierce defense, which culminated in the supreme sacrifice of his life, saved not only the lives of his three comrades but provided for the successful evacuation of the remaining survivors of the base." Since it hadn't happened on Nixon's watch, Laird recommended that the names not be released so long after the fact. The widows themselves had been sworn to secrecy.

20. Elliot Richardson, "Dear Dave" letter to deputy secretary of defense David Packard, 5/29/70.

21. David Packard, "Prairie Fire Operations in Laos," memorandum for the chairman, JCS, 6/18/70.

22. John R. Stevenson, "Prairie Fire Operations—The President's Statement on the Church Amendment," Opinion of the Legal Adviser, attached to 7/17/70, State Department letter to Packard.

23. U. Alexis Johnson, undersecretary of state for political affairs, State Department, "Dear Dave" letter to Packard, 7/17/70.

24. Kissinger, "Participation of U.S. Personnel in the Exploitation Phase of Prairie Fire Operations in Laos," memorandum for secretaries of defense and state, and CIA director, 10/13/70.

25. MRL, "Participation of U.S. Personnel in the Exploitation Phase of Prairie Fire Operations in Laos," memorandum for the president, 12/7/70.

26. According to Michael Maclear, the Hanoi strategist Ha Van Lau maintained after the war that "it was a road system of more than 13,000 kilometers," which is more than twice the size of the 5,645 kilometers (3,500 miles) that American military computers had mapped. Maclear, *Ten Thousand Day War*, 173.

27. This is the figure used by North Vietnamese journalist Khanh Van, writing after the war in Hanoi's military newspaper, *Quan Doi Nhan Dan*, as paraphrased by Maclear, *Ten Thousand Day War*, 186–87.

28. Maclear, *Ten Thousand Day War*, 185. He asserts, "In World War II, two million tons of air ordnance were dropped. From 1965 to 1971, 2,235,918 tons of bombs were dropped over Laos infiltration routes."

29. Secretary of defense schedule, 12/23/70; Kissinger, *White House Years*, 994.

30. MRL, memorandum of conversation, President Nguyen Van Thieu and MRL, 1/11/71.

31. The American portion of the operation was called "Dewey Canyon II." The first such operation in the Laotian panhandle had actually been misspelled, and that mistake continued in 1971. It was supposed to be "*Dewy* Canyon," in reference to the dew-like mists that covered the Ho Chi Minh Trail. The evocation of the fifteenth-century Lam Son victory had such historic significance for the South Vietnamese that Admiral Moorer advised in a memo that U.S. military should not engage in "any action to terminate the use of the term Lam Son" in connection with any future RVNAF operations. Adm. T. H. Moorer, chairman, JCS, "U.S. Support for RVNAF Cross-Border Operations," memorandum for MRL, 4/1/71.

32. "The two sides of this sign embody both the facts and the goal of the current action," Laird said. MRL, "Address by the Honorable Melvin R. Laird, Secretary of

Defense, Before the Rotary Club of Phoenix," Phoenix, AZ, 2/12/71; "Indochina: A Cavalry Man's Way Out," *Time,* 2/15/71.

33. Laird referred to his remarks during his weekly senior staff meeting held shortly after the cabinet meeting on February 16, according to the minutes.

34. Vietnam Military History Institute, *History of the People's Army of Vietnam.*

35. MRL and Lt. Gen. John W. Vogt, director, JCS, "News Conference at Pentagon," 2/24/71.

36. "Laos Drive on Schedule, Laird Says," *Washington Post,* 2/25/71.

37. MRL, "Department of Defense Appropriations for 1972," Hearing before a Subcommittee of the Committee on Appropriations, House of Representatives, 209–12, 3/4/71.

38. Art Buchwald, "The Pentagon's Little Lies," *Washington Post,* 3/9/71.

39. Minutes, senior staff meeting, 3/1/71.

40. Minutes, senior staff meeting, Moorer briefing, 3/8/71.

41. Nalty, *Vietnam War,* 253.

42. Minutes, senior staff meeting, 3/29/71.

43. Haig with McCarry, *Inner Circles,* 273–78.

44. Sorley, *Better War,* 270.

45. Ibid., 256 and 261.

46. Gen. Bruce Palmer Jr., "U.S. Intelligence and Vietnam," *Studies in Intelligence,* CIA (1984), 90.

47. Minutes, Moorer briefing, senior staff meeting, 3/29/71.

48. UPI, 1/28/71; "Thousands in U.S. Protest on Laos," *New York Times,* 2/11/71.

49. Jack Vessey, interview, 2/25/02.

CHAPTER 20. THE HAWKS HAVE FLOWN

1. From Laird's own recollection of the evening as well as a contemporary account in *Newsweek,* which described Laird as being "alone in a roomful of friends." "End of the Tunnel Remains Blurred," *Washington Post,* 4/8/71; "White House, Scott Split on Pullout Date," *Washington Post,* 4/9/71; "'You Don't See Any Hawks around Here,'" *Newsweek,* 4/19/71. Remarking on the differing accounts, Pentagon press chief Dan Henkin wrote Laird on 4/14: "It needs to be borne in mind that in any dinner with eleven [*sic*] Senators, there will be eleven different versions reported to the press. Witness the *Newsweek* stories of Javits's not-so-private dinner."

2. MRL, "Tempo of the War," memorandum for the president, 4/6/71.

3. MRL, "Redeployment of U.S. Forces from Southeast Asia," memorandum for the president, 4/3/71.

4. "Eavesdropping Some More on Nixon in the Oval Office," *Chicago Tribune,* 10/31/99.

5. Richard Nixon, "Discussion of Vietnam Plans," memorandum for the secretaries of state and defense, and CIA director, 4/9/71.

6. "U.S. Plans Air, Sea Asia Role: Laird Cites 'Deterrent' after Pullout," *Washington Post,* 4/14/71.

7. "Veterans Discard Medals in War Protest at Capitol," *New York Times,* 4/24/70; "Vets Leave; Mass March Slated Today," *Washington Post,* 4/24/71.

8. *Washington Post,* 2/21/85.

9. Joe Zaice, interview, 8/31/01.

10. "The Cost of the War after It's 'Over,'" *Time*, 4/19/71.

11. Minutes, senior staff meeting, 6/14/71; both the *New York Times* and Secretary of State William Rogers, in June 1971, said that "thirty-six persons" authored the study.

12. Ungar, *Papers*, 31.

13. The title used by Pentagon officials in transmitting the documents to Congress was different: "United States-Vietnam Relations, 1945–1967."

14. At the 6/14/71 senior staff meeting, Laird generally outlined the location of the fifteen copies. A more detailed list was in the "FBI Checking All Having Access to Known 15 Copies of Viet Study," *Washington Post*, 6/16/71. In a memo of the same day to Laird referring to the *Post* story, his spokesperson Dan Henkin called their list "rather complete." See also, Ungar, *Papers*, 40–41.

15. Laird was among four hundred invited guests to the event. The eighteen-minute ceremony was conducted by the House of Representatives chaplain, even though not one member of Congress had been invited. It was the eighth wedding of a president's daughter in White House history.

16. National Archives, White House tapes, 6/14/71: "Conversation no. 519-7," Alexander Haig, 12:27–1:09 p.m.; "Conversation no. 521-7," Henry Kissinger, 3:19–3:31 p.m.; "Conversation no. 521-9," John N. Mitchell and John D. Erlichman, 3:45–4:30 p.m.

17. Minutes, senior staff meeting, 6/21/71.

18. "Pentagon Calls Study 'The McNamara Papers,'" *Washington Star*, 6/22/71.

19. Ungar, *Papers*, 207, 229–30.

20. National Archives, White House tape, "Conversation no. 533-1," 6/30/71.

21. National Archives, White House tapes, "Conversation no. 534-3," 10:28–11:49 a.m., 7/1/71, Oval Office, Nixon, Haldeman, and Colson.

22. National Archives, White House tapes, "Conversation no. 260-21," 5:39–6:29 p.m., 7/2/71, Old Executive Office Building; Nixon, Ehrlichman, and Haldeman.

23. National Archives, White House tape, "Conversation no. 538-15," 11:50 a.m.–12:15 p.m., 7/6/71; Nixon, Mitchell, Ehrlichman, and Haldeman.

24. Minutes, senior staff meeting, 7/12/71.

25. The survey was conducted July 9 and 12, and reported to Laird by Air Force Secretary Robert C. Seamans Jr. in a 7/15/71 memorandum.

26. National Archives, "Conversation No. 533-1."

27. National Archives, White House tapes, "Conversation no. 533-1," 8:49–9:52 a.m., Oval Office; Nixon, Haldeman, and Kissinger.

28. Ford, interview, 8/28/97.

29. This dictum was so hard-and-fast that the Pentagon press corps was aware of it. Bob Schieffer, who was the CBS Pentagon correspondent from 1970 to 1974, recalled that even though Laird "never put out a press release on it, we all knew that Laird would not let anybody at the White House talk to anybody at the Pentagon unless they went through him." Schieffer, interview, 7/25/01.

30. Barry Shillito, interview, 8/8/00; Dr. Johnny Foster, interview, 4/23/01.

31. Stanley Kutler, interview, 7/14/00.

32. Shillito, interview, 8/8/00.

33. Minutes, senior staff meeting, 8/31/70.

34. Robert Seamans, interview, 10/12/00.

35. Robert Froehlke, interview, 7/23/00.

36. Dick Capen, interview, 8/8/00; Robert Pursley, interview, 10/28/97; Norman Augustine, interview, 11/7/00; Rep. Pierre (Pete) Du Pont, interview, 4/4/01.

37. Sen. John Chafee, interview, 10/22/99.

38. Sen. John Warner, interview, 11/10/99; Laird also confirmed the event.

CHAPTER 21. WITHDRAWAL SYMPTOMS

1. MRL, "Press Conference," Fort Campbell, KY, 9/2/71.

2. MRL, "Address before the Rotary Club of Phoenix, Arizona," 2/12/71; minutes, senior staff meetings, 11/29/71 and 12/27/71; MRL, "Press Conference," Pentagon, 9/1/71.

3. Gen. William C. Westmoreland, acting chairman, JCS, "RVNAF Improvement and Modernization Program," memorandum for MRL, 4/6/71.

4. Hammond, *Military and the Media,* 503.

5. MRL, "Your Memorandum of April 28, 1971," memorandum for Kissinger, 5/4/71.

6. Minutes, senior staff meeting, 11/29/71.

7. Kissinger, "Air Activities over Southeast Asia: FY 1972 and FY 1973," memorandum for MRL, 8/6/71.

8. Phil Odeen, ISA, "Vietnamization Meeting with Secretary Laird," 8/18/71.

9. This memo was referred to in the minutes of a Vietnam Task Force meeting. Phil Odeen, ISA, "Vietnamization Meeting with Secretary Laird," memorandum, 8/26/71.

10. Minutes, senior staff meeting, 5/3/71.

11. MRL, "Protective Reaction Strikes in North Vietnam," memorandum for the president, 2/26/71, with attachment: Adm. T. H. Moorer, chairman, JCS, "Protective Reaction Strikes in North Vietnam," 2/25/71.

12. MRL, "Protective Reaction Strikes against North Vietnam," memorandum for chairman, JCS, 3/6/71.

13. Moorer, chairman, JCS, "Protective Reaction Strikes against North Vietnam," memorandum for MRL, 3/19/71.

14. Phil Odeen, ISA, "Vietnamization Meeting with Secretary Laird," memorandum for the Record, 7/23/71.

15. MRL, "Request for Strikes," memorandum for the chairman, JCS, 10/21/71; Gen. John D. Ryan, acting chairman, JCS, "Air Strikes against North Vietnam Air Defenses," memorandum for MRL, 11/13/71; MRL, "Air Strikes against North Vietnam Air Defenses," memorandum for the chairman, JCS, 11/15/71; Moorer, chairman, JCS, "Operations against Targets in North Vietnam," memorandum for MRL, 11/30/71.

16. Moorer, chairman, JCS, "Arc Light," cable to General Holloway and Adm. John McCain.

17. Adm. E. R. Zumwalt Jr., acting chairman, JCS, "Reaction to MIG Activity—3 December 1971," memorandum for the Deputy Secretary of Defense David Packard, 12/4/71.

18. MRL, "Air Strikes against North Vietnam," memorandum for the president, 12/9/71.

19. Moorer, chairman, JCS, "Proud Deep/Hai Cang Tudo II," cable to Adm. John McCain, 12/19/71.

20. UPI, "Christmas Truce Ends in Vietnam," *Baltimore Sun,* 12/27/71.

21. MRL, "Trip to Paris, Bangkok, South Vietnam, and CINCPAC, January 5–15, 1971," memorandum for the president, 1/16/71.

22. Hersh, *Price of Power,* 432–33.

23. Report prepared for MRL, "The Vietnam War: Chronology of Significant Events since 20 January 1969," 164; minutes, senior staff meeting, 10/4/71; "Thieu Gets 95% as 87% vote," *Washington Star,* 10/4/71.

24. "Laird Takes Self Out of Race for Office in 1972," *Stevens Point Daily Journal,* 10/19/71.

25. Laird reported that at the 10/12/71 cabinet meeting, it was tentatively decided at first that Health, Education, and Welfare secretary Elliott Richardson go instead of Laird—according to the minutes Phil Odeen recorded of the 10/13 "Vietnamization Meeting with Secretary Laird."

26. Minutes, senior staff meeting, 6/21/71.

27. MRL, "RVNAF Leadership," memorandum for the chairman, JCS, 6/23/71.

28. MRL, "Trip to Vietnam, November 2–8, 1971," memorandum for the president, 11/8/71.

29. Minutes, senior staff meeting, 9/7/71.

30. Minutes, senior staff meeting, 11/8/71.

31. Saigon police said McGovern was unwittingly meeting with Viet Cong agents, who were mingling with the South Vietnamese antiwar leaders at the school building. Phil Odeen, "Vietnamization Meeting with Secretary Laird," memorandum, 9/14/71; "McGovern Rescued after Saigon Riot," *New York Times,* 9/15/71; "The Vietnam War: Chronology of Significant Events since 20 January 1969," 155.

32. Odeen, "Vietnamization Meeting," memoranda, 10/5/71 and 10/7/71.

33. Ibid., 10/14/71.

34. MRL, "U.S. Force Planning, Southeast Asia," memorandum for the chairman, JCS, 8/26/71.

35. Sorley, *Better War,* 282.

36. MRL, memorandum for the president, 11/8/71.

37. Transcript, NBC's *Meet the Press,* 11/14/71.

38. Moorer, chairman, JCS, "U.S. Redeployments from the RVN," memorandum for MRL, 12/30/71.

39. MRL and David Packard, "News Conference at Pentagon," 11:30 a.m., 12/13/71.

40. Sorley, *Better War,* 282.

41. MRL, "Appointment of a Deputy Secretary of Defense," memorandum for the president, 1/6/72.

42. Laird recalled that Sen. John Tower, an influential member of the Senate Armed Services Committee, also heavily pressured him to take Clements and was quite disappointed when Laird discounted his candidate. Clements was later elected governor of Texas in 1978.

43. MRL, "Press Conference," Milwaukee, WI, 3/23/72.

44. MRL, "Remarks and Question-Answer Session at TV Correspondents' Breakfast," Harvard Club, New York, 4/26/72.

45. Dr. Alfred Goldberg, chief historian for the office of the secretary of defense, agreed: "If McNamara had left in 1965, he would have been hailed as probably the most effective secretary of defense we had. If (Caspar) Weinberger had left several years earlier, he would have left with a better reputation. They overstayed." Goldberg, interview, 10/19/99.

46. Hearings before the Committee on Armed Services, U.S. Senate, "Fiscal Year 1973 Authorization for Military Procurement, Research, and Development, Construction Authorization for the Safeguard ABM, and Active Duty and Selected Reserve Strengths," 2/15/72.

47. Donald Rumsfeld, interview, 2/28/01.

48. Jerry Friedheim, interview, 7/19/00.

49. Nixon to MRL, 11/17/72.

50. There is no independent confirmation of the incident available. It was not recounted in Ginsberg's voluminous writings, nor in biographies on him. "That sounds like something Allen might have done," laughed the late poet's stepbrother Harold Collen. "I really don't remember this particular incident. But knowing Allen, he could easily have peed on Melvin Laird's doorstep and followed it up with a defecation." Neither Collen nor Ginsberg's most noted biographer, Michael Shumacher, nor Peter Hale of the Ginsberg Trust, could confirm the specific incident. On the other hand, they could not absolutely say that Ginsberg had *not* done it—especially if that's the way Laird remembered it. "Allen did a lot of things and it may have just very well have gotten lost in all the other madness that was going on at the time," Collen added. Harold Collen, interview, 8/31/01; Michael Shumacher, interview, 8/31/01; Peter Hale, interview, 8/31/01.

51. John Laird, interview, 2/27/01.

52. David Laird, interview, 2/27/01; David Laird, speech in Marshfield, WI, 9/12/97.

53. MRL, "U.S. Force Levels in the Republic of Vietnam," memorandum for the president, 1/11/72.

54. MRL, "Press Conference at the White House, Following Announcement by President of Further Withdrawal of U.S. Troops from Vietnam," 1/13/72.

55. Minutes, senior staff meeting, 1/17/72.

56. Minutes, senior staff meeting, 3/6/72.

57. Kissinger, "Additional Authorities for Southeast Asia," NSDM 149, 2/4/72.

58. Adm. T. H. Moorer, chairman, JCS, "Urgent Request for Air Authorities," memorandum for MRL, 3/9/72.

59. MRL, "Request for Operating Authorities to Counter the North Vietnamese Threat," memorandum for the president, 3/14/72.

60. Nixon, memorandum for MRL, 3/18/72.

61. This timing was noted by Air Force Secretary Robert Seamans at the 6/12/72 senior staff meeting.

62. MRL, memorandum for the record about the 3/27 meeting, dated 5/15/72.

63. MRL, "Rules of Engagement and 1968 Bombing Halt Understandings," memorandum for the chairman, JCS, 3/28/72.

64. MRL, "Command of Air Elements in Southeast Asia," memorandum for the chairman, JCS, 3/30/72.

65. Whether Congress was informed in a timely manner and adequately about the Lavelle "irregularities" became a minor controversy. Gen. John Ryan had testified in June that, early on, he recommended that he brief Congress about the episode, but Laird turned him down. What Ryan didn't know was that at that point, Laird had already privately briefed senators Stuart Symington and Clifford P. Case in his Pentagon office. Always favoring disclosure, Laird informed the relevant committee chairs about the Lavelle matter over the following week. Secretary of defense schedule for 4/6/72; "Hill

Groups Got Private Briefing on Lavelle Raids," *Washington Star,* 9/26/72; MRL, "Interview on CBS Program *Capitol Cloakroom,*" 9/27/72.

66. "Air Force Relieved Its Vietnam Chief for 'Irregularities,'" *New York Times,* 5/17/72.

CHAPTER 22. EASTER OFFENSIVE

1. "8 Bases Near DMZ Heavily Attacked by North Vietnam," *New York Times,* 3/31/72; "Saigon's Forces Said to Abandon 6 Bases Near DMZ," *New York Times,* 4/1/72; Adm. Thomas Moorer, chairman, JCS, "Daily Report, Enemy Land Campaign," memorandum for MRL, 4/1/72; Sorley, *Better War,* 321–22.

2. MRL, memorandum to chairman, JCS, 5/24/72.

3. Hearings before the Committee on Foreign Relations, U.S. Senate, "Foreign Assistance Act of 1972," 110–12, 114, 117–18, 4/18/72.

4. MRL, memorandum for Kissinger, 4/21/72; Kissinger, memorandum for MRL, 4/28/72.

5. Kissinger, memorandum for MRL, 4/28/72.

6. Messages for CINCPAC (Adm. John McCain) from COMUSMACV (Gen. Creighton Abrams), "Redeployment of US Forces from the RVN," 4/16 and 4/21/72.

7. MRL, "US Force Redeployments from SVN," memorandum for the president, 4/21/72; MRL, "US Force Deployments from SVN," 4/24/72.

8. The Abrams cable was quoted in MRL, "Personal Assessment of the Situation in RVN as of 26 April 1972," memorandum for the president, 4/26/72.

9. Quoted by MRL, "Personal Assessment of the Situation in RVN as of 1 May 1972," memorandum for the president, 5/1/72; "Saigon Weak in Military Leaders," *Christian Science Monitor,* 5/3/72; Sorley, *Thunderbolt,* 323.

10. MRL "Personal Assessment of the Situation in RVN as of 1 May 1972," memorandum for the president, 5/1/72.

11. MRL, "General Abrams' Supplementary Assessment," memorandum for the president, 5/2/72.

12. Minutes, secretary of defense staff meeting, 5/8/72; Sorley, *Better War,* 340–41.

13. MRL statements and press releases, 6/14, 7/30, 8/21, 8/25, 9/8, and 9/10/65. He continued to make similar pro-mining statements from 1966 to 1968.

14. MRL, "Contingency Plans for Operations against North Vietnam," memorandum for Kissinger, 4/6/72; Kissinger, *White House Years,* 1116; Kimball, *Nixon's Vietnam War,* 303.

15. "President Took Nearly a Week to Reach His Vietnam Decision," *New York Times,* 5/10/72; Zumwalt, *On Watch,* 384–87; Kissinger, *White House Years,* 1174–84; Haldeman, *Haldeman Diaries,* 453–56; Kimball, *Nixon's Vietnam War,* 314–15.

16. Cdr. B. B. Traweek, USN, "Mining of Haiphong Harbor," Fact Sheet (for MRL), 11/28/72; Sorley, *Better War,* 327.

17. Sorley, *Thunderbolt,* 324–25.

18. Ayers, *Fugitive Days,* 124, 256–63, 284–85.

19. "Bomb Explodes Inside Pentagon," *Washington Post,* 5/19/72; "Ho Chi Minh's Birthday Marked in Pentagon by Bomb," *ABC News,* 5/19/72; "Bombing Fails to Disrupt Pentagon," *Washington Post,* 5/20/72; "The Pentagon: Huge Building Is No Fortress," *Washington Post,* 5/20/72; "March Organizers Deny Knowledge of Pentagon Bombing," *Washington Post,* 5/20/72; "Who Are Weather People?—Ask FBI," *Washington Post,* 5/20/72;

UPI, "F.B.I. Scanning Fingerprints for Clues to Pentagon Blast," *New York Times*, 5/21/72; "Protest: Blast at the Pentagon," *Newsweek*, 5/22/72.

20. Dan Henkin, "News Items of Special Interest," memorandum to MRL, 5/19/71; minutes, senior staff meeting, 5/22/72.

21. Minutes, senior staff meeting, "Demonstrations," 5/22/72; AP, 5/22/72; UPI, 5/22/72; "800 Protest at Pentagon," *Washington Star*, 5/22/72; "Pentagon Police Rout Protesters," *New York Times*, 5/23/72; "Police Arrest 224 Antiwar Demonstrators Outside Pentagon," *Washington Post*, 5/23/72; "Protesters: How Do You Blockade Pentagon?" *Washington Post*, 5/23/72; "War Protest a Slim Copy of 1970," *Christian Science Monitor*, 5/23/72; "Antiwar," UPI, 5/23/72.

22. "Hanoi's Red River Dikes Called Underpinning of Nation's Life," *Washington Post*, 7/11/72; "Dikes in Hanoi Area Represent 2,000-Year Fight to Stem Floods," *New York Times*, 7/14/72; Reuters, "Dikes," 7/15/72.

23. Minutes, senior staff meetings of 9/7, 9/27, 10/18, 11/1/71, and 8/21/72.

24. The Defense Intelligence Agency study was included as an attachment to a 7/3/72 memorandum from the chairman of the Joint Chiefs to Laird.

25. MRL, "News Conference at the Pentagon," 7/6/72.

26. Minutes, senior staff meeting, "Alleged Bombing of Dikes and Dams in North Vietnam," 7/31/72; MRL, "Targeting in North Vietnam," memorandum for the president, 7/31/72. Dan Henkin, "News Items of Special Interest," memorandum to MRL, 8/1/72.

27. Jane Fonda, interview, 2/16/98; Reuters, "Indochina-Fonda," 7/8/72; Dan Henkin, "News Items of Special Interest," memorandum to MRL, 7/10/72.

28. Reuters, "State Dept. Reprimands Jane Fonda," *Washington Post*, 7/15/72; "Jane Fonda Hits U.S. on War," *New York Daily News*, 8/2/72; Fonda, *My Life So Far*, 291–324.

29. Dan Henkin, "News Items of Special Interest," memorandum to MRL, 7/24/72; Fonda, *My Life So Far*, 291, 295, 314–18, and 324.

30. North Vietnamese News Agency, "Hanoi Press Conference Statement," 7/20/72; Dan Henkin, "News Items of Special Interest," memorandum to MRL, 7/29/72.

31. MRL, "News Conference at the Pentagon," 7/17/72; "Laird Again Raps McGovern," *Washington Post*, 7/18/72; "U.S. Won't Prosecute Jane Fonda," *Washington Post*, 8/26/72; Fonda, *My Life So Far*, 304–6, 325.

32. Minutes, senior staff meeting, 7/31/72.

33. "U.S. Feels Vindicated by Hanoi's Low Flooding," *Baltimore Sun*, 8/28/72; Dan Henkin, "News Items of Special Interest," memorandum to MRL, 12/11/72.

34. "Laird May Aid Nixon Drive," *Washington Star*, 3/4/72.

35. MRL interview, 8/11/00; AP, "Laird Climbs Off Perch," *Marshfield News Herald*, 1/14/72; Nixon, *Memoirs*, 513.

36. Hearings before a Subcommittee of the Committee on Appropriations, United States Senate, "Foreign Assistance and Related Programs Appropriations for Fiscal Year 1973," 858–59, 898–901, and 914, 6/5/72; "Laird Projects Big Rise in Cost of Vietnam War," *New York Times*, 6/6/72.

37. Adm. T. H. Moorer, chairman, JCS, memorandum to MRL, 6/21/72.

38. MRL, "Redeployments from SVN," memorandum for the president, 6/23/72.

39. MRL, "Volunteer Force in Vietnam," memorandum for the president, 2/8/70.

40. MRL, "Assignment of Draftees to Duty in Vietnam," memorandum for the president, 8/21/70; MRL, "An All-Volunteer/No Draftee Force in Vietnam," memorandum

for Kissinger, 5/6/71; Adm. T. H. Moorer, chairman, JCS, "All-Volunteer Force for Vietnam," memorandum for MRL, 5/31/71.

41. "Pentagon Seems to Shelve Plan to Keep Draftees Out of Vietnam," *Baltimore Sun*, 10/24/71; MRL, "An All-Volunteer/No Draftee Force in Vietnam," memorandum for Kissinger, 10/29/71; "Draftee Duty in Vietnam Falling Off," *Washington Post*, 1/10/72; Kenneth E. BeLieu, acting secretary of the Army, "All-Volunteer Force for Vietnam," memorandum for MRL, 1/13/72; Robert F. Froehlke, secretary of the Army, "Draftees for Vietnam," memorandum for MRL, 3/27/72; MRL, "Evaluation of a Policy to Stop Sending Draftees to Vietnam," memorandum for the president, 4/25/72; Kissinger, "No Draftees to Vietnam," memorandum for MRL, 5/10/72.

42. MRL, "US Force Redeployments from SVN," memorandum for the president, 6/23/72.

43. Robert Froehlke, interview, 7/23/00; Robert Pursley, interview, 12/26/00; Stan Resor, interview, 10/30/01; Perry, *Four Stars*, 136–37.

44. MRL, "Remarks at the Retirement Ceremonies for General William C. Westmoreland, U.S. Army," Fort Myer, VA, 6/30/72; "Westmoreland Gets Full-Dress Army Farewell," *Baltimore Sun*, 7/1/72; "Westmoreland Retires with All the Honors," *Washington Post*, 7/1/72.

45. "The General v. 'The System,'" *Time*, 2/15/71; "Abrams Profile," AP, 6/20/72.

46. MRL, "Unforgettable Creighton Abrams," *Reader's Digest*, 7/76.

47. MRL, "Telephone Conversation (3/21/72) with General Creighton Abrams," undated memorandum of conversation.

48. "Abrams Is Choice as Chief of Staff," *New York Times*, 6/1/72.

49. MRL, memorandum for the president, 6/15/72.

50. *New York Times*, 7/2/72.

51. "Abrams Leaves Vietnam after Transforming War," *New York Times*, 7/2/72.

52. Minutes, senior staff meeting, 5/1/72.

53. Shillito, quoted by MRL in both "Third" and "Fifth and Final Interim Report from Barry Shillito," memoranda for the president, 5/8 and 5/9/72.

54. MRL appearance on *Today*, 7/20/72.

55. UPI, "Last American Ground Combat Unit Is Deactivated in South Vietnam," *New York Times*, 8/12/72; MRL, "Press Conference Prior to Luncheon Remarks," Sacramento, CA, McClellan Air Force Base, 8/22/72; AP, "No U.S. Combat Deaths," *Washington Post*, 9/22/72.

CHAPTER 23. NO TIME FOR QUITTERS

1. "Platform," UPI, 2/15/72; MRL, "News Conference by Secretary of Defense at Pentagon," 7/6/72.

2. "McGovern Vows Total Pullout of Troops," *Washington Post*, 7/14/72.

3. Some criticized the defense secretary for this "partisan" appearance, but Laird reminded interrogators that when he was chairman of the GOP Platform Committee in 1964, he invited Defense Secretary Robert McNamara to speak to the group on defense spending. McNamara declined, but later spoke before the Democratic Platform Committee. MRL, memorandum to correspondents, 8/15/72; "Laird Bids G.O.P. Back Nixon Policy," *New York Times*, 8/16/72; "Nixon's 'Dramatic Success' Recited," *Washington Post*, 8/16/72.

4. AP, "McGovern Calls Rogers, Laird 'Fright Mongers,'" *Baltimore Sun,* 8/13/72; David S. Broder, "McGovern Hits Nixon Letting 'Lackeys' Do His 'Dirty Work,'" *Washington Post,* 9/26/72.

5. Safire, *Before the Fall,* 651.

6. UPI, "Clark, in Hanoi, Is Said to Find U.S. Prisoners in Good Health," *New York Times,* 8/13/72; "Ramsey Clark Says POWs Are Healthy," *Washington Post,* 8/13/72; MRL, "Press Conference," Miami, FL, 8/15/72; MRL, "Press Conference Prior to Luncheon Remarks," McClellan Air Force Base, 8/22/72; "War Prisoners: Center of a Political Fight," *U.S. News and World Report,* 8/28/72.

7. "'Begging Is Better Than Bombing,'" *Washington Post,* 6/30/72; MRL, appearance on NBC's *Today Show,* 7/20/72.

8. MRL, "Interviewed on NBC's *Meet the Press,*" 9/24/72; MRL, "Statement on Senator McGovern's Comments Regarding Delay in Return of POW's," 9/24/72; "McGovern: Nixon 'Using' POWs," *Washington Post,* 9/25/72; UPI, "Laird Rips McGovern on POW Issue," *Washington Star,* 9/25/72.

9. Sorley, *Better War,* 349.

10. MRL, "Attack Sorties in North Vietnam," memorandum to chairman, JCS, 10/14/72.

11. Haldeman, *Haldeman Diaries,* 531–32.

12. MRL to Nixon, 11/8/72; Nixon, *Memoirs,* 717.

13. Memorandum, "Post-Election Activities," White House, with attachments, 11/8/72.

14. Minutes, senior staff meeting: "The Next Sixty Days," "Mr. Laird's Selection as Secretary of Defense," "*Pro Forma* Resignations of Statutory Appointees," and "*Pro Forma* Resignations of Non-Career Executive (Schedule C) Personnel," 11/9/72; also, Gardiner L. Tucker, handwritten notes of the same meeting, 11/9/72; Georgiana (Sheldon) Sharp, interview, 1/16/02.

15. "A Two-Star General Is Favored for Second-Highest Army Post," *New York Times,* 9/2/72; "Haig, Kissinger Aide, Jumps to No. 2 Army Job," *Washington Post,* 9/8/72; "Generals," UPI, 9/8/72; Dan Henkin, "News Items of Special Interest," memorandum to MRL, 9/8/72.

16. Sen. John Chafee, interview, 10/22/99; James Marshall, interview, 4/18/02; "Chafee," UPI, 3/23/72; "Chafee Resigns Post as Secretary of Navy," *Washington Post,* 4/5/72; "How John Chafee, Ex-Navy Secretary, Runs Against War," *Wall Street Journal,* 8/15/72; "Man in the Middle," *Providence Sunday Journal,* 9/12/93.

17. MRL, "Press Conference before Remarks to Secondary School Administration Association," Oshkosh, WI, 11/2/72; "Laird Says Draft Will Call Fewer Than 10,000 in '73," *New York Times,* 11/29/72; "Final Draft Put at Fewer Than 10,000," *Baltimore Sun,* 11/29/72.

18. Nixon to MRL, 11/17/72.

19. MRL, "Approval of the TRIDENT System as a Program of Highest National Priority," memorandum for the president, 11/21/72; Kissinger, "Approval of Trident as a Program of Highest National Priority," memorandum for MRL, 12/3/72; "The Next Missile Gap: Trident Delays, Costs May Halve Undersea Missile Force in 1980s as Poseidons Retire," *Washington Post,* 3/19/78; "Depth Charge: Cost Overruns on America's New Trident Sub Make Wry History," *Washington Post,* 10/4/81.

20. "March 6 Starts '73 Draft List," *Washington Post,* 2/3/72; "50,000-Man Draft Limit Announced for All of '72," *New York Times,* 5/14/72.

21. MRL, "Progress in Ending the Draft and Achieving the All-Volunteer Force," report to the president, 7/28/72; MRL, "Secretary Laird's Remarks on the All-Volunteer Force," memorandum for correspondents, 8/28/72; "President to End Draft Next July if Pay Bill Wins," *New York Times*, 8/29/72; "President Sets End of Draft," *Washington Post*, 8/29/72; UPI, 8/29/72.

22. AP, "Uncertainties Cloud All-Volunteer Army," *Baltimore Sun*, 1/11/71; minutes, senior staff meeting, "All Volunteer Force" (8/21/72), "FY 1973 Budget" (9/11/72), and "FY 1973 Budget Reclama" (9/18/72); "War Curb Vote Loses in House," *Washington Post*, 9/15/72; "House Votes to End K.P. Duty," *Chicago Tribune*, 9/15/72.

23. Dr. Richard Wilbur, interviews, 2/20 and 10/28/01; MRL, report to the president, 7/28/72.

24. The American Medical Association also opposed the creation of a military medical academy. Laird hinted in his staff meetings that one of their former prominent officials, Dr. Richard Wilbur, who happened to be the Pentagon's chief medical official now appeared to oppose it as well. With a wink and a smile, he jibed Wilbur with the observation more than once that the good doctor had not personally supported the university during congressional testimony. Instead, Wilbur had carefully always quoted his boss's statement of support when pressed by congressmen. William K. Brehm, "Ongoing, Planned and Other Actions to Reduce Reliance on the Draft," memorandum for assistant secretary of defense Roger Kelly (Manpower & Reserve Affairs), 7/12/69; William Raspberry, "Doctors for the Military," *Washington Post*, 10/27/71; minutes, senior staff meeting, "H.R. 2—Military Medical Academy," 8/7/72; "Area Medical School for Military Gains," *Washington Post*, 9/24/72; "On the Way . . . a 'West Point' for Doctors," *U.S. News and World Report*, 10/9/72.

25. In its 1995 report, "Military Physicians—DoD's Medical School and Scholarship Program," the General Accounting Office reported that "43 out of 44 commanders of the major military medical units perceived that physicians from [USU] have a greater overall understanding of the military, better preparation for operational assignments, and better preparation for leadership roles. [USU military-unique training includes] between 784 and 889 hours of initial military education and medical readiness training compared to that provided to [civilian medical school] graduates whose (related) training ranges from 50 to 132 hours." Harold Brown, interview, 2/20/01; MSgt. Gary Carpenter, Office of University Affairs, USU, interview, 11/1/01; "Military Medical School Appears to Be Aborted on Hill," *Washington Post*, 2/26/77; "A First-Class Federal Medical School," *Washington Post*, 3/19/95.

26. Gardiner Tucker, interview, 4/23/01; Roger Kelley, interview, 7/27/01; Project Volunteer Committee, "Plans and Actions to Move Toward an All Volunteer Force," report to MRL, 8/14/70; "Pentagon to Cut Use of Draftees in Fast Build-Ups," *New York Times*, 9/9/70; Roger Kelley, "Achieving the All-Volunteer Force," summary essay for the record, memorandum for MRL, 12/11/72; "Taking Stock" memoranda to MRL from the Joint Chiefs of Staff, 12/12/72, Warren Nutter (International Security Affairs), 12/72, and Gardiner L. Tucker (Systems Analysis), 1/30/73.

27. MRL, "Accounting for US Servicemen Missing in Southeast Asia," memorandum for Kissinger, 7/26/72; MRL, "Essential Negotiating Points" with attachment, "Essential Elements of Agreement," memorandum for Kissinger, 11/10/72; minutes, senior staff meeting, 11/20/72.

28. Laird explained that this was not his position alone but that also held by Deputy Secretary Ken Rush and Adm. Thomas Moorer—with whom he "had long and detailed discussions" about the peace negotiations. In conclusion, he stated that together "Ken Rush, Tom Moorer, and I strongly recommend" signing an agreement sooner than later. MRL, "Ceasefire Agreement," memorandum for the president, 12/12/72.

29. Kenneth Rush, deputy secretary of defense, on behalf of MRL, "North Vietnam Contingency Plan," memorandum for the president, 12/7/72.

30. Minutes, senior staff meetings: 8/28, 9/5, 9/11, 9/18, 10/16, 11/27, and 12/18/72; MRL, "Assessment of the Air and Naval Campaign against North Vietnam," memoranda for the president, 9/8 and 10/25/72; Adm. T. H. Moorer, JCS chairman, "Objectives of the LINEBACKER/POCKET MONEY Campaign," memorandum for MRL, 10/11/72; Cdr. B. B. Traweek, USN, "Mining in Haiphong Harbor," Fact Sheet, 11/28/72; Zumwalt, *On Watch*, 387–88.

31. At a press conference at Pearl Harbor on December 29, Laird responded carefully when asked if Linebacker II was designed to wipe out Hanoi's military might. "No, I don't believe that would be a fair assessment of the situation, because North Vietnam depends largely upon supplies and military equipment that are not produced within the borders of North Vietnam." MRL, "North Vietnam," memorandum for Kissinger, 12/18/72; MRL, "News Conference at the Pearl Harbor (Hawaii) Enlisted Club," 12/29/72; minutes, senior staff meeting, 1/2/73. In the end, Laird respected Nixon's right to try the bombing as a tactic that Kissinger thought would bring Hanoi back to the table. Nixon to MRL, 12/24/72.

32. "A 'Family' Farewell," *Washington Star*, 12/16/72.

33. "U.S. Could Now Quit Vietnam, Laird Says," *Washington Post*, 1/9/73.

34. MRL, "Press Conference at Pentagon," 1/19/73.

35. That afternoon, Secretary Laird recounted the confidential morning conversation with Kissinger to *Milwaukee Journal* reporter John W. Kole during a ninety-minute end-of-service interview. "Laird Was a Skillful Politician as Secretary," *Milwaukee Journal*, 2/4/73. "Kissinger in Paris; Ceremonial Site Chosen for Talks," *New York Times*, 1/23/73.

36. Minutes, secretary of defense staff meeting, 1/15/73.

37. Laird brought a typewritten statement he intended to paraphrase at the cabinet meeting. Laird hand-wrote a note on the 1/23/72 document after the meeting: "Used substance but did not read—I spoke after Pres. paid special tribute to Vietnamization Program and how it made this night possible." Also, Nixon speech writer William Safire provided a detailed account of the cabinet meeting, *Before the Fall*, 675–78.

38. The message was publicly announced in a 1/27/73 Department of Defense News Release.

39. Gerald Ford, interview, 8/28/97; Richard Holbrooke, interview, 8/11/00; Dick Cheney, interview, 2/20/01.

40. Donald Rumsfeld, "Dear Mel" note to MRL, 1/27/73.

41. Nixon to MRL, 2/20/73.

CHAPTER 24. WATERGATE

1. *Green Bay Press-Gazette*, 2/7/73.

2. Rogers C. B. Morton, secretary of the interior, to MRL, 11/30/72; James R. Schlesinger, chairman, U.S. Atomic Energy Commission, to MRL, 1/29/73.

3. "Laird to Head N.Y. Stock Exchange?" *Washington Star*, 1/27/72; "Big Seat on the Big Board," *Newsweek*, 4/26/72; "Washington Whispers," *U.S. News and World Report*, 5/15/72; "Laird," UPI, 1/19/73.

4. "What's to Become of Laird?" *Washington Star*, 12/12/72.

5. "'74 Speculation Rises on Laird," *Milwaukee Sentinel*, 11/28/72.

6. David S. Broder, "The Domestic Vacuum," *Washington Post*, 11/21/72; "Mr. Laird's Past—and Future?" *Christian Science Monitor*, 11/29/72; "From Pentagon to White House?" *Chicago Tribune*, 12/7/72; UPI, 1/19/73; "Is Laird Looking at White House?" *Appleton Post-Crescent*, 1/23/73.

7. Ehrlichman, *Witness to Power*, 94.

8. Nixon to MRL, 11/17/72. Nixon wrote Laird a steady stream of thank-you letters after Laird's resignation. A letter in March was accompanied by a large gift. "The Cabinet chair of the Secretary of Defense has been filled by some of our country's great public servants. Few of them however, could match the record of dedicated, devoted service of my first Secretary of Defense whose selfless work for the past four years has meant so much to me. (Therefore,) I want you to have the chair you occupied with such distinction at the Cabinet table," Nixon wrote. Nixon to MRL, 3/1/73.

9. Jack Mills, interviews, 11/12/99 and 10/6/00.

10. Nick Thimmesch, "Last 3 Years Have Been Grueling for the Pentagon's Melvin Laird," *Baltimore Sun*, 10/24/72; "Laird: 'No Regrets,'" *Stevens Point Journal*, 3/30/73.

11. "Laird Denies He Will Take Nixon Job," *Wausau (WI) Record Herald*, 4/26/73.

12. "Laird Says Nixon Musn't Be Tried, No Matter What," *Madison Capital Times*, 5/2/73.

13. "Packard May Be Next Defense Chief," *Chicago Daily News*, 5/1/73; "Packard Queried on Defense Job," *Washington Star*, 5/1/73; "Packard Is Undecided on Heading Pentagon," *Washington Post*, 5/4/73; UPI, "Packard Said to Reject Top Post at Pentagon," *Washington Post*, 5/10/73.

14. Cannon, *Time and Chance*, 171; Burke and Thompson, *Bryce Harlow*, 277–79.

15. Though more than one historical account suggests that Laird and Harlow asked Nixon about his involvement, Harlow himself disputed that in a late 1970s interview with *Reader's Digest* senior editor Trevor Armbrister, who was working on Gerald Ford's autobiography. Armbrister pointedly asked him if he, like Laird, made working at the White House conditional on Nixon's innocence regarding Watergate. "No," Harlow said, "I didn't ask him." And then Harlow expressed initial doubt that Laird had asked the question. "I don't want to challenge what Mel says to you at all, but I just find that amazing because Mel and I were talked to together by the President and Haig in an attempt to bring us in there. . . . We spent two or three hours up there at Camp David and I don't recall that we discussed that. . . . As far as I was concerned, I don't recall that." But then, vouching for his friend Laird's honesty, he added, however, that "if Mel says it was, it was." The most likely thing is that Laird asked him when Harlow was out of the room. For more than three decades, Laird has maintained that he did ask the president pointedly about it. "Bryce didn't ask that question," he explained. "I did, because I told my wife I would." The fact that Laird soon referenced the "personal assurance [of] noninvolvement" from Nixon in his announcement press conference seems good evidence that it happened.

16. Alexander Haig, interview, 1/21/02.

17. Osborne's column was published 6/23/73 and reprinted in his book. Osborne, *Fifth Year of the Nixon Watch*, 104–5.

18. "Laird Takes Ehrlichman White House Job; Haig to Quit Army to Hold Haldeman Post as Civilian," *New York Times*, 6/7/73.

19. "Press Conference of MRL, Counselor-Designate to the President for Domestic Affairs," Office of the White House Press Secretary, 6/6/73.

20. Rowland Evans and Robert Novak, "The Self-Bugging of Mr. Ehrlichman," *Washington Post*, 7/22/73.

21. White, *Breach of Faith*, 245–47.

22. "J. Fred Buzhardt: To the White House, Low Key, Experienced . . . ," *Washington Post*, 5/11/73.

23. Joseph Kraft, *Washington Post*, 7/22/72.

24. MRL, "Press Conference," Roosevelt Room, White House, 7/26/73.

25. MRL, "Remarks at the National Legislative Conference," Chicago, IL, 8/10/73.

26. MRL, "Press Conference," Roosevelt Room, White House, 7/26/73.

27. MRL appearance on NBC's *Today Show*, 7/31/73.

28. Oval Office conversation between Nixon and Haig, 3:26–4 p.m., 7/12/73. Kutler, *Abuse of Power*, 630–32.

29. Evans and Novak, "Can Laird Decentralize the Power?" *Washington Post*, 6/25/73.

30. Caspar Weinberger, interview, 1/25/01; MRL, "Informal Meeting," 6/29/73.

31. In his memoirs, Adm. Elmo Zumwalt, chief of naval operations, observed at a meeting he attended in which George Shultz, then the director of the Office of Management and Budget, participated: "There was another [White House meeting] that dissolved in confusion when Tom Moorer made a passing reference to the effect of one or another budgetary decision on the economy and George Shultz . . . snapped that the economy was none of the military's business." Zumwalt, *On Watch*, 314; George Shultz, interview, 2/6/01; "White House Weighs Plan for Tax Rise, with Refund When the Economy Slows," *New York Times*, 9/14/73; Reuters, "Shultz to Laird: 'Keep Hands Off' in Economic Area," *New York Times*, 9/14/73; "'Refundable' Increase in Taxes Considered," *Washington Post*, 9/14/73; "Proposal for Increase in Taxes Draws Stiff Opposition in the Administration," *New York Times*, 9/15/73; "Tax Raise Issue Clouded," *Washington Post*, 9/15/73; Evans and Novak, "Tax Increase Turmoil," *Washington Post*, 9/19/73; MRL, *Washington Post* interview, 9/19/73; Evans and Novak, "Mr. Nixon's Long, Cold Winter," *Washington Post*, 9/23/73.

32. Rady Johnson, interview, 8/22/00.

33. MRL, "Press Conference," Briefing Room, White House, 8/13/73; "Nixon Signs $22 Billion Highway Bill," *Washington Post*, 8/14/73; MRL, "Meeting with Sarah McClendon Press Group," Roosevelt Room, White House, 11/29//73; "House Passes Budget for HEW and Labor," *Washington Post*, 12/6/73; "Nixon Gets $33 Billion HEW Money Bill," *Wall Street Journal*, 12/8/73.

34. "Congress vs. Nixon, How It Came Out," *Wall Street Journal*, 12/24/73.

35. Joseph Kraft, "Regrouping at the White House," *Washington Post*, 7/22/73.

36. Kissinger, interview, 1/10/01; William Safire, "Let Henry and Al and George and Mel Do It: Who's What around the White House," *New York Times Magazine*, 11/11/73; Kissinger, *Years of Upheaval*, 370–72, 420.

37. Minutes, senior staff meeting, "Letter Bombs," 9/25/72; "Israelis Intercept Letter

Bombs Mailed to Nixon, Rogers and Laird," *New York Times*, 10/26/72; "Israel Says Syrian-Run Ring Mailed Letter Bomb to Nixon [and Laird, Rogers]," *New York Times*, 2/1/73; Reuters, "Israel Holding 14 as Spies for Syria," *New York Times*, 2/2/73.

38. Nixon, *Memoirs*, 922, 926–28; Seamans, *Aiming at Targets*, 167; McLucas and Benson, *Confessions*.

39. "Nixon to Reveal Stiff Fuel Curbs in Talk Tonight," *New York Times*, 11/25/73.

CHAPTER 25. PICKING A PRESIDENT

1. Hartmann, *Palace Politic*, 8–12.

2. Cohen and Witcover, *Heartbeat Away*, 3–11, 92–96, 116, 127–30, 214.

3. Program, "Launching *Glenard P. Lipscomb*," Groton, CT, 8/4/73; Passenger Manifest, thirty-five-passenger SAM VC-131H, 8/4/73; Ford, *Time to Heal*, 101; Cannon, *Time and Chance*, 189.

4. No formal deal could be made except between Richardson, representing the prosecution, and Agnew's lawyers. However, behind the scenes, Laird and Harlow—either personally or through their White House point man, special counsel Fred Buzhardt—effectively brought both sides closer to a compromise that Nixon also favored. Meanwhile, Haig acted as the "bad cop" with Agnew. On September 18, Laird denied that he had personally talked with Agnew about resignation. "I have been in communication with the vice president," he told an inquiring reporter. "Matter of fact, I played golf with him last Tuesday and I can assure you that I am not the source of that particular [resignation] information because I had a long visit with the vice president and do keep in touch with him, and the question of resigning has never been discussed with me." "Some Aides Hint That Agnew Ought to Resign," *New York Times*, 9/19/73. MRL interview with *Washington Post* editors, 9/19/73; MRL on CBS's *Face the Nation*, 9/23/73; Burke and Thompson, *Bryce Harlow*, 233–36.

5. A summary of the national coverage about Laird as Nixon's possible vice president was in his local newspaper, the *Marshfield (WI) News-Herald*, "Laird Rates High among Potentials," 10/11/73. Alexander Haig, interview, 1/21/02; James Reston, "A New Problem for President," *New York Times*, 10/11/73; "Congress to Vote," *New York Times*, 10/11/73.

6. Cannon, *Time and Chance*, 197–98.

7. Connally with Herskowitz, *In History's Shadow*, 282–83, 288–89.

8. Ford, interviews 8/28 and 9/12/97; Ford, *Time to Heal*, 103–4; Hartmann, *Palace Politics*, 17–18; Cannon, *Time and Chance*, 205–7.

9. Barber Conable, interview, 4/5/01.

10. Laird had an uphill battle. While Ford was the first choice among his fellow Republican House members, he fell far behind in the Senate and Republican National Committee totals. From the members of the committee, the chairman, George H. W. Bush tallied the following results: Rockefeller (30), Connally (27), Goldwater (22), Reagan (17), Bush (15), and Ford (4). Ford wasn't even among the top four recommended by Republican senators—Rockefeller (6), Goldwater (5), Connally (4), and Reagan (4). Cannon, *Time and Chance*, 207–10.

11. In his memoir, Nixon maintained that during his morning meeting with Ford, "I revealed nothing of my decision about the vice presidency." Ford's memoir says that Nixon revealed everything. Ford's chief aide, Bob Hartmann, reported that his boss

returned to the office unusually exuberant after the meeting, which was a tip-off to Hartmann that the nomination was Ford's. Nixon's memory may have been confused by the fact that he explained to Ford and others at the time that his final choice would get a call at 7:30 p.m. that evening. Ford took that to mean he would be called in the evening with a confirmation of the offer Nixon had already extended him at the morning meeting. In reality, Nixon could have changed his mind any time before the public announcement that night. Nixon, *Memoirs*, 926; Ford, *Time to Heal*, 105–6; Hartmann, *Palace Politics*, 21–23.

12. Ford, interview, 8/28/97.

13. Nixon, *Memoirs*, 909–11, 929–30.

14. MRL appearance on *Meet the Press*, 10/21/73; "Nixon Defended," *New York Times*, 10/22/73; Clifton Daniel, "White House Strategy," *New York Times*, 10/22/73; Ball and NBC News, *Meet the Press*, 120.

15. William Archer, interview, 7/13/00; "Leon Jaworski: Biographical Data," White House press release, 11/1/73.

16. Nixon, *Memoirs*, 929–30.

17. "Nixon Names Saxbe Attorney General; Jaworski Appointed Special Prosecutor," *New York Times*, 11/2/73; Jaworski, *Right and the Power*, 1–7; Doyle, *Not Above the Law*, 234–37.

18. Kutler, *Wars of Watergate*, 426–29.

19. "Talk of Impeachment in Surprising Circles," *New York Times*, 10/21/73.

20. David S. Broder, "Laird Warns Nixon of Bid to Impeach," *Washington Post*, 10/17/73; Evans and Novak, "Mr. Nixon: Determined to Defy the Supreme Court?" *Washington Post*, 10/17/73.

21. Jaworski, *Right and the Power*, 25–30; Nixon, *Memoirs*, 918–20, 948–51.

22. "Melvin Laird, Available for Comment," *Newsday*, 11/14/73.

23. MRL, "Meeting with Sarah McClendon Press Group," Roosevelt Room, White House, 11/29/73; "Impeachment Drive Loses Steam—Laird," *Washington Post*, 11/30/73; UPI, "Laird Plans to Resign When Ford Takes Over," *New York Times*, 11/30/73.

24. "A Watershed for Nixon," *New York Times*, 12/7/73.

25. MRL to Nixon, 12/17/73.

26. MRL, "Press Conference," Briefing Room, White House, 12/19/73; "Laird Quits, Urges Speed on Impeachment Question," *New York Times*, 12/20/73; Peter Lisagor, "Departure of Laird Is Big Loss," *Denver Post*, 12/22/73.

27. Nixon to MRL, undated [ca. 12/17/73].

CHAPTER 26. KITCHEN CABINET

1. Class of '75, "Press Statement," 1/27/74; UPI, "Laird Praised by Ford for 'Perceptive Genius,'" *New York Times*, 1/28/74; "Vice President Ford Given Warm Welcome despite Protesters," *Providence Journal-Bulletin*, 1/28/74; "Ford, Laird at PC: Elegance and Protest," *Providence Journal-Bulletin*, 1/28/74; "Protesters Hurl Eggs, Insults," *Pawtucket (RI) Times*, 1/28/74; News Release, Providence College, 1/29/74; "Demonstrators Protest Laird's Credibility" and "Class of '75 Denounces Demonstration," *Cowl* (Providence College student newspaper), 1/30/74; Maj. Stephen M. Maroney, acting chief of police, and The Attica Brigade, letters to the editor, *Cowl*, 2/6/74.

2. Minutes, senior staff meeting, "Europe," 1/15/73.

3. MRL appearance on Maury Povich's *Panorama* TV show, 1/15/74; "Schlesinger, Laird Differ on Vietnam," *Washington Post*, 1/17/74; "One Year Later, Peace in Vietnam Remains Elusive," *Washington Post*, 1/27/74; MRL, "Press Conference," Roosevelt Room, White House, 1/29/74; "Exit Mel Laird Firing a Few Parting Shots," *Philadelphia Inquirer*, 1/30/74.

4. "Laird Bars Amnesty on Draft Now," *Washington Post*, 2/4/72; MRL, "Question-answer Period Following Remarks to Rotary Club of Brooklyn," New York City, 4/26/72.

5. Robert Froehlke, interviews, 9/10/97 and 7/23/00; "Ex-Army Secretary Now Backs Amnesty," *Madison Capital Times*, 12/1/73; "Laird Airs Amnesty Plan Discussed During War," *Washington Star*, 1/5/74; UPI, "Laird Says He Favors Some Kind of Amnesty," *New York Times*, 1/9/74; "Time for Amnesty?" *St. Louis Post-Dispatch*, 1/10/74.

6. "Exchange of Remarks between the President and MRL, Counsellor to the President, at the Presentation of the Medal of Freedom Award to MRL," 3/26/74; "Hail from the Chief," *Washington Post*, 3/27/74; AP, "Laird Is Beribboned," *Washington Star*, 3/27/74; *Washington Post*, 3/31/74.

7. Jaworski, *Right and the Power*, 45–47, 57, and 276–77.

8. "President Hands Over Transcripts," *Washington Post*, 5/1/74; Jaworski, *Right and the Power*, 131–33; G. H. W. Bush, *All The Best*, 77.

9. Gulley with Reese, *Breaking Cover*, 226–27.

10. Jaworski, *Right and the Power*, 203–4; Nixon, *Memoirs*, 1051–52; Cannon, *Time and Chance*, 282; Kutler, *Abuse of Power*, 639.

11. Albert Quie, interview, 4/5/01; "Ford and Friends Meet for Prayer," *New York Times*, 8/8/74; Ford, *Time to Heal*, 26–27; Cannon, *Time and Chance*, 267 and 275.

12. Jaworski, *Right and the Power*, 17, 263–67, and 286–87; Connally with Herskowitz, *In History's Shadow*, 271, 273, 281, and 283–86.

13. MRL, manuscript, "The President I Know," 8/19/74, subsequently revised for publication in the 11/74 issue of *Reader's Digest*.

14. "Mel Laird's Friends Are Said to Be a Big and a Wary Group," *Wall Street Journal*, 5/11/76.

15. In recalling his side of the conversation to Robert Hartmann years after the fact, Rockefeller reportedly quoted Laird as saying: "My year is 1980"—meaning that he (Laird) would run for president if a Democrat won in 1976. Laird maintained that he neither uttered those words or ever had such a plan. Hartmann, *Palace Politics*, 222–23.

16. Donald Rumsfeld, interview, 2/28/01; "What Happened to Our 'Wise Men'?" *U.S. News and World Report*, 11/10/75.

17. Dick Cheney, interview, 2/20/01; "A Ford Interview," *New York Times*, 8/8/74; "The 'Cronies' Ford Turns to When He Wants to Relax," *U.S. News and World Report*, 9/29/75; Ford, *Time To Heal*, 188–89, 261–62.

18. Clarence Brown, interview, 8/1/01.

19. Jack Mills, interviews, 6/2/00 and 2/13/01.

20. Evans and Novak, "Jerry Ford's Friend Melvin Laird: The Man of the Ear," *New York Magazine*, 9/74.

21. Ultimately, only 6 percent of the eligible men ever applied for the program. It was easier for draft evaders and military deserters to turn themselves into appropriate authorities and take their chances that they would not be prosecuted. Most weren't. Once the Vietnam War was over for Americans, neither the Justice nor the Defense

Departments were interested in wasting resources on jailing them. As one of his first acts in office, President Jimmy Carter in 1977 made amnesty unconditional. President Ford, interview, 8/28/97; Baskir and Strauss, *Chance and Circumstance,* 215; Ford, *Time to Heal,* 181–82; Cannon, *Time and Chance,* 367.

22. On the morning of Ford's first press conference, he received a memo from one of Nixon's lawyers, Leonard Garment, urging that he announce a pardon for the former president. Consistent with his conversation with Laird, Buchen counseled Ford: "I think it's premature, don't you?" "Yes," Ford agreed. "I'm going to say [at the press conference] we'll just let the matter go on for a while." Cannon, *Time and Chance,* 371.

23. "Ford Says He Views Nixon as Punished Enough Now; Pardon Option Kept Open," *New York Times,* 8/29/74; Ford, *Time to Heal,* 157–58.

24. Gerald Ford interviews with Trevor Armbrister, 1977–79; Cannon, *Time and Chance,* 371–73.

25. Ford, interview, 8/28/97; Ford, *Time to Heal,* 175–78; Kutler, *Wars of Watergate,* 567–68; Cannon, *Time and Chance,* 382–84.

26. "Ford's Gallup Rating Off 21 Points after Pardon," *New York Times,* 10/13/74; Witcover, *Marathon,* 43–44; Ford, *Time to Heal,* 178–81; Kutler, *Wars of Watergate,* 564–66; Cannon, *Time and Chance,* 384–86.

27. William Archer and Melvin Laird, interview, 7/13/00; Jaworski, *Right and the Power,* 99–101, 108, 224–30, 237–38, and 243–45; Doyle, *Not Above the Law,* 349–50; Kutler, *Wars of Watergate,* 568–69.

28. MRL, "Is *This* Detente?" *Reader's Digest,* 7/75; Henry Kissinger, "Mel Laird's *Reader's Digest* Article, 'Is *This* Detente,'" memorandum for the president, 7/75.

29. Colonel Bui Tin was the highest-ranking officer on the scene in Saigon on April 30 to accept Saigon's surrender. "How North Vietnam Won the War" (interview with Bui Tin), *Wall Street Journal,* 8/3/95; Sorley, *A Better War,* 374.

30. "Why Did the ARVN Break?" *Newsweek,* 4/7/75; "Reporter's Notebook," *New York Times,* 3/17/75.

31. AP, 5/27/06.

32. Ford, *Time to Heal,* 233–35; Isaacson, *Kissinger,* 640–43.

33. Shawcross, *Sideshow,* 365–69; Isaacson, *Kissinger,* 635–40.

34. Snepp, *Decent Interval,* 563.

35. Record, *Wrong War;* Sorley, *Better War,* 383.

36. Alexander Haig, interview, 1/21/02.

37. Agnew, *Go Quietly . . . or Else,* 27.

38. Evans and Novak, "Jerry Ford's Friend Melvin Laird: The Man of the Ear," *New York Magazine,* 9/74.

CHAPTER 27. A SECOND CAREER

1. Hugh Carey, interview, 10/24/01; Ford, *Time to Heal,* 314–19, 331; Cannon, *Time and Chance,* 404.

2. "Laird Won't Head Ford's Campaign," AP, 4/2/75; Ford, *Time to Heal,* 295–97.

3. "Ready on the Right," *Newsweek,* 3/24/75; "Laird Expects Challenge to Rockefeller," *New York Times,* 5/14/75; "Laird Sees 'Dump Rocky' Bid in 1976," *Washington Post,* 5/14/75; Joseph Kraft, "Family Politics," *Washington Post,* 5/14/75; "Laird Moves to Assuage Reagan Wing," *Los Angeles Times,* 5/14/75; Mary McGrory, "Rockefeller, the Puzzle for

1976," *Washington Star,* 5/19/75; Rowland Evans and Robert Novak, "The Laird Ploy That Backfired," *Washington Post,* 5/21/75; Witcover, *Marathon,* 51.

4. "The Countdown," *Newsweek,* 11/17/75; Hartmann, *Palace Politics,* 360.

5. John Walker, Air France representative who was on the Paris trip with Laird, interviews, 7/24 and 7/25/01; "Detente Can Be U.S. Delusion, Former Defense Chief Warns," *Arizona Republic,* 12/5/75; "Mel Laird's Friends . . . ," *Wall Street Journal,* 5/11/76.

6. "Enter Reagan, Stage Right," *Economist,* 11/15/75; "The Countdown," *Newsweek,* 11/17/75; "The Vice Presidency: With Rockefeller Out, a Wide-Open Choice," *U.S. News and World Report,* 11/17/75; Witcover, *Marathon,* 82–83.

7. Rumsfeld, interview, 2/28/01; James Schlesinger, interview, 7/27/01.

8. Ford, interview, 8/28/97; Trevor Armbrister interviews with President Ford, 1977–79, referenced in Cannon, *Time and Chance,* 406–7.

9. Both Laird and Kissinger also thought that Nelson Rockefeller would make a good secretary of state. Kissinger also mentioned Elliot Richardson as a good choice. "Clouds Over Kissinger," *Newsweek,* 12/8/75; "Pssst—Looks Like Henry May Be On the Way Out," *Chicago Tribune,* 3/7/76; John Osborne, "Kissinger's Future," *New Republic,* 4/76; "Laird Slams Reagan on 'Demagogic' Speech," *Milwaukee Sentinel,* 4/2/76; "Talking with Beleaguered Henry K.," *Forbes,* 4/15/76; "If Republicans Win . . . What President's New Team Would Look Like," *U.S. News and World Report,* 8/30/76; "Laird Sees Rockefeller in Kissinger's Job," *Milwaukee Journal,* 10/26/76.

10. AP, "Rockefeller Backed as No. 2 (by Laird)," *New York Times,* 8/15/76.

11. Ford, *Time to Heal,* 440–41.

12. Heidenry, *Theirs Was the Kingdom,* 13–18, 212.

13. Laurie Hawley, interview, 8/12/99; Kathy Weaver, interview, 7/11/02; *Wall Street Journal,* 5/11/76; Heidnry, *Theirs Was the Kingdom,* 388–90; MRL, "Personal Notes on Life after Politics and Government," 2000.

14. MRL, "Let's Stop Undermining the CIA," *Reader's Digest,* 5/76.

15. "Laird Collection Appraisal," Chestnut Court Appraisal Associates, 4/29/98.

16. Jeanne Dugan, *Business Week,* 7/14/97.

17. Quoted by Steve Hannah, columnist, "Secret of Fund-raising—Give Yourself," *Madison Capital Times,* 8/16/97.

18. "Laird Research Center Unveiled," *Marshfield News Herald,* 10/25/94; "Secretary Shalala Calls for Increased Commitment to Rural Health Care," *PR Newswire,* 10/25/94.

19. Kissinger, interview, 1/10/01; Reed Hall, interviews, 5/8 and 5/23/06; Meldon Maguire, interview, 5/22/06; AP, 9/12/97; *Marshfield News Herald,* 9/13/97; *Madison Capital Times,* 19/4/97.

20. Reed Hall, interview, 5/8 and 5/23/06; "Healing the World," *World Traveler,* Northwest Airlines magazine, 5/97; "Replanted in Larger Pot, Clinic Research Programs Ready to Take Off," *Marshfield News Herald,* 9/10/97; program, "Dedication Ceremony: Melvin R. Laird Center," 9/12/97; "Laird Center for Medical Research," brochure, 1/06; "The Strength of Our System: 2005 System Review," Marshfield Clinic booklet, 4/06.

21. "Thank You, Bill Agee," *Forbes,* 3/11/85; "Martin Marietta's Stunning Comeback," *Dun's Business Month,* 3/86; "Thomas Pownall, 83: Executive Popularized the 'Pac-Man Defense,'" obituary, *Los Angeles Times,* 7/1/05.

22. *New York Times,* 2/25/75; *New York Times,* 2/19/76; "Phillips to Revamp Directorate," *Washington Post,* 2/20/76; "Outside Directors Take Over at Phillips," *Business*

Week, 3/1/76; "A Year's Time Turns Phillips' Meeting from Jeers to Cheers," *Wall Street Journal*, 4/28/76; *United States of America*, Plaintiff, v. *Phillips Petroleum Company, Stanley Learned, William F. Martin, William W. Keeler*, Defendants, U.S. District Court ruling, 7/5/77; "Conspiracy Charge Voided," *Washington Post*, 7/6/77.

23. "Thousands Rally in Support of Oil Company," AP, 12/13/84.

24. David Heebner, interview, 8/28/00.

25. Colin Powell, interview, 12/18/01; "Gen. Roscoe Robinson Dies," *St. Louis Post-Dispatch*, 7/23/93; "Gen. Roscoe Robinson Jr., Ex-NATO Envoy, Dies at 64," 7/23/93; "Gen. Roscoe Robinson Jr.," *Los Angeles Times*, 7/24/73; "COMSAT Corporation Establishes a Four-year Scholarship in Memory of Gen. Roscoe Robinson," *PR Newswire*, 12/10/93; Phillips, "A Loud Hurrah for an Unsung Member of Our Military History," *Austin American-Statesman*, 2/23/03.

26. Dick Cheney, interview, 2/20/01.

27. "Fine Arts Grant Awarded to Center," *Marshfield News Herald*, 8/13/92; "$600,000 Pledged to the Laird Endowment Fund for the Arts at the University of Wisconsin Center–Marshfield/Wood County," press release, 8/18/92; "Laird Gives Two Big Gifts," *Marshfield News Herald*, 8/19/92.

CHAPTER 28. WAR AND PEACE AND WAR

1. "Reveille for the Reserves," *Newsweek*, 9/3/90; "Weekend to Full-Time Warriors," *Time*, 9/10/90.

2. "Meet Mr. Tomahawk," *Washington Times*, 1/24/91.

3. Robert C. Moot, ASD (Comptroller), "How the Budget Battles Were Won, FY 1970-FY 1973," memorandum for MRL, 12/4/72.

4. MRL testimony, "Department of Defense Appropriations for 1970," House Appropriations Defense Subcommittee, 11/17/69.

5. MRL, "News Conference at Pentagon," 12/27/71; minutes, secretary of defense staff meeting, 1/19/70.

6. "Air War on Hill: 3 Planes for 1 Job?", *Washington Post*, 3/22/71.

7. David Packard, deputy secretary of defense, "Systems for Air Delivered Fire Support of Ground Forces," memorandum for secretary of the Army and secretary of the Air Force, 1/22/70.

8. Stanley R. Resor, secretary of the Army, and Robert C. Seamans Jr., secretary of the Air Force, "Systems for Air Delivered Fire Support of Ground Forces," memorandum for Deputy Secretary of Defense Packard, 3/26/70.

9. Seamans, *Aiming at Targets*, 174–75.

10. David Heebner, interview, 8/28/00.

11. Minutes, secretary of defense staff meeting, "Close Air Support," 3/27/72; UPI, "Army Terminates Copter Program," *New York Times*, 8/10/72.

12. Dan Henkin, "A-X Proposals Received," news release, 8/10/70; Robert C. Seamans, Jr., "A-X Source Selection Decision," memorandum for MRL, 12/17/70; Henkin, "A-X Prototypes Designated," news release, 3/1/71; Jack Anderson and Dale Van Atta, "The Hero That Almost Missed the War," *Washington Post*, 3/5/91; Seamans, *Aiming at Targets*, 175; McLucas and Benson, *Confessions*, 1/1/03.

13. "Saddam Can Hold On for Months, Laird Says," *Marshfield News Herald*, 10/30/90; Rowland Evans and Robert Novak, columnists, *Record* (NJ), 11/8/90.

14. "Seven Former Defense Secretaries Discuss Gulf Crisis," AP, 12/1/90; "Mideast Tensions; Ex-Defense Secretaries Advise Patience in Gulf," *New York Times*, 12/3/90; "Military Force Needed to Evict Iraq from Kuwait, Officials Say," AP, 12/14/90.

15. George H. W. Bush, interview, 10/14/97.

16. Colin Powell, interview, 12/18/01.

17. Robert Pursley, interview, 12/19/00; "Singlaub's Fellow Officers also Oppose Troop Pullout," *Washington Post*, 5/21/77; MRL, "Statement at the Request of the White House in Support of President Carter's Comments at His Press Conference," 5/26/77; "President Defends His Korea Policy," *Washington Post*, 5/27/77; transcript, Carter news conference, *Washington Post*, 5/27/77.

18. Jimmy Carter, interview, 10/23/97.

19. Helmut Schmidt, interviews, 2/4/01 and 6/29/01.

20. John Laird, interview, 2/27/01.

21. MRL, "Arms Control: The Russians Are Cheating!" *Reader's Digest*, 12/77.

22. Harold Brown, interview, 2/21/01.

23. "Laird Plans a Haven for Ex-GOPers," Scripps-Howard news service, 8/2/71; "Ford Accepts Position with a Think Tank," *Washington Post*, 2/3/77; "The Dominant Washington Think Tanks—AEI and Brookings Institution—Are Widening Their Focus and Trying to Broaden Their Financial Support," *National Journal*, 2/25/78; "Conservative Brain Trust," *New York Times Magazine*, 1/81; "Right-of-Center Defense Groups—The Pendulum Has Swung Their Way," *National Journal*, 1/24/81; J. A. Smith, *Idea Brokers*, 176–80.

24. David S. Broder, "Stumping Ford Unlikely to Run in '80," *Washington Post*, 9/29/78; Broder, "GOP Game: Will Ford Deal Himself In?" *Washington Post*, 3/6/80; "Ford's Stance Worries Friends, Rivals," *Washington Post*, 3/8/80.

25. For example, MRL, "Defense Secretaries Shouldn't Play Politics," *Washington Post*, 8/17/80.

26. "Shultz Thinks Weinberger Kept Him Out of Initial Reagan Cabinet," *Washington Post*, 7/4/82; "Shultz, at Swearing-in, Speaks of His Optimism," *New York Times*, 7/17/82.

27. MRL, "Not a Binge, but a Buildup," *Washington Post*, 11/19/80; MRL, "What Our Defense Really Needs," *Washington Post*, 4/12/82; "Military Costs Trouble Conservatives," *New York Times*, 4/19/82; MRL, "Defense: Bad Cuts," *Washington Post*, 2/21/83.

28. Caspar Weinberger, interview, 1/25/01.

29. Frank Aukofer, "Laird & Friends," *Wisconsin*, 7/12/87.

30. "The Role of Political Parties in the Nomination Process," *Commonsense*, 1981; "Another Reform Group Starts," AP, 1/27/82; *Report of the Commission on the Presidential Nominating Process*, 3/82; "Reduce Presidential Primaries, Commission Proposes," AP, 3/17/82.

31. "Reagan, with New Backing, Faces Foreign Policy Decisions," AP, 10/31/83; *U.S. News and World Report*, 11/21/83; Rowland Evans and Robert Novak, "Laird Turned Down Job as Mideast Troubleshooter," 11/28/83.

32. Charles Bowsher, comptroller general of the United States, 1981–96, and later POB chairman, 8/30/00; "Hill Unit Plans Probe of Auditing Industry," *Washington Post*, 1/5/85; "Panel Calls for Tougher Auditing Standards," *Washington Post*, 3/5/93.

33. MRL, chairman, Diego C. Asencio, Richard M. Helms, and John W. Vessey Jr.,

Report of the Assessment Review Panel for the United States Missions in the Soviet Union, 7/87, 3–4; "At Moscow Embassy, Continuous Shadow War," *Washington Post,* 8/22/85; Kessler, *Moscow Station,* 4–5, 26–28, and 92–97.

34. "President Orders Inquiry in Moscow into Embassy Site," *New York Times,* 4/8/87.

35. Jack Vessey, interview, 2/25/02.

36. State Department, "Action Taken," The Laird Report Recommendations, 9/17/87.

37. MRL to George P. Shultz, secretary of state, 7/6/87; MRL et al., *Report,* 5–8; "Envoy Is Blamed in Moscow Spying," *New York Times,* 1/20/88; "Ambassador, State Department Hit for Marine Spy Case," AP, 2/25/88; Kessler, *Moscow Station,* 13–14, 84, 136, 262–63.

38. MRL et al., *Report,* 2, 5, 7, 22, and 28.

39. "Reagan Decides to Raze New Moscow Embassy," *New York Times,* 10/28/88; "U.S. Embassy in Moscow to Be Razed," *Washington Post,* 12/21/89; "Moscow Embassy Opens after Years of Delay," *Philadelphia Inquirer,* 5/13/00; "Bug-free U.S. Embassy Building in Moscow Opens for Business," *Baltimore Sun,* 7/7/00; "Brick, Bars, Art Adorn New U.S. Embassy in Moscow," *Boston Globe,* 7/7/00.

40. William Perry, interview, 1/18/02.

41. MRL to Sen. John Warner, chairman, Senate Armed Services Committee, 2/17/98.

42. Donna Shalala, interview, 2/10/05.

43. Sen. John Warner to MRL, 6/10/04.

CHAPTER 29. ANOTHER VIETNAM?

1. Much of the February 28 meeting, which Laird had arranged in part as an interview for this author, was taped. The author also accompanied Laird and Rumsfeld's aide, Susan Wallace, on the tour of the Pentagon.

2. Mel Cunningham, interview, 9/11/01.

3. Drew Lindsay, "71 People the President Should Listen To," *Washingtonian,* 11/01.

4. "Designing a Pentagon Tribute; Thousands Enter," *Washington Post,* 8/29/02; "Families Look to Memorial to Ease Grief," *Army Times,* 9/16/02; "Pentagon Memorial Design Selection Announced," Department of Defense news release, 3/3/03.

5. "Ex-defense Chiefs Cautious on Iraq," *Atlanta Journal-Constitution,* 5/2/02.

6. Scowcroft confirmed some of the elements of his pre-invasion efforts in interviews with reporter Jeffrey Goldberg. "Breaking Ranks: What Turned Brent Scowcroft against the Bush Administration?" *New Yorker,* 10/31/06.

7. MRL to Secretary of Defense Rumsfeld, 2/11/04.

8. Rumsfeld to MRL, 6/6/04.

9. "This Atrocity Thing," *Harper's Magazine,* 8/1/04.

10. "Kissinger Tapes Describe Crises, War and Stark Photos of Abuse," *New York Times,* 5/27/04; *Weekend Edition,* National Public Radio, 5/30/04; "This Atrocity Thing," *Harper's Magazine,* 8/1/04.

11. MRL to Kissinger, 1/8/02.

12. MRL, "Iraq: Learning the Lessons of Vietnam," *Foreign Affairs,* November/December 2005, 21–43 (freelance writer Daryl Gibson collaborated with Laird on the article).

13. "Visited by a Host of Administrations Past, Bush Hears Some Chastening Words," *New York Times,* 1/6/06; Maureen Dowd, "Reach Out and Touch No One," *New York Times,* 1/7/06.

14. "This Time Around, Bush Lets Former Secretaries Speak," *New York Times,* 5/13/06.

15. MRL, "Don't Downsize the Guard," *Washington Post,* 2/6/06.

16. MRL and Robert Pursley, "Why Are They Speaking Up Now?" *Washington Post,* 4/19/06.

17. Robert Novak, *Chicago Sun-Times,* 8/6/06; "Round 2 for Rumsfeld," *USA Today,* 9/25/06.

18. "Election 2006: Voters Side with Democrats," *Los Angeles Times,* 11/9/06.

19. MRL, "Purse Strings and Pragmatism," *Washington Post,* 1/17/07.

20. MRL, "A Model for Responsible Withdrawal; The Vietnam Plan Worked Until Aid Was Cut Off," *Washington Post,* 6/29/07.

21. "President Compares Vietnam, Iraq Wars; Innocents Would Perish if US Pulled Out, He Says," *Boston Globe,* 8/23/07.

22. "As Iraq War Drags On, Comparisons with Vietnam Grow," AP, 1/25/07.

EPILOGUE

1. Gerald R. Ford, speech at dedication of Laird Center, Marshfield, WI, 9/12/97.

2. David Broder, speech at dedication of Laird Center, Marshfield, WI, 9/12/97; Broder, "'Fraternizing with the Enemy,'" *Washington Post,* 9/17/97.

BIBLIOGRAPHY

Abernathy, Ralph David. *And the Walls Came Tumbling Down.* Harper and Row, 1989.

Adamson, Hans Christian, and George Francis Kosco. *Halsey's Typhoons.* Crown Publishers, 1967.

Agnew, Spiro T. *Frankly Speaking: A Collection of Extraordinary Speeches.* Public Affairs Press, 1970.

———. *Go Quietly . . . Or Else.* William Morrow, 1980.

———. *Where He Stands: The Life and Convictions of Spiro T. Agnew.* Hawthorn Books, 1968.

Albert, Carl, with Danney Goble. *Little Giant: The Life and Times of Speaker Carl Albert.* University of Oklahoma Press, 1990.

Ambrose, Stephen E. *Eisenhower: The President.* Simon and Schuster, 1984.

———. *Eisenhower: Soldier, General of the Army, President-Elect.* Simon and Schuster, 1983.

———. *Nixon: The Education of a Politician 1913–1962.* Touchstone, 1987.

———. *Nixon: The Triumph of a Politician 1962–1972.* Simon and Schuster, 1989.

———. *The Wild Blue: The Men and Boys Who Flew the B-24s Over Germany.* Simon and Schuster, 2001.

Amme, Carl H., Jr. *NATO without France: A Strategic Appraisal.* Hoover Institution, 1967.

Anderson, Jack, with Daryl Gibson. *Peace, War, and Politics.* Forge, 1999.

Anderson, Jack, and Ronald W. May. *McCarthy: The Man, the Senator, the "Ism."* Beacon Press, 1952.

Anderson, Martin. *The Making of the All-Volunteer Armed Force.* Hoover Institution, 1991.

Anson, Robert Sam. *McGovern: A Biography.* Holt, Rinehart and Winston, 1972.

Aukofer, Frank, and William P. Lawrence. *America's Team: The Odd Couple: A Report on the Relationship between the Media and the Military.* Freedom Forum First Amendment Center, 1995.

Ayers, Bill. *Fugitive Days: A Memoir.* Beacon Press, 2001.

Ball, Rick, and NBC News. *Meet the Press: 50 Years of History in the Making.* McGraw-Hill, 1998.

Baskir, Lawrence, and William Strauss. *Chance and Circumstance: The Draft, the War and the Vietnam Generation.* Knopf, 1978.

Bates, Tom. *Rads: The 1970 Bombing of the Army Math Research Center at the University of Wisconsin and Its Aftermath.* HarperCollins, 1992.

BeLieu, Kenneth E. *The Captains and the Kings.* Gateway Press, 1999.

Benson, Ezra Taft. *Cross Fire: The Eight Years with Eisenhower.* Doubleday, 1962.

Berger, Jason, ed., *The Military Draft.* H. W. Wilson Company, 1981.

Beschloss, Michael R. *Reaching for Glory: Lyndon Johnson's Secret White House Tapes, 1964–1965.* Simon and Schuster, 2001.

———. *Taking Charge: The Johnson White House Tapes, 1963–1964.* Simon and Schuster, 1997.

Beschloss, Michael R., and Strobe Talbott. *At the Highest Levels: The Inside Story of the End of the Cold War.* Little, Brown, 1993.

Beyer, Don E. "The Marshfield Clinic: A History, 1916–1970." Master's thesis, University of Wisconsin, 1975.

Boettcher, Thomas D. *Vietnam: The Valor and the Sorrow.* Little, Brown, 1985.

Boyle, Richard. *GI Revolts: The Breakdown of the U.S. Army in Vietnam.* United Front Press, 1973.

Boyne, Walter J. *Beyond the Horizons: The Lockheed Story.* St. Martin's Press, 1998.

Brayman, Harold. *The President Speaks Off-the-Record. Gridiron Club.* Dow Jones Books, 1976.

Brendon, Piers. *Ike: His Life and Times.* Harper and Row, 1986.

Brock, Ted, and Larry Eldridge Jr. *25 Years: The NFL since 1960.* Simon and Schuster, 1985.

Broder, David S. *Behind the Front Page.* Simon and Schuster, 1987.

Brodie, Fawn. *Richard Nixon: The Shaping of His Character.* W. W. Norton, 1981.

Brownell, Herbert, with John P. Burke. *Advising Ike: The Memoirs of Attorney General Herbert Brownell.* University Press of Kansas, 1993.

Buchanan, Patrick J. *The New Majority: President Nixon at Mid-Passage.* Girard Company, 1973.

———. *Right from the Beginning.* Little, Brown, 1988.

Bundy, William. *A Tangled Web: The Making of Foreign Policy in the Nixon Presidency.* Hill and Wang, 1998.

Burk, Robert F. *Dwight D. Eisenhower: Hero and Politician.* Twayne Publishers, 1986.

Burke, Bob, and Ralph G. Thompson. *Bryce Harlow: Mr. Integrity.* Oklahoma Heritage Association, 2000.

Burns, Diane L. *Cranberries: Fruit of the Bogs.* Carolrhoda Books, 1994.

Bush, George H. W. *All The Best, George Bush: My Life and Other Writings.* Scribner, 1999.

Bush, George H. W., with Vic Gold. *Looking Forward.* Doubleday, 1987.

Calhoun, Raymond. *Typhoon: The Other Enemy; The Third Fleet and the Pacific Storm of December 1944.* United States Naval Institute, 1981.

Campbell, Shepherd, and Peter Landau. *Presidential Lies: The Illustrated History of White House Golf.* Macmillan, 1996.

Cannon, James. *Time and Chance: Gerald Ford's Appointment with History.* HarperCollins, 1994.

Caro, Robert A. *The Years of Lyndon Johnson: Master of the Senate.* Alfred A. Knopf, 2002.

———. *The Years of Lyndon Johnson: Means of Ascent.* Alfred A. Knopf, 1990.

Carroll, James. *An America Requiem: God, My Father and the War That Came between Us.* Houghton Mifflin, 1996.

———. *House of War*. Houghton Mifflin, 2006.

Castle, Timothy N. *War in the Shadow of Vietnam: United States Military Aid to the Royal Lao Government, 1955–1975*. Columbia University Press, 1993.

Chambers, John Whiteclay II. *To Raise an Army: The Draft Comes to Modern America*. Free Press, 1987.

Chester, Lewis, Godfrey Hodgson, and Bruce Page. *An American Melodrama: The Presidential Campaign of 1968*. Viking Press, 1969.

Clifford, Clark, with Richard Holbrooke. *Counsel to the President: A Memoir*. Random House, 1991.

Clinton, Hillary Rodham. *Living History*. Simon and Schuster, 2003.

Cohen, Richard M., and Jules Witcover. *A Heartbeat Away: The Investigation and Resignation of Vice President Spiro T. Agnew*. Viking Press, 1974.

Colodny, Len, and Robert Gettlin. *Silent Coup*. St. Martin's Press, 1991.

Congressional Quarterly Almanac, 1961. CQ Press, 1962.

Conlan, Timothy. *New Federalism: Intergovernmental Reform from Nixon to Reagan*. Brookings Institution, 1988.

Connally, John, with Mickey Herskowitz. *In History's Shadow: An American Odyssey*. Hyperion Books, 1993.

Crowe, William J., with David Chanoff. *The Line of Fire*. Simon and Schuster, 1993.

Crowley, Monica. *Nixon Off the Record*. Random House, 1996.

Cunningham, Mary, with Fran Schumer. *Power Play: What Really Happened at Bendix*. Simon and Schuster, 1984.

Curtis, Richard. *The Berrigan Brothers*. Hawthorn Books, 1974.

Dallek, Robert. *Flawed Giant: Lyndon Johnson and His Times, 1961–1973*. Oxford University Press, 1998.

———. *Nixon and Kissinger: Partners in Power*. HarperCollins, 2007.

Daniel, Clifton. *Lords, Ladies and Gentlemen: A Memoir*. Arbor House, 1984.

Davis, James Kirkpatrick. *Assault on the Left: The FBI and the Sixties Antiwar Movement*. Praeger, 1997.

Davis, Vernon E. *The Long Road Home: U.S. Prisoner of War Policy and Planning in Southeast Asia*. Historical Office, Office of the Secretary of Defense, 2000.

Dean, John W., III. *Blind Ambition*. Simon and Schuster, 1976.

Dever, John P., and Maria C. Dever. *Women and the Military*. McFarland, 1995.

Dorough, C. Dwight. *Mr. Sam*. Random House, 1962.

Doyle, James. *Not Above the Law: The Battles of Watergate Prosecutors Cox and Jaworski*. William Morrow, 1977.

Edwards, Lee. *Goldwater: The Man Who Made a Revolution*. Regnery Publishing, 1995.

———. *The Power of Ideas: The Heritage Foundation at 25 Years*. Jameson Books, 1997.

Ehrlichman, John. *Witness to Power*. Simon and Schuster, 1982.

Eisenhower, Dwight D. *At Ease: Stories I Tell to Friends*. Doubleday, 1967.

———. *Mandate for Change*. Signet Books, 1963.

———. *Post-Presidential Appointment Books*. Unpublished manuscripts, 1961–67.

———. *White House Years: Waging Peace, 1956–1961*. Doubleday, 1965.

Eisenhower, John S. D. *Strictly Personal*. Doubleday, 1974.

Eisenhower, Milton S. *The President Is Calling*. Doubleday, 1974.

Emery, Fred. *Watergate: The Corruption of American Politics and the Fall of Richard Nixon.* Simon and Schuster, 1994.

Encyclopedia of the Vietnam War. Simon and Schuster/Prentice Hall International, 1996.

Ervin, Sam J., Jr. *Preserving the Constitution.* Michie Company, 1984.

Etheridge, Elizabeth W. *Sentinel for Health: A History of the Centers for Disease Control.* University of California Press, 1992.

Evans, Rowland, Jr., and Robert D. Novak. *Nixon in the White House: The Frustration of Power.* Random House, 1971.

Fairclough, Adam. *Better Day Coming: Blacks and Equality, 1890–2000.* Viking, 2001.

Ferejohn, John A., and Barry R. Weingast, eds. *The New Federalism: Can the States Be Trusted?* Hoover Institution Press, 1997.

Ferrell, Robert H., ed. *The Eisenhower Diaries.* W. W. Norton, 1981.

Fields, Howard. *High Crimes and Misdemeanors: The Dramatic Story of the Rodino Committee.* W. W. Norton, 1978.

Fitzgerald, A. Ernest. *The High Priests of Waste.* W. W. Norton, 1972.

Fitzgerald, Frances. *Fire in the Lake: The Vietnamese and the Americans in Vietnam.* Vintage Books, 1972.

Fleming, Dan B., Jr. *Kennedy vs. Humphrey, West Virginia, 1960.* McFarland, 1992.

Flynn, George Q. *Lewis B. Hershey, Mr. Selective Service.* University of North Carolina Press, 1985.

Fonda, Jane. *My Life So Far.* Random House, 2005.

Ford, Gerald R. *A Time to Heal.* Harper and Row, 1979.

Fowler, Verna. *The Menominee.* Raintree Steck-Vaughn Publishers, 2001.

Friedman, Milton, and Rose D Friedman. *Two Lucky People.* University of Chicago Press, 1998.

Fulbright, J. W. *The Pentagon Propaganda Machine.* Liveright, 1970.

Gardner, John W. *On Leadership.* Free Press, 1990.

Garthoff, Raymond L. *Detente and Confrontation: American-Soviet Relations from Nixon to Reagan.* Brookings Institution, 1985.

Gellman, Irwin G. *The Contender: Richard Nixon, the Congress Years: 1946–1952.* Free Press, 1999.

Gergen, David. *Eyewitness to Power: The Essence of Power: Nixon to Clinton.* Simon and Schuster, 2000.

Gettleman, Marvin E., Jane Franklin, Marilyn B. Young, and H. Bruce Franklin. *Vietnam and America: A Documented History.* Grove Press, 1995.

Gibbs, James A. *Shipwrecks of the Pacific Coast.* Binford and Mort Publishing, 1957.

Godson, Joseph, ed. *35 Years of NATO.* Dodd, Mead, 1984.

Goldwater, Barry M. *With No Apologies.* William Morrow, 1979.

Goldwater, Barry M., with Jack Casserly. *Goldwater.* Doubleday, 1988.

Goodman, Richard A., Karen L. Foster, and Michael B. Gregg. *Highlights in Public Health: Landmark Articles from the MMWR, 1961–1996.* Centers for Disease Control and Prevention, 1996.

Gough, Michael. *Dioxin, Agent Orange: The Facts.* Plenum Press, 1986.

Gould, Alberta. *First Lady of the Senate: A Life of Margaret Chase Smith.* Windswept House Publishers, 1990.

Goulding, Phil G. *Confirm or Deny: Informing the People on National Security.* Harper and Row, 1970.

Greenstein, Fred I. *The Hidden-Hand Presidency: Eisenhower as Leader.* Basic Books, 1982.

Gruening, Ernest, and Herbert Wilton Beaser. *Vietnam Folly.* National Press Inc., 1968.

Gulley , Bill, with Mary Ellen Reese. *Breaking Cover.* Simon and Schuster, 1980.

Hackworth, David H., and Julie Sherman. *About Face.* Simon and Schuster, 1989.

Haig, Alexander M., Jr., with Charles McCarry. *Inner Circles: How America Changed the World, a Memoir.* Warner Books, 1992.

Halberstam, David. *The Best and the Brightest.* Random House, 1969.

Haldeman, H. R. *The Haldeman Diaries: Inside the Nixon White House.* G. P. Putnam's Sons, 1994.

Haldeman, H. R., with Joseph DiMona. *The Ends of Power.* Times Books, 1978.

Hamilton-Merritt, Jane. *Tragic Mountains: The Hmong, the Americans, and the Secret Wars.* Indian University Press, 1993.

Hammond, William M. *United States Army in Vietnam: Public Affairs: The Military and the Media, 1968–1973.* Government Printing Office, 1996.

Hardeman, D. B., and Donald C. Bacon. *Rayburn: A Biography.* Madison Books, 1987.

Harrington, Denis J. *The Pro Football Hall of Fame: Players, Coaches, Team Owners and League Officials, 1963–1991.* McFarland, 1991.

Harris, David. *The League: The Rise and Decline of the NFL.* Bantam Books, 1986.

Hartmann, Robert. *Palace Politics.* McGraw-Hill, 1980.

Heidenry, John. *Theirs Was the Kingdom: Lila and DeWitt Wallace and the Story of Reader's Digest.* W. W. Norton, 1993.

Hendrickson, Paul. *The Living and the Dead: Robert McNamara and Five Lives of a Lost War.* Alfred A. Knopf, 1996.

Hersh, Seymour M. *The Price of Power: Kissinger in the Nixon White House.* Summit Books, 1983.

Hillin, Hank. *Al Gore Jr.: His Life and Career.* Birch Lane Press, 1988.

Historical Office, Office of the Secretary of Defense. *Department of Defense Key Officials 1947–1995.* Historical Office, Office of the Secretary of Defense, 1995.

Hoff, Joan. *Nixon Reconsidered.* BasicBooks, 1994.

Holm, Jeanne. *Women in the Military: An Unfinished Revolution.* Presidio, 1992.

Hoxie, R. Gordon. *Command Decision and the Presidency: A Study in National Security Policy and Organization.* Reader's Digest Press, 1977.

Humble, Richard. *World War II Aircraft Carriers.* Franklin Watts, 1989.

Humphrey, Hubert H. *The Education of a Public Man: My Life and Politics.* Doubleday, 1976.

Isaacson, Walter. *Kissinger: A Biography.* Simon and Schuster, 1992.

Jaworski, Leon. *The Right and the Power: The Prosecution of Watergate.* Reader's Digest Press, 1976.

Johnson, Lyndon Baines. *The Vantage Point: Perspectives of the Presidency, 1963–1969.* Holt, Rinehart and Winston, 1971.

Kaiser, Charles. *1968 in America: Music, Politics, Chaos, Counterculture, and the Shaping of a Generation.* Weidenfeld and Nicholson, 1988.

Kaiser, David. *American Tragedy: Kennedy, Johnson and the Origins of the Vietnam War.* Belknap Press, 2000.

Kalb, Marvin, and Bernard Kalb. *Kissinger.* Little, Brown, 1974.

Kaplan, Lawrence S. *NATO and the United States.* University Press of Kentucky, 1984.

Karnow, Stanley. *Vietnam: A History.* Viking Press, 1983.

Kelley, Roger. *Letters to My Children.* Roger Kelley, 1999.

Kerry, John, and Vietnam Veterans against the War. *The New Soldier.* Collier Books, 1971.

Kessler, Ronald. *Moscow Station: How the KGB Penetrated the American Embassy.* Scribner, 1989.

Kimball, Jeffrey. *Nixon's Vietnam War.* University Press of Kansas, 1998.

———. *The Vietnam War Files: Uncovering the Secret History of Nixon-Era Strategy.* University Press of Kansas, 2004.

Kinnard, Douglas. *The Secretary of Defense.* University Press of Kentucky, 1980.

Kissinger, Henry. *Diplomacy.* Simon and Schuster, 1994.

———. *Ending the Vietnam War: A History of America's Involvement in and Extrication from the Vietnam War.* Simon and Schuster, 2003.

———. *White House Years.* Little, Brown, 1979.

———. *Years of Upheaval.* Little, Brown, 1982.

Korb, Lawrence J. *The Joint Chiefs of Staff: The First Twenty-five Years.* Indiana University Press, 1976.

Kutler, Stanley I. *Abuse of Power: The New Nixon Tapes.* Simon and Schuster, 2000.

———, ed. *Encyclopedia of the Vietnam War.* Simon and Schuster, 1996.

———. *The Wars of Watergate: The Last Crisis of Richard Nixon.* W. W Norton, 1990.

LaBlanc, Michael L., ed. *Professional Sports Team Histories.* Gale Research Inc., 1994.

Laird, Helen. *A Mind of Her Own: Helen Connor Laird and Family, 1888–1982.* University of Wisconsin Press, 2006.

Laird, Melvin R., ed. *The Conservative Papers.* Quadrangle Books, 1964.

———. *A House Divided.* Henry Regnery Co., 1962.

———, ed. *Republican Papers.* Frederick A. Praeger, 1968.

Lampert, Hope. *Till Death Do Us Part: Bendix vs. Martin Marietta.* Harcourt Brace Jovanovich, 1983.

Langguth, A. J. *Our Vietnam: The War, 1954–1975.* Simon and Schuster, 2000.

Larson, Arthur. *Eisenhower: The President Nobody Knew.* Charles Scribner's Sons, 1968.

Lehman, John. *Making War: The 200-Year-Old Battle between the President and Congress over How America Goes to War.* Charles Scribner's Sons, 1992.

Lieberman, Adam J., and Simona C. Kwon. *Facts versus Fears: A Review of the Greatest Unfounded Health Scares of Recent Times.* American Council on Science and Health, 1997.

Link, Albert N. *A Generosity of Spirit: The Early History of the Research Triangle Park.* Research Triangle Foundation, 1995.

Logistics Management Institute. *The Cost Analysis Improvement Group: A History.* Logistics Management Institute, 1998.

Lord, Carnes. *The Presidency and the Management of National Security.* Free Press, 1988.

Lott, Arnold S. *Brave Ship Brave Men.* United States Naval Institute, 1986.

Lyon, Peter. *Eisenhower: Portrait of the Hero.* Little, Brown, 1974.

Maclear, Michael. *The Ten Thousand Day War: Vietnam, 1945–1975.* Avon, 1981.

Magruder, Jeb Stuart. *An American Life: One Man's Road to Watergate.* Atheneum, 1974.

Mann, Robert. *Legacy to Power: Senator Russell Long of Louisiana.* Paragon House, 1992.

Maraniss, David. *When Pride Still Mattered: A Life of Vince Lombardi*. Simon and Schuster, 1999.

Maraniss, David, and Ellen Nakashima. *The Prince of Tennessee: The Rise of Al Gore*. Simon and Schuster, 2000.

Marchetti, Victor, and John D. Marks. *The CIA and the Cult of Intelligence*. Dell, 1974.

Marshall, Don. *Oregon Shipwrecks*. Binford and Mort Publishing, 1984.

Marshfield History Project. *The Marshfield Story, 1972–1997: Piecing Together Our Past*. Palmer Publications, 1997.

Martin, Joe, as told to Robert J. Donovan. *My First Fifty Years in Politics*. McGraw-Hill Book Company, 1960.

Mason, John T., ed. *The Pacific War Remembered: An Oral History Collection*. U.S. Naval Institute Press, 1986.

McCain, John, with Mark Salter. *Faith of My Fathers*. Random House, 1999.

McCloud, Bill. *What Should We Tell Our Children about Vietnam?* University of Oklahoma Press, 1989.

McCormick, Joseph B., and Susan Fisher-Hoch, with Leslie Alan Horvitz. *Level 4: Virus Hunters of the CDC*. Turner Publishing, 1996.

McGovern, George. *Grassroots: The Autobiography of George McGovern*. Random House, 1977.

McGovern, James R. *Black Eagle: General Daniel "Chappie" James, Jr.* University of Alabama Press, 1985.

McLucas, John, and Lawrence Benson. *Confessions of a Technocrat*. unpublished manuscript autobiography.

McMaster, H. R. *Dereliction of Duty: Johnson, McNamara, the Joint Chiefs of Staff and the Lies That Led to Vietnam*. HarperCollins, 1997.

McNamara, Robert S., with Brian VanDeMark. *In Retrospect: The Tragedy and Lessons of Vietnam*. Vintage Books, 1995.

Meir, Golda. *A Land of Our Own: An Oral Autobiography*. G. P. Putnam's Sons, 1973.

———. *My Life*. G. P. Putnam's Sons, 1975.

Members of Congress for Peach through Law. *The Economics of Defense: A Bipartisan Review of Military Spending*. Praeger, 1971.

Michener, James A. *Kent State: What Happened and Why*. Random House, 1971.

Mills, Jack. *Caddy*. unpublished memoir, 2007.

Milton, Joyce. *The First Partner: Hillary Rodham Clinton*. William Morrow, 1990.

Mollenhoff, Clark R. *George Romney: Mormon in Politics*. Meredith Press, 1968.

———. *The Man Who Pardoned Nixon*. St. Martin's Press, 1976.

Molzahn, Arlene Bourgeois. *The Green Bay Packers*. Enslow Publishers, 1999.

Morin, Relman. *Dwight D. Eisenhower: A Gauge of Greatness*. Associated Press, 1969.

Morison, Samuel Eliot. *History of United States Naval Operations in World War II*. Vols. 9, 12–15. Little, Brown, 1954, 1958–62.

Morris, Roger. *Haig: The General's Progress*. Playboy Press, 1982.

Murray, David. *Charles Percy of Illinois*. Harper and Row, 1968.

Nakasone, Yasuhiro. *The Making of the New Japan: Reclaiming the Political Mainstream*. Translated by Lesley Connors. Curzon, 1999.

Nalty, Bernard C., ed. *Vietnam War: The History of America's Conflict in Southeast Asia*. Smithmark Publishers, 1996.

National Party Conventions, 1831–2000. CQ Press, 2001.

Neft, David S., and Richard M. Cohen. *The Football Encyclopedia.* St. Martin's Press, 1991.

Nelson, W. Dale. *The President Is at Camp David.* Syracuse University Press, 1995.

Newhouse, John. *Cold Dawn: The Story of SALT.* Holt, Rinehart and Winston, 1973.

The NFL's Official Encyclopedic History of Professional Football. Macmillan Publishing, 1973.

Nitze, Paul H., with Ann M. Smith and Steven L. Rearden. *From Hiroshima to Glasnost: At the Center of Decision.* Grove Weidenfeld, 1989.

Nixon, Richard M. *In the Arena: A Memoir of Victory, Defeat and Renewal.* Simon and Schuster, 1990.

———. *RN: The Memoirs of Richard Nixon.* Grosset and Dunlap, 1978.

———. *Six Crises.* Doubleday, 1962.

Novak, Robert D. *The Prince of Darkness: 50 Years of Reporting in Washington.* Crown Forum, 2007.

Nutter, G. Warren. *Kissinger's Grand Design.* American Enterprise Institute, 1975.

Oberdorfer, Donald. *Tet.* Doubleday, 1971.

O'Brien, Lawrence F. *No Final Victories: A Life in Politics—from John F. Kennedy to Watergate.* Doubleday, 1974.

O'Donnell, Kenneth, and David Powers, with Joe McCarthy. *"Johnny, We Hardly Knew Ye": Memories of John Fitzgerald Kennedy.* Little, Brown, 1972.

Ognibene, Peter J. *Scoop: The Life and Politics of Henry M. Jackson.* Stein and Day, 1975.

Olson, James S., and Randy Roberts. *Where the Domino Fell: America and Vietnam, 1945 to 1990.* St. Martin's Press, 1991.

Osborne, John. *The Fifth Year of the Nixon Watch.* Liveright, 1974.

———. *The Fourth Year of the Nixon Watch.* Liveright, 1973.

———. *The Second Year of the Nixon Watch.* Liveright, 1971.

———. *White House Watch: The Ford Years.* New Republic Books, 1977.

Packard, David. *The HP Way: How Bill Hewlett and I Built Our Company.* Harper-Business, 1995.

Palmer, Bruce, Jr. *The 25-Year War: America's Military Role in Vietnam.* Simon and Schuster, 1984.

Peroff, Nicholas. *Menominee DRUMS: Tribal Termination and Restoration, 1954–1974.* University of Oklahoma Press, 1982.

Perret, Geoffrey. *Eisenhower.* Random House, 1999.

Perry, Mark. *Four Stars.* Houghton Mifflin, 1989.

Phelps, J. Alfred. *Chappie: America's First Black Four-Star General.* Presidio, 1991.

Pickens, T. Boone, Jr. *Boone.* Houghton Mifflin, 1987.

Polmar, Norman, and Thomas B. Allen. *Rickover.* Simon and Schuster, 1982.

Powell, Colin L., with Joseph E. Persico. *My American Journey.* Random House, 1995.

Powers, Thomas. *The Man Who Kept the Secrets: Richard Helms and the CIA.* Alfred A. Knopf, 1979.

Price, Raymond. *With Nixon.* Viking Press, 1977.

Quie, Albert. *Riding the Divide.* Quie Publications, 2003.

Rather, Dan, and Gary Paul Gates. *The Palace Guard.* Harper and Row, 1974.

Ravenel, Marion Rivers. *Rivers Delivers.* Wyrick, 1995.

Record, Jeffrey. *Dark Victory: America's Second War against Iraq.* Naval Institute Press, 2004.

———. *The Wrong War: Why We Lost in Vietnam.* Naval Institute Press, 1998.

Reeves, Richard. *A Ford, not a Lincoln.* Harcourt Brace Jovanovich, 1975.

———. *President Nixon: Alone in the White House.* Simon and Schuster, 2001.

Reeves, Thomas C. *The Life and Times of Joe McCarthy.* Stein and Day, 1982.

Regis, Ed. *Virus Ground Zero: Stalking the Killer Viruses with the Centers for Disease Control.* Pocket Books, 1996.

Rettig, Richard A. *Cancer Crusade: The Story of the National Cancer Act of 1971.* Princeton University Press, 1977.

Reuss, Henry S. *Revenue-Sharing: Crutch or Catalyst for State and Local Governments?* Praeger, 1970.

———. *When Government Was Good: Memories of a Life in Politics.* University of Wisconsin Press, 1999.

Richardson, Elliot. *Reflections of a Radical Moderate.* Pantheon, 1996.

Richey, George. *Britain's Strategic Role in NATO.* Macmillan, 1986.

Richie, Jason. *Secretaries of War, Navy and Defense: Ensuring National Security.* Oliver Press, 2002.

Ricks, Thomas E. *Fiasco: The American Military Adventure in Iraq.* Penguin, 2006.

Rochester, Stuart I., and Frederick Kiley. *Honor Bound: The History of American Prisoners of War in Southeast Asia, 1961–73.* Historical Office, Office of the Secretary of Defense, 1998.

Rudenstine, David. *The Day the Presses Stopped: A History of the Pentagon Papers Case.* University of California Press, 1996.

Rusch, Harold P., MD. *Something Attempted, Something Done: A Personal History of Cancer Research at the University of Wisconsin, 1934–1979.* Wisconsin Medical Alumni Association, 1984.

Safire, William. *Before the Fall: An Inside View of the Pre-Watergate White House.* Doubleday, 1975.

Salinger, Pierre. *With Kennedy.* Doubleday, 1966.

Schecter, Jerrold L., and Nguyen Tien Hung. *The Palace File.* Harper and Row, 1986.

Schemmer, Benjamin F. *The Raid.* Avon, 1976.

Schieffer, Bob. *This Just In: What I Couldn't Tell You on TV.* G. P. Putnam's Sons, 2003.

Schlesinger, Arthur M., Jr. *A Thousand Days: John F. Kennedy in the White House.* Houghton Mifflin, 1965.

Schmidt, Helmut. *Men and Powers: A Political Retrospective.* Translated from the German by Ruth Hein. Random House, 1989.

Schuck, Peter H. *Agent Orange on Trial: Mass Toxic Disasters in the Courts.* Belknap Press, 1986.

Seamans, Robert C., Jr. *Aiming at Targets: The Autobiography of Robert C. Seamans, Jr.* NASA History Office, 1996.

Segal, David R. *Recruiting for Uncle Sam: Citizenship and Military Manpower Policy.* University Press of Kansas, 1989.

Shapley, Deborah. *Promise and Power: The Life and Times of Robert McNamara.* Little, Brown, 1993.

Shawcross, William. *Sideshow: Kissinger, Nixon and the Destruction of Cambodia.* Simon and Schuster, 1979.

Sheehan, Neil. *A Bright Shining Lie: John Paul Vann and America in Vietnam.* Random House, 1988.

Shillito, Barry J. *A Memoir.* Shillito Publications, 1997.

Shorter, Edward. *The Health Century.* Doubleday, 1987.

Shultz, George P. *Turmoil and Triumph: My Years as Secretary of State.* Charles Scribner's Sons, 1993.

Shultz, George P., and Kenneth W. Dam. *Economic Policy beyond the Headlines.* Stanford Alumni Association, 1977.

Sims, Robert B. *The Pentagon Reporters.* National Defense University Press, 1983.

Singlaub, John K., with Malcolm McConnell. *Hazardous Duty: An American Soldier in the Twentieth Century.* Summit Books, 1991.

Sloan, Allan. *Three Plus One Equals Billions: The Bendix-Martin Marietta War.* Arbor House, 1983.

Smith, James Allen. *Brookings at Seventy-Five.* Brookings Institution, 1991.

———. *The Idea Brokers: Think Tanks and the Rise of the New Policy Elite.* Free Press, 1991.

———. *Strategic Calling: The Center for Strategic and International Studies, 1962–1992.* CSIS, 1993.

Smith, Kevin B. *The Iron Man: The Life and Times of Congressman Glenn R. Davis.* University Press of America, 1994.

Snepp, Frank. *Decent Interval: An Insider's Account of Saigon's Indecent End Told by the CIA's Chief Strategy Analyst in Vietnam.* Vintage Books, 1978.

Sorensen, Theodore C. *Kennedy.* Harper and Row, 1965.

Sorley, Lewis. *A Better War: The Unexamined Victories and Final Tragedy of America's Last Years in Vietnam,* Harcourt Brace, 1999.

———. *Thunderbolt: General Creighton Abrams and the Army of His Times.* Simon and Schuster, 1992.

Stacewicz, Richard. *Winter Soldiers: An Oral History of the Vietnam Veterans against the War.* Twayne Publishers, 1997.

Stans, Maurice H. *One of the Presidents' Men: Twenty Years with Eisenhower and Nixon.* Brassey's, 1995.

Stockdale, Jim, and Sybil Stockdale. *In Love and War: The Story of a Family's Ordeal and Sacrifice during the Vietnam Years.* Naval Institute Press, 1990.

Strickland, Stephen P. *Politics, Science, and Dread Disease.* Harvard University Press, 1972.

Stubbing, Richard. *The Defense Game.* HarperCollins, 1986.

Sulzberger, Cyrus. *An Age of Mediocrity.* Macmillan, 1973.

Summers, Anthony, with Robbyn Swan. *The Arrogance of Power: The Secret World of Richard Nixon.* Viking, 2000.

Talbott, Strobe. *Endgame: The Inside Story of SALT II.* Harper and Row, 1979.

———. *The Master of the Game: Paul Nitze and the Nuclear Peace.* Vintage, 1988.

Tarr, Curtis W. *By the Numbers: The Reform of the Selective Service System, 1970–1972.* National Defense University Press, 1981.

Tedeschi, Anthony Michael. *Live Via Satellite: The Story of COMSAT and the Technology That Changed World Communication.* Acropolis Books, 1989.

TerHorst, J. F., and Ralph Albertazzie. *The Flying White House: The Story of Air Force One.* Coward, McCann and Geoghegan Inc., 1979.

Thomas, Helen. *Dateline: White House.* Macmillan, 1975.

———. *Front Row at the White House: My Life and Times.* Scribner, 1999.

Thomas, Lately. *When Even Angels Wept: The Senator Joseph McCarthy Affair—A Story without a Hero.* William Morrow, 1973.

Todd, Jack. *Desertion in the Time of Vietnam.* Houghton Mifflin, 2001.

Tower, John G. *Consequences: A Personal and Political Memoir.* Little, Brown, 1991.

Trask, Roger R., and Alfred Goldberg. *The Department of Defense, 1947–1997: Organization and Leaders.* Historical Office, Office of the Secretary of Defense, 1997.

Turque, Bill. *Inventing Al Gore: A Biography.* Houghton Mifflin, 2000.

Ungar, Sanford J. *The Papers and the Papers.* E. P. Dutton, 1972.

U.S. Army Office of Chief of Information. "Biography: General Earle G. Wheeler," ca. 1969.

Valeriani, Richard. *Travels with Henry.* Houghton Mifflin, 1979.

Vallin, Marlene Boyd. *Margaret Chase Smith: Model Public Servant.* Greenwood Press, 1998.

Vandiver, Frank E. *Shadows of Vietnam: Lyndon Johnson's Wars.* Texas A&M University Press, 1997.

Volkan, Vamik, Norman Itzkowitz, and Andrew Dod. *Richard Nixon: A Psychobiography.* Columbia University Press, 1997.

Walker, Samuel. *In Defense of American Liberties: A History of the ACLU.* Southern Illinois University Press, 1990.

Wallace, Patricia Ward. *Politics of Conscience: A Biography of Margaret Chase Smith.* Praeger, 1995.

Weinberger, Caspar W. *Fighting for Peace: Seven Critical Years in the Pentagon.* Warner Books, 1990.

Wells, Tom. *The War Within: America's Battle over Vietnam.* University of California Press, 1994.

Westmoreland, William C. *A Soldier Reports.* Doubleday, 1976.

Wetterhahn, Ralph. *The Last Battle: The Mayaguez Incident and the End of the Vietnam War.* Plume, 2002.

White, Theodore H. *Breach of Faith: The Fall of Richard Nixon.* Atheneum, 1975.

———. *The Making of the President, 1960.* Atheneum, 1961.

———. *The Making of the President, 1964.* Atheneum, 1965.

———. *The Making of the President, 1968.* Atheneum, 1969.

Wicker, Tom. *One of Us: Richard Nixon and the American Dream.* Random House, 1991.

Wilcox, Fred A. *Waiting for an Army to Die: The Tragedy of Agent Orange.* Vintage Books, 1983.

Willbanks, James H. *Abandoning Vietnam: How America Left and South Vietnam Lost Its War.* University Press of Kansas, 2004.

Witcover, Jules. *Marathon: The Pursuit of the Presidency, 1972–1976.* Viking Press, 1977.

Witherspoon, Ralph Pomeroy. "The Military Draft and the All-Volunteer Force: A Case Study of a Shift in Public Policy." PhD dissertation, Virginia Polytechnic Institute and State University, 1993.

Woodward, Bob. *Bush at War.* Simon and Schuster, 2002.

————. *The Commanders.* Simon and Schuster, 1991.

————. *Plan of Attack.* Simon and Schuster, 2004.

————. *State of Denial.* Simon and Schuster, 2006.

Woodward, Bob, and Carl Bernstein. *All the President's Men.* Simon and Schuster, 1974.

————. *The Final Days.* Simon and Schuster, 1976.

Wool, Harold. *The Military Specialist: Skilled Manpower for the Armed Forces.* Johns Hopkins Press, 1968.

Wright, Jim. *Balance of Power: Presidents and Congress from the Era of McCarthy to the Age of Gingrich.* Turner Publishing, 1996.

Zaffiri, Samuel. *Hamburger Hill: May 11–20, 1969.* Presidio, 1988.

————. *Westmoreland.* William Morrow, 1994.

Zaroulis, Nancy, and Gerald Sullivan. *Who Spoke Up? American Protest against the War in Vietnam, 1963–1975.* Holt, Rinehart and Winston, 1984.

Zelnick, Bob. *Gore: A Political Life.* Regnery, 1999.

Zumwalt, Elmo R., Jr. *On Watch: A Memoir.* Quadrangle, 1976.

Zumwalt, Elmo R., Jr., and Elmo Zumwalt III, with John Pekkanen. *My Father, My Son.* Macmillan, 1986.

INDEX

ABMs (antiballistic missiles): ABM Treaty, 193, 199–200, 558–59n60; debate over, 188–200, 191–92; Safeguard missile system, 187, 197–98, 556n25, 557n35

Abrams, Creighton: air war in Vietnam and, 383–84; Cambodian invasion and, 174, 179, 260, 261, 263, 350; chain of command in Vietnam, 153–54, 155; death of, 350; Green Beret murder case and, 238–40; Laird's relationship with, 175–76, 415–16; Laotian operations and, 346, 349–50; on long-term outlook for war, 160, 234; McCain and, 408–9; personality and personal integrity of, 414–15; pictured, *354;* Vietnamization process and, 173, 203, 234–35, 257–58, 339, 346, 348, 388, 390, 405, 415; Westmoreland replaced with, 149; withdrawal of troops and, 173, 175–76, 203, 261, 366, 397, 405

Abshire, David, 56

Abu Ghraib prison, 522

Adams, K. S. "Boots," 495

Afghanistan, 244, 426, 509, 525, 529n61

AFL-CIO, 227

Agee, William, 494

Agency for International Development (AID), 117

Agnew, Spiro Theodore "Ted," 128–29, 155, 369, 436, 441, 450, 561–62n39;

ethics scandal and resignation of, 452–55, 593n4; on Laird, 481; Laird's relationship with, 209, 450, 481; on POW releases, 209; Vietnamization and, 481

agricultural issues, 26–27, 36, 37–38, 46–47, 470

Airlie Foundation, 498

air war in Southeast Asia: ban on North Vietnam bombing runs, 134, 151, 269, 384; Cambodian offensives, 174–77, 179–82, 187, 259, 264; "Christmas Bombing" (Operation Linebacker II), 430–31, 590n31; collateral damage, 409; costs of, 268, 383, 390; dikes and dams damaged by, 408–11; "Easter Offensive" and, 398–99, 403; escalation of, 100, 106–7, 383–84; as ineffective, 178, 184, 243, 268, 383; Johnson and, 100, 106–7, 134; Laird's opposition to, 134, 184, 243, 268–69, 383–84, 390; Laotian offensives, 177, 342–43, 383; media reporting of, 175; as negotiating tool, 384, 386, 421, 430–31; Nixon as enthusiastic supporter of, 409; Nixon's enthusiasm for strategy, 390; "Operation Rolling Thunder," 100, 102, 105; as political campaign issue, 419; "protective reaction missions," 383–85, 398–401, 415–16, 584–85n65; public opinion and, 180–82;

Coffee stain p 151, 11/17/17